HQ1075.5.U6 R46 1992
NRG
33663003078744
Women, men, and society

W9-CAN-210

WOMEN, MEN, AND SOCIETY

Second Edition

Claire M. Renzetti
St. Joseph's University

Daniel J. Curran
St. Joseph's University

Allyn and Bacon

Boston   London   Toronto   Sydney   Tokyo   Singapore

To our parents—
Clara and Joseph Renzetti
and Nancy and Daniel Curran
—with thanks

Executive Editor: Susan Badger
Series Editor: Karen Hanson
Series Editorial Assistant: Laura Lynch
Production Administrator: Susan McIntyre
Composition Buyer: Linda Cox
Manufacturing Buyer: Megan Cochran
Cover Designer: Suzanne Harbison
Editorial-Production Service: Kathy Smith

Copyright © 1992, 1989 by Allyn and Bacon
A Division of Simon & Schuster, Inc.
160 Gould Street
Needham Heights, MA 02194

All rights reserved. No part of the material protected by this copyright notice may be reproduced or utilized in any form or by any means, electronic or mechanical, including photocopying, recording, or by any information storage and retrieval system, without the written permission of the copyright owner.

Photo Credits: 1, Stock, Boston, © Elizabeth Crews; 15, Stock, Boston, © Frank Siteman MCMLXXX; 39, Photo Researchers, Inc., © Ivan Massar; 56, Photo Researchers, Inc., © Alice Kandell; 74, Stock, Boston, © Elizabeth Crews; 101, Stock, Boston, Michael Weisbrot; 126, Stock, Boston, Michael Weisbrot; 175, Stock, Boston, © Hazel Hankin; 219, Stock, Boston, © Gale Zucker; 250, Stock, Boston, © Bob Daemmrich; 278, Stock, Boston, © Barbara Alper; 306, Stock, Boston, © J. Berndt/ 1983; 352, Stock, Boston, © Addison Geary 1983.

Library of Congress Cataloging-in-Publication Data

Renzetti, Claire M.
    Women, men, and society / Claire M. Renzetti, Daniel J. Curran.—
2nd ed.
        p. cm.
    Includes bibliographical references and index.
    ISBN 0-205-13258-8
    1. Sex role—United States. 2. Women—United States—Social
conditions. 3. Women—United States—Socialization. I. Curran,
Daniel J. II. Title.
    HQ1075.5.U6R46 1992   91-22592
    305.3—dc20   CIP

Printed in the United States of America

10 9 8 7 6 5 4 3 2 1   96 95 94 93 92 91

AUSTIN COMMUNITY COLLEGE
LIBRARY SERVICES

Contents

PART II
TEACHING US TO KNOW OUR
RESPECTIVE PLACES

Chapter 8   Gender, Employment, and the Economy   175

Preface

The primary purpose of any textbook is to summarize and explain the rich body of knowledge that constitutes a specific discipline or subdiscipline. It is impossible, however, to do this with complete objectivity, especially given the constraints of space and time. Authors bring to their writing projects personal and paradigmatic biases with respect to what should as well as what must be covered in a text. In addition, they infuse the presentation with, at the very least, a particular theoretical perspective. Since we certainly cannot claim to be exceptions to this, we would like to define the goals, methods, and perspectives of this text.

Our first objective remains to assist students in connecting a central element of their personal lives—their gendered experiences—with the social and political world in which they live. To do so, we present them with a broad sampling of the wealth of recent scholarship on gender and gender-related issues. Most of this research is sociological, but we have also drawn on the work of biologists, psychologists, anthropologists, economists, historians, and others. This material will often affirm students' observations that women and men *are* different in many ways—although perhaps less so than students might suppose. Clearly, women and men are treated differently in most societies, and much of the research we examine addresses this differential treatment and its significance in the everyday lives of women and men within the context of particular structural or institutional arrangements. The new material in the second edition that addresses these issues includes: a section on early peer group socialization (Chapter 4), a section on women's and men's communication styles (Chapter 6), a boxed insert on female sports reporters (Chapter 6), an expanded discussion of reproductive freedom (Chapter 7), and a section on the women's movement internationally, which discusses not only European feminism but also Third World feminism (Chapter 13).

Our second objective is closely intertwined with the first. Specifically, we wish to persuade students to look beyond the boundaries of their own lives so as to understand the complexity and diversity of gendered experiences in terms of race, social class, sexual preference, age, and cultural differences. The book is written from a feminist perspective, and although our primary focus is a critical assessment of gender inequality, we also emphasize the interdependence of multiple inequalities. We want students to understand how the constraints imposed on women and men by specific social constructions of gender may be tightened when one also has a devalued racial status, sexual preference, age, or economic status.

Although we cannot claim to provide a fully balanced picture of the experiences of all groups, we have tried to incorporate into every chapter research that examines how gender inequality intersects with inequalities based on race, social class, age, and/or sexual preference to produce *multiple oppressions* that differentially impinge on the lives of specific groups of women and men. We also include cross-cultural research on the social constructions of gender and on gender-related issues in other societies, often non-Western ones. In these ways, we hope to encourage students to question their own beliefs about what is true or correct with regard to sex and gender, and to expose them to experiences and conditions with which they may not be personally familiar. Most of the new material in this edition speaks to these issues: a section on elder abuse (Chapter 7); a section on the earnings gap, poverty, and welfare policy, along with a boxed insert on gender and welfare (Chapter 8); a boxed insert on homosexuals in the military (Chapter 10); and a boxed insert on life expectancy in the Third World (Chapter 12).

Finally, we hope to accomplish these two objectives by presenting the material in a way that students find stimulating, clear, and highly readable. Together, we have brought to this project more than 25 years of experience teaching the sociology of gender, women's studies, marriage and family, and similar courses. During these years in the classroom, we have observed that our students typically come from diverse academic backgrounds. Although most are juniors and seniors, many have had only one or two introductory-level social science courses. With this in mind, we have incorporated into the text a number of useful pedagogical tools. For instance, key terms or concepts are emphasized in boldface within each chapter, allowing students to study each in the context in which it is introduced. These key terms are also grouped at the end of each chapter, where they appear with a brief definition. At the end of the book, all of the concepts are alphabetized and defined in a glossary. Each chapter also concludes with a brief list of suggested readings. The exercises that introduced each chapter in the first edition are now incorporated into an expanded *Instructor's Manual* that also contains film suggestions, a test bank, and other resources.

We are fortunate to be writing at a time when scholarship, especially feminist scholarship, in gender studies continues to flourish. In fact, research in the field is so prolific that it can be difficult to keep abreast of all the very latest findings. We are also lucky, therefore, to have had the support and assistance of many colleagues who read all or part of the manuscript, made insightful comments and criticisms, suggested additional references, shared journals and other publications, or passed along relevant information that crossed their desks. In particular, we wish to thank Diana Anhalt and Raquel Kennedy Bergen. Thanks also to librarians Barbara Lang, Deborah Thomas, and Chris Dixon.

Many others contributed in various ways to this second edition. Our special thanks to Karen Hanson, senior editor at Allyn and Bacon, for her expert advice and cherished friendship. Thanks also to Kathy Smith, our copyeditor, who made the production process a pleasure. We also wish to acknowledge those who reviewed the manuscript: Donna Eder, Betty Dobratz, Judy Aulette, Victoria Swigert, Alice Abel-Kemp, Diana Kendall, Carol Wharton, Judith DiIorio, and Kathleen Blee.

Finally, a message to our sons, Sean and Aidan: Thanks for your patience.

Chapter 1

Studying Gender: An Overview

We describe ourselves in many different ways. One of the most fundamental ways is to say "I am a man" or "I am a woman"—that is, to describe oneself in terms of biological sex. However, the information conveyed by these simple phrases goes beyond the mere description of one's anatomy. It also conjures up a configuration of personality traits and behavior patterns. Without ever having seen you, others are likely to draw conclusions about you—about the clothes you wear, the way you express yourself, and the various activities you pursue.

If you are a woman, for example, people may picture you wearing slacks, but they would not be surprised to see you in a dress. Most expect you to be rather passive and dependent, also emotional and given to crying easily. They will think of you as nurturing and happiest when you are caring for children, preocccupied with your appearance, disinterested in business affairs and world events, and inept with things mechanical.

If you are a man, though, people will picture you wearing slacks, and they would be shocked, maybe even frightened, to see you in a dress. Most expect you to be assertive and independent, always in control of your emotions. They will think of you as ambitious and happiest when pursuing your career, preoccupied with your studies or your job, well informed about business and world affairs, and mechanically inclined.

In other words, a biological given, **sex** (i.e., maleness or femaleness) is used as the basis for constructing a social category that we call **gender** (i.e., masculinity or femininity). It may be that few of the socially defined characteristics of your respective gender describe you accurately, but this is perhaps less important than the fact that people believe these assumptions to be true or appropriate and that they act on their beliefs, treating women and men differently, even as opposites.

Significantly, this differentiation occurs not only on an interpersonal level between individuals, but also on a structural level within a given society. Every society prescribes traits, behaviors, and patterns of social interaction for its members on the basis of sex. These prescriptions are embedded in the institutions of the society—in its economy, political system, educational system, religions, family forms, and so on. This institutionalized pattern of gender differentiation is referred to as a society's **sex/gender system,** and an examination of sex/gender systems, as well as their consequences for women and men, forms the major focus of this book.

As we will learn, sex/gender systems vary historically and cross culturally, but each system includes at least three interrelated components:

1. the social construction of gender categories on the basis of biological sex.
2. a sexual division of labor in which specific tasks are allocated on the basis of sex, and
3. the social regulation of sexuality in which particular forms of sexual expression are positively or negatively sanctioned (Thorne 1982; Rubin 1975).

Of special concern to us will be the ways in which a sex/gender system functions as a system of *social stratification*; that is, the extent to which women and men, and the traits and behaviors respectively associated with them, are valued unequally in a society.

Given that social institutions are imbued with the power to reward and punish—to bestow privileges as well as to impose obligations and restrictions—a sex/gender system has a profound impact on the lives and life chances of women and men. Consider, for example, that although "women represent 60 percent of the world population, they perform nearly two thirds of all working hours, receive only one tenth of the world income and own less than one percent of world property" (United Nations Commission on the Status of Women 1980). These startling statistics reflect the fact that most women and men worldwide live in societies with patriarchal sex/gender systems. A **patriarchy** is a sex/gender system in which men dominate women, and that which is considered masculine is more highly valued than that which is considered feminine. Yet, as we will learn in this text, patriarchy is by no means universal. Thus, one of our tasks here will be to examine alternative, more egalitarian sex/gender systems. We will also find that patriarchy does not benefit all groups of men equally, just as it disadvantages some groups of women more than others.

Before we undertake our analysis of gender and sex/gender systems, however, we should realize that not all sociologists agree on how to study gender or on what aspects of sex/gender systems are most important to study. Why the disagreement? To understand it better, let's look at some of the research on gender and the various theoretical perspectives that have informed it.

SOCIOLOGICAL PERSPECTIVES ON GENDER

Sociology may be defined very broadly as "the scientific study of human society and social behavior" (Robertson 1987:3). Not all sociologists undertake this work in the same way, however. Rather, a single social phenomenon—gender, for instance—may be researched and explained differently by various sociologists. This may be a bit puzzling, since it is commonly assumed that all sociologists by virtue of being sociologists share the same perspective. Certainly, the traditional image of science itself is one of a cumulative enterprise. That is, each scientist, whatever his or her specific field, supposedly works to solve the problems that the members of the discipline have agreed are most important. Each scientist's work progressively builds on that of others until the answer or truth is attained. The fact of the matter is, though, that scientists, including sociologists, conduct their research within the framework of a particular paradigm.

What is a *paradigm*? Ritzer (1980:7) defines it as "a fundamental image of the subject matter within a science. It serves to define what should be studied, what questions should be asked, and what rules should be followed in interpreting the answer obtained." In other words, a paradigm is a school of thought that guides the scientist in choosing the problems to be studied, in selecting the methods for studying them, and in explaining what is found. This implies that research carried out within a specific framework is, to some degree, predetermined. The paradigm, in focusing the researchers' attention on certain issues, simultaneously blinds them to the significance of other issues and also colors their view of the social world. Still, this is not to say that there is no objective social reality or that sociology is simply what our favorite paradigm tells us it is. Instead, it indicates that sociological research, like all scientific research, is subjective as well as objective. This is an important point to which we will return shortly.

Sociology is a multiple-paradigm science; that is, it comprises a number of competing paradigms (Ritzer 1980). Thus, we solve our earlier puzzle of how a single social phenomenon can be researched and explained differently by different sociologists. At any given time, however, one paradigm tends to dominate the discipline. This does not mean that other paradigms are ignored or not utilized, but rather that one paradigm seems to better explain current social conditions. Consequently, the majority of sociologists at that time will carry out their work within the framework of the dominant paradigm.

For much of sociology's recent past—especially from the 1940s to the 1960s—the dominant paradigm was structural functionalism. The structural functionalist perspective has been particularly influential in the study of gender, so it behooves us to examine it carefully.

Structural Functionalism

The **structural functionalist paradigm** depicts society as a stable, orderly system in which the majority of members share a common set of values, beliefs, and behavioral expectations that may be referred to collectively as *societal consensus.* The social system itself is composed of interrelated parts that operate together to keep the society balanced or, as a functionalist would say, in equilibrium. Each element of the society functions in some way to maintain social order. Change, then, must come about slowly, in an evolutionary way; rapid social change in any element would likely be disruptive and, therefore, dysfunctional for the system as a whole.

In their analysis of gender, structural functionalists begin with the observation that women and men are physically different. Of special significance are the facts that men tend to be bigger and stronger than women and that women bear and nurse children. According to functionalists, these biological differences have led to the emergence of different *gender roles.* More specifically, a social role, not unlike a theatrical role, includes a set of behavioral requirements or expectations that the person who occupies the role is supposed to play. The concept of gender roles refers to the behaviors that are prescribed for a society's members depending on their sex.

Functionalists maintain that for much of human history, women's reproductive role has dictated that their gender role be a domestic one. Given that women bear and nurse children, it makes sense for them to remain at home to rear them. It then follows that if women are at home caring for children, they will assume other domestic duties as well. In contrast, men's biology better suits them for the roles of economic provider and protector of the family. As one prominent functionalist theorist put it:

> In our opinion the fundamental explanation for the allocation of the roles between the biological sexes lies in the fact that the bearing and early nursing of children establishes a strong and presumptive primacy of the relation of mother to the small child and this in turn establishes a presumption that the man who is exempted from these biological functions should specialize in the alternative [occupational] direction (Parsons 1955:23).

Adherents to this perspective point out that the work women do in the home is functional. In many ways, women reproduce society: by giving birth to new members, by teaching or socializing them to accept the culture's agreed-upon values and norms, and by providing men and children with affection and physical sustenance. However, functionalists simultaneously devalue traditional women's work, referring to it as a "duty" or "pseudo-occupation" and designating men as the instrumental leaders of their families.

Setting aside for the moment the inherent sex bias in this approach, let's consider two of functionalism's central themes. First is functionalists' emphasis on gender differences as *natural* phenomena deriving from human biology. Portraying masculinity and femininity as natural, however, confuses gender with sex and suggests immutability. The implicit message is that efforts to reconstruct our definitions of masculinity and femininity are futile at best in terms of their effects on behavior. Moreover, in this perspective, men and women are opposites; what men are, women are not, and efforts to alter this natural dichotomy will likely do more harm than good. Yet, the fact is that gender is quite amenable to change; what constitutes masculinity and femininity varies tremendously throughout history and across cultures. That is because gender as we defined it at the outset is a social creation, not a biological given. Even if biological factors play some part in producing gender differences, available evidence shows that biologically determined traits can be modified or completely overridden by environmental influences. We will discuss this point further throughout the text, especially in Chapters 2 and 3.

Another serious consequence of depicting gender differences as natural is that such a position traditionally has been used to justify inequality and discrimination on the basis of sex. History is replete with examples. In the fifth century B.C., for instance, the Chinese philosopher Confucius declared that while women are human beings, they are of a lower state than men (Peck 1985). In 1873, Myra Bradwell was denied admission to the Illinois bar and the right to practice law on the ground that "the natural and proper timidity and delicacy which belong to the female sex evidently unfits it of many for the occupations of civil life" (quoted in Goldstein 1979:50). More recently, a social scientist has argued that men inevitably surpass women in the competition for the most prestigious positions in society because men secrete more testosterone (the hormone associated with aggressive behavior) and this gives them "an insuperable headstart" over women (Goldberg 1974).

It may well be the case that biological factors are responsible for many of the personality and behavior differences that we may observe between women and men. However, that does not mean that one sex or gender is better than the other or that members of one sex deserve a disproportionate share of society's resources and rewards because of their sex. In Chapter 2, we will more thoroughly evaluate claims regarding biologically-based differences between the sexes; however, the problems of gender inequality and discrimination will occupy us throughout the text.

This brings us to a second major theme in the structural functionalist perspective: the conception of gender in terms of roles. Although this position recognizes the importance of social learning in the development of gender, it also presents several difficulties. Stacey and Thorne (1985:307) succinctly summarize these:

> The notion of "role" focuses attention more on individuals than on social structure, and implies that "the female role" and "the male role" are complementary (i.e., separate or different, but equal). The terms are depoliticizing; they strip experience from its historical and political context and neglect questions of power and conflict. It is significant that sociologists do not speak of "class roles" or "race roles."

A key concept in this critique is *power.* Power is one's ability to impose one's will on others. The most powerful members of a society are usually those who control the largest share of societal resources, such as money, property, and the means of physical force. In hierarchically structured societies such as our own, these resources may be distributed unequally on the basis of characteristics over which individuals have no control, such as race, age, and *sex.* In overlooking the issue of power relations, then, the structural functionalist perspective neglects significant dimensions of gender: the structural causes of gender-based inequality and the consequences this inequality has for women and men in society.

This point of view also has serious implications with regard to social change. If we put too much emphasis on the process of individual learning, we may be tempted to assume that the solution to gender inequality lies simply in teaching people new social roles. Although much has been accomplished by individuals learning to reject the social constructions of gender that they find oppressive, we will see in the chapters that follow that far-reaching and effective social change requires a fundamental restructuring of society's basic institutions. A fatal inadequacy of the structural functionalist analysis of gender is its defense of the status quo.

A Paradigm Revolution

We noted earlier that structural functionalism was the dominant paradigm in sociology from the 1940s to the 1960s. Like most dominant paradigms, however, structural functionalism began to wear out; that is, it could no longer adequately explain social conditions or problems without being revised in some fundamental way (Harding 1979). When this occurs, a *paradigm revolution* is likely. This means that the members of a scientific discipline reject the dominant paradigm in favor of a competing paradigm that is better able to explain prevailing conditions (Kuhn 1970). Specifically what prompted a paradigm revolution in sociology during the 1960s?

The popularity of structural functionalism during the years following World War II is understandable, given the conservative climate of the time. During the 1960s, however, structural functionalism began to lose its status as the dominant sociological paradigm. The *turbulent sixties,* as the decade is often called, was a period of social protest and activism. Although opposition to the Vietnam War is usually viewed as the focal point of this unrest, other social problems mobilized many people for collective action. At the heart of their concern was the widespread inequality that characterized American society. Poverty and malnutrition in the United States, for instance, demonstrated that American affluence was not as widely shared as was commonly believed (Harrington 1962). The black civil rights movement and the women's liberation movement raised public awareness of the fact that many Americans were systematically denied both full participation in their society and equal access to its resources and rewards simply on the basis of their race and/or sex.

Sociologists began to question the accuracy of depicting society as an orderly, harmonious social system. Many also rejected the notion of societal consensus and instead undertook an examination of the development of dominant ideologies as products of the struggles between the haves and have-nots in a society. At the center of their analysis was the issue of power relations.

A number of different paradigms have emerged out of the turmoil. Particularly important to the sociological study of gender has been the development of the feminist paradigm. Although it has been argued that feminism has had less revolutionary effects on sociology than on other disciplines, its impact nonetheless has been far reaching (Chafetz 1988; Stacey and Thorne 1985). Let's take a closer look, then, at the feminist paradigm.

A Feminist Sociology of Gender

We must begin this discussion with a caveat: it is somewhat inaccurate to speak of feminism as a single, unified perspective. It is more appropriate, as Delmar (1986:9) argues, to think in terms of a "plurality of feminisms." Although we will consider this point more carefully in a moment, there are several points that virtually all feminist-identified perspectives share, and these will be our initial focus.

The **feminist paradigm** acknowledges the importance of both nature and learning in the acquisition of gender. However, feminist sociologists stress that it is virtually impossible to separate out the precise influences of biology because, as we will see in Chapter 4, the learning process begins immediately after birth. The complex interrelation between biological and cultural factors is also emphasized. Our genes, they tell us, "do not make specific bits and pieces of a body; they code for a range of forms under an array of environmental conditions. Moreover, even when a trait has been built and set, environmental intervention may still modify [it]" (Gould 1981:156).

The feminist perspective, therefore, begins with the assumption that gender is essentially socially created, rather than innately determined. Feminists view gender, in part, as a set of social expectations that is reproduced and transmitted through a process of social learning. In this way, the expectations become fundamental components of our personalities. But feminists also recognize that a complete understanding of gender requires more than an analysis of this learning process. They point out, in fact, that what we learn is itself a social product that is generated within the context of a particular political and economic structure. Consequently, feminist sociologists seek to answer research questions that set them apart from structural functionalists and other nonfeminist sociologists.

Feminists take issue with the inherent sex bias or **sexism** in traditional sociological research that we noted earlier. Sexism involves differentially valuing one sex, in this case, men, over the other. Historically, sexism in sociology has been in large part the result of the relatively low numbers of women faculty and students at academic and research institutions. However, it also reflects a broader societal prejudice against women, which is embodied in the assumption that what women do, think, or say is unimportant or uninteresting.

The influence of these factors on sociological research has been threefold:

1. Most sociological studies were conducted by men, using male subjects, although findings were generalized to all people.
2. Gender was considered an important category of analysis only in a limited number of sociological subfields, such as marriage and family, whereas in all others (e.g., sociology of work, complex organizations, or sociology of law), it was ignored.
3. When women were studied, their behavior and attitudes were analyzed in terms of a male standard of normalcy or rightness.

A few examples should make these points clearer.

Consider, for instance, the classic research in the subfield of urban sociology. In her review of this literature, Lyn Lofland (1975:145) found that "[women] are part of the locale or neighborhood or area—described like other important aspects of the setting such as income, ecology, or demography—but are largely irrelevant to the analytic *action*." Thus, although urban sociologists claimed to be studying community, their focus was limited to empirical settings in which men were likely to be present (e.g., urban street corners or neighborhood taverns). They completely overlooked the areas of urban life where women were likely to be found (e.g., in playgrounds with their children or at grocery stores), though few of us would deny that these locales are also central components of human communities.

Sociologist Dale Spender (1981) offers another example. Studies on sex and language have shown differences in women's and men's speech. Spender found in her examination of the extant research that many studies were designed to discover deficiencies in women's speech. The underlying assumption of such research is that there is something wrong with women's speech because it is different from that of men. That is, men's speech is taken as normative; therefore, speech that is different must be deficient.

In short, "most of what we have formerly known as the study of society is only the male study of male society" (Millman and Kanter 1975:viii). Feminists, in contrast, include gender as a fundamental category of analysis in their research because they view the understanding of gender relations as central to understanding other social relations. This, in turn, has important implications for the research process and its outcomes. For one thing, it means that although feminist researchers strive to uncover similarities and differences in women's and men's behaviors, attitudes, and experiences, they do so not for the sake of estimating the value of one relative to the other. Rather, their goal is to develop a holistic view of how women and men, because of their different locations in the social structure, encounter differential opportunities and constraints, and how they resist or respond to their relative circumstances (Offen 1988; Hess and Ferree 1987).

We are speaking here of the differential consequences of particular social arrangements on the lives of women and men, and of women and men as agents of social change. We will return to each of these issues momentarily. Notice first, however, that feminists do not exclude male experiences and perspectives from their research, but they do insist on the inclusion of female experiences and perspectives. Feminists deliberately seek to make women's voices heard in sociological research where previously they have been silenced or ignored. To do this, feminists reject the traditional model of science "as establishing mastery over subjects, as demanding the absence of feeling, and as enforcing separateness of the knower from the known, all under the guise of 'objectivity' " (Hess and Ferree 1987:13; Maguire 1987). Feminist researchers instead take an empathic stance toward their research subjects. They frequently utilize more inclusive research methods that allow subjects to express their feelings and to speak for themselves, rather than imposing the researchers' own ideas or categories of response on their respondents.

The experiential emphasis in feminist research has frequently drawn charges of bias from traditional sociologists. However, feminists do not deny the partiality of their work; on the contrary, they acknowledge that it is intended. "To talk of a feminist methodology is clearly political, controversial, and implies personal and/or political sympathies on the part of the researcher which inform, but do not constitute the sociological approach" (Roberts 1981:16). What feminists are telling us here is that sociological research is *dualistic*: it has both subjective and objective dimensions. On the one hand, no research, including that conducted within the structural functionalist paradigm as we have seen, is completely unbiased or "value free." No matter how objective sociologists may like to think they are, they cannot help but be influenced by values, personal preferences, life experiences, and aspects of the cultural setting in which they live. On the other hand, this does not mean that research is completely subjective either. While a researcher may be influenced by *values* (i.e., judgments or appraisals), her or his goal is the collection of *facts* (i.e., phenomena that can be observed or empirically verified). Two social theorists expressed it this way: "It's one thing to find out what the state of affairs is in the world, another thing to decide whether we think it is good or bad, just or unjust, beautiful or ugly" (Collins and Makowsky, 1989:7). The former involves the pursuit of facts, the latter a statement of values.

The dualistic nature of sociological research makes it especially challenging, particularly for those of us interested in the study of gender. This is because of our intimate tie to what we are studying—after all, each of us has gender. But this duality also makes gender research very promising. Just as our values affect what we choose to study and how we choose to study it, they can also guide us in deciding how the facts we gather can be put to practical use. As we will argue shortly, the scientific knowledge we acquire through the research process can empower us to act to change behaviors and conditions that are harmful or oppressive.

Let's return now to the issue of consequences. Feminist sociologists are fundamentally concerned with the question of how specific social constructions of gender impinge upon the lives of women and men. The feminist research we will review in this text documents the serious and far-reaching effects of sexism in our society and in others. In Chapter 8, for example, we will learn that sexist beliefs that devalue women's labor have served as justifications for paying women less than men, and often as excuses for not paying them at all. This, in turn, is one of the major reasons women outnumber men among the ranks of the world's poor. Similarly, in Chapter 7, we will see that the notion that women are the natural caretakers of children has been used to deny fathers custody of their children in divorce settlements.

This latter example highlights an important point that we raised earlier, but that bears repeating here. Specifically, although many people tend to think of feminism as applicable only to so-called women's issues, feminists themselves see their paradigm as relevant to the experiences of both sexes. Certainly, feminists' primary concern has been to study the position of women in society largely because, as we have already noted, women and women's experiences have long been devalued or ignored in scientific research. Nevertheless, they have not left the social construction of masculinity unanalyzed. In fact, "as feminist scholars have studied men's lives, they find that although men benefit from institutionalized power and privilege, they, too, are subjected to sexist cultural expectations of masculinity that affect their emotions, identities, and social roles" (Andersen 1988:8).

Significantly, feminists also recognize that the consequences of sexism are not identical for all groups of women and men. Instead, the effects of gender inequality are made worse by racism, ageism, social class inequality, and discrimination on the basis of sexual preference. Consider, for example, the likely dissimilarities in the lives of a white, middle-class, middle-aged, gay man and a poor, black, pregnant teenager. Both may think of themselves as oppressed, but their objective circumstances are very different. Feminist research, therefore, attempts to account for the gender-based experiences of many diverse groups of women and men in our society. It analyzes the inextricable links among *multiple* oppressions: sexism, racism, classism, ageism, and heterosexism (King 1988). An examination of these complex interrelationships is a central theme of this text.

Finally, just as other sociological models, such as structural functionalism, have implications for social change, so does the feminist paradigm. Feminist sociologists, in fact, are advocates of social change. They seek to develop effective means to eradicate gender inequality and to change those aspects of our social constructions of gender that are harmful or destructive.

An important first step in this process is for people to develop a *group consciousness;* that is, they must begin to see that their problems are not personal ones, but rather are shared by others like them. Until a group consciousness develops, change is likely to be limited to the individual level. As one observer explained, "People tend to think that personal problems can be solved simply by working harder. Personal problems become political demands only when the inability to survive, or to attain a decent life, is seen as a consequence of social institutions and social inequality rather than personal failure, and the system is blamed" (Klein 1984:3). Once a group consciousness emerges and institutional arrangements are identified as the source of the problem, collective action can be taken to bring about *structural* change.

Feminist research serves to raise our consciousness about gender inequality, and it has spurred many people to work together for social change. This collective effort is usually fittingly referred to as the *feminist movement.* Throughout this text we will examine the extent to which feminists have been successful in their efforts to reconstruct gender, and in Chapter 13 we will give special attention to feminist social movements and other social movements that share similar goals. Importantly, we will see that although feminists share similar views with regard to the themes we have discussed so far, they also are quite diverse, comprising heterogenous factions with different interests and perspectives. In Chapter 13, we will focus on how this diversity gives rise to different tactics or strategies within feminism to achieve various objectives. Now, though, we will briefly discuss differences in feminist theory.

A plurality of feminisms   Although it appears at first that feminism is a single, unified approach, we have noted that there are actually several feminist perspectives or theories. As Chafetz (1988) points out, one of the most fundamental areas of difference among feminists lies with the questions of what causes gender inequality and what mechanisms operate to maintain unequal sex/gender systems. Jaggar and Rothenberg (1984) have identified at least four feminist approaches to these questions, although Chafetz (1988) argues that there are even more (see also Tong 1989; King 1988; Offen 1988).

One perspective, known as *liberal feminism,* equates gender equality with equality of opportunity. Liberal feminists maintain that gender oppression is caused by unequal access to civil rights and the resources and rewards of certain social institutions, such as education and work. Interestingly, however, they offer no analysis of why such opportunities became blocked in the first place (Jaggar and Rothenberg 1984). Their concern is providing all individuals with a chance to succeed regardless of their sex (or other social characteristics). If each person is given the same chance to try to accomplish his or her objectives, then failure will be caused by personal inadequacies, not socially imposed ones. The liberal feminist perspective underlies many mainstream programs and policies aimed at ending sex-based discrimination, including laws prohibiting sex discrimination in the workplace.

Other feminist theories are more far reaching. *Marxist feminists,* for example, see gender inequality as rooted in social class inequality. It is the capitalist system of production that generates social class inequality as well as women's economic dependence on men. From this perspective, gender inequality can only be eliminated by replacing capitalism with socialism; then, social classes will be abolished and women along with men will be fully integrated into the economy. Once women are equal economic contributors, equality in other areas will follow, although some resocialization may be necessary to change entrenched sexist attitudes (Jaggar and Rothenberg 1984). Marxist feminism, however, has been criticized for downplaying the importance of sex and gender as well as race in its analysis of capitalism. "While Marxism theorizes a genderless mode of production and genderless classes, capitalism is very aware of workers' sex and race and uses the subordinate groups to its advantage in the labor market" (Danner 1989:4).

In contrast, *socialist feminists* take issue with the notion of the primacy of social class inequality and point out that some forms of gender oppression cut across class boundaries. Socialist feminists maintain that capitalism and patriarchy are interdependent systems; consequently, both must be overthrown if gender inequality is to be eliminated (Hartmann 1984). "The essence of socialist feminism is seen in two major points. First, the mode and relations of production and *re*production are interconnected, indeed, inseparable. And second, gender, class, and race intersect in ways that result in important differences in life experiences in both the productive and reproductive realms for persons" (Danner 1989:4).

Finally, *radical feminism* sees women's oppression as primary relative to all other oppressions and maintains that gender inequality is rooted in the nature of traditional heterosexual interpersonal relationships as well as in the structure of social institutions. Sexism, then, must be addressed not only in the public sphere, but also in the private sphere; both are seen as arenas of political struggle (Jaggar and Rothenberg 1984). Some radical feminists go so far as to advocate separatism, recommending the establishment of female-only communities free of male dominance. Radical feminism, though, has been criticized for ignoring the significant differences in power and privilege among various groups of women, such as those between white women and women of color (Danner 1989; King 1988).

Although this brief overview can hardly do justice to the complexity of any of these perspectives, it does provide some sense of the diversity that permeates feminism. In the chapters that follow, these diverse views will be seen in more detail as we examine gender relations within specific areas of social life.

THE PERSPECTIVE OF THIS TEXT

We have spent so much time discussing the feminist paradigm because it is the paradigm that informs this text. Although we recognize that there are different approaches that may each be labeled feminist, we have also outlined several themes that seem to be shared by all feminists. We think these common themes, coupled with diverse interests and emphases, illustrate the richness of the feminist model. The fact that it is interdisciplinary—that feminist sociologists share their research with and learn from the work of feminist psychologists, biologists, historians, and others—adds to its ability to account for the variations of gender that we will observe. In short, we think that the feminist paradigm, taken as a whole, offers a comprehensive and insightful framework for the analysis of gender and gender inequality.

Of course, feminism is not perfect. It is sometimes criticized for what is called *structural determinism,* namely, blaming the system or society for social problems such as gender inequality, while downplaying the role of individuals in creating and maintaining their circumstances. Feminist sociologists must be wary of falling into the trap of structural determinism, for it runs counter to our goal of mobilizing people to act for social change. Structural determinism depicts individuals as passive victims of oppression and gives us the sense that society is something over which we have no control. Still, feminists recognize that societies are made up of people, and people have the distinctively human ability to transform their environment to better meet their needs. As we proceed with our study of gender, therefore, we must not lose sight of the fact that although we are born into a particular social structure that in many ways constrains us, we in turn can act back on this structure and change it.

KEY TERMS

feminist paradigm   explains gender in terms of the political and socioeconomic structure in which it is constructed; emphasizes the importance of taking collective action to eradicate sexism in sociology as well as in society, and to reconstruct gender so that it is neither a harmful nor oppressive social category

gender   socially generated attitudes and behaviors, usually organized dichotomously as masculinity and femininity

patriarchy   a sex/gender system in which men dominate women, and that which is considered masculine is more highly valued than that which is considered feminine.

sex   the biologically determined physical distinctions between males and females

sex/gender system   the institutionalized traits, behaviors, and patterns of social interaction that are prescribed for a society's members based on sex; the system incorporates three interrelated components: (1) the social construction of two dichotomous genders on the basis of biological sex, (2) a sexual division of labor, and (3) the social regulation of sexuality

sexism   the differential valuing of one sex over the other

structural functionalist paradigm   explains gender as being derived from the biological differences between the sexes, especially differences in reproductive functions

SUGGESTED READINGS

Each chapter of this text will conclude with a list of books that we feel will enhance your understanding of the issues just discussed. We begin with a list of anthologies that provide a good introduction to the study of gender and to the theoretical perspectives that inform it.

Brod, H. (Ed.) 1987. *The Making of Masculinities.* Boston: Allen and Unwin.

Hansen, K.V., and I.J. Philipson (Eds.) 1990. *Women, Class, and the Feminist Imagination.* Philadelphia: Temple University Press.

Hess, B.B., and M. Marx Ferree (Eds.) 1987. *Analyzing Gender: A Handbook of Social Science Research.* Newbury Park, CA: Sage.

Jaggar, A.M., and P.S. Rothenberg (Eds.) 1984. *Feminist Frameworks.* New York: McGraw-Hill.

Kimmel, M.S., and M.A. Messner (Eds.) 1989. *Men's Lives.* New York: Macmillan.

Rothenberg, P.S. (Ed.) 1988. *Racism and Sexism: An Integrated Study.* New York: St. Martin's Press.

Simms, M.C., and J.M. Malveaux (Eds.) 1986. *Slipping Through the Cracks: The Status of Black Women.* New Brunswick: Transaction Books.

For a review of various feminist perspectives within sociology, see:

Chafetz, J.S. 1988. *Feminist Sociology: An Overview of Contemporary Theories.* Itasca, IL: F.E. Peacock.

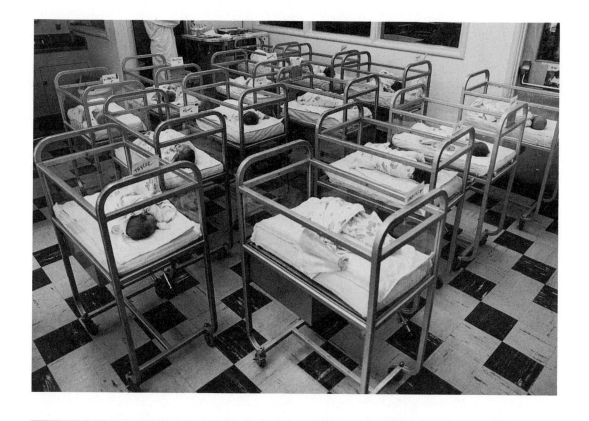

Chapter 2

Sex Differences: The Interaction of Nature and Environment

We all probably have childhood memories of meeting some of our parents' friends for the first time and of having to stand by with a tolerant smile while they chattered on about how much we resembled Mom or Dad or Aunt Tilly or Uncle Ned. Thinking about it for a moment, you can probably recall innumerable instances of being told you have your mother's eyes or your father's chin.

In recollecting these experiences, we are doing more than just reminiscing about the little indignities of childhood. Rather, we are beginning to get an inkling of the extent to which most people incorporate the idea of inheritance into their understanding of the world around them. Not only do we learn from others how much we physically resemble our kin, but we also often hear about the behavioral traits we have inherited as well. You may have been told, for instance, that you are stubborn like your father, or outgoing like your mother. Of course, this kind of explanation for our actions and appearance can come in handy at times. It allows us to rationalize, for example, that the inability to find a pair of jeans that fits properly is because of the large bone structure passed on from our mother's side, rather than recent overindulgence in pepperoni pizza.

Undoubtedly, the notion that genetics is responsible for who we are socially, as well as physically, holds considerable appeal. Not surprisingly, it has been very popular as a way of explaining many of the differences we observe between men and women. In this chapter, we will examine some of the available scientific evidence on the genetic causes of these sex differences. We will review research on both animals and humans, and will discuss the significance of studies of genetic abnormalities for our understanding of sex differences. We will also examine the possible effects of other biological factors on gender, particularly the role of hormones, and the influence of the size and structure of our brains. In short, we will be discussing in greater detail the relationship between (biological) sex and (social) gender that we introduced in Chapter 1. To make sense of all this, however, we need some knowledge of how we become male or female in the first place. Let's begin, therefore, by discussing the process of sexual differentiation—a process that begins not long after conception.

THE SEX CHROMOSOMES AND SEXUAL DIFFERENTIATION

Human development is extraordinarily complex. Consider the process of sexual differentiation, for example. Typically—although not always, as we'll see shortly—a person is born with forty-six chromosomes arranged in twenty-three pairs, one of each pair contributed by the individual's mother and one by his or her father. One pair of chromosomes is referred to as the *sex chromosomes* because it plays the primary role in determining whether a fertilized egg will develop into a male or a female fetus. The sex chromosomes of a genetically normal male consist of one X and one Y chromosome, while genetically normal females have two X's. Thus, since the mother of a child always contributes an X to the sex chromosome pair, it is the father's genetic contribution that determines the child's sex.

It is not until the sixth week of embryonic development that the process of sexual differentiation begins. This means that from the moment of conception until the sixth week of their development, all embryos, be they XX or XY, are *sexually bipotential*; they are anatomically identical, each possessing the necessary parts to eventually develop as a male or a female. One scientist explains it this way:

> During this early period each develops an embryonic gonad dubbed the "indifferent gonad" because of its sameness in both XX and XY embryos. In similar fashion the other internal structures of both the male and female reproductive systems begin to form, so that by the first month and a half of embryonic development all the embryos, regardless of which sex chromosomes are inside their cells, have a set of female (müllerian) ducts as well as a set of male (wolffian) ducts . . . (Fausto-Sterling 1985:78).

What happens during week six? Scientists are not entirely certain, but with regard to the development of a male fetus at least, they do know that the Y chromosome is involved. The presence of a Y chromosome, it seems, triggers a chain reaction during the sixth week of embryonic growth which eventually results in the development of a fully recognizable male fetus. More specifically, the genetic information on the Y chromosome helps to stimulate the production of a protein called *H-Y antigen,* which in turn appears to promote the transformation of the indifferent gonad into fetal testes. The fetal testes then begin to synthesize a whole group of hormones called *androgens.* Two of the most important androgens are müllerian inhibiting substance (MIS) and testosterone. MIS causes the degeneration of the female duct system, whereas testosterone promotes the further growth of the male (wolffian) duct system. (It is testosterone that will figure prominently in our discussion of behavioral and personality differences between the sexes.) Meanwhile, the secretion of the hormone dihydrotestosterone during week eight prompts the formation of the external genitals. The genital tubercule (another bipotential structure like the indifferent gonad) develops into a penis, and the surrounding tissue becomes a scrotum (Fausto-Sterling 1985; Baker 1980).

What about the development of a female fetus? Unfortunately, scientists are less clear about this process. Traditionally, it was argued that the absence of a Y chromosome and the subsequent lack of testosterone production prompt the indifferent gonad of an XX embryo to transform into ovaries at about the twelfth week of gestation. Recent research, however, suggests an alternative hypothesis. There is evidence that the gonad of an XX embryo begins to synthesize the hormone estrogen (often referred to as one of the "female sex hormones") around the same time that an XY embryo starts to produce testosterone. Some scientists now theorize that fetally synthesized estrogen may be responsible for the development of the female genitalia in much the same way that androgens are involved in male genital development (Fausto-Sterling 1985). Much more research is needed before the entire puzzle of sexual differentiation is solved.

Figure 2.1 summarizes the process of sexual differentiation in the human embryo. We know that males and females are identical in their development until the sixth week of gestation. At that point, it appears that the chromosomes, along with various hormones, come into play to help produce those physical differences between the sexes of which we are all very aware. However, the question remains as to whether chromosomes and hormones contribute in any way to the behavioral and personality differences we often observe between males and females. One of the ways scientists have attempted to uncover the effects of these two factors on gender is to study cases involving genetic and hormonal abnormalities. Let's take a brief look at some of this research.

Prenatal Mishaps: What Can They Teach Us about Gender?

What if a female fetus is somehow exposed to androgens? When she is born, will she behave like a girl or a boy? Or, suppose that because of a genetic malfunction, the cells of a male fetus are insensitive to the androgens it secretes—will that child grow up to be masculine or feminine? Mishaps such as these actually do occur, although fortunately they are rare. When they occur, however, they provide researchers with a unique opportunity to gauge the effects of the sex chromosomes and hormones on the development of gender. The classic research in this area has been conducted by John Money, Anke Ehrhardt, and their associates at the Johns Hopkins University Gender Identity Clinic.

The first situation we have described here is referred to as *adrenogenital syndrome* (AGS). It is caused by a malfunction in the mother's or the female fetus's adrenal glands or from exposure of the mother to a hormone that acts upon the fetus like an androgen. The result is a baby whose chromosomal sex is female and who has the internal reproductive organs of a female, but whose external genitals are masculinized (i.e., the clitoris is enlarged and resembles a small penis).

Money and Ehrhardt interviewed twenty-five fetally androgenized females who came to the Gender Identity Clinic for treatment. The researchers questioned the girls (who ranged in age from four to sixteen) about their clothing preferences, how they liked to spend their leisure time, their goals for the future, and so on. They then compared the girls' responses with those of twenty-five other girls, similar to the research subjects in age and other social characteristics, but without AGS. The findings did reveal some striking differences between AGS patients and normal girls. For one thing, AGS girls described themselves as tomboys more often than normal girls did, and they preferred to dress the part, wearing slacks and shorts more often than dresses. They also expressed a preference for toys considered more appropriate for boys and showed a greater interest in pursuing a career than did non-AGS girls. Nevertheless, AGS girls were not more physically aggressive than normal girls, and each expressed a desire for romance, marriage, and motherhood in the future (Baker 1980; Money and Ehrhardt 1972).

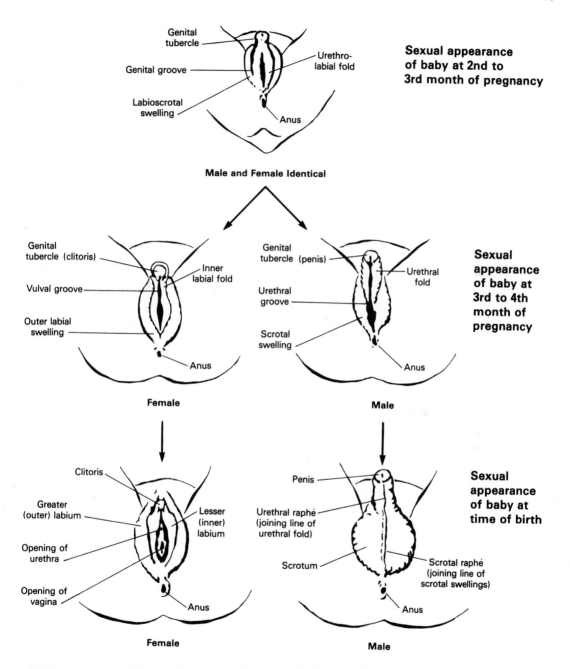

FIGURE 2.1 External Genital Differentiation in the Human Fetus. Source: Money, John and Anke A. Ehrhardt. *Man and Woman, Boy and Girl.* The Johns Hopkins University Press, Baltimore/London, 1973, Fig. 3.2, p. 44.

What about boys who prenatally were insensitive to androgens? They have a condition known as *androgen-insensitive syndrome*. Individuals who are androgen-insensitive are sometimes referred to as "*XY* females" owing to the fact that, although they possess the sex chromosomes of normal males (*XY*), their testes do not descend and they are born with the external genitalia of females. Because they look like girls at birth, they are typically raised as girls by their parents. But do their *XY* chromosomes predispose them to behave masculinely? According to Money, Ehrhardt, and others, androgen-insensitive individuals are as feminine (and sometimes more feminine) than normal *XX* females. In one study, for example, androgen-insensitive subjects expressed as pronounced an interest in dolls, dresses, housewifery, and motherhood as did normal girls who were identical to them in terms of age, race, social class, and IQ (Baker 1980; Brooks-Gunn and Matthews 1979; Frieze, et al. 1978; Money and Ehrhardt 1972).

In a moment we will discuss the strengths and weaknesses of this kind of research. First, though, let's look at two other types of prenatal mishaps and whether they appear to influence the gender of individuals affected by them. One such condition is called *Turner's Syndrome*; it occurs when a fertilized egg receives only one sex chromosome, an *X,* as opposed to the normal pair. "Since these individuals have neither a *Y* chromosome nor two *X* chromosomes, they have no gonadal tissue and consequently are unable to produce gonadal hormones" (Frieze, et al. 1978:89). Yet research with Turner's Syndrome females reveals an exaggerated femininity in their behavior and personalities. Turner's Syndrome females showed "a lower frequency of being labeled a 'tomboy,' preferring or content to be a girl, a higher interest in 'frilly dresses,' extensive preference for girls rather than boys as playmates, play only with dolls versus boys' toys, and a strong, actively expressed interest in infant care" (Baker 1980:87; Money and Ehrhardt 1972).

Finally, we may consider the condition known as *hermaphroditism*. Hermaphrodites are individuals in whom sexual differentiation is ambiguous or incomplete. In one case studied by Money and Ehrhardt, for instance, a chromosomally normal (*XY*) male was born with a penis just one centimeter long (resembling an enlarged clitoris) and a urinary opening similar to that of a female. The parents opted to surgically "reassign" the child's sex and rear it as a girl. Following up on the case three years later, Money and Ehrhardt reported on the child's overt femininity. She preferred "girlish toys" (such as Cinderella's glass slippers) and especially enjoyed dancing with her father when he arrived home from work (Money and Ehrhardt 1972).

What, if anything, can these studies of prenatal mishaps teach us about gender? Many scientists urge caution in interpreting the findings because of the serious weaknesses inherent in the research itself (Rogers and Walsh 1982). We can easily see, for example, that the researchers had to rely on information from very small, atypical groups of individuals. What is more, although they frequently matched the research subjects with a control group similar in various social characteristics, other important factors were ignored. The research on AGS females, in particular, has been strongly criticized for this reason. For instance, the AGS subjects were familiar with the researchers and were already comfortable with the clinical setting in which the research took place. "Thus, it is possible that the results reflect a greater willingness of the androgenized girls to mention cross-sex-typed attitudes and behaviors more than this being a true behavioral difference between the patient group and the control group" (Frieze, et al. 1978:88). In addition, the researchers themselves were aware of which subjects were AGS females and which were normal girls. "Such knowledge could lead to nonconscious but nevertheless inaccurate assessments of the behavior of AGS patients" (Fausto-Sterling 1985:137; Logino and Doell 1983).

Despite these and many other problems, however, this research does offer us an important lesson with regard to the relationship of chromosomes and hormones to gender. It suggests that the development of a masculine or feminine gender identity is quite independent of either the presence of a pair of *XY* or *XX* sex chromosomes, or the production of particular hormones. Indeed, this research highlights the important distinction that we made in Chapter 1 between sex and gender. It should be clear to us at this point that sex is a biological given; it is the result of a complex interaction between chromosomes and hormones, which ultimately determines whether an individual will develop *physically* as a male or a female. Gender, on the other hand, refers to attitudes and behaviors—what we generally call masculinity and femininity. Far from being an either/or phenomenon, though, gender embraces a broad spectrum of behaviors and social expectations that we acquire during our lifetimes through interactions with one another and our experiences in various environments. As Money and Ehrhardt's research illustrates, what appears to be more important in the acquisition of gender than our specific sex chromosomes is the sex that our parents assign to us and use as a guide in rearing us. This is a topic to which we will return in Chapter 4.

Of course, there's more to the debate over the effects of chromosomes and hormones on gender than what we have discussed so far. To understand the controversy a bit better, we will next examine some of the research on sex differences between genetically normal males and females.

SEX DIFFERENCES IN INFANTS: MUCH ADO ABOUT NOTHING?

A considerable amount of the research on sex differences utilizes infants as subjects under the assumption that the younger the subject, the lesser the impact of environmental influences on his or her behavior. "If sex differences in behavior are found at or near birth, there is reason to suspect that biology contributed to this difference. In contrast, if the sex differences do not appear until later in life it is difficult to determine whether biology is responsible for behavioral differences or not" (Frieze, et al. 1978:73).

Most of the differences scientists test for are those suggested by adult gender stereotypes. A *stereotype* is an oversimplified summary description of a group of people. There are positive and negative stereotypes, and virtually every group in our society has been stereotyped at one time or another; the sexes are not exceptions. **Gender stereotypes,** then, are simplistic descriptions of the supposedly "masculine male" or "feminine female." Most people conceive of these in bipolar terms, that is, a normal male supposedly lacks any feminine traits, and a normal female lacks masculine traits (Deaux and Kite 1987). Thus, gender stereotypes are all-inclusive; every member of one sex is thought to share the characteristics that constitute their respective gender stereotype. The reality, as we will learn in this chapter, is that many members of each sex do not conform to their stereotyped images. Sometimes this may be looked upon favorably by others, but often a nonconformist is labeled deviant, abnormal, or bad and is treated as such.

Some commonly held gender stereotypes include the beliefs that males are supposed to be independent, females dependent; males are better at spatial tasks, females at verbal skills; and males are aggressive, females passive. Do little babies behave this way? To find out, let's consider the evidence for each hypothesized sex difference in turn. Keep in mind, however, that difference does not imply inequality. Prevalent stereotypes may predispose us to rank any differences we observe, but the differences themselves have no inherent hierarchical order.

Independence vs. Dependence

According to Eleanor Maccoby and Carol Jacklin (1974), two social scientists who have extensively researched sex differences, dependence is one of the two most frequently studied behaviors that is presumed to be associated with sex. (The other, aggression, will be discussed shortly.) Scientists usually measure dependency in terms of what is called **separation anxiety**: the level of distress exhibited by a child if its parent leaves the room, and the extent to which the child clings to its parent or seeks the parent's help when placed in novel situations.

In one famous study of dependency, researchers Goldberg and Lewis (1969) reported findings that affirmed the female/dependent, male/independent gender stereotype. Goldberg and Lewis's observations revealed that eleven-month-old girls tended to play quietly, close by their mothers in the laboratory setting, whereas same-age boys were more active and tended to venture away from their mothers to explore their new environment. In addition, when the children were separated from their mothers by a barrier, the little girls usually just stood and cried, while the little boys tried to figure a way to remove the barrier.

Fascinating as the Goldberg and Lewis study may be, research by numerous other scientists contradicts their findings. For example, Maccoby and Jacklin (1974) reviewed twenty studies of dependency behaviors in children under two years of age. Twelve of the studies showed no sex differences. The results of the remaining eight were inconsistent—boys were more dependent in some cases; girls were more dependent in others. Similarly, another study reported by Brooks-Gunn and Matthews (1979) found that although girls do tend to play close to their mothers, boys are not as adventurous as the Goldberg and Lewis research made them out to be. The boy infants in this study played just a few feet from their mothers, and they also got more upset than the girls at the prospect of their mothers leaving them.

Given the inconsistent nature of the research findings, there does not seem to be much evidence to support the notion that girl infants are any more dependent than boy infants. Instead, we agree with the conclusions drawn by Maccoby and Jacklin almost two decades ago:

> [T]he picture as a whole is quite clearly one of sex similarity rather than sex difference. . . . Clinging to parents or other caretakers, or remaining near them under conditions of uncertainty or anxiety, is a characteristic of *human* children . . . (1974:201, emphasis added).

Visual Ability vs. Verbal Ability

In Chapter 5, we make note of the fact that few female college graduates are awarded degrees in fields such as architecture and engineering. Rather, they are concentrated in majors such as literature, education, and library science. Some observers of this trend maintain that it is because of men's superior visual-spatial skills and women's greater verbal prowess. Certainly it is the case among adults that men outperform women in solving visual-spatial problems, whereas women are the higher scorers on tests of verbal ability. But are these differences present in very young children, thereby suggesting a biological basis for their development? To answer that question, researchers have focused their attention on the visual and auditory responses of male and female infants.

Studies of infants' visual abilities use a variety of different measures. Often, the infant's eye movements are recorded as he or she is shown some visual stimulus. In addition, the infant's interest in the visual stimulus is frequently measured in terms of the length of time he or she looks at it. Such studies, however, yield few findings of sex differences. Maccoby and Jacklin (1974), for instance, reviewed nine studies of newborns and thirty-three of infants from one to twelve months old. They report no difference for the newborns, but inconsistent findings with regard to the infants: "For most samples and most stimuli, sex differences are not found. When a difference is found, it favors one sex nearly as often as the other, with a slight balance in favor of boys" (Maccoby and Jacklin, 1974:28). There is some evidence that males are more sensitive than females to bright light and are better able to detect subtle differences in lighting, but it is unclear how this may influence their visual-spatial skills (McGuinness 1985).

Significantly, other tests using older children (from age two) and including a spatial component (e.g., asking subjects to find certain objects camouflaged in a larger picture) show no significant sex differences *until adolescence* (Fausto-Sterling 1985; Maccoby and Jacklin 1974). We will offer an explanation for this "late-blooming" difference in Chapter 5. For now, however, we wish to note that while adolescent and adult males in the United States display stronger visual-spatial skills than their female counterparts, this pattern is not found in all societies. For example, studies of Canadian Eskimos show no sex differences in males' and females' visual-spatial skills, indicating that the pattern observed in our own society may be more culturally than biologically induced (Harmatz and Novak 1983). Even among Americans, actual sex differences in visual-spatial ability are not large, with studies reporting less than 5 percent variation. In addition, the amount of difference discovered varies significantly depending on the type of spatial test used in the research (Deaux and Kite 1987).

What about sound and vocalization? Everyone is probably familiar with the stereotype that women are naturally talkative so that, on some level, the idea that girls are more responsive to sound and vocalize earlier than boys makes sense. In looking at available scientific evidence, however, we once again find more similarity than difference between the sexes. With regard to responsiveness to sound (audition), for example, the research findings either are inconsistent or reveal no differences. In most studies, male and female infants respond similarly to sound, but in a few studies the results depended on what the sounds were and how responsiveness was measured. In some cases, boys appeared more responsive, whereas in others, girls were more responsive (Maccoby and Jacklin 1974).

There is some evidence that girls vocalize earlier and more often than boys, but the large number of studies reporting no differences makes this finding less impressive (Sherman 1978; Maccoby and Jacklin 1974). There is some evidence that females vocalize more in response to human faces, whereas males verbalize to inanimate objects and blinking lights (McGuinness 1985), thus lending support to the notion that females are naturally more social than males. However, it appears that environmental influences may be at the root of any differences that are observed. For instance, cross-cultural research again indicates that female verbal superiority is not universal (Safir 1986; Harmatz and Novak 1983). Studies in the United States have also found that male infants tend to babble as much as female infants, but that female infants vocalize more in response to their mothers. However, they also report that mothers talk more to infant daughters than to infant sons. "This raises the age-old question—which came first: girls' interest in and responsivity to speech or mothers' more loquacious style with their daughters?" (Brooks-Gunn and Matthews 1979:70). We will return to this question in Chapter 4, but for now the research findings lead us to conclude that the differences in visual-spatial ability and verbal skills that we observe in adult men and women are not present to any significant degree in infants.

Aggression vs. Passivity

Research on aggression has yielded some of the most consistent findings of sex differences in behavior, at least among school-age children. The results of these studies repeatedly show males to be more aggressive than females. The research findings of infant studies are less clear, however, and a large part of the ambiguity rests with the problem of measuring aggressiveness in infants. Many of us would probably define aggression as actions intended to hurt other people, either physically or psychologically. It is difficult, though, to imagine an infant harboring such motives.

Consequently, scientists have had to rely on other (often questionable) indicators of aggression in infants. One commonly used measure is the infant's activity level. Researchers have counted the number of hours a baby sleeps, how much the baby moves when awake, the vigor of the movements, and so on, under the assumption that the highly active baby may grow into the aggressive youngster or adult. You may already have detected some of the weaknesses in this kind of research, but before we discuss them, let's review the findings.

Early research indicated that male infants, on average, sleep approximately one hour less than female infants do, although the findings of subsequent studies are inconsistent (Frieze, et al. 1978; Maccoby and Jacklin 1974). What is more certain is that when children are awake, there are no significant sex differences in their activity levels. This appears to be the case for both infants and toddlers. Female infants kick and wave their arms as often and as vigorously as male infants do, and male and female toddlers tend to engage in equal amounts of running, tricycle riding, and fidgeting during quiet times (Maccoby and Jacklin 1974; Pedersen and Bell 1970). As two astute observers concluded, it's hard to imagine a healthy eight-month-old who just sits quietly in a living room without reaching for stereo knobs, lamp cords, magazines, or knicknacks (Brooks-Gunn and Matthews 1979). By the time the children are preschool age, greater difference has emerged—boys tend to move more quickly from one activity to another, whereas girls have a longer attention span (McGuinness 1985)—but by this age, environmental influences have surely come into play.

Of course, one obvious, but nonetheless serious problem with this sort of research concerns whether or not activity level is a valid measure of aggression. There is considerable evidence that suggests that it is not. Various studies have found infant activity level to be a poor predictor of later childhood behavior (Maccoby and Jacklin 1974). One study, for instance, discovered that the most active newborn baby boys grew up to be rather passive preschoolers who preferred to quietly watch other children play rather than join in group activities (Bell, et al. 1971).

A second serious methodological weakness in this research concerns the extensive use of observers to record activity level as well as other indicators of aggression. Although some researchers use mechanical devices such as *actometers* in their studies, most rely on their own perceptions or on the judgments of observers to determine whether a specific behavior is exhibited by a subject. Observers are trained as to what to look for, but because they usually know the sex of the child they are watching, it is possible that nonconscious stereotyping comes into play, influencing what they see. Consider the case of "Baby X," for instance. In this experiment, one group of observers was told that the three-month-old baby they were watching was a boy, while another group was told that it was a girl. In fact, the baby was a boy, but the observers' descriptions of the behavior they saw depended on what sex they thought the child was. Those who believed they were observing a girl described the child as friendly, satisfied, and accepting, and "saw" the baby smile more than they thought a boy baby would (Sidorowicz and Lunney 1980).

In a similar study, male and female college students were shown a videotape of a baby reacting to a jack-in-the-box. At first, the baby is startled, and then it becomes agitated and starts to cry. Interestingly, observers who were told the baby was a boy described the reactions as anger, but those who thought it was a girl described the baby as frightened. The authors of this study conclude—and we find it difficult to disagree—that observed sex differences are frequently "in the eye of the beholder" (Condry and Condry 1976).

This point raises another important issue with regard to research on aggression. More objective indicators of aggression, such as hitting or name-calling, can easily be observed among older children. By that time, however, boys and girls have had considerable exposure to a variety of environmental influences, including television programs, the examples of their older brothers and sisters, and the rewards and punishments meted out by their parents. Thus, it is virtually impossible to sort out the extent to which these later sex differences are biologically determined or learned. Moreover, sex differences in aggression among adults are extremely small: "less than one-third of a standard deviation in the direction of greater aggression by men than women" (Eagly and Steffan 1986:323). This perhaps would not be worth emphasizing were it not for the fact that many scientists have tried to build their strongest case for innate sex differences using aggression research. Because their work generally is given a lot of media attention, it deserves a closer look from us.

The most common argument in favor of a biological basis for sex differences in aggression centers around the fact that men secrete higher levels of the hormone testosterone. (It is important to note here that both males and females produce the same sex hormones, but in different amounts; males secrete more testosterone and other androgens, while females produce more estrogen and progesterone.) The evidence linking testosterone to aggression comes largely from animal studies. Typically, in these experiments, laboratory animals (rats, mice, or monkeys) are injected with testosterone. The usual outcome is that, regardless of their sex, the animals show a significant increase in rough-and-tumble play and fighting behavior. A variation on this theme involves castrating newborn rats with the result that as they mature, they display little aggressive behavior.

Some people accept such findings as strong indicators that males are biologically programmed to be aggressive. However, there are many good reasons to be cautious about interpreting these results. First, further research has discovered a number of aggressive animal behaviors (e.g., offensive sideways movements) that appear to be unrelated to testosterone levels. Second, it has been shown that abnormally high levels of various hormones, not just testosterone, also increase fighting behavior in animals (Frieze, et al. 1978).

A third reason for caution is that while the research with rats provides the strongest evidence of a link between testosterone and aggression, we must keep in mind that there is tremendous variation in behavior among different animal species. Female gerbils and hamsters, for instance, are just as aggressive as the males of their species, without being injected with hormones (Fausto-Sterling 1985). Clearly, this variation points to the difficulty in generalizing about behavior from one species of rodents to another, let alone from rodents to human beings (Frieze, et al. 1978).

Moreover, the kind of experimental research that is possible with animals cannot be undertaken with humans for obvious ethical reasons. Reinisch's (1983) research, which studied twenty-five boys and girls who had been exposed to unusually high levels of androgens in utero, did show these subjects to be more aggressive than a group of control subjects. However, Reinisch used a paper-and-pencil test to measure aggression, which raises some serious methodological questions. Other researchers have measured testosterone levels in subjects' blood and then correlated this with various psychological tests of hostility or aggression. Rubin (1987:245) reports, though, that "there is no consistent correlation between various measures of hostility, aggression, and similar behavior, as determined both by rating scales and observed behavior, and circulating testosterone levels" (see also Jacklin 1988).

At the same time, studies abound which demonstrate that human social behavior is highly governed by the situation or context in which it occurs, and that this, in turn, may easily override the potential effects of hormones. In one experiment, for example, human subjects were injected with a hormone that was supposed to induce aggression, but they were subsequently placed in a peaceful environment. The result was that their observed behavior was also peaceful and sociable (Richardson 1981). Other studies show that females can be just as aggressive as males in certain situations—for instance, when they are rewarded for behaving aggressively or when they think no one is watching them (Hyde 1984; Frieze, et al. 1978). This research suggests that females may simply inhibit aggression because of social pressures to conform to a feminine or lady-like ideal; in the absence of such pressures, they may be as likely as males to express aggression. Additional research also indicates that females are more likely than males to perceive aggressive behavior on their parts as posing a danger to themselves and, therefore, may inhibit aggression when the likelihood of retaliation is high (Eagly 1987; Eagly and Steffan 1986).

Finally, it is important to understand that the relationship between a single hormone and specific behaviors, such as aggression, is neither as simplistic nor as direct as many of the animal studies would lead us to believe. Anne Fausto-Sterling (1985:130–131) provides an example worth quoting at length:

> Mired in the morass of arguments about testosterone and aggressive behavior, it is easy to forget that our bodies have a number of different hormonal systems, all of which interact with one another. . . . For example, people sometimes say in referring to a situation that made them angry, "that really got the adrenalin flowing." What they meant, of course, was that their brains translated their psychological state of anger into a chemical message which traveled through the

bloodstream to their adrenal glands. The glands responded by producing adrenalin, which in turn enabled people, quite literally (because of the dilated blood vessels), to get "hot under the collar," to become agitated, excited, to scream loudly—that is, to act angrily. . . . Under stress, during a fight, when angry, when engaging in behavior some might label aggressive, many different hormone levels change in the body.

It is erroneous, then, to conclude that it is the change in one hormone that causes behavioral changes, when in fact, several hormones may be changing simultaneously. It is also important to point out that a correlation between testosterone and aggression does not prove that the former causes the latter. In fact, there is evidence that the relationship may be the opposite: aggression leads to elevated testosterone levels (Jacklin 1988; Fausto-Sterling 1985).

Summing Up the Research on Early Sex Differences

Table 2.1 summarizes the findings on infant sex differences that we have discussed here. Contrary to popular stereotypes, male and female babies are more alike than they are different. This is not to say that there are no differences between them except anatomical ones, but interestingly, most of these run counter to the stereotypes too. For example, although we tend to think of males as physically stronger than females, boy babies are actually weaker and more vulnerable. Males are more likely to die of birth trauma and to suffer birth injuries and congenital defects, and they are more susceptible to infectious diseases during the first year of life. Males are also anywhere from one to six weeks less skeletally mature at birth than females (Jacklin 1988; Harmatz and Novak 1983; Brooks-Gunn and Matthews 1979). We will further explore some of the sex differences in males' and females' health in Chapter 12.

Virtually all of the well-known and much-discussed sex differences in behavior do not appear until later in life—some at nursery-school age and many not until adolescence—thus suggesting that we should turn our attention to the issue of how gender is *learned.* But before we do that, we are going to discuss two other popular topics in which a link between biology and gender has been hypothesized: brain lateralization and premenstrual syndrome.

THE CASE FOR HIS AND HERS BRAINS

The notion that men and women have different brains is an old one. Nineteenth-century scientists maintained, for instance, that women were less intelligent than men because their brains are smaller. When it was pointed out that elephants, then, should be more intelligent than men given the relative size of their brains, the argument was quickly modified. It was subsequently argued that the best estimate of intelligence could be obtained by dividing brain size by body weight.

TABLE 2.1
Infant Sex Differences: Fiction versus Fact

Fiction	Fact
Boys are independent; girls are dependent.	Few studies (e.g., Goldberg and Lewis 1969) support this gender stereotype. The vast majority of studies reveal either no sex differences or are inconsistent as to which sex is more or less independent (Maccoby and Jacklin 1974; Brooks-Gunn and Matthews 1979).
Boys have stronger visual abilities than girls do.	Studies of newborns report no sex differences in visual abilities, whereas studies of infants provide inconsistent findings (Maccoby and Jacklin 1974; Fausto-Sterling 1985; McGuinness 1985).
Girls are more verbal than boys are.	Studies of infants' responsiveness to sound either provide inconsistent findings or show no sex differences. The research on vocalization is also inconsistent in its findings, but most studies show no significant sex differences (Maccoby and Jacklin 1974; Sherman 1978; Brooks-Gunn and Matthews 1979; McGuinness 1985).
Boys are aggressive; girls are passive.	As measured by activity level, there are no sex differences in aggression among infants (Pedersen and Bell 1970; Maccoby and Jacklin 1974; Frieze, et al. 1978; Brooks-Gunn and Matthews 1979).

However, this hypothesis, too, was abandoned when it was discovered that by this measure, women were more intelligent than men (Harrington 1987; Fausto-Sterling 1985; Gould 1980). Today, the controversy centers not on the size or weight of men's and women's brains, but rather on how our brains are organized (Gornick 1982). Consider, for instance, the recent debates over the phenomenon of brain lateralization and its hypothesized effects on men's and women's behaviors and personalities.

This debate originated during the late 1960s as a result of research by Dr. Roger Sperry and his colleagues. Sperry knew that the human brain is divided into hemispheres, one left and one right, and that the hemispheres are connected by a mass of tissue and nerve fibers called the *corpus collosum.* What happens, Sperry asked, if the two halves of the brain are somehow disconnected?

To answer this question, Sperry studied a group of patients suffering from severe epileptic seizures who, as part of their treatment, had had their corpus collosa surgically cut. What he discovered from working with these "split-brain" patients was that each half of the brain appears to "specialize" in certain functions or tasks. This specialization is referred to as *hemispheric asymmetry* or **brain lateralization.** The left hemisphere (which controls the right side of the body) seems to be responsible for speech, among other things, whereas the right hemisphere (which controls the left side of the body) is thought to be responsible for such functions as visual perception.

Let's consider some of Dr. Sperry's findings. In one experiment, he asked tha patients to verbally identify or describe the object (a pencil) that they were holding in their left hands. The patients were unable to respond until the pencil was moved to their right hands. Yet, when blindfolded, each patient could pick out a pencil from an assortment of other objects (Sperry 1982).

What does all this have to do with gender? You may recall that earlier we mentioned that females tend to score higher than males on tests of verbal ability, whereas males on average outperform females on visual-spatial tasks. It was not long after Sperry's work was first published that some scientists began to speculate that these sex differences may be caused by the differential lateralization of males' and females' brains (Lambert 1978).

However, intriguing though it is, the phenomenon of brain lateralization is still poorly understood, and the research on its relationship to sex differences tends to be characterized by confusion and unresolved contradictions (Gornick 1982; Star 1979; Lambert 1978). First of all, scientists have relatively little knowledge of how the human brain works: "We have yet to understand how the brain thinks, and we know nothing about how, or even whether, the brains of two individuals . . . differ" (Fausto-Sterling 1985:48). In addition, scientific studies of brain lateralization and sex have yielded few consistent findings and seem to have generated more disagreement than understanding of the issues.

Still, let's assume for the moment that there is a relationship between brain lateralization and sex. For the sake of argument, we will say that females are "left-brain dominant" (giving them superior verbal skills) and males are "right-brain dominant" (giving them an edge in visual-spatial skills). Unfortunately, we are now confronted with the task of reconciling our gender stereotypes with the fact that "the left hemisphere, as well as being verbal, has also been characterized as intellectual, analytic, and business-like, while the right hemisphere has been characterized as spontaneous, intuitive, and experiential, as well as spatially skilled" (Frieze, et al. 1978:93). Clearly, the relationship between brain lateralization and sex is neither simplistic nor direct, even if such a relationship does indeed exist (Kimura 1987; Alper 1985; Springer and Deutsch 1985).

What seems to have been lost in the heat of the controversy over brain lateralization is one of Roger Sperry's most valuable insights. According to Sperry, the left and right hemispheres of healthy males and females function *independently,* and neither hemisphere is more complex nor more important than the other. Given this observation, it may be that scientists' time would be better spent pursuing answers to more fundamental questions about how the *human* brain works, instead of how men's and women's brains are different.

Nevertheless, there is evidence that suggests that, apart from the issue of lateralization, male and female brains may develop and be structured differently (Treadwell 1987). Much of this evidence comes from animal studies. Research on rats, for example, shows that the presence or absence of testosterone secretion during fetal development affects the cell structure of the *hypothalamus* (the part of the brain that controls the release of hormones at sexual maturity) and produces a male or female pattern of brain functioning. More specifically, at sexual maturity, females release hormones in a cyclic pattern, whereas male hormone levels remain relatively stable. "The extent to which this applies to humans, however, may be seriously questioned," and researchers caution us about the potential errors involved in drawing conclusions about human behavior based on such animal studies (Harmatz and Novak 1983:97). To date, there is little evidence indicating that sexual differentiation of the brain consequently predisposes human males and females to behave in gender-specific ways (Treadwell 1987).

Research on humans in this area is based on small, nonrandom samples and the results are preliminary. However, at least two studies have found that the corpus collosum (or part of it) is larger in women's brains than in men's brains. It is hypothesized that this may allow greater communication between the brain's two hemispheres and thus help to explain why women recover from strokes more quickly than men and are less likely to suffer certain types of brain damage (Witelson 1989). Still, other studies have failed to confirm this finding, and the significance of the research with respect to other sex differences in behavior remains purely speculative.

"MY HORMONES MADE ME DO IT": PREMENSTRUAL SYNDROME

In December 1980, in a town fifty-two miles northeast of London, thirty-seven-year-old Christine English drove her car at full speed directly at her boyfriend, pinning him to a telephone pole and killing him. She was subsequently convicted of manslaughter instead of murder, and she was released on probation because of a mitigating factor in her case: at the time of the crime, her defense attorney argued, English was suffering from a condition known as premenstrual syndrome

(PMS), which may cause those afflicted to behave violently. That same year, twenty-nine-year-old Sandie Smith was convicted of killing a co-worker at the London pub where she tended bar, but she too was sentenced to probation on the basis of the premenstrual syndrome defense. As a condition of probation, both English and Smith were required to receive monthly hormone injections to control their PMS symptoms (Glass 1982; Parlee 1982).

Understandably, these cases generated considerable controversy, not only in Great Britain, but also in the United States. Legal scholars worried that the courts would be flooded with cases in which female defendants would try to escape punishment for serious crimes by claiming that their behavior was a product of the stress caused by the onset of their monthly periods. Others used the cases to bolster their argument that women are naturally unfit for positions of responsibility and leadership. Dr. Edgar Berman, once the personal physician of Senator Hubert Humphrey, was often quoted on this matter. Said Berman:

> If you had an investment in a bank, you wouldn't want the president of your bank making a loan under those raging hormonal influences at that particular period. . . . There just are physical and psychological inhibitants that limit a female's potential (quoted in Parlee 1982:126).

This, of course, generated alarm among feminists. As one physician pointed out:

> I don't think anything is going to set back women's causes more than [PMS] . . . To let women think they become criminal once a month as a result of their

---

Postpartum Depression Syndrome   BOX 2.1

In early January 1989, Tanya Dacri, a twenty-year-old Philadelphia woman, told police her seven-week-old son had been kidnapped by two men at a shopping center. Within twenty-four hours, Ms. Dacri had been charged with the murder of the infant whom she had drowned in the bathtub, dismembered, and whose body parts she then disposed of in area rivers. Ms. Dacri's attorney asked that she be found not guilty by reason of insanity; she was suffering, it was argued, from *postpartum depression syndrome.*

By the time Ms. Dacri went to trial, there were about twenty-five similar cases in the United States, less than half of which had successfully used this defense. In England and Canada, however, a woman charged with killing her infant within one year of its birth cannot be found guilty of murder if it is determined that she was suffering from postpartum depression syndrome. Instead, she may only be found guilty of a special category of infanticide similar to manslaughter which carries a less severe sentence than murder (Conrad 1989).

Depression after the birth of a child, also called the "baby blues," is not uncommon and is thought to be caused by the sudden drop in estrogen levels in the woman's body that begins immediately after delivery. For a few weeks after giving birth, many women report feeling sad or irritable, and the major adjustments that accompany the onset of caregiving likely add to the feelings of stress. For most, the depression passes

physiology is to really debase the status of women. This is to say women are criminal by nature (quoted in Glass 1982:8C).

Several years have passed since the English and Smith trials. Much of the sensationalism surrounding PMS has died down, but the treatment of PMS has become a thriving business. In 1987, the American Psychiatric Association included PMS in its revised edition of the *Diagnostic and Statistical Manual of Mental Disorders,* arguing that sufferers of the condition could benefit from psychiatric treatment. More than seventy-five PMS treatment clinics are operating in the United States, and articles on PMS as a medical problem continue to appear in popular magazines (Chisler and Levy 1990). At the same time, other hormonally related syndromes are receiving increasing attention (*see* Box 2.1). However, a number of important questions remain unanswered: What is PMS? What causes it? and What are its real effects on women's personalities and behavior? The remainder of this section will address each of these questions.

Premenstrual syndrome has been called "the disease of the eighties," but it is not that new (Eagan 1983). In 1931, Dr. Robert T. Frank defined it as a " 'feeling of indescribable tension' occurring from 7 to 10 days before a period and causing 'unrest, irritability . . . and a desire to find relief by foolish and ill-considered actions' " (Vrazo 1983a:1K). PMS was further popularized in the 1950s through the work of Dr. Katharina Dalton. Dalton has claimed that her work demonstrates that women in the premenstrual phase of their monthly cycles

---

fairly quickly, but for about one in 1,000 new mothers, the depression turns into a psychosis involving hallucinations and delusions which requires hospitalization. It is estimated that about one percent of these women kill their babies; some kill themselves (Yen 1988).

Postpartum depression syndrome is still poorly understood and is not yet listed in the *Diagnostic and Statistical Manual of Mental Disorders* because it is not officially recognized as a distinct illness. Researchers warn that obstetricians can easily fail to see the psychosis developing because they usually send women home within three days of the birth and also because a case of the "blues" at this time is considered normal. However, researchers argue that if it is diagnosed early, postpartum depression syndrome can be treated effectively with medication (Gitlin and Passnau 1990; Yen 1988).

The warning signs of postpartum depression syndrome include sleeplessness (even when someone else is caring for the baby), irrationality, and panic attacks. It also appears that the disorder is more common after the birth of a second child. As one psychiatrist put it, "Dividing attention between an infant and a toddler increases the stress not just twofold but many times" (quoted in Yen 1988:18). Women who are isolated in the home and who lack family and social support networks also may be more prone to postpartum depression syndrome, illustrating again the link between biology and environmental conditions (Gjerdingen, et al. 1990).

become unreliable, irresponsible, accident-prone, and even violent and suicidal. She and others have estimated that anywhere from 20 to 100 percent of the female population suffers from premenstrual syndrome, with approximately 20 to 40 percent being mentally or physically incapacitated by it (Fausto-Sterling 1985; Frieze, et al. 1978).

Despite these sweeping claims, a *precise* definition of PMS has eluded scientists and physicians. Today, many define it simply as a "menstrual disorder," but one which encompasses up to 150 disparate symptoms, including headaches, bloating, cravings for salty or sweet foods, skin disorders, depression, shortness of temper, an inability to concentrate, and execution of sloppy housework (Chisler and Levy 1990; Fausto-Sterling 1985). Supposedly, "the key to recognizing PMS and differentiating it from anything else that might cause some or all of a woman's symptoms is timing. The symptoms appear at some point after ovulation (around mid-cycle) and disappear at the beginning of the menstrual period" (Eagan 1983:28). However, some women apparently experience symptoms throughout menstruation, leading some physicians and therapists to diagnose "perimenstrual (around menstruation) syndrome" (Young 1990), an even more vague term.

There is little consensus regarding the cause of PMS. One theory proposed by Dalton explains PMS as a hormone imbalance or deficiency. Several days before menstruation, production of the hormone progesterone by the adrenal glands drops. Since the adrenal hormones regulate such body functions as fluid retention, allergic reactions, and blood-sugar level, a drop in progesterone, and the subsequent imbalance this may cause relative to the other adrenal hormones, may provoke the physical and psychological symptoms of PMS (Frieze, et al. 1978). However, "there is *nothing* in the medical literature showing clearly what causes PMS; and there has never been a well-designed, controlled study here or in England of the effect of progesterone on PMS" (Eagan 1983:28, author's emphasis).

Other physical factors thought to be related to PMS are nerve irritability, an unbalance in electrolyte metabolism, and an increase in the enzyme monoamine oxidase (MAO). Research on the influence of this third factor is especially promising because MAO, found throughout the body and in the brain, has been linked to depression. Studies indicate that changes in estrogen and progesterone levels late in the menstrual cycle are associated with increases in MAO activity which, in turn, may cause negative moods, including depression (Frieze, et al. 1978; Paige 1975). But MAO activity is poorly understood, and "no physiological explanation has yet been adequately researched" (Frieze, et al. 1978:200). Another theory that has received some empirical support argues that PMS is caused by disturbances in circadian rhythms or what are typically called the body's "biological clocks." However, the most promising test of this theory to date utilized a sample of only sixteen women (eight with PMS and eight controls) (Parry, et al. 1991).

Physiological studies of the causes of PMS are lacking, and much of the available research is plagued by serious methodological flaws. For example, the majority of studies have relied on subjects' self-reports in determining the onset of premenstrual symptoms. However, this method is highly unreliable for several reasons. First, there is evidence that retrospective studies dependent on subjects' recall produce exaggerated results compared with prospective studies which begin with a sample of women who subsequently chart their cycles over several months (Sommer 1983; Koeske 1980). Second, Widom and Ames (1988:319) cite several studies that show that "there is a tendency for women with randomly occurring chronic mood changes to selectively remember those changes occurring during the premenstrual phase of the cycle." Third, and perhaps most important, several recent studies indicate that some PMS symptoms may be caused by social psychological factors. It has been argued, for example, that the attitudes toward menstruation prevalent in a particular culture may affect women's reactions to their monthly periods (Woods, et al. 1982). In the United States, menstruation has long been viewed as a negative event in a woman's life—at best it is an inconvenience, at worst, a "curse." Women have also been led to believe that they should restrict their behavior during their periods; they should not swim, bathe, or have sexual relations during that time.

Clarke and Ruble (1978) report that negative attitudes toward menstruation are learned by both girls and boys at an early age. Indeed, there is evidence that mothers often pass on to their daughters negative attitudes toward menstruation and these become manifested in negative menstrual experiences. Debra Neff's study of 101 mothers and daughters found that daughters whose mothers viewed menstruation as a debilitating, bothersome event report more pain, anxiety, and other negative changes during their periods than daughters whose mothers held more positive or neutral views (*Glamour* 1989).

Thus, it appears that if women are expected to be negatively affected by menstruation, then the negative expectations themselves may account for PMS. Additional research lends support to this argument. One researcher, for instance, asked a group of students to evaluate the behaviors of several hypothetical female patients. Included with each case was information about the patient's menstrual cycle. When the students thought that the patient was in the premenstrual phase of her cycle, they attributed any hostile, aggressive, or negative behaviors to biological causes; interestingly, they attributed positive behaviors during the same period to nonbiological factors (Koeske 1980). In a second experiment, psychologist Diane Ruble (1977) told a group of female subjects that physical tests indicated that they were in the premenstrual phase of their cycles. In reality, all the women were in another cycle phase, but they began to report PMS symptoms. "Expectations became reality, apart from actual bodily state" (Parlee 1982:127).

Given these findings, what actual behavioral or personality changes have been found to be related to the menstrual cycle, especially the premenstrual phase? The question is a difficult one to answer largely because the results of most studies are inconsistent. Some of the research on mood swings, for example, has found that women tend to feel less able to cope with everyday problems during the premenstrual phase of their cycles than during the ovulatory phase (Friedman, et al. 1980). But others report that negative changes in mood have more to do with stressful external events (e.g., the approach of final exams) than with the phase of the menstrual cycle (Golub 1980; Wilcoxon, et al. 1976). One study even found cyclical changes in mood to be correlated with the "social week": both male and female subjects tended to feel down on Tuesdays and Wednesdays, but happy and healthy on weekends. Interestingly, in this study, men reported more days per month that they experienced physical discomfort than women did (Rossi and Rossi 1977).

There is no evidence to support the notion that women's academic or work performance declines during the premenstrual phase of their cycles. In fact, a few studies show improved task performance premenstrually. Stewart and her colleagues, for example, report that of the 100 healthy women they studied, 66 reported at least one positive premenstrual change, including a higher energy level, greater creativity, and increased efficiency in getting work done (cited in Young 1990). The majority of studies, though, report no relationship between academic or work performance and menstrual cycle phase (Sommer 1983; Friedman, et al. 1980). Some researchers have observed a relationship between menstrual cycle phase and such psychophysiological functions as visual, auditory, and olfactory sensitivity; galvanic skin response; and spontaneous body movement. "However, the variations among findings are such that one could select studies to support almost any hypothesis one chose . . ." (Sommer 1983:82).

Certainly, these studies neither prove nor disprove the existence of PMS, but, taken together, they do allow us to roughly gauge the current state of scientific knowledge about the problem. In a nutshell, there are few definitive findings on PMS as a medical entity. Nevertheless, thousands of women seek treatment for PMS symptoms each year, and research in this area indicates that the side effects of many treatment programs may be worse than the condition itself. The most common treatment for PMS is the administration of the hormone progesterone, usually throughout the premenstrual phase of the cycle. Women who take progesterone, however, report a number of serious side effects, including chest pains, vaginal and rectal swelling, a lessened sex drive, and bleeding between periods. What concerns researchers even more are the long-term effects of progesterone treatments since laboratory tests have linked progesterone injections with increased rates of breast tumors and cervical cancer (Eagan 1983). In addition, some doctors report cases of progesterone addiction among their patients who begin to demand ever-increasing dosages because of the euphoric feelings it gives them (Vrazo 1983a).

Among the other common PMS treatments is the administration of megadoses of vitamin B_6, but this, too, is not without side effects. High doses of vitamin B_6 have been shown to cause nerve damage, leading to a loss of feeling in the fingers and toes (Fausto-Sterling 1985). And, of course, there is the issue of whether any of these treatments really work. In a careful review of the research on treating PMS, Dr. Judith Abplanalp (1983) discovered that placebos (inactive substances with no medicinal content) are just as successful in relieving PMS symptoms as are vitamins, hormones, and other drugs. What this means is that patients are as likely to report feeling better after taking sugar pills as they are after a dosage of vitamin B_6 or progesterone.

We must be careful not to interpret these findings to mean that what women experience during their menstrual cycles is "all in their heads." Nor is it to say that biological factors are insignificant in women's menstrual experiences; the menstrual cycle is clearly rooted in biology (Parlee 1982). Instead, the point we are trying to make is that, in light of our poor understanding of PMS and its effects, and given the impact of social factors on women's menstrual experiences, some caution should be exercised in pursuing a PMS "cure." Research on premenstrual syndrome has been conducted for more than fifty years, and scientists are still unsure of precisely what it is or what causes it. Meanwhile, thousands of women have been encouraged to seek treatment for PMS, using substances that *are known* to be detrimental to their health. Unfortunately, in our zeal to rid ourselves of the "disease of the eighties," we may end up producing more serious health problems for the 1990s.

THE INTERACTION OF BIOLOGY AND CULTURE

The issues we have explored in this chapter may best be summed up in a question: What is the direct evidence for hormonal or genetic control of specific gendered behaviors or personality traits? The answer, it appears, is very little, if any (Gould 1976). That this is the case in no way denies the vital role that biological factors play in the lives of men and women. Male or female, humans are a biological species. Too often, however, we conceive of the biological and the social as mutually exclusive categories, or as polar opposites when, instead, they are better understood as two essential parts of an interconnected system (Fausto-Sterling 1985). As one researcher concluded:

> I am suggesting, then, that children are born with personality characteristics that
> lead to behaviors, and that these behaviors are reacted to evaluatively by
> parents. . . . It is not, then, that children are born with a built-in set of responses
> that will determine their behaviors irrespective of environmental reactions. Nor is
> it true that children are "tabula rasa," or blank clay, destined to be molded solely
> by the imprint of a parental (and heavy) hand (Bardwick 1973:35).

In other words, biology, rather than *determining* who we are as males and females, instead establishes for us the broad limits of *human potential*. How each of us eventually thinks and behaves as a man or a woman is a product of the inescapable interaction between that potential and the opportunities and experiences to which we are exposed in our social environments. That these environments are diverse and that humans as a species exhibit great adaptability account for wide variations in behaviors and personalities not only *between* the sexes, but also *within* each sex.

It should be clear at this point that recognizing the potential influence of biology on gender is not incompatible with a feminist perspective (Rhode 1990; Koeske 1983). To focus only on the biological or the social is, at best, to tell just half the story. What feminists challenge, though, is the use of biological theories to justify gender inequality. As Janet Sayers (1987:68) has observed, "Preoccupation with sexual difference and inequality has tended to be particularly intense at those times when prevailing differences between the sexes seem most likely to be eroded." We may only speculate on the motives that underlie some scientists' tenacious attempts to establish that behavioral and personality differences between women and men are biologically based. To reiterate a point that we made at the outset of this chapter: the existence of difference, even if biologically caused, does not imply a hierarchical ordering, nor does it imply that one behavior or trait is inherently superior to another. That women and men are different in many ways is an observable fact; however, that either is discriminated against on the basis of these differences is a social injustice.

Feminists also object to *biological reductionism,* the tendency to reduce all sex differences to the level of biological imperatives. Were this the case, all men as a group would think and behave more or less identically. The same would be true for women as a group. And, perhaps more importantly, purposeful social change would be difficult, if not impossible. But men and women can and do act to change the conditions that they find harmful and oppressive about their existence; and we respond to our biological needs in a stunning variety of ways. In the next chapter, we will examine some of these diverse responses through a discussion of the social construction of gender in different cultures.

KEY TERMS

brain lateralization (hemispheric asymmetry)   the theory that the two sides of the brain (the right and left hemispheres specifically) control particular functions or skills

gender stereotypes   summary descriptions of masculinity and femininity that are oversimplified and generalized

premenstrual syndrome (PMS)   a menstrual disorder, the exact causes of which are unknown; there are up to 150 disparate physical, psychological, and behavioral symptoms

separation anxiety   the level of distress exhibited by a child if left alone by a parent; the extent to which the child clings to its parent or seeks the parent's help when placed in new situations; used as a measure of dependency in infants

SUGGESTED READINGS

Benderly, B. L. 1987. *The Myth of Two Minds.* New York: Doubleday.

Fausto-Sterling, A. 1985. *Myths of Gender.* New York: Basic Books.

Hare-Mustin, R., and J. Marecek. 1990. *Making a Difference.* New Haven, CT: Yale University Press.

Harrington, A. 1987. *Medicine, Mind, and the Double Brain.* Princeton, NJ: Princeton University Press.

Rhode, D. L. 1990. *Theoretical Perspectives on Sexual Difference.* New Haven, CT: Yale University Press.

Chapter 3

Ancestors and Neighbors:
Social Constructions of Gender at
Other Times, in Other Places

None of us was alive 5 million years ago when humans as a species diverged from the apes, but all of us probably think we have a pretty good idea of what life was like for our prehistoric ancestors. For most of us, the quintessential symbol of prehistory is the caveman: a hairy, club-wielding cross between a man and an ape, who fiercely protected the homefront and hunted wild animals to provide food for his dependents. Where do women fit into this scenerio? "If women appear at all, they are at the edge of the picture, placid-looking, holding babies, squatting by the fire, stirring the contents of a pot" (Bleier 1984:116).

"The theory that humanity originated in the club-wielding man-ape, aggressive and masterful, is so widely accepted as scientific fact and vividly secure in our popular culture as to seem self-evident" (Bleier 1984:115). Yet, this theory has been challenged recently by scientists uncovering new data and reexamining existing data. In this chapter, we will discuss the *Man the Hunter* theory of human evolution more fully, and we will review some of the major scientific criticisms that have been leveled against it. Our discussion will be based on evidence from three sources:

1. the archeological record, which includes fossil remains;
2. primatology, especially studies of living non-human primates, such as chimpanzees; and
3. anthropological studies of preindustrial societies which scientists believe may be replicas of the earliest human communities.

To begin, then, let's turn to the archeological evidence.

BONES AND STONES: THE ARCHEOLOGICAL RECORD

Scientists confront a number of problems when attempting to reconstruct evolutionary history. For one thing, archeological finds are relatively sparse and fragmentary and, as Ruth Hubbard (1990:67) points out, "behavior leaves no fossils." Scientists must rely on a few, very general clues—a jaw or skull (but often just pieces of them), some teeth, or chipped stones—as they try to solve the puzzle of how our early ancestors lived hundreds of thousands of years ago. The farther back in time we go, the less evidence we have and the more geographically spread out the puzzle is. For some periods, there is a "fossil gap"; for instance, no fossil remains have been discovered for the period between 8 or 9 million years ago and 4 or 5 million years ago—a gap of about 4 million years (Bleier 1984; Hubbard 1979). Adding to the difficulty is the fact that only certain types of material such as bone and stone can be preserved. Organic materials, such as reeds and other plants as well as wood and bark, decay (Bleier 1984; Tanner and Zihlman 1976). Consequently, "the fossil record available for study in no way represents an adequate sample of human populations once inhabiting the planet," nor of the foods they ate nor of the tools they used. "Even armed with the maximum amount of information currently available for study . . . the amount of knowledge we do *not* possess is so vast that no one can claim a definitive theory of human origin and evolution, either morphological or cultural" (Bleier 1984:122–123, author's emphasis). Theories about the history and process of human evolution remain, as John Dupre (1990:57) notes, at the level of "origin myths."

Despite these difficulties, however, archeologists and anthropologists have provided us with what by now has become a familiar account of prehistory focusing on Man the Hunter. According to this traditional reconstruction, some time between 12 and 28 million years ago, our ape ancestors were forced down out of the trees as the climate became dryer, causing their subtropical forest habitat to recede. One of their most important adaptations to life on the ground was **bipedalism:** the ability to walk upright on two feet. This freed their hands for reaching, grasping, and tearing objects; for carrying; and eventually, for using tools. However, bipedalism had other significant consequences as well. "Walking upright produced a narrower pelvis to hold the guts in position. Yet as language developed, brains and hence heads grew much bigger relative to body size" (Gough 1975:61). To compensate for these anatomical changes, offspring were born at an earlier stage of development than had previously been the case, making them more dependent on their mothers' care for survival. Obviously, females burdened with helpless infants could not roam very far in search of food, so the role of breadwinner was taken up by the males.

In assuming the responsibility of breadwinner, males faced a special challenge: the spread of indigestible grasses in their new savanna habitat made foraging for vegetation an unreliable food source. Gradually, hunting replaced foraging as the primary subsistence strategy, and meat became a central part of the early human diet. The most successful hunts were cooperative, so men banded together on hunting expeditions. This, in turn, led to the further evolution of their communication skills (in particular, language) and to the invention of the first tools (weapons for hunting and for defense). After a successful hunt, the men would share the kill and carry it back to their home bases where the women would prepare it for eating (Gough 1975).

This sexual division of labor—women as caretakers of home and children, and men as breadwinners and protectors—was adaptive; those who conformed to it enjoyed a distinct advantage in the struggle for survival. In addition, these mutually exclusive female and male roles gave rise to particular personality traits; women grew to be empathic, nurturing, and dependent, whereas men were daring, unemotional, and aggressive. Over time, these adaptive characteristics were also naturally selected for in the evolutionary process (Lovejoy 1981; Tiger and Fox 1971; Ardrey 1966).

It is hardly a coincidence that this depiction of prehistoric social life bears an uncanny resemblance to the traditional, middle-class nuclear family of Western societies. Anthropology, like most scientific disciplines, has been dominated by white, middle- and upper-middle-class men from Western industrialized countries, primarily the United States, Great Britain, and France. As we argued in Chapter 1, the values and beliefs of our society, as well as those of the specific groups to which we belong in that society, can strongly influence or bias our understanding of the world around us. Indeed, feminist anthropologists have identified two types of bias in the traditional Man the Hunter theory of human evolution: **ethnocentrism** and **androcentrism.**

To be ethnocentric means that one views one's own cultural beliefs and practices as superior to all others. Looking again at the Man the Hunter argument, we can see that it is ethnocentric in two ways. First, it inaccurately depicts contemporary Western gender relations as universal, both historically and cross culturally. In other words, it makes it seem as if the behaviors and traits that are typically viewed as masculine or feminine in modern industrial societies like the United States are the same for men and women everywhere and that they have remained basically unchanged throughout human history. Second, and perhaps more importantly, this argument implies that the contemporary Western model of gender relations is the only correct or appropriate model because it is natural and adaptive. We will return to these criticisms shortly, but for now let's examine the second type of bias inherent in the Man the Hunter perspective.

Androcentric means male-centered. The Man the Hunter theory clearly emphasizes male behavior, "with females having little or no part in the evolutionary saga except to bear the next generation of hunters" (Tanner and Zihlman 1976:585). Cooperation and sharing, competition and aggression, communication and the development of material technology are all seen as deriving from the exclusively male role of hunter. "Because both sexes are not included, because the interaction of their roles is not examined except in the most rudimentary sense, traditional reconstructions have been incomplete and misleading" (Tanner and Zihlman 1976:585).

Can the archeological record be interpreted in less androcentric terms? Feminist anthropologists think so. By reexamining existing evidence and uncovering new data, they have developed an alternative reconstruction of our prehistoric past which highlights the female role in human evolution. To begin, they point out that "the old notion of apes being forced into open country as forests receded is no longer tenable" (Tanner and Zihlman 1976:596). Instead, they maintain that our ape ancestors moved away from the forests as their numbers grew so as to avoid competition with the various species of monkeys and other animals living there. On the forest fringe and the open savanna, they found not just indigestible grasses, but a plentiful variety of foods, including nuts and seeds, fruits and berries, roots and tubers, eggs and insects, and several species of small animals, some of which burrowed underground. However, the successful exploitation of these food resources, as well as the need for protection and defense in the open savanna habitat, required the development of new survival strategies (Tanner and Zihlman 1976). One important adaptation was bipedalism, which freed the hands for other tasks, as discussed earlier.

Feminist anthropologists agree that the change to bipedalism prompted other physiological changes, including the birth of offspring at an earlier stage of development. But rather than forcing mothers and children to become dependent on males, these changes spurred females to be more innovative in their quest for food and in the defense of their young against predators (Bleier 1984). More specifically, males and females without offspring could forage at will, eat the food they found on the spot, and maybe save a little for later use. In contrast:

> Mothers with dependent infants and juvenile offspring needed to obtain larger amounts of food in order to feed them. Initially mothers probably shared premasticated food with relatively young offspring to supplement nursing. As the transitional hominids came to rely more fully on savanna foods, mothers collected more and came to share plant food with older offspring as well (Tanner and Zihlman 1976:599; Slocum 1975).

The mothers' food-gathering task was made more difficult by other physiological changes that were occurring, especially the loss of body fur. This meant that infants had to be carried, since they could no longer cling to the fur on their mothers' backs and abdomens the way ape offspring do. Consequently, "it would have been very important for mothers to invent baby slings to carry nursing babies on their backs, leaving their hands free for gathering" (Bleier 1984:131; Slocum, 1975). There were certainly plenty of natural resources from which to fashion such slings: vines, leaves, ostrich eggshells, and even human hair. Furthermore, "the idea and techniques for carrying babies could then have been extended to the idea of carrying food when it became possible or necessary to collect and carry more food than could be eaten on the spot" (Bleier 1984:131; Tanner and Zihlman 1976; Slocum 1975).

What feminist anthropologists are suggesting is that the first material technology was not weapons for hunting invented by males, but rather slings for carrying babies and food invented by females with dependent offspring. In addition:

> Because mothers had more reason to collect and carry food consistently, they would be most likely to select and modify appropriate objects regularly for use as digging tools and containers in order to make the job easier and quicker.
> Expansion of lever use combined with the idea of termiting probes formed a basis for exploiting underground food sources with an appropriately shaped piece of wood, stone, or bone. Such an implement, even if crude, could effectively dig out small burrowing animals and pry up roots and tubers that were close to the surface (Tanner and Zihlman 1976:599).

It appears, then, that meat probably made up a fairly small portion of the early human diet. The meat that was eaten came from small animals that were easily trapped and killed. Rarely was meat obtained from larger animals, but even then it was not necessarily the product of a successful, systematic hunt. Rather, it was more likely a fortuitous find, and the animal was sick, mired, or already dead (Gailey 1987; Bleier 1984). This hypothesis is clearly supported by the archeological record. For instance, the earliest archeological evidence for the hunting of large animals with weapons is only 100,000 years old. (Bows and arrows appeared just 15,000 years ago.) Older tools—small hand-sized stones dating as far back as about 2.5 million years ago—might have been used for cutting and scraping meat, but would not have made good weapons for killing animals (Bleier 1984; Longino and Doell 1983; Zihlman 1978). Moreover, archeological finds of early hominid teeth indicate that they were used primarily for grinding, most likely "to process tough or gritty food from the ground, characteristic of much vegetable food" (Tanner and Zihlman 1976:598).

In sum, a very different picture of human evolutionary history emerges from feminist anthropological theory. Females, far from being passive, dependent childbearers, were active technological innovators. They provided food for themselves and for their young, and defended against predators. Through the mother-infant bond, sharing and cooperation also developed. As offspring matured, mothers taught them basic foraging techniques. Both sons and daughters reciprocated their mother's early care by sharing the food they gathered with her as well as with their siblings and by helping her care for the very young. Instead of nuclear families, our early human ancestors probably lived in mother-centered kin groups with flexible structures. Mature group members of both sexes foraged for food, aided in group protection, and shared child care.

> Thus male and female kin contributed to the survival of their young relatives. With this support, mothers could have another offspring before the previous one was entirely independent. Without this involvement of kin—a social solution to a physical problem—birth spacing would have been extended to more than three or four years, leaving little time for reproduction in a species whose life span may have been little more than twenty years (Zihlman 1978:9; Gailey 1987; Tanner and Zihlman 1976; Slocum 1975).

Which reconstruction of prehistory is the correct one—Man the Hunter theory or feminist theory? We may never know, but the feminist perspective is of special value to us "since it opens the mind to the possibility of alternative arguments that are at least as plausible and logical as traditional androcentric versions" (Bleier 1984:133; Dupre 1990; Hubbard 1990). Equally important, feminist theory is not simply a counter theory to Man the Hunter, for it emphasizes the cooperative and interdependent nature of early gender relations in which members of *both sexes* were food providers, defenders of the social group, and caregivers to the very young (Bleier 1984; Haraway 1978). And finally, the feminist reconstruction receives considerable support from other data sources, including primatology and anthropological studies of contemporary foraging societies. Let's examine some of this evidence now.

OUR RELATIVES, THE CHIMPS

Because of the many gaps in the archeological record, scientists have sought additional sources of data to help them piece together our evolutionary past. Research on living, nonhuman primates has been especially useful in this regard.

Recent studies have identified close biological similarities between humans and various species of monkeys and apes, particularly chimpanzees. For example, the genes of humans and chimps are almost 99 percent identical (Tanner and Zihlman 1976). Therefore, "observing what living primates do as they adapt to the various environments in which they live should, in theory, throw some light on the social behavior of our ancestors" (Leibowitz 1975:23).

Of course, this approach is not without problems too. For one thing, "The women and men who have contributed to primate studies have carried with them the marks of their own histories and cultures. These marks are written into the texts of the lives of monkeys and apes, but often in subtle and unexpected ways" (Haraway 1989:2). Second, primate species vary widely in the extent to which there are both anatomical and behavioral differences between the sexes. Consequently, one can cite examples of virtually any behavior one is looking for simply by choosing a particular animal (Dupre 1990; Hubbard 1990). And third, "most scientists find it convenient to forget that present-day apes and monkeys have had as long an evolutionary past as we have had, since the time we went our separate ways millions of years ago" (Hubbard 1979:30). Nevertheless, keeping the limitations of these data in mind, many scientists, feminists included, maintain that much can be learned about human evolutionary history by studying present-day primates, especially our closest primate relatives, the chimps.

Early primate studies were much in the tradition of Man the Hunter theory (Haraway 1989). They characterized the primates ancestral to humans as killer apes, with the males of the species competing aggressively with one another for food and sexual access to females. Chimpanzee groups, like other primate herds, were said to be organized into *dominance hierarchies* with the largest male assuming the role of "leader" and being accorded special sexual privileges as well as top priority in the ordering for food distribution (Lovejoy 1981; Ardrey 1966). But more recent research raises serious doubts about the accuracy of these findings. For instance, we now know that chimpanzees are very sociable creatures and that they live in flexibly organized communities. Rather than a rigid hierarchical structure, it appears that "leadership" shifts frequently along with the composition of the group as a whole. The largest male is not necessarily "dominant" and has no prerogatives over others. Females, in fact, are often the initiators of sexual activity and may choose to mate with several males who each patiently wait their turn (Tanner and Zihlman, 1976; Leibowitz, 1975).

Both male and female chimps participate in food acquisition activities, and both prepare and use tools for these tasks. Contrary to earlier reports, chimpanzees are neither strict carnivores nor pure vegetarians. Like humans, they are *omnivores*—that is, they eat both vegetable foods and meat—although approximately 95 percent of their diet is made up of plants and fruits (Bleier, 1984; Teleki, 1975). Importantly, some of the meat that is eaten is obtained by "hunting"; groups of two to five adult chimps may cooperatively pursue, capture, and kill small prey (Teleki 1975). In any event, chimpanzees share food with one another, and it is age, genealogical relationship, and friendship that govern the distribution of food, not physical size or "dominance." Males share with members of both sexes, while females share almost exclusively with their offspring. Indeed, mother-offspring bonds, as well as sibling relationships, remain strong for chimps throughout their lives (Tanner and Zihlman 1976).

What does all of this tell us about the evolution of human gender relations? Some scientists remain skeptical about the value of primatological studies, and again we are reminded of the dangers of making generalizations about human behavior from observations of chimpanzees. Still, given that chimps are our closest primate relatives, studies of their behavior and modes of social organization may provide us with clues—albeit limited ones—about our ancestral roots. At the very least, such research raises the possibility that our prehuman ancestors, quite unlike "killer apes," lived in nonhierarchical groups characterized by sociability and cooperation among males and females. Interestingly, such gender relations are not unknown among contemporary human societies, as we will see next.

WOMEN AND MEN ELSEWHERE: ARE WESTERN CONSTRUCTIONS OF GENDER UNIVERSAL?

Earlier we discussed the ethnocentric bias of Man the Hunter theory. This perspective portrays male dominance and female subordination as historical and cultural universals. It assumes that men everywhere and at all times have been women's superiors and that the work men do is more important or more highly valued than women's work. Not surprisingly, this theory was developed largely by Western male anthropologists who were viewing other societies through the tinted lenses of their own culture. Assuming male dominance, they often overlooked women's roles in the societies they were observing, or they relied on male informants for data on women (Gailey 1987; Rogers 1978). The question, then, bears re-asking: Are Western constructions of gender universal?

More than fifty years ago, the pioneering anthropologist Margaret Mead answered that question in the negative based on her field research among three societies in New Guinea. Mead observed cultures in which men were expected to be timid and nurturant, but women could be described as aggressive and competitive (Mead 1935). Since Mead's work was published, more research has been done on cross-cultural variations in gender. Rather than lending support to the notion of the universality of Western constructions of gender or gender inequality, these studies reveal a rich assortment of patterns of gender relations throughout the world.

Every known society has a division of labor by sex (and also by age). However, what is considered men's work versus what is considered women's work varies dramatically from society to society. In some cultures, for instance, women build the houses; in others, this is men's work. In most societies, women usually do the cooking, but there are societies in which this is typically men's responsibility. In fact, looking at Table 3.1, we see that there are very few tasks

TABLE 3.1
The Division of Labor by Sex for 50 Tasks in 185 Societies

	Number of Societies in Which Task is Done By:					
TASK	Men Only	Men Predom- inantly	Both Sexes Equally	Women Predom- inantly	Women Only	% Male
1. Hunting large sea animals	48	0	0	0	0	100.0
2. Smelting of ores	37	0	0	0	0	100.0
3. Metalworking	85	1	0	0	0	99.8
4. Lumbering	135	4	0	0	0	99.4
5. Hunting large land animals	139	5	0	0	0	99.3
6. Woodworking	159	3	1	1	0	98.8
7. Fowling	132	4	3	0	0	98.3
8. Making musical instruments	83	3	1	0	1	97.6
9. Trapping small land animals	136	12	1	1	0	97.5
10. Boatbuilding	84	3	3	0	1	96.6
11. Stoneworking	67	0	6	0	0	95.9
12. Work with bone, horn, or shell	71	7	2	0	2	94.6
13. Mining/quarrying	31	1	2	0	1	93.7
14. Bonesetting/surgery	34	6	4	0	0	92.7
15. Butchering	122	9	4	4	4	92.3
16. Collecting wild honey	39	5	2	0	2	91.7
17. Clearing land	95	34	6	3	1	90.5
18. Fishing	83	45	8	5	2	86.7
19. Tending large animals	54	24	14	3	3	82.4
20. Housebuilding	105	30	14	9	20	77.4
21. Preparing soil	66	27	14	17	10	73.1
22. Netmaking	42	2	5	1	15	71.2
23. Ropemaking	62	7	18	5	19	69.9
24. Generating fire	40	6	16	4	20	62.3
25. Bodily mutilation	36	4	48	6	12	60.8
26. Preparing skins	39	4	2	5	31	54.6
27. Gathering small land animals	27	3	9	13	15	54.5
28. Planting crops	27	35	33	26	20	54.4
29. Making leather goods	35	3	2	5	29	53.2
30. Harvesting	10	37	34	34	26	45.0
31. Tending crops	22	23	24	30	32	44.6
32. Milking	15	2	8	2	21	43.8
33. Basketmaking	37	9	15	18	51	42.5
34. Burden carrying	18	12	46	34	36	39.3
35. Matmaking	30	4	9	5	55	37.6
36. Tending small animals	19	8	14	12	44	35.9

continued

TABLE 3.1 (*Continued*)

	Number of Societies in Which Task is Done By:					
TASK	Men Only	Men Predom- inantly	Both Sexes Equally	Women Predom- inantly	Women Only	% Male
37. Food preservation	24	2	3	3	40	32.9
38. Loom weaving	18	0	6	8	50	32.5
39. Gathering small sea animals	11	4	1	12	27	31.1
40. Gathering fuel	25	12	12	23	94	27.2
41. Making clothes	16	4	11	13	78	22.4
42. Preparing drinks	15	3	4	4	65	22.2
43. Pottery making	14	5	6	6	74	21.1
44. Gathering wild vegetables	6	4	18	42	65	19.7
45. Dairy production	4	0	0	0	24	14.3
46. Spinning	7	3	4	5	72	13.6
47. Laundering	5	0	4	8	49	13.0
48. Fetching water	4	4	8	13	131	8.6
49. Cooking	0	2	2	63	117	8.3
50. Preparing vegetables	3	1	4	21	145	5.7

Source: Adapted from G. P. Murdock and C. Provost, "Factors in the Division of Labor by Sex: A Cross-Cultural Analysis," *Ethnology* 12:207; and D.S. Eitzen, *In Conflict and Order,* Boston: Allyn and Bacon, Inc.

from which either sex is completely excluded. The exceptions appear to be hunting, the smelting of ores, metalworking, and lumbering. According to the table, there are no societies in which women smelt ores and very few in which women participate in hunting, metalworking, and lumbering. Some researchers also have argued that in virtually all societies men hold a monopoly on the use of physical violence (e.g., Konner 1982), but others have reported on female warriors and soldiers (e.g., Sacks 1979). There is also considerable evidence that women may behave as aggressively as men, especially when competitiveness and verbal abusiveness are included as measures of aggression (e.g., Frodi, et al. 1977).

Of particular interest to us, however, are gender relations in contemporary **foraging societies.** Anthropologists maintain that these societies are probably most like the communities of our earliest human ancestors (O'Kelly and Carney 1986). This is not to say that the present-day foraging society is an exact replica of prehistoric social organization; these societies, like all others, have experienced numerous environmental and social changes throughout their histories, not the least of which came through contact with European and American colonizers during the past 600 years (Bleier 1984; Etienne and Leacock 1980). But as the smallest (25 to 200 members) and least technologically developed of all human societies, contemporary foraging peoples may offer us further clues as to how our early ancestors lived, while teaching us valuable lessons about the diversity of social constructions of gender today.

Gender Relations in Contemporary Foraging Societies

The **foraging society** is also referred to as the *hunting-gathering society* because its members meet their survival needs by hunting game (and often by fishing) and by gathering vegetation and other types of food in their surrounding environment. Just who performs each task, however, varies somewhat from society to society. The pattern most frequently observed is one in which men hunt large animals and go deep-sea fishing if possible, while women take primary responsibility for gathering and for hunting small animals as well as for food preparation, home building, and child care (O'Kelly and Carney 1986). In most societies, though, in spite of a clear division of labor by sex in principle, in practice there is actually considerable overlap in what men and women do and there are "crossovers in role," as Gilmore (1990) refers to them, without shame or anxiety for women or men.

O'Kelly and Carney (1986:12–21) have identified six different patterns of the gendered division of labor among hunting and gathering societies:

1. men hunt, women process the catch;
2. men hunt, women gather;
3. men hunt, men and women gather;
4. men hunt and fish, women hunt and gather;
5. men and women independently hunt, fish, and gather;
6. men and women communally hunt and gather.

In the first type, which is common among Eskimo groups, meat and fish are the dietary staples, and men are the chief food providers. This puts women at a disadvantage relative to men; they are dependent on men for food as well as for goods obtained through trade with non-Eskimos. Consequently, men in these societies have more power and prestige than women, but this does not mean that women are powerless or that women's work is considered unimportant. Women may secure power and prestige as shamans, and elderly women may act as political and military advisors. What is more, women are responsible for making the clothing and much of the equipment men need to hunt and fish (O'Kelly and Carney 1986). As a result, "the skills of women are as indispensable to survival as are those of men, and they are so perceived by men. . . . The question, 'Which is better (or more important), a good hunter or a good seamstress?' is meaningless in Eskimo; both are indispensable" (quoted in Sacks 1979:89–90).

Despite the complementarity of gendered behaviors in hunting-gathering societies of this first type, they are the least egalitarian of all hunter-gatherers. Women who live in societies characterized by one of the five other previously listed patterns take a more direct and active role in food acquisition, which in turn affords them more equal access to their societies' resources and rewards. Among the !Kung bush-living people of the Kalahari Desert, for example, women provide from 60 to 80 percent of the society's food through their gathering activities. The !Kung division of labor conforms to the second type on our list, but the game hunted by men is a much less dependable food source than the plant and small animal food obtained by women. !Kung women are respected for their specialized knowledge of the bush; "successful gathering over the years requires the ability to discriminate among hundreds of edible and inedible species of plants at various stages in their life cycle" (Draper 1975:83). In addition, women return from their gathering expeditions armed not only with food for the community, but also with valuable information for hunters:

> Women are skilled in reading the signs of the bush, and they take careful note of animal tracks, their age, and the direction of movement. . . . In general, the men take advantage of women's reconnaissance and query them routinely on the evidence of game movements, the location of water, and the like (Draper 1975:82).

The !Kung have a clear division of labor by sex, but it is not rigidly adhered to, and men and women sometimes do one another's chores. This is especially true of men, who frequently do "women's work" without any shame or embarrassment. Childcare is viewed as the responsibility of both parents, and "as children grow up there are few experiences which set one sex apart from the other" (Draper 1975:89). In fact, !Kung childrearing practices are very relaxed and nonauthoritarian, reflecting !Kung social relations in general; among the !Kung, aggressive behavior on the part of men or women is strongly discouraged (Shostak 1981; Draper 1975).

Egalitarian gender relations like those of the !Kung are also characteristic of the other types of hunting-gathering societies remaining on our list. In these societies, one sex is not intrinsically valued over the other. Rather, an individual wins respect and influence within the community based on his *or her* contribution to the general well-being of the group (Bleier 1984). The Mbuti Pygmies of Zaire (type 6 in the preceding list) provide another example. In Mbuti society, work is a collective enterprise, and few tasks are assigned exclusively to one sex. Men and women share childcare, forage together, and even hunt cooperatively. The Agta of the Philippines also have this type of division of labor. Both Agta women and men hunt, using knives or bows and arrows. They fish with spears while swimming underwater, an activity that requires considerable skill and physical stamina. Although hunting and fishing supply most of the Agta's food, members of both sexes gather vegetation as well (Estioko-Griffin 1986). As O'Kelly and Carney (1986:13) observe, "This cooperative interdependence is associated with highly egalitarian gender roles."

It should be noted that egalitarian gender relations are not limited to hunting and gathering societies, although they are more common in these types of societies than in others. Lepowsky (1990) reports on a horticultural society, the people of Vanatinai (a large island southeast of mainland New Guinea), where the division of labor and other social relations are highly egalitarian. Both Vanatinai women and men plant, tend, and harvest garden crops. Although hunting with spears is a male monopoly, women also hunt game by trapping. Women have primary responsibility for caring for children, but men share this task quite willingly. Members of both sexes learn and practice magic; participate in warfare, peacemaking, and community decision making; and undertake sailing expeditions in search of ceremonial valuables. In short, Vanatinai society "offers every adult, regardless of sex or kin group, the opportunity of excelling at prestigious activities such as participation in traditional exchange or ritual functions essential to health and prosperity" (Lepowsky 1990:178).

Several important points can be drawn from these cross-cultural data. First, it should be clear to us by now that contemporary Western constructions of gender are not universal. The research indicates that there is a wide range of gender relations cross culturally and that in some societies, gender relations are highly egalitarian. Furthermore, if contemporary foraging societies do resemble the communities in which our earliest ancestors lived, they do not lend support to the reconstruction offered by Man the Hunter theory. Instead, they reinforce archeological and primatological data that indicate that our early ancestors probably lived in groups characterized by cooperation and reciprocity and in which adults of both sexes actively contributed to group survival.

A second significant point that can be gleaned from these anthropological studies is that a gendered division of labor does not necessarily produce gender inequality. The key intervening variable appears to be the *value* that the members of a society attach to a particular role or task. In our own society, the work women do is typically viewed as less important than the work men do. But in the societies discussed here, women are seen as "essential partners" in the economy and in decision making, even though women and men may be responsible for different tasks or have different spheres of influence (Gailey 1987; O'Kelly and Carney 1986). As Sacks (1979:92–93) observes, "Many nonclass societies have no problem in seeing differentiation without having to translate it into differential worth."

A third and final point concerns women's capacity to bear children. We noted earlier in the chapter that some scholars maintain that women's reproductive role prevents them from fully participating in other acitivities, such as food acquisition. However, the anthropological studies reviewed in this section suggest that women are not automatically excluded from certain activities because they bear children. Nor are men automatically excluded from childrearing simply because they cannot bear children.

> It is important to see that, unlike breathing, for example, the biological capacity to reproduce does not necessarily mean that one *has* to reproduce or even be heterosexually active, nor does it dictate the social arrangements for child nurturance and rearing or determine how child rearing affects one's participation in other cultural activities. Whether or not we bear, nurse or mother children is just as much a function of cultural, social, political, economical, and, no more importantly, biological factors as whether we are poets or soccer players (Bleier 1984:146, author's emphasis).

In preindustrial societies, like those we have discussed so far, childbearing and childrearing do not isolate mothers as they frequently do in societies like our own. "The tasks are absorbed by a broader range of people, and children are more incorporated into public activities . . . Moreover, motherhood (either through childbirth, adoption, or fosterage) often conveys an *increase* in status, giving women a greater say in matters than when they were not fully adult" (Gailey 1987:45–46, author's emphasis).

It appears, then, that nonbiological factors—among them environmental resources, size of the group, the economy, and, of course, ideology—play a more significant part in determining what the members of a society define as appropriate "men's work" and "women's work" than do biological factors. Contrary to Sigmund Freud's assertion, anatomy is *not* destiny. This point is made even clearer when we consider examples of multiple genders.

Multiple Genders

Thus far we have discussed gender as a dichotomous social category. Anthropological research, however, offers fascinating evidence for the existence of multiple genders; for instance, in some societies there are three, and in others four. The Navajo provide an example. In traditional Navajo societies, one could be male/masculine, female/feminine, or *nadle,* a third gender set apart from masculinity and femininity. The *nadle* status was ascribed to anyone whose sex is ambiguous at birth, but individuals could also choose to become *nadle. Nadle* could perform the tasks and duties of both women and men, although according to research reports, they typically behaved and were treated as women (e.g., they danced as women, and kin used female terms to address them). Significantly, *nadle* had the social and legal status of women (which in traditional Navajo societies is higher than that of men), but they were also accorded special rights and privileges, including extensive sexual freedom, the right to control the property of their relatives, status as mediators in disputes between men and women, and the option to marry someone of either sex (Martin and Voorhies 1975).

A more extensively studied example is that of the *berdache* of some Asian, South Pacific, and North American Indian societies. *Berdaches* are individuals who adopt the gender ascribed to members of the opposite sex. While women may become *berdaches,* it is more common for men. Historical research indicates that men who chose to become *berdaches* often did so at puberty as an alternative to becoming warriors. *Berdaches* lived, worked, and dressed as members of the opposite sex (Gailey 1987; Whitehead 1981). They also were frequently believed to possess supernatural powers. Among traditional Plains Indian groups, for instance, all *berdaches* were shamans and enjoyed high social and economic status as the spiritual guardians of their societies (Williams 1986). Significantly, Walter Williams (1986) reports that *berdachism* is beginning to reappear in some North American Indian societies. He attributes this to the combined efforts of the Native American rights movement and the gay rights movement.

The Mohave also allowed men and women to cross genders. Boys who showed a preference for feminine toys and clothing would undergo an initiation ceremony at puberty during which they became *alyha*. As *alyha*, they adopted feminine names, painted their faces as women did, performed female tasks, and married men. When they married, *alyha* pretended to menstruate by cutting their upper thighs. They also simulated pregnancy. "Labor pains, induced by drinking a severely constipating drug, culminate in the birth of a fictitious stillborn child. Stillborn Mohave infants are customarily buried by the mother, so that an *alyha*'s failure to return to 'her' home with a living infant is explained in a culturally acceptable manner" (Martin and Voorhies 1975:97).

A Mohave female who wished to pursue a masculine lifestyle underwent an initiation ceremony to become a *hwame*. *Hwame* dressed and lived much like men; they engaged in hunting, farming, and shamanism, although they were not permitted to assume leadership positions or participate in warfare. They did, though, assume paternal responsibility for children; some women, in fact, became *hwame* after they had children. Again, it is important to note that like *nadle* and *berdaches*, neither *hwame* nor *alyha* were considered abnormal or deviant within their cultures (Martin and Voohies 1975).

Other examples of such gender crossing can also be found in Tahitian culture (Gilmore 1990) and among the Omani Muslims (Wikan 1984). Meigs (1990) and Gailey (1987), however, report on a society in which gender is regarded as a process rather than as a stable social category. Among the Hua of Papua New Guinea, gender is perceived as changing throughout an individual's life. The Hua bestow high status on masculine people, but view them as physically weak and vulnerable. Feminine people are regarded as invulnerable, but polluted. When children are born, they are all at least partially feminine because the Hua believe that women transfer some of their own femininity to their offspring. Thus, the more children a woman has, the more femininity she loses. After three births, she is no longer considered polluted. She may participate in the discussions and rituals of men and share their higher status and authority, but she must also observe their diet and sanitation customs since she has now become vulnerable.

Hua men, meanwhile, gradually lose their masculinity by imparting it to young boys during growth rituals. As this happens, they become regarded as physically invulnerable, but polluted. Consequently, old men work in the fields with young women and have little social authority. "Among the Hua, then, gender is only tangentially related to sex differences; it is mutable and flows from person to person. The process of engendering is lifelong, and through it males and females shed the gender they were born with and acquire the opposite characteristics" (Gailey 1987:36).

Each of these examples illustrates the fluidity of gender as well as the creativity that humans bring to the process of social organization. While "our society typecasts women and men from birth through death . . . other societies exist where gender differences are not extended beyond adult reproductive roles" (Gailey 1987:35).

GENDER, EVOLUTION, AND CULTURE

In this chapter, we examined evolutionary perspectives of gender. The traditional view—Man the Hunter theory—rests on the assumption that the gender inequality and asymmetry attached to masculinity and femininity in modern Western industrial societies are historical and cultural universals. This position maintains that contemporary Western constructions of gender evolved from a prehistoric past in which women were necessarily dependent on men for food and protection as a result of the burdens of pregnancy and motherhood. Women, then, were relegated to the "home," whereas men assumed the public roles of defender and food provider. They fulfilled the latter primarily by hunting together in groups, and it was through these hunting activities that the hallmarks of the human species—in particular, language and the invention of material technology—supposedly developed.

In contrast to Man the Hunter theory, we also presented a feminist perspective of the evolution of gender. Feminist social scientists have sought new evidence and reexamined existing evidence from three main sources—the archeological record, primatology, and studies of contemporary foraging societies—in an effort to develop a perspective that overcomes the ethnocentric and androcentric biases of the traditional approach. Standing alone, each of these data sources has serious drawbacks, but taken together they provide us with an alternative reconstruction of our prehistoric past. The feminist account depicts early human communities as cooperative, flexible units centered around mother-infant and sibling bonds. Women were hardly passive and dependent; instead, they were active food providers who invented a material technology that included carrying devices and digging sticks to make their tasks easier and more productive.

Not unlike our closest primate relatives and probably very similar to members of contemporary foraging societies, our early human ancestors of both sexes were hunters and gatherers, although it is likely that gathering was the more successful subsistence strategy. In any event, the research reviewed in this chapter suggests that if we are to develop a more balanced account of the evolution of gender, we need to explore further the very strong possibility that both females and males were full and active participants in the struggle for survival. A presumption of gender inequality appears to be unfounded and misleading. Moreover, the existence of multiple genders in some societies underlines the point that sex and gender are distinct and sometimes independent categories, one biological and the other social. Gender is not an either/or category, but rather a fluid one that can best be conceptualized in terms of a continuum instead of a dichotomy.

One question that remains unanswered is how did we get here from there? That is, if gender relations in some societies were (and still are) highly egalitarian, what factors gave rise to the pervasive gender inequality characteristic of societies like our own? Any answer remains speculative, but scientists who have addressed this question have identified a number of related factors, including population growth, increased environmental danger owing to ecological changes or warfare, the establishment of trade or exchange relations between societies, a change from a nomadic to a sedentary lifestyle, and technological advances allowing for the accumulation of a surplus of food and other goods (Lepowsky 1990; Gailey 1987; O'Kelly and Carney 1986; Bleier 1984; Gough 1975). Certainly, much more research is needed to clarify the relationship between each of these conditions and the emergence of gender inequality. However, what the available evidence does indicate is that specific gender relations appear to arise largely in response to external circumstances—economic, political, and social—not biological imperatives. In succeeding chapters, we will focus on how particular gender relations are reinforced and perpetuated.

KEY TERMS

androcentrism   male-centered; the view that men are superior to other animals and to women

bipedalism   walking upright on two feet

ethnocentrism   the view that one set of cultural beliefs and practices is superior to all others

foraging societies (hunting and gathering societies)   small, technologically undeveloped societies whose members meet their survival needs by hunting and trapping animals, by fishing (if possible), and by gathering vegetation and other types of food in their surrounding environment; characterized by highly egalitarian gender relations

SUGGESTED READINGS

Gilmore, D. O. 1990. *Manhood in the Making.* New Haven, CT: Yale University Press.

Haraway, D. 1989. *Primate Visions.* New York: Routledge.

Sanday, P. R., and R. G. Goodenough (Eds.) 1990. *Beyond the Second Sex: New Directions in the Anthropology of Gender.* Philadelphia: University of Pennsylvania Press.

Williams, W. L. 1986. *The Spirit and the Flesh: Sexual Diversity in American Indian Culture.* Boston: Beacon Press.

Chapter 4

Early-Childhood Gender Socialization

Imagine that it is ten years from now. You are married and would like to start a family, but you and your spouse have just been told that you can have only one child. Which would you prefer that child to be: a boy or a girl?

If you are like most college students in the United States, you would prefer your only child to be a boy. Indeed, since the 1930s, researchers have documented that Americans in general have a clear "boy preference" (Coombs 1977; Williamson 1976a). Not only do we prefer boys as only children, but also in larger families, we prefer sons to outnumber daughters, and we have a strong preference for sons as firstborns. There is some evidence to suggest that this may be weakening a bit in the United States; for instance, several recent studies have reported an increasing tendency for people to express no preference rather than an explicit son or daughter preference (Steinbacher and Gilroy 1985; Gilroy and Steinbacher 1983; Rent and Rent 1977; Williamson 1977). There also appears to be a strong desire among most American couples to have at least one child of each sex (Teachman and Schollaert 1989). Outside the United States, however, boy preference remains so strong that in some countries, such as India and Egypt, it is estimated that if parents could choose the sex of their offspring, the resulting ratio of boys to girls would range from 162:100 to as high as 495:100 (Williamson 1976a).

It appears, then, that children are born into a world that largely prefers boys over girls. Some of the more common reasons that adults give for this preference are that boys carry on the family name (assuming that a daughter will take her husband's name at marriage) and that boys are both easier and cheaper to raise. The small minority that prefers girls seems to value them for their traditionally feminine traits: they are supposedly neater, cuddlier, cuter, and more obedient than boys (Williamson 1976b). Although it is uncertain whether children perceive their parents' sex preferences (Williamson 1976a), it is clear that these attitudes are closely associated with parental expectations of children's behavior and tend to reflect gender stereotypes.

In this chapter, we will discuss how parents transmit these expectations to their children through **socialization.** Socialization is the process by which society's values and norms, including those pertaining to gender, are taught and learned. This is a life-long process, but in this chapter, we will concentrate on the socialization that occurs mostly in the early childhood years. We will see that gender socialization is often a conscious effort in that expectations are reinforced with explicit rewards and punishments. Boys in particular receive explicit negative sanctions for engaging in what adults consider gender-inappropriate behavior. Gender socialization may also be more subtle, however, with gender messages relayed implicitly through children's clothing, the way their rooms are decorated, and the toys they are given for play. In addition, children may socialize one another through their interactions in peer groups. To begin our discussion, we will examine some of the theories that have been put forward to explain how young children acquire their gender identities.

LEARNING GENDER

Research indicates that children as young as two years old are aware of their gender and already adhere to gender stereotypes (Cowan and Hoffman 1986; Kuhn, et al. 1978). Obviously, children are presented with gender messages very early in their lives, but how do they come to adopt this information as part of their images of themselves and their understanding of the world around them? In other words, how do little girls learn that they are girls, and how do little boys learn that they are boys? Perhaps more importantly, how do both learn that only boys do certain (masculine) things, and only girls do other (feminine) things? A number of theories have been offered in response to such questions. We will discuss the three major ones: identification theory, social learning theory, and cognitive-developmental theory.

Identification Theory

Identification theory is rooted in the work of the famous psychoanalyst Sigmund Freud (1856–1939). According to Freud, children pass through a series of stages in their personality development. During the first two stages, referred to respectively as the *oral* and *anal* stages, boys and girls are fairly similar in their behavior and experiences. For both boys and girls, their mother is the chief object of their emotions since she is their primary caretaker and gratifies most of their needs. It is around age four, however, that an important divergence occurs in the personality development of girls and boys. It is at this age that children become aware both of their own genitals and of the fact that the genitals of boys and girls are different. This realization signals the start of the third stage of development, the *phallic stage*. It is during the phallic stage that **identification** takes place; that is, children begin to unconsciously model their behavior after that of their same-sex parent, thus learning how to behave in gender-appropriate ways. Significantly, identification does not occur for girls the same way it occurs for boys.

For boys, identification is motivated by what Freud called *castration anxiety.* At this age, a boy's love for his mother becomes more sexual and he tends to view his father as his rival (the *Oedipus complex*). What quickly cures him of this jealousy is a glimpse of the female genitalia. Seeing the clitoris, the little boy assumes that all girls have been castrated for some reason, and he fears that a similar fate may befall him if he continues to compete with his father. Boys perceive the formidable size and power of their fathers and conclude that their fathers have the ability to castrate competitors. Consequently, instead of competing with his father, the little boy tries to be more like him and ends up, in a sense, with the best of both worlds:

> [I]n choosing to be like his father, the boy can keep his penis. The boy, however, may still [vicariously] enjoy his mother sexually, through his father. As a result of this . . . identification, the boy begins to take on his father's characteristics, including his [gender] role behaviors (Frieze, et al. 1978:98).

In contrast, a girl's identification with her mother is motivated by what Freud called *penis envy.* Penis envy develops in girls upon first sight of the male genitals. Seeing the male's "far superior equipment" as Freud put it (1983/1933:88), the little girl also thinks she has been castrated. She becomes overwhelmed by her sense of incompleteness, her jealousy of boys, and her disdain for her mother and all women since they share her "deformity." Instead, she shifts her love to her father, who does possess the coveted penis, and begins to identify with her mother as a means to win him. Eventually, the girl realizes that she can have a penis in two ways: briefly through intercourse and symbolically by having a baby, especially a baby boy. "The original penis-wish is transformed into a wish for a baby which leads to love and desire for the man as bearer of the penis and provider of the baby" (Freize, et al. 1978:31). However, a female never fully overcomes the feelings of inferiority and envy which leave indelible marks on her personality:

> Thus, we attribute a larger amount of narcissism to femininity, which also affects women's choice of object, so that to be loved is a stronger need for them than to love. The effect of penis envy has a share, further, in the physical vanity of women, since they are bound to value their charms more highly as a late compensation for their original sexual inferiority. Shame, which is considered to be a feminine characteristic *par excellence* but is far more a matter of convention than might be supposed, has as its purpose, we believe, concealment of genital deficiency. . . . The fact that women must be regarded as having little sense of justice is no doubt related to the predominance of envy in their mental life (Freud 1983/1933:90,92).

Now before you start looking askance at every four-year-old you meet, let us point out that identification theory has received considerable criticism. For one thing, the theory maintains that identification is an unconscious process. As such, we have no objective means to verify it. Instead, we must rely on either the psychoanalyst's interpretation of an individual's behavior or the individual's memories of childhood. Even if we are willing to trust the memories of individuals, we are still left with the problem of observer bias. Because the methods of psychoanalysts are extremely subjective, we may question whether their interpretations of individuals' experiences are accurate or whether they simply reflect what the psychoanalyst expects to find in light of identification theory. Other than clinical reports of psychoanalysts themselves, there is little evidence of the existence of castration anxiety in boys or penis envy in girls (Frieze, et al. 1978; Sherman 1971). Moreover, research indicates that children do not understand the relationship between gender and genitalia until at least the ages of seven to nine, or perhaps even later (McConaghy 1979).

Identification theory also portrays the gendered behaviors acquired in early childhood as fixed and stable over time. In other words, the theory leaves little room for personal or social change. However, while it is certainly the case that gender is resilient, it is also true that social learning continues throughout our lives and that we may modify our behavior and attitudes as we are exposed to new situations and models.

Finally, it is impossible to overlook the antifemale bias in Freudian identification theory. Females are defined as inadequate; they are jealous, passive, and masochistic according to this perspective. In short, identification theory asserts that women are clearly men's inferiors. At its best, the theory legitimates gender inequality; at its worst, it is misogynistic and harmful to women.

In light of these serious weaknesses, it is not surprising that some identification theorists have revised Freud's original argument (Chodorow 1990). Erik Erikson (1968), for instance, has offered the provocative suggestion that males harbor some jealousy toward females for their unique ability to bear children. Referring to this phenomenon as *womb envy,* he views it as the underlying reason for men's apparent need to dominate women. Others, such as Karen Horney (1967) and Clara Thompson (1964), place the notion of penis envy in a social context. That is, women are jealous of the male organ only in that it is a symbol of male power in our society. From this point of view, then, women are actually envious of men's higher status and greater freedom.

More recently, Nancy Chodorow (1990; 1978) has revised identification theory in an effort to explain why females grow up to be the primary caretakers of children and to develop stronger affective ties with their children than males do. She suggests that identification is more difficult for boys since they must psychologically separate from their mothers and model themselves after a parent who is largely absent from the home, their fathers. Consequently, boys become more emotionally detached and repressed than girls. Girls, in contrast, do not experience this psychological separation. Instead, mothers and daughters maintain an intense, ongoing relationship with one another. From this, daughters acquire the psychological capabilities for mothering, and "feminine personality comes to define itself in relation and connection to other people more than masculine personality does" (Chodorow 1978:44).

There are several other feminist psychoanalytic theories besides Chodorow's (Chodorow 1990). Even though each raises some interesting possibilities for our understanding of gender acquisition, all remain largely speculative because of their untestability and lack of supporting evidence (Lorber, et al. 1981). In addition, they have been critiqued as ethnocentric. As we saw in Chapter 3, the sexual division of labor in which only women care for infants is not present in all societies, yet children in all societies acquire gender, whatever its specific content. Thus, the developmental sequence described by Chodorow and others applies only to Western families, and not all Western families at that (Lorber, et al. 1981).

Identification theory is not the only explanation of gender acquisition that has been developed. We will turn now to two other theories.

Social Learning Theory

Social learning theory is more straightforward than identification theory in that it focuses on observable events and their consequences rather than on unconscious motives and drives (Bandura 1986). The basic principles of social learning theory derive from a particular school of thought in psychology known as *behaviorism*. You are probably somewhat familiar with at least one important idea of behaviorism, the notion of **reinforcement**: a behavior consistently followed by a reward will likely occur again, whereas a behavior followed by a punishment will rarely reoccur. So, for example, your dog will probably learn to play frisbee with you if you give it a biscuit every time it runs to you with the plastic disk in its mouth. Conversely, the dog will stop urinating on your houseplants if you spank it with a rolled newspaper and put it outside each time it squats or lifts a leg near the indoor foliage. According to behaviorists, this same principle of reinforcement applies to the way people learn, including the way they learn gender.

More specifically, social learning theory posits that children acquire their respective gender by being rewarded for gender-appropriate behavior and punished for gender-inappropriate behavior. Often the rewards and punishments are direct and take the form of praise or admonishment. For instance, on a recent shopping excursion, one of the authors overheard a little girl asking her father to buy her a plastic truck. Looking at her with obvious displeasure, he said, "That's for boys. You're not a boy, are you?" Without answering, the little girl put the toy back on the shelf. (Interestingly, research indicates that boys actually receive harsher disapproval for cross-gender behavior than do girls; see, for example, Martin 1990; Fagot 1985; Feinman 1981). Children learn through indirect reinforcement as well; for example, they may learn about the consequences of certain behaviors just by observing the actions of others (Bronstein 1988).

This latter point raises a second important principle of social learning theory: children learn not only through reinforcement, but also by imitating or **modeling** those around them. Of course, the two processes—reinforcement and modeling—go hand-in-hand. Children will be rewarded for imitating some behaviors and punished for imitating others. At the same time, children will most likely imitate those who positively reinforce their behavior. In fact, social learning theorists maintain that children most often model themselves after adults whom they perceive to be warm, friendly, and powerful (i.e., in control of resources or privileges that the child values). More importantly, these theorists predict that children will imitate individuals most like themselves (Bussey and Bandura 1984; Margolin and Peterson 1975; Mischel 1966). Obviously, this includes same-sex parents and older same-sex siblings, but as we will see in Chapters 5 and 6, teachers and media personalities also serve as effective models for children.

Social learning theory is appealing. Chances are that we have seen reinforcement in practice, and we know that children can be great imitators (sometimes to the embarrassment of their parents). However, social learning theory is not without difficulties. First, studies of same-sex modeling indicate that children do not consistently imitate their same-sex parent more than their opposite-sex parent (Raskin and Isreal 1981). Rather, sex may be less important in eliciting modeling than other variables, especially the perceived power of the model (Jacklin 1989). For instance, "both boys and girls imitate a cross-sex model when that model controls rewards . . . [and] children imitate the dominant parent, regardless of sex" (Frieze, et al. 1978:111). In addition, children tend to imitate a same-sex model only if that model is engaged in gender-appropriate behavior (Jacklin 1989; Perry and Bussey 1979). This finding suggests that children have some knowledge of gender apart from what they acquire through modeling. Finally, social learning theory depicts children as passive recipients of socialization messages; "socialization is seen as a unilateral process with children shaped and molded by adults" (Corsaro and Eder 1990:198). There is evidence, though, that children actively seek out and evaluate information available in their social environment (Bem 1983).

One theory that attempts to address each of these criticisms is called cognitive-developmental theory. Cognitive-developmental theory is the third explanation of gender learning that we will examine in this chapter.

Cognitive-Developmental Theory

Based on the work of psychologists Jean Piaget and Lawrence Kohlberg, cognitive-developmental theory holds that children learn gender (and gender stereotypes) through their mental efforts to organize their social world, rather than through psychosexual processes or rewards and punishments. For the young child who is literally new to the world, life must seem chaotic. Thus, one of the child's first developmental tasks is to try to make sense of all the information he or she receives through observations and interactions in the social environment. According to cognitive-developmental theorists, the child accomplishes this by creating **schema** or mental categories. Psychologist Sandra Bem (1983:603–604) explains in more detail:

> A schema is a cognitive structure, a network of associations that organizes and guides an individual's perception. A schema functions as an anticipatory structure, a readiness to search for and assimilate incoming information in schema-related terms. Schematic information processing is thus highly selective and enables the individual to impose structure and meaning onto a vast array of incoming stimuli.

Sex is a very useful schema for young children. Why sex? The answer lies in a second major proposition of cognitive-developmental theory: children's interpretations of their world are limited by their level of mental maturity. Early on in their lives, children's thinking tends to be concrete; that is, in organizing their observations and experiences, they rely on simple and obvious cues. Sex is a category that has a variety of obvious physical cues attached to it, such as anatomy, hair length, body and facial hair, dress, and so on. Children first use the schema to label themselves and to organize their own identities. They then apply the schema to others in an effort to organize traits and behaviors into two classes, masculine or feminine, and they attach values to what they observe—either gender appropriate ("good") or gender inappropriate ("bad").

Cognitive-developmental theory helps to explain young children's strong preferences for sex-typed toys and activities and for same-sex friends, as well as why they express rigidly stereotyped ideas about gender (Cann and Palmer 1986; Cowan and Hoffman 1986; O'Brien and Huston 1985). Studies indicate, too, that as children get older and as their cognitive systems mature they appear to become more flexible with regard to the activities that males and females pursue, at least until they reach adolescence (Stoddart and Turiel 1985; Archer 1984; however, for a contrasting view see Carter and McClosky 1983).

Still, cognitive-developmental theory has not escaped criticism. One difficulty centers around the question of the age at which children develop their own gender identities. Cognitive-developmental theorists place this development between the ages of three and five, but their critics point to research that shows that it may appear sooner and that children as young as two years old subscribe to gender stereotypes (Cowan and Hoffman 1986; Kuhn, et al. 1978). In addition, recent research indicates that not everyone develops sex and gender schemas; there are some individuals who may be considered gender "aschematic," although they themselves have developed gender identities (Skitka and Maslach 1990). Thus, the process by which gender schemas form needs to be better understood.

Another serious criticism is the charge that, by portraying gender learning as something children basically do themselves, cognitive-developmental theory downplays the critical role of culture in gender socialization (Corsaro and Eder 1990). We may agree that children actively seek to organize their social world, but that they use the concept of sex as a primary means for doing so probably has more to do with the culture of the society in which they live than with their level of mental maturity. There are other organizing categories available with obvious physical cues, but children use sex instead—not because it is easier, but because in the culture of their society, sexual distinctions are emphasized. As Bem (1983:608–609) explains:

> Nearly all societies teach the developing child two crucial things about gender: first . . . they teach the substantive network of sex-related associations that can come to serve as cognitive schema; second, they teach that the dichotomy between male and female has intensive and extensive relevance to virtually every domain of human experience. The typical American child cannot help observing, for example, that what parents, teachers, and peers consider to be appropriate behavior varies as a function of sex; that toys, clothing, occupations, hobbies, the domestic division of labor—even pronouns—all vary as a function of sex.

This point is especially significant if one values social change for it "implies that children would be far less likely to become gender schematic and hence sex-typed if the society were to limit the associative network linked to sex and to temper its insistence on the functional importance of the gender dichotomy" (Bem 1983:609).

Those who take this approach often refer to it as *gender schema theory,* but rather than treating it as a separate explanatory model, we see it as an important and much-needed revision to cognitive-developmental theory. In the remaining sections of this chapter, we will examine more carefully the various ways that children's worlds are structured in terms of sex and gender. We think you will come to agree on the basis of this discussion that the "gender schema criticism" is well-taken.

GROWING UP FEMININE OR MASCULINE

If you ask parents whether they treat their children differently simply on the basis of sex, most would probably say "no." However, there is considerable evidence that what parents *say* they do and what they *actually* do are often not the same.

It appears, in fact, that gender socialization gets underway shortly after a child is born. Although there are few physiological or behavioral differences between males and females at birth, parents do tend to respond differently to their newborns on the basis of sex. For example, when asked to describe their babies within twenty-four hours of birth, new parents frequently use gender stereotypes. Infant girls are described as tiny, soft, and delicate, but parents of infant boys use adjectives such as strong, alert, and coordinated to describe their babies. Interestingly, fathers provide more stereotyped descriptions than mothers (Lake 1975; Rubin, et al. 1975).

It is not unreasonable for us to suspect that parents' initial stereotyped perceptions of their children may lay the foundation for the differential treatment of sons and daughters. Maccoby and Jacklin (1974), for example, found that parents tend to elicit more gross motor activity from their sons than from their daughters, but there appears to be little if any difference in the amount of affectionate contact between mothers and their sons and daughters. Additional research indicates that parents tend to engage in rougher, more physical play with infant sons than with infant daughters (MacDonald and Parke 1986). This is especially the case with respect to father-infant interactions. Studies show that fathers play more interactive games with infant and toddler sons and also encourage more visual, fine-motor, and locomotor exploration with them, whereas they promote vocal interaction with their daughters. At the same time, fathers of toddler daughters appear to encourage closer parent-child physical promixity than fathers of toddler sons (Bronstein 1988). In this way, parents may be providing early training for their young sons to be more independent and aggressive than their daughters.

This pattern continues through the preschool years. For example, Fagot, et al. (1985) discovered that adults respond differently to boys' and girls' communicative styles. Although thirteen- and fourteen-month-old children showed no sex differences in their attempts to communicate, adults tended to respond to boys when they "forced attention" by being aggressive, or by crying, whining, and screaming. Similar attempts by girls were usually ignored, but adults were responsive to girls when they used gestures or gentle touching, or when they simply talked. Significantly, when Fagot and her colleagues observed these same children just eleven months later, they saw clear sex differences in their styles of communication; boys were more assertive, whereas girls were more talkative.

In studies with a related theme, researchers have found that parents communicate differently with sons and daughters. Gleason reports that parents speak more to their daughters about feelings and emotions than they do to their sons (cited in Shapiro 1990). When parents tell stories to their children, they also tend to use more emotion words with daughters than sons, except that they speak more about anger in stories told to boys (Goleman 1988). Not surprisingly, by the age of two, girls typically use more emotion words than boys.

Finally, Weitzman and her colleagues (1985) found that mothers tend to speak to their sons more explicitly, teach and question them more, and use more numbers and action verbs in speaking to them. Others have reported similar findings with respect to father-son communication (Bronstein 1988). This indicates that parents provide more of the kind of verbal stimulation thought to foster cognitive development to their sons than to their daughters. What is also interesting with respect to Weitzman, et al.'s study, however, is that the researchers included mothers who professed not to adhere to traditional gender stereotypes. Although the differential treatment of sons and daughters was less pronounced among these mothers, it was by no means absent.

It is significant to note that the studies discussed so far have been based almost exclusively on samples of white, middle-class, two-parent families, making generalizations with regard to other types of families' socialization practices unreliable at best. Despite the limitations of such studies, they do help to explain why sex differences that are absent in infancy (see Chapter 2) begin to emerge during early childhood. However, as we have already mentioned, gender socialization is accomplished not only through parent-child interaction, but also through the ways parents structure their children's environment. Let's turn, then, to a discussion of this latter aspect of the socialization process, keeping in mind that this research, too, tends to be race- and class-specific. We will examine more carefully the variables of race and social class later in the chapter.

The Gender-Specific Nature of Children's Environments

What is the easiest and most accurate way for a stranger to determine the sex of an infant? According to Madeline Shakin and her associates (1985), a baby's clothing provides the best clues. Ninety percent of the infants they observed in suburban shopping malls were dressed in sex-typed clothes. The color of the clothing alone supplied a reliable clue for sex labeling: the vast majority of the girls wore pink or yellow, while most boys were dressed in blue or red. The style of children's clothing also varies by sex. On special occasions, girls wear dresses trimmed with ruffles and lace; at bedtime, they wear nighties with more of the same; and for leisure activities, their slacks sets may be more practical, but chances are they are pastel in color and decorated with hearts or flowers. In contrast, boys wear three-piece suits on special occasions; at bedtime, they wear astronaut, athlete, or super-hero pajamas; and for leisure activities, their overalls or slacks sets are in primary colors with sports or military decorations.

All of this may seem insignificant, even picky, to you. However, what we must emphasize here is that clothing plays a significant part in gender socialization in two ways. First, by informing others about the sex of the child, clothing sends implicit messages about how the child should be treated. "We know . . . that when someone interacts with a child and a sex label is available, the label functions to direct behavior along the lines of traditional [gender] roles" (Shakin, et al. 1985:956). Second, certain types of clothing encourage or discourage particular behaviors or activities. Girls in frilly dresses, for example, are discouraged from rough-and-tumble play, whereas boys' physical movement is rarely impeded by their clothing. Boys are expected to be more active than girls, and the styles of the clothing designed for them reflect this gender stereotype. Clothing, then, serves as one of the most basic means by which parents organize their children's world along gender-specific lines.

Parents also more directly construct specific environments for their children with the nurseries, bedrooms, and playrooms that they furnish and decorate. The classic study in this area was conducted by Rheingold and Cook (1975), who actually went into middle-class homes and examined the contents of children's rooms. Their comparison of boys' and girls' rooms is a study of contrasts. Girls' rooms reflected traditional conceptions of femininity, especially in terms of domesticity and mother-hood. Their rooms were usually decorated with floral designs and ruffled bed-spreads, pillows, and curtains. They contained an abundance of baby dolls and re-lated items (e.g., doll houses) as well as miniature appliances (e.g., toy stoves). Few of these items were found in boys' rooms, where, instead, the decor and con-tents reflected traditional notions about masculinity. Boys' rooms had more animal motifs and were filled with military toys and athletic equipment. They also had build-ing and vehicular toys (e.g., blocks, trucks, and wagons). Importantly, boys had more toys overall as well as more types of toys, including those considered educa-tional. The only items girls were as likely to have as boys were musical instruments and books (although, as we will see shortly, the content of children's books is rarely gender-neutral). Given that similar findings were obtained more than ten years later (Stoneman, et al. 1986), it appears that Rheingold and Cook's conclusion remains applicable, at least with regard to the socialization of middle-class children:

> The rooms of children constitute a not inconsiderable part of their environment. Here they go to bed and wake up; here they spend some part of every day. Their rooms determine the things they see and find for amusement and instruction. That their rooms have an effect on their present and subsequent behavior can be assumed; a standard is set that may in part account for some differences in the behavior of girls and boys (1975:463).

The Rheingold and Cook study also highlights the importance of toys in a young child's environment. Toys, too, play a major part in gender socialization. Toys not only entertain children, but they also teach them particular skills and encourage them to explore through play a variety of roles they may one day occupy as adults. Thus, if we provide boys and girls with very different types of toys, we are essentially training them for separate (and unequal) roles as adults. What is more, we are subtly telling them that what they *may* do, as well as what they *can* do, is largely determined (and limited) by their sex.

Are there clear differences in the toys girls and boys are expected to play with and, if so, just what are these differences? Rheingold and Cook's research already answered these questions to some extent, but a quick perusal of most contemporary toy catalogs further addresses the issue. The toys for sale are frequently pictured with models; pay careful attention to which toys are pictured with female models and which are shown with males. In the catalog we picked up (Toys to Grow On 1990), most of the toys were obviously gender-linked. We found, for instance, that little girls were most frequently shown with dolls or household appliances. The only "dolls" boys were pictured with were "giant vinyl dinosaurs as tough as the real thing." Costumes for dressing up also were featured in gender-specific ways. On one page, a boy was shown dressed as a cowboy in "the perfect outfit for wild West adventures." A little girl was pictured on the opposite page wearing "a dreamy gown for brides-to-be." For this costume one could also purchase a kit to "complete the fantasy": accessories that included wedding invitations with envelopes, a bouquet, dainty gloves, a lace garter, a bride and groom cake topper, a "just married" sign, a marriage certificate, bell decorations, and a wedding ring set. On other pages, little boys were shown putting together a pirate ship, learning to tie knots, or playing doctor, while little girls were pictured making hair bows, decorating clothing, or playing ballerina.

Even though toy catalogs are directed primarily to parents—in the United States, parents make over 70 percent of all toy purchases (Kutner and Levinson 1978)—many children spend considerable time looking at the catalogs and often ask their parents to buy specific toys they see advertised. If the catalog we examined is typical of toy catalogs in general—and we have no reason to doubt that it is—then children are receiving very clear gender messages about the kinds of toys they are supposed to want. These messages are reinforced by the pictures on toy packaging, by the way toy stores often arrange their stock in separate sections for boys and girls (Shapiro 1990; Schwartz and Markham 1985), and by sales personnel who frequently recommend gender-stereotyped toys to potential customers (Ungar 1982; Kutner and Levinson 1978). It is no wonder that by two and a half years of age, children request mostly gender-stereotyped toys (Robinson and Morris 1986). Are they ever really given a choice?

The toys themselves foster different traits and abilities in children, depending on their sex. Toys for boys tend to encourage exploration, manipulation, invention, construction, competition, and aggression. In contrast, girls' toys typically rate high on manipulability, but also creativity, nurturance, and attractiveness (Miller 1987; Bradbard 1985; Peretti and Sydney 1985). As one researcher concluded, "These data support the hypothesis that playing with girls' vs. boys' toys may be related to the development of differential cognitive and/or social skills in girls and boys" (Miller 1987:485). Certainly the toy manufacturers think so; the director of public relations for Mattel, Inc. (which makes the Barbie doll) stated in a recent interview that, "Girls' play involves dressing and grooming and acting out their future—going on a date, getting married—and boys' play involves competition and conflict, good guys versus bad guys" (quoted in Lawson 1989:C1).

Apart from toys, what other items stand out as a central feature of a child's environment? You may recall from the Rheingold and Cook study that books are one of only two items that boys and girls are equally likely to have. Unfortunately, children's literature has traditionally ignored females or portrayed males and females in a blatantly stereotyped fashion. For example, Lenore Weitzman and her colleagues (1972) found in their now-classic analysis of award-winning picture books for preschoolers that males were usually depicted as active adventurers and leaders, while females were shown as passive followers and helpers. Boys were typically rewarded for their accomplishments and for being smart; girls were rewarded for their good looks. Books that included adult characters showed men doing a wide range of jobs, but women were restricted largely to domestic roles. In about one third of the books they studied, however, there were no female characters at all.

In a recent replication of the Weitzman research, Williams, et al. (1987) noted significant improvements in the visibility of females. Only 12.5 percent of the books published in the 1980s that they examined had no females, while a third had females as central characters. Nevertheless, although males and females are now about equal in their appearance in children's literature, the ways they are depicted remain largely unchanged. According to Williams, et al. (1987:155), "With respect to role portrayal and characterization, females do not appear to be so much stereotyped as simply colorless. No behavior was shared by a majority of females; while nearly all males were portrayed as independent, persistent, and active. Furthermore, differences in the way males and females are presented is entirely consistent with traditional culture." In short, the gender stereotypes fostered by much toy play continue to be promoted in children's books.

Considerable attention has been given to the problem of sexism in children's literature, resulting in an effort to change it. Publishers, for instance, have developed guidelines to help authors avoid sexism in their works, and a number of authors' and writers' collectives have set to work producing egalitarian books for youngsters. Research on the success of these endeavors is limited, and the findings are mixed. On the one hand, it has been argued that the so-called nonsexist picture books frequently advantage female characters at the expense of male characters, thus simply reversing traditional depictions of gender rather than portraying gender equality (St. Peter 1979). On the other hand, Davis (1984) praises the nonsexist books for their depictions of females as highly independent and males as nurturant and nonaggressive. However, he also points out that the nonsexist books continue to reinforce some traditional gender stereotypes in that they still tend to portray females as more emotional and less physically active than males. It remains to be seen, therefore, whether this new genre can overcome the gender biases that have traditionally pervaded children's literature.

One way that writers and publishers have tried to overcome sexism in children's literature is to depict characters as genderless or gender neutral. However, recent research casts doubt on the potential success of this approach since it has been found that mothers who read these books to their children almost always label the characters in gender-specific ways. In 95 percent of these cases the labeling is masculine (DeLoache, et al. 1987). In this study, the only pictures that prompted feminine labels were those showing an adult helping a child, an interpretation consistent with the gender stereotypes that females need more help than males and that females are more attentive to children. Based on this research, then, it appears that "picturing characters in a gender-neutral way is actually counterproductive, since the adult 'reading' the picture book with the child is likely to produce an even more gender-biased presentation than the average children's book does" (DeLoache, et al. 1987:176).

To summarize our discussion so far, we have seen that virtually every significant dimension of a child's environment—his or her clothing, bedroom, toys, and books—is structured according to cultural expectations of appropriate gendered behavior. If, as cognitive-developmental theorists maintain, young children actively try to organize all the information they receive daily, their parents and other adults are clearly providing them with the means. Despite their claims, even parents who see themselves as egalitarian tend to provide their children with different experiences and opportunities and to respond to them differently on the basis of sex. Consequently, the children cannot help but conclude that sex is an important social category. By the time they are ready for school, they have already learned to view the world in terms of a dichotomy: his and hers. Parents are not the only socializers of young children, however; recent research has demonstrated the importance of peers in early childhood socialization. Let's consider, then, the ways in which young children help to socialize one another.

Early Peer Group Socialization

Corsaro and Eder (1990) emphasize that socialization is not a one-way process from adults to children. Rather, childhood socialization is a collective process in which "children creatively appropriate information from the adult world to produce their own unique peer cultures" (Corsaro and Eder 1990:200).

Children socialize one another through their everyday interactions in the home and at play. Research indicates, for example, that one of young children's first attempts at social differentiation is through increasing sex segregation. Observations of young children at play indicate that they voluntarily segregate themselves into same-sex groups and that when compared with girls, boys tend to interact in larger groups, be more aggressive and competitive, and engage in organized sports (Corsaro and Eder 1990; Thorne 1986).

Thorne (1986) is critical of much of this research for focusing solely on sex differences and ignoring sex similarities and cross-sex interaction. She gives a number of examples in which young children work cooperatively and amiably in sex-integrated groups (*see also* Goodenough 1990). She also points out that children frequently engage in "borderwork"; that is, they attempt to cross over into the world of the other sex and participate in cross-gender activities. There is considerable evidence, however, that children reward gender-appropriate behavior (Goodenough 1990; Carter and McClosky 1983; Langolis and Downs 1980).

Unfortunately, the research on peer cultures in early childhood is limited; much more is needed before we can fully appreciate the ways that children actively participate in the socialization process. Available data do indicate, however, that at the very least, children should be considered partners with parents in childhood socialization, including gender socialization.

The Intervening Variables of Race and Social Class

We must emphasize again that much of the research on early-childhood gender socialization has recruited subjects from white, middle- and upper-middle-class, two-parent families. There are indications that the findings of such studies may not be representative of the socialization practices of families of other races and social classes. The work of Janice Hale-Benson (1986) is instructive on this point.

Hale-Benson has studied the socialization goals and practices of black families. She emphasizes the dual nature of the socialization that takes place in black households. "One of the challenges Black families must face in socializing their children is to understand and assist their children to function within their peer group. In addition, Black parents must also provide them with the skills and abilities they will need to succeed in the outside society" (1986:64). For both male and female children, black parents stress heavily the importance of hard work, ambition, and achievement. Thus, black children of both sexes tend to be more independent and self-reliant than their white peers. They are also imbued at an early age with a sense of financial responsibility to earn income for themselves and to contribute to the support of their families.

Still, the socialization experiences of young black males and females is not identical. Hale-Benson points out, for example, that among the traits and skills taught to black boys (largely in the context of their peer group) are the ways to move their bodies distinctively, athletic prowess, sexual competence, and street savvy, including how to fight. In contrast, black girls are socialized into "a very strong motherhood orientation," although this does not preclude the general expectation that they will also work outside the home. The development of personal uniqueness or distinctiveness is also emphasized, with special attention given to sexuality, clothing, and body movement.

Black children are often exposed to women and men sharing tasks and assuming collective responsibility. A number of studies indicate that in two-parent black families, women are typically employed outside the home and men participate in child care (Colletta 1981; Johnson 1981), although there is also evidence that disputes the finding of role-sharing in black households (Wilson, et al. 1990). Over half of black children live with just one parent, usually their mother, compared with 19 percent of white children and 30 percent of Hispanic children (U.S. Department of Commerce 1990; see also Chapter 7). In black single-parent households, the parent may be aided in the care and socialization of the children by an extended kin and friendship network (Reid 1982). In addition, Hale-Benson (1986:53) notes that the black church offers "a kind of extended family fellowship that provides other significant adults to relate to the children, and it also provides material and human resources to the family."

In light of these data, it is not surprising that Hale-Benson and others (e.g., McAdoo 1988; Lewis 1975) have found that black children are not taught to perceive gender in completely bipolar terms. Instead, both males and females are expected to be nurturant and expressive emotionally as well as independent, confident, and assertive. Reid (1982) reports that black girls more than black boys are encouraged to be high achievers, and Carr and Mednick (1988) have found that this nontraditional gender socialization leads to high achievement motivation in black female preschoolers. Bardwell, et al. (1986) have also found that black children are less gender stereotyped than white children. Importantly, Isaaks (1980) obtained similar results in a comparison of Hispanic and white children. However, there is some research that reports contradictory findings. For instance, Gonzalez (1982) and Price-Bonham and Skeen (1982) found at least as much, if not more, gender stereotyping among blacks and Hispanics as among whites. Similarly, in her study of Mexican fathers' interactions with their seven- to twelve-year-old children, Bronstein (1988) reports that, similar to white fathers, these men interacted more socially with daughters than with sons, but encouraged their sons' cognitive achievement more than their daughters'.

The picture becomes blurred or more complex when social class is taken into account. For example, there is modest support for the hypothesis that gender stereotyping decreases as one moves up the social class hierarchy (Brooks-Gunn 1986; Seegmiller, et al. 1980). However, if parental educational level may be used as an indicator of a family's social class, it appears that, at least among whites, gender stereotyping may be greater the higher a family's social class position (Bardwell, et al. 1986). Most studies of black and Hispanic or Chicano socialization practices, though, still utilize middle-class samples (e.g., Bronstein 1988; McAdoo 1988) and there is little research that examines the interaction of social class with race and ethnicity. One study that did address this interaction indicates that the latter is the more important variable; that is, race and ethnicity have a stronger influence on child-rearing practices than does social class, although this research did not examine gender socialization specifically (Hale-Benson 1986). We can only conclude that much more research is needed to elucidate the rich diversity of gender socialization practices and their outcomes among various races and social classes.

BY THE TIME A CHILD IS FIVE

At the outset of this chapter, we argued that children are born into a world that largely favors males. Throughout much of the remainder of our discussion, we examined research that indicates that this male preference carries over into parents' and other adults' interactions with children. We have seen here that during

early childhood, boys and girls—at least those from white, middle-class families—
are socialized into separate and unequal genders. Little boys are taught independence, problem-solving abilities, assertiveness, and curiosity about their environment—skills that are highly valued in our society. In contrast, little girls are taught
dependence, passivity, and domesticity—traits that our society devalues. Children themselves reinforce and respond to adults' socialization practices by socializing one another in peer groups.

We also discussed three theories or explanations of how the process of
gender socialization takes place. The first, Freudian identification theory, argues
that all children pass through a series of psychosexual stages, with the phallic
stage being the most critical for the development of gender identity. It is during
this phase that boys and girls attempt to resolve their respective gender-identity
complexes by identifying with their same-sex parents. However, identification
theory's emphasis on the unconscious nature of this process makes it virtually
impossible to verify objectively.

The other two theories—social learning theory and cognitive-developmental
theory—have been tested and both have received empirical support. Social learning theory maintains that children learn gender the same way they learn other
behaviors and attitudes—through reinforcement (i.e., rewards and punishments
for specific behaviors) and by imitating adult models. Cognitive-developmental
theory contends that children acquire gender as they try to make sense of their
everyday observations and experiences. Sex is an easy and obvious category or
schema for them to use in their organization efforts, especially given that adults
themselves differentially structure children's environments according to sex. We
have seen here that gender-typed clothing, room furnishings, toys, and books
serve both to organize children's environments in terms of a gender dichotomy
and to reinforce children for stereotypic gender-appropriate behavior. Taken together, then, social learning and cognitive-developmental theories are helpful in
explaining why children as young as two years old already adhere to gender
stereotypes and why preschoolers exhibit such strong preferences for gender-
typed toys and activities as well as same-sex friends.

May we conclude from this that nonsexist socialization is impossible? Certainly not. Considerable research is underway to evaluate a variety of nonsexist
socialization techniques (Lorber 1986). One of the most interesting proposals has
been offered by psychologist Sandra Bem (1983:613), who has suggested two
strategies for nonsexist socialization. First, she advises parents to retard their
young child's knowledge of our culture's traditional messages about gender, while
simultaneously teaching him or her that the only definitive differences between
males and females are anatomical and reproductive. Second, she suggests that
parents provide the child with an alternative schema for organizing and compre-
hending information. Instead of a sex schema, for example, parents could substitute an "individual differences" schema that emphasizes the "remarkable variabil-
ity of individuals within groups." We think proposals such as these have merit and
deserve further exploration. However, we must keep in mind that parents are not

the only ones responsible for gender socialization. Indeed, as we will see in Chapters 5 and 6, schools and the media take up where parents leave off, and peers remain active socializers throughout our lives.

KEY TERMS

identification   a central concept of the Freudian-based theory of gender socialization; the process by which boys and girls begin to unconsciously model their behavior after that of their same-sex parent in their efforts to resolve their respective gender-identity complexes

modeling   the process by which children imitate the behavior of their same-sex parent, especially if the parent rewards their imitations or is perceived by them to be warm, friendly, or powerful; a central concept of the social learning theory of gender socialization

reinforcement   a central principle of the social learning theory of gender socialization which states that a behavior consistently followed by a reward will likely occur again, whereas a behavior followed by a punishment will rarely recur

schema   a central concept of the cognitive-developmental theory of gender socialization; a mental category that organizes and guides an individual's perception and helps the individual assimilate new information

socialization   the process by which a society's values and norms, including those pertaining to gender, are taught and learned

SUGGESTED READINGS

Here we will break with our usual pattern of recommending a number of scholarly works and instead suggest a few practical guides to the issues that we have raised in this chapter. One work, however, that is both scholarly and practical is Sandra Bem's article, "Gender Schema Theory and Its Implications for Child Development: Raising Gender-aschematic Children in a Gender-schematic Society" (*Signs* 8:598–616). We recommend it for its review of the theories of gender socialization we have examined here as well as for its provocative suggestions for nonsexist childrearing.

A useful reference source for nonsexist children's books is *Books for Today's Children* compiled by Jeanne Bracken and Sharon Wigutoff (published by the Feminist Press at the City University of New York). The Feminist Book Mart of New York provides a catalog of nonsexist children's books, and author Jack Zipes has compiled an anthology of sixteen feminist retellings of classic fairy tales entitled, *Don't Bet on the Prince: Contemporary Feminist Fairy Tales in North America and England* (New York: Methuen, 1986). See also *Tatterhood and Other Tales* edited by Ethel Johnston Phelps, and *My Mother the Mail Carrier* by Inez Maury (with a Spanish translation by Norah Alemany) from the Feminist Press at the City University of New York.

Finally, for toy catalogs that picture models engaged in cross-gender behavior, consult "Constructive Playthings" available from the company of the same name, 1227 East 119th Street, Grandview, Missouri 64030, and "Hand in Hand" available from First Step, Ltd., 9180 LeSaint Drive, Fairfield, Ohio 45014.

Chapter 5

Schools and Gender

In a speech before a group of educators in 1980, Florence Howe, herself an educator, began by quoting from the writings of Frederick Douglass, the famous abolitionist. In the passage she selected, Douglass recalls his childhood as a slave on a Southern plantation and relays a conversation he overheard between his master and his master's wife. Said the master to his wife, "If you teach that . . . nigger how to read, there would be no keeping him. It would forever unfit him to be a slave. He would at once become unmanageable, and of no value to his master. As to himself, it could do him no good, but a great deal of harm. It would make him discontented and unhappy" (quoted in Howe 1984:247). Howe selected this passage because it aptly illustrates what she calls the power of education. Both Douglass and his master recognized that education may enable us to understand our social position and thus empower us to act to change it.

To this observation we must add another: education is powerful in the sense that it may also serve to keep us in our respective places. More specifically, schools are officially charged with the responsibility of equipping students with the knowledge and skills they need to fill various roles in their society. This is accomplished primarily by requiring students to study subjects (e.g., reading, writing, mathematics, and history) known collectively as the **formal curriculum.** But schools also teach students particular social, political, and economic *values.* This instruction, too, may be done explicitly (by punishing students for being late, for instance), but just as often these value messages are implicit in the curriculum materials used to teach traditional academic subjects. They constitute, in other words, a kind of **hidden curriculum** that operates alongside the more formal one. However, the subtle nature of the hidden curriculum in no way lessens its significance. Through it, students learn to view the world in particular ways. More importantly, they learn what they can expect for themselves in that world and, for certain groups of students, this may result in very low aspirations.

In this chapter, we will examine the kinds of messages both the formal and informal curricula send about gender, and we will assess their impact on the aspirations and achievements of male and female students. In addition, we will explore some of the recent efforts to transform the educational experience into a richer, more equal one for students of both sexes. Before we examine the current relationship between schools and gender, however, let's begin with a brief discussion of how this relationship has developed and changed over time.

AN HISTORICAL OVERVIEW OF WOMEN AND MEN IN EDUCATION

The word *school* derives from an ancient Greek word that means "leisure." This makes sense when one considers that until relatively recent times, only the very wealthy had enough free time on their hands to pursue what may be considered a formal education. Literacy was not a necessity for the average person; most people acquired the knowledge they needed to be productive citizens either on their own, or from parents, other relatives, coworkers, or tradespeople. However, even the education of the privileged few was somewhat haphazard. The educated man—for formal education was restricted to males until 1786—was schooled in the classics, moral philosophy, mathematics, and rhetoric, although he acquired this knowledge through private study, tutoring, and travel as well as in a classroom (Graham 1978). Those who went to college were trained in self-discipline and moral piety as much as in academic subjects, for upon graduation they were to take their places among the white "ruling class" as ministers, lawyers, and other professionals (Howe 1984).

Upper-class white women, when educated, were taught at home, but what they learned was far more restricted than the knowledge imparted to men. Women learned music and were given "a taste" of literature and a foreign language. Their education was to prepare them not to assume public leadership positions, but rather to better fulfill their "natural" role in life as demure, witty, well-groomed partners for their elite husbands. Even when schools for girls began to open in America—the first, the Young Ladies Academy, established in Philadelphia in 1786—the rationale behind them centered on women's domestic roles. In the post–Revolutionary War period, it was argued that American women would play a vital role in the future of the republic, not as political leaders, but as the first educators of sons who would grow up to be citizens. If women were to be good teachers of civic virtue, they needed to be better educated themselves (Schwager 1987). Still, these early educational opportunities for females were offered largely by private schools and thus remained available only to the well-to-do.

With increasing industrialization in the United States during the nineteenth century, basic literacy and numeracy skills came to be viewed not only as desirable, but also as necessary for most jobs. During the first half of the century, free public schools for girls and boys began to open, especially in the northeastern cities. This produced two major consequences. The first was that white female literacy rates, at least in the northeastern part of the country, began to match white male literacy rates by mid-century. Nevertheless, black literacy rates remained substantially lower (Schwager 1987).

Second, the proliferation of elementary schools provided women with new career opportunities as teachers. In the early 1800s, men dominated teaching and looked upon it as a good sideline occupation that provided extra income. The school year was relatively short and was structured around the farm calendar, with classes held during the winter months when farm chores were light. However, with urbanization and growing demands for higher educational standards in an industrialized society, teaching became a full-time job, albeit one that carried a salary too low to support a family. As a result, educational administrators employed women as a cheap and efficient means to implement mass elementary education (Strober and Landford 1986). Women were paid 40 percent less than their male counterparts on the (often false) assumption that they had only themselves to support (Schwager 1987). Their "maternal instincts" made them naturally suited to work with young children, and if a disciplinary problem arose, they could enlist the aid of the school principal or superintendent who was invariably a man. Valued, too, were their supposed docility and responsiveness to male authority since male-dominated school boards were handing down strict guidelines for instruction and a standardized curriculum (Strober and Lanford 1986; Strober and Tyack 1980). Given such attitudes, as well as the fact that few other occupational opportunities were open to women, it is not surprising that female teachers outnumbered male teachers by 1860 (Schwager 1987).

Most of the women who became teachers were trained in *normal schools* (precursors to teacher training colleges) or in female seminaries, such as the Troy Female Seminary established in 1821. It was not until 1832 that women were permitted to attend college with men. Oberlin College in Ohio was the first coeducational college in the United States; it was, incidentally, the first white college to admit black students. Lawrence College in Wisconsin followed suit in 1847, and by 1872, there were ninety-seven coeducational American colleges (Leach 1980). Still, the more prestigious institutions, such as Harvard, Yale, and Princeton, continued to deny women admission on a number of grounds. It was widely believed, for example, that women were naturally less intelligent than men, so that their admission would lower academic standards. A second popular argument was that women were physically more delicate than men and that the rigors of higher education might disturb their uterine development to such an extent that they would become sterile or bear unhealthy babies. Others argued that women would distract men from their studies, or that college would make women more like men: loud, coarse, and vulgar (Howe 1984). (Interestingly, Yale and Princeton did not admit women as undergraduate students until 1969).

Even at coeducational colleges, however, women and men had very different educational experiences. At liberal Oberlin, for instance, female students were expected to remain silent at public assemblies; in addition, they were required to care not only for themselves, but also for the male students by doing their laundry, cleaning their rooms, and serving them their meals (Flexner 1971). Moreover, there, and at virtually every other coeducational college, women and men were channeled into different areas of study. Men specialized in fields such as engineering, the physical and natural sciences, business, law, and medicine. Women, in contrast, studied home economics, nursing, and, of course, elementary education (Howe 1984). In fact, a teaching degree or certificate remained one of the few avenues of upward mobility for white, black, and immigrant women well into the twentieth century (Giddings 1984).

Nevertheless, some women did earn degrees in nontraditional or male-dominated fields, and many of them graduated from women's colleges. Wheaton College, established in 1834, was the first women's college, and in the late 1880s, the elite "Seven Sisters" colleges (Mount Holyoke, Vassar, Wellesley, Smith, Radcliffe, Bryn Mawr, and Barnard) were opened. What is perhaps most significant about these institutions is that they offered women the traditional men's curriculum in a highly supportive environment that fostered their ambitions and encouraged achievement. Consequently, "these institutions produced an exceptional generation of women during the 1890s who, nurtured by the collective female life of the women's college, emerged with aspirations to use their educations outside the confines of women's domestic sphere as it was narrowly defined in marriage" (Schwager 1987:362). Many of these women became leaders of the various social reform movements, including the suffrage movement, that grew during the early 1900s. A substantial percentage pursued further training or entered the professions. Even midway through the twentieth century when, as we will soon see, the overall percentage of female Ph.D.'s dropped considerably, the women's colleges continued to graduate exceptional female students who often went on to graduate and professional schools (Tidball 1980).

Women and Men in Education During the Twentieth Century

The emphasis on mass education did not diminish during the early decades of the twentieth century, fueled in large part by widespread concern over the influx of European immigrants into the United States. Special efforts were made to teach immigrants English and basic literacy skills, for according to many social reformers, education would help solve the social problems associated with immigrant life (e.g., poverty, alcoholism, and juvenile delinquency). This, coupled with continuing industrialization, promoted a steady rise in elementary and secondary school enrollments throughout the first half of the century.

Still, as Table 5.1 indicates, an education gap between males and females persisted, especially at the higher educational levels. To some extent, this was because of the popular belief that education was less important for females. Although Tyack and Hansot (1990) maintain that gender was rarely a major factor in the development of educational policy, there is evidence that in the often overcrowded public schools, administrators appeared quite willing to let girls drop out, since their departure would open more spaces for boys. In the 1930s, however, many states enacted laws that made school attendance until age sixteen mandatory. This, in turn, narrowed the gap at the secondary school level, but other factors operated to preserve it in colleges and graduate programs.

Looking again at Table 5.1, we see that, until the 1980s, women have consistently comprised less than half the undergraduate student body in the United States, despite the fact that they make up slightly more than 50 percent of the country's population. Interestingly, in 1920, they did approach the 50 percent mark, but by 1930, their numbers had dwindled, continuing to fall until 1960. A similar pattern can be seen with regard to graduate school as measured by the percentage of doctoral degrees awarded to women. The percentage of doctorates who were women peaked in 1930, but then dropped considerably until 1970 when it began to rise steadily once again.

How can we account for this kind of roller coaster pattern in women's representation in higher education? As we mentioned previously, a number of factors appear to be involved. The early growth in female college and graduate

TABLE 5.1
The Education Gap Between the Sexes, 1870–1984

Year	% of Population Enrolled in Elementary & Secondary School (M/F)	Females as Undergrads (%)	Females as Bachelor's Degree Recipients (%)*	Females as Master's Degree Recipients (%)	Females as Doctorates (%)
1870	49.8/46.9	21	15	n.a.	0
1880	59.2/56.5	32	19	n.a.	6
1890	54.7/53.8	35	17	n.a.	1
1900	50.1/50.9	35	19	n.a.	6
1910	59.1/59.4	39	25	n.a.	11
1920	64.1/64.5	47	34	n.a.	15
1930	70.2/69.7	43	40	n.a.	18
1940	74.9/69.7	40	41	n.a.	13
1950	79.1/78.4	31	24	29.3	10
1960	84.9/83.8	36	35	32	10
1970	88.5/87.2	41	41	39.7	13
1980	95.5/95.5	52.3	47.3	49.3	29.8
1987	95.6/95.9	52.5	51.5	51.2	35.2

*Includes first professional degrees from 1870 to 1970.
Sources: U.S. Department of Commerce 1990, 1985, and 1975; Graham, 1978.

school enrollments was probably due, at least in part, to the first feminist movement and the struggle for women's rights (*see* Chapter 13). In addition, with males off fighting World War I, colleges may have looked to (tuition-paying) females to take their places (Graham 1978). The Great Depression of the 1930s dashed many young people's hopes of attending college, but it is likely that women more often sacrificed further schooling given the old belief that education (particularly a college education) is less important for them. World War II sent men abroad once again to fight, while women were recruited for wartime production jobs (*see* Chapter 8). After the war ended, an unprecedented number of men entered college thanks to the GI bill. For women, though, the dominant postwar ideology idealized marriage and motherhood and promoted a standard of femininity by which women were judged according to how well they cared for their families, their homes, and their appearance. As Graham (1978:772) reports:

> The women of the forties and fifties absorbed the new values and withdrew from the professional arena. They married at very high rates at more youthful ages and had lots of babies. The birth rate reached its peak in 1957, at which time the average age for first marriage for women was just over 20.

Those women who did attend college were often accused of pursuing an *Mrs.* instead of a *B.S.*, for the college campus came to be seen as the perfect setting for meeting a promising (i.e., upwardly mobile) mate. Not infrequently, women dropped out of school to take jobs to help support their student-husbands.

This pattern appears applicable only with regard to the educational history of white women, however. When race is taken into account, a different historical overview emerges. According to Giddings (1984:245), for example, during the time that white women began to drop out of or not attend college, the number of black women in college, especially in black colleges, increased:

> By 1940, more black women received B.A. degrees from Black colleges than Black men (3,244 and 2,463 respectively). By 1952–53, the surge of Black women had increased significantly. They received 62.4 percent of all degrees from Black colleges when, in all colleges, the percentage of women graduates was 33.4 percent. The percentage of Black women graduates was in fact just a little below that of *male* graduates in all schools (66.6 percent) and substantially higher than that of Black men (35.6 percent). An important dimension of this was that a large proportion of these women were the first in their families to receive college degrees.

Also significant is the fact that many of these women went on to graduate school. By the early 1950s, the number of black women with master's degrees exceeded the number of black men with this level of education. However, black male Ph.D.'s and M.D.'s still outnumbered their female counterparts by a considerable margin (Giddings 1984). Interestingly, Smith (1982) reports that black females' educational aspirations are higher than those of black males until college, when they begin to decline. This is a point to which we will return shortly.

Since the 1970s, the percentage of women and minority undergraduates and graduate students has risen substantially, and considerable attention has been given to the problems of sexism and racism at every level of schooling. Undoubtedly, the Civil Rights Movement and the resurgence of the feminist movement during the sixties and seventies played a major part in bringing about these changes. With respect to sex descrimination, in particular, feminist lobbying efforts were instrumental in the passage of the Education Amendments Act of 1972, which contains the important provisions known as **Title IX.** Simply stated, Title IX forbids sex discrimination in any educational program or activity that receives federal funding. This law has resulted in a number of beneficial reforms in education, especially in school athletic programs for women and girls (*see* Chapter 12.) Nevertheless, the educational experiences of males and females remain quite different and, more significantly, unequal. In the remainder of this chapter, we will examine the various structural factors that serve to perpetuate this inequality, from elementary school through graduate school.

EDUCATING GIRLS AND BOYS: THE ELEMENTARY SCHOOLS

Just like parents, when elementary school teachers are asked, they will state that they treat all their students fairly regardless of their sex. Research findings indicate, however, that in practice, teachers typically interact differently with their male and female students. For one thing, most teachers continue to use various subtle forms of sex segregation in their classrooms. For example, they seat girls on one side of the room and boys on the other; they ask girls and boys to form separate lines; or they may organize teams for a spelling competition according to students' sex. It is also not uncommon for teachers to assign girls and boys different classroom chores; for instance, girls may be asked to dust or water the plants, whereas boys are asked to carry books, rearrange desks, or run equipment (Thorne and Luria 1986; Sadker and Sadker 1985a).

Subtle though they may be, these kinds of sex segregation have at least three interrelated consequences. First, sex segregation in and of itself prevents boys and girls from working together cooperatively, thus denying children of both sexes valuable opportunities to learn about and sample one another's interests and activities. Second, it makes working in same-sex groups more comfortable than working in mixed-sex groups—a feeling that children may carry with them into adulthood and which may become problematic when they enter the labor force (*see* Chapter 8). And finally, sex segregation reinforces gender stereotypes, especially if it involves diffferential work assignments (Lockheed 1986; Sadker and Sadker 1985b).

Separating students by sex is not the only, nor is it the most significant way that teachers treat their male and female pupils differently. It also appears that teachers respond more to boys than girls, in both positive and negative ways. For example, one recent study of fourth, sixth, and eighth grade classes in the Washington, D.C., and New England areas found that "Teachers were more likely to provide remediation and challenge for male students. They gave boys more help in finding errors and correcting problems. They were also more likely to challenge a male student to achieve the best possible academic response"(Sadker and Sadker 1985a:451). Other studies confirm these findings. Boys get more praise for the intellectual quality of their work, whereas girls are praised more often for the neatness of their work (Dweck, et al. 1978). In addition, teachers typically provide boys with detailed instructions for completing a complex task, but they are more likely to simply do the task for girls, thereby depriving girls of the valuable experience of independent learning through doing (Sadker and Sadker 1985b).

Although boys in general engage in more positive interactions with teachers, they are also more likely than girls to incur their teachers' wrath. Boys are subject to more disciplinary action in elementary school classrooms, and their punishments are harsher and more public than those handed out to girls. Of course, this may be because boys misbehave more than girls. In Chapter 4, we pointed out that preschool boys are encouraged to be active and aggressive, while preschool girls are rewarded for quiet play and passivity. It may be that the early childhood socialization of girls better prepares them for the behavioral requirements of elementary school. Yet, this fails to explain why, when boys and girls are being equally disruptive, it is the boys that teachers most frequently single out for punishment (Serbin, et al. 1973). The one exception appears to be when answers are called out in class: When boys call out comments without raising their hands, teachers accept their answers. However, when girls call out, teachers reprimand this 'inappropriate' behavior with messages such as, 'In this class we don't shout out answers, we raise our hands' " (Sadker and Sadker 1985b:56). Clearly, gender stereotypes have a strong influence on teacher-student interactions.

It is hardly surprising that teachers respond to their students in these ways given that few teacher preparation programs do anything to prevent it. In one study of teacher-education textbooks, for instance, researchers found that the problem of sexism in the schools is rarely addressed. In fact, the authors of these texts are sometimes guilty of sexism themselves (Sadker and Sadker 1980).

Gender stereotypes are not the only prejudices that may affect teacher's interactions with their students, however. Race and social class prejudices may interact with sexism to have an especially pernicious effect on some students' educational experiences. In her thorough review of the literature, Reid (1982) cites a study in which the reinforcement practices of sixty female black and white teachers were observed. The researchers found that teachers tended to reinforce children of their same race less than opposite-race children and to reinforce boys more often than girls. However, the study showed that black girls received the least reinforcement of any group of children. A study by Jensen and Rosenfeld (1974) indicated that children's social class mediated this pattern to some extent in that middle-class children, regardless of race, receive more favorable evaluations from teachers than lower-class class children. "Interestingly, however, academic ability has a reverse effect upon teachers' reinforcement of black children. Black girls with high academic ability were ignored even more than those with lesser abilities. The same effect was true to some extent for black boys. It seems as though teachers prefer black children to conform to expectations of low academic ability" (Reid 1982:144). This is one of the reasons that the Milwaukee school board voted in 1990 to establish two African-American Immersion Schools. The controversial pilot program is designed to "emphasize black culture, build self-esteem and promote the rewards of responsible male behavior" (Johnson 1990). Given teachers' unresponsiveness to black females, though, it may be a mistake to structure learning in these schools around a black male perspective.

The gender messages that teachers send to students are reinforced by the traditional curricular materials available in elementary schools. We noted at the outset of this chapter that students learn not only the academic subjects of their school's formal curriculum, but also a set of values and expectations of a hidden curriculum. We can see the hidden curriculum at work in the selective content of textbooks and other educational materials. Even though the United States is a country with citizens of both sexes who share a rich and varied racial and ethnic heritage, there is a conspicuous absence of racial minorities and women in elementary school textbooks. In history texts, for example, Native Americans and Chicanos are rarely mentioned apart from such events as Custer's last stand or the Alamo, and in both cases, it is made abundantly clear who the "bad guys" were. Blacks are typically discussed in the context of slavery, the Civil War, and perhaps the Civil Rights Movement, but Harriet Tubman and Rev. Martin Luther King, Jr., are often the only blacks singled out as history makers. When women are mentioned, it is usually in terms of traditional feminine roles: for example, for nursing, Florence Nightingale; for sewing, Betsy Ross; and for being married to famous men, Dolly Madison and Jackie Kennedy Onassis. The heterosexist bias of the texts goes without saying.

The use of history texts as an example is not meant to imply that a hidden curriculum is prevalent only in the material taught to older children. Researchers have found the hidden curriculum at work even in the early grades. Consider the books used to teach children to read. As the following example illustrates, these books may also teach children particular lessons about gender:

> A book in the easy-to-read section of the library taught the children that: "Boys eat, girls cook; boys invent things, girls use what boys invent; boys build houses, girls keep house" (Best 1983:62).

Just as their later history texts will implicitly teach them that racial minorities and women rarely make significant contributions to our society, early readers also teach young children that there are things only boys can do and things only girls can do. Some publishers of children's readers have made a serious effort in recent years to eliminate gender as well as racial stereotyping from these texts. There is evidence that the readers now available are significantly improved, although there continue to be imbalances in favor of males with regard to rate of portrayal and the types of roles assigned to males and females in the stories (e.g., girls need to be rescued more than boys; boys are more adventurous than girls) (Purcell and Stewart 1990). The importance of using nonsexist curriculum materials is underlined by evidence that indicates that children do learn their lessons quite well. Consider, for instance, the findings of one researcher who asked a group of second and third graders what they wanted to be when they grew up. Typical responses from boys included: "A pro football player because I would make a lot of money"; "A spy chief, I like to spy"; and "A motorcycle racer, it is fun." In contrast, the girls replied: "I want to be a plain old woman wife, it is fun"; "A mother, I want to have a baby, it is fun"; "I want to be a nurse so I can help people when they are sick"; and "I want to be a teacher, I just like it" (Best 1983:67–68).

Finally, children receive messages about gender simply by the way adult jobs are distributed in their schools. While approximately 86 percent of elementary school teachers and 84 percent of teachers' aides are women, only 21 percent of principals and assistant principals are women (U.S. Department of Commerce 1990). Research indicates that the sex of a school principal does have a measurable effect on children's gender-role perceptions. According to one study of first graders, for instance, children who attended a school headed by a female principal held fewer gender stereotypes than those who went to a school with a male principal (Paradise and Wall 1986).

In light of our discussion so far, it is hardly surprising to find that, although girls outperform boys academically in the early grades, their achievement test scores decline significantly as they progress through school (Sadker and Sadker 1985a). As we will see next, this pattern continues in high school.

EDUCATING TEENAGE GIRLS AND BOYS: THE SECONDARY SCHOOLS

Both parents and teenagers will attest that adolescence is one of the more stressful periods of the life cycle. As one's body changes and matures, so do one's interests, and the opinions of friends take on greater significance in the formation of one's self-concept. Young men and women both feel the need to be popular with their peers, but the means and measures of their success at this are somewhat different.

For teenage boys, the single most important source of prestige and popularity is athletic achievement. The teenage boy tends to measure "himself by what he can do physically compared to others his age, and how he stacks up determines to a great extent his social acceptance by others and his own self-esteem" (Richardson, 1981:69). The "non-jock" is at an obvious disadvantage, socially and psychologically. It is the athlete who is looked to as a leader, not only by his peers, but also by teachers and parents. Moreover, on the court or on the playing field, boys are taught a variety of stereotypically masculine skills and values: aggression, endurance, competitiveness, self-confidence, and teamwork (Messner 1989).

It is also in high school that young men are expected to formulate their career goals. For those not planning to attend college, there are vocational training programs that provide the educational background needed for jobs in the skilled trades or in preparation for technical school. Most boys, though, study an academic or college prep curriculum, which may seem a bit surprising given their greater likelihood for academic difficulties in the lower grades. However, boys' academic performance usually improves during high school—to such an extent, in fact, that their SAT scores are higher on average than those of girls (U.S. Department of Commerce 1990).

And what about girls? How does their high school experience differ from that of boys? For one thing, physical prowess and athletic ability are not their chief sources of prestige and popularity. Indeed, most teenage girls learn that to be athletic is to be unfeminine and, as we will discuss in Chapter 12, schools reinforce this message with inadequate funding for girls' sports programs. Instead, what contributes most to a teenage girl's prestige and popularity is having a boyfriend. "A girl may be bright, friendly, competent, and attractive, but without a boyfriend she lacks social validation of these positive attributes. It is as though being selected by a boy tells others that a girl is worthwhile" (Lott 1987:71; Bush 1987).

Of course, it is during high school that young women also begin to plan for their futures. However, the career aspirations of teenage girls appear to be significantly lower than those of teenage boys with similar backgrounds and abilities (Bush 1987). Even though teenage girls now see the majority of adult women around them working full-time outside the home (*see* Chapter 8), they continue to expect a rather traditional future for themselves. A number of studies have found that while many high school girls today express a preference for an egalitarian division of labor in the household, most still favor an arrangement in which the husband is the primary breadwinner and the wife is responsible for housework and childcare, especially when there are young children at home (Canter and Ageton 1984; Herzog, et al. 1983; Sherman 1983).

These traditional expectations are reflected in the coursework teenage girls most often undertake in preparation for their future careers. Those not planning to attend college are typically enrolled in sex-typed vocational training courses, such as home economics, cosmetology, and secretarial programs that prepare them to be homemakers or to take jobs with salaries far lower than the skilled trades that employ mostly men. But even college-bound girls shy away from courses such as those in advanced mathematics and science that will prepare them to pursue further study for the most highly paid and prestigious professions (Bush 1987; Sherman 1982; *see also* Box 5.1).

The low career aspirations of teenage girls are usually unrelated to their academic achievement. For example, Bernice Lott (1987:71) reports that in one study of midwestern high school students, "the girls who anticipated working in the lowest status occupations had higher grade point averages than the boys who anticipated working in medium status occupations." Thus, girls tend to underestimate their academic ability which, in turn, may lead them to lower their educational and career plans for the future (Eccles 1985; Danzinger 1983; Stanworth 1983). In her recent study of adolescents at a private girls school in New York, Carol Gilligan (1990) reports that by age fifteen or sixteen, girls who had earlier exuded confidence become less outspoken and more doubtful about their abilities.

An obvious question at this point is why do young women develop such perceptions of themselves? One explanation, offered by psychologist Matina Horner (1972), is that women fear success. In her research, Horner asked female and male subjects to write stories based on information she provided them; in some cases, the story theme was success. She found that 62 percent of the women, but only 9 percent of the men, wrote stories containing negative imagery in response to success-related cues. She subsequently discovered that these women tended to perform better on word-game tasks when they worked alone rather than in mixed-sex groups. This led her to conclude that women's fear of success was related to a discomfort they experienced when competing with men. Horner argued that women may deliberately, though perhaps unconsciously, underachieve because they fear the consequences that success in high achievement situations might bring—specifically, that they will appear unfeminine and, therefore, be rejected socially.

Empirical research on the "fear of success" theory, however, has yielded inconsistent findings. There is evidence that girls tend to feel uneasy and embarrassed about academic success (Sherman 1982), and that they often avoid subjects defined as masculine because they think boys will not like them (Tobias and

---

BOX 5.1   Are Boys Naturally Gifted with Greater Math Ability Than Girls?

Fact: On average, males score significantly higher than females on math tests. Is this difference the result of some inborn talent in males, or are there social factors at work that foster math achievement for males but hamper it for females? This question has long been the focus of a heated and still-unresolved debate. Although we certainly cannot hope to settle the argument here, we can review some of the evidence that has been gathered.

You may recall that in Chapter 2 we discussed differences in the spatial abilities of girls and boys; boys tend to outperform girls on tasks involving spatial skills (Maccoby and Jacklin 1974). Since many math problems require a strong spatial orientation, some observers argue that boys do better at math because of their greater visual spatial ability. Is this ability natural, or is it nurtured? In Chapter 2 we noted that sex differences in spatial ability are actually small and appear to be developmental; that is, they emerge over time as children get older (Tartre 1990; Hyde 1984). Consequently, some researchers maintain that these differences may be caused by the fact that "boys more than girls may be allowed to explore and manipulate their environment and/or encouraged to play with materials, such as mechanical toys, that develop spatial skills" (Frieze, et al. 1987:63). Would sex differences in spatial abilities, and hence math achievement, disappear if girls were given the same opportunities? Unfortunately, we know of no research to date that provides a definitive answer, although Tartre's (1990) work is a useful starting point.

Other factors associated with sex differences in math achievement are: (1) the extent to which math is oriented to males; (2) teacher-student interaction; and (3) parental encouragement. With regard to the first factor, several observers have noted that math word problems are often oriented toward traditionally masculine-typed areas and interests. Frieze and her colleagues (1978) cite as a typical example a problem that involves mixing cement—an activity girls rarely (are permitted to) engage in. Research, however, indicates that girls perform significantly better on problems with feminine-typed content, so they suggest varying the gender-orientation of word problems by changing the focal activity, for instance, from cement mixing to cake mixing.

More recent research has pointed to the masculine orientation of much computer software, particularly computer games, as well as the male-dominated environment of most public game rooms (Crawford 1990; Lockheed 1985). Hess and Muira (1985) also found that the educational software programs most likely found in math and science classes center around male themes of violence and adventure. Consequently, girls may come to see math, science, and computer-related activities as masculine—a perception that may affect not only their performance, but also their career aspirations. In addition, research indicates that girls may pay a heavy social cost for computer proficiency. When interviewing adolescents, for example, Crawford (1990:25) heard many stories from

---

Weissbrod 1980). There is also evidence that their concerns are not unfounded. Pfost and Fiore (1990) report that females described as masculine and seeking traditionally masculine jobs were considered by research subjects as undesirable heterosexual partners and friends, although subjects' responses to males described in gender-incongruent ways were not consistently negative.

Box 5.1 continued

female achievers in computer studies "of the boys being 'jealous' of [the girls'] knowledge of electronics and of 'hassling' the girls in class. The boys confirmed their view."
Not surprisingly, then, as one young woman reported about girls who pursue computer
science, "It's usually the brave that do it" (quoted in Crawford 1990:25).

Fennema and Sherman (1977) discovered that the major difference between males
and females with regard to mathematics is not math ability per se, but rather extent of
exposure to mathematics. Girls and boys with identical math backgrounds show little
difference in performance on math tests. Yet girls are less likely than boys to pursue
math training beyond their schools' requirements for graduation, and two critical factors
influencing their decisions appear to be their interactions with teachers and the encouragement of their parents (Crawford 1990). Sherman (1982), for example, reports that
girls (33 percent) are much more likely than boys (10 percent) to cite a teacher as the
factor that most discouraged them from studying math. Research on teacher-student
interaction indicates that there are various ways that teachers differentially reinforce
math achievement in male and female students: by perceiving and conveying the belief
that math is more important for boys than for girls, by encouraging girls to become
proficient at computational math and boys at problem solving, and by calling on boys
more than girls to solve problems in class (Fennema 1990; Koehler 1990; Leung 1990).

Girls who pursue math training tend to be closer to their parents and more influenced by them (Sherman 1983). Although few parents openly discourage their daughters
from studying math or math-related fields, the message may be communicated indi-
rectly. For instance, recent research indicates that parents are much less likely to enroll
daughters than sons in computer camps, especially when the cost of the camps is high
(Hess and Muira 1985). Importantly, although girls and boys both recognize that computers will have a significant impact on their personal futures, boys are more likely to
report having access to computers at home (Crawford 1990; Lockheed 1985).

In summary, the weight of the evidence points to a variety of social factors as
being responsible for observed differences in math achievement between males and females. In one sense, this is encouraging since, as we have argued previously, socially
induced conditions are more easily changed than those that are biologically caused. Indeed, the solution seems obvious: educators and parents must consciously commit themselves to providing a more supportive and less sex-segregated learning environment for
both girls and boys. Until such steps are taken, math will probably remain a "critical
filter" that blocks females' advancement into the lucrative and prestigious scientific professions (Leder and Fennema 1990; Chesterman 1990; The McClintock Collective 1990;
Sherman 1982).

Fear of success seems to decrease as girls progress through adolescence,
however (Ishiyama and Chabassol 1985), and it is certainly the case, too, that
girls do excel in many areas; the fact that our male-centered culture devalues
what it defines as feminine accomplishments should not detract from their successes. In addition, replications of Horner's research have produced no significant

differences between females and males in their use of negative imagery in response to success-related cues. In other words, male subjects in subsequent experiments were just as likely as female subjects to exhibit fear of success (Tresemer 1977).

By focusing on the psychology of the adolescent girl, the fear of success argument also ignores the "invisible ceiling" that others frequently impose on young women's ambitions. This invisible ceiling takes a variety of forms. First, there is the widespread belief that girls are not as intellectually gifted as boys and, therefore, cannot be expected to do as well in school. Research reveals, for example, that both parents and teachers tend to attribute boys' academic achievements to intellectual prowess and to explain their failures in terms of factors such as "bad luck." They do just the opposite for girls; if they are successful, they were lucky or the task itself was easy; if they do poorly, it is because they are not smart (Deaux 1976). Consequently, teachers appear to offer male students more encouragement, to publicly praise their scholastic abilities, and to be friendlier toward them than they are toward female students. Importantly, as Bush (1987:15) notes, "These findings are analogous to those for teacher expectations linked to class and/or race" in which teachers respond more positively to middle- and upper-class students than to working class and poor students or to white students relative to minority students. We can only speculate on the impact that the intersection of teachers' sexism, racism, and classism may have on students, but there is evidence that students internalize these beliefs which, if one is female, could reasonably lead to a scaling down of aspirations—not for fear of success, but for fear of failure (Bush 1987; Vollmer 1986; Smith 1982; Dweck, et al. 1978).

Curriculum materials and school personnel may also place a ceiling on girls' ambitions. Reskin and Hartmann (1986) cite research that shows gender stereotyping in math and foreign language texts as well as in other higher educational materials (*see also New York Times* 4 March 1990:35). At the same time, high school guidance counselors may channel male and female students into different (i.e., gender stereotyped) fields and activities. There is evidence that gender stereotyping is common among counselors (Petro and Putnam 1979), and that they often steer female students away from certain college prep courses, particularly in mathematics and the sciences (Marini and Brinton 1984). Finally, although elementary school girls can at least identify with their teachers, whom we have noted are almost all women, this becomes more difficult in senior high school where 53 percent of teachers are men (U.S. Department of Commerce 1990). High school students are especially likely to have a male teacher for their math courses (57.7 percent) and science courses (65.4 percent) (Commission on Professionals in Science and Technology 1989).

Given the rather discouraging nature of their high school experience, it is somewhat surprising that so many young women choose to go on to college. Nevertheless, as shown in Table 5.1, they now constitute a slight majority of college students. Unfortunately, as we will find next, the education they receive continues to differ from that of their male peers in many important respects.

EDUCATING WOMEN AND MEN:
COLLEGES AND GRADUATE SCHOOLS

"What's your major?" is certainly a question college students get asked a lot. The next time you are in a group and that question comes up, compare the responses of the male students with those of the female students. Chances are you will discover an interesting sex-specific pattern, for as Table 5.2 shows, men and women continue to be concentrated in very different fields of study. Male students tend to pursue degrees in engineering, architecture, the physical and natural sciences, computer science, and business. Women, in contrast, are heavily concentrated in nursing, home economics, library science, education, the social sciences, and humanities. Among the few exceptions in the latter two areas are political science, criminology, philosophy, and theology, which each have a higher percentage of male than female degree recipients.

This imbalance persists and, in fact, worsens at the graduate level. Again, the graduate degrees of men and women tend to be concentrated in different fields. For example, men earn 93 percent of the Ph.D.'s in engineering, but less than 10 percent of the Ph.D.'s in nursing. Conversely, women earn 78 percent of the doctorates in home economics, but just 9 percent of the doctorates in physics (Commission on Professionals in Science and Technology 1989).

An even more disturbing trend also emerges at the graduate level: the number of female degree recipients declines dramatically. Consider that although women represent half of all bachelor's and master's degree recipients, they constitute only one-third of all doctorate recipients. More importantly, male Ph.D.'s outnumber female Ph.D.'s in many fields that have a higher concentration of women undergraduates or in which there is a relative balance between the sexes at the undergraduate level. Sociology is a good example; men receive only 31 percent of the bachelor's degrees in sociology, but 60 percent of the doctorates. Similarly, in international relations, men are awarded 45 percent of bachelor's degrees and 87 percent of doctorates; in music, 47 percent of bachelor's degrees and 64 percent of doctorates; and in mathematics, 54 percent of bachelor's degrees and 83 percent of doctorates (Commission on Professionals in Science and Technology 1989). Table 5.3 provides a distribution of recent doctoral degree recipients by race as well as sex. Here we see that the overwhelming majority of Ph.D's are awarded to whites of both sexes, while the numbers for men and women of other racial groups are significantly lower. We will see shortly that this has a substantial impact on the number of minorities, especially minority women, in university faculties who may then serve as role models for students.

An important point that must be made with regard to sex is that these figures actually represent a better balance between women and men in higher education than in the recent past. For instance, in 1970, women constituted only 13 percent of the doctoral recipients in the United States, up from 10 percent in 1960 (U.S. Department of Commerce 1985). It is especially noteworthy that women have made their greatest gains in some of the fields that have had the

TABLE 5.2
Percentage of Bachelor's Degrees Conferred by U.S. Institutions to Men and Women in Selected Fields of Study, 1986–87

Major Field of Study	%Bachelor's Degrees Conferred to Men	%Bachelor's Degrees Conferred to Women
Accounting	49	51
Agriculture	67	33
Anthropology	36	64
Architecture	75	25
Astronomy	84	16
Banking & Finance	65	35
Biology	51	49
Business Management & Admin.	55	45
Chemistry	63	37
Computer & Info. Sciences	65	35
Communications	40	60
Criminology	60	40
Economics	70	30
Education	24	76
Engineering	85	15
English	33	67
Foreign Languages	27	73
Geology	77	23
History	62	38
Home Economics	7	93
International Relations	45	55
Library Science	14	86
Mathematics	54	46
Military Science	93	7
Music	47	53
Nursing	5	95
Philosophy & Religion	64	36
Physics	84	16
Political Science & Government	60	40
Psychology	31	69
Public Affairs	32	68
Sociology	31	69
Theology	76	24

Source: Commission on Professionals in Science and Technology 1989:60–62.

TABLE 5.3
Doctorates Conferred by U.S. Universities for Selected Fields, by Race and Sex, 1986–87

Field	Total	White		Black		Hispanic		Asian		Native American	
		M	F	M	F	M	F	M	F	M	F
Physical Sci	3671	1985	456	22	4	43	17	129	37	3	0
Engineering	3807	1502	170	26	3	65	3	240	18	3	0
Mathematics	723	285	64	8	1	7	2	24	13	1	0
Life Sciences	3417	1703	921	30	23	36	23	83	66	4	1
Social Sciences	2915	1328	723	57	38	50	18	59	18	2	2
Psychology	3056	1436	1289	35	62	23	48	22	29	6	10
Letters	1181	405	545	6	22	17	9	5	16	3	3
Education	6909	2412	3083	177	291	87	120	59	45	25	24

Source: Commission on Professionals in Science and Technology 1989:63

fewest female students, such as the physical sciences and engineering. Although still small, the number of doctorates earned by women in engineering increased rapidly in recent years, more than tripling between 1978 and 1988 (Commission on Professionals in Science and Technology 1989). Still, some nagging questions remain: Why does sex segregation in particular fields persist, and why is the education gap between the sexes still so large?

In addressing the first question, we must consider not only why women are largely absent from certain fields, but also why there are so few men in fields such as nursing, home economics, and library science. We can say with some certainty that the scarcity of men in the female-dominated fields has less to do with discrimination against them than with their unwillingness to pursue careers in areas that typically have lower prestige and lower salaries than the male-dominated fields. We have already noted that activities and topics deemed feminine are systematically devalued in our society. Until fields such as nursing and home economics are viewed as being equally important as accounting or public administration—and are rewarded with comparable salaries—it will remain difficult to attract men to major in them. However, in solving the puzzle of women's relative absence from the more prestigious and higher paying male-dominated fields, the issue of discrimination is central.

It is widely thought that sex discrimination in education has virtually disappeared, thanks to Title IX. You may recall that Title IX is the provision of the 1972 Education Amendments Act that forbids discrimination in any educational program or activity that receives federal funding. However, Title IX has not eliminated sex discrimination in education for a number of reasons. One important reason for the less than total success of Title IX is that, while the law abolished most overtly discriminatory policies and practices, it left more subtle forms of sex discrimination intact (Sandler and Hall 1986). Sandler and Hall (1986:3) refer to these subtle, everyday types of discrimination as **micro-inequities.** Micro-inequities single out, ignore, or in some way discount individuals and their work or ideas simply on the basis of an ascribed trait, such as sex. "Often the behaviors themselves are small, and individually might even be termed 'trivial' or minor annoyances, but when they happen again and again, they can have a major cumulative impact because they express underlying limited expectations and a certain discomfort in dealing with women" (Sandler and Hall 1986:3).

Hall and Sandler (1985) have documented more than 35 different kinds of micro-inequities experienced by female undergraduate and graduate students, including the following:

Male students are called on more than female students and are interrupted less when they are speaking (*see also* Lewis and Simon 1986).

Professors may use sex stereotyped examples when discussing men's and women's social or professional roles (e.g., always referring to physicians as "he" and nurses as "she").

References are made to males as "men" but to females as "girls" or "gals," or the generic "he" or "man" is used to refer to both men and women (*see* Chapter 6).

Comments are made about a female student's physical attributes or appearance, especially while she is discussing an academic matter or an idea (e.g., "did anyone ever tell you how big your eyes get when you're excited about something?").

Comments are made that disparage women in general (e.g., references to single, middle-aged women as "old maids"), that disparage women's intellectual abilities (e.g., "You girls probably won't understand this"), or that disparage women's academic commitment and seriousness (e.g., "You're so cute; why would you ever want to be an engineer?").

It is difficult to imagine such comments being made to or about men or male students, but they are not infrequently made to or about women. Granted, "these behaviors do not happen in *every class,* nor do they happen all the time. But they happen often enough that they contribute to a pattern—a pattern of behavior that dampens women's ambition, lessens their class participation, and diminishes their self-confidence" (Hall and Sandler 1985:506, authors' emphasis). More importantly, it appears that these inequities are more common in courses and fields of study traditionally dominated by men, and that they intensify in graduate school (Hall and Sandler 1985). Clearly, this helps to explain the relative absence of women in the sciences and business and also at the doctoral level.

There are, though, at least two other serious barriers to equality for women in higher education: the lack of mentors and the incidence of sexual harassment. We will discuss each of these in turn.

Women Faculty and Administrators: Still Too Few

Despite the gains that women have made in terms of the percentage of advanced degrees awarded to them, they still constitute a small minority of university faculty and administrators. The national average of women in senior administrative positions on college and university compuses is 1.1, and women represent only about 27 percent of full-time faculty (American Association of University Professors, hereafter AAUP, 1990; Weis 1987). In general, the more prestigious the institution or department, the fewer the women. Similarly, the higher the academic rank, the fewer the women. For instance, less than 5 percent of full-time female faculty hold the rank of full professor compared with about 31 percent of male faculty; women constitute less than 12 percent of full professors. At the same time, 46 percent of female faculty are at the rank of assistant professor or below compared with 25 percent of male faculty (AAUP 1990; Commission on Professionals in Science and Technology 1989). One might expect the percentage of women in higher ranks to increase as more women enter academic employment. However, given that women are less likely than men to be tenured, there is not much room for optimism. The tenure rate for women is less than 50 percent, whereas for men it is almost 75 percent (Rohter 1987). Regardless of rank or tenure status, however, women faculty are paid less than men and, as Table 5.4 shows, the gap is widest at the highest academic rank.

Female faculty and administrators, like female students, confront innumerable inequities—some subtle, some overt—on the campuses where they work (Sandler and Hall 1986). They may find, for example, that male colleagues or students feel free to address them as "honey" or "dear," or that their male colleagues are consistently called "Dr." while they are "Miss" or "Mrs." At department or committee meetings, they may be expected to record the minutes or, as the "token woman," to provide the "women's point of view" as if one woman can speak for all. Their personal lives may be scrutinized (e.g., "Who takes care of

TABLE 5.4
Average Salaries for University Faculty by Rank and Sex, 1989–90

Academic Rank	Salary		Salary Difference
	Men	*Women*	*M/F*
Professor	$67,760	$59,590	$8,170
Associate Professor	46,540	43,170	3,370
Assistant Professor	39,810	36,020	3,790
Instructor	30,090	29,360	730

Source: American Association of University Professors 1990:6.

her kids?"), and their appearance commented on (e.g., "With legs like those, why don't you wear skirts more often?"). But perhaps most frustrating and damaging of all, their work may be devalued even when it is equal or superior to that of a man. Sandler and Hall (1986:6) report some of the research findings on this issue:

> In one study, first done in 1968 and then replicated in 1983, college students were asked to rate identical articles according to specific criteria. The authors' names attached to the articles were clearly male or female, but were reversed for each group of raters: what one group thought had been written by a male, the second group thought had been written by a female, and vice versa. Articles supposedly written by women were consistently ranked lower than when the very same articles were thought to have been written by a male. In a similar study, department chairs were asked to make hypothetical hiring decisions and to assign faculty rank on the basis of vitae. For vitae with male names, chairs recommended the rank of associate professor; however, the identical vitae with a female name merited only the rank of assistant professor.

Discrimination such as this effectively keeps women out of academia and prevents those already there from moving up. Once again, the problem is most acute in the academic disciplines traditionally dominated by men, but it has its greatest impact on minority women regardless of department. This is because they face a kind of double jeopardy—discrimination on the basis of both race and sex—that is often perpetrated by white women as well as men (Sandler and Hall 1986). This accounts in large part for the even greater absence of minority women from academe which we noted earlier. Of a total of 464,072 full-time university faculty, just 14,980 are women of color. Table 5.5 shows their distribution across the academic ranks. Clearly, they are not only few in number, but they are also concentrated at the bottom of the academic hierarchy.

A net result of all this for female students, especially female minority students, is a lack of mentors. A **mentor** is a role model and more; as an older,

TABLE 5.5
Percentage of Full-Time Female Faculty in Institutions of Higher Education, by Academic Rank and Race, 1985

Rank	Percent Female				
	White	*Black*	*Hispanic*	*Asian*	*Native American*
Professors	2.9	.17	.05	.08	.007
Associate Professors	5.0	.34	.10	.15	.012
Assistant Professors	7.5	.64	.14	.26	.02
Instructors	6.1	.53	.14	.15	.03

Source: Commission on Professionals in Science and Technology 1989:123.

established member of a profession, a mentor shows young, new members "the ropes" by giving advice and providing valuable contacts with others in the field. However, since mentors tend to choose protegés who are most like themselves, and since there are so few women in the upper echelons of the academic hierarchy, female students (and junior faculty) may have fewer opportunities to establish mentoring relationships and thereby lose out on the benefits such relationships provide (Nevels 1990). They may even come to doubt the realism of their own ambitions, as one student's account illustrates:

> I had a man advisor . . . there was only one woman who taught in the graduate school. . . . [T]he whole time I never did work with any women professors. . . . And I began to think, "Where do I fit in the system if there are no women in it, or very few?" (Quoted in Sandler and Hall 1986:16; *see also* Arundel 1989).

Although some have questioned the necessity of a mentor for individual success (Speizer 1981), we maintain that at the very least, the presence of senior female faculty and administrators communicates to students and other members of the campus community that women are as capable, productive, and serious professionally as their male counterparts. Of course, it may be argued that male faculty can also mentor female students and, in fact, they often do. But abundant evidence indicates that male faculty typically interact differently with male and female students. They sometimes feel uncomfortable with female students, or they may relate to them paternalistically rather than professionally. Worse still, they view their female students as potential sexual partners and use their positions of power and authority to coerce sexual favors. As we will see next, this is not an uncommon experience for college women.

Sexual Harassment

Sexual harassment involves any unwanted leers, comments, suggestions, or physical contact of a sexual nature, as well as unwelcome requests for sexual favors. Studies conducted on campuses throughout the country indicate that between 20 and 49 percent of female faculty have experienced some form of sexual harassment along with 20 to 30 percent of female students (Dzeich and Weiner 1990; Project on the Status and Education of Women 1986a; Reilly, et al. 1986; Sandler and Hall 1986). Although only 2 to 3 percent of female undergraduates are victims of the most serious forms of harassment (e.g., threats or bribes involving grades or letters of recommendation in exchange for sex), a sizeable minority experience unwanted touching and verbal harassment (Reilly, et al. 1986; Sandler and Hall 1986).

Most of these incidents go unreported to school authorities. Instead, victims try to handle the problem by simply avoiding the harasser whenever possible, or they tell family members and friends about it. Neither of these tactics may be helpful, particularly the latter one since family and friends may blame the victim or just tell her to ignore the harassment (Reilly, et al., 1986). Even when victims choose to report incidents of sexual harassment to school officials, administrators often downplay it and, despite frequently voiced faculty fears of overly harsh sanctions, harassers usually are dealt with informally, with the most common sanction being a verbal warning from a superior (Robertson, et al. 1988). A recent federal appeals court ruling may cause school officials to be more responsive to complaints, however. In *Stoneking* v. *Bradford Area School District* (1989), the Third U.S. Circuit Court of Appeals ruled that school administrators who fail to stop sexual harassment of students by teachers can be held liable for the inaction.

Inevitably, when the issue of sexual harassment is discussed, someone will feel obliged to point out that male students can be victimized too, or that female students sometimes approach faculty with offers of sex in exchange for grades. It is also sometimes argued that female students may make false complaints against faculty members whom they dislike or who have spurned their sexual advances. Although such incidents certainly do occur, there are several important factors that distinguish them from the sexual harassment experienced by female students at the hands of male faculty which, research indicates, constitutes the majority of sexual harassment incidents (Robertson, et al. 1988). First, the sexual harassment of male students is relatively rare and appears to take rather mild forms, such as suggestive looks and gestures, or unwanted sexual teasing by female staff and graduate assistants, rather than by faculty (Reilly, et al. 1986). Moreover, "when a man is harassed, the event is an isolated incident at odds with conventional norms about appropriate forms of sexual expression for men and women and about appropriate gender-related patterns of assertiveness and deference [on campus]." The sexual harassment of women by men is more systematic and, as we will see shortly, functions as a form of social control (Hoffman 1986:110).

Despite widespread concerns among faculty regarding the possibility of false accusations, evidence indicates that these are rare. In fact, in their survey of 668 U.S. colleges and universities, Robertson and her colleagues found among the 256 administrators who responded to a question about how many false complaints of sexual harassment they had *ever* received, only 64 complaints were identified as proven to have been intentionally fabricated compared with 425 documented incidents of sexual harassment and 760 estimated complaints of sexual harassment made at these institutions. "A rough extrapolation from the numbers given would make the false complaints less than 1 percent of annual complaints. This is a maximum estimate that does not take into account that some complaints listed as false by administrators may actually have been genuine according to our definition" (Robertson, et al. 1988:800).

With regard to female students propositioning faculty, we must question whether such incidents actually constitute sexual harassment. As McCormack (1985) points out, what is askew here is the direction of the asymmetrical power relationship between male professor and female student. There is little with which a student can threaten a faculty member—a poor teaching evaluation perhaps, but in many schools these do not count for much or a complaint brought to the department chairperson maybe, but as we have already noted, the institution usually operates to protect faculty more than students. Consider, on the other hand, that faculty control students' grades and recommendations and thus, to some extent, their futures. Viewed in this light, we conclude with McCormack (1985:30) that "to make assertions that students sexually harass faculty is to attribute power to the powerless."

However, Benson (1984:517) and others (e.g., Reilly, et al. 1986) have documented what they call *contrapower sexual harassment* which "occurs when the victim has formal power over the abuser." Contrapower harassment, then, would involve a male student propositioning or abusing a female faculty member. For instance, Reilly, et al. (1986:354) report that one of the male students in their study recounted an incident in which he asked a female professor for a cigarette and when she did not have one, he said, he "smacked the bitch." Contrapower sexual harassment clearly illustrates how some men in our society, by virtue of their sex, may feel free to exercise power and control over women even if their other statuses indicate a relatively lower social standing (Reilly, et al. 1986; Benson 1984).

What impact does sexual harassment have on women's educational experience? Research findings indicate that sexual harassment has serious negative consequences for female students. Victims report declines in their academic performance, discouragement about studying a particular field, lowered self-esteem, and emotional disturbance, physical illness, or both (Dzeich and Weiner 1990, Reilly, et al. 1986). In addition, sexual harassment fosters tension-filled relationships rather than mentoring relationships between female students and male faculty. Students consciously avoid certain professors, and some professors, afraid that their interest may be misinterpreted, distance themselves from female students. The outcome is "limitations on students whose academic success often counts on developing a close working relationship with their instructors" (McCormack 1985:30). In short, sexual harassment creates an unpleasant and hostile learning environment for female students which, in turn, affects their performance, their personal and professional growth, and ultimately, their future careers.

Structuring More Positive Learning Environments

It seems clear that women are shortchanged in their educational experiences, but the question of how to redress the inequities continues to be debated by educators. Interestingly, some observers advocate sex segregated schools as a solution. This is not to say that these educators favor channeling women and men into "gender appropriate" fields. To the contrary, their position is that single-sex institutions make it easier for both women and men to pursue fields of study not traditionally dominated by members of their sex. This is especially true at all-female schools where women can major in such traditionally male-dominated fields as physics, engineering, and business without the discomfort of being in the minority and without discouragement from male peers and faculty. As we noted earlier in this chapter, graduates of all-female schools have historically excelled in many fields, including male-dominated ones, and recent research continues to bear this out (Rice and Hemmings 1988; Lyall 1987; Tidball 1980).

Opponents of sex segregated schooling are quick to point to its various disadvantages, but unfortunately the issue may soon be moot. The school-age, and in particular, college-age population has been declining during the past two decades, forcing many single-sex institutions to become coed in the hopes of attracting more new students. Between 1965 and 1990, the number of all-female colleges in the United States dropped from 281 to 94; by 1987, there were fewer than 20 all-male colleges remaining (Bishop 1990; Lyall 1987).

A second method for balancing the educational experiences of the sexes is the integration of material about women into the curricula of both single-sex and coeducational institutions. One way this has been accomplished is through women's studies programs. According to the National Women's Studies Association, there were more than 600 such programs at U.S institutions of higher learning in 1990.

One of the original goals of women's studies was to add women to the traditionally "womanless" curriculum (McIntosh 1983). This gave rise to what may be called the *women-in* courses: women in history, women in literature, and so on. As Andersen (1987:235) points out, however, the difficulty with this approach is that, "while [it] leads to some documentation of women's experience, it tends to see a few women as exceptions to their kind and never imagines women and other underclasses as central or fundamental to social change and continuity." In other words, it accepts male-defined standards of "rightness" and excellence and examines the work of women who fit this model.

More recently, women's studies has moved away from treating women and women's experiences as problematic or as special cases, and instead examines how "women's experiences and perspectives create history, society, and culture as much as those of men do" (Andersen 1987:236). Perhaps more importantly, feminist educators are working to transform the traditional curriculum so that women's experiences and perspectives are not the material just of women's studies courses, but are taught as knowledge in their own right—as half the *human* experience studied in all courses.

Research indicates that women's studies courses have a positive impact on students. For example, one researcher found that after completing a women's studies course, students expressed less stereotyped attitudes toward women, greater self-esteem, an expanded sense of their options and goals in life, and a greater ability to understand their personal experiences in terms of a broader social context (Howe 1985).

Despite such outcomes, however, feminist educators warn that women's studies and curriculum revision programs are currently being threatened by conservative policy makers and scholars who see them as academically weak and politically biased (Andersen 1987). Alan Bloom (1987) and Roger Kimball (1990) have been perhaps the most vitriolic complainants against women's studies and similar programs on these grounds. In addition, there is considerable resistance to curriculum revision among some academics who resent being told what to cover in their courses or who simply refuse to undertake the work that revising their courses would entail (Aiken, et al. 1988). Others continue to view the issue of gender as unimportant. This attitude is typified in the answers one of your authors received when she surveyed the faculty at her institution about whether they incorporate women's experiences and perspectives into their courses. The near-unanimous response was, "Only when they're relevant." When, may we ask, are the ideas and experiences of half of humanity not relevant?

Women's studies has spurred the development of another subfield: men's studies. According to the National Education Association, men's studies was offered on almost 200 college campuses by 1986 (Project on the Status and Education of Women 1986b). Harry Brod (1987), a leader in the area of men's studies, sees it as complementary to women's studies and as informed by feminist scholarship. "As women's studies brought women into history, men's studies began to ask how men had experienced history *as men,* as carriers of masculinity" (Stimpson 1987:xii). In addition, men's studies seeks to revise the traditional view of men's experience as homogenous and to elucidate the diversity of men's lives, particularly in terms of race, social class, and sexual preference. Newer still is the addition of gay and lesbian studies on a few college campuses. Although too recent to evaluate, such programs at least hold the promise of making valuable contributions to our understanding of gender.

GENDER, EDUCATION, AND POWER

In this chapter we have learned how the educational experiences of female and male students—from elementary school through graduate school—are different and, more importantly, unequal. Although females now constitute a slight majority of students, they continue to confront a number of structural barriers that serve to impose a ceiling on their aspirations and achievement. We have seen, for example, that women are underrepresented in textbooks and course material. They are interrupted and silenced in classroom discussions. They are channeled into relatively low-paying, low-prestige fields that have been devalued simply because they are female-dominated. They lack mentors and role models and, not infrequently, they are sexually harassed by male faculty. Indeed, given the rather dismal educational environment provided to most female students, we may begin to marvel at the many who do succeed in spite of the disadvantages.

We also briefly discussed here some means to remedy these inequities, particularly through women's studies, men's studies, and curriculum revision programs. Although there has been some resistance to such efforts, their thrust has been to insure that the educational process is a democratic one that is not "merely technical and task-oriented [but also addresses] the facts of a multiracial and multicultural world that includes both women and men" (Andersen 1987:233). It is only when this vision becomes reality that we may speak of education as an empowering agent of social change rather than as a preserver of the status quo.

KEY TERMS

formal curriculum   the set of subjects officially and explicitly taught to students in school

hidden curriculum   the value preferences children are taught in school that are not an explicit part of the formal curriculum, but rather are hidden or implicit in it

mentor   an older, established member of a profession who serves as a kind of sponsor for a younger, new member by providing advice and valuable contacts with others in the field

micro-inequities   subtle, everyday forms of discrimination that single out, ignore, or in some way discount individuals and their work or ideas simply on the basis of an ascribed trait, such as sex

sexual harassment   involves any unwanted leers, comments, suggestions, or physical contact of a sexual nature, as well as unwelcome requests for sexual favors

Title IX   the provisions of the Education Amendments Act of 1972 that forbid sex discrimination in any educational programs or activities that receive federal funding

SUGGESTED READINGS

Aiken, S. H., K. Anderson, M. Dinnerstein, J. N. Lensink, and P. MacCorquodale (Eds.)1988. *Changing Our Minds: Feminist Transformations of Knowledge.* New York: State University of New York Press.

Dzeich, B. W. and L. W. Weiner 1990. *The Lecherous Professor: Sexual Harassment on Campus.* Boston: Beacon Press.

Fennema, E., and G. C. Leder (Eds.)1990. *Mathematics and Gender.* New York: Teachers College Press.

Holland, D. C., and M. A. Eisenhart. 1991. *Educated in Romance: Women, Achievement, and College Culture.* Chicago: University of Chicago Press.

Weis, L. (Ed.) 1988. *Class, Race, and Gender in American Education.* New York: State University of New York Press.

For a review of innovative educational equity programs being implemented in Great Britain, consult Burchell, H., and V. Millmen (Eds.), 1989. *Changing Perspectives on Gender: New Initiatives in Secondary Education.* Milton Keynes, England: Open University Press.

In addition, three journals have recently published special issues of relevance:

Sex Roles, Volume 13, No.3/4, 1985 is devoted to research on "Women, Girls, and Computers."

Signs, Volume 12, No.2, 1987 provides essays and research on "Restructuring the Academy."

Refractory Girl, a feminist journal published in Australia, devoted its May 1990 issue to the theme of "Women and Technology," with articles on girls and computers and gender-inclusive science and technology education.

Chapter 6

The Great Communicators: Language and the Media

Each year, Americans spend more than $70 billion on various media. An estimated $26 billion is spent on books, newspapers, and magazines, while much of the remainder goes to audio-visual media, such as records, tapes, and movies. Without a doubt, one of the most popular forms of media is television. More than 98 percent of U.S. households have at least one television set, almost 65 percent have videocassette recorders, and 52 percent subscribe to cable television (U.S. Department of Commerce 1990). In the average American home, the television is on six hours a day (Staples and Jones 1985).

Obviously, the mass media are an important part of our everyday lives. Through them, we are both entertained and informed. In either case, however, we are mistaken if we think that the media are simply transmitting neutral or objective information and messages. Rather, as we will learn in this chapter, much of what is conveyed to us through the mass media is infused with particular values and norms, including many about gender. In other words, the media serve as gender socializers, and our focus will be on what various media communicate about gender and how they communicate it. We will examine the gender images depicted in print media (newspapers and magazines) and an audio-visual medium (television), as well as a communication form common to both (advertisements). Although we will not discuss music, film, or theater, much of our analysis is applicable to those media too.

Before we look at the content of specific media, however, it would be instructive for us to examine the primary means by which media messages are conveyed—that is, through language. While "a picture paints a thousand words," the English language itself expresses our culture's underlying values and expectations about gender. Let's see how.

SEXISM AND LANGUAGE: WHAT'S IN A WORD?

"Sticks and stones may break my bones, but words will never hurt me!" How many times did you recite that chant as a child? In response to jeers or name-calling, we tried to tell our taunters that what they said had no effect on us. Yet, as we have grown older, we have come to realize that although words do not have the same sting as sticks and stones, they can indeed inflict as much harm. That is because words are symbols with meaning; they define, describe, and *evaluate* us and the world in which we live. The power of words lies in the fact that the members of a culture share those meanings and valuations. It is their common language that allows the members of a society to communicate and understand one another, and thus makes for order in society.

Language is a medium of socialization. Essentially, as a child learns the language of his or her culture, he or she is also learning how to think and behave as a member of that culture. How, then, does language shape our thoughts about women and men? That is a complex question that warrants a detailed answer.

To begin, consider the first group of word pairs in Part A of Box 6.1. In each

---

Sexism and Language   **BOX 6.1**

A. Connotations   **B. Generic He/Man**
   governor—governess   policeman
   mister—mistress   spokesman
   patron—matron   manpower
   sir—madam   Social Man
   bachelor—spinster   mankind
                   workman's compensation
Word Pairs   "Man the oars!"
   brothers and sisters   he, him, his
   husband and wife
   boys and girls
   hostess and host
   queen and king
   Eve and Adam

    Source: Compiled from Smith 1985; Strauss-Noll 1984.

---

case, a word associated with men appears on the left and a word associated with women appears on the right. What does each word connote to you? The words associated with men have very different connotations than those associated with women, and the latter are uniformly negative or demeaning. The male words connote power, authority, or a positively valued status, while most of the female words have sexual connotations. Interestingly, many of these words originally had neutral connotations; *spinster,* for example, meant simply "tender of a spinning wheel." Over time, though, these words were debased, a process known as **semantic derogation.** "[L]exicographers have noted that once a word or term becomes associated with women, it often acquires semantic characteristics that are congruent with social stereotypes and evaluations of women as a group" (Smith 1985:48). Reflecting on the words we have been discussing, what do their contemporary connotations tell us about the status of women in our society?

    Another form of semantic derogation is illustrated by the second group of word pairs in Part A of Box 6.1. When you read each word pair, chances are that the word pairs in which the female term precedes the male term sound awkward or incorrect. The tradition of placing the female term after the male term further signifies women's secondary status and is hardly accidental. Eighteenth-century grammarians established the rule precisely to assert that, "the supreme Being. . . . is in all languages Masculine, in as much as the masculine Sex is the superior and more excellent" (quoted in Baron 1986:3). Thus, according to them, to place women before men was to violate the natural order. What is perhaps more alarming is that, with the exception of "ladies and gentlemen," contemporary speakers of English perpetuate this rule usage—and its traditional connotation—in their everyday communications.

Semantic derogation is just one dimension of the larger problem of **linguistic sexism.** Linguistic sexism refers to ways in which a language devalues members of one sex, almost invariably women. In addition to derogating women, linguistic sexism involves defining women's "place" in society unequally and also ignoring women altogether. With respect to the former, for example, we may consider the commonly used titles of respect for men and women in our society. Men are addressed as *Mr.,* which reveals nothing about their relationship to women. But how are women typically addressed? The titles *Miss* and *Mrs.* define women in terms of their relationships to men. Even when a woman has earned a higher status title, such as *Dr.,* she is still likely to be addressed as Miss or Mrs. (Henley, et al. 1985). A couple we know, both Ph.D's, often get mail from friends and relatives addressed to Dr. and Mrs. To a large extent, a woman's identity is subsumed by that of her husband, particularly if she adheres to the custom of adopting her husband's family name when she marries. She will find that she not only acquires a new surname, but also a new given name, since etiquette calls for her to be addressed as, for instance, Mrs. John Jones rather than Mrs. Mary Jones (Smith 1985).

The most blatant way that our language ignores or excludes women is through the use of the supposedly generic *he* and *man.* From our first grammar class on, we are told that these two terms should be used to refer not only to males specifically, but also to human beings generally. Recent research, however, raises serious doubts as to whether this he/man approach is really neutral or generic (Martyna 1980).

To understand the issue better, read the words in Part B of Box 6.1. What image comes to mind with each word? Do you visualize women, women and men together, or men alone? If you are like a majority of people, these words conjure up images only of men (Treichler and Frank 1989a; Wilson and Ng 1988; Silveira 1980; Schneider and Hacker 1973). Of course, it could be argued that these words lack context; provided with a context it would be easier to distinguish whether their referents are specifically masculine or simply generic. Perhaps, but research indicates that context is rarely unambiguously generic and, consequently, the use of "he/man" language frequently results in "cognitive confusion" or misunderstanding. Richardson (1981:20), for instance, cites the case of a beginning anthropology student who "believes (incorrectly) that all shamans ('witch-doctors') are males because her textbook and professor use the referential pronoun 'he.' " Similarly, Adams and Ware (1989:481) recount an incident that occurred at the conclusion of a popular television series on human evolution: the host of the program questioned the guest anthropologist about "what women were doing during this early period in the ascent of man."

There are those who feel that this emphasis on language is trivial or misplaced. Some maintain, for example, that a focus on language obscures the more serious issues of the physical and economic oppression of women. (Blaubergs (1980), provides an excellent summary of this and other, less compelling arguments against changing sexist language.) But others counter that "one of the really important functions of language is to be constantly declaring to society the psychological place held by all of its members" (quoted in Martyna, 1980:493; Treichler and Frank 1989a). Given that women are denigrated, unequally defined, and often ignored by the English language, it serves not only to reflect their secondary status relative to men in our society, but also to reinforce it. Changing sexist language, then, is one of the most basic steps we can take toward increasing awareness of sexism and working to eliminate it.

How can sexist language be changed? A variety of simple, but effective usage changes has been instituted by individuals and organizations. Substituting the title Ms. for Miss and Mrs. is one example. Alternating the order of feminine and masculine nouns and pronouns is another. Perhaps most controversial has been the effort to eliminate the generic he/man. Instead of he, one may use she/he, or he and she, or simply they as a singular pronoun. Nouns with the supposedly generic *man* are also easily neutralized—for example, police officer, rather than policeman; spokesperson, rather than spokesman. Humanity and humankind are both sex-neutral substitutes for man and mankind (Frank 1989; Treichler and Frank 1989b; Baron 1986; Henley, et al. 1985).

Those who have made an effort to overcome linguistic sexism in their own communications report that the changes required are not difficult to make (Blaubergs 1980). We share Baron's (1986:219) optimism, therefore, "that if enough people become sensitized to sex-related language questions, such forms as generic *he* and *man* will give way no matter what arguments are advanced in their defense." Nevertheless, how words and ideas are conveyed may be as important as the words and ideas themselves. Consequently, it is important that we also consider the issue of communication styles.

Do Women and Men Speak Different Languages?

According to linguist Deborah Tannen (1990), women and men have different styles of communication and different communication goals. Just as people from different cultures speak different dialects, women and men speak different *genderlects*. Women, maintains Tannen, speak and hear a language of intimacy and connection, whereas men speak and hear a language of status and independence. In addition, women's and men's differing communication styles reflect differences in their life experiences and the power imbalances between them (Henley, et al. 1985; Nichols 1986).

In cross-sex conversations, men tend to dominate women in at least three ways: "(1) they actually do more of the talking; (2) they interrupt women, in the sense of seizing the floor, more often than women interrupt them; and (3) they more often succeed in focusing the conversation on topics they introduce. . . . In all these respects, the conversational relation between women and men parallels that between children and adults, employees and employers, and other power-differentiated groups" (McConnell-Ginet 1989:41; Edelsky 1981). The nonverbal communication of men in cross-sex interaction also tends to be characterized by dominance; men control more space than women and they invade women's personal space more than women invade men's by standing closer to them, and by touching and staring at them more. Women, in contrast, tend to avert their eyes when stared at by men, but they also smile more than men whether they are happy or not, a gesture that can be viewed as both social and submissive (Henley, et al. 1985).

These findings fly in the face of the common stereotype that women are more talkative than men. Research on same-sex conversation, however, does show that in all-female groups women talk more than men do in all-male groups. In addition, studies of same-sex talk indicate that woman's conversations have a cooperative character, "enlarging on and acknowledging one another's contributions, responding to conversationalists' attempts to introduce topics, and signaling active listening by nods and *mmhmms* during a partner's turn" (McConnell-Ginet 1989:42). Men's conversations are more competitive, less social, and more individualistic. In short, "the evidence shows that men generally aim at individual conversational control, whereas women aim at social conversational collaboration" (McConnell-Ginet 1989:43; Tannen 1990; Stanback 1985).

What are some of the consequences of the clash between these different communication styles? Tannen (1990) argues that women and men frequently misinterpret one another's words and gestures, which causes interpersonal conflict in intimate relationships and misunderstandings in public and professional interactions. For instance, she points out that in the workplace, a woman's connective style of communication (a positive attribute) may be misjudged by her male colleagues as a lack of independence, which they associate with incompetence and insecurity (negative traits).

This example raises two other important points:

> First, men are more likely than women to have a chance to express their perspective on situations, not only because they have more frequent access to the floor but also because they are more actively attended to. This distinction is especially important, since comprehension goes well beyond simple recognition of the linguistic structures used. In other words, where the sexes have somewhat different perspectives on a situation, the man's view is more likely to be familiar to the woman than hers is to him. This observation leads directly to the second point: men are much more likely than women to be unaware that their own view is not universally shared. As a result, women and men may well be in different positions regarding what they believe to be commonly accepted (or accessible) in the speech community (McConnell-Ginet 1989:43).

Indeed, the negative consequences associated with sex differences in communication styles have been borne almost exclusively by women, since men have had greater power to define acceptable standards of speech. In this way, women's styles of communication have been judged not only as different from the male standard, but also typically as inferior.

Henley and her colleagues (1985) offer several suggestions for breaking sex-specific communication habits; for instance, they urge men to be more cognizant of women's personal space and to interrupt women less in conversations. They also encourage men to be more emotionally expressive and women to be more assertive. However, they are quick to point out that changing personal communication styles is not enough, for these habits are simply indicators of power in our society. What must also change is the power structure, which is further reflected in various institutions of social control, such as the mass media.

GENDER AND THE MEDIA

Raise the question of media portrayals of men and women, and someone will invariably argue that the media only give the public what it expects, wants, or demands. This popular view is known in technical terms as the **reflection hypothesis.** Simply stated, the reflection hypothesis holds that media content mirrors the behaviors and relationships, and values and norms most prevalent or dominant in a society. There is certainly some truth to this position. After all, sponsors (the media's most important paying customers) want to attract the largest audience possible, and providing what everyone wants or expects seems like a logical way to do this. However, media analysts also point out that, far from just passively reflecting culture, the media actively shape and create culture. How?

Consider the network news. In a brief twenty-two minutes (accounting for commercials), these programs purport to highlight for us the most significant events that took place throughout the world on a given day. Obviously, decisions must be made by the program staff as to what gets reported, and that is precisely one of the subliminal ways the media shape our ideas and expectations. "The media select items for attention and provide rankings of what is and is not important—in other words they 'set an agenda' for public opinion. . . . The way the media choose themes, structure the dialogue and control the debate—a process which involves crucial omissions—is a major aspect of their influence" (Baehr 1980:30).

In addition to their role as definers of the important, the media are the chief sources of information for most people, as well as the focus of their leisure activity. There is considerable evidence indicating that many media consumers, particularly heavy television viewers, tend to uncritically accept media content as fact. Although there are intervening variables, such as the kinds of shows one watches and the behavior of the real-life role models in one's immediate environment, the media do appear to influence our worldview, including our personal aspirations and expectations for achievement, as well as our perceptions of others. Not surprisingly, therefore, feminist researchers have been especially concerned with media portrayals of gender. If these depictions are negative and sexist, or if they distort the reality of contemporary gender relations, they may nevertheless be accepted as accurate by a large segment of the general public (Courtney and Whipple 1983).

It has been argued that with respect to their treatment of women, the media are guilty of **symbolic annihilation** (Tuchman, et al. 1978). That is, the media traditionally have ignored, trivialized, or condemned women. In the sections that follow, we will investigate this charge more carefully. In addition, however, we will discuss the ways in which men have been exploited and denigrated by media portrayals. Although they typically fare better than women, men's media roles are also limited by stereotypes that are not always positive or flattering.

The Written Word: Gender Messages in Newspapers and Magazines

Although research indicates that women are close readers of newspapers, a quick perusal of just about any news daily gives one the impression that it is surely a man's world. News of women-centered activities and events or of particular women (with the exception of female heads of state and women notable for their association with famous men) is usually reported as *soft* news and relegated to a secondary, "non-news" (often back) section of the paper. One recent study of twenty U.S. newspapers, for example, found that women were just 14 percent of the people quoted as sources in front page news stories and only 32 percent of front page photos included women (Women's Institute for Freedom of the Press, hereafter WIFP, 1990a). Women fare even worse in news magazines (e.g., *Time, Newsweek,* and *U.S. News and World Report*), where they average just 13 percent of story references and appear in only 27 percent of photos (WIFP 1989a). This implicitly sends the message that women are not newsmakers and that women's news is unimportant or not of general interest.

Perhaps more telling, though, is the way news about women is treated when it is reported as *hard* news. A study by Karen Foreit and her colleagues (1980) is enlightening on this point. Foreit, et al. found that in female-centered news stories, reporters were likely to mention an individual's sex (e.g., "the female attorney"), physical appearance (e.g., "the petite blonde"), and marital status or parenthood (e.g., "Dr. Smith is the wife of" or "the feisty grandmother"). Such details were rarely provided in male-centered stories, however. A recent letter to the editor of the *New York Times* illustrates this further. The writer complained about the sexist reporting on the only female included in an article about "super stock brokers." The reporter had written about the female stock broker's marital status, her husband and his occupation, her hair, its color, and "how feminine she could be while earning almost half a million." The reporter had also noted that this woman keeps three bottles of nail polish and a make-up mirror in her desk. No comparable information had been provided about the male stock brokers featured in the story (*New York Times,* 26 August 1984:10F).

Feminists both here and abroad have long complained about media portrayals of themselves, as well as negative reporting of the women's movement. For instance, at a recent conference in London, British journalists argued that, although so-called acceptable topics, such as equal pay, are given limited coverage, the media "ghettoize" stories on feminism. One speaker at the conference cited as an example a recent newspaper story that argued that since the women's movement had "knocked women off a pedestal," women now deserve to be exploited (WIFP 1986a).

In an attempt to explain this symbolic annihilation of women by newspapers, many analysts have emphasized the overwhelming male dominance of newspaper staffs. A 1989 survey found that women held just 16.2 percent of directing editorships, including 11.9 percent of top editor posts, 21.1 percent of news editor positions, and 13.9 percent of editorial page editor positions. Women did make gains in newspaper publishing during the late 1980s, but these were modest and occurred most often at smaller circulation newspapers (WIFP 1990b). (Female journalists in the United States do seem to have better opportunities than their sisters abroad, however, although women from some countries, such as Nicaragua or Malaysia, report that for them the major problem is freedom of the press, not the gender gap in journalism; Toner 1986).

Other observers maintain that having women in top editorial positions is no guarantee against sexism in the papers. For example, in a study that compared the representation of women in the business sections of two newspapers, one edited by a man and the other by a woman, the latter was found to have five and a half more stories bylined by women than the former. Nevertheless, there were no significant differences in the number of articles that featured women, that cited them as news sources, or that showed them in photographs; in both newspapers, women were underrepresented. More importantly, as one sociologist of the media has pointed out, "Women frequently create 'sexist' content. . . . [Their] judgments about general news resemble those of men. . . . According to [one] study of journalism students, women seem to have the same stereotypes of women as men do" (Tuchman 1978:534–535). This problem becomes more evident, in fact, when we examine women's magazines, for the editorial staffs of these periodicals are often predominantly female.

Magazines, of course, are different from newspapers in many ways. Of particular interest to us is the fact that while newspapers seek a broad, general readership, magazines try to appeal to specific segments of the population. There are women's magazines (e.g., *Redbook, Ladies' Home Journal, and Seventeen*), and there are men's magazines (e.g., *Esquire, Sports Illustrated, and Playboy*). Even within these two large groups, there are various subgroups that specialty magazines target as potential readers. Subscribers to *Ms.: The World of Women,* for instance, are likely to have very different attitudes and interests than subscribers to *Cosmopolitan,* although both groups are almost exclusively female and both may see themselves as "liberated." Generally speaking, however, how do magazines expressly designed for women differ from those for men?

BOX 6.2   Female Reporters in Men's Locker Rooms

On September 17, 1990, Lisa Olson, a reporter for the *Boston Herald,* entered the locker room of the New England Patriots football team to interview players after a game. While interviewing one player, several others began to verbally abuse her and another paraded naked in front of her, making sexual remarks. When she complained, she found herself insulted by the team's owner and booed by the team's fans, who seemed to suggest that it was her fault the players behaved as they did. Yet Lisa Olson is hardly the first female sports reporter to be sexually harassed by male players. During the summer of 1990, for example, Jennifer Frey, a reporter for the *Detroit Free Press,* attempted to interview Detroit Tigers pitcher, Jack Morris, who rebuffed her with the comment, "I don't talk to people when I'm naked, especially women, unless they're on top of me or I'm on top of them." (Morris was not nude at the time.) Like Olson, Frey did not get a sympathetic response from the team's president about her complaints about Morris. Similarly, in September 1989, a forum between professional athletes and sports reporters was organized after Melody Simmons, a writer for the *Baltimore Evening Sun,* was verbally harassed by Baltimore Orioles players in their locker room.

It was Lisa Olson's experience in the Patriots' locker room, however, that sparked the public debate over whether female reporters should be permitted in men's locker rooms. A number of people, including athletes, who have expressed an opinion on the issue, argue that female reporters go into the men's locker rooms primarily "to check out the nude men" and they cite as evidence the fact that the women frequently can be seen looking around the room while they're talking with a player. At least one athlete, though, commented that that's not why he thought the female reporter was looking around. Said Rolando Blackman of the Dallas Mavericks basketball team, "I just figured reporters look around to make sure one of my teammates doesn't dress quickly and leave before they can ask some questions" (quoted in WIFP 1990c:3).

Blackman's deduction certainly makes sense; after all, that's one of the reasons for conducting locker room interviews—to get players' and coaches' immediate feedback on the game. Unfortunately, judging by the negative responses to Olson's and other female reporters' complaints of harassment, many players, coaches, and fans continue to sexualize the professional interactions of these women. They also ignore the deliberateness of some players' abuse. For instance, Blackman and his teammate, Sam Perkins, noted that some players intentionally remain naked when female reporters are in the locker room "just to get a reaction or to see if the expression changes on the reporter's face" (quoted in WIFP 1990c:3).

For now, the controversy may have been resolved, at least within the National Football League. A special counsel appointed to investigate Lisa Olson's complaint concluded that the reporter was sexually harassed and that the team as a whole and its management personnel were at least partially responsible since they did nothing to remedy the problem. The individual players who were directly involved were punished with substantial fines. The team itself was fined $50,000, half of which will go to help pay for instructional materials for all NFL personnel on how to interact with representatives of the news media. It remains to be seen whether this outcome will send the message to those involved in other sports that women must be given an equal opportunity to report on the teams and that sexual harassment or other behavior that impedes their opportunities will not be tolerated.

According to Marjorie Ferguson (1983), women's magazines promote what she calls a "cult of femininity." Central to the notion of femininity as defined by these magazines is a narcissistic absorption with oneself—with one's physical appearance ("the business of becoming more beautiful"), with occupational success, and with success in affairs of the heart ("getting and keeping your man"). Interestingly, Ferguson found few changes in women's magazines over a thirty-one-year period (1949 to 1980). In 1980, even though establishing one's own identity displaced getting and keeping a man as the number one theme of these periodicals, the goals they set for their readers were little changed from those of thirty years before. The goals included personal happiness (e.g., by winning romance, losing weight, or getting a satisfying job); personal achievement (whether in the kitchen or at the office); having a happy family (including one-parent families); and physical attractiveness (the triumph of nurture over nature). Not surprisingly, the magazines themselves promise to provide advice and sometimes even step-by-step instructions to help their readers accomplish these goals.

Ferguson's study focuses chiefly on British magazines, but she maintains that the analysis is applicable to most women's magazines in other countries. Similar research in the United States supports her claim (Cantor 1987; Glazer 1980; Phillips 1978). However, a recent study of U.S. women's magazines from the nineteenth century to the present shows that in their early years, many of these periodicals took what may be considered feminist stands on serious women's issues, including women's education, suffrage, and financial support for widows and orphans. According to Mary Ellen Waller-Zuckerman (forthcoming), the emphasis in women's magazines on women as housewives and sex objects is a product of the powerful growth of advertising in the twentieth century.

In the first edition of this text, we undertook our own unscientific test of Ferguson's argument about women's magazines. We examined the contents of two issues of three of the most popular U.S. women's magazines: *Cosmopolitan* and *Glamour* (which are targeted primarily for a white female readership), and *Essence* (which is designed for black women). We found that relationships with men was clearly the dominant theme in these magazines, with becoming beautiful the second most prevalent theme. The goals of personal happiness and achievement were prominent in these articles—for example, "I Lost 65 Pounds and Became a Poet Too," or "Building a Better Bosom" (which was accompanied by photos of barebreasted models and the caption, "Unhappy with the bosom nature gave you? Plastic surgery—quite simple—has created zillions of breathtaking breasts!"). Although all three magazines contained columns about careers and occupational success, the multitude of advertisements insured that readers never lost sight of the main themes. In fact, even more than Ferguson (1983), we found the ideal of femininity projected in these magazines to be embodied in the woman who first and foremost attracts men.

In revising this text, we decided to see, again unscientifically, if the predominant themes of these magazines had changed over the past two years. We found that they have not. Relationships with men remain the central focus of the feature articles with *Glamour* asking, "Do You Think About Sex Too Much?" *Essence* advising on "Loving a Younger Man" and *Cosmopolitan* reporting on "What Smart Women Know," which turns out to be things like "men respect women who retain their boundaries" and "some relationships just weren't meant to be." Becoming more beautiful remained the second most prevalent theme, although insecurity about one's body seemed to be emphasized more than personal achievement. *Cosmopolitan* advised readers about "Coping with the Worst Part of Your Body," and *Glamour* gave instructions on how to shape up one's legs for "short skirt confidence." The beauty feature in *Essence* was entitled, "They Shoot Models, Don't They?" and gave readers advice about what it takes to be a "hot model." Little had changed with respect to advertising either; the themes of physical attractiveness and "getting and keeping a man" were intertwined and often indistinguishable. Thus, advertisements for personal hygiene products [forty-six in *Cosmopolitan;* twenty-five in *Glamour;* and thirty-six in *Essence* (which were primarily for hair care products)] and cosmetics (thirty-five in *Cosmopolitan;* thirty-three in *Glamour;* but only fourteen in *Essence,* although this was still the second highest advertising category) not only promise to make the buyer more beautiful, but also sexier and irresistible to men. In short, the woman idealized in these magazines remains a "superwoman": beautiful, alluring, talented, and energetic—successful in virtually every endeavor, be it business or pleasure. Occupational achievement is a priority, but it too is often presented as being dependent on physical appearance, as in "dressing for success," applying the right make-up, or fixing one's hair a particular way.

Men's magazines provide some glaring contrasts to the women's periodicals. For one thing, men's magazines tend to be more specialized. Most can be placed in one of three categories: finance/business, sports/hobbies, and sex. Sex, which as we have seen is by no means absent from the women's magazines, is almost always discussed in the context of interpersonal relationships. Sex-oriented magazines for men objectify and depersonalize sex (*see* Chapter 9). That is, the emphasis is almost exclusively on the physical aspects of sexuality and the articles are generally devoid of emotions and interpersonal involvement.

Apart from these three types of magazines, however, what are the dominant themes in more general periodicals designed for men? In our 1989 analysis, and again for this second edition, we examined two men's magazines—*Esquire* (which claims on the cover to represent "Man at His Best") and *Gentlemen's Quarterly* ("For the Modern Man")—which we felt were especially comparable to *Cosmopolitan* and *Glamour* (although we could not find a magazine similar to *Essence* that was targeted primarily to black men). Overall, the predominant theme in these magazines, then and now, is living a leisurely lifestyle which is made possible by one's financial success. (Not surprisingly, *GQ* also contained about thirty-five pages on men's clothing and accessories.) Articles about music, art, and sophisticated men (often celebrities of some sort) were also common. However, conspicuous by their absence were articles about male/female relationships. In our most recent perusal, we found that between the two magazines there was just one article on the topic: a satiric essay in *Esquire* about a man's term in a "feminist prison" because he had made fun of women. There were three other articles that focused on women: "Women We Love: Robin Wright," which consisted of one paragraph and two photos of the actress (in *Esquire*), "Les Girls," about the women who perform nude at the Crazy Horse Saloon in Paris, and "What to Wear When She's Wearing Almost Nothing" (both in *GQ*).

The low priority men's magazines give to interpersonal relationships is reinforced by the advertisements most prevalent on their pages. Judging only by the ads, one might easily conclude that men spend the majority of their time alone, driving their cars, listening to their stereos, looking at their watches, and drinking alcohol, much to the neglect of their personal hygiene. Apart from clothing advertisements in *GQ*, the most common ads in both magazines were for liquor and wristwatches. Equipment, especially stereos, ranked second, followed by cars, but ads for cosmetics and personal hygiene products were relatively few (three in *Esquire*, nine in *GQ*). Interestingly, the two women's magazines contained more ads for cigarettes (twelve) than did the men's magazines (five), probably reflecting efforts by the tobacco industry to target the only group that has shown an increase in smoking in recent years—young women (*see* Chapter 12).

Like women's magazines, then, periodicals intended for men generate their own gender images and ideals. Modifying Ferguson's concept a bit, we may say that in the cult of masculinity, getting and keeping a woman is not a priority. Instead, the *real* man is free and adventurous. He is a risk-taker who pursues his work and his hobbies—including in this latter category relationships with women—with vigor. He is concerned about his personal appearance, but not in an all-consuming sense as women seem to be. The magazines, of course, promise to help their readers achieve these goals with articles and ads on muscle tone and hair retention among others. In this respect, they are not at all unlike the magazines for women.

Despite their continuing appeal, magazines like those we have been discussing have shown declines in sales in recent years. Media analysts report that consumers appear to be turning away somewhat from print media and utilizing more electronic, audiovisual media. Television remains the most popular form of electronic media, especially since the advent of the cable networks, which now claim more than 47 million subscribers (U.S. Department of Commerce 1990). A critical question that arises, therefore, is whether the gender messages of television programming are any less sexist or exploitative than those we have found in the print media. Or do television programs simply reinforce the cults of femininity and masculinity promoted by the popular women's and men's magazines? These are questions that we will address next.

Television: The Ubiquitous Media Socializer

It has been argued that television is the most important media socializer. We will discuss the effectiveness of television shortly, but for now we must agree that the sheer pervasiveness of television sets, as well as television's unique characteristics, do make this claim plausible. Consider, for example, that "by the time the average American child reaches eighteen years of age he [or she] has watched 22,000 hours of TV, as compared to 11,000 hours of school; and has seen 350,000 commercials" (Staples and Jones 1985:17). The average school-age child watches about twenty-seven hours of television a week (Tracy 1990).

Richardson (1981) delineates the special characteristics of television that add to its potency as an agent of socialization. It is free, for instance, it is available to just about everyone, and it does not even require viewers to leave their homes, as movies and theater do. It requires no special skills, such as literacy, to watch it, and everyone, regardless of sex, race, age, social class, and often geographic location gets the same visual and verbal messages.

What are the standard messages of television with regard to gender? We will first discuss prime-time television, then briefly examine news broadcasts and a new genre of television programming, music videos.

A recent study of thirty years (1955 to 1985) of prime-time television found that gender portrayals on these programs for the most part remain traditional, although new themes, such as women's rights and equality, have been introduced (WIFP 1986b). This study, noteworthy for its magnitude as well as its findings, analyzed 620 episodes and more than 7,000 individual characters from over 20,000 programs. The researchers report that women continue to be "the second sex" on prime-time television in that they are still outnumbered by men two to one (67 percent of prime-time characters versus 33 percent, and this has changed little since 1955).

Female characters also tend to be younger and less mature than male characters and, therefore, are less authoritative. Another study, for example, found that although 35 percent of the female characters in the shows the researchers rated were less than twenty-six years old, only 16 percent of the male characters were in this age group. Fifty percent of the males were older than thirty-five, but only 22 percent of females were so evaluated (Silverstein, et al. 1986). As Condry (1989:73) notes, "It is especially bad to be old on television, and it is terrible to be an old woman." Young female characters are typically thin and physically attractive. In the Silverstein, et al. study (1986), for instance, 69 percent of the female characters were rated thin compared with just 17.5 percent of male characters, but only 5 percent of female characters were rated as heavy compared with 25.5 percent of male characters.

In general, then, male television characters are given more leeway in terms of their appearance. At the same time, female characters are still typically portrayed at home or in family situations. If they do work outside the home, they are rarely shown on the job. Even when depicted at work, their focus is still on family matters or interpersonal relationships (Condry 1989; Wober and Gunter 1988). A recent review of the 1989 prime-time television season argues, in fact, that female characterization and representation on these programs have actually worsened (WIFP 1990d).

The relative number of appearances of males and females on prime-time television does vary somewhat by type of program. Women are least visible on action/drama programs, but appear at about the same rate as men on situation comedies. Not surprisingly, the latter type of program often centers on family life and the problems associated with it. Regardless of number of appearances, however, women's and men's behavior on all types of prime-time programs usually reflects gender stereotypes. One recent study found that teenage girls are depicted especially negatively. According to Steenland (1988), teenage female characters typically are shown as obsessed with shopping, dating, and grooming themselves and are rarely portrayed as concerned with academics or their future careers. Adult female characters do not fare much better, however.

Men are still far more likely to solve problems than women; in fact, women usually need help from others to solve problems. Men are more powerful and less enotional; rarely do male characters cry. Women, though, express emotions easily and are seven times more likely than men to use sex or romantic charm to get what they want (Condry 1989; WIFP 1986b; Downs 1981). But there is one way that men are depicted clearly less favorably than women: they are the "bad guys." Male characters are twice as likely as female characters to use force and violence, and they commit twice as many crimes (WIFP 1986b). Women, especially old women, are the usual victims. "Old women are the most victimized category of individuals on television, being thirty times more likely to be caught up in a violent act than older women actually are in reality" (Condry 1989:73).

These findings are confirmed by small-scale studies as well (Theroux 1987; Downs 1981; Baehr 1980). The results, however, may be a bit surprising, since to many viewers, women seem to be more prominent on television nowadays. This may be because one of the biggest changes in prime-time programming has been the incorporation of women's rights and gender equality themes. According to the study reported by the WIFP (1986b), programs that raise these issues overwhelmingly take a feminist position. In addition, several prime-time specials have sensitively addressed such topics as sexual assault, spouse abuse, and incest.

The illusion of more women in prime-time may also be due to a few well-placed female characters—what the U.S Commission on Civil Rights (1977) referred to as "window dressing on the set." A small number of prominently placed female characters may give the impression that there are more women on television than are actually there. Importantly, however, the women who do appear in lead roles are still typically white. Female or male, racial minorities continue to be largely absent from television (Condry 1989; WIFP 1982a; U.S Commission on Civil Rights 1979). One study which coded the race of 6,663 characters found that 90.3 percent were white, 7.7 percent were African American, 1.3 percent were Asian, and 0.6 percent were Hispanic; only one character out of the 6,663 was a Native American (Williams and Condry 1988).

When minorities do appear on prime-time television, it is usually in supporting rather than starring roles, and the roles are often demeaning, negatively stereotyped, and distorted. There are exceptions, of course, such as the enormously popular *Cosby Show* and *A Different World,* which have demonstrated "that the American public will watch a television show about unstereotyped black Americans" (Staples and Jones 1985:14). Apart from these programs and a few others, however, nonwhites usually are cast in less prestigious occupations than whites (despite the fact that the occupational levels of most TV characters are significantly higher than those of the actual population). Williams and Condry (1988) report that nonwhites are likely to be cast as blue-collar workers and as public safety personnel, and are less likely than whites to be depicted as friends and neighbors. One recent study of a single national network's prime-time programming found that 49 percent of the black characters portrayed were criminals, servants, entertainers, or athletes (Staples and Jones 1985). In Williams and Condry's (1988) research, none of the Hispanic characters was cast as a friend or neighbor, and their criminality rate was the highest of all racial groups.

Negative stereotypes also are common in portrayals of minority women, especially childless, black women. One recent study found, for instance, that childless, black female characters are typically depicted as unskilled, unpolished, and lacking in decorum; rarely in control of situations; financially dependent on a parent or even a white family; never giving information unless it is about child care or housekeeping; and, if single, desperately preoccupied with finding a husband (WIFP 1990e).

Although little positive change appears to have taken place in prime-time entertainment, more progress has been made in news programming. Indeed, the greatest move toward equality of the sexes on television has taken place on local news programs. All-male news desks are now rare on local televised news shows, and the trend is clearly toward male-female anchor teams (WIFP 1986c). By 1982, 92 percent of local TV stations had a female anchor for at least one of their regular news programs (Steenland 1987). Unfortunately, female co-anchors often confront a double standard on the job. As the case of Christine Craft illustrated, higher standards of physical attractiveness and dress are sometimes set for them compared to their male partners, and they may be expected to look younger and act friendlier than male anchors (Craft 1988; Smith 1983). Most are, in fact, younger. More than a third of local television news anchors are women, but just 3 percent of them are over age forty; 50 percent of male local television news anchors are over forty and 16 percent are over fifty years old (Sanders and Rock 1988).

At the same time that women have made gains on local television news, they have had far less success at the networks. There are no women anchors on the weekday news of the three major networks, although women do anchor the weekend news programs. Much attention has been given to the lucrative contracts recently awarded to several female news anchors, such as Jane Pauley, Diane Sawyer and Connie Chung. Some analysts argue, though, that this too is little more than window dressing—that these women are being paid for their "star appeal" and have little say about what news gets aired. (Only the three major network news anchors—Dan Rather, Tom Brokaw, and Peter Jennings—have editing privileges with regard to their broadcasts.) At the same time, research indicates that the percentage of female correspondents reporting news on the three major networks rose between 1974 and 1989, but only by 6 percent. Women constitute 23 percent of the correspondents at CBS, 14 percent at NBC, and 10.5 percent at ABC. Yet, at two of these networks, one quarter of the news broadcasts have no female correspondents reporting (Nash 1989). Joe S. Foote, a radio and television specialist, annually ranks the news correspondents by the number of on-air stories they report. In 1989, there were only eight women among the top one hundred correspondents, compared with fifteen in 1988. What is more, there were no African American correspondents, male or female, ranking in the top fifty and only two Hispanic correspondents, both male (WIFP 1990f). Similarly, a month-long analysis of the major networks' newscasters in March 1986 found that stories filed by minority female correspondents constituted just nine-tenths of one percent of the on-air news that month (Steenland 1987).

Off-camera, women, particularly women of color, have fared worse. Nationwide, women constitute just 18.5 percent of TV news directors; racial minorities make up only 7.9 percent. The double discrimination confronted by women of color is clear in Table 6.1 where we see the distribution of news directors by both sex and race. Similarly, while women make up about 37 percent of the commercial broadcasting labor force, few hold top executive and professional positions. In 1985, women constituted 28 percent of station officers and 29 percent of station

TABLE 6.1
Race and Sex of Commercial Television
News Directors, 1988

	Estimated Number	Percent
Total Male	603	81.5
Total Female	137	18.5
Total White	682	92.1
Total Minority	58	7.9
White Men	566	76.5
White Women	115	15.6
Black Men	4	5.0
Black Women	10	1.3
Hispanic Men	24	3.2
Hispanic Women	7	1.0
Asian Men	6	.8
Asian Women	2	.3
Native American Men	4	.5
Native American Women	2	.3

Source: WIFP 1989b:6

managers; of these women, 84 percent were white, 9 percent black, 5 percent Hispanic, and only 2 percent Asian. Of all television professionals in 1985, 36 percent were women, but only 18 percent of these were women of color. Interestingly, it is in the sales divisions of commercial television that white women are best represented, but it is in sales that minority women have the lowest representation. About 90 percent of female television sales personnel are white, compared with 4 percent black, 4 percent Hispanic, and less than 1 percent Asian (Steenland 1987). Although all three major networks and many local stations have had sex discrimination complaints to the Federal Communications Commission filed against them, the FCC has adopted a hands-off approach to the problem, claiming that market forces will regulate the industry (WIFP 1986d; Eddings 1980). Thus, it is likely that television, like printed media, will remain largely a man's world.

In closing this section on television, we want to briefly discuss a new genre of television programming that has generated considerable controversy: the music video. Parents and others have expressed concern about the violent and sexual content of many music videos broadcast by the cable station MTV and on such programs as *Friday Night Videos* and *Video Soul.* In addition, the decision in some communities to ban the sale of the album "As Nasty as They Wanna Be," and to arrest and prosecute members of the rap group *2 Live Crew* on obscenity charges added to the controversy over whether to permit the performance of music that blatantly degrades women and graphically describes sexual violence or to invoke censorship. Although little research has been done on music videos themselves, the few available findings are worth noting.

In one study, Sherman and Dominick (1986:89) concluded that music videos tend to reflect "the chauvinism of rock culture" in general. Women appear significantly less often than men do. When they are shown, they are typically white and frequently portrayed as "upper-class sex objects for lower-class males with visions of sexual conquest." More than half the women were provocatively dressed, and sex was usually depicted in physical terms with little emotional involvement. Violence was a common theme, with men the likely aggressors and victims. Interestingly, however, when females were involved in violence, they were more often aggressors than victims, leading these researchers to conclude that "the predatory female is a popular music TV stereotype" (Sherman and Dominick 1986:90).

Other studies report similar results. Brown and Campbell (1986), for instance, obtained virtually identical findings with regard to the roles of men and women as aggressors. In addition, when they compared white videos (from MTV) with black videos (from Black Entertainment Television's *Video Soul*), they found that regardless of race, women are relatively rare on music videos. When they are shown, black women are usually dancing, rather than singing or playing an instrument. White women, on the other hand, frequently wander aimlessly or try to get the attention of a man who is ignoring them.

In sum, the gender messages communicated by music videos appear to be negative for both sexes. Women tend to be portrayed as sex objects or predators, while men are frequently aggressors or victims of aggression. Given that this genre is targeted to an adolescent audience and that it seems to be growing in popularity (Sherman and Dominick 1986), there is reason to be concerned about its impact on the development of particular gender stereotypes among teenagers. At the same time, however, research that has examined adolescents' understanding of rock music lyrics has found that a large percentage of adolescents and preadolescents interpret the songs quite differently than adults do. While adults see and hear explicit sexual themes, many young people interpret the songs in terms of "Love, friendship, growing up, life's struggles, having fun, cars, religion, and other topics that relate to teenage life" (Prinsky and Rosenbaum 1987:393). Other research indicates that music videos are less stimulating to the imagination and are enjoyed less than the music heard alone (Greenfield, et al. 1986). Obviously, considerably more research must be undertaken before the influence of music videos can be more accurately assessed.

We will return to the issue of the effects of television in general, but for now we turn to an examination of gender portrayals in advertising.

Gender Messages in Advertisements: Does Sexism Sell?

A woman changes her clothes from business suit to housedress to evening gown while singing in a husky voice about how she can "bring home the bacon, fry it up in a pan," and still make her husband "feel like a man" all because she uses a particular perfume.

A young man stands beside his car, discussing its merits, while beautiful women pass by and ask for a ride. Visibly proud of his ability to attract women, he soon realizes that it is not him they find attractive, but the car.

These scenarios are quite familiar to us. They come, of course, from the contrived world of advertising and, like most advertisements, they are selling us more than a specific product. Indeed, they are peddling needs and desires. In the first example, the implicit message is that every woman can have a successful career, be a good homemaker, and find sexual fulfillment by using the advertised product which, realistically, is designed only to make her smell good. In the second, men are told that regardless of what they look like or how socially inept they are, they too can attract beautiful women if they buy the advertised car, the real purpose of which is just to provide them transportation. Just about everyone wants to be successful, physically attractive, even sexy. What advertisers often do is play on these desires by implying that their products may serve not only their intended purposes, but also offer bonuses as well. In this way, "advertisements portray an image that represents the interpretation of those cultural values which are profitable to propagate" (Courtney and Whipple 1983:192).

Advertisements also portray images of gender that the advertising industry deems profitable. According to two advertising analysts, for male consumers the message is to buy a particular product and get the "sweet young thing" associated with it, whereas for female consumers the message is to buy the product in order to be the sweet young thing (Masse and Rosenblum 1988). This has resulted in ads rife with sexist stereotypes because, as Courtney and Whipple (1983) and others (e.g., Lazier-Smith 1989) point out, the dominant philosophy of the industry proclaims that "sexism sells." Before we evaluate the accuracy of this belief, let's look at some of the common gender stereotypes in print and television advertising.

Occupational stereotyping by sex pervades advertisements. Men hold positions of authority—they are the so-called experts—while women receive advice, usually from men, or are shown in traditional female occupations. For example, in a recent analysis of pictorial representations of the sexes in popular computer magazine ads, the researchers found that females were overrepresented as sales and clerical workers, and were often depicted in a passive role—for example, as an onlooker or as learner rather than teacher. Males, on the other hand, were portrayed as active computer users and were overrepresented as managers, experts, and technicians (Ware and Stuck 1985).

Occupational stereotyping is endemic in less specialized advertising too. Suppose we told you that we were about to show you ten advertisements featuring male models, and we asked you to guess what jobs they would most likely be doing. You would probably have little difficulty coming up with answers because men in advertisements are shown in a wide range of roles—from white collar professionals such as scientists, physicians, and business executives, to blue-collar workers such as plumbers, electricians, and exterminators. Less often, they are shown in family roles as husbands and fathers. But what if we asked the same question using ads with female models? Chances are you would have a tougher time varying your answers; two of the most common roles for women depicted in advertisements remain housewife and mother (Lazier-Smith 1989; Courtney and Whipple 1983).

In television commercials, women most often demonstrate household cleaning products, personal care items, and food. Yet the announcers and background voices (known as voice-overs) in these ads are almost always male. Nine out of ten voice-overs, in fact, are male. The rationale of the advertising industry is that female voices are neither authoritative nor believable. Consumers, they maintain, trust a male voice; "the male voice is the voice of authority" (quoted in Courtney and Whipple 1983:136). Marketing research refutes this argument, however. Studies, for instance, show no differences in the persuasiveness of female and male voice-overs (Mosedale 1987; Courtney and Whipple 1983). Other studies have also found that female spokespersons are more trusted by the public than male spokespersons (Steenland 1987; WIFP 1982b). Given these findings, we might expect female voice-overs to be used even more than male voice-overs, but it appears that advertisers are still unconvinced about their effectiveness.

Another frequent role for women in advertising is as sex objects. Usually this is purely a decorative role; in other words, the model has no clear relationship to the product and is shown simply because of her physical attractiveness and sex appeal. Typically, models are scantily dressed (e.g., in bathing suits) and provocatively posed. While many consumers have come to expect these portrayals in personal care or cosmetics ads—indeed they dominate such advertisements—they are also prevalent in nonappearance-related advertising (Downs and Harrison 1985). For instance, in magazine ads for computers, women are often shown dressed in evening gowns and seductively draped across equipment (Ware and Stuck 1985). "In many industrial advertisements women are employed to call attention to parts and equipment. In those advertisements it is not uncommon to see bikini-clad women lounging on new machine tools or electronic equipment" (Courtney and Whipple 1983:103). In a comparison of magazine ads from 1973 and 1986, Lazier-Smith (1989) found that there has been a 10 percent increase in ads depicting women as sex objects or in decorative roles.

Research indicates that the percentage of advertisements depicting men in decorative roles also has increased in recent years (Skully and Lundstrom 1981). It appears that the response of the advertising industry to complaints of sexism in ads using decorative female models has not been to eliminate such ads, but rather to demean men by increasing portrayals of them as sex objects too. This approach reflects the industry's confusion of gender equality with sexual permissiveness and exploitation. Consider, for instance, the recent print advertisement for Charlie perfume in which a "liberated" businesswoman publicly patted the behind of her businessman companion. Other forms of confusion appear in ads that show "liberated husbands" trying ineptly to help with housework, or that depict "liberated women" as domineering types who like to put down men (Courtney and Whipple 1983).

There are other, more subtle ways that sexism permeates advertisements. One, for example, is the way models are posed. In a study that compared the ways women and men are depicted in magazine advertisements, Masse and Rosenblum (1988) found that female models are significantly more likely than male models to be depicted in subordinate poses. Female models are more frequently solitary and also appear more often as "partials," that is, only a part of their bodies such as their legs, is shown. Models are sometimes diminished in advertisements, although this is more common in men's magazines. Masse and Rosenblum found that almost a quarter of the female figures were not fullsized, in these magazines, as compared with less than 7 percent of the male figures. (In women's magazines, 6.5 percent of female models and 7 percent of male models were diminished.) Overall, 27 percent of the female models, but just 3.8 percent of the male models, in the magazine ads were subordinated in some way.

Despite industry claims that sexism sells, research demonstrates otherwise. Consumers consistently express a preference for advertisements that show women and men in non-sex-stereotyped roles. "Whether the portrayal is an occupational or a family role, it should be contemporary and nonsexist" to effectively sell a product (Whipple and Courtney 1985:6). Consumers do like to see attractive models of both sexes in advertisements, but the use of nudity, semi-nudity, and sexual innuendo actually inhibits their recall of the products and the advertisements (Courtney and Whipple 1983). Sometimes, in fact, such sexism offends and angers consumers. Such was the case in 1989 when a Miller beer advertising supplement designed as a "humorous take-off on spring break," was distributed in college newspapers throughout the United States. The ad depicted women as mindless objects and men as only interested in sex and drinking. At some schools, students were so offended by the ad that they called for a boycott of Miller products and demanded an apology from the company, which they got almost immediately (*New York Times* 13 March 1989). Nevertheless, many industry representatives continue to deny that sexism is a problem in advertising, and they have openly resisted change. As we have seen here, in fact, the changes that have been made frequently perpetuate sexism by distorting liberation and increasingly demeaning men.

IMAGES OF GENDER IN THE MEDIA: WHAT ARE THEIR EFFECTS?

Defenders of the media sometimes argue that while media portrayals are often sexist, their effects are benign. "That only happens on television," they say, "People don't really believe that stuff." There is considerable evidence, though, that appears to contradict this argument; many people, it seems, do believe that stuff.

The majority of research on media effects has focused on television, largely because of its popularity, particularly with children, and because of the unique characteristics that we outlined earlier. A central issue has been the effects of violent television programming. Since the 1970s, more than 2,500 research reports have been published on this topic, and the conclusion drawn by most of them is that watching violence and aggression on television can lead to violent and aggressive behavior in children, both during their younger years and later in life (Corry 1985; WIFP 1982c). In addition, in its review of the available literature, the National Institute of Mental Health reported that, "[P]eople who look at a great deal of television tend to believe that there is more violence in the real world than do those who do not look at much television. . . . Exposure to televised violence has also been found to lead to mistrust, fearfulness of walking alone at might, a desire to have protective weapons, and alienation" (quoted in WIFP 1982c:8; *see also* Condry 1989; Wober and Gunter 1988).

We will take up the issue of the effects of reading about and seeing violence against women in Chapter 9. Suffice it to say here, however, that at least with regard to violent behavior in general, television's impact hardly seems benign. Is there a similar relationship between television viewing and perceptions of appropriate roles for women and men? Current research provides no conclusive answers. In their review of the literature, for example, Courtney and Whipple (1983) found evidence that heavy television viewers are more sexist than light or occasional viewers. Still, they caution that this finding does not reveal which variable, the heavy television viewing or the sexist attitudes, is the causal factor in the relation-ship. Additional research indicates that children tend to choose programs that conform to gender stereotypes they have already learned. In other words, the media reinforce gender stereotypes that children are taught both by their parents and in school because children will select those media presentations that confirm what they have previously learned (Liebert, et al. 1982). Similarly, Johnson and Ettema (1982) used a specially produced television series to try to alter children's beliefs about gender, but found that change depended upon additional external reinforcement of the programs' content.

More definitive research exists with regard to television commercials (Baran and Blasko 1980). For instance, Geis and her colleagues (1984) showed groups of students a series of commercials, some of which were gender stereo-typed and others that portrayed gender role reversals. They then asked the students to write a short essay about how they pictured their lives ten years into the future. Women who saw the stereotyped commercials tended to stereotype their futures; they emphasized homemaking and expressed few aspirations for achievement outside the home. In contrast, women who saw the role-reversed commercials wrote essays similar to those of male subjects; their essays were achievement oriented and had few homemaking themes. The researchers con-cluded that gender depictions in television commercials may be understood as gender *prescriptions* by female viewers and may have a cumulative effect on their real life aspirations, especially given that, as children, they watch an estimated 22,000 to 25,000 commercials a year.

Clearly, the Geis, et al. (1984) study points to the detrimental effects of gender-stereotyped commercials, but it is significant for a second reason: it also indicates that nonstereotyped commercials can have a positive impact on women's aspirations. Similar results have been obtained by other researchers. The National Institute of Mental Health concluded in its report, "The clear and simple message derived from the research on prosocial behavior is that children learn from watch-ing television and what they learn depends on what they watch. . . . Television can have beneficial effects; it is a potential force for good" (quoted in WIFP 1982c:8; *see also* Condry 1989; Wober and Gunter 1988; Courtney and Whipple 1983). Unfortunately, so little research in this area has been done using print media that we cannot comment on whether it, too, may have such effects, but based on the findings of television studies, it is an issue that deserves more attention.

LANGUAGE AND MEDIA AS SHAPERS OF GENDER

In this chapter we have examined the gender images communicated by the pri-mary means by which we give and receive information: language and the mass media. Far from simply reflecting the values and norms of our culture, we have learned here how language and media shape and recreate culture. In this way, language and the media socialize us, and with respect to gender, much of this socialization takes place through *symbolic annihilation*: symbolically ignoring, trivializing, or demeaning a particular group, which in this case has traditionally been women. We have found, for example, that language "tells a woman she is an afterthought, a linguistic variant, an 'et cetera' " (Butler and Paisley 1980:50). Newspapers convey a similar message. Rarely are women or women-centered events and issues considered to be worthy of serious attention as *hard* news; instead, they are ghettoized or distorted.

Magazines, television, and the advertisements that dominate both, promote what may be called cults of femininity and masculinity. Women, they seem to say, must be all things to all people, although men come first in their lives. They are depicted as homemakers and sex objects, interested primarily in serving men and children. Occupational success is secondary, but when it appears, women are usually limited in their occupational choices. Men, on the other hand, are stereotyped as aggressive and selfish, and in this way they, too, are symbolically annihilated by the media. They are depicted as being somewhat concerned with their physical appearance, but they are not as obsessed with it as women are shown to be. Sex appeal is important, but so are power and authority. Men's foremost concern is material success, and they are offered a wide spectrum of occupations in which to achieve it. If they cannot get what they want through work or competition, force and violence are held up as alternatives.

We have discussed evidence in this chapter indicating that such depictions do have a negative impact on men's and women's behaviors and self-concepts. But we have also reviewed research that shows that the media, particularly television, can be a powerful force in breaking down sexist stereotypes by sensitively and realistically portraying women and men in nontraditional roles. Some observers have argued that this latter consequence is likely only if more women are hired for policy making posts at newspapers, television stations, and advertising agencies. We, too, advocate a balanced representation of the sexes in these jobs; however, evidence we have discussed in this chapter suggests that this is not enough. In addition, a concerned public must take action. Successful strategies have included letter-writing campaigns to newspapers and television stations, and boycotts of products promoted in sexist advertisements (*New York Times* 13 March 1989; Courtney and Whipple 1983). At the very least, we must adopt the practice of using nonsexist language in our own communication. If language and the media help to construct what comes to be defined as reality, we must act to insure that the reality constructed is a nonsexist one.

KEY TERMS

linguistic sexism   ways in which language devalues members of one sex
reflection hypothesis   the belief that media content mirrors the behaviors, relationships, values, and norms most prevalent or dominant in a society

semantic derogation   the process by which the meaning or connotations of words are debased over time

symbolic annihilation   symbolically ignoring, trivializing, or condemning individuals or groups in the media

SUGGESTED READINGS

Condry, J. 1989. *The Psychology of Television.* Hillsdale, NJ: Lawrence Erlbaum Associates.

Creedon, P.J. (Ed.) 1989. *Women in Mass Communication: Challenging Gender Values.* Newbury Park, CA: Sage.

Frank, F.W., and P.A. Treichler (Eds.) 1989. *Language, Gender, and Professional Writing: Theoretical Approaches and Guidelines for Nonsexist Usage.* New York: The Modern Language Association of America.

Sanders, M., and M. Rock 1988. *Waiting for Prime Time: The Women of Television News.* Urbana, IL: University of Illinois Press.

In addition, the Women's Institute for Freedom of the Press publishes a bimonthly newsletter, "Media Report to Women," which reprints excerpts from research reports and articles covering virtually every dimension of the topic of gender and the media. It is available from Communications Research Associates (10606 Mantz Road, Silver Spring, MD 20903-1228) at a nominal charge.

We also recommend for a compilation of further suggested readings, G.H. Hill and S. Saverson Hill, *Blacks on Television: A Selectively Annotated Bibliography,* which was published by The Scarecrow Press (Metuchen, NJ) in 1985.

Chapter 7

Gender and Intimate Relationships

In Chapter 4, we saw how parents teach their children gender. We learned that gender socialization can occur not only by what is said, but also through what is left unsaid but demonstrated (i.e. through modeling). In this chapter, our focus is on how family organization itself helps to shape, and in turn is shaped by, a society's sex/gender system. We will address two central and inseparable questions:

1. How do relations of production *and* reproduction in the home serve to reinforce or undermine gender relations in the larger society?
2. At the same time, how do the nonfamilial institutions and dominant normative ideology of a particular society impinge upon home life and relationships among intimates?

These are obviously complex questions, and the task of answering them is made more difficult by the fact that much of our thinking about families is colored by the culturally prescribed ideals of our society. Before we discuss contemporary family relations, therefore, we need to critically examine some of our taken-for-granted assumptions about families and home life.

FAMILIES: MYTHS AND REALITIES

"More are doing it and they're doing it bigger and better!" So proclaims a recent newspaper advertisement for diamond engagement rings. The "it" referred to, of course, is getting married. The ad bubbles on:

> Since 1976, the marriage rate has been climbing steadily and 1980 set the record with 2,396,000 marriages, an even higher figure than the post–World War II peak reached in 1946. Riding the crest of this wave is the traditional formal wedding with all the trimmings. Out are the 60's style weddings in the park, in are the religious ceremonies performed in a church, chapel, or synagogue with elaborate reception following. The 80's bride is opting for a white or ivory formal wedding gown and the popular fashions this fall are lavished with lace and traditional detailing that harkens back to the Victorian era.

Indeed, more scientific evidence indicates that bridal attire is not the only thing reminiscent of an earlier age. Surveys of high school and college students reveal that prevalent attitudes toward sex, marriage, and parenting are hardly nontraditional. For example, in a 1987 opinion poll conducted by a popular national magazine, 61 percent of the 1,200 male and female college students questioned expect to marry (up from 56 percent in 1980) and 94 percent wish to have children (compared with 81 percent in 1980). What is more, these students are overwhelmingly optimistic about the future success of their marriages, with 81 percent of the men and 95 percent of the women anticipating only one wedding during their lifetimes (*Glamour,* August 1987; *see also* Bezilla 1988). Other researchers have found that both young men and women prefer husbands to be the primary breadwinners and wives to be homemakers, especially after children are born (Canter and Ageton 1984; Herzog, et al. 1983).

Such attitudes stand out in startling relief against a background of official statistics on sexual activity, marriage, and family life in the United States. Although the marriage rate is high—about 94 percent of men and 96 percent of women marry by age 35—a substantial proportion of marriages are remarriages. For instance, of the 2,413,000 marriages performed in 1985, just slightly more than half involved first-time brides and grooms. The divorce rate has been slowly declining; nevertheless, couples in the United States continue to divorce at a high rate, and half of all marriages in the United States end within seven years (U.S. Department of Commerce 1990). In addition, a declining divorce rate does not necessarily mean a corresponding increase in healthy, enduring marital relationships. Rather, there is evidence that some couples are simply postponing divorce for economic reasons. As one divorce lawyer explained, "Divorce in the eighties is divorce on hold . . . When we subtract taxes and figure out what's the minimum amount they need to live on, and they see what's left, a lot of them are saying: 'Maybe when the kids are grown-up.' And they stay in the marriage" (quoted in Kantrowitz 1987:53)

As we will learn later in this chapter, the economics of divorce impinge most on women and children, who tend to experience a precipitous drop in their standard of living. Divorced women, especially those with children, rarely have the option of being full-time homemakers. The majority, including those with children under five years of age, are employed at least part-time outside the home. Even among married women, however, 56.5 percent are in the labor force, and a substantial proportion of these have children. As Table 7.1 shows, the percentage of employed married women with children has increased significantly since 1970;

TABLE 7.1
Trends in Employment of Married Mothers

Percentage of Married Mothers (of Children Under 18) in the Labor Force					
Age of Youngest Child	*1970*	*1975*	*1980*	*1985*	*1988*
1 year or younger	24%	31%	39%	49%	51.9%
2 years	31	37	48	54	61.7
3 years	35	41	52	55	59.3
4 years	39	41	51	60	61.4
5 years	37	44	52	62	63.6
Total: under 6 years	30%	37%	45%	54%	57.4%
Total: 6 to 17 years	49%	52%	62%	68%	72.5%
Total: with children under 18 years	40%	45%	54%	61%	65.2%

Source: U.S. Department of Commerce 1990:385.

by 1988, 65.2 percent of married women with children under 18 were in the labor force. Even more striking is the percentage of employed married women with infants and toddlers. Of course, many of these women, like their divorced sisters, are working out of sheer economic necessity, but as we will see in Chapter 8, many also find employment satisfying and psychologically rewarding. Regardless of their reasons for working, though, it is clear that employed wives and mothers outnumber full-time homemakers in the United States today.

What, if anything, does this comparison of attitudes with statistical summaries of behaviors tell us? Certainly it shows that what people say they believe and what they actually do are frequently quite different; sociologists have recognized and studied such disparities for years. More than that, however, we think the contrast illustrates the continuing tendency on the part of most men and women to romanticize marriage and family life and to view the home as a refuge or haven from the harsher, depersonalized public world. Despite the realities of contemporary marital and family life, many people, but particularly the young, still hold idealized images derived from their society's normative dictates of what a marriage or family should be like (*see also* Larson 1988). However, sociologists have not been immune to these prejudices; their work, in fact, has often reinforced as well as reflected them. Let's look, then, at some of the traditional sociological literature on marriages and families. There we will find quite explicitly the glorification of certain family forms and roles as right and normal, whereas others are denounced as "deviant." Subsequently, much of the remainder of this chapter will examine the consequences that this traditional model has had for the everyday lives of women and men.

SOCIOLOGY CONSTRUCTS *THE* FAMILY: THE WORK OF TALCOTT PARSONS

Writing in 1955, the sociologist Talcott Parsons described what he called the **isolated nuclear family.** According to Parsons, the contemporary nuclear family, that is, husband, wife, and their dependent children, is isolated in the sense that the members not only live apart from other relatives (such as the spouses' parents or siblings), but also they are economically independent from them as well. To Parsons, the nuclear family is also isolated to a large degree from other societal institutions because it no longer performs many of its earlier functions. More specifically, Parsons maintains that prior to industrialization, many of the services now provided externally by social institutions—for example, education, care of the sick, production of food and clothing—were done at home by family members. In contrast, the contemporary family has just two vital functions: "first, the primary socialization of children so that they can truly become members of the society into which they have been born; second, the stabilization of the adult personalities of the population of the society" (Parsons 1955:16).

From this functionalist perspective, the best way to accomplish these tasks is for the two spouses to carry out distinct specialized roles—one instrumental, the other expressive. The **instrumental family role** entails leadership and decision-making responsibilities, and it is filled by the spouse who is the economic provider for the family, traditionally the husband/father. The wife/mother, then, assumes the **expressive role,** which means she does the housework, cares for the children, and sees to it that the emotional needs of family members are met. Although Parsons acknowledges that some married women, even a few with small children, are employed outside the home, he maintains that they hold jobs in the lowest occupational categories so as not to compete with or displace their husbands as chief "status-givers" and wage earners. Thus, Parsons argues:

> It seems quite safe in general to say that the adult feminine role has not ceased to be anchored primarily in the internal affairs of the family, as wife, mother, and manager of the household, while the role of the adult male is primarily anchored in the occupational world, in his job and through it by his status-giving and income-earning functions for the family. Even if, as seems possible, it should come about that the average married woman had some kind of job, it seems most unlikely that this relative balance would be upset; that either the roles would be reversed, or their qualitative differentiation in these respects completely erased (1955:14–15).

A logical question at this point is why does this particular role differentiation exist? Why can't men sometimes be expressive and women sometimes be instrumental leaders? For Parsons, the answer is simple and obvious:

> In our opinion the fundamental explanation for the allocation of the roles between the biological sexes lies in the fact that the bearing and early nursing of children establish a strong presumptive primacy of the relation of mother to the small child and this in turn establishes a presumption that the man, who is exempted from these biological functions, should specialize in the alternative instrumental direction (1955:23).

Although written in the 1950s, Parson's work warrants a careful look first, because much of the sociological literature on families that followed it bears the imprint of his functionalist analysis, and second, because we hear his ideas today echoed in the "pro-family" rhetoric of the political right (*see* Chapters 11 and 13). Not surprisingly, his perspective has also had its critics, and feminists have been among the most vociferous.

To begin, the historical accuracy of Parson's argument has been called into question. As Allan (1985:5–6) points out, it is unlikely that families were ever able to provide the services that Parsons claimed they did before industrialization. For instance, given that most families had limited resources at their disposal, typically lived under poor conditions, and lacked any specialized medical knowledge, the extensive health and welfare needs of their members could rarely be met adequately in the home. Similarly, "it is questionable whether families had an educational function as distinct from a socialization function [since] most of the knowledge imparted in schools was simply not available to the majority of people."

Parsons's emphasis on the isolation of the contemporary nuclear family from other kin has also been criticized. Implicit in his position is an image of the preindustrial family as an extended one—that is, grandparents, parents, children, and perhaps other relatives sharing a common household and its attendant economic burdens. Although cross-cultural research indicates that such arrangements are common in many non-Western preindustrial societies, historical evidence shows that in the preindustrial societies of the Western world, extended families were rare, except maybe among the aristocracy. A short life expectancy precluded the possibility of even a three-generation family for most people. Rather, it is more likely that "three-generation families actually developed as a consequence of industrialization rather than being destroyed by it" (Allan, 1985:6). Moreover, recent research indicates that contemporary families are not nearly as isolated from extended kin as Parsons made them out to be. It has been estimated, for example, that about 80 percent of the ever-married now in their late 50s and early 60s have living children, not to mention grandchildren, and the vast majority (80 to 90 percent) see at least one of these children once a week. This interaction includes socializing, but family members also turn to their kin for advice and emotional support as well as for financial help (Kammeyer 1987; Cicirelli 1983). Among minorities, especially African Americans and Asian Americans and among the working class and the poor in particular, researchers have found extensive kin and friendship networks in which resources are pooled so that families can survive hard times (Chatters, et al. 1989; Height 1989; Jewell 1988; Glenn 1987; Stack 1974).

Harsher criticism has been leveled against Parsons's rigid differentiation of roles between the sexes. In Chapter 1, we critiqued the role concept as depoliticizing the analysis of gender. Here we take up other problematic aspects of how functionalists depict the roles men and women are supposed to play. First, this erroneously separates public life—what Parsons sees as the masculine world of work, government, and so on—from what he claims is the private (feminine) world of the family. Critics refer to this false dichotomy as the **public/private split.** In their everyday lives, however, family members do not experience these two spheres as separate. For one thing:

> Men *and* women are bound to their jobs out of the family's need for economic survival, and in many ways—evident, for example in power relations between husbands and wives and in their use of leisure time—the nature of paid work shapes the daily experience of families. Moreover, activities in the home (housework, consumption, child care), which are mostly done by women, serve to maintain and reproduce the labor force (Thorne 1982:16, emphasis added).

There are, of course, social class differences. Poor families must frequently interact with the state, through social service agencies and the welfare system, in an effort to meet their daily survival needs, whereas middle-class families can utilize savings, pensions, or bank loans to handle financial demands. In addition to care of family and home, middle- and upper-middle class wives are often expected to help advance their husbands' careers by participating in community events, entertaining clients and colleagues, and serving as unpaid secretaries. In spite of these variations, however, it is quite clear that families of all social classes "are in continuous interaction with other institutions" (Thorne 1982:17; Rapp 1982; Margolis 1979; Zaretsky 1976).

The notion of the public/private split poses other problems as well. In particular, it masks the reality that work performed in the home—housework—is socially and economically necessary work. By labeling housework private and expressive, Parsons not only legitimates the fact that it is unpaid labor—it should be, in his view, a labor of love—but also that the burden of this unpaid labor falls squarely on the shoulders of women. Unfortunately, placing primary responsibility for housework on women makes their participation in the paid labor force more difficult, and this, in turn, helps keep them in a position of dependence and inequality vis-á-vis men. In addition, the image of the home as a private, emotionally nurturing world also serves to hide the conflict and physical and psychological abuse that frequently takes place there, with women and children being the most common victims. These two issues—the division of labor in the home and domestic violence—are, in fact, central to an accurate understanding of family relationships, so we will discuss them in greater detail shortly.

Another major difficulty with Parsons's rigid role differentiation is that it portrays instrumental and expressive activities as being mutually exclusive and thus assumes that their assignment on the basis of sex is natural. In other words, we are offered *the* male role and *the* female role, which are biologically based, and from this it follows that this arrangement is both normal and unchanging (*see* Chapters 1 and 3). His concept of the natural extends to family forms and thus constructs *the* family as well. He argues, for example, that "by and large a 'good' marriage from the point of view of the personality of the participants is likely to be one with children" (Parsons 1956:21). Similarly, he contends that "in the 'normal' case it is both true that *every adult* is a member of a nuclear family and that every child must begin his [sic] process of socialization in a nuclear family" (Parsons 1956:17, author's emphasis). One outcome of this is that individuals and families who by choice or chance do not conform to these models come to be seen as deviant or abnormal. Attention, therefore, is focused on treating them, rather than on solving the structural problems that confront them, such as prejudice and discrimination.

In the preceding chapters of this text, we learned that gender and family arrangements are not biologically given, but rather culturally prescribed and socially learned. In Chapter 3, for instance, we examined extensive cross-cultural evidence that demonstrates wide variation in gender norms and family forms. But we need not look to other societies for alternatives, for within the United States itself there are variations in forms of intimate relationships. In fact, as we see in

TABLE 7.2
Households in the United States, 1988

Type of Household	Percent
Married couple with dependent children: husband sole wage earner, wife full-time homemaker	14.0
Married couple with dependent children: dual wage earners	17.3
Married couple, childless or without children at home	30.9
Single-parent, female head	7.1
Single-parent, male head	1.2
Unrelated persons living together	4.6
Individuals living alone	24.8
Total	99.9*

*Percentages do not add up to 100 because of rounding.
Source: U.S. Department of Commerce 1990.

Table 7.2, the type of family described by Parsons as universal and natural represents only a minority of households in the United States today (14 percent). More prevalent are families with dependent children and both spouses in the labor force, as well as households of married couples without dependent children. Several other types of households have been increasing in recent years: single-parent, female-headed households; unrelated persons living together; and individuals living alone.

This last category has grown partly as a result of the growing population of elderly, particularly elderly widows (*see* Chapter 12). At the same time, however, the increase reflects the larger number of women and men who are choosing to remain single or, more typically, who are delaying marriage longer than in the past. Included in the category of unrelated persons living together are the more than 2 million heterosexual couples who are cohabiting, but more significantly, it also includes a percentage of the estimated 24 million homosexual women and men, since many live with their partners (*see* Box 7.1)

In short, diversity rather than uniformity seems to be the best way to characterize family composition in the United States. Even the governments and courts of some large cities and states are officially recognizing alternative family forms as legitimate. For instance, in a landmark case in 1989, the New York Court of Appeals ruled that a homosexual couple who had lived together for ten years could be considered a family under New York City's rent control regulations. In explaining its decision, the court expanded the traditional definition of the family by considering such factors as the exclusivity and longevity of a relationship as well as the level of emotional and financial commitment of those involved in the relationship (Gutis 1989).

BOX 7.1   Cohabitation: Trial Marriage, Substitute Marriage, or Neither?

Cohabitation, or "living together" without marriage, appears to be an increasingly appealing lifestyle for many U.S. couples. The Census Bureau estimates that in 1988 there were 2.6 million unmarried couples living together in the United States, an increase of more than 600,000 couples from 1985. Since 1980, the number has risen by about one million (U.S. Department of Commerce 1990). Although the number is still small compared with other countries—in Sweden and Norway, for instance, it is estimated that 12 percent of all couples cohabit (Blanc 1987; Kammeyer 1987)—the increase is nevertheless substantial. Still, its meaning remains unclear. Is cohabitation becoming a substitute for marriage, or is it a "trial marriage," a kind of test run before making the full (and legally binding) commitment? Perhaps it serves some other purpose altogether—for example, it is convenient, or economical.

Unfortunately, most research on cohabiting couples has focused on college students or other young people. Although two-thirds of cohabitors are under age thirty-five, and more than 80 percent are younger than forty-five years old, 12.6 percent are forty-five to sixty-four, and almost 5 percent are sixty-five or older (U.S. Department of Commerce 1990). Thus, as Blumstein and Schwartz (1983:38) conclude, "When we consider the effect age has on lifestyles and personal needs, we can see how misleading it would be to think of all cohabitors as wanting the same things or behaving in the same ways for the same reasons." Still, there are some general trends in cohabitation that may provide us with at least tentative answers to our questions.

Blumstein and Schwartz (1983) and other researchers have found that most cohabiting relationships are of relatively short duration, that is, two years or less. Most cohabiting couples, then, either marry or break up instead of adopting cohabitation as a permanent lifestyle, which appears to be the trend in Sweden and Norway (Blanc 1987). In addition, most cohabiting couples in the United States are childless, although there may be children in the home from a previous marriage of one or both partners. "[A]ll evidence points to the fact that when cohabitors consider adding children to their relationship, they are very reluctant to do so without first becoming legally married" (Blumstein and Schwartz 1983:36).

A majority of cohabitors (54.1 percent) have never been married, but if the couples do eventually marry, research indicates that they are more likely to separate and divorce than couples who did not cohabit before they married. According to one sociologist, this may be because cohabitors have higher expectations of what marriage should offer in terms of intimacy, friendship, and similar factors (Barringer 1989).

A substantial percentage (34.5 percent) of cohabitors are divorced (U.S. Department of Commerce 1990). Many of these report that they prefer cohabitation to traditional marriage, at least for the time being, because it affords them the benefits of intimacy without the legal or economic entanglements that marriage entails. However, cohabiting partners may have more legally binding ties to one another than they think, especially if they acquire property and other assets together. This was made clear in the much publicized "palimony" suit brought by Michelle Triola against actor Lee Marvin, with whom she had cohabited for seven years. In deciding in favor of Ms. Triola, the California Supreme Court ruled that simply because a couple does not participate in a

Box 7.1 continued

valid marriage ceremony, it does not necessarily mean that their intent is to be independent of each other and to keep their earnings and assets separate. Although Ms. Triola was awarded significantly less "palimony" than she sued for, many observers have interpreted the outcome of this case as an indication that the courts are coming to view cohabitation as "an unspoken business partnership, at the very least" (Blumstein and Schwartz 1983:39).

Still, the courts have been inconsistent in their rulings. Even though many attorneys advise cohabiting couples to draw up contracts, some courts have been reluctant to enforce such agreements because they see them as potentially undermining the institution of marriage. Consequently, if a cohabiting couple decides to separate, one partner may lose out financially, or a battle may ensue over the division of assets. But even if the relationship endures, other difficulties may surface. "If one partner becomes ill, for example, the mate may be barred from visiting that person in the hospital or from participating in decisions about medical care. And if the person dies without a will, property that the deceased may have wanted to go to his or her partner may go instead to estranged family members" (Rankin 1987:F11).

One final note: our discussion has concentrated on heterosexual couples, but the problems outlined here are exacerbated for gay and lesbian couples. Although cohabitation among straight couples has become increasingly legitimatized in our society, the stigma attached to homosexuality remains intact. Most courts have refused to recognize such unions, and only a handful of large city governments have permitted homosexual couples to officially register their relationships. Thus, as we will learn later in this chapter, our legal system is designed not simply to protect marriages and families, but, more specifically, traditional heterosexual marriages and families.

Still, it remains true that most Americans do eventually marry in the conventional way, and many have children. We will therefore examine marriage and parenting, focusing especially on marital power, the division of labor in the home, and the problem of domestic violence. We will also include in our discussion single-parent families and gay and lesbian families. It is the latter two groups who have been most misunderstood and much maligned in the traditional literature. They also have suffered the most in the hands of a patriarchal and heterosexist sex/gender system.

MARRIAGE, INTIMACY, AND POWER

The origin of the word *family* has important implications for the nature of contemporary marital and family relations. *Family* derives from the Latin word *famulus* meaning "household servant or slave." This notion of the family was sanctioned by custom and law throughout most of the Western world, for a man's family—his wife, children, and slaves—were, like his material possessions, defined as his property. His legal obligation was to provide their economic support at a standard he saw fit in exchange for their service to him.

Certainly, few of us today think of the family in these terms, but we may still discern in contemporary marital and family relations remnants of this supposedly bygone theme. We can see this best by examining the institution of marriage. For example, our government continues to regulate marriage and to define the rights and responsibilities of spouses. Every state has a set of laws specifying who may marry in terms of age, sex, and health requirements. In addition, the states formulate the conditions of the *marriage contract.* Like any contract, the marriage contract is a legally binding agreement, but unlike most other contracts, its conditions cannot be changed by the two parties involved—only the state has that right. In fact, the contracting parties rarely, if ever, have the opportunity to even review the conditions of their agreement before entering into it. The marriage contract is imposed, rather than negotiated.

Although there is a tremendous variation among the fifty states as to the specific conditions of their marriage contracts, several common assumptions that underlie these contacts have been identified (Kammeyer 1987; Weitzman 1981). Interestingly, they ring of that original meaning of the word *family.* One assumption, for instance, is that the husband is the family head. Thus, although a wife is no longer expected to take her husband's surname, in most states the husband typically retains the right to decide domicile (place of residence). Consequently, "when a woman marries, her husband's legal domicile automatically supersedes her own. If her husband's legal domicile was different from her premarital domicile, she must re-register to vote; she may be subjected to unfavorable state income tax consequences; she may lose the right to attend a university in her own state as a resident student; and she may lose the privilege of running for public office in her home state" (Kay 1988:203). Exceptions have been made by some courts and state legislatures; one court, for instance, ruled that if the wife is the chief breadwinner, she may determine her domicile. Under most circumstances, however, it is the husband's legal right to choose the family's domicile. Although in the 1970s the U.S. Supreme Court handed down a number of rulings that considerably equalized spouses' marital privileges and obligations (Mansbridge 1986), laws such as that regarding domicile retain the Common Law standard of *coverture,* that is, the notion that a wife is under the protection and influence of her husband (Kay 1988).

In short, marital relations are fundamentally power relations—usually the power of husbands over wives. Because this assessment clearly runs contrary to the romanticized view of marriage so commonly held, we need to explore the issue of marital power more fully.

Marital Power

As we noted in Chapter 1, when we speak about power, we are essentially speaking about the ability to influence others so that they do what we want them to do whether they want to do it or not. It is the ability to get one's own way. When we think of marriages, however, we think of partnerships, not power struggles. We like to think that each spouse has equal input and, if there is a disagreement, the two compromise. To what extent does available research support such a view?

In answering this question, we are immediately confronted with another: how do we measure marital power? Most studies of marital power use a strategy developed in 1960 by sociologists Robert Blood and Donald Wolfe. Blood and Wolfe looked at decision making by married couples to determine which spouse has more power. They asked more than 900 wives who had the final say in such decisions as where to go on vacation, what car to buy, how much money to spend on food, whether the wife should get a job, where to live, or what doctor to consult. In general, their findings showed husbands to be more powerful than wives in that it was they who made most family decisions even though they usually talked matters over with their wives. There were conditions, however, under which this tended to vary. More specifically, the spouse who brought more "resources" to the marriage—for example, income, social status, or education—was likely to be more powerful. Typically, this was the husband, but Blood and Wolfe discovered that as a wife's resources increased, she gained leverage relative to her husband.

Although Blood and Wolfe's study was conducted more than a quarter century ago, their findings have been substantiated by more recent research. For example, in their 1983 study of more than 12,000 couples in the United States, Blumstein and Schwartz found that in most cases, the partner who earns more money tends to be the more powerful as measured by decision making. Like Blood and Wolfe, the researchers report that at least among married and cohabiting heterosexual couples, the more women earn relative to their partners, the more power they acquire in the relationship; the full-time homemaker tends to be relatively powerless. An important exception to this general rule occurs among couples who adhere to the belief that men should be the primary family breadwinners. In these relationships, men are the more powerful regardless of the earnings of either partner. The prevailing logic in such relationships is that if it is the man's role to be the family provider, then he should have the final say in most decisions. In fact, Thompson and Walker (1989:857) report that among couples in which the wives earn more than the husbands, most exhibit traditional attitudes and behaviors with respect to men's and women's roles in marriage.

> Such wives, especially younger ones, attempt to be more attractive and sexual with their husbands and report catering to their husbands' whims and salving their egos. The division of domestic labor in these families tends toward the traditional. If earnings are a source of power, these wives are not using their power to push for a fair distribution of labor at home.

This latter finding alerts us to the fact that there is more to marital power than can be discerned by simply asking questions about family decision making. Indeed, this method of measuring marital power has been amply criticized on this and related grounds. For one thing, the decision-making measure tends to treat all decisions as if they carry equal weight. But as Allan (1985:81) points out, some decisions must be made fairly regularly, whereas others may be made only once or twice in a lifetime. Obviously, such decisions vary in their consequences and in their import: "Is it really sensible to consider decisions about whether the wife is employed as equivalent to ones about which doctor should be consulted when someone is ill?"

A second criticism centers around the nature of power itself. Power includes not only authority in decision making, but also the right to *delegate* responsibility for certain decisions to others. For instance, Blumstein and Schwartz (1983) found that among the married couples they surveyed, wives frequently made the decisions about the purchase of expensive items, such as furniture for the home. However, they also discovered that in most cases, the wives were acting as *agents* for the couple; the husbands *assigned* the wives this responsibility. The words of one husband they interviewed illustrates this nicely:

> We don't argue about money because she pays all the bills. I don't have to worry about it, do I? I don't see the bills so I don't worry about them, so it's a copout on my part. I let her worry about them. . . . I'm giving her all the responsibility and she enjoys it, apparently, it gives her a sense of power. It's beautiful.

As Blumstein and Schwartz (1983:65) accurately conclude, this husband "regards the delegation of control to his wife as giving her a *false* sense of power" (emphasis added).

A third related criticism can be summed up in the old adage, "Actions speak louder than words." More precisely, critics have pointed out that some social practices are so taken-for-granted, so deeply embedded in ideology and family structure, that decisions do not have to be made about them. Rather, they are automatically carried out and rarely questioned (Allan 1985). From this perspective, more can be learned about marital power by observing the division of labor in the home and who benefits from it than from asking couples who decides what. Maintaining that this criticism has considerable merit, we turn now to a discussion of the division of household labor.

Gender and the Politics of Housework

Several years ago, one of the authors was part of a research team working on a project that involved telephone interviewing. One of the last questions asked in each interview was, "What kind of work do you do?" In call after call, literally hundreds of women replied, "I don't work; I'm just a housewife."

What is so striking in such a response is that despite the fact that housework is socially and economically necessary work, it is not considered real work, not even by the women who have primary responsibility for doing it. First, housework is unspecialized work—covering, by some estimates, more than eighty different tasks—but it is also repetitive work. By repetitive we mean that housework is never fully finished in the traditional sense of the word; no sooner is a chore completed than it must be done again. This is because housework involves production for immediate consumption: "Freshly laundered articles quickly become soiled; dust begins to settle as soon as it is swept away, children and husbands quickly sully newly tidied living areas." There is, though, another sense in which housework never ends:

> Unlike industrialized workers who sell their labor power for a fixed period of time, the housewife cannot watch the clock in the sure knowledge that work will soon be over. There is no formal end to the working day. It has no beginning, it has no end—it is merely a continuing set of tasks that need doing more or less adequately (Allan 1985:35).

Homemakers, then, rarely get time off, not even holidays—who, for instance, cooks those large holiday meals? What is more, homemakers tend to be on twenty-four-hour call: who usually gets up in the middle of the night to tend to a sick or frightened child?

There are several other reasons housework is not typically viewed as "real" work. One is that it is intertwined with love and feelings of caring. Another is that it is privatized. We see people leaving their houses *to go to work;* we see them in public on the job. But housework is done in isolation in the home, and much of it is done while other family members are elsewhere (e.g., in the labor force or at school). A third reason that housework is not considered "real" work is because it is *unpaid.* In a society like ours, individuals' status—how much persons are valued by others as well as by themselves—is measured largely by how much money they make. Homemakers do not receive wages in exchange for their labor; rather, they are "provided for" by a family wage earner. "Their work is not worth money, is therefore valueless, is therefore not even real work" (Benston 1969:282).

The absence of a rigid hourly schedule and the privatized nature of housework do give it an advantage over many jobs outside the home in that they afford homemakers a fair degree of autonomy. It is this freedom that homemakers report as one aspect of housework they appreciate most (Doyal 1990b; Thompson and Walker 1989; Allan 1985). In addition, most homemakers derive some satisfaction from meeting the needs of those they love (Thompson and Walker 1989). Still, the homemaker status is a devalued one, and the actual tasks that constitute much housework are menial, monotonous, stressful, and often unappreciated (Doyal 1990b; Thompson and Walker 1989).

Of course, whenever complaints about housework are raised, someone is usually quick to point out how much easier it is today compared with the past; after all, contemporary homemakers have a vast array of labor-saving appliances at their disposal. Interestingly, however, research indicates that the 1980s homemaker spent about as much time on household chores as the 1780s homemaker did (Ogden 1986; Cowan 1984). This is largely because of two factors. First, our standard of living has risen dramatically, and with it, so have our expectations with regard to the comfort and cleanliness of our household environment. To this we may also add that we have become a society of consumers. For example, the average family dwelling today is much larger than that of two centuries ago, with the consequence that there are more rooms to clean. Within its walls, we find far more personal possessions, all of which we expect to be well maintained—along with the house and ourselves. Contemporary middle-class family members may routinely change clothes several times a day and expect to sit down each evening to a tasty meal served on china so shiny they can see themselves. In contrast, "even on a good day in the eighteenth century, you would have been lucky to wear dirty, smelly clothes and eat a boring, nutritionally incomplete meal in a cramped one- or two-room house" (Stobaugh 1985:41). Thus, household chores have perhaps become more sophisticated over the last two hundred years, but they have not seemed to lessen or to grow less time-consuming.

Historian Ruth Schwartz Cowan (1984) offers a second reason why housework remains demanding: women's chores in the home have multiplied over the years, whereas men's chores have largely been industrialized. In eighteenth century households, for example, wives cooked meals and baked bread, while husbands grew and milled the grain, butchered the meat, and cleaned the hearth. Today, we rely on commercially produced food, a convenience that benefits both husbands and wives, but wives retain responsibility for cooking and now have the added task of cleaning the oven.

Lest we be misunderstood, our intent here is not to romanticize the past, nor are we suggesting that families would be better off if we could turn back the clock. Rather, our point is that housework, despite technological advances and modern convenience, continues to be arduous and time-consuming work, and it is women's time that is consumed by it.

To understand this better, consider the number of hours wives and husbands contribute to housework. Studies conducted for more than a decade have yielded consistent findings: Wives spend an average of fifty to sixty hours per week on housework; husbands contribute about eleven hours a week (Levant, et al. 1987; Hartmann 1981). This may not seem so unfair if spouses are exchanging services according to the traditional marriage contract—she does the housework and child care, he works in the paid labor force and financially supports the family—but we have already seen that this model applies to only a minority of contemporary families in the United States. Most married women are employed, and the vast majority of them, along with their husbands, say that in two-earner households housework should be divided more equally between spouses. Importantly, however, the division of labor in such homes does not reflect this belief (Hochschild 1989; Thompson and Walker 1989; Hiller and Philliber 1986). Although employed wives spend fewer hours on housework than full-time homemakers, their husbands' contributions do not increase significantly (Thompson and Walker 1989; Berardo, et al. 1987; Levant, et al. 1987; Johnson and Firebaugh 1985; Hartmann 1981). "Even if a husband is unemployed, he does much less housework than a wife who puts in a forty-hour week" (Blumstein and Schwartz 1983:145). Employed wives, then, carry a **double work load**: they are wage earners *and* they continue to hold almost exclusive responsibility for housework.

Arlie Hochschild (1989) refers to this double work load as *the second shift*. In her study of fifty couples, Hochschild found that husbands do about one-third of household chores, although these are usually not *daily* chores. Wives do most of the *daily* chores, such as cooking and routine cleaning. A major difference, then, between women's work in the home and men's work in the home lies not only in the relative contributions each spouse makes to housework, but also in the amount of control they have over when they do the work. The jobs women do in the home are those that tend to bind them to a fixed schedule, whereas men's household chores are done less regularly. Thus, for example, meals must be prepared every day, but the lawn needs mowing only about once a week (Hochschild 1989; Thompson and Walker 1989).

There are a number of other factors that influence the amount of time spouses spend on housework, although the research findings are far less consistent. With regard to age, for instance, some studies indicate that older husbands spend more time on housework than younger husbands, but other studies show just the opposite (Thompson and Walker 1989). In Hochschild's (1989) study, for example, the spouses were in their late twenties and early thirties. Social class variations have also been reported, with at least one researcher finding that higher-income husbands do more housework than lower-income husbands, but most others maintain that the reverse is true (Berardo, et al. 1987). In fact, Thompson and Walker (1989) maintain that high-income husbands are the least likely to participate in housework when their wives are also employed. Although the research on nonwhite couples is limited, some show that minority husbands are significantly more likely than white husbands to share housework with their wives, although other researchers have been unable to substantiate this (Wilson, et al. 1990; Thompson and Walker 1989). Hartmann (1981) found that neither social class nor race and ethnicity had a significant impact on the number of hours devoted to housework, even among full-time homemakers. However, it does appear that as a wife's own earnings increase, the amount of time she spends on housework decreases. Keep in mind, though, that this is not necessarily because her husband is doing more, but rather because she can afford to hire another person—usually a poor, minority *woman* (*see* Chapter 8)—to do the housework for her (Thompson and Walker 1989; Bernardo, et al. 1987; Blumstein and Schwartz 1983). In a fascinating study of couples in which husbands and wives do equally share housework, Coltrane (1989) found that one of the most important factors influencing an equal division of household labor was husbands' and wives' beliefs that housework is not "women's work," but rather something family members should do for one another.

Of course, the presence of children in a household increases housework time, although the amount varies by the number and ages of the children. Once again, however, it is women's time that is most significantly affected. A wife with an infant, for example, typically spends about seventy hours a week on house-work, thirty of which go to child care alone, while her husband spends about sixteen hours on chores and child care combined. If she is also employed, her housework time will decrease to fifty hours a week including twenty on child care, but her husband's contribution increases by only four hours (Hartmann 1981).

Much attention has been given recently in both the academic and popular literature to the supposedly increasing number of "househusbands" in the United States and the greater egalitarianism in the division of household labor between spouses in contemporary marriages (e.g., Pleck 1983). A careful review of avail-able evidence, however, indicates that "househusbandry" is not common nor is it even growing in popularity. Many "househusbands," it appears are either tempo-rarily out of work or are actually wage earners who have offices in their homes (Johnson and Firebaugh 1985; Beer 1983). Certainly the research we have re-viewed here does not suggest that the traditional division of labor in the home is on the wane. To the contrary, not only do women do more housework than men, but it is still taken for granted that housework is their responsibility regardless of whatever other demands they have on their time. Men who do household chores are often said to be "helping" their wives. Fathers frequently refer to taking care of their own children as "babysitting." Men appear to resist doing tasks they consider "feminine." The work men typically do around the house is less repeti-tious and more long-term than "women's work"; for example, men repair the car, paint, and make "do-it-yorself" home repairs (Coltrane 1989; Hochschild 1989; Thompson and Walker 1989; Levant, et al. 1987).

The notion of housework as "women's work" is part of the traditional family ideology that we outlined earlier. In Chapter 8, we will examine how an uncritical acceptance of this ideology may be used to deny women employment opportuni-ties and to relegate them to low-paying, low-prestige jobs. For now, we will focus on how it affects the balance of marital power.

We have already noted the relationship between money and power, but the nature of housework—in particular, that it is unpaid and privatized—means that the spouse chiefly responsible for it (almost invariably wives) is denied an important resource for balancing power in the marriage. Even if they are employed, however, most wives earn less than their husbands do (Chapter 8 discusses why), so the balance of power remains tipped in their husbands' favor. The wife/homemaker–husband/provider dichotomy ensures that the imbalance remains that way, for if a woman's first responsibility is supposed to be household and family care, then her job and earnings will likely be devalued and considered secondary to her husband's. Ironically, the employed wife often finds herself precariously balancing a double work load rather than marital power: if she devotes too much attention to her family she may become trapped in a relatively unrewarding low-paid job or be in danger of losing the job altogether, but if she spends too much time on her paid job, she may experience guilt or complaints from family members about her neglect of them (Vannoy-Hiller and Philliber 1989; Hochschild 1989; Thompson and Walker 1989; Barnett and Baruch 1988). Compounding the problem is another axiom of traditional family ideology, namely, that women are natural childbearers; therefore, they should also be the primary childrearers. A woman's power in the marital relationship decreases with the birth of children, since childrearing imposes severe limitations on her ability to pursue other activities, especially paid employment outside the home. Let's continue our discussion, then, with a look at parenting.

PARENTING: TO MOTHER AND/OR TO FATHER

Having a child has long been thought of as the next logical step for a couple after marriage. Until fairly recently, most couples in the United States had their first child only one to three years into their marriages (Kammeyer 1987). Becoming parents was not something over which couples spent much time deliberating; it was something they were automatically expected to do. The childless couple was either pitied because of their barrenness or scorned for their selfishness.

Nowadays, social pressures on couples to have children still exist, and research indicates that there remains some stigma attached to infertility (Miall 1986). Nevertheless, the prevalent attitude seems to be that childbearing is a private matter and a personal choice. Not only are women and men delaying marriage—the median age at first marriage was 23.3 for women and 25.1 for men in 1986 compared with 20.3 and 22.8 respectively in 1960—but also, once married, they are waiting longer to have children. These delays, in turn, have affected family size; as Table 7.3 shows, the average number of children born to women in the United States has declined significantly since 1800 so that small families with one or two children has become the norm. In addition, many married couples are voluntarily remaining childless, whereas many single heterosexual women and men, as well as gay and lesbian couples, are choosing to parent.

Three factors have contributed most to making childbearing more a matter of choice: greater availability of effective means of contraception, the legalization of abortion, and scientific advances in reproductive technology. Importantly, however, none of these is equally available to everyone, so that childbearing remains less a matter of choice for some than it is for others. Before discussing the actual care of children, therefore, it is imperative for us to consider the issue of *reproductive freedom* and the factors that impinge upon it.

Reproductive Freedom

The desires to prevent pregnancy and to control family size are not recent concerns. Historical and archeological evidence provides abundant proof that contraceptive methods and abortive techniques have been known and widely practiced for thousands of years. In the United States, though, most methods of contraception, along with abortion, were made illegal by 1850. It has been argued that the outlawing of abortion was in part the result of efforts by professionally trained physicians to take control of the provision of health care by, at least initially,

TABLE 7.3
Average Number of Births for White Women in the United States,
1800–1987*

Year	Average Number of Births per Woman
1800	7.0
1810	6.9
1820	6.7
1830	6.6
1840	6.1
1850	5.4
1860	5.2
1870	4.6
1880	4.2
1890	3.9
1900	3.6
1910	3.4
1920	3.2
1930	2.5
1940	2.1
1950	3.0
1960	3.5
1970	3.3
1980	1.8
1987	1.9

*Data for black and other minority women are incomplete, but based on what is available, it appears that their birth rates have also shown sharp declines, although the drop began somewhat later (around 1880) than for white women. However, the birth rate of black women is still higher than that of white women, and Hispanic women have a birth rate approximately 50 percent higher than non-Hispanics (Gordon 1976; U.S. House of Representatives 1987).
Sources: U.S. Department of Commerce 1990; The World Bank 1987; Gordon 1976.

displacing midwives (*see* Chapter 12). Historically, midwives performed or assisted with abortions as well as attended to women during childbirth. Outlawing abortion eliminated a substantial proportion of midwives' medical practice. In addition, some analysts have pointed out that abortions were most common among middle- and upper-class white women and that they were increasing at a time when racist fears about the growing numbers of foreign immigrants and African Americans was widespread. Thus, the outlawing of abortion was a means to prevent "race suicide" among women of "native" (i.e., white middle- and upper-class) stock. In both cases, however, the abortion controversy was clearly political, rather than moral or religious (Luker 1984; Mohr 1978; Gordon 1976).

Women have long taken—some would say, have been forced to take—responsibility for birth control, so it is hardly surprising that they have led the social movements for planned parenthood and the legalization of contraception and abortion. Many women became active on these issues because they or someone close to them had experienced the stigma of illegitimacy or had suffered the painful, often tragic, consequences of illegal abortions. Minority women, in particular, frequently contributed to these causes with their health and lives as the knowing or unwitting subjects in early medical research on the Pill, the IUD, and other contraceptive devices (*see* Chapter 12).

Supporters of reproductive freedom won major victories in the 1970s when the U.S. Supreme Court ruled in a series of cases that the decision to bear a child is part of an individual's constitutionally protected right to privacy. The Court's landmark ruling in *Griswold* v. *Connecticut* (1971) served as a precedent for later cases. In *Griswold,* the Court invoked the right to privacy in invalidating laws that prohibit the use of contraceptives by married couples. One year later, the Court applied this principle in a case involving the distribution of contraceptives to unmarried adults (*Eisenstadt* v. *Baird*). Finally, in 1977, the Court ruled in *Carey* v. *Population Services International* that minors, too, are protected by the same constitutional right to privacy. Therefore, the state cannot interfere in their decision not to bear children by denying them access to contraceptives.

Many young people now find it hard to believe that the distribution and use of contraceptives in the United States was illegal only about thirty years ago—and relatively few would like to see these decisions reversed. However, other Supreme Court rulings have generated more controversy, especially those dealing with abortion. The most important abortion case—*Roe* v. *Wade*—was decided in 1973 with the Court ruling seven to two that women have a constitutionally protected right to choose abortion, and that the state cannot unduly interfere with or prohibit that right. In this much misunderstood and hotly debated case, the Court actually made three rulings, one for each trimester of pregnancy. More specifically, the Court ruled that during the first trimester, the decision to abort is a strictly private one to be made by a woman in consultation with a physician; the state has no authority or compelling reason to interfere at this point. During the second trimester, however, abortion involves more health risks to women, so the state may impose some restrictions, but only if they are intended to safeguard women's health. It is in the third trimester that the state's role is greatest; then, the Court ruled, the state may prohibit abortions (except when necessary to preserve a woman's life or health) because of the *viability* of the fetus—that is, the ability of the fetus to survive outside a woman's womb. Importantly, though, in a companion case—*Doe* v. *Bolton*—the Court ruled that any restrictions imposed by the state must be reasonable and cannot inhibit a physician's duty to provide medical care according to his or her professional judgment. Thus, in *Doe* v. *Bolton,* the Court invalidated a number of state restrictions, including two-doctor concurrence in the abortion decision and committee approval of the decision (Babcock, et al. 1975).

Undoubtedly, legalization of contraception and abortion has provided women with greater control over their sexual and reproductive lives. However, legalization has not meant that contraception and abortion are equally available to all women. Who has greater reproductive freedom and why?

To begin to answer these questions, we must first understand that although the courts have declared the decision to bear children a personal and private one, it is nevertheless a decision made in the context of structural (i.e., social, political, and economic) constraints. One of the most frequently cited examples of this is the national one-child family policy of China, instituted in 1980. The policy was adopted because population growth was inhibiting the country's economic development and threatening to keep its people in poverty. But one need not look as far away as China to find structural constraints on reproductive freedom; they are extensive in the United States as well.

One of these constraints is imposed by religion. The Catholic Church, for example, forbids its members to use any form of artificial contraception. In addition, Catholic authorities and others vehemently oppose abortion, believing that life begins at conception and abortion is, therefore, murder. Since surveys show that a majority of Catholics do not support the Church's teachings on contraception, and that many (more than 50 percent in some surveys), including some members of religious communities, take a pro-choice position on abortion, Catholics face considerable strain and difficulty in reconciling their loyalty to their church with their desire to exercise reproductive freedom (Ferraro and Hussey 1990; Greeley 1990; Gallup and Castelli 1989).

Contraception and abortion are also political issues. Political conservatives have argued, for instance, that allowing young people access to contraceptives encourages immorality and premarital sex. They favor, instead, teaching youth to abstain from sex, and they have taken an active stand against the distribution of contraceptives to minors. At the same time, public opinion polls show that our attitudes toward abortion are fairly complex. One 1989 general survey, for instance, showed that 58 percent of U.S. citizens questioned were supportive of a woman's right to choose abortions as provided by the *Roe* v. *Wade* decision. However, 52 percent also favored a viability test for the fetus at five months into the pregnancy before abortion is permitted at that time, and 67 percent favored parental consent requirements for minors seeking abortions (Gallup 1989).

Despite these diverse (and frequently ambivalent) public opinions, anti-abortion groups, such as the National Right to Life Committee, have been somewhat successful in winning support for their conservative position through intense lobbying of state and federal politicians. One of their recent victories was the imposition in 1988 of new regulations that prohibit recipients of federal family planning funds from providing their clients with abortion referrals and counseling. Clinics that receive government funding, such as the 171 affiliates of Planned Parenthood, serve primarily young and poor women; thus the reproductive freedom of these groups was considerably curtailed. The regulations were upheld by U.S. Supreme Court in 1991.

The Court has acted in other ways to curtail reproductive freedom in recent years. Although the Supreme Court reaffirmed *Roe* v. *Wade* in 1986, a number of its recent decisions have served in effect to rescind the reproductive rights of some groups of women. In 1977, for example, the Court ruled in two cases—*Beal* v. *Doe* and *Maher* v. *Roe*—that states are not statutorily nor constitutionally required to provide welfare or Medicaid funds to pay for the abortions of poor women. Since these cases were decided, a number of states have enacted laws prohibiting Medicaid funding for abortions. In 1989, the Court stopped just short of overturning *Roe* v. *Wade* in its decision in the case of *Webster* v. *Reproductive Health Services, Inc.* In its five to four ruling in *Webster*, the Court indicated that it is now willing to uphold state restrictions on abortions that formerly had been declared unconstitutional. Immediately following *Webster*, a number of states enacted stringent abortion restrictions, such as a requirement that the father be notified of the abortion decision before the procedure is performed. Many observers, in fact, have interpreted the *Webster* decision as an ominous sign that within a few years, abortion may once again be outlawed in many states. In 1990, the Court's decisions in two cases—*Hodgson* v. *Minnesota* and *Ohio* v. *Akron Center for Reproductive Health*—placed further restrictions on the reproductive rights of young women under the age of eighteen. In *Hodgson*, the Court upheld by a vote of five to four a state requirement that minors must inform both parents before having an abortion. The Court maintained that, since the Minnesota law allows for a judicial hearing as an alternative to parental permission, it does not totally prevent minors from obtaining abortions. Similarly, in a six to three ruling, the Court upheld an Ohio law that requires notification of one parent, but also provides the judicial alternative.

Thus, in response to our question of which women have greater reproductive freedom, we must answer first, those who are adults who can afford it. Second, however, we must remember that since African Americans and other racial minorities are disproportionately represented among the poor, it is women of color whose reproductive freedom has been most severely curtailed. A large percentage of poor women live in urban areas, but many also live in rural regions of the country. A recent survey of abortion providers found that women who live in rural communities have more difficulty obtaining abortions than urban women. Between 1985 and 1988, the number of rural hospitals offering abortion services decreased by 19 percent and the number of rural abortion clinics dropped by 7 percent; in fact, 93 percent of all rural counties have no abortion provider (Henshaw and Van Voort 1990). Consequently, many rural women must travel long distances to get an abortion, and this imposes further hardship if they are poor.

What are some of the consequences of this inequality? Certainly, the high rate of teenage pregnancy is one of them. The United States currently has the highest rate of teenage pregnancy among Western industrialized countries—almost one million per year—and it is the only one of these countries where the rate is increasing. Although teens in other countries appear to be as sexually active as youths in the United States, they have easier access to contraceptives and better educational programs and counseling services available to them (Jones

---

BOX 7.2   Children Having Children: The Problems of Unwanted Teen Pregnancy and Parenthood

The United States has the dubious distinction of having one of the highest teen pregnancy and birth rates among the Western industrialized nations. The rates of pregnancy and birth among U.S. teens are twice those in England, Wales, and Canada; three times those in Sweden; and seven times those in the Netherlands. Yet, as we have already noted, U.S. teens are not more sexually active than their European peers.

Even more important perhaps is the fact that although the overall number of teen births in the United States declined during the 1970s, the proportion of births to unmarried teens rose sharply and continued to rise during the 1980s. In 1985, 60 percent of babies born to teens were born to unwed mothers, compared with 50 percent in 1980 and 30 percent in 1970. Between 1970 and 1985, the number of births to teens decreased by 178,000, but the number of births to unmarried teens increased by 80,000. In 1985, there were about 9 million fifteen- to nineteen-year-old girls in the U.S. population, 4.2 million of whom were sexually active. Only 2.1 million, though, used some form of contraception. Not surprisingly, 980,000 became pregnant, 850,000 of whom were not married. About 470,000 of these young women gave birth, 270,000 as unmarried mothers. Remarkably, however, 110,000 had given birth at least twice previously.

As alarming as these statistics are, the general public remains largely misinformed or uninformed about adolescent pregnancy and parenthood. A number of prevalent myths, in fact, cloud our understanding of these problems. For instance, it is commonly believed that most teen pregnancies occur among youth who live in large urban centers. However, the ten states ranking highest for births to unmarried teens are mostly in the South and are less urbanized than the northern states.

It is also widely thought that teen pregnancy is a problem primarily among racial minorities. Although minority adolescents are disproportionately represented among teen parents, they do not account for the majority of teen births. In 1985, there were approximately 323,000 births to white teens, compared with 140,000 to African American teens and 62,000 to Hispanic teens. Of unmarried teen mothers in 1985, only about 16 percent were African Americans or Hispanics under the age of eighteen. Nevertheless, given their relative numbers in the general population, an African American teenager is five times more likely than a white teenager to become an unwed parent.

Finally, one often hears the argument that the availability of welfare, in particular Aid to Families with Dependent Children (AFDC), encourages teen pregnancy and parenthood. However, research has found no relationship between the level of welfare benefits in a state and the number of teen pregnancies and births in that state. In addition, such an argument overlooks the fact that our European allies have lower rates of teen pregnancies and births, yet their welfare benefits typically are far more gener-

---

1989). The impact of adolescent pregnancy and parenthood on both the parents and their child can be financially and emotionally devastating (*see* Box 7.2), but what choice do some women—particularly poor women—have other than to carry their pregnancies to term? One recent study found that the cut-off of Medicaid funds for abortions has led to a rise in the number of poor women trying to

Box 7.2 continued

ous than those in the United States. Although teen pregnancy and parenthood may lead to long-term welfare dependency, the availability of welfare is not a cause of these problems. Instead, it appears that poverty and below-average academic skills are strongly related to adolescent pregnancy and parenthood in that "poor teens with poor basic skills are less likely to have other more positive life options that make early parenthood an unattractive and irrational choice" (Children's Defense Fund 1988:26). Poverty and low academic skills are also strongly related to high unemployment, especially among teens and racial minorities. Recent research shows that employed men are twice as likely to marry the mother of their children as unemployed men are (Schmidt 1989; Connor 1988; Wilson 1987).

Whatever the causes, the consequences of pregnancy and childbirth can be devastating for teens and their offspring. For one thing, pregnant teens are less likely than older pregnant women to receive early and adequate prenatal care. Consequently, while teens are responsible for 13 percent of all births, they have 18 percent of low-birth-weight babies. Low-birth-weight babies are twenty times more likely to die in their first year than normal-birth-weight babies, and they also have a greater chance of suffering from a number of serious handicaps and health problems. In addition, children born to teens have a greater probability of living in poverty. About 66 percent of children under the age of three who live in a household headed by someone younger than twenty-two-years-old are poor. Moreover, in families headed by white women under the age of twenty-two, 80 percent are poor; in young Hispanic female-headed families, 75 percent are poor; and in young African American female-headed families, 91 percent are poor.

The poverty of these young families is directly related to the fact that teens who become parents are more likely than other teens to come from poverty-level households themselves. In addition, adolescent pregnancy and parenthood are major causes for dropping out of school for both females and males. This returns us to the relationship between poverty, low academic skills, and unemployment and single teen parents; school drop-outs lack marketable job skills and therefore experience either high levels of unemployment or employment in low-paying jobs.

Given these data, we must concur with the Children's Defense Fund (1987:15) that, "Teen pregnancy is a symptom of the lukewarm national commitment to the young that can only continue at our peril. The survival and quality of our children and youths and our families are the single most important determinant of the quality of our national future. No moral or sensible nation can dare write off a quarter of its human assets."

Sources: Statistics compiled from Children's Defense Fund 1988; 1987.

perform dangerous, self-induced abortions with coat hangers or by drinking large amounts of quinine (Paolantonio 1987).

Before concluding our discussion of reproductive freedom, we must consider one other group in our society: infertile couples. It is estimated that 15 percent of couples in the United States are unable to conceive or maintain a pregnancy

(Diamond 1988). For them, there are a number of options available—some conventional, such as adoption, but others quite revolutionary, including *in vitro* fertilization, artificial insemination, and surrogacy. Box 7.3 briefly explains these alternatives. Here we wish to emphasize that these reproductive decisions are also not without constraints. Religion is again a factor; for example, the Catholic Church has condemned all forms of *in vitro* fertilization, artificial insemination, and surrogate mothering (*see* Chapter 11). Apart from religious concerns, there are many serious ethical and legal questions still to be resolved (Raymond 1990; Rothman 1989; Diamond 1988). Consider, for instance, a situation in which an infertile couple attempts *in vitro* fertilization and several embryos are produced in the laboratory and frozen for later implantation in the mother's uterus. Meanwhile, however, the couple separates and eventually divorces. Who should be awarded custody of the embryos? What about sperm and egg donors; do they have any parental rights? In the case of surrogacy, do women have a legal right to rent their bodies to infertile couples? Under what circumstances do surrogate mothers have parental rights? Do fetuses have rights independent of their parents?

Several state legislatures and courts have begun to address questions such as these. In 1990, for example, the Tennessee Court of Appeals awarded joint custody of seven frozen embryos and equal say in their disposition to a divorced couple, thereby overturning an earlier ruling that had awarded custody solely to the mother. Most states, however, have been grappling with problems arising from surrogacy. In the controversial *Baby M* case, William and Elizabeth Stern entered into a contract with Mary Beth Whitehead in which Ms. Whitehead agreed to bear a child fathered by Mr. Stern through artificial insemination in exchange for $10,000. But when the baby was born, Ms. Whitehead changed her mind about relinquishing custody of the child to the Sterns and a court battle ensued. In February 1988, the New Jersey Supreme Court, in a unanimous decision, voided the Sterns–Whitehead surrogacy contract. The court did not outlaw surrogacy completely, but argued instead that surrogacy arrangements could be legal only if there was no fee paid to the gestational mother and if she retained the prerogative to change her mind about giving up the baby after birth. The Sterns were awarded custody of the baby, but Ms. Whitehead was given visitation rights.

Following the *Baby M* case, measures were introduced in every state legislature to regulate or outlaw surrogacy, but few have been enacted. Surrogacy is banned in Michigan and Florida, and in five other states, surrogacy contracts are considered legally unenforceable. In November 1990, a California court denied parental rights to a surrogate mother who had no genetic relationship to the baby she had agreed to bear. In this case, the egg had been taken from Crispina Calvert and the sperm from her husband Mark Calvert; after *in vitro* fertilization, the embryo was surgically implanted in Anna Johnson who had agreed to carry the child to term and then relinquish custody to the Calverts. Like Mary Beth Whitehead, though, Ms. Johnson changed her mind when the baby was born, but in this case the judge ruled that Ms. Johnson was similar to a foster parent: "her womb was little more than a home in which she had sheltered and fed the legal offspring of the genetic parents" (Mydans 1990a:6E).

Reproductive Strategies   **BOX 7.3**

For infertile couples, homosexual couples, and singles who wish to have children, there is currently a wide range of reproduction options available. Among them are:

Adoption   a traditional choice, but one that has become more difficult given that there are an estimated 3 million couples seeking to adopt healthy, white infants, of which there are only about 50,000 available. Alternatives include interracial adoptions, international adoptions, adoptions of physically or psychologically impaired children, adoptions of toddlers or older children, and adoptions of sibling groups. Increasing in popularity are private adoptions in which the adoption is arranged through an attorney rather than an agency; sometimes the couple seeking to adopt advertises for a prospective birth mother. Private adoptions may be closed or open. In a closed adoption, the adoptive parents and the birth parents do not meet. In an open adoption, the adoptive and biological parents meet and arrive at a mutual agreement concerning the adoption; the adoptive parents may invite the birth mother to live with them during the pregnancy and they may even be present at or assist in the birth. In any event, in private adoptions, the adoptive parents are expected to pay all legal and medical expenses, as well as any advertising, telephone, and travel expenses. They may also be expected to pay for the birth mother's living expenses during the pregnancy.

Artificial Insemination   a solution for male infertility and an option for single heterosexual women and lesbians. Sperm from a donor (usually anonymous) is injected into a woman to fertilize the egg. At sperm banks, the sperm are screened for infections and genetic diseases, and recipients sometimes can select sperm from donors with physical or social characteristics (e.g., high intelligence) that they value.

In Vitro Fertilization   also known as "test-tube" fertilization. Eggs are removed from the woman seeking to get pregnant, fertilized in the laboratory, and then returned to the uterus to be carried to term. Variations on this include eggs donated by another woman (usually anonymously) if the woman seeking to get pregnant does not have eggs. The donated eggs are fertilized in the laboratory, then implanted in the uterus of the woman who wants to have the child. In 1990, physicians reported that this latter option now makes it possible for post-menopausal women to become pregnant.

Surrogacy   the most controversial reproductive option, surrogacy usually involves a contract between a couple and a woman in which the latter agrees to be artificially inseminated with the male partner's sperm, carries the pregnancy to term, and then gives the child to the couple at birth. She usually does this for a substantial fee. A second form of surrogate mothering may be used when a woman's uterus does not allow a fertilized egg to implant itself and develop. In this arrangement, an egg from the female partner is fertilized with her male partner's sperm, but then implanted in the uterus of another woman to be carried to term. In some cases, the surrogate, or gestational mother as she is sometimes called, is a relative of the female partner—in one instance, she was the woman's mother. It is estimated that there have been more than 600 successful surrogacy arrangements completed in the United States.

Sources: Compiled from Mydans 1990a; Rothman 1989; Diamond 1988; Quindlen 1987; Mezzacappa 1986.

The Calvert-Johnson case raised concerns among many observers, including many feminists, who see the judge's opinion as classifying women's bodies as "interchangeable fetal containers," with little regard for the emotional attachment that a gestational mother may develop to the fetus she is carrying (Mydans 1990a). Such an image also worries those who see increasing attention being given by the courts and government to the rights of the fetus over the rights of the mother (*see also* Chapter 12). This issue was dramatically highlighted in 1988, when a judge in the District of Columbia ordered a Caesarian section performed on Angela Stoner Carder, who was dying of lung cancer, in an effort to save her twenty-six-week-old fetus, despite the fact that Ms. Carder could not consent to the operation and her husband, her parents, and her personal physicians were opposed to it. Both Ms. Carder and the baby died, but Ms. Carder's family nevertheless appealed the decision. In April 1990, the District of Columbia Appeals Court, in a seven to one decision, ruled that the surgery had violated Ms. Carder's right to bodily integrity and that individuals cannot be forced to undergo significant medical intrusions for the medical benefit of another, even if that other is her fetus. Importantly, the court did not explicitly address the issue of whether the fetus is a part of a woman's body or an individual trapped within a woman's body, which is a central issue in the maternal rights versus fetal rights debate (Rothman 1989).

Clearly, the questions surrounding reproductive alternatives are difficult ones, not only for the courts, but also for the families and couples involved. For many infertile couples, though, these issues are moot—they cannot afford any of the alternatives, even the more conventional ones such as adoption. The costs of adoption, for example, are estimated at between $5,000 and $12,000 (Cole 1987), although private adoptions may be even more costly, especially if there are medical complications. *In vitro* fertilization ranges from $4,000 to $7,000 per pregnancy attempt, with an average success rate of about 11 percent (Leary 1989). Few insurance plans cover *in vitro* fertilization or other reproductive technologies. Surrogate mothering costs at least $10,000, but may exceed $25,000 (Mydans 1990a; Quindlen 1987).

In short, social class plays a major role once again in determining who will and who will not bear children. It is doubtful that many poor, infertile couples will be able to utilize any of these reproductive strategies. Rather, it is more likely that poor women who can have children and are in desperate need of income will be vulnerable to exploitation by wealthier couples who are seeking to have children. Indeed, although some feminists see the new reproductive technologies as potentially liberating for women by giving them greater control over the reproductive process, others are deeply concerned that such technologies turn children into commodities and may also give rise to a "breeder class" of women composed primarily of poor women who rent their bodies to the wealthy (Raymond 1990; Rothman 1989; Diamond 1988). The debate, even among feminists, is unlikely to be resolved soon.

Among people who do have children, we find that structural and ideological constraints further impinge on their parenting. We will discover in what ways in the section that follows.

Caregiving

Despite the widespread belief that the birth of a child brings marriage partners closer together, sociologists, as well as marriage and family counselors, have learned from research conducted over the past two decades that the addition of children to a household increases stress and lowers marital satisfaction (Larson 1988; Cox 1985). If we think about it for a moment, we can see that this observation is really not puzzling. Although new parents are typically excited about the birth of their baby, they are rarely prepared for the level of disruption that a baby causes in their lives. For example, their sleep is frequently interrupted and lessened. There is, by necessity, less spontaneity in the relationship and less time to pursue outside interests. Financial pressures increase, as do household chores and, as the couple become immersed in parental roles, the partner/lover roles get "squeezed" (Cowan, et al. 1985).

Importantly, however, just as we have seen that within every marriage there are really two marriages, his and hers (Bernard 1972), so we will see here that men and women experience parenthood differently. Although men may be present at the birth of their children, they are rarely involved in early infant care. They tend to see themselves as lacking the competence required for infant care and, instead, tend to place more emphasis on their roles as family providers and protectors (Entwisle and Doering 1988). Their involvement usually increases when children are around eighteen months old and walking and talking. Even then, however, the time fathers spend with their children is more oriented to recreation—playing, reading to them, teaching them something—than to primary care giving (Thompson and Walker 1989). It is mothers who provide primary care for children in addition to caring for their husbands and their homes. We have already seen that having children substantially increases the amount of time women spend on housework, while men's housework hours change very little. Significantly, recent studies show that this pattern is consistently found in "egalitarian" households as well as traditional ones. In fact, there is evidence that "egalitarian" marriages tend to become more traditional in terms of role division once children are born (Cox 1985; Eiduson, et al. 1982, but for an exception, see Coltrane 1989).

Before we discuss the consequences of this division of labor, let's first consider some of the reasons for it. Most likely we are all familiar with the age-old notion of "maternal instinct." This is the belief that women are the primary caregivers because their biological childbearing capacity gives them a natural childrearing capacity—that is, women automatically know how to mother. Few scientists nowadays would admit they accept such a notion, but the argument that parenting is an innate ability in women has not disappeared, even among feminists. Among the best known work from this perspective is that of feminist sociologist Alice Rossi (1984; 1977). Rossi cites as evidence to support her theory of innate sex differences in parenting ability, research from endocrinology and neurophysiology that shows, for example, that women are more sensitive to such stimuli as infants' soft skin or their nonverbal communication, and that women are more responsive physiologically to pictures of babies. Unfortunately, such findings, while clearly provocative, do not provide conclusive evidence for an innate biological basis to caregiving behaviors and abilities. Women, after all, may be responding to learned cues that reflect their lifelong socialization to mother—training men do not receive. Furthermore, as we learned in Chapter 3, "whatever biological tendencies there may be that influence parenting, they can be exaggerated or reduced in any particular culture" (Kammeyer 1987:351; Gross, et al. 1979).

Other social scientists emphasize the psychological and social learning components of parenting. For instance, Nancy Chodorow (1978), whose work we briefly discussed in Chapter 4, argues that a social system like ours that vests women with primary responsibility for parenting, ensures that family caregiving will continue to be gender-specific because being mothered has different developmental consequences for boys and girls. As we noted previously, Chodorow maintains that in order for boys to develop an appropriate gender identity, they must break their attachment to their mothers and identify with their fathers who, in most households, are oriented outward or away from the family. In contrast, the development of girls' gender identity requires no such break; they maintain an ongoing attachment to the mother, which orients them inward to the family. Thus, through their intense interpersonal relationship with their own mothers, girls become psychologically programmed to mother themselves.

An analysis such as Chodorow's alerts us to the possibility of deeper, unconscious motivations that may underlie our gender-specific system of parenting. However, it has also been critiqued for its reliance on clinical data and for its neglect of social structural factors (Lorber, et al. 1981). There is evidence, for example, that some men welcome greater involvement in the care of their children, but that the structure of work in our society makes this difficult, if not impossible, for most (Cohen 1987). As we will see again in Chapter 8, and as we have already discussed, the occupational structure of our society operates on the ideology that men are the economic providers of families, women the caretakers. Men are expected to invest time and energy in their jobs, women in their families. If one accepts this "men only" model of employment, then there is no need for child care facilities, paternity and maternity leaves, and equal pay for women and men. This latter factor is particularly relevant, for even in two-earner households, few families could afford to have fathers assume primary caregiving responsibility given that women, on average, earn only about 70 percent of what men earn. Hence, a gender-specific parenting arrangement is left intact.

Shortly we will learn that this gendered parenting/employment model is especially detrimental for single-parent families. But it is not without consequences for two-parent families either; women and men in these families are both advantaged and disadvantaged by it.

On one hand, women reap the benefits of developing close bonds with their children, and of watching and contributing to their children's growth and development. These are experiences most mothers find gratifying and emotionally fulfilling. At the same time, through their ties to their children, and through ties to their own parents and siblings, women are also *kinkeepers* in families; that is, they link the generations within the families and, therefore, are instrumental in preserving family cohesion. Kranichfeld (1987:48) has identified this kinkeeping role as a source of family power in that as kinkeepers "women do not just change the behavior of others, they shape whole generations of families."

However, this almost exclusive responsibility for child rearing and caregiving also denies women much personal autonomy. Housework can at least be postponed, but a child's needs must be met immediately. Child rearing, then, imposes severe limits on a mother's time and ability to pursue other interests, such as paid employment, and this, in turn, we have noted, lowers her power in the marital relationship. The woman who mothers full-time may also come to feel isolated and trapped by her caregiving responsibilities, which helps to explain why full-time mothers, particularly those with preschool children, often report bouts of severe depression (Doyal 1990b). But women who combine mothering with paid employment, either by choice or necessity, may experience role strain or overload, especially given that the structure of work in our society is hardly accommodating to the needs of families.

Also noteworthy is the stress that can stem from the kinkeeper role. For instance, women's mid-life options may be constrained because their adult children need assistance with their own households and families, or because elderly parents need care (Gerson, et al. 1984). Ninety-five percent of the elderly and 90 percent of the disabled elderly live at home and rely on family members to provide virtually all of their care. Recent research shows that women are 75 percent of caregivers to elderly family members. More than half are between the ages of 35 and 64 with a median age of 45. More importantly perhaps, 42 percent are employed full-time and an additional 13 percent are employed part-time; 39 percent still have their own children in their households. This responsibility adds significantly to women's caregiving burden; as one study pointed out, women now spend an average of seventeen years of their lives caring for their children and eighteen years assisting their elderly parents (Montgomery and Datwyler 1990; *New York Times* 26 January 1989; Older Women's League 1989; Sanchez-Ayendez 1986).

Men, on the other hand, escape many of the burdens of family care. They are relieved of the drudgery and the time constraints so that they may join the labor force to financially support their families. Besides the provider role, parenting for most men is typically limited to occasionally playing with and disciplining the children. But if fathers are freer to give their time and energy to their jobs, the trade-off is social and emotional distance from their children. One study, for example, reported that 50 percent of the preschoolers questioned said they would rather watch television than be with their fathers. Among seven- to eleven-year-olds, one in ten told researchers that their father is the person they fear the most (Pogrebin 1982). Although we are speaking here of intact two-parent families, there is a sense in which they are "father-absent." The loss for men can perhaps best be found in the words of fathers who have taken responsibility for the care of their children; according to these men, child care has made them more sensitive, less self-centered, and more complete as human beings (Coltrane 1989; Greif 1985). And what if fathers do not have jobs that adequately meet the financial needs of their families? Stress, health problems, shame, guilt, lowered self-esteem, and increased family conflict are all likely outcomes (Glenn 1987).

In our society, then, and in many others, parenting has traditionally been synonymous with mothering; fathers have been, at best, marginal participants in the parenting process. Of course, many fathers—and mothers—prefer this arrangement (Thompson and Walker 1989; Barnett and Baruch 1988), but others have made serious efforts to become involved parents by, for example, joining fathers-only groups with their children or by drawing the line at work in order to spend more time at home and to more equally participate in child care (Coltrane 1989; Cohen 1987). These fathers, though, are still the exceptions, and many fathers simply accept uncritically, or resist changing, their marginal parental involvement.

It is important to keep in mind here that "men's [and women's] notions of appropriate role behaviors are produced and then reinforced or challenged by a culture that is still less than wholehearted in embracing the idea of family-oriented men" (Cohen 1987:72). We have noted many times how the structure of employment in our society reinforces a traditional gender ideology. The legal system has also played a significant part, which is perhaps most evident in the assumptions historically used by the courts in awarding custody of children in divorce cases.

Prior to the Industrial Revolution, fathers were far more likely than mothers to be given legal custody of their children in the event of divorce, basically for two reasons. First, fathers had the economic means to support their children. Second, "there existed between a father and his children an unwritten but binding contract; children were entitled to a father's economic support and protection during minority in exchange for services at maturity and for products of labor during minority" (Brown 1984:203). However, as the Industrial Revolution progressed, moving much production away from home, and as compulsory schooling was introduced, the ideology of childhood changed. Children were no longer viewed as miniature adults, but rather as helpless dependents in need of nurturing. The so-called childrearing experts began to emphasize the superiority of the mother in child care, so that by the turn of the twentieth century, it was commonly accepted that a child needs to be with its mother. The courts also adopted this principle; this resulted in a dramatic shift in custody decisions against fathers and for mothers. "The bias toward the mother during the middle fifty years of this century was such that the only way the father could obtain custody was to prove her unfit" (Greif 1985:7), which was extremely difficult to do.

Today, mothers continue to receive custody of their children in most divorce cases, typically because fathers do not contest it. Even in joint custody agreements where both parents have equal decision-making authority regarding the rearing of their children, one parent is usually given physical custody with responsibility for the everyday care of the children; nine times out of ten the physical custodian is the mother. However, more fathers are now requesting custody, and researchers estimate that they are awarded it in about one-half to two-thirds of such cases (Hanson 1988; Grief 1985; Brown 1984). Importantly, just as we have seen that parenting is not the same for men and women in two-parent families, so too we find that the experiences of solo fathers and solo mothers are quite different. Moreover, recent changes in divorce and child support laws exacerbate these differences. Let's turn, then, to a discussion of single-parent families.

Single-Parent Families

Although one may become a single parent because of a partner's death or by choosing to rear children while unmarried, one of the most frequent causes of single parenthood is divorce. The divorce rate, along with the rise in births to unmarried women, accounts for most of the increase in single-parent households in recent years (Kamerman and Kahn 1988). In 1970, single-parent families constituted only about 11 percent of U.S. households with children; in 1988, they represented 23 percent. Among white children, almost 19 percent lived with only one parent, but for minority children, single-parent households were even more common: 30 percent of Hispanic children and 54 percent of African American children lived with just one parent (U.S. Department of Commerce 1990).

Just about 3 percent of children in the United States live with their fathers only: 3 percent of white children, 3 percent of African American children, and 3 percent of Hispanic children. In 1988, there were 1,047,000 male-headed single-parent households in the United States, about 14 percent of all single-parent families (U.S. Department of Commerce 1990). The solo fathers in these families are typically middle- or upper-class and well-educated, so financial difficulties in rearing children alone is not one of their common complaints. In addition, they often receive considerable support from friends, relatives, and neighbors who tend to view them as somewhat extraordinary for parenting alone, but as needy when it comes to handling housework and children. In fact, single fathers' most frequent complaints are that others treat them as incompetent parents (for example, teachers may ask to meet with an ex-wife instead of the father) and that they feel constrained in their social lives and careers due to the demands of parenting (Hanson 1988; Greif 1985). As one researcher explained with regard to the latter:

> When the father is no longer able to pursue job progression at work with his old vigor because he is raising the children, he has to change his view of himself. For many men, abandoning long-held career goals is hard. His boss may also be unhappy with his parenting status. She may have hired him with the expectation that he could work late, travel or change his shift at her request. When the father begins to balk at such requests because of parenting responsibilities, the boss may begin to look elsewhere to get the job done, bypassing the father (Grief 1985:157).

Single mothers also confront many problems in parenting alone. For one thing, they may receive little or no help and support; many report feelings of isolation (Kamerman and Kahn 1988). Second, given the number of women in the labor force who have children, it is clear that most single mothers, like their male counterparts, also must struggle to fulfill employment responsibilities without sacrificing the well-being of their children. Some of these women encounter career dilemmas similar to those of single fathers, but because women are less likely than men to hold high-status, high-income occupations (*see* Chapter 8), their employment constraints are more often inflexible work schedules and inadequate salaries. Simply finding a job is frequently difficult for a single mother, particularly if she has been out of the labor market as a full-time homemaker for many years, has little work experience, and has developed few salable skills. Not surprisingly, then, the biggest problem of single mothers is money (Quinn and Allen 1989).

We get some sense of the dimensions of this problem by looking at Table 7.4. Here we see that the median income of female-headed families is substantially lower than that of two-parent families. What is more, we find that after controlling for inflation, the incomes of all families have *declined* since 1979, but that the loss tends to be larger for female-headed families, especially black female-headed families.

The low median incomes of female-headed families alerts us to the extent of poverty among them. Mother-only families represent almost 60 percent of poor families with children under 18 (Kamerman and Kahn 1988). Of the almost 6.3 million female-headed households with children under 18 in 1987, more than half (54.7 percent) were living below the poverty line. When race is taken into account, the figures are even more alarming: 45.2 percent of white female-headed families, 66.9 percent of black female-headed families, and 72.4 percent of Hispanic female-headed families live in poverty (U.S. Department of Commerce 1990; 1989; U.S. House of Representatives 1987). But, as Ruth Sidel (1986:xvi)

TABLE 7.4
Median Income* of Families with Children under 18 by Race 1979, 1988

	Husband-Wife Families		Solo-Mother Families	
	1979	*1988*	*1979*	*1988*
All races	$36,180	$38,164	$12,571	$11,865
White	36,922	32,153	14,724	11,296
Black	28,234	24,867	10,671	7,267
Hispanic	26,918	21,415	9,645	7,368

*In constant 1988 dollars
Source: U.S. Department of Commerce 1990.

reminds us, "Statistics are 'people with the tears washed off.' " The suffering that the poor experience can perhaps best be understood in terms of its impact on the lives of children. For example, children in low-income families have higher morbidity and mortality rates than other children and are more likely to be hospitalized. They are hospitalized for ailments that do not normally require hospitalization, and they stay in the hospital longer than nonpoor children. According to researchers, this may be due to the fact that poor children have less access to routine primary care than nonpoor children. It may also indicate that poor children are taken to hospitals for treatment later in the courses of their illnesses than nonpoor children and therefore are sicker when they do arrive at a hospital (Perrin, et al. 1989). Racial minorities are disproportionately represented among the poor; thus, black infants die at a rate more than double that of white infants, a situation that has existed for almost four decades. In fact, the black infant mortality rate is about equal to what the white rate was in 1965. Black children aged one to four die at a rate almost 72 percent higher than their white peers (U.S. Department of Commerce 1990; 1987a; Children's Defense Fund 1988; U.S. Department of Health and Human Services 1988).

Some observers blame **no-fault divorce** laws for the poverty of many female-headed households. Under no-fault statutes, either husband or wife may file for divorce on the grounds of "irreconcilable differences," and neither is blamed for the failure of the marriage. However, although elimination of the question of fault has made divorce somewhat easier and maybe a bit less painful, it has also changed the economic outcome. No longer is the wronged or offended spouse compensated, for example. Instead, financial awards such as alimony and child support are determined primarily by the spouses' ability to work and, if neither is disabled, the courts typically assume that each is equally capable. As we have already learned, though, husbands and wives are rarely equal. Sociologist Lenore Weitzman (1985:xi) explains further:

> Since a woman's ability to support herself is likely to be impaired during marriage, especially if she is a full-time homemaker and mother, she may not be "equal to" her former husband at the point of divorce. Rules that treat her as if she is equal simply serve to deprive her of the financial support she needs. In addition, rules that require an equal division of property often force the sale of the family home, and compound the financial dislocation and impoverishment of women and children. When the legal system treats men and women "equally" at divorce, it ignores the very real economic inequalities that marriage creates. It also ignores the economic inequalities between men and women in the larger society.

Adding to this is the fact that in dividing marital property, the courts usually take into account only tangible assets, which besides a house may include items like furniture and cars. Given that most divorcing couples, like most married couples, have mortgages and other debts, by the time the bills are paid, there may be little left to divide. However, as Weitzman points out, there are other types of assets— for example, pensions and retirement benefits, licenses to practice a profession, medical insurance, or the value of a business—that the courts only infrequently figure into property settlements. "They thereby allow the major wage-earner, typically the husband, to keep the family's most valuable assets" (Weitzman 1985:xiii). Based on her research on the impact of no-fault statutes, Weitzman (1985:323) concludes that within the first year after a divorce, women and their dependent children suffer a 73 percent drop in their standard of living, while men enjoy a 42 percent rise.

Some researchers have challenged Weitzman's contention that no-fault statutes per se are responsible for the substantial decline in the standard of living of divorced women and their children. Instead, they maintain that inadequate child support laws and other gaps in public policy are more likely to blame for these circumstances (Jacob 1989; Kamerman and Kahn 1988). Child support payments historically have done little, if anything, to offset the financial decline that women and children experience after divorce. For one thing, only 50 to 60 percent of all single mothers are awarded child support by the courts. Second, the average award in 1985 was $2,215 a year, about one tenth the average earnings for men over 18 in 1985. When controlling for inflation, the average child support payment declined by 25 percent between 1978 and 1985. But even among those who are awarded child support, fewer than half (48.2 percent) receive the full amount due; 26 percent receive none at all. Fathers, in fact, pay child support only for an average of about six months. White women and women with college degrees are more likely than minority women and less educated women to be awarded child support and to actually receive payments (Hinds 1989; Kamerman and Kahn 1988; U.S. Department of Commerce 1987b).

It was expected that the Child Support Enforcement Amendment passed by Congress in 1984 would help remedy widespread defaulting on child support. These regulations allowed states to withhold wages and tax refunds from anyone delinquent on support payments. However, unforeseen difficulties in administering the law made it largely unsuccessful. In 1988, as part of a welfare reform package, Congress passed a new law that allows states to automatically deduct child support payments from the paychecks of parents who are behind in their support payments; by 1994, all child support payments will automatically be withheld from parents' paychecks. In addition, the new law requires the states to set and utilize consistent formulas for determining the amount of an award so that they are not only fair, but also do not vary from judge to judge.

Still, some observers are skeptical, emphasizing that no-fault divorce and a long history of nonenforcement of support laws have been major contributing factors in the **feminization of poverty.** The feminization of poverty refers to the recent economic trend of a steady increase in the percentage of the total poverty population composed of women and their children (*see* Chapter 8). Swelling the ranks of the poverty population are the *new poor:* a group of people, largely women, who were not born into poverty but who have been forced into it by recent events in their lives. In fact, according to researchers, a change in family composition, such as separation, divorce, marriage, remarriage, or becoming a parent, is the single most important factor affecting the economic well-being of families; the second most important factor is the labor market decisions of a family, that is, who will work outside the home (Kamerman and Kahn 1988). Consequently, Bane (1986) refers to the poverty of many recently divorced women and their children (especially white women and children) as "event-driven poverty."

The feminization of poverty and the notion of the new poor are important ingredients in our understanding of the consequences of gender inequality in our society, and in particular, the forms it takes in marriage and divorce. Nevertheless, these concepts have been criticized for being both color-blind and class-blind. More specifically, critics charge that the feminization of poverty perspective assumes that women are a homogeneous group. Clearly, they are not, and one significant factor that divides them is social class:

> It is true that, in the case of divorce, [middle- and upper-class women] may experience a fairly dramatic drop in income and standard of living. However, many of these women have the independent property, financial resources, education and skills to live comfortably with or without men. Furthermore, the majority of these women remarry. And when they do, it is generally to men of their class. . . . There are, to be sure, millions of women whose lives are shaped by sex-segregated, low-paying, low-status jobs; unemployment; and cutbacks in social services. But these are not women in general—they are women of the working class (Allegiance Against Women's Oppression [AAOW] 1986:241).

Even within the working class, though, there are divisions; the most important is race. Women of color not only suffer the indignities of sexism, but of racism as well. These women are disproportionately more likely than white women to be poor; regardless of the type of family in which they live. Their poverty status is often independent of their marital and family status and, in this sense, they have more in common with minority men than with white women (AAOW 1986; *see also* Chapter 8). Thus, as Bane (1986) points out, the poverty of many minority female-headed families is "reshuffled poverty." In other words, poor families dissolve and the women and children form new, but still poor families. The considerable economic differences among female-headed households of different races become apparent when we consider the total net worth of these households instead of simply income. In 1988, the median net worth of white female-headed households was $22,100 compared with $760 for African American female-headed households and $740 for Hispanic female-headed households. These figures largely reflect the fact that white female householders are more likely to live in a house in which they have established some equity (U.S. Department of Commerce 1991). As Bane (1986:277) points out, "Reshuffled poverty as opposed to event-caused poverty for blacks challenges the assumption that changes in family structure have created ghetto poverty. This underscores the importance of considering the ways in which race produces different paths to poverty."

This is not an insignificant point, for sociologists and others have long equated female-headed families in general, and minority female-headed families in particular, with pathology. It has been argued that the female-headed family form itself causes poverty as well as a variety of other social problems, including juvenile delinquency, drug abuse, and alcoholism. According to this perspective, the "deviant" subcultural values of minorities are said to cause the high percentage of female-headed families in these groups. But recent research has failed to uncover anything inherently "pathological" or "abnormal" in the female-headed family structure. In fact, researchers have argued that the black female-headed family has historically been a source of strength and resistance to oppression (Height 1989; Jewell 1988; McAdoo 1986; Ladner 1971). Sociologists who emphasize a particular family form or subculture as the source of social problems are blaming the victim and reinforcing institutionalized discrimination. Indeed, available evidence indicates that the key to understanding the rise of female-headed minority households, as well as the plethora of social problems that disproportionately affect minority families of all types, lies with institutionalized discrimination itself (Baca Zinn 1989; Collins 1989; Gresham 1989; Wilson 1987; The Center for the Study of Social Policy 1986). Thus, an analysis of single-parent households must take into account not only the impact of gender inequality, but also social class and racial inequalities. The kinds and levels of stress experienced by single-parent families, and the families' methods and chances of success in dealing with them, are intimately tied to these variables (Brewer 1988; McAdoo 1986).

From this discussion it is clear that there is an imbalance of power *between* families. Much of the chapter so far, however, has focused on the imbalance of power *within* families. We return to this emphasis in the next section which examines one of the most extreme consequences of power differences among family members: domestic violence. "The least powerful members of families—children and women—are the most likely to be victims of violence" (Thorne 1982:13).

THE DARK SIDE OF FAMILY LIFE: DOMESTIC VIOLENCE

It has only been in the last twenty-five years that social scientists have given serious attention to the problem of domestic violence among family members. The early clinical work in the 1960s done by C. Henry Kempe and his colleagues with children who had been battered by a parent or foster parent helped raise public and professional awareness about child abuse (Gelles and Maynard 1987). The women's movement has been instrumental in focusing attention on spouse abuse as well as incest and sexual abuse of children. Today, research on domestic violence has mushroomed, but even though more is now known about its causes and effects, the problem remains widespread. Although some of us may comfort ourselves with the belief that domestic violence is rare and only occurs in families in which a parent or spouse is "sick" or mentally ill, we will learn here that this problem is more common than we would like to think and is usually perpetrated by people who are thought to be quite normal. We will begin with a discussion of child abuse, and then examine spouse abuse and briefly elder abuse.

Child Abuse

We have already pointed out that historically children have been regarded as the property of their parents, in particular their fathers. The view of children as property, coupled with the notion that children will behave like wild animals if they are not subdued and tamed, has through much of Western history served as a justification for beating them. Consider, for example, the thirteenth century statute that maintained that "If one beats a child until it bleeds, then it will remember, but if one beats it to death, the law applies" (de Mause 1974:42). In Puritan America, parents were instructed to "beat the devil" out of their children (Gelles and Cornell 1985). Kammeyer (1987) reports that the beating of children with rods, straps, paddles, and other instruments by caretakers and parents was routine in the United States and Europe into the first half of the nineteenth century. Importantly, this was a childrearing practice common among families of all social classes, as a 1755 journal entry by Ester Burr, wife of the president of Princeton College, indicates. According to Kammeyer (1987:343), Burr wrote that she had "whipped" her ten-month-old daughter for doing something wrong and " 'tis time she should be taught." Although changes in ideology about childhood and childrearing during the nineteenth and twentieth centuries helped to discourage severe and routine beatings, corporal punishment continued to be viewed, as it is today, as an acceptable method of disciplining children. Most people still believe that children need to be hit (Dibble and Straus 1990; Gelles and Cornell 1985).

There is, of course, a major difference between a light pat on the behind and physical abuse. In addition, children may be harmed as much by neglect as by physical punishment. How prevalent, then, are incidents in which children are killed, injured, or put at serious risk of injury? Based on available data, it is estimated that about 6.9 million children are abused by parents each year in the United States and 1.5 million are seriously assaulted by their parents (Straus and Gelles 1990). These estimates were based on a national survey of the general U.S. population; other estimates are considerably lower, ranging from 500,000 to 1.5 million cases of child abuse and neglect annually. However, most analysts agree that the latter figures are conservative estimates since they are usually derived from cases known to police, social service agencies, and health-care professionals. As many as one third of all abuse and neglect cases may go unreported or undetected, particularly if they involve middle-class or wealthy families. Even the conservative estimates, though, are alarming, but they help to explain why homicide is the fifth highest cause of death among children.

Most studies show that male and female children are equally susceptible to neglect and abuse with just one exception: girls are significantly more likely than boys to be sexually abused. Although the sexual exploitation of children may be perpetrated by strangers, most victims know their abusers; abusers are frequently a relative, stepparent, family friend, or close neighbor. Again, estimates of child sexual abuse vary, but it has been argued that conservatively, about 19 percent of girls and 9 percent of boys have been sexually abused by the time they turn 18, about 40 percent of them by a relative (Hodson and Skeen 1987; Finkelhor 1984). In one study, sociologist Diana Russell (1986) found that 16 percent of a random sample of 930 adult women had been sexually victimized as children by a relative, including 4.5 percent who had been abused by their fathers or stepfathers. Russell's work is especially important because it helps refute the myth that incest occurs only in lower-class households; in her study, more than half the victims were from middle-class families.

What are the factors associated with child abuse and neglect? Although it is beyond the scope of this text to examine all of these, we will focus on the ones that are related to the issues we have been discussing in this chapter. For instance, there is considerable evidence that unwanted or unplanned children are at high risk for abuse and neglect (Zuravin 1987). Recognizing this, participants in the 1985 Surgeon General's Workshop on Violence and Public Health concluded that "the starting point for effective child abuse prevention is pregnancy planning" (Cron 1986:10). Most studies also show that mothers are as likely or more likely than fathers to abuse their children, even though as we will see in Chapter 9, women's rates of violence in general are significantly lower than those of men. This finding may simply be an artifact of the amount of time mothers spend with their children. But it may also be due to the greater social isolation of women in the home, since research indicates that parents who are socially isolated are more likely to abuse their children (Straus and Smith 1990; Gelles and Cornell 1985). In addition, although mothers more often than biological fathers abuse their children, stepfathers and boyfriends of single mothers are also frequent abusers, especially sexual abusers (Gordon and Creighton 1988; Hodson and Skeen 1987).

Finally, we must not forget that child abuse occurs in a specific historical and social context. Contemporary approval of parental control over children is rooted in our history. Moreover, we live in a society in which the credo "might makes right" guides much social interaction as well as public policy, and in which females are routinely objectified sexually (*see* Chapter 9). People learn that violence is a way to solve problems and that the powerless are appropriate victims.

Spouse Abuse

The issue of spouse abuse has been much more hotly debated than child abuse. On one hand, the controversy has been fueled by the notion of *mutual battering*; that is, the argument that spouse abuse, far from being a one-sided attack, involves an exchange of physical and psychological abuse between husbands and wives. In fact, one sociologist has claimed that "husband abuse" is the most underreported form of family violence (Steinmetz 1978). On the other hand, the public and many professionals have been far less sympathetic to spouse abuse victims than child abuse victims. This is largely due to the fact that in child abuse cases, the helplessness and dependence of victims is more obvious. With respect to spouses, people typically ask, "If it's really as bad as they say, why don't they leave?" (Pagelow 1981:278). We will address each of these issues in turn.

Research indicates that as many as one out of eight wives report having been violent towards their husbands (Straus and Gelles 1990). The difficulty, however, is that it is impossible to determine how many of these women are acting in self-defense or retaliating against abusive husbands. Studies show that husbands initiate the violence in the majority of cases, and if they kill their partners, it is less often in self-defense than wives who kill their partners (Saunders 1989). In addition, given the differences in size, strength, and resources between husbands and wives, some have questioned the appropriateness of labeling wives' abusive behavior toward their husbands as "battery" (Saunders 1989; Gelles and Cornell 1985). Certainly, in terms of the damage inflicted, it is wives who are most victimized. Battery is the single major cause of injury to women in the United States. What is more, 2,000 to 4,000 women are killed each year by their husbands and lovers. Women are undoubtedly the most frequent victims of domestic violence: 2 to 6 million women annually are abused by their partners; a woman is beaten in the United States every 18 seconds. So widespread is the problem of battery that a woman has a higher probability of being assaulted by her partner in her own home than a police officer has of being attacked on the job (U.S. House of Representatives 1988; Browne 1987; Saline 1984).

One other aspect of spouse abuse that is evident from research is that it is rarely an isolated incident. Instead, spouse abuse tends to follow a pattern or a cycle in a relationship. After the first incident, the batterer is likely to be remorseful and loving, but researchers warn that once the inhibition against violence is broken, the likelihood of subsequent abuse is high. As it becomes more frequent, it may also become more severe (Gelles and Cornell 1985).

So, then, why do women remain in abusive relationships for any length of time? Raising this question has traditionally brought the response that they must enjoy the violence if they stay. A corollary to this is that women also cause the violence, and certainly women often accept blame if they are battered. They frequently try to change themselves or the circumstances that they think led to the abuse, and most hold out hope that their husbands will change. However, they usually find that the abuse is unpredictable and that virtually anything may trigger it; as one battered wife reported, "If the coffee was too hot, he'd say I was trying to aggravate him and I'd get punched" (quoted in Saline 1984:146). It is not difficult to understand that living under such conditions lowers self-esteem and generates feelings of helplessness (Dutton 1988; Walker 1979). Intimidation and the threat of violence are often sufficient to keep women paralyzed with fear in an abusive relationship (Edelson, et al. 1985).

A second dimension of this intimidation arises when battered wives assess their chances of financially supporting themselves and their children. In Chapter 8, we will learn how various forms of employment and wage discrimination keep women in low-paying, low-status jobs. We noted earlier in this chapter that women experience a substantial drop in their standard of living when they separate from their husbands. Not infrequently, women's economic dependence on men helps keep them trapped in violent family relationships.

In order for abused women to leave their batterers, they must also have viable alternatives available. This point is underscored by research that shows that women who are quick to escape abusive marriages tend to be gainfully employed or have high chances for employment, possess above-average resources, and have relatives nearby who are willing and able to help them (Pagelow 1981). Many women also turn to battered women's shelters, which provide temporary housing for abused women and their children. Unfortunately, most shelters can accommodate less than half of the women who come to them.

Finally, Loseke and Cahill (1984:304–305) argue that many battered wives remain with their abusers because of a personal commitment to the relationship. They point out that experts and others who appear preoccupied with the question of why battered women stay assume that the "normal" or rational response to abuse is to simply leave the marriage. Yet, in our society a high value is placed on marital stability and women are the ones who are expected to keep the family together, even at great cost to themselves. Many marriages remain intact even though the partners may have lost their admiration or respect for one another. "Because a large portion of an adult's self is typically invested in their relationship with their mate, persons become committed and attached to this mate as a uniquely irreplaceable individual. Despite problems, 'internal constraints' are experienced when contemplating the possibility of terminating the relationship with the seemingly irreplaceable other. . . . [If] this is the case, then women who remain in relationships containing violence are not unusual or deviant; they are typical."

In sum, it should be clear that battered women do not precipitate their abuse, nor do they enjoy it. Many try to escape, some eventually do, and more would probably leave sooner if realistic options were available or if their personal commitment to the relationship was weaker. However, it should also be clear from this discussion that the appropriate question to be asked is not why do battered women stay, but rather what factors make it possible—even permissible—for their husbands to abuse them? We will conclude this section by addressing that question.

Much of the initial research on the causes of spouse abuse focused on the personal characteristics of batterers. One hypothesis was that batterers were uneducated, lower-class men who, because of their poor status, could assert their dominance in relationships only through violence. Subsequent research has shown that although spouse abuse among lower-class couples is more likely to be reported, the problem crosses all socioeconomic and educational lines. According to one observer, "Educated, successful, sophisticated men—lawyers, doctors, politicians, business executives—beat their wives as regularly and viciously as dock workers" (Saline 1984:82).

A second popular argument is that alcohol and drug abuse cause battering. There is a relationship between substance abuse and family violence, but it does not appear to be causal. Rather, drinking and drug abuse tend to justify or excuse battering—for example, "I didn't know what I was doing; I was drunk." Most batterers are not alcoholics or drug addicts (Herman 1988; Edelson, et al. 1985; Gelles and Cornell 1985). But perhaps they are psychologically disturbed? The evidence for this is contradictory; although some studies find that batterers tend to have a variety of psychological difficulties, such as depression and poor self-concepts, others report no significant psychological differences between batterers and nonbatterers (Edelson, et al. 1985). The dangers with this hypothesis, as well as the two others, are that they exonerate batterers from responsibility for their behavior and they isolate spouse abuse from the social context in which it occurs. "[M]en's violence toward their partners has been part of world culture for most of written history and should be understood both as an individual and as a sociocultural phenomenon (Edelson, et al. 1985:238; Dobash and Dobash 1979).

Like the beating of children, wife beating historically has been condoned in Western societies. English Common Law permitted husbands to "correct" their wives through "domestic chastisement in the same manner that a man is allowed to correct his apprentices or children" (quoted in Kay 1988:192). The law even prescribed the method for doing so: with a stick no thicker than the husband's thumb, hence the phrase "rule of thumb" (Browne 1987; Dobash and Dobash 1979). In the United States, until the late 1800s, husbands could legally beat their wives.

Although the laws have changed, prevalent attitudes remain remarkably similar. Violence in our society is viewed by many as a normal part of everyday life; research shows that violence between husbands and wives is often seen as a positive and necessary component of marriage. Consider, for example, that in one national survey, more than a quarter of the respondents (27.6 percent) indicated that slapping a spouse is necessary, normal, or good (Dibble and Straus 1990). This approval extends to premarital relationships, too. Research indicates that one out of ten high school students and two to three out of ten college students experience courtship violence, but 29 to 36 percent of them interpret the abuse as love and as helping to improve their relationships (Flynn 1987).

To this we must add the notion of family privacy. Among the general public, social science agencies, police, and judges, there is a continuing reluctance to violate the privacy of the home and family life. There seems to be an unwritten rule that what goes on between family members, even if it is violent, is no one else's business. This unwillingness to intervene makes it difficult for wives to get help and also sends husbands the message that they will rarely be held accountable for their violence. Medical staff, for example, often do not believe spouse abuse is a legitimate medical problem and frequently are reluctant to label the women they treat as battering victims (Kurtz 1987).

In most states, spouse abuse is considered simple assault and police cannot make an arrest unless they witness the crime or the victim files a criminal complaint and a warrant is issued. But even if an arrest is made, husbands are usually released after a few hours; they go home, and the violence typically resumes during the long delay before the trial. Some states have revised their laws to require mandatory arrests of batterers and to have the police, instead of the victims, prosecute them. There are also provisions for evicting violent husbands from the home to ensure the safety of wives and children. When enforced, there are indications that such laws do help to prevent repeated incidents of abuse (Dutton 1987; Sherman and Berk 1984). However, there is evidence of widespread noncompliance with such laws (Ferraro 1989). According to a report by the Select Committee on Children, Youth and Families of the U.S. House of Representatives (1988:2), "A battered wife who kills her husband to protect the lives of her children or herself is more likely to be convicted of murder than the husband who beats his wife to death." It is also not uncommon for judges, in an effort to preserve the marriage, to try to convince victims to give their batterers another chance or to suggest that couples receive psychological counseling rather than legal assistance (*New York Times* 16 December 1990:31 and 3 May 1987:51). In 1991, a federal bill, The Violence Against Women Act, was introduced in Congress in an effort to improve official responses to domestic violence. The proposed legislation would mandate harsher penalties for batterers, impose federal penalties on batterers who cross state lines in pursuit of a fleeing partner, offer incentives to states that arrest batterers, and triple federal funding for battered women's shelters.

Meanwhile, however, spouse abuse continues to thrive in a context of social approval and one in which violent husbands will suffer few consequences for their actions. In fact, it is safe to say that batterers have been afforded more protection in our society than their victims. We will see this pattern again in Chapter 9 when we examine other forms of violence against women. Now, though, we will conclude this section with a brief discussion of another type of domestic violence: elder abuse.

Elder Abuse

Research on child abuse and spouse abuse has prompted interest in other forms of violence between intimates, including *elder abuse*. Although experts disagree on a precise definition of elder abuse, for our purposes the term refers to physical or psychological maltreatment or neglect of a senior citizen by an adult caretaker. Obviously, such abuse can be inflicted by anyone entrusted with the care of an elderly person—for example, nurses, physicians, bankers, or lawyers—but research indicates that the typical abuser is a family member (Kosberg 1988; Pillemer and Finkelhor 1988).

Much less is known about elder abuse than child or spouse abuse largely because the research is more recent, most of it undertaken during the 1980s. In addition, many of these studies failed to yield generalizable findings because they are based on small, nonrandom samples or official police and social service agency reports (Callahan 1988; Kosberg 1988). The only large-scale random survey published to date produced an estimate of between 700,000 and one million abused elderly in the United States (Pillemer and Finklehor 1988).

Despite the serious theoretical and methodological weaknesses of the available research, it nevertheless provides us with clues as to who is at greatest risk of being abused and who are the likely abusers. Of particular interest to students of gender relations is the observation that women aged seventy-five and older who are infirm and physically or financially dependent on others for meeting their basic daily needs are most susceptible to abuse (Kosberg 1988; Pillemer and Finklehor 1988). Women may have higher rates of victimization simply because they outnumber elderly men (*see* Chapter 12), but it is also likely because of their inability to resist abuse, their greater vulnerability to sexual assault (*see* Chapter 9), and their devalued status in our society. One study, however, reported little difference in the victimization rates of women and men, but found that women suffered more serious physical and psychological harm from the abuse (Pillemer and Finklehor 1988).

Evidence regarding abusers is less conclusive. Initial research findings showed that although frequently the abuser is an adult son, it is more often an adult daughter who has taken on the difficult task of caring for a severely impaired aged parent. As we noted earlier in this chapter, women are significantly more likely than men to assume responsibility for the care of an elderly relative and they add this burden to other daily responsibilities, including paid employment, care of their own children, and housework. Typically they receive little or no outside assistance. Eventually, the stress induced from these circumstances becomes so great that some caregivers grow angry and resentful and lash out against their elderly parent (Steinmetz and Amsden 1983).

More recent research supports these findings, but also shows greater diversity among abusers than was originally thought. For example, a sizeable percentage of abusers are the victims' spouse. The violence may be a continuation of a pattern of abuse in the marriage or, as it has been hypothesized in the case of abusive wives, revenge for previous abuse by the husband. Pillemer and Finklehor (1988), however, point out that more elderly people live with a spouse than with an adult child, and when this is taken into account, the data show children to be more likely abusers than spouses. Some of these adult children were themselves abused when they were growing up and thus learned that violence toward intimates is acceptable behavior, or they may be acting in retaliation against their abusive parents (Kosberg 1988). Others, rather than having an elderly parent dependent on them, are instead still dependent on their parent for income or housing. Consequently, the abuse may stem from "the relative dependency and sense of powerlessness of the abuser. In fact, powerlessness experienced by a child who is still dependent on an elderly parent may be especially acute, as such a situation goes so strongly against society's expectations of normal adult behavior" (Pillemer 1985:155), especially for men.

At least thirty-seven states have enacted laws to deal with elder abuse by making reporting of incidents of abuse or neglect of senior citizens mandatory. Callahan (1988) and others (e.g., Kosberg 1988), though, question the effectiveness of such laws, given that they address the problem only after the fact and the programs they create are usually too underfunded to adequately meet the needs of elderly victims. A more successful strategy might be preventive measures, such as providing adult children with greater institutional assistance and support in caring for their elderly parents. In addition, given the evidence examined here, it is unlikely that elder abuse can be eliminated unless other forms of family violence are also dealt with effectively. Finally, the elderly, like women and children, in our society are ascribed a devalued status and this, in turn, increases their vulnerability to abuse. Research and public policy, therefore, must focus on how gender inequality intersects with ageism to produce and perpetuate domestic violence.

BREAKING DOWN THE CLOSET: GAY AND LESBIAN RELATIONSHIPS

In Chapter 1, we defined sex/gender systems as having three interrelated components: the social construction of gender categories on the basis of biological sex, a gendered division of labor, and the social regulation of sexuality by which some forms of sexual expression are encouraged and others are negatively sanctioned. In our discussion of traditional theoretical accounts of intimate relationships in this chapter, we have noted the emphasis placed by structural functionalists and others on the traditional nuclear family as the ideal of intimacy. Within the traditional nuclear family, there are two mutually exclusive, but complementary roles: the male instrumental role and the female expressive role. Although this type of intimate relationship is not predominant in our society, we have seen that many people regard it as the ideal. Importantly, however, the division of the sexes in this type of relationship "can also be seen as a taboo against sexual arrangements other than those containing at least one man and one woman, thereby enjoining heterosexual marriage" and stigmatizing homosexual unions (Rubin 1975:167).

Consequently, accurate knowledge and genuine appreciation of gay and lesbian relationships are still goals, rather than realities. Most of what has been written is based on a psychoanalytic or psychiatric perspective which historically has assumed that homosexuality is pathological and that homosexuals are "sick, perverted, inverted, fixated, deviant, narcissistic, masochistic, and possibly biologically mutated" (Krieger 1982:93). Based largely on clinical work with patients who sought treatment for a variety of psychological troubles, this position maintains that homosexuals, though not responsible for their "condition," are nevertheless in need of a "cure," such as aversion therapy, hormone injections, and psychotherapy (Berliner 1987). According to one analyst, "Thirty percent of male homosexuals who come to psychotherapy for any reason (not just for help with their sexual preference) can be *converted* to the heterosexual adaptation" (Barnhouse 1977:95, emphasis added). Another commentator makes the claim that "the prospects for *heterosexual readjustment* are often apt to be better than we have widely assumed" (Williams 1987:275, emphasis added; *see also* Kristof 1990).

In a word, such an approach can best be described as **heterosexist**: it views heterosexuality as superior to homosexuality, not because heterosexuality is culturally prescribed and enforced as part of our patriarchal sex/gender system, but because it is supposedly the central component of the "natural plan" of human life. Unfortunately, the work undertaken from this perspective has done little more than fuel myths and reinforce stereotypes about homosexuals and *the* homosexual lifestyle. For example, it is commonly assumed that gays and lesbians are sexually promiscuous. Recent research, however, indicates that although male homosexuals do have more partners on average than male heterosexuals, most do establish enduring relationships. Lesbian couples as a group appear to have more stable relationships than heterosexual couples or male homosexual couples (Blumstein and Schwartz 1983).

A second popular misconception is that since homosexuals are attracted to partners of the same sex, they must really wish they were members of the opposite sex. Individuals who subscribe to this belief typically look for cross-gender clues in the behavior or appearance of others to detect their sexual orientation—for example, signs of femininity in men and masculinity in women. Outward appearances, though, are poor guides, and the majority of homosexuals are quite satisfied with their sex and do not have confused gender identities. As one lesbian psychologist said, "There has never been any question about my gender or my femininity. I am quite feminine. If I try to be unfeminine, it's hard for me to do—even on a softball field" (quoted in Sifford 1984:8E).

Myths surrounding the relationships between homosexual adults and children abound. For instance, many people think that male homosexuals in particular frequently try to seduce young children, but a careful look at the data on child molesters reveals that about 90 percent are heterosexual men (Gelles and Cornell 1985). The erroneous belief that homosexuals try to "recruit" children to their lifestyle has been used to prevent gays and lesbians from becoming foster or adoptive parents and to deny them custody of or visitation rights to their own children (Polman 1985). Researchers, however, have found no evidence that being raised by homosexual parents causes any gender-identity conflict or confusion in children (Bozett 1988; Greer 1986).

These ill-founded concerns reflect a long-standing preoccupation in both the popular and professional literature with the question, "What *causes* homosexuality?" Since the 1960s, work has begun to appear, much of it by gays and lesbians, that recognizes this question as misguided. For some men and women being gay is a conscious choice—for many lesbians, the choice is a political one—and for others, their homosexuality is simply a given, a fact of who they are as individuals (Bozett 1988; Sifford 1984; Bunch 1978). Regardless, this new work has redirected our attention to other, more appropriate questions, such as how is heterosexuality enforced in our society, and what are the consequences of this enforcement (Rich 1980)? In other words, among some researchers the focus is no longer on homosexuality as a social problem, but rather on institutionalized discrimination against homosexuals as a social problem.

This institutionalized discrimination takes many forms. We have already noted that gays and lesbians can be denied the right to parent. They can also be denied equal access to housing, employment, credit, and other civil rights. Few city and state governments have enacted laws banning discrimination on the basis of sexual preference, and the courts typically have refused to extend the constitutional protection of the Fourteenth Amendment to homosexuals. In fact, the U.S. Supreme Court gave its tacit approval to this discrimination when, in 1986, it ruled in the case of *Bowers* v. *Hardwick* that the states may criminalize homosexual acts such as sodomy even if they are engaged in by consenting adults in the privacy of their own homes. Twenty-three states and the District of Columbia have such laws. However, a few cities and the state of California have recently enacted laws that permit homosexual couples and other nontraditional families to register their relationships as domestic partnerships. Although the registration is largely symbolic, some observers see it as an important first step toward winning family benefits, such as family membership rates and, more importantly, housing rights, insurance benefits, and bereavement leave. Currently, only about six U.S. cities provide such benefits for nontraditional families and then only on a limited basis (Lewin 1990a and b; Gutis 1989). (In 1989, Denmark became the first country in the world to legalize homosexual unions; it extended to legally registered homosexual couples all but a few of the rights and responsibilities of legally married heterosexual couples.)

With discrimination against homosexuals officially condoned in most parts of the United States, it is hardly surprising that violence against gays and lesbians has been increasing. National surveys indicate that 15 to 20 percent of homosexuals have been violently attacked simply because of their sexual preference, and most studies show a dramatic increase in these attacks during the last several years (Berrill 1990; Greer 1986). Some observers blame the AIDS epidemic (*see* Chapter 12) for the rising violence, arguing that the disease gives already homophobic people an excuse to attack. **Homophobia** is an unreasonable fear of and hostility toward homosexuals, and although it is clearly present among individuals, our public policies reveal its existence at the institutional level as well. It is likely that institutionalized discrimination reinforces—or perhaps promotes—individual acts of violence.

What are the effects of all this on homosexual relationships? It is difficult to say because there is as much diversity among gay and lesbian couples as there is among straight couples; there is no homosexual lifestyle. It is clear that some homosexuals internalize homophobia themselves, which produces self-hatred and may cause self-destructive behavior, such as substance abuse (Margolis, et al. 1987; Nicoloff and Stiglitz 1987). Obviously, this will also generate hostility toward partners and could even lead to violence in the relationship (Renzetti 1988; Lobel 1986). There is, of course, no way to determine just how prevalent such responses are, but there is no evidence that they are typical. Instead, most gays and lesbians seem to cope with public homophobia and discrimination by living a double life; that is, being open about their sexual preference with those they trust and concealing it from others. Their partners and the gay and lesbian community usually provide the support needed to effectively deal with the stress this produces.

Recent opinion polls show that homosexuals are gaining more acceptance among the general public in the United States, although among most segments of the population the attitude can at best be described as tolerant. Our culture is still a long way from affirming homosexuality (Kagay 1989). However, homosexuals are becoming more visible in the United States and, more importantly, they are taking a stronger, more active stand in demanding protection of their human rights. We will take up this topic in Chapter 13.

INTIMATE RELATIONSHIPS: THE IDEAL AND THE REAL REVISITED

The material presented in this chapter illuminates for us the disparity between traditional images of ideal intimate relationships and their reality in everyday life. We have seen that the social construction of *The Family*—that is, the isolated, nuclear household of husband/breadwinner, wife/homemaker, and dependent children—is not only an inaccurate depiction of the majority of families in the United States, but also promotes the misconception that other family arrangements and relationships, including homosexual ones, are inherently deviant or abnormal.

Compounding this image is the notion of the family as a private retreat from the harsh public world. First, this idea masks the very serious problems that family members, in particular, women and children, confront as the gender inequality of the larger society is replicated and preserved in the home: the power imbalance between husbands and wives, an unequal division of household labor and parenting responsibilities, women's double work load, the economic difficulties of female-headed families, and domestic violence. Many of these problems are made worse by racism, ageism, heterosexism, and social class inequality, creating power differences between families in addition to those within them. Second, this idea of family privacy ignores the many ways in which other social institutions impinge upon intimate relationships. For example, we have seen here that the official policies of governments and churches serve to constrain even the most personal and private decisions, including how and with whom we may have sexual relations and whether or not we will bear children.

Similarly, a recurring theme in this chapter has been the intersection of family and work. Indeed, we have argued that one cannot examine the family in isolation from employment issues. In the next chapter, we turn to the topic of gender and the occupational work world, but our discussion will often require us to reiterate many of the points made here.

KEY TERMS

double work load   a problem faced by women who are in the paid labor force but who also maintain primary responsibility for housework and caregiving

expressive family role   the role of women in the traditional nuclear family; structural
functionalists define women's natural role to include reproduction, housework, and
care of husband and children

feminization of poverty   the position that poverty is increasingly becoming a problem affecting primarily women and their dependent children

heterosexism   the belief that heterosexuality is a superior lifestyle to homosexuality

homophobia   an unreasonable fear of and hostility toward homosexuals

instrumental family role   the male role in the traditional nuclear family; structural
functionalists define men's natural role to include that of breadwinner and protector

isolated nuclear family   a family form in which the husband/father, wife/mother, and
their dependent children establish a household separate from other kin, and private in the sense that production no longer takes place there

no-fault divorce   a form of marital dissolution that allows either spouse to divorce the
other on the ground of irreconcilable differences and without fixing blame for the
marital breakdown

public/private split   the notion that the world of the family is private and therefore
separate from and uninfluenced by the public world of work and other social institutions

SUGGESTED READINGS

Bronstein, P., and C. P. Cowan (Eds.) 1988. *Fatherhood Today: Men's Changing Role in the
Family.* New York: John Wiley.

Gordon, L. 1989. *Heroes of Their Own Lives: The Politics and History of Family Violence.*
New York: Penguin.

Greenberg, D. F. 1988. *The Construction of Homosexuality.* Chicago: University of Chicago
Press.

Hochschild, A. 1989. *The Second Shift.* New York: Viking.

Kamerman, S. B., and A. J. Kahn 1988. *Mothers Alone.* Dover, MA: Auburn House
Publishing Company.

Rothman, B. K. 1989. *Recreating Motherhood.* New York: W. W. Norton and Company.

In addition, two journals recently published special issues on topics of relevance to the
issues raised in this chapter: *Social Problems,* Volume 37 (February 1990), on "Moral
Problems in Reproduction," and *The Nation,* Volume 249 (July 24/31, 1989), on "Scape-
goating the Black Family: Black Women Speak."

Chapter 8

Gender, Employment,
and the Economy

When we speak of a society's **economy,** we are referring to its system of managing and developing its resources, both human and material. The human resources of the economy constitute the labor force. Sociologists have long emphasized the significance of work in humans' lives. At the most basic level, work is necessary to meet one's survival needs. Most work, though, is not done by individuals laboring in isolation, but rather entails the coordination of the activities of a group. Work, in other words, is social as well as economic, and in the United States, as in other industrialized capitalist societies, the social organization of work is hierarchical. People do different jobs that are differentially valued and rewarded. Ideally, the value and rewards attached to a particular job should reflect its intrinsic characteristics: for example, the degree of skill required, the amount of effort expended, the level of responsibility involved, and the conditions under which it is performed. In practice, however, the value and rewards of a job often have more to do with the ascribed traits of workers—their race, for instance, and/or their sex.

Our focus in this chapter is on the different economic and employment experiences of women and men and the differential values and rewards that have been attached to their work. Both men and women have always worked, but the kinds of work opportunities available to them and the rewards they have accrued have typically depended less on their talents as individuals than on culturally prescribed and enforced notions of "women's work" and "men's work." We know from our discussion in Chapter 3 that such prescriptions vary from society to society. They also vary historically within a single society. We will begin our discussion here, then, with a brief historical overview of men's and women's labor force participation in the United States.

U.S. WORKING WOMEN AND MEN IN HISTORICAL PERSPECTIVE

Men's and women's participation in the wage labor force has been shaped by a number of factors, not the least of which have been changes in production and demographic changes. These, too, have influenced prevailing gender ideologies of men's and women's appropriate work roles.

Undeniably, one of the most important changes occurred during the nineteenth century when the American economy shifted from being predominantly agricultural to becoming industrialized, moving production off the farms and into factories. Interestingly, industrialization is frequently discussed only in terms of its effects on male workers, the common assumption being that women did not accompany men into the factories, but instead remained at home as family caretakers. This, though, was true only in certain households. Overall, men entered the paid labor force in significantly greater numbers than women. At the same time, dominant middle-class ideology dictated that the so-called true woman was the woman at home who supposedly did not work. But of women in poor and working class families, women rearing children alone, minority women, and white immigrant women, few could afford to stay at home. The exigencies of survival required that they find paid employment, and the harsh reality of their work world stood sharply juxtaposed to the prosperous middle-class image of genteel womanhood (Stansell 1986).

A substantial number of early factory workers were women. In the New England textile mills, for instance, most of the labor force was female by 1850 (Werthheimer 1979). In urban areas such as New York City women were heavily concentrated in the garment industry as seamstresses (Stansell 1986). Other women did piece work, such as folding books, rolling cigars, or making flowers for wealthier ladies' hats. They labored fourteen to eighteen hours a day under extraordinarily unsafe conditions for a daily wage of 10 to 18 cents. Of course, factory work for men was unpleasant and dangerous too, but from the outset men and women were largely segregated into different jobs with the more skilled—and better paid—work open only to men. Widespread stereotypes about women's innate passivity and physical weakness and their greater tolerance for tedium legitimated offering women work that was usually the most boring and repetitive. In addition, despite the fact that many women's wages were crucial to their families' welfare, the belief that women worked only temporarily until they married was used to justify their lower wage rates (Kessler-Harris 1990; Reskin and Hartmann 1986). Labor organizers and male workers themselves capitalized on the notion that paid work was "unladylike" and argued that no woman would have to work if men were provided a "family wage." Trade unions systematically excluded women or organized them into separate unions. Far fewer women than men were unionized, "but even when women did join unions in large numbers, as in the garment industry, those unions were for the most part directed and controlled by men" (Sidel 1986:62).

Jobs in manufacturing, however, were available primarily to white women. Minority women, though more likely than white women to be in the paid labor force, historically have found their employment opportunities largely limited to agricultural work (e.g., fruit and vegetable harvesters), domestic work (e.g., house maids), and laundry work. For instance, in 1890, 38.7 percent of black female workers held agricultural jobs, 30.8 percent were domestics, 15.6 percent were laundresses, but only 2.8 percent worked in manufacturing. Three decades later, agriculture, domestic service, and laundries still employed 75 percent of black female workers and, although more black women were in manufacturing, they faced widespread segregation and discrimination in the factories: "White women were sometimes able to start work one hour later, and when amenities such as lunchrooms, fresh drinking water, and clean toilets were available, they were available primarily to white women" (Sidel 1986:60).

The experiences of Asian and Hispanic women workers were similar to those of black women with the important exception, of course, that black women had also been enslaved in the United States (Zavella 1987; Glenn 1980). It is true, too, that the dirtiest, most menial, and lowest paying jobs went to minority men as well as minority women, but while minority men received considerably lower wages than white men, they were paid more than minority women (*see,* for example, Zavella 1987). Historically, minority women have been the lowest paid members of the labor force.

Ironically, one can argue that the social disorganization wrought on many groups by nineteenth century industrialization, urbanization, and immigration, actually created new job opportunities for white middle-class women, especially the college educated. Extending their domestic roles to the larger society, they took up "civic housekeeping" and lobbied for a variety of social welfare reforms, including wages and hours laws, child labor prohibitions, improved housing for the poor, and public health measures. Some supported these causes by forming or joining voluntary organizations, but others made a career of it by entering the "female professions" of nursing, teaching, and social work (Evans 1987). Such jobs were not perceived as a threat to genteel womanhood since women were expected to perform good works and to nurture and care for others. To these were added other stereotypes when, as production expanded and the need for service workers grew, women were recruited for secretarial and other clerical positions. It was argued, for instance, that women's natural dexterity and compliant personalities made them ideally suited for office work (Kessler-Harris 1982). The ideology that women's work was temporary or secondary to men's remained intact and helped to keep jobs sex segregated and women's wages depressed.

Table 8.1 shows men's and women's labor force participation rates from 1900 to 1988. The early decennial statistics, however, mask some important changes in the labor force during the first half of this century, especially during the Great Depression. You will notice in Table 8.1 that between 1920 and 1930, men's labor force participation rate declined slightly, whereas women's rose slightly. During the Depression, many married women entered the paid labor force to support their families when their husbands were out of work. Unfortunately, these women were often accused of stealing jobs from men, although "in reality, the pervasive sex segregation of the labor force meant that women and men rarely competed for the same jobs" (Evans 1987:46). In fact, the clerical and service jobs in which these women were concentrated have traditionally been less sensitive to economic downturns than male blue-collar jobs in manufacturing and the building trades (Reskin and Hartmann 1986). Nevertheless, "numerous states, cities, and school boards passed laws prohibiting or limiting the employment of married women. And since cultural norms still ascribed the breadwinner's role to men, those women who lost paid jobs, or were unable to find paid work, found that relief programs for the unemployed consistently discriminated against them" (Evans 1987:47).

With the outbreak of World War II, the U.S. economy reversed itself, and the wartime production boom created jobs for millions of Americans, but especially for women. The enlistment of a large percentage of men into the military resulted in critical labor shortages and forced employers to recruit women to take men's places. Women entered the labor force in unprecedented numbers between

TABLE 8.1
Labor Force Participation Rates by Sex, 1900–1988
(% of population 16 and older)*

Year	Male	Female
1900	53.7	20.0
1920	54.3	22.7
1930	53.2	23.6
1940	55.2	27.9
1945	61.6	35.8
1950	59.9	33.9
1955	60.4	35.7
1960	60.2	37.8
1965	59.7	39.3
1970	61.3	43.4
1975	78.4	46.4
1980	77.8	51.6
1985	76.3	54.5
1988	76.2	56.4

*Prior to 1947, the Census Bureau included in these figures all persons 14 years and older in the labor force.
Source: U.S. Department of Commerce 1990; 1976; Taeuber and Valdisera 1986.

1940 and 1945 but, more importantly, they were given jobs previously held only by men—for example, welding, riveting, ship fitting, tool making, and so on. Minority women, though still severely discriminated against, also had new job opportunities opened to them during the war, not only in blue-collar work, but in clerical fields and in nursing as well. For the duration of the war, the federal government campaigned aggressively to recruit women for the labor force by appealing to their sense of patriotism—but also on a more practical level by urging employers to pay them the same wages men would have received and by sponsoring public day care centers (Gluck 1987; Milkman 1987; Bergmann 1986; Banner 1984).

Once the war ended, women were laid off to make room in the labor force for returning servicemen. Federal war programs, such as public child care facilities, were abruptly discontinued, and new government-issued propaganda told women to return to their "normal" roles as wives and mothers at home. Some women did quit their jobs, and marriage and birth rates soared in the early postwar years. But public opinion polls showed that as many as 80 percent of the women who held jobs during the war wished to keep them, and a substantial number simply moved into the traditionally female-dominated—and lower paying—service sector rather than leave the labor force altogether (Evans 1987; Milkman 1987; Banner 1984).

As we see in Table 8.1, women's labor force participation rate never returned to its prewar level. In fact, since 1950, even though men's labor force participation rate has fluctuated in response to dips in the economy and calls to service during military conflicts, women's labor force participation rate has risen steadily. The greatest increase, however, occurred after 1965. To some extent, this was due to an important demographic change: women's life expectancy increased and their fertility rate (even during the baby boom years) decreased compared with earlier generations. This has meant that middle-class women who have been full-time homemakers can expect to spend fewer years rearing children, thus being freer to pursue other activities, including paid employment. The rising divorce rate coupled with changes in divorce laws discussed in the previous chapter also resulted in more women being forced to support themselves and their children without the financial help of a spouse. In addition, recent economic changes have played a major part. For one thing, the service sector of the economy expanded rapidly after the war and much of the job growth occurred in fields labeled "women's work"—primarily clerical work, but also health care and education. Later economic recessions fueled women's labor force participation as two incomes became a necessity to make ends meet in many families (Smith 1987). Finally, political and social changes were important, particularly those prompted by the feminist movement. The feminist movement itself called into question traditional notions of women's "proper place" and encouraged women to redefine their roles and to seek paid employment. Moreover, feminist activists were instrumental in securing the passage of legislation that facilitated women's greater participation in the labor force.

Today, the typical woman, like the typical man, is in the paid labor force and is working full-time, year-round (Taeuber and Valdisera 1986). It does appear that women's labor force participation rates leveled off at around 57.7 percent by 1990, because of several factors. One is the most recent downturn in the economy, which, unlike previous recessions, hit hardest the service industries in which women are heavily represented, such as retail sales and financial services. In addition, there has been a rise in the birth rate along with an increase in the number of women taking time off from work to remain at home to rear their children, especially given the lack of affordable child care facilities (Uchitelle 1990).

This latter point highlights one of the significant differences that remain between the experiences of women and men who are employed outside the home. For example, one of the most dramatic increases in labor force participation has been among married women with children under the age of six; only 12 percent of such women were employed in 1950 compared with 57.4 percent in 1988 (U.S. Department of Commerce 1990). But, as we pointed out in Chapter 7, employed married women, especially those with children, carry a double work load; unlike employed married men, they not only hold jobs outside the home, but also shoulder primary responsibility for housework and child care. We will see momentarily how such an arrangement constrains women's employment opportunities.

A second important difference between women's and men's employment experiences lies in the kinds of jobs they do. Women and men remain largely segregated in different occupations which are considered women's work and men's work respectively. And, as Reskin and Hartmann (1986:1) point out, despite tremendous changes in the U.S. labor market historically, "the overall degree of sex segregation has been a remarkably stable phenomenon; it has not changed much since at least 1900." Occupational sex segregation has serious consequences for both female and male workers, so we turn now to examine it more closely.

SEX SEGREGATION IN THE WORKPLACE

It should be clear from our discussion so far that **occupational sex segregation** refers to the degree to which men and women are concentrated in occupations in which workers of one sex predominate. A commonly used measure of occupational sex segregation is the **dissimilarity index,** also called the **segregation index.** Its value is reported as a percentage that tells us the proportion of workers of one sex that would have to change to jobs in which members of their sex are underrepresented in order for the occupational distribution between the sexes to be fully balanced (Reskin and Hartmann 1986).

Using the index of dissimilarity in Table 8.2, we see the extent of occupational

TABLE 8.2
Occupational Sex Segregation in Twelve Industrialized Nations

Country	Index of Dissimilarity
Japan	27.6
Austria	37.4
Finland	41.2
Norway	41.8
Germany	42.6
Northern Ireland	43.6
Israel	45.8
United States	46.8
Netherlands	50.2
Denmark	50.4
Great Britain	51.1
Sweden*	60.0

*The index of dissimilarity for Sweden was calculated with data available before that country established national policies and programs designed to reduce occupational sex segregation. It is not yet clear to what extent these reforms have succeeded in reducing Sweden's dissimilarity index, but some recent research indicates that it remains high (Bohen 1984).
Source: Adapted from Roos 1985.

sex segregation in the United States as well as eleven other industrialized countries. First, we find that the United States ranks eighth on the list, with a high dissimilarity index of 46.8. This means that nearly 47 percent of the female labor force in the United States would have to change jobs in order to equalize their representation across occupations. For the most part, however, occupational sex segregation is extensive in all these industrialized countries, with the exception of Japan. The low level of sex segregation in the Japanese labor force, though, may simply be a function of the way occupations are classified there. Japan uses very broad occupational categories (such as, professional, technical, and managerial), while the other countries use more detailed ones (such as, physician or nurse) (Roos 1985). A major weakness of the index of dissimilarity is its sensitivity to types of occupational classifications: the broader the occupational categories, the lower the index tends to be (Sokoloff 1988; Reskin and Hartmann 1986). Thus, in the United States alone, the dissimilarity index was only 40 when ten broad occupational categories were used, but rose to 62.7 on the basis of 426 detailed occupational categories (Jacobs 1983). A second serious problem with the index of dissimilarity is that it masks both industry-wide and establishment sex segregation, a point to which we will return later.

Another way to gauge occupational sex segregation is simply to look at the percentage of workers of each sex that holds a specific job. Table 8.3 provides us with such information by showing the ten occupations employing the largest numbers of men and women. One of the most striking features of this table is the lack of overlap in the jobs held by men and women. Men, we find, are concentrated in the skilled crafts, operative jobs, and labor (e.g., construction). Women, in contrast, are primarily in clerical, sales, and other service occupations. Indeed, five of the top ten occupations employing women are clerical and sales positions: secretary, sales worker, bookkeeper, office clerk, and cashier. One in every nine full-time women workers is a secretary and, as was the case just after World War II, the service sector continues to be an area of high job growth for women as well as racial minorities (Rothschild 1988; Taeuber and Valdisera 1986; Smith 1984).

A second significant point to be made with regard to Table 8.3 is the extent to which the jobs listed employ one sex relative to the other. Of the ten largest occupations for women, eight were more than 75 percent female, compared with a total civilian labor force in 1988 that was 45 percent female. Of the ten largest occupations for men, seven were more than 85 percent male and 6 were more than 90 percent male. Moreover, if we exclude private household workers (96.3 percent female) from the category of janitors and cleaners, it becomes almost 70 percent male. Men also tend to be concentrated in supervisory positions, even in areas that otherwise are predominantly female, such as sales and clerical work. In the former category, 66.5 percent of supervisors and proprietors are male; similarly, 42 percent of clerical supervisors are male, although 98.2 percent of clerical staff (secretaries, typists and stenographers) are female (U.S. Department of Commerce 1990; Reskin and Hartmann 1986).

According to Rytina and Bianchi (1984), 48 percent of female employees

TABLE 8.3
Top Ten Occupations for Men and Women, 1988*

Men	No. Employed	% Occupation Male
Truckdrivers, heavy & light	2,852,443	95.7
Janitors & cleaners	1,629,115	56.3
Salespersons, retail	1,506,762	39.3
Carpenters	1,064,785	98.5
Farmers	969,850	85.0
Freight, stock, & material movers, hand	804,664	88.6
Auto mechanics	765,603	98.3
Cooks, except short order	551,698	50.2
Electricians	534,954	98.7
Construction helpers	531,135	95.7

Women	No. Employed	% Occupation Female
Secretaries	3,342,643	99.1
Salespersons, retail	2,327,238	60.7
Bookkeepers, accounting & auditing clerks	2,074,092	92.1
General office clerks	2,047,947	81.3
Cashiers	1,898,820	82.2
Registered nurses	1,491,842	94.6
Waitresses	1,475,236	82.6
Food counter & fountain workers	1,273,158	78.3
Janitors & cleaners	1,265,115	43.7
Elementary & kindergarten teachers	1,152,432	84.8

*The Department of Labor does not provide data by sex for all occupations; consequently, several occupations, such as manager, in which a large percentage of the population are employed, had to be excluded from the calculations for this table.
Source: Adapted from U.S. Department of Labor 1990:20–29.

hold jobs in fields in which 80 percent or more of the workers are women, while 71 percent of male employees are in occupations where 80 percent or more of the work force is composed of men. Interestingly, this occupational segregation persists across educational levels. For instance, among full-time female workers ranging in age from thirty-five to forty-four with five or more years of college education, 50 percent are employed in eight different occupations, including elementary school teacher, a category that applies to one in every six women in this group. In contrast, 25 percent of full-time male workers aged thirty-five to forty-four with five or more years of college education are employed in just three occupations: managers and administrators, lawyers, and physicians (Taeuber and Valdisera 1986). Notice, too, that female-dominated occupations, regardless of the education they require, tend to pay substantially less than male-dominated occupations—an important point that will be given further attention shortly.

In short, the labor market in the United States continues to be a **dual labor market,** that is, a labor market characterized by one set of jobs employing almost exclusively men and another set of jobs, typically viewed as secondary, employing almost exclusively women. The extent of this occupational sex segregation may come as a surprise to some readers in light of the extensive media coverage recently being given to "the new professional women" and to women now holding nontraditional blue-collar jobs (e.g., carpenters, and miners) Certainly we are not suggesting here that women have not made inroads into the high-status, high-paying professions as well as the skilled trades. To the contrary, available data indicate that they have. For instance, between 1962 and 1988, the percentage of female engineers increased from 1 to 7.3 percent, the percentage of female physicians from 6 to 20 percent, and the percentage of female college and university teachers from 19 to 38.5 percent (U.S. Department of Commerce 1990; Sidel 1986). In just ten years, from 1974 to 1984, the percentage of female attorneys increased more than fivefold—from less than 3 percent to 15 percent (Serrin 1984). In 1988, women constituted 19.3 percent of attorneys (U.S. Department of Commerce 1990). Perhaps the most dramatic gain can be found among underground miners: in 1978, 1 in every 10,000 underground miners was a woman, while in 1980, owing largely to pressure on mine operators from the federal Equal Employment Opportunity Commission, 1 in every 12 underground miners was a woman (Reskin and Hartmann 1986).

Still, what we must keep in mind here is that the number of women in many occupations historically has been so low that to say it doubled, tripled, or even increased fivefold does not mean that large numbers of women now hold these jobs or that the jobs are no longer male-dominated. For example, women constituted 19.3 percent of lawyers in 1988, but that translated into less than 140,000 female lawyers in the United States (U.S. Department of Commerce 1990). Similarly, between 1970 and 1980, the number of black female attorneys in the United States rose from about 446 to 4,272—a tenfold increase—but this is put into perspective when we consider that there were more than 500,000 attorneys in the United States in 1980 (Sokoloff 1988). Even though the number of women employed in skilled trades increased by almost 80 percent between 1960 and 1970, by 1988 women constituted only 1.5 percent of carpenters, 1.3 percent of electricians, 0.7 percent of auto mechanics, 0.6 percent of plumbers, and 4.9 percent of painters (U.S. Department of Labor 1990; Sidel 1986).

In addition, although the dissimilarity index decreased significantly during the seventies and eighties (from 67.7 in 1970 to 59.3 in 1980), several female-dominated occupations grew even more so. For instance, women went from being 56.8 percent of food counter and fountain workers in 1970 to being 78.3 percent of such workers in 1988. Women were 77.7 percent of bookkeepers in 1950, but

92.1 percent in 1988 (U.S. Department of Labor 1990; Reskin and Hartmann 1986). Thus, although media reports may sometimes give the impression that substantial numbers of women and men are now working side by side in the same jobs, these data indicate that such a claim is largely overstated (*see also* Burris 1989; Robinson and McIlwee 1989; Blum and Smith 1988). These, though, are not the only qualifiers that must be made with regard to the claim that occupational sex segregation has declined in recent years.

More specifically, we find important differences in the degree of occupational sex segregation among various groups of workers. First, the ages of workers are significant. Young workers new to the full-time labor force show a moderately lower dissimilarity index than older workers. Among women workers from twenty to twenty-four years old, for example, the index of dissimilarity has been reported at 51.1, and it is women in this age group who are most likely to enter the male-dominated fields of engineering, science, management and administration (Reskin and Hartmann 1986). Nevertheless, women aged twenty-five to thirty-four, still considered younger workers, remain concentrated in female-dominated fields, even if they have five or more years of college education (Taeuber and Valdisera 1986).

A second factor to be considered is race. Dramatic drops in the dissimilarity index have been reported for racial minorities, particularly for Hispanics and Asian Americans, among whom the index declined from 75.6 in 1971 to 64.6 in 1981. Unlike whites, however, only a small part of this decrease appears to be due to minority women moving into professional occupations, "indicating that much of the increase in integration by sex for nonwhites occurred at the lower end of the occupational distribution" (Reskin and Hartmann 1986:23).

In addition, a good deal of the occupational shifting among minority women workers in recent years has been from one female-dominated job to another. For instance, while Hispanic women remain concentrated in poorly paying, female-dominated jobs in food processing, electronics, and garments (sewing and stitching), their numbers have increased in female-dominated white-collar work, especially in secretarial and clerical jobs (Zavella 1987). Such shifts have been greater among African American women who went from being 70 percent of domestics in 1940 to just 3.6 percent of such workers in 1987, and from 1 percent of clerical workers to 26.4 percent during the same time frame. African American women, though, have made less progress than white women in moving into male-dominated professions. Overall, only 14 percent of African American women hold professional jobs; they are just 1.5 percent of lawyers and judges, 1.9 percent of college and university teachers, and 3.8 percent of managers and business executives (Commission on Professionals in Science and Technology 1989; Edwards 1987; Jones 1986; Taeuber and Valdisera 1986).

According to Sokoloff (1988), between 1960 and 1980, African American men made the greatest gains in the professions relative to African American and white women. However, she cautions that this progress is mitigated by the fact that during the same period, African American men experienced a drop in their labor force participation rate by more than 10 percent. Collins (1989) further cautions that the gains of many African Americans in the business professions were racially oriented. They were also in such fields as personnel and public or urban relations, which makes these executives marginal and uniquely vulnerable to economic recessions. According to Collins (1989:329):

> Black entry into these specialties during the 1960s and 1970s occurred in an atmosphere of economic expansion and intense social upheaval. In the 1980s, upheaval has been quelled, and competition for market share has intensified; racial functions especially have lost their value. In an era of corporate mergers and acquisitions, heavily leveraged debt will be reduced by reducing the cost of management. The lack of a strong push by government on the one hand and the need to reduce staff costs on the other will eradicate these positions.

Collins's emphasis on changing economic conditions and the government's severely curtailed commitment to ensuring racial and gender equity in employment are important points to which we will return later in the chapter.

A third issue worth raising here is the extent to which occupational shifts have occurred among workers of both sexes. Up to this point, we have been discussing declines in occupational sex segregation because of women moving into male-dominated jobs. But occupational sex segregation may also be reduced by increases in male employment in female-dominated jobs. This latter scenerio, though, has been far less frequent than the former. Although women made gains of 20 percentage points or more in twenty-one male-dominated occupations between 1970 and 1980, men's representation in most female-dominated occupations rarely increased by more than 2 or 3 percentage points during the same period. This pattern remained unchanged during the 1980s. For example, men constituted 2.7 percent of registered nurses in 1970, 4.1 percent in 1980, and 5.4 percent in 1988. In some cases, slight gains in male representation in female-dominated occupations were lost during the 1980s. For instance, men increased their employment as prekindergarten and kindergarten teachers from 2.1 percent to 3.6 percent between 1970 and 1980, but by 1988, men were just 1.8 percent of prekindergarten and kindergarten teachers. Some notable exceptions were chief communications operators, which went from 18.2 percent male in 1970 to 65.6 percent male in 1980 to 89.4 percent male in 1988, and hand engravers and printing operators, which during the same periods rose from 18.4 to 68.3 to 86.2 percent male (U.S. Department of Commerce 1990; U.S. Department of Labor 1990; Reskin and Hartmann 1986).

Occupational shifts like these last two have caused concern among some observers about trends toward occupational *resegregation.* As Reskin and Hartmann (1986:31) explain, "Perhaps after reaching some 'tipping point' integrated occupations become resegregated with members of one sex replaced by members of the other." Historically, this has most frequently occurred as a result of men leaving occupations as women entered them. Why this occurs remains open to speculation, although some analysts attribute it to the belief among male workers that the presence of large numbers of women workers would lower the prestige and pay of the occupations. Strober and Arnold (1987) report that bank telling shifted from a male to a female occupation as men were lured to other jobs by higher salaries and as bank telling was de-skilled to entail fewer responsibilities and thus less prestige. We also saw an example of this in Chapter 5 where we discussed the transition of teaching from a male-dominated to a female-dominated profession. It was certainly the case that female teachers were paid less than their male counterparts, but it is unclear whether the entrance of women into teaching prompted men's exodus from the profession. Further research is needed with regard to this and other occupations, such as secretary and computer programmer, in order to better understand the phenomenon of occupational resegregation (Reskin and Hartmann 1986).

Finally, any beneficial effects on workers from declines in occupational sex segregation may be undermined by other forms of workplace sex segregation, in particular *industry sex segregation* and *establishment sex segregation*. For example, about half of all assemblers in manufacturing are women, indicating at first glance that employment in this occupation is balanced between the sexes. Upon closer examination, however, we find that within the manufacturing industry, women are 70 percent of electrical assemblers, but only about 17 percent of motor vehicle assemblers, the latter being better paid than the former (U.S. Department of Labor 1990; Reskin and Hartmann 1986). Similarly, although women and men may be employed in the same occupation, such as lawyer, they may work for different types of firms, with men being hired at the larger, more prestigious, and better paying firms (Sokoloff 1988; Epstein 1981; Blau 1977). Other researchers have documented the emergence of "female ghettos" within various fields, such as medicine, management, and the insurance industry, in which women have fewer opportunities for promotion and little authority or power (Hartmann 1987; Rosenfeld 1984; Harlan and O'Farrell 1982). Some companies hire workers of only one sex, or they hire men and women for totally different jobs or work shifts (Bielby and Baron 1986; 1984). Also common within an individual establishment is for men and women to be segregated into different departments, such as in department stores where men typically sell "big ticket" items like large appliances and furniture and women sell clothing and housewares (Hartmann 1987; Reskin and Hartmann 1986).

In sum, although occupational sex segregation seems to have declined somewhat in recent years, it has declined more for certain groups than for others; for the majority of workers, it remains a fact of everyday work life. Moreover, what gains have been made are frequently minimized by industry-wide and establishment sex segregation. At this point, most readers are probably wondering why this is true, especially since so much public attention has been given to policies such as affirmative action that are supposed to remedy employment discrimination. However, before we explore the reasons behind the persistance of workplace sex segregation, let's examine some of its most serious consequences.

Consequences of Workplace Sex Segregation

Workplace sex segregation limits the employment opportunities of both sexes, but it is most disadvantageous to women workers. This is because what is typically labeled "women's work" has some very negative features attached to it. For one thing, there is considerable evidence that much of women's work, such as secretarial and clerical tasks, is more stressful than most male-dominated jobs. Reskin and Hartmann (1986) report, for instance, that secretaries have the second-highest incidence of stress-related diseases among workers in 130 different occupations studied by the National Institute of Occupational Safety and Health (NIOSH). Data-entry clerks, whose jobs involve the full-time use of video display terminals, have the highest stress levels according to NIOSH—higher than air traffic controllers. The vast majority of data-entry clerks are women. Jobs such as these provide workers with minimal opportunities for creativity and autonomy and require them to complete tasks under pressure, within a limited period of time, and with minimal errors. These jobs also offer few rewards in the forms of compensation, mobility, benefits, or prestige. Workplace sex segregation keeps women, not men, locked into such jobs (*see also* Doyal 1990a; Burris 1989).

Workplace segregation is also associated with greater susceptibility to unemployment for women workers. This is somewhat paradoxical given that, as we noted earlier, female-dominated occupations, such as clerical and sales jobs, historically have been less affected by cyclical dips in the economy than male-dominated jobs in manufacturing and construction. As we noted at the outset of this chapter, however, this is beginning to change, and the most recent recession is expected to negatively affect the female-dominated service sector of the economy. In addition, when women in female-dominated occupations do lose their jobs, they tend to be unemployed longer than women in sex-neutral or male-dominated jobs. Since female-dominated jobs, especially those in the service sector, have high labor turnover rates, women workers tend to have put in less time on a specific job than men workers, making them more vulnerable to layoffs. "Thus, in the short run, reducing segregation would place women in more cyclically sensitive sectors or occupations, but in the long run it would probably increase their labor force attachment and thereby reduce the male-female unemployment differential and the overall sex difference in labor force participation" (Reskin and Hartmann 1986:14; Smith 1984).

At the same time, however, it is important to consider the effect of race on both occupational segregation and unemployment. In her study of a large insurance firm, for example, Hartmann (1987) found that race had a greater negative impact on occupational segregation than sex, but that black female workers experienced the greatest segregation, being relegated primarily to "back office" jobs that entailed little or no contact with clientele. Looking at unemployment rates, we also find that race has a stronger negative effect than sex. In 1988, the unemployment rates of white males and white females were equal: 4.7 percent. The unemployment rates of black males and black females were also equal: 11.7 percent (U.S. Department of Commerce 1990).

It is important to note that a history of sex segregation in the workplace also negatively affects those who obtain employment in jobs nontraditional for their sex. Men, for instance, who become nurses or dental hygienists often find that their masculinity is questioned by their clients, colleagues, and supervisors. However, since women have been more likely than men to cross the sex line in occupations, it is they who usually confront suspicion and hostility on the job. Femaleness is frequently a devalued trait in the workplace, and employers, clients, and colleagues tend to relate to women workers on the basis of their sex rather than on their individual qualifications and job performance. In her classic analysis of women and men in corporate management, Rosebeth Moss Kanter (1977:209) discussed this problem in terms of *tokenism,* the marginal status of a category of workers—in this case women—who are relatively few in number in the workplace. Tokens, according to Kanter, are "often treated as representatives of their category, as symbols rather than as individuals."

Kanter identifies a number of serious consequences for token workers. For instance, because of their conspicuousness in the workplace, they are more closely scrutinized by others. This places intense pressure on them to perform successfully, creating a work situation that is highly stressful. In addition, tokens experience what Kanter calls *boundary heightening;* that is, dominant workers tend to exaggerate the differences between themselves and the tokens and to treat the tokens as outsiders. Thus, researchers have noted that women workers frequently find themselves excluded from formal information networks that help them do their jobs. More often, they are shut out of informal social networks that may be just as crucial for their job performance and advancement. As male workers are well aware, important business is conducted not only in board rooms or at union meetings, but also on golf courses and in local taverns. However, it is these sorts of informal social/business activities in which women workers are least likely to be included by their male co-workers or supervisors (Couric 1989; Schur 1984; Epstein 1981).

Kanter makes the argument that tokenism is a problem of numbers and, therefore, the situation of female corporate managers should improve as more women enter the managerial ranks. Zimmer (1988:72) and others (e.g., Blum and Smith 1988; Franklin and Sweeney 1988), however, maintain that "men's negative behavior toward women in the workplace . . . seems to be much less motivated by women's presence in a numerical minority than by men's evaluation of women as a social minority—an opinion based on notions of inferiority rather than scarcity."

Certainly, this view of women as inferior, as well as easily intimidated and controllable, is reflected in the incidence of sexual harassment that women experience in the workplace. You may recall that in Chapter 5 we defined sexual harassment as any unwanted leers, comments, suggestions, or physical contact of a sexual nature, as well as unwelcome requests for sexual favors. Studies in the United States and Great Britain reveal that from one-fifth to four-fifths of female workers have experienced sexual harassment while at work. In a 1989 study of 918 female attorneys in the United States, among whom one-third earned more than $100,000 a year, 60 percent reported that they had experienced unwanted sexual attention at work. Thirteen of these respondents stated that they had been victims of rape, attempted rape, or assault while at work; the assailants in most cases were their supervisors (Couric 1989). In another study of 23,000 U.S. female federal employees in 1981, 12 percent reported experiences of mild harassment (e.g., suggestive remarks or pressure for dates), 29 percent experienced severe harassment (e.g., touching, pressure for sexual favors, and letters and phone calls), and 1 percent reported attempted or completed acts of rape or sexual assault (Stanko 1985). In an earlier survey of 9,000 women, more than 92 percent characterized sexual harassment as a problem in the workplace, and nine out of ten reported that they themselves had been sexually harassed on their jobs (Farley 1978).

Although women in all types of occupations confront sexual harassment, some observers claim that it is especially pervasive in male-dominated jobs to which women are new hires, since it may serve as a means for male workers to assert dominance and control over women who otherwise would be their equals (Gruber and Bjorn 1982; Westley 1982; Enarson 1980). However, regardless of the types of jobs in which it occurs, the consequences of sexual harassment for female workers are serious and harmful. Harassed women report a number of physical responses to the harassment, including chronic neck and back pain, upset stomach, colitis and other gastrointestinal disorders, and eating and sleeping disorders. Harassed women also become nervous and irritable. Psychologically,

> they feel humiliated; they feel they cannot control the encounters with the harasser(s) and thus feel threatened and helpless. Many develop techniques to protect themselves, through, for example, avoidance (particularly difficult if the woman works in the same location as the harasser(s) or through changing their dress or behavior (acting 'coolly'). These women describe the daily barrage of sexual interplay in the office as psychological rape (Stanko 1985:61).

Such feelings of powerlessness often intensify when women workers attempt to report the harassment. Although sexual harassment is a violation of equal employment laws, enforcement is difficult given an employer's economic power to reward or punish a female employee on the basis of her response to his sexual overtures. Employers also tend to prefer to handle harassment of co-workers quietly, through private mediation. Thus, many harassers are left publicly unaccountable for their actions. Not surprisingly, then, most women do not report incidents of sexual harassment on the job. In the 1989 study of female attorneys reported earlier, for example, only 7 percent reported the incidents to their law firms (Couric 1989). Instead of filing reports, many women feel forced to quit their jobs in order to end the harassment, although even this is no guarantee that they will not encounter similar problems at another work site.

In Chapter 9, we will again take up the issue of sexual assault and violence against women. For now, however, we wish to emphasize that sexual harassment serves to objectify women workers, and it undermines the goal of gender equality in the workplace. "In each instance, a woman is no longer made to feel like an employee or a colleague; she is immediately transformed into a sexual object" (Stanko 1985:61).

Each of the issues discussed here demonstrates convincingly the negative effects of workplace sex segregation on workers—particularly women workers. But there is one additional consequence that deserves special attention because of the harm it, in turn, produces. This is the economic impact of sex segregation, or what is perhaps better known as the *wage gap*.

THE MALE/FEMALE EARNINGS GAP

In their longitudinal analysis of the economic well-being of women and children, Corcoran, et al. (1984:233–234) quote a biblical verse in which God, speaking to Moses, said, "When a man makes a special vow to the Lord which requires your valuation of living persons, a male between twenty and sixty years old shall be valued at fifty silver sheckels. If it is a female, she shall be valued at thirty sheckels." As Corcoran and her colleagues subsequently note, this biblical custom of valuing women's labor at three-fifths that of a man appears to have carried over into the contemporary work world. Today, full-time, year-round female workers earn on average 70 percent of what male workers earn. In other words, for every dollar a male worker makes, a female worker makes on average just 70 cents. What is more, this ratio has remained remarkably stable over the past thirty years. Between 1960 and 1988, the male-female wage gap fluctuated between 59 and 70 percent (U.S. Department of Commerce 1990; Taeuber and Valdisera 1986; Serrin 1984) In fact, looking at Table 8.4, we find that, compared with nine other industrialized countries, the United States ranks among the lowest in terms of women's average earnings relative to those of men, and it has not made much progress in closing the wage gap.

The wage gap is especially acute when race is taken into consideration, as we can see by examining Figure 8.1. More specifically, the median annual income of white men in 1988 was $24,180 ($21,230 in constant 1984 dollars); for minority men, it was more than $7,000 less: $17,004 ($14,930 in constant 1984 dollars). Still, white and minority women had even lower median incomes in 1988: $16,536 ($14,519) and $14,248 ($12,510) respectively. By grouping all minorities together, however, Figure 8.1 masks the substantial differences in median income between different minority groups. For example, in 1980, the most recent year for which comparable statistics are available, the median annual income of Native American women was $10,069. Hispanic women had the lowest median annual income, but when the Hispanic population is disaggregated into specific ethnic groups, we find that median income for Puerto Rican women was $10,171, whereas for Cuban and Mexican-American women, median incomes were $9,703 and $9,217 respectively. In comparison, the median annual income of white women in 1980 was $11,189; the median for African American women was $10,381 (Smith and Tienda 1988).

TABLE 8.4
Average Earnings of Full-Time Female Workers as a Percentage of Those of Men in 10 Industrialized Countries, Nonagricultural Activities, 1980–1988

Country	Earnings Ratio (1980)	Earnings Ratio (1988)
Australia	85.9	87.9
Denmark	84.5	82.1
France	79.2	81.8*
Netherlands	78.2	76.8
Belgium	69.4	75.0
West Germany	72.4	73.5
United Kingdom	69.7	69.5**
United States	66.7***	70.2
Switzerland	67.6	67.4
Japan	53.8	50.7

*1987 data
**1984 data
***1983 data
Sources: International Labor Organization 1990:759–764; U.S. Department of Commerce 1990:405.

At the same time, recent statistics indicate that minorities, especially minority women, are more likely than whites to be hired as temporary employees or to be employed in minimum-wage as opposed to salaried occupations. In 1987, 65 percent of women compared with just 35 percent of men held jobs that paid the minimum wage. Among hourly wage workers, 8.7 percent of African Americans were paid at the minimum wage, whereas 9.1 percent of Hispanics and 7.8 percent of white hourly workers were minimum-wage earners. The minimum wage in 1987 was $3.35 per hour, unchanged since 1981, although due to inflation its spending power was only $2.68 if measured in 1981 dollars (Stout 1988).

The monetary rewards to employers are obvious; not only do temporary and minimum-wage employees receive lower salaries, but they also typically are not entitled to costly employment benefits such as medical insurance plans, disability, and paid vacations. Labor union policies have served to further reinforce this pattern. "Temporary help are expected to pay union dues, but, if their positions are lost within 90 days, they are not considered union members and, therefore, are not entitled to support during their lay-offs" (Richardson 1981:214).

Regardless of the economic benefits of such policies for employers and unions, the effects on women workers are overwhelmingly negative. Indeed, given these data, it is hardly surprising that women, particularly minority women, are disproportionately represented among the poor. We turn our attention now to this impact of the male/female earnings gap.

(1984 constant dollars)

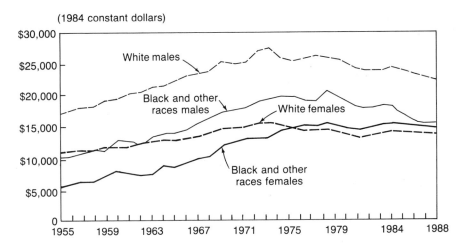

FIGURE 8.1 Median Income of Year-Round, Full-Time Workers by Sex and Race, 1955–1984. Sources: U.S. Dept. of Commerce 1990:409; Taeuber and Valdisera 1986:29.

The Earnings Gap, Poverty, and Welfare Policy

As we learned in Chapter 7, more than half (54.7 percent) of female-headed households were living below the poverty line in 1987; this is a poverty rate more than four times that of male-headed households (U.S. Department of Commerce 1990). About 45 percent of white female-headed families live in poverty, but almost 67 percent of African American and 72 percent of Hispanic female-headed families live below the poverty line (U.S. House of Representatives 1987). Importantly, the majority of women who head households work, and 85 percent of those who work, work full-time. In 1988, female heads of households had median earnings of $269 per week or $13,988 per year. If we take into account deductions for social security tax and employment-related expenses (e.g., child care, transportation, food, and clothing) disposable income is significantly reduced, placing these families precariously close to, if not below, the official poverty line (in 1988 it was $9,436 for a family of three and $12,092 for a family of four). It is important to emphasize that we are speaking here of *median* earnings, which means that half of all females who head households and work full-time, year round earn less than $13,988 annually. In contrast, median earnings for married-couple families in 1988 were $668 per week or $34,736 per year; for men who maintained families, median earnings were $486 per week or $25,272 per year.

Of course, race is again a major factor to be considered. Families maintained by minority women have median annual earnings of about $3,000 less than families maintained by white women. Although married-couple families and families maintained by men have median earnings higher than those of families maintained by women regardless of race, minority married-couple families have median annual earnings from about $5,200 to $9,500 less than white married-couple families; families maintained by minority men have median annual incomes of $3,400 to $4,000 less than families maintained by white men (U.S. Department of Commerce 1990). These inadequate wages may make welfare benefits more appealing than jobs to some women who head households (*see* Box 8.1).

BOX 8.1   The Myths and Realities of Welfare

Underlying recent debates about the pros and cons of government assistance programs to the poor are a number of widely held stereotypes about welfare recipients and myths about the nature of welfare programs themselves. For instance, there is a common perception among the general public that welfare rolls are excessively long because many of those receiving benefits are defrauding the government. In fact, however, between 1980 and 1988, although the official number of poor people in the United States increased dramatically, revised welfare guidelines and budget cuts significantly reduced assistance to the poor. After 1981, for instance, when eligibility requirements for Aid to Families with Department Children (AFDC) were tightened, a half-million low-income families lost AFDC benefits as well as Medicaid coverage (health insurance for the poor). Only about one-third of officially poor families receive cash welfare or unemployment benefits (U.S. House of Representatives 1989; O'Hare 1985). Although government officials repeatedly express strong concerns about welfare fraud, abuses by welfare administrators may be more common than fraud by recipients (Miller 1990).

Each year, about one-fourth of those who apply for welfare or Medicaid are turned down and do not receive assistance. Although one might assume that the main reason for this is that the applicants have too much income or other assets, the primary reason people are turned down for welfare is problems with paperwork or documentation. In 1986, for example, of the 2,602,236 people whose requests for welfare were rejected, 59.7 percent were denied because of application problems (Tolchin 1988). The factors that prevent eligible individuals from securing needed benefits are quite basic: illiteracy or language barriers, lack of transportation to obtain help, and difficulty in providing necessary records.

It is also believed by some that welfare benefits are so generous that recipients can live relatively lavish lifestyles. The fact of the matter is that once an individual meets the stringent eligibility requirements, the amount of aid given falls well below the poverty line. Consider, for example, that the typical AFDC family consists of three members, usually a mother and her two dependent children. In 1988, the average monthly AFDC payment nationwide was $370, with average payments by state ranging from a low of $114 to a high of $594. Consequently, almost all AFDC recipients fall below the official poverty line, which in 1988 was an annual income of $9,056 for a family of three (Miller 1990).

continued

Box 8.1 continued

Perhaps the most pervasive stereotype about welfare recipients is that most are able-bodied adults who, because they receive welfare payments, have no incentive to work. First, it must be pointed out that most poor adults aged twenty-two to sixty-four are working or looking for work. In 1987, for instance, 2.1 million people worked full-time year-round but were still living below the poverty line. Another 6.9 million worked either full-time or part-time for a portion of the year. However, the jobs held by the poor are menial, low-paying ones. Even with a federal minimum wage set at at least $3.35 per hour, a full-time worker, working forty hours a week year-round, would have a pre-tax annual income of only $6,968, still considerably below the poverty line for a family of three.

However, in considering the argument that welfare recipients are able-bodied adults capable of, but too lazy to work, one must also consider the sex bias inherent in our nation's welfare policies. Until quite recently, most welfare programs excluded men and intact families under the assumption that the availability of benefits would induce men to shirk from their responsibility of working to support their families. Such policies "assume that most women are mothers, that children need their mothers' exclusive care, and that fathers should support both" (Miller 1990:2).

According to Miller (1990), in fact, our nation's welfare system has been designed to enforce the norm of the traditional nuclear family, and in particular women's place in it. While excluding most men, U.S. welfare programs simultaneously have provided women with few incentives or supports for obtaining employment. An example may make this clearer. The following list reports the welfare benefits that an unemployed mother of two would have received in 1987. (The figures are based on the Pennsylvania allowance since that state's AFDC benefits closely approximate the national averages.)

Earnings	0
Earned income tax credit	0
AFDC	$4,584
Food stamps	$1,549
Disposable income	$6,133
Plus Medicaid	$1,537 (estimated value)
Total value of benefits	$7,670

Although most people agree that it is impossible for a family of three to survive on $7,670 a year, little is done to address this problem. Instead, most people ask, why doesn't this woman go out and get a job? The fact of the matter is that she is economically better off staying on welfare than taking a minimum-wage job. The statistics that follow assume that the mother of two has been working for over one year at a job that pays $8,000 a year, a sum slightly above the minimum wage rate. However, this causes the woman to be ineligible for certain benefits. Here is her financial situation based on federal estimates:

Earnings	$8,000
Earned income tax credit	$742
AFDC	0
Food stamps	$1,306
Social Security and income tax	−$740
Child care and other work-related expenses	−$2,400
Disposable income	$6,908

continued

Box 8.1 continued

We can see here that first, while the woman receives an earned income tax credit, it basically serves to offset taxes paid. Second, she has lost an important benefit, Medicaid; it is unlikely that she can afford to purchase health insurance and it is equally unlikely that she is employed in a job that provides health insurance as a benefit of employment. Finally, child care becomes a major expense; adequate and affordable child care services are scarce in the United States. In reality, employment for this mother must be considered a financial loss (*see also New York Times* 5 March 1989:E6).

Although recent welfare "reforms," such as the Family Support Act of 1988, were designed to promote (if not require) employment training, education, and job placement for welfare recipients, they have not adequately addressed such problems as the need for child care (a need of 60 percent of AFDC recipients) or transportation. Nor do they require that a specific level of skills training be offered to ready potential workers for nonpoverty level jobs, or safeguard against the payment of poverty level wages. Thus, while it is still too early to fairly evaluate these recent policy changes, preliminary data indicate that "large numbers of women will remain unserved, excluded, given short-term training or meaningless experience in low-paying jobs, provided with few or no auxiliary services, and remain poor" (Miller 1990:66).

In short, as Miller (1990:3) concludes, "Programs function so that men and women are differently rewarded or punished for different circumstances and behaviors." The welfare system operates to keep women dependent—either dependent on the government or, more preferable in the eyes of policy makers, dependent on husbands.

Women are also disproportionately represented among individuals living in poverty, and a large percentage are elderly women living alone. Although the poverty rate of the elderly population in general has declined significantly during the last two decades—from 25 percent or twice the rate of the general population in 1970, to 12.2 percent, just under the 13.5 percent rate for the general population, in 1987—improvement has been slower for elderly women. About 63 percent of the elderly population is female, but females constitute 73 percent of the elderly poor and 82 percent of the elderly poor who live alone. Two-thirds of the elderly who live alone are widows and, in contrast with the stereotype of the "old, rich widow," most elderly widows are poor. Overall, the poverty rate of elders who live alone is 19 percent, five times higher than the poverty rate of elderly couples. In 1987, 1.9 million elderly women were poor, and of these, 1.4 million lived alone. Importantly, however, sex puts one at greater risk of being poor than simply living alone, since 15 percent of men who lived alone in 1987 were poor, compared with 20 percent of women. As Davis and her colleagues (1990:43–45) conclude:

> As these figures suggest, elderly women living alone, often nonwhite widows of advanced age and declining health, are most vulnerable to poverty. . . . When elderly people living alone are categorizied by sex, age, and race, the lowest poverty rate is for white men aged 65–74, at 9 percent, and the highest is for nonwhite women age 85 and above, at 59 percent. . . . Even more troubling is

evidence indicating that the concentration of poverty among elderly women living alone will worsen as we move into the next century. . . . While most of the older population will fare well economically over the next 30 years, the proportion of women with incomes below 150 percent of poverty will remain high: 45 percent in 1987, and 38 percent in 2020. . . . Among widows the situation is slightly worse, with the proportion who are poor or near-poor rising until the turn of the century. . . . [B]y 2020 poverty among the elderly will be almost exclusively a problem among elderly women.

The economic difficulties of these women are directly related to their employment patterns, the wages they earned during their work lives, and their job benefits. For example, women are less likely than men to be employed in jobs that have private pension plans. In addition, since women earn less than men, their Social Security benefits, as well as any other retirement benefits they may have accrued, will also be lower (Reskin and Hartmann 1986). Women must frequently interrupt their labor force participation because of caregiving responsibilities (*see* Chapter 7); in fact, women on average spend 11.5 years out of the paid labor force because of caregiving, whereas men spend an average 1.3 years out for the same reason. Employment interruptions not only limit job opportunities, but also prevent women from accruing sufficient retirement benefits (Davis, et al. 1990). At the same time, government programs such as Social Security and Supplemental Security Income (SSI) have been found in some cases to actually increase widows' risks for poverty. More specifically, when her spouse dies, a widow's Social Security benefits decline substantially, from one-third to one-half of their previous level when the spouse was alive. "At lower levels of income, then, the survivor's benefit may be inadequate to meet the remaining spouse's needs" (Davis, et al. 1990:44), and because women typically outlive men (*see* Chapter 12), this policy disproportionately affects them. Although SSI was designed to assist those not covered by Social Security or those for whom Social Security benefits are inadequate, the program has stringent eligibility requirements that disqualify many individuals even though they are poor. This, coupled with the fact that many eligible persons do not apply for SSI because they are unaware of the program or do not understand it, explains why less than one-third of the elderly poor who live alone receive SSI (Davis, et al. 1990).

Clearly, the male/female wage gap presents pervasive and serious problems. But how is it related to sex segregation in the workplace? To answer this question, we need to explore possible reasons for the wage gap itself.

Explaining the Gender Gap in Wages

Table 8.5 shows average weekly earnings of selected occupations in 1990. The table contains a broad range of jobs that require different levels of training, skill, effort, and responsibility, but one consistent observation that can be made is that female-dominated occupations typically pay significantly less than male-dominated occupations. Recent research indicates, in fact, that occupational sex segregation

TABLE 8.5
Average Weekly Earnings of Selected Male-Dominated and Female-Dominated Occupations, 1990

Occupation	Female(%)	Average Weekly Earnings ($)
Secretary	99.1	343
Dental assistant	98.7	300
Receptionist	97.1	273
Child care worker	96.1	203
Private household worker	95.6	190
Registered nurse	94.6	608
Bookkeeper	92.1	338
Bank teller	91.0	273
Textile sewing machine operator	90.1	214
Nursing aide	89.8	251
Data entry keyer	88.2	316
Librarian	85.4	489
Elementary school teacher	84.8	519
Cashier	82.2	215
Architect	14.6	695
Police officer or detective	13.4	645
Engineer	7.3	814
Furnace operator	6.9	467
Truck driver	4.3	430
Logger	4.2	314
Material-moving equipment operator	4.1	415
Airplane pilot or navigator	3.1	898
Fire fighter	2.9	595
Aircraft engine mechanic	.7	576

Source: U.S. Department of Labor 1991.

alone accounts for about 35 to 40 percent of the difference in men's and women's earnings. For example, Trieman and Hartmann (1981) found a strong inverse relationship between the extent to which women were represented in a specific job and that job's median annual earnings. More specifically, the higher the percentage of female representation, the lower the salary. According to these researchers, for each additional percentage point of female dominance in an occupation, there was a corresponding $42 drop in median annual earnings. Thus, they calculated that in an occupation composed totally of women workers, the median annual salary would be $3,946, or less than half the median annual salary of $8,185 calculated for an occupation filled exclusively by men.

Many employers, economists, and public policy makers acknowledge that "women's work" almost always pays less than "men's work," but they maintain that the reason particular jobs have become female-dominated is because large numbers of women have freely chosen to enter them. Central to their argument is the assumption that women's primary allegiance is to home and family; thus, they seek undemanding jobs that require little personal investment in training or skills acquisition so that they can better tend to their household responsibilities. In other words, women choose to invest less than men in employment outside the home, so they get less in return. This explanation is called **human capital theory.**

In evaluating human capital theory, we will focus first on the issue of women's "choice" of occupations. It is certainly the case, as we learned in Chapter 7, that women bear primary responsibility for home and family care, but what is less clear is the extent to which this is voluntary. A major weakness in human capital theory is that it fails to distinguish between self-imposed job restrictions and structurally imposed ones. For instance, are nonemployed mothers who cannot find affordable and reliable child care really making a "free choice" to stay out of the labor market? Studies indicate that five of every six nonemployed women would enter the labor force if they could find adequate child care (Barrett 1987; Reskin and Hartmann 1986). The decision to remain at home or to accept low-paying jobs because they better suit one's child care responsibilities is most often a response to a structurally imposed constraint on women's occupational opportunities—that is, our government's failure to enact a national child care policy (*see* Box 8.2).

Who Cares for the Children? BOX 8.2

Work in the United States is still organized under the assumption that workers are men who, if they have children, also have a wife at home to care for them. As we have learned in this and the preceding chapter, however, this is not the case; the number of single-parent families in the United States has increased significantly during the last twenty years alone, and women with preschool-aged children have been the fastest growing segment of the labor force. Nevertheless, both the federal government and employers have been largely unresponsive to these demographic changes. The United States, unlike at least 117 other countries, has no official government policy mandating paid maternity leave, and we are one of the few advanced industrialized countries that lacks a government-mandated child care system (Hewlett 1986). It is estimated that almost 10 million preschool children in the United States are in need of child care along with 2 to 5 million older children between the ages of six and thirteen. According to one recent survey, about 23 percent of working parents must regularly leave their children without adult supervision (Rubin 1987; Hewlett 1986).

To better understand the current crisis in child care, let's compare conditions in the United States with those of one of our industrialized allies, Sweden. In Sweden, the government has mandated a system of parental insurance whereby a parent, mother or

continued

Box 8.2 continued

father, may remain at home after the birth of a child while still receiving 90 percent of his or her salary. "In addition to parental leave during the first year of life, Swedish fathers are entitled to a ten-day parents' allowance at the time of the birth of the baby to help care for the mother and the new baby or other children in the home; either parent may take up to sixty days' leave per year per child if the child or its regular caretaker is ill" (Sidel 1986:181). Worth emphasizing here is the point that these policies are designed to encourage and maximize paternal involvement in child care. However, statistics indicate that only 25 to 30 percent of fathers utilize their parental leave when their children are born, although almost as many men as women take advantage of parental leave to care for sick children (Sidel 1986).

In addition to parental insurance, Sweden has established an extensive system of public child care. "The options range from municipal day-care mothers (who care for three to four children in their homes and are paid for and licensed by the municipalities) to various types of day care centers (Hewlett 1986:127). Preschool care was estimated to cost the equivalent of about $5,000 per year per child in 1981, but the government subsidized almost half of this amount. In addition, parents' fees are determined by income, but part-time preschools are provided free. After-school care is also available at a nominal charge.

By all accounts, the quality of public child care in Sweden is exceptionally high. "Close attention is paid not only to the children's physical environment but to their individual development, to their health and well-being, and to their social development" (Sidel 1986:185). Still, it is estimated that public child care fills the needs of only about 30 percent of Swedish families, although the government has made a strong commitment to establishing new centers at a pace that will not compromise their quality (Sidel 1986).

How does the United States compare? First, as we have already noted, the United States has no federally mandated policy for paid maternity leave. In 1990, Congress passed the Parental and Medical Leave Act that required employers of fifty or more employees to provide up to ten weeks of unpaid leave over a twenty-four month period to parents of newborns, newly adopted, or seriously ill children. (The bill also allows the same leave for employees to care for seriously ill parents.) President Bush, however, vetoed the legislation.

Currently, 37 percent of workers at U.S. companies with 100 or more employees are offered unpaid maternity leave; 18 percent of workers at such companies are provided unpaid paternity leave (Holmes 1990a). Not surprisingly, few U.S. men take advantage of paternity leave when it is available largely because of the fact that, since men's salaries typically are higher than those of women, the unpaid nature of the leave makes it impractical for most to utilize it (Churchman 1985).

Most U.S. employers continue to treat pregnancy as a short-term disability with maternity leaves typically ranging from one to six months. Many women, however, work in low-paying service positions or in unskilled labor jobs that provide few, if any, disability benefits. These women must either quit their jobs or return to work within days of their child's birth, arranging for some form of child care for the infant.

We have already noted that public child care is extremely limited in the United States, although we have made more progress in this area than with regard to parental leave. Most child care facilities and nursery schools are private, with costs ranging from as little as $1,500 to as much as $10,000 per child per year, depending on the facility

continued

Box 8.2 continued

(Hewlett 1986). Most private child care centers have waiting lists of parents who wish to enroll their children, but the cost is prohibitive for many families. Consequently, most parents in the United States have depended on a patchwork of care providers that includes relatives and friends as well as unlicensed home-based "centers." In fact, home-based child care—care given in a private home by an unlicensed provider, usually a neighbor—is estimated to account for about 94 percent of child care in the United States (Nelson 1988).

Some major corporations have opened their own child care centers, in recognition of the importance of family concerns and as means to attract and retain workers. Other corporations provide child care referral services or a child care subsidy as a job benefit. Still others permit "flextime" (i.e., employees may set their own work schedule as long as a requisite number of hours are worked per day or week) and "flexplace" (i.e., employees may work out of their own homes during at least part of the work day or week). In 1989, one business analyst even urged companies to establish two separate (and unequal) career tracks for their female employees. One track would be for career-oriented women who, like men, are willing to commit themselves completely to meeting their employers' needs and demands. A second, slower track—which has come to be called the "mommy track"—would be for family-oriented women who prefer to put the needs of their spouses and children before those of their employers (Schwartz 1989). This recommendation has sparked a heated debate. Many corporations praised the suggestion, arguing that it highlights a significant difference between male and female workers. However, critics point out that this proposal encourages employers to track their female employees into dead-end jobs and it reinforces the notion that caregiving is women's responsibility (Lewin 1989).

While there are advantages and disadvantages to each of the options we discuss here (Rubin 1987), the more important point is that they are exceptions; most employers continue to view the parenting needs of their employees as a "private" rather than a business matter. Only about 6,000 of the nearly 6 million employers in the United States offer their employees any kind of child care assistance (Lawson 1990).

The federal government's response to the child care crisis until 1990 was the Child and Dependent Care Tax Credit, which allowed families to deduct up to 30 percent of child care costs (at a maximum of $2,400 for one child and $4,800 for two or more children) from their annual taxes. A major problem with this program, however, was that it did not address the needs of the working poor; if a family did not earn enough income to pay taxes, then it did not receive the benefit regardless of its child care costs. According to one report, "[i]n 1988, 77 percent of the $3.6 billion in credits went to families with annual incomes above $30,000, and 43 percent went to families making more than $50,000 (Holmes 1990b).

The federal government did provide grants to states for various social programs for the poor that included child care, but budget cuts during the Reagan administration caused the families of at least 200,000 children to lose their federal child care benefits during the 1980s. In 1990, however, national child care legislation was passed by Congress and signed by President Bush mandating state grants and tax credits to provide low-income families with $22 billion of federal support between 1991 and 1996. Through an expansion of the Earned Income Tax Credit program, poor working parents whose credits are more than their taxes are refunded the difference, thus alleviating the

continued

Box 8.2 continued

problem with this program identified earlier. In addition, the states have been allocated more money to subsidize child care, especially for poor families, and the Entitlement Funding for Child Care Services program enables states to give money to welfare families or families about to go on welfare because they cannot afford child care.

According to the Children's Defense Fund (1990), this new legislation provides child care for approximately 400,000 more children than were served during the 1980s. Nevertheless, given the number in need, many families will continue to piece together child care services or simply go without. And unfortunately, the United States still lags behind at least one of its industrialized allies, Sweden, with regard to parental work leaves and child care. In fact, a comparison of the United States with other industrialized nations would yield similar results (Hewlett 1986). However, our objective here is not to suggest that the Swedish model or that of any other country is flawless or that these should be transplanted to the United States. Rather, we wish only to suggest that the strategies and experiences of other countries demonstrate that the problem of child care provisions can be addressed by government policy makers in diverse and creative ways. The U.S. child care legislation of 1990 is perhaps an indication that our federal government is at last ready to explore some of these options so as to more effectively meet the needs of the nation's families.

Similarly, research shows that workers' decisions to take specific jobs reflect the occupational opportunities available to them. Historically, women have not been hired for jobs such as coal mining or shipbuilding, but evidence indicates that once employers began to open job opportunities in these fields, women responded by seeking such jobs. The more that women were hired, the more other women applied for the jobs. "It seems likely, then, that women's aspirations and preferences change as their perception of opportunities changes and that the occupational opportunity structure is an important determinant of their preferences" (Reskin and Hartmann 1986:79). The number of women already working in a particular job is also important because they may serve as role models and mentors to other female job aspirants (*see* Chapter 5). If few or no women hold particular jobs then "[t]he impression would be that these jobs are off-limits for women, and so other women would be less likely to aspire to them. Perhaps they thought their chances of success were low simply because few other women had succeeded before them" (Riger 1988:898–899). Or, as Riger goes on to point out, perhaps some women choose not to enter certain occupations because they do not want to subject themselves to discrimination on the job and a working environment that is hostile to women.

Although evidence we have discussed so far does not support it, let's assume for the moment that human capital theory is correct: women choose jobs that involve fewer skills and time demands, and less training than the jobs men choose. To what extent does this explain the differential in women's and men's wages? Based on the findings of recent studies, the answer is very little. Corcoran, et al. (1984), for example, tested human capital theory by calculating how much differences in men's and women's education, work experience, work continuity, self-

imposed restrictions on work hours and location, and rates of absenteeism contributed to differences in their salaries. Significantly, they found that self-imposed
restrictions on work hours and location explained almost none of the wage gap.
Large differences in patterns of job tenure between male and female workers also
explained little of the wage gap. "Although discontinuous employment [caused, for
example, by temporary withdrawal from the labor force to bear and raise children]
did reduce women's work experience, they apparently were not handicapped by
having 'rusty' skills when they returned to the work force. After adjusting for the
effects of lost experience, we found that labor force interruptions never significantly lowered wages for either women or white men (Corcoran, et al. 1984:238).
In fact, all of the factors they analyzed, taken together, accounted for less than a
third of the wage gap between white men and white women and only about a
quarter of the wage gap between white men and African American women.

Additional research supports their finding that sex differences in education
have little to do with the wage gap. In a recent study of engineers, for instance,
Robinson and McIlwee (1989) found that educational attainment, as well as experience in the work force and job tenure, failed to explain the lower status of the female
engineers in their sample relative to the male engineers. With respect to education,
the women and men in this study were virtually identical. In fact, Robinson and
McIlwee note that female engineering students typically outperform male engineering students in their classes and have slightly higher grade point averages. Yet, for
their sample, "[t]he educational achievements of these women . . . appear to yield
fewer occupational rewards than do the men's" (Robinson and McIlwee 1989:463).

As Table 8.6 shows, women's earnings are significantly lower than men's
across educational levels. Women with college degrees can expect to earn on
average just slightly more than male high school dropouts and less than men with
only high school diplomas. Race is also a significant factor in wage differentials

TABLE 8.6
**Mean Money Earnings by Sex and Educational Attainment of Full-Time, Year-Round
Workers, 1987**

	Earnings	
Level of Educational Attainment	*Female Workers*	*Male Workers*
Less than 8 years	$10,163	$16,883
8 years	12,655	18,946
1–3 years of high school	13,136	21,327
Graduated high school	16,223	24,745
1–3 years of college	19,336	29,253
Graduated college	23,506	38,117
1 or more years of postgraduate training	30,255	47,903

Source: U.S. Department of Commerce 1990:455

irrespective of employees' educational levels. White males at every level of education have higher incomes than African American men and both African American and white women. Asian women have a higher educational attainment level than women in any other racial group, yet 70 percent of them work in clerical, service, and blue-collar occupations which, as we have already seen, pay low salaries (Taeuber and Valdisera 1986; U.S. Department of Commerce 1986).

This leads us to another difficulty in human capital theory: it assumes that women's work automatically entails lower skill, effort, and responsibility than traditional men's work. It fails to account for the fact that female-dominated jobs that require basically the same (and sometimes more) skill, effort, and responsibility as male-dominated jobs still pay less. To understand this point, return to the figures in Table 8.5. Here we find, for instance, that a child care worker earns $127 less per week than a truck driver and $264 less than a furnace operator. Additional examples are abundant. In Illinois, mental health technicians (disproportionately female) earned $446 less per year than auto mechanics (disproportionately male). In Minnesota, behavior analysts (also predominantly female) were paid $218 less per year than game wardens (predominantly male). And in New York, where kindergarten teachers—almost all of whom are female—are required to have a bachelor's degree, the average starting salary of $15,250 was found to be more than $4,000 less than the starting salary of zookeepers, who are predominantly men and have no educational requirements for their jobs (Mydans 1984; Lewin 1984).

Disparities such as these have prompted many women workers throughout the country to demand through the courts that their salaries be set on the basis of **comparable worth.** We will return to the issue of comparable worth shortly, but suffice it to say here that this refers to the principle of equal pay for different jobs of similar value. "It argues that people should be paid according to the worth of the work they perform—its value to the employer—regardless of sex, race, or other characteristics" (Feldberg 1984:312). A problem arises, however, in that the job evaluation systems typically used to determine wages are themselves highly subjective and often contain many common gender stereotypes (Hartmann, et al. 1985; Steinberg and Haignere 1985; Beatty and Beatty 1984). For example, skills that are utilized in predominantly female occupations, such as teaching, nursing, and social work, are frequently not recognized as compensable skills in job evaluation systems at least in part because they are viewed as an extension of women's unpaid work in the home. Historically, women's work in the home "was taken for granted, looked simple, and was not thought to need any particular formal education or training." The incorporation of such stereotypes into job evaluation programs has sometimes produced nonsensical results—for example, the rating of nursery school teachers' skills as lower than those of dog trainers (Briggs 1975:204; Feldberg 1984).

In sum, what we have found here has little to do with the preferences or free choices of individual workers. Instead, it appears that:

> The structure of the market incorporates historic customs, prejudices, and
> ideologies that connect the worth of different kinds of work with ideas about the

inherent worth of workers who vary by sex, race, age, ethnicity, and other social characteristics. It is these customs, prejudices, and ideologies, modified by the effects of struggles between workers and employers, rather than the nature of work or any natural economic laws, that have shaped the basic framework of wage determination. This process has systematically disadvantaged women, who have been seen as people whose primary attachments are or ought to be to home and family (Feldberg 1984:319–320).

Let us continue our discussion, then, by examining these ideologies and discriminatory practices further.

THE WORK WORLD: IDEOLOGY AND THE ROLE OF LAW

It is clear that workplace sex segregation is a major contributor to the male/female wage gap. The question that remains, however, is what factors allow for workplace sex segregation. In this section we will address two important factors—sexist ideology and legal limitations—but we caution our readers to keep in mind that workplace sex segregation is a complex phenomenon produced and perpetuated by a variety of interrelated variables.

Gender Stereotypes at Work

In our earlier discussion, we saw how beliefs about women's and men's "appropriate" roles historically helped give rise to a dual labor market. To review, the prevalent ideology was that a "proper lady" did not work unless she was unmarried or, if married, then childless. A wide range of occupations were open to men, but women entered a limited number of jobs that supposedly matched their "natural" traits and talents and simply extended their family roles into the public arena. These, as we have noted, were occupations in the "helping professions" and in blue-collar and low-level service fields (e.g., clerical work, sewing, assembling, and canning). This ideology gave rise to a corollary set of beliefs: that women did not need to work; that they worked only briefly until they married or had children (things all women should do); and that if they worked after marriage or the birth of children, it was only for "pin money" or to "help out" financially.

In short, employers and employees alike, women as well as men, came to see women's employment as secondary to that of men and to view women workers as less serious about or less committed to their jobs. The fact that such ideas stood in stark contrast with the reality of many women's everyday lives did not make these beliefs any less powerful or any less widely held. To the majority, it appeared that women deserved to be relegated to the lower rungs of the job hierarchy and to be paid less than men. What is more, the ideology of "true womanhood" was never extended to minority women. As Glenn (1987:359–360) notes, "Racist ideology triumphed over sexist ideology. Women of color were not deemed truly women, exempting them from the protective cloaks of feminine frailty or womanly morality."

Interestingly, in recent discussions with students, the attitude that is often expressed is that these ideas are "old-fashioned" and no longer prevalent in the work world. "People just don't think like that anymore," we are frequently told. However, research indicates that these ideologies have not disappeared from the workplace, although they may now be more subtle than in the past. Reskin and Hartmann (1986), for example, review a number of studies that show that both the public and employers continue to believe that there are certain jobs for which women and men are naturally unsuited. One researcher found, for instance, that construction firms often justified not hiring women for certain jobs because they assumed that women are not physically strong enough for the work (Westley 1982). Employers also sometimes make hiring decisions on the basis of stereotypes about men's and women's supposed job preferences. Thus, in a study that examined factors influencing hiring decisions for entry-level, semi-skilled jobs, employers made remarks such as, "Women wouldn't like this [job]," and "The work is clean and women like that" (Harkess 1980). Obviously, such ideas bias personnel decisions by predisposing employers to hire men and women for different kinds of jobs, thereby perpetuating workplace sex segregation. As Riger (1988:901) points out, "The more ambiguous the evaluation process [for hiring], the more likely it is that gender bias will operate. The more the job involved is stereotyped as appropriate for the opposite sex, the more likely it is that gender bias will operate."

Reskin and Hartmann (1986:66) also discuss how *statistical discrimination* contributes to workplace sex segregation. Statistical discrimination "refers to decision making about an individual on the basis of characteristics believed to be typical of the group to which he or she belongs. . . . According to this model, employers do not hire anyone who is a member of a group thought to have lower productivity; statistical discrimination serves for them as a cheap screening device." On the face of it, statistical discrimination may not seem unfair; it certainly does not appear to be inherently sex-biased. However, as Reskin and Hartmann convincingly demonstrate, it is often premised on gender stereotypes. "For example, employers may refuse to hire a woman in the childbearing years for certain jobs—especially those that require on-the-job training—because they assume that many young women will leave the labor force to have children, irrespective of any individual applicant's childbearing or labor market intentions" (Reskin and Hartmann, 1986:66). It also assumes that men have little interest in or responsibility for childrearing—that men who have children also have a spouse to care for them. Although such assumptions may reflect the family lives of a majority of men, they nevertheless disregard individual circumstances and work against single fathers and men who prefer an equal or primary parenting role (*see* Chapter 7).

Sexist workplace ideology also operates to preserve industry-wide sex segregation. Because femaleness, as we noted previously, is a devalued trait in some workplaces, a concern over loss of prestige or status may prompt some firms or businesses to restrict their hiring of women (and racial minorities) either to "back office" jobs that have little contact with clientele (Hartmann 1987) or to a few "tokens" (Reskin and Hartmann 1986). An example of this was provided recently by a colleague who works in a department of three men and three women at a small, private college. She recounted to us how one of her co-workers had objected to the hiring of another woman on the ground that the department would then be female-dominated and consequently lose status within the institution.

There is evidence that some work-related gender stereotypes have weakened in recent years and that women who have entered male-dominated occupations have positively changed many workplaces (*see,* for example, Lunneborg 1990). Consequently, it is sometimes argued that sexist workplace ideology, although slow to change, will eventually break down as more women and men enter occupations nontraditional for their sex. However, there is also evidence that as particular gender stereotypes are refuted, new ones may develop to replace them. As Reskin and Hartmann (1986:65–66) explain, "A single woman worker who violates the stereotype can be explained as an exception; when the behavior of many women clearly belies a particular stereotype, a different one may emerge to maintain the gender homogeneity with which members of an occupation have become comfortable." Ironically, traits or behaviors admired in workers of one sex may be negatively redefined when exhibited by workers of the opposite sex so as to make the latter fit the stereotyped image. Box 8.3 provides some examples.

Although attitudes and stereotypes appear fairly resilient, change is not impossible. One important method of bringing about change is the enactment of legislation. Several laws were enacted during the past three decades in an effort to remedy workplace sex segregation and its consequences, especially the wage gap. However, as we shall learn next, there frequently has been a disparity between the written law and the law in action.

Legislation for Equality in the Workplace

Until the 1960s, the legal system functioned largely to reinforce gender discrimination in the workplace, rather than to remedy it. For the most part, law and judicial actions simply codified widespread gender stereotypes about women's innate weaknesses, which as Justice Bradley argued in 1872, "unfits [women] for many of the occupations of civil life" (*Bradwell* v. *Illinois* 1872). Legislators and judges maintained that women were a "special class" of citizens in need of protection: "That her physical structure and a proper discharge of her maternal functions— having in view not merely her own health, but the well-being of the race—justify legislation to protect her from the greed as well as the passion of man" (*Muller* v. *Oregon,* 1908). Consequently, most states enacted laws restricting women's working hours and the kind of work women could do. In many states, for instance, women were prohibited from working at night or from performing a work task that involved lifting more than a prescribed maximum weight. Other states forbade employers from hiring women for jobs ruled dangerous or morally corrupting

---

BOX 8.3   How to Tell a Business Man from a Business Woman

A businessman is aggressive; a businesswoman is pushy.

A businessman is good with details; a businesswoman is picky.

He loses his temper because he's so involved in his job; she's a bitch.

When he's depressed or hungover, everyone tiptoes past his office. If she's moody, it must be her time of the month.

He follows through; she doesn't know when to quit.

He's confident; she's conceited.

He stands firm; she's hard.

His judgments are her prejudices.

He's a man of the world; she's been around.

If he drinks it's because of job pressures; she's a lush.

He's never afraid to say what he thinks; she's always shooting off her mouth.

He exercises authority diligently; she's power mad.

He's closed-mouthed; she's secretive.

He's a stern task master; she's hard to work for.

He climbed the ladder of success; she slept her way to the top.

Source: Doyle 1983:154.

(e.g., bartending). Initially, a variety of reform groups, including suffrage and feminist organizations, endorsed protective labor laws in the belief that they would benefit women workers, but as the decades passed, it became clear that such legislation usually served to severely restrict women's employment (Christensen 1988; Babcock, et al. 1975).

In the 1960s, owing largely to the efforts of the feminist and civil rights movements, the federal government acted to outlaw sex discrimination in employment. The first important piece of legislation in this regard is **Title VII of the 1964 Civil Rights Act.** Title VII forbids discrimination in hiring, benefits, and other personnel decisions (such as promotions or layoffs) on the basis of sex, race, color, national origin, or religion, by employers of fifteen or more employees. There are, though, a few exceptions permitted by the law. For instance, an employer may hire an employee on the basis of sex (or religion or national origin, but never race or color) if the employer can demonstrate that this is a *bona fide occupational qualification* (BFOQ), that is, a qualification "reasonably necessary to the normal operation of that particular business or enterprise." However, since the courts have interpreted the BFOQ exception narrowly, there are few occupations to which it applies (Christensen 1988: Babcock, et al. 1975). According to guidelines issued with the law, for example, sex is considered a bona fide occupational qualification in those instances where authenticity and genuineness are required, such as roles for actors and actresses (Kay 1988). Title VII has been implemented and enforced by the Equal Employment Opportunity Commission (EEOC), which can bring suit on behalf of an employee or class of employees who have been discriminated against by their employer. It is estimated that an average of 50,000 new charges of discrimination are filed with the EEOC each year (Reskin and Hartmann 1986).

A second important federal anti-discrimination policy is **Executive Order 11246,** better known as **Affirmative Action,** which was amended in 1968 to prohibit sex discrimination in addition to discrimination on the basis of race, color, national origin, and religion. Executive Order 11246 applies to employers who hold contracts with the federal government. It provides that such contracts can be terminated and employers barred from future contracts if discrimination is found. But Executive Order 11246 goes beyond the mere prohibition of employment discrimination by requiring employers to take affirmative actions to recruit, train, and promote women and minorities. Since 1978, contractor compliance has been monitored by the Office of Federal Contract Compliance (OFCCP) in the Department of Labor. Besides this enforcement agency, the U.S. Department of Justice may also bring suit against discriminating employers, although it has rarely done so (Babcock, et al. 1975).

The impact of both Title VII and Executive Order 11246 is visible and far-reaching. Peruse the "want ads" of your local newspaper and you will see one result: employers may no longer advertise sex-labeled or sex-specific jobs. Employers also may not use customer preference as a justification for sex discrimination. For instance, in *Diaz* v. *Pan American World Airways, Inc.* (1971), the Fifth Circuit Court ruled that men could not be denied employment as flight attendants on the ground that passengers expect and prefer women in this job (*see also* (*Wilson* v. *Southwest Airlines Co.,* 1983). In addition, employers may not: utilize sex-based seniority lists; administer discriminatory pre-employment selection tests; set different retirement ages for workers of each sex; utilize double standards of employment, such as policies requiring only female employees to remain unmarried; penalize women workers who have children; or discriminate on the basis of pregnancy (Christensen 1988; Reskin and Hartmann 1986; Renzetti 1983; Thomas 1982). Under these regulations, the courts have also struck down most state protective labor laws and have ruled that sexual harassment is a form of employment discrimination.

Research indicates that these laws have helped to reduce workplace sex segregation and its consequences. For example, "when the EEOC pursued systemic cases involving large employers, the visibility of such cases presumably had a deterrent effect, and, in fact, a survey of major employers revealed that managerial awareness of enforcement efforts at other companies was positively related to having effective programs to enhance women employees' opportunities at their own companies" (Reskin and Hartmann 1986:84). What puzzles us, however, is why, more than twenty-five years after the passage of this legislation, workplace sex segregation is still pervasive.

At least part of the solution to this paradox lies with the limitations of the laws and the inconsistency with which they have been enforced. For one thing, Title VII and Executive Order 11246 define employment discrimination in limited, but complex terms, leading judges to arrive at varying interpretations of both these regulations and appropriate affirmative measures to remedy past discrimination (Greene 1989). For instance, in 1984, the U.S. Supreme Court ruled that judges cannot order preferential treatment of women or racial minorities to protect them from job layoffs if an employer utilizes a legitimate seniority system. Subsequently, however, many federal judges interpreted this opinion narrowly as applying only to layoffs. In 1985, the Supreme Court ruled in *Johnson* v. *Transportation Agency of Santa Clara County* that employers may give preference to employees on the basis of sex or race "as long as the purpose is to erase a 'manifest imbalance in traditionally segregated job categories' " (*New York Times* 29 March 1987:1E). Some observers have argued that this opinion did more to cloud the issue than to clarify it.

In 1989, the Court handed down two 5–4 decisions that civil rights experts have argued will seriously limit the further progress of affirmative action and other anti-discrimination employment legislation. In one case, *Ward's Cove Packing Company* v. *Atonio,* the Court ruled that employees must prove that specific employment practices of their employers caused sex or racial discrimination in their employment. The Court also made it easier for employers to defend themselves against charges of sex or race discrimination. In effect, this decision reverses eighteen years of anti-discrimination employment guidelines which the Court itself established. In a second case, *Martin* v. *Wilks,* the Court gave white males who claim to be adversely affected by affirmative action programs new authority to challenge those plans in court by filing "reverse discrimination" suits. The impact of this decision is expected to be a curtailment of affirmative action programs, especially by government agencies where, we have noted, they have been most successful in the past. Recognizing the potential negative consequences of these decisions, Congress attempted to modify them by passing the Civil Rights Act of 1990, but President Bush vetoed the legislation.

It is also significant that lawsuits brought under the anti-discrimination regulations discussed here, particularly Title VII class action suits, are typically complex and may drag on for a number of years before a settlement is reached (Reskin and Hartmann 1986). Consider, for example, the recently decided case *EEOC* v. *Sears, Roebuck and Co.* (1986). Sears was first charged in 1973 with discriminating against women in hiring for and promotion to commission sales positions, but the case was not heard until 1984. During this eleven-year delay, at least two relevant changes took place. First, Sears instituted an affirmative action program in 1974 that helped increase the number of women in commission sales jobs by the time the case was actually heard (although the EEOC maintained that Sears continued to discriminate between 1974 and 1980). Second, the administration of the federal government shifted to the political right. The conservative Reagan administration voiced its opposition to class action suits such as the *Sears* case, favoring instead cases in which individual victims of discrimination could be identified. The director of the EEOC in 1984 was a Reagan appointee who himself openly supported the administration's position. The federal district judge who eventually decided the case *in favor of Sears* was also a Reagan appointee (Madden and Erikson 1987; Cooper 1986; Lewin 1986; Milkman 1986).

This latter issue is important, too, because it alerts us to the fact that law enforcement is directly influenced by changes in government and political climate. This point is underscored by available statistics on funding and staffing at the agencies responsible for Title VII and Executive Order 11246. Between 1977 and 1981, the EEOC, with an increased budget and staff along with the adoption of more efficient procedures, reduced a huge backlog of cases while simultaneously increasing case settlements and lowering the number of cases dismissed for no cause. In 1981, however, the Reagan administration cut the EEOC's budget and staff with the result that the settlement rate dropped from 43 percent in 1980 to 28 percent by 1983, while the no-cause dismissal rate rose from 29 percent to 43 percent during the same period. The total number of suits filed by the EEOC was halved by 1983. A similar pattern is found at the OFCCP with a similar outcome: "Less thorough attention is given to an increased number of cases. The agency has decreased its use of its more stringent enforcement tools" (Reskin and Hartmann 1986:87; Burbridge 1984).

Clearly, then, while Title VII and Executive Order 11246 have made visible dents in our society's discriminatory work structure, the effects of these policies have been limited for at least two reasons. First, the inherent weaknesses and complexities of the laws themselves promote lengthy litigation with sometimes negative consequences; they also give judges considerable discretion, which frequently produces contradictory decisions in obviously similar cases. Second, and more significantly, these policies, like all public policies, are vulnerable to political change. Given the antifeminism and hostility to affirmative action displayed by the Reagan administration, it is not surprising that the modest, but hard-won employment gains of the 1960s and 1970s were eroded during the 1980s. The Bush administration has provided no indication that this trend will be reversed during the first half of the 1990s.

A note about other anti-discrimination laws   We have focused here on laws that primarily address the problem of workplace sex segregation. Since we know that workplace sex segregation contributes to the male/female wage gap, we may expect that laws designed to remedy the former will also have a positive impact on the latter and, indeed, there is evidence to support this hypothesis (Reskin and Hartmann 1986). But the wage gap has also been attacked directly by legislation that outlaws discriminatory pay policies. Perhaps the best known and most frequently utilized law of this type is the **Equal Pay Act of 1963.**

The Equal Pay Act prohibits employers from paying employees of one sex more than employees of the opposite sex when these employees are engaged in work that requires equal skill, effort, and responsibility and that is performed under similar working conditions. This prohibition extends to other forms of discrimination in compensation, such as overtime. However, pay need not be equal if the difference is based on employees' relative seniority, merit, the quantity or quality of their production, or "any other factor other than sex" such as the profitability of their work (Christensen 1988; Thomas 1982).

The courts have determined that the work performed by employees of the opposite sex does not have to be identical to require equal pay, but must only be *substantially equal.* In addition, the courts have ruled that employers may not justify unequal pay for their male and female workers by creating artificial job classifications that do not substantially differ in content. The major difficulty with the Equal Pay Act, however, is that it "does not prohibit sex segregated employment, with higher paying positions reserved for men, but only requires equal pay for substantially equal work assignments once the men and women are hired" (Thomas 1982:209). The benefits of a law designed to provide equal pay for equal work are limited, therefore, if, as we have found, men and women are largely segregated into different jobs and predominantly female jobs are systematically devalued.

Of course, it is for this reason that women workers and others have increasingly called for comparable worth, which we defined earlier as equal pay for different jobs of similar value. Since 1985, several comparable worth cases have been brought on behalf of women workers, but in general, the courts have not looked favorably upon comparable worth as a means to remedy gender inequities in pay. According to Christensen (1988:340), their reluctance is due to two reasons: they do not wish "to punish employers who rely on the market in setting wages and who are not individually responsible for societal discrimination" and they do not wish "to become involved in trying to evaluate the worth of different jobs."

The first, and probably the most well known comparable worth suit was *AFSCME* v. *State of Washington.* In 1983, a federal district judge ruled in this case that the state of Washington had discriminated against its female employees who worked in female-dominated jobs by paying them less than male employees who worked in comparable, but male-dominated jobs. The state appealed, however, and subsequently won the case in 1985, when the Ninth Circuit Court of Appeals ruled that "comparable worth is not a viable theory under our present laws and that employers are not required to remedy societal wage disparities that they did not create" (Christensen 1988:341). Nevertheless, the state did agree to make pay equity adjustments in its female employees' salaries. Washington and Minnesota both have laws requiring the implementation of comparable worth, but only in public sector employment.

Although we must wait for more definitive evaluations of the impact of comparable worth, preliminary research indicates that it may make a significant contribution to closing the wage gap between male and female workers (Hartmann 1985). It is unlikely to be adopted widely, however, given the open hostility voiced by recent federal administrations and agencies toward it (Christensen 1988). Importantly, though, some analysts caution against seeing comparable worth, as well as Title VII and affirmative action, as panaceas for solving gender inequality in the workplace. Steinberg and Cook's (1988:326) conclusions in this regard are worth quoting at length:

> [E]qual employment requires more than guaranteeing the right to equal access, the right to equal opportunity for promotion, or the right to equal pay for equal, or even comparable worth. Additionally, it warrants a broader policy orientation encompassing social welfare laws that assume equality within the family; widespread use of alternative work arrangements that accommodate the complexities of family life within two-earner families; and a rejuvenated union movement, with female leadership more active at work sites in defending the rights of women workers. Social welfare laws, family policy, and government services must create incentives toward a more equal division of responsibilities for family and household tasks between men and women. Increasing child care facilities, as well as maintaining programs to care for the elderly, would help alleviate some of the more pressing demands made on adults in families. . . . This also means that tax policy, social security laws, and pension programs must be amended to make government incentives to family life consistent with a family structure in which husbands and wives are equal partners.

Few countries have even attempted such ambitious reforms, let alone been successful in implementing them. However, in socialist societies, policies such as these have been set as goals at least in terms of official rhetoric; realizing them, as we will see next, has proved difficult at best.

CAN SOCIALISM LIBERATE WOMEN?

The preceding discussion highlights some of the problems inherent in attempts to legislate equality in the workplace. There are, though, a number of countries that have pursued this strategy more aggressively than the United States. Among them are socialist societies, and their approach to the "woman question" is useful in developing a thorough understanding of the relationships among gender, employment, and economies.

Writing more than a century ago, Karl Marx and Frederick Engels recognized women as an oppressed and exploited group. Their plan for women's liberation depended upon women's mass participation in the paid labor force and a concomitant decline in the time they spent on unremunerated household tasks (Engels 1942). Consequently, in countries that have adopted some form of socialism—for example, the Soviet Union, various Eastern European nations, Cuba, the People's Republic of China, and several African countries—political leaders have promoted these goals and have even codified them into law. Available evidence, however, indicates that in practice, most countries have found this easier said than done.

It is certainly the case that in most socialist societies, women make up a significant proportion of the paid labor force. For example, "one of the most striking features of the Soviet economy is the number of women in waged labor and their central position not only in the industrial and professional work force but in agriculture as well" (Croll 1981a:375; Bystydzienski 1989; Gray 1989). Still, nearly half of all Soviet women workers are unskilled manual laborers or low-skilled industrial workers, and despite their high representation in the labor force, they are concentrated in fields labeled "women's work" in Soviet society (e.g., teaching, medicine, child care, food processing, janitorial work, highway construction, and warehouse work) (Gray 1989). Even in the professions, women are concentrated at the lower levels and have little representation in decision-making positions. For example, more than 80 percent of school teachers are women, but two thirds of school superintendents are men. Seventy percent of engineers and skilled technical workers are women, but 94 percent of the work collectives' leadership posts are held by men (Gray 1989; Andors 1983).

It appears that, as in the United States, those jobs considered to be women's work in the Soviet Union are systematically devalued. For instance, most people in the United States are impressed by the fact that the majority of Soviet physicians (about 77 percent) are women. However, in contrast to the United States, the medical profession in the Soviet Union has little prestige and physicians there are overworked and underpaid, each typically tending to thirty patients a day for a relatively low salary. Most physicians, in fact, cannot afford to hold just one job (Morgan 1980).

Indeed, in most socialist societies, despite laws requiring equal pay for equal work, female workers on average are paid less than male workers. In Poland, for instance, women earn about 60 percent of what men earn; in the Soviet Union, their wages are 65 to 70 percent of male wages (Bystydzienski 1989; Gray 1989). The earnings gap between women and men holds for both the industrial and agricultural sectors and is true regardless of the criteria used to evaluate specific jobs (Holland 1985; Andors 1983; Croll 1981b; Scott 1974). Thus, it appears that in these societies, too, there is a dual labor market. Although the specific jobs that constitute the secondary labor market are often different from those in the United States, they share similar characteristics—low wages, poor working conditions, little opportunity for advancement, and few benefits—and they are dominated by women.

Even more resistant to change than the gender division of labor in paid employment has been the gender division of labor in the home (Gray 1989; Holland 1985; Mamanova 1984). To free women from domestic chores and thus facilitate their labor force participation, many socialist societies initially attempted to socialize housework and child care by opening public nurseries, dining rooms, and other services. Unfortunately, such programs quickly became prohibitively expensive for governments with limited resources and developing or underdeveloped economies. As a result, housework and child care remain primarily the responsibilities of social- ist women in addition to their paid employment. The average working mother in the Soviet Union, for instance, spends about forty hours per week shopping, preparing meals, cleaning house, and doing laundry, whereas the average Soviet working man spends less than five hours per week on domestic chores, doing mostly shopping (Gray 1989). As Croll (1981b:367) discovered:

> [These women] shoulder a "double burden" and experience evident tensions in combining the dual, and often conflicting, demands that productive and repro- ductive activities place on their time and energies. This conflict is perhaps sharpest in the Soviet Union where women have been exhorted both to enter into production on a full-time basis and to have more children to counter the declining birth rate. To mitigate this conflict, the governments of the Soviet Union, China, and Cuba have frequently taken steps to reduce slightly the demands made on women in the collective labor force (for example, requiring fewer labor days per month or year or fewer hours per day), but in each case these policies have ultimately discriminated against and financially penalized women in the productive sector.

This double work load has led some analysts to conclude that socialist women are not more liberated than their sisters in capitalist societies, just more tired (Gray 1989; Scott 1974).

In most socialist countries, the government has made little effort to encour- age men to participate in household work short of exhortations now and then. An exception, though, is Cuba, where in 1975, the Family Code was adopted, making men legally responsible for an equal share of housework and child care. The Cuban strategy is an interesting one in that it tries to dissolve the gendered division of labor by requiring an alteration in men's personal lives, rather than by placing a drain on the national budget. Men have resisted this law, however, and recent research shows that they have not assumed family responsibilities on an equal footing with women (Nazzari 1983).

Their reluctance stems in part from the persistence of sexist prejudices, but it is also a result of certain economic constraints inherent in Cuban society. More specifically, although Cuba has a policy of guaranteed employment for all of its citizens, a severe job shortage has meant that, in practice, jobs are available primarily to men and to female heads of households. Other women are hired only as needed, causing them to be treated as "reserve labor," which depresses their wages and increases their economic dependence on men. This problem is com- pounded by the contradiction between the country's maternity law and the require- ment that business enterprises show an annual profit. Employers must provide pregnant workers with a fully paid leave of absence six weeks before and twelve weeks after childbirth, but the dent this policy makes in profits actually acts as an incentive for hiring men over women (Nazzari 1983). Like their sisters in the United States, then, unemployed and underemployed Cuban women do not have the economic leverage in their families to force their spouses to do an equal share of the domestic chores.

The Cuban experience is certainly not unique. Among the socialist nations of Africa, for example, one finds that the serious problems of economic underdevelopment, coupled with ethnic customs and Islamic religious traditions, work against the enforcement of laws that have been passed in women's interests (Renzetti and Curran 1986). The question remains, then, can socialism liberate women workers? In light of our brief discussion, the answer appears to be an uncommitted maybe, rather than a definitive yes or no. "While levels of participation in the labor force . . . have increased significantly for women [in socialist societies], they are not equal to those of men. Nor has there been any significant reduction of the sexual division of labor within the family" (Andors 1983:7). This is due at least in part to the resilience of sexist prejudices and customs in these countries, but it is also the result of serious economic constraints that have made women's liberation a noble, but unrealistically expensive goal. As Scott (1974:208) concluded in her study of the status of women in Czechoslovakia:

> The abolition of private ownership of the means of production does not bring about the end of the single family as the economic unit of society, nor the transformation of private housekeeping into a social industry. Even when the best intentions are present, there must also be an economic base sufficiently strong to assume those economic functions. . . . So far no socialist country has met these conditions.

Still, we must be cautious in concluding that women's liberation will necessarily follow from economic development in socialist societies. In the Soviet Union, for instance, current development efforts include *glasnost* or an openness to other societies and cultures. One byproduct of this openness, however, has been a glorification of traditional women's roles in the West and the inauguration of Western-style beauty pageants, complete with swimsuit and evening gown competitions. Consequently, the effects of economic development on women's status in the Soviet Union and other socialist countries is yet to be determined.

THE INTERSECTION OF HOME AND THE WORK WORLD

Our discussion of the difficulties faced by women workers in socialist societies highlights one of the major themes of this and the preceding chapter: the interrelationship between family life and the work world. Men and women possess different levels of power in the family, with women typically being the less powerful partners. In Chapter 7, we learned that differences in power between intimate partners are directly related to differences in their income and other resources.

The work women do in the home is unremunerated and, therefore, not even regarded as "real" work. As we saw in this chapter, however, the division of labor in the home also often constrains women's opportunities to earn outside income.

For one thing, since employed women continue to bear primary responsibility for housework and child care, they shoulder a double work load compared with employed men, but receive fewer rewards. The unavailability of adequate and affordable child care, we have learned, is a major obstacle to employment for many women. But regardless of their objective circumstances, the widespread belief among employers and co-workers that "a woman's place is in the home" serves to justify discrimination against women in hiring, promotion, and other employment-related opportunities. In fact, the evidence discussed in this chapter shows that persistent stereotypes about women's and men's "appropriate" roles reinforce and perpetuate workplace sex segregation and its attendant consequences, including the male/female earnings gap. The prevailing assumption seems to remain that the public world of work is men's domain, whereas the private world of home belongs to women. If women are in the labor force, their employment is secondary to that of men. From our discussions in Chapters 7 and 8, we know that these assumptions are patently false. We know, too, that both women and men suffer negative consequences from blind adherence to them.

Legislation such as Title VII, Executive Order 11246, and the Equal Pay Act is designed to protect workers of both sexes and racial minorities. It has, in fact, primarily benefitted white women as well as men of color. Although this legislation has fallen far short of equalizing the job opportunities and salaries available to female and male workers, and among workers of different racial groups, there is evidence that when it is stringently enforced, it can help to lessen employment inequities. Still, this legislation was not designed to alter the gender division of unpaid household labor. Since we know that this is directly tied to sex-based employment discrimination, we cannot expect women or men to be free to choose the work that best suits them as individuals unless the simultaneous elimination of both these inequities becomes a central goal of our nation's public policy.

KEY TERMS

comparable worth   the policy of paying workers equally when they perform different jobs that have similar value

dissimilarity index (segregation index)   a measure of occupational sex segregation, reported in percent, that indicates the proportion of workers of one sex that would have to change to jobs in which members of their sex were underrepresented to achieve a balanced occupational distribution between the sexes

dual labor market   a labor market characterized by one set of jobs employing almost exclusively men and another set of jobs, typically lower paying with lower prestige, employing almost exclusively women

economy   the system for the management and development of a society's human and material resources

Equal Pay Act of 1963   forbids employers from paying employees of one sex more than employees of the opposite sex when these employees are engaged in work that requires equal skill, effort, and responsibility and is performed under similar working conditions, although exceptions, such as unequal pay based on seniority, merit, the quality or quantity of production, or any other factor besides sex, are allowed

Executive Order 11246 (Affirmative Action)   forbids federal contractors from discriminating in personnel decisions on the basis of sex, as well as race, color, national origin, and religion, and requires employers to take affirmative measures to recruit, train, and hire women and minorities; since 1978, implemented and enforced by the OFFCP

human capital theory   explains occupational sex segregation in terms of women's free choice to work in jobs that make few demands on workers and require low personal investment in training or skills acquisition based on the assumption that women's primary responsibility is in the home

occupational sex segregation   the degree to which men and women are concentrated in occupations that employ workers of predominantly one sex

Title VII of the 1964 Civil Rights Act   forbids discrimination in employment on the basis of sex, race, color, national origin, or religion, by employers of fifteen or more employees, although exceptions, such as the BFOQ, are allowed; implemented and enforced by the EEOC

SUGGESTED READINGS

Gray, F.D. 1989. *Soviet Women: Walking the Tightrope.* New York: Doubleday.

Kessler-Harris, A. 1990. *A Woman's Wage: Historical Meanings and Social Consequences.* Lexington, KY: University Press of Kentucky.

Miller, D.C. 1990. *Women and Social Welfare: A Feminist Analysis.* New York: Praeger.

Ozawa, M.N. (Ed.) 1989. *Women's Life Cycle and Economic Insecurity.* New York: Praeger.

Reskin, B.F., and H.I. Hartmann (Eds.) 1986. *Women's Work, Men's Work: Sex Segregation on the Job.* Washington, D.C.: National Academy Press.

Zavella, P. 1987. *Women's Work and Chicano Families.* Ithaca, NY: Cornell University Press.

Chapter 9

Gender, Crime, and Justice

Equality before the law is a constitutional guarantee in the United States. Yet, we know from our discussions so far that the laws of our land have allowed—indeed, even prescribed—discriminatory treatment of different groups of citizens. Women, for example, were historically defined by law as men's property and were systematically denied their civil rights, including the right to vote. In fact, in 1894, the U.S. Supreme Court ruled that women were not "persons" under the law. The case, *In re Lockwood,* was heard on appeal from the State of Virginia where Belva A. Lockwood had been denied a license to practice as an attorney even though state law permitted any "person" licensed as an attorney in any other state to practice in Virginia. The Supreme Court upheld a lower court opinion that the word "person" meant "male." Consequently, "from 1894 until 1971 states could maintain that women were not legally 'persons' by virtue of this single Supreme Court decision" (Hoff-Wilson 1987:8; Sachs and Wilson 1978).

Most of the court cases we discuss in this text fall within the realm of civil law, that is, "the body of law concerned with resolving private conflicts, particularly those concerning private property such as contracts, as well as divorce, child support, and so on" (Sokoloff and Price 1982:18). In this chapter, however, we will focus on gender and *criminal law.* Criminal law "applies to acts which are considered so serious and important to the general welfare that the state initiates prosecution" (Sokoloff and Price 1982:18). In other words, the violation of a criminal law is viewed, in theory at least, as a transgression against society as well as against an individual citizen.

What gets defined in law as criminal, though, does not necessarily represent the interests of all segments of society. Rather, criminal law typically represents the interests of lawmakers. Historically, those who have had the power to make laws in the United States have been wealthy white men (*see* Chapter 10). Not surprisingly, therefore, the experiences of women and men in the criminal justice system tend to be different. Compounding these sex differences are differences in race, social class, age, and sexual preference.

This chapter begins with a discussion of men and women as offenders. First, we will examine men's and women's relative crime rates. In addition, we will address their differential processing through the criminal justice system—from arrest to prosecution to conviction to sentencing to imprisonment. In studying the administration of justice, we will also have the opportunity to discuss issues pertaining to men's and women's roles as criminal justice professionals. Finally, we will conclude the chapter by examining differences in the criminal victimization of men and women, with special attention given to sexual assault and other violent crimes against women.

WOMEN AND MEN AS OFFENDERS

Among the questions most often addressed by criminologists, two in particular seem most relevant to our present discussion: Who commits crime? and Why?

There Oughtn't Be A Law   **BOX 9.1**

Historically, the laws of our land, rather than ensuring the liberty of all citizens, have often served to unfairly restrict it for some, particularly the liberty of female citizens. The following is a list of laws—some still on the books, but none any longer enforced—compiled from the statutes of cities and towns throughout the United States. We wonder how many of these laws our female readers have broken:

A Dyersburg, Tennessee, law prohibits women from phoning men for dates.

In Oxford, Ohio, women are prohibited from undressing in front of a photograph of a man.

In Providence, Rhode Island, a law forbids women from wearing transparent clothing, including silk and nylon stockings.

If a woman leaves her husband in Michigan, the law permits him to follow her and publicly remove her clothes, piece by piece, because they are his property.

And in Kentucky, a female cannot appear on a public highway wearing a bathing suit unless she is accompanied by at least two officers or is armed with a club. However, this statute does not apply to "females weighing less than 96 pounds, nor exceeding 200 pounds; nor shall it apply to female horses."

Even though such laws seem ridiculous to us now, they demonstrate how the law can be used not only to restrict the liberty of some citizens, but also to impose a double standard of morality—one standard for women, another for men. In this chapter we will learn how the law and the criminal justice system continue to uphold this double standard by their differential treatment of female and male criminals and crime victims.

Source: Miles 1983:24.

Traditionally, a common response to the first question has been men, especially young men. Indeed, a careful survey of criminological research conducted prior to the mid-1970s would probably lead you to conclude that women are rarely criminal. The little attention that was given to female offenders was largely limited to three contexts: (1) comparisons to underscore women's low crime rates relative to those of men; (2) studies of prostitution; and (3) analyses of the depravity of violent women, the rationale being that since "normal" women are passive, the few women who do commit violent crimes must be "sick" (Edwards 1986). Clearly, in the minds of criminologists and the general public, "criminal" was equated with "male".

In 1975, however, this perception began to change, owing largely to the publication of two books—Freda Adler's *Sisters in Crime* and Rita James Simon's *Women and Crime* —each of which received widespread attention in both the academic and popular presses. A central theme in both books is that women's crime had begun to change both in its nature and in the number of offenses committed. In fact, according to Adler, the United States at that time was in the midst of a female crime wave. Although men were still committing a greater absolute number of offenses, the female crime *rate* was increasing more than the male crime rate. Thus, for example, Adler cites statistics from the F.B.I. *Uniform Crime Reports* (UCR) that show that between 1960 and 1972, women's arrest rates for robbery increased 277 percent compared with a 169 percent increase for men. Statistics on juvenile offenders revealed similar changes. What is more, Adler argued that females were not only engaged in more crime than previously but also their criminal activity had assumed a more serious and violent character: women were committing crimes that traditionally had been committed by men. In this respect, Simon's work closely resembles Adler's, with the exception that Simon saw the increase in women's crime limited primarily to property offenses rather than violent crimes against persons. Still, she maintained that women were committing more crimes generally characterized as masculine, particularly white-collar and occupationally related offenses such as fraud and embezzlement.

These claims did not cause the greatest stir, however. Indeed, what received the most attention, especially from the popular media, were Adler's and Simon's explanations of their findings. Specifically, both argued that the changes they uncovered in the rate and character of female crime were logical outcomes of the women's liberation movement. As Adler (1975:10) phrased it, "Is it any wonder that once women were armed with male opportunities they should strive for status, criminal as well as civil, through established male hierarchical channels?" Simon's position was a bit more complex. She argued that violent crimes by women had actually decreased because of feminism. "As women feel more liberated physically, emotionally, and legally, and less subjected to male power, their frustrations and anger decrease . . . [which results] in a decline in their desire to kill the usual objects of their anger or frustration: their husbands, lovers, and other men upon whom they are dependent, but insecure about" (Simon 1976:40). The down side, however, is that the feminist movement, by encouraging women's participation in the paid labor force, had also contributed to the rise in female property crime. "As women increase their participation in the labor force their opportunity to commit certain types of crime [e.g. white-collar and occupational crimes] also increases" (Simon 1976:40). Because of its emphasis on the women's movement, Adler's and Simon's perspective has become known as the **emancipation theory** of female crime.

Actually, this argument is not totally new; as Meda Chesney-Lind (1986:78) points out, "Since the 1800s, criminologists have been issuing warnings that the emancipation of women would result in a dramatic change in the character and frequency of women's crime." What is of greatest value in Adler's and Simon's work is that it forced a contemporary reassessment of the relationship between gender and participation in criminal activity. In critiquing Alder and Simon, subsequent analyses shed light on the extent to which female crime had actually changed in recent years, and the degree to which the women's movement may have contributed to such a change.

One of the most serious weaknesses in both Adler's and Simon's work is their reliance on official crime statistics. First, "it is well known that these official records are not a true representation of criminal behavior; there are many omissions, an overemphasis on certain types of offenses and an under-representation of white-collar crime. In addition, there are the influences and modifications in policing and prosecution policies and the effects of moral panics on particular crime rate figures" (Smart 1982:108). A second difficulty stems from the way Adler, in particular, utilizes the UCR data. In comparing male and female rates of increase for specific crimes, she fails to control for the large difference in the absolute base numbers from which the rates of increase are calculated. Consequently, if one base figure is small, even a slight rise will exaggerate the rate change. Conversely, a sizeable increase in a large base figure is likely to appear as only a minor change (Smart 1982; Terry 1978). An example should make the point clearer. Between 1965 and 1970, the number of arrests of women for homicide increased almost 79 percent; during the same period, the number of homicide arrests for men increased 73 percent. However, in absolute terms, the number of homicides committed by women rose from 1,293 to 1,645, whereas for men, the figures were 6,533 and 8,858 respectively. Clearly, if we look only at percent changes without taking into account these major absolute base differences, we end up with a very distorted picture of men's and women's involvement in crime.

A more accurate measure of changes in men's and women's criminal activity is to calculate sex-specific arrest rates, that is, the number of men arrested for a crime per 100,000 of the male population and the number of women arrested for the same crime per 100,000 of the female population. Subsequently, the sex differential in arrest rates can be determined by calculating women's share of all arrests, male and female, for a specific offense. In a careful analysis using this method, Steffensmeier (1982:120–121) discovered that for the period from 1965 to 1980, "in the majority of offense categories the sex differential has remained stable. Figures for this period also demonstrate the *parallel* changes, in arrest rates of males and females over the past decade." In other words, "relative to males, the profile of the female offender has not changed." Moreover, additional data sources show a similarly stable pattern in reported delinquency among male and female adolescents.

In the area of property crime, though, Steffensmeier finds several exceptions to the generally stable sex differential in arrest rates. In particular, he reports that women's share of arrests for larceny increased significantly between 1965 and 1980, from 25.2 percent to 33.4 percent. Smaller, but also significant increases occurred in women's share of arrests for fraud, forgery, and embezzlement (although embezzlement arrests for both men and women are low). Given that Simon also found women's share of arrests for these crimes rising, we may ask to what extent the data support the contention that these are occupationally related offenses committed by "liberated" women in the labor force?

Evidence in response to this question derives from at least three sources. First, studies of female offenders reveal that they are "least likely to respond to ideologies of sex-role equality" (Sarri 1986:91). Rather, these women tend to be quite traditional in terms of gender orientations (Campbell 1984; Giordano and Cernkovich 1979; Crites 1976). In fact, Adler's (1975) own work indicated that female offenders often expressed a strong dislike of the women's movement and not infrequently considered feminists "kooks".

Second, as we saw in Chapter 8, although women's labor force participation has risen dramatically over the past two decades, women remain segregated in low prestige, low-paying clerical, sales, and service occupations. These are not the types of jobs that afford women workers opportunities to commit white-collar crimes, such as false advertising or product fraud. Nor are women well represented in blue-collar occupations such as truck driver, warehouse or dock worker, or delivery person, occupations that would provide them with opportunities for grand larceny, drug dealing, or the fencing of stolen merchandise (Steffensmeier 1982).

Finally, in his analysis, Steffensmeier (1982) found that increases in female crime are accounted for almost completely by rising female arrest rates for *petty property offenses,* including shoplifting, passing "bad checks," and engaging in credit card fraud. Importantly, these are crimes which women have traditionally committed and are unrelated to changes in their employment opportunities.

In sum, the claims of the emancipation theorists seem overstated at best. With the exception of petty property offenses, women have not made significant gains on male rates of crime, nor do they appear to be engaged in more violent, masculine, or serious offenses. Larceny-theft, which includes crimes traditionally committed by women (e.g., shoplifting), remains the crime for which females are arrested most often. In 1989, this offense alone accounted for 19 percent of all female arrests (U.S. Department of Justice 1990a). As Table 9.1 indicates, crime remains, for the most part, a male enterprise, virtually untouched by feminism and the women's movement. Eighty-two percent of those arrested in the United States in 1989 were males; males accounted for 89 percent of those arrested for violent crimes and 76 percent of those arrested for property crimes (U.S. Department of Justice 1990a). Recent research indicates, in fact, that most of the increase in arrests between 1960 and 1990 can be accounted for by the rise in arrests of fifteen to twenty-nine-year-old nonwhite males. Particularly in urban areas of the United States, it is this group that has for several decades dominated official arrest statistics, although the debate continues as to why this has been so. Is it because young black males are engaged in more criminal behavior than members of other demographic groups (Byrne and Sampson 1986)? Or, are they more susceptible to arrest and criminal justice processing because of their race

TABLE 9.1
Male and Female Arrest Rates by Offense Charged, United States, 1980–1989

Offense Charged	Males			Females		
	1980	*1989*	*% Change*	*1980*	*1989*	*% Change*
Murder & Non-negligent man-slaughter	11,148	12,434	11.5	1,588	1,676	5.5
Forcible rape	19,966	23,352	17.0	166	254	53.0
Robbery	95,427	101,385	6.2	7,394	9,567	29.4
Aggravated assault	158,131	242,399	53.3	22,252	36,553	64.3
Burglary	313,108	252,673	19.3	21,704	25,747	18.6
Larceny/Theft	542,147	660,274	21.8	227,248	297,334	30.8
Motor vehicle theft	87,859	129,483	47.4	8,327	14,424	73.2
Arson	11,337	9,853	−13.1	1,550	1,558	2.5
Total Index Crime*	1,239,123	1,431,853	15.6	290,229	387,143	33.4
Other Assaults	271,329	465,552	71.6	44,009	87,159	98.0
Forgery & counter-feiting	35,701	41,475	16.2	16.063	21,176	31.8
Fraud	110,133	124,713	13.2	78,017	102,570	31.5
Embezzlement	4,308	6,581	52.8	1,689	4,252	151.7
Stolen property (buying, receiv-ing, possessing)	77,936	103,302	32.5	9,056	13,632	50.5
Vandalism	151,996	166,520	9.6	14,391	20,435	42.0
Weapons	98,828	122,471	23.9	7,329	10,085	37.6
Prostitution & Com-mercialized vice	18,916	21,274	12.5	38,366	47,289	23.3
Drug abuse viola-tions	326,050	710,802	118.0	51,125	141,303	176.4
Gambling	26,913	10,831	−59.8	3,077	2,081	−32.4
Offenses against family/children	29,182	31,878	9.2	3,383	6,707	98.3
Driving under the influence	811,636	877,297	8.1	87,624	120,806	37.9
Drunkenness	698,853	463,305	−33.7	58,334	50,174	−14.0
Disorderly conduct	346,652	374,538	8.0	61,597	90,002	46.1
Vagrancy	19,216	19,924	3.7	2,714	2,745	1.1
All other offenses (except traffic)	979,416	1,531,171	56.3	166,654	292,207	75.3
Total Crime	5,608,028	6,950,843	23.9	1,044,420	1,544,336	47.9

*The Index Crimes are the eight crimes considered most serious by the F.B.I.
Source: U.S. Department of Justice, Federal Bureau of Investigation, 1990:177.

and sex? That is, do their higher arrest rates simply reflect racism and sexism inherent in the American criminal justice system (Flowers 1988)?

We will return to these questions shortly, but first we have the dramatic rise in female property crime to explain. Some researchers suggest that at least part of this increase is due to changes in consumption patterns in the United States and technological innovations in housework (Steffensmeier 1982). It has been argued that contemporary homemakers spend less time on traditional household chores (e.g., cleaning and cooking) and more time on managerial tasks, such as shopping and bill paying. In fact, it is estimated that 80 percent of the money spent on goods in the United States in spent by women (Glazer-Malbin 1976). Logically then, changes such as these might increase women's opportunities for shoplifting, credit card fraud, and bad-check passing. Unfortunately, evidence in support of this hypothesis is sparse and inconsistent. For instance, although the greatest increases in female arrests have been for shoplifting, it appears that the typical shoplifter is less likely than in the past to be a housewife (Silverman, et al. 1976). In addition, as we noted in Chapter 7, recent research indicates that women are spending as much and sometimes more time on housework than previous generations had (Ogden 1986; Cowan 1984). Technological innovations, moreover, have benefitted primarily middle and upper-class women. The fact that the vast majority of women processed through the criminal justice system are poor minority women makes this explanation less tenable.

A more plausible argument centers around the worsening economic conditions of women, especially minority women (Carlen 1988; Chapman 1980). In Chapters 7 and 8, we examined the increasing feminization of poverty, particularly among women of color who head households. Significantly, research indicates that the typical female offender is young, nonwhite, poor, a high school dropout, and an unmarried mother. "[S]ome researchers are now speculating that the severe economic discrimination all women confronted in the last decade was particularly hard on young, single, minority women, perhaps propelling them directly into property crimes" (Chesney-Lind 1986:94; Carlen 1988; Messerschmidt 1986; Chapman 1980). In other words, rising rates of female petty property crimes may be indicative of the increasingly difficult struggle for survival for some groups of women.

A third explanation holds that the rise in female arrest rates is simply an artifact of an increased willingness among criminal justice personnel to apprehend and prosecute women. Proponents of this argument contend that historically, police, attorneys, and judges have been reluctant to process women through the criminal justice system. Those women who were prosecuted were supposedly treated leniently or "chivalrously." However, the recent emphasis on gender equality in society could not help but penetrate the criminal justice system, with the result that male and female offenders are now more likely to be treated similarly.

This position, known as the **chivalry hypothesis,** rests on the assumption that traditionally female offenders have been afforded more leniency before the law than their male counterparts. To evaluate the chivalry hypothesis, therefore, we must examine the administration of justice in the United States.

WITH JUSTICE FOR ALL?

Criminologists emphasize that crime and criminals are, to a large extent, socially and legally produced or constructed. Edwin Schur (1984:224) explains:

> The production of "criminals" involves the creation of crime definitions by legislation, and the application of those definitions to particular persons through the various stages of criminal justice processing. At every stage decisions are being made by ordinary fallible, and sometimes biased human beings.

Thus, in assessing the issue of differential treatment of male and female offenders, one should first consider some of the relevant characteristics of those charged with administering justice.

The Administration of Justice

One of the most salient features of the criminal justice system in the United States is male dominance. Historically, the overwhelming majority of police, attorneys, judges, corrections officers, and other law enforcement personnel have been white men. As Table 9.2 indicates, the contemporary picture is much the same.

Traditionally, a variety of reasons were offered to justify the exclusion of women from careers in law. It was said, for instance, that women were too weak and timid to enforce the law or to serve as corrections officers. Others maintained that women were too emotional and sentimental, easy "push-overs." Still others claimed that women were too "good" or righteous for such work; shortly before the turn of the century, one judge said, "Our profession has essentially and habitually to do with all that is selfish and extortionate, knavish and criminal, coarse and brutal, repulsive and obscene. Nature has tempered women as little for the judicial conflicts of the courtroom as for the physical conflicts of the battlefield" (quoted in Reid 1987:225).

Of course, there were those who used similar arguments to promote women's involvement in law enforcement, the legal professions, and prison reform. It was argued, for example, that women would have a civilizing influence on the courtroom and the prison because of their "higher morality" and their innate need to help relieve the suffering of others. Interestingly, this conception of female morality and sentiment is still with us in scholarly as well as popular literature (Kerber, et al. 1986; Gilligan 1982). It also remains prevalent in law enforcement agencies and courtrooms throughout the country. For instance, studies indicate that police administrators' ratings of female officers are frequently colored by stereotypes of women as sympathetic, warm, and nonaggressive in

---

TABLE 9.2
Criminal Justice Personnel by Sex

Full-Time Police Officers (Sworn)	% Female (1989)
All agencies	8.3
(N = 12,218; population = 229,678,000)	
All cities	7.9
(N = 9,295; population = 153,189,000)	
Suburban counties	11.3
(# agencies = 667; population = 45,397,000)	
Rural counties	6.2
(# agencies = 2,256; population = 31,092,000)	
Suburban areas	8.3
(# agencies = 5,487; population = 92,021,000)	

Correctional Officers	% Female (1988)
All institutions	13.7

Judges (Federal)*	% Female (1986)*
Supreme Court	11.5**
Circuit Courts of Appeal	10.7
District Courts	10.7

Judges (State)*	% Female (1985)
Courts of last resort	6.8
Intermediate Appellate Courts	6.5
Other full-time courts	7.3

*Includes all judges in criminal and civil courts.
** Of a total of nine Supreme Court Justices, one is a woman, Sandra Day O'Connor.
Sources: Administrative Office of the United States Courts 1990; U.S. Department of Justice 1990a and b; Reid 1987; Rix 1987

---

contrast with the image of the male police officer as tough, authoritarian, and aggressive. Consequently, the administrators tend to rate female officers lower than male officers in terms of patrol effectiveness even though objective measures show the officers to be equally effective on patrol (Reid 1987; Townsey 1982). Female officers do seem to have a less aggressive style of policing than do their male counterparts in that they tend to use reason and verbal negotiation more often than physical force to resolve disputes and diffuse potentially violent situations (Price, et al. 1989). Although police administrators may view this negatively, evidence indicates that citizens hold a different view; women police are judged by citizens who have interacted with them as more competent, pleasant, and respectful than their male peers (Sichel, et al. 1977).

Similarly, studies of female guards in male correctional facilities reveal that women confront more resistance from prison administrators and male co-workers than from inmates.

> One study found that female guards were tested more often by male officers than by inmates, that male officers were uneasy and unaccepting of female officers in male prisons; and that male officers believed females were not physically strong enough for the job. . . . In spite of the negative attitudes in their work environment, it appears that female correctional officers are able to establish and maintain personal authority in a prison setting; they are not manipulated by inmates any more often than male officers (Reid 1987:428; Zimmer 1986; Owen 1985).

Women in more prestigious positions, female attorneys, for instance, are no less likely to escape such prejudices and discriminatory treatment. Recent research, in fact, demonstrates a pervasive bias against women in our nation's law firms and courtrooms (Gold 1989; Couric 1989; Morello 1986; Epstein 1981). For example, a 1989 report for the state of Massachusetts noted that female attorneys are three times more likely than male attorneys to be addressed by their first names or by terms of endearment which, the investigating committee found, affects the outcome of cases. In addition, it was reported that female litigants and witnesses are subjected to inappropriate comments, unwanted touching, and verbal harassment (Gold 1989). Similarly, a 1986 report by the New York Task Force on Women in the Courts concluded that "female lawyers were 'routinely' demeaned and treated patronizingly by male judges and attorneys. And it was found that the credibility of female witnesses was sometimes questioned because women were viewed by some judges as emotional and untrustworthy" (Schmalz 1986:1). Minority women often fare worse. As one black female attorney recently recounted, "I once appeared before a judge in Middlesex Superior Court [Massachusetts] who refused to address me until I showed proof that I was a lawyer, something not requested of any other attorney there that day" (quoted in the *New York Times* 10 August 1986:37).

To what extent, then, do such attitudes affect the disposition of cases? Do prejudices like these disadvantage male offenders by affording their female counterparts greater leniency before the law? Or are male offenders advantaged by sexism in the criminal justice system? As a preliminary response we can say that the sex of the offender does appear to play a part in the disposition of a case. However, a number of other factors interact with sex in producing certain outcomes. These include the offender's age and race as well as the offense with which he or she is charged and the number of previous criminal convictions. We can understand this better by comparing sentencing patterns for male and female offenders.

Do the Punishments Fit the Crimes?

Little more than a decade ago, criminologist Clayton Hartjen (1978:108) observed that, "Although a suspect's behavior is of primary importance in determining his or her chances of being arrested, in most cases the decision to arrest a person is based on factors that have little to do with the degree of a person's behavioral criminality. . . . It is not so much what a person does as what kind of person he [or she] is (or is seen by the police to be) that affects official labeling." Hartjen's argument can be extended to the practice of sentencing criminal offenders. Who or what kind of person the offender is perceived to be by the courts influences the sentence he or she receives. This leads to **sentencing disparity**: the imposition of different sentences on offenders convicted of similar crimes. Sentencing disparity is problematic because it typically results in unfair and inappropriate sentences. Sentences are then disproportionate to the severity of the crime or the offender's criminal history, and are based instead on irrelevant factors, such as the offender's sex and race.

Early studies of sentencing disparities between male and female offenders reported that women were given preferential treatment by the courts and were less likely than men to receive prison sentences for their crimes (Faine and Bohlander 1976; Nagel and Weitzman 1972). However, as Chesney-Lind (1986) points out, the difficulty with much of this early research is that it did not control for the less serious nature of female criminality. More recent research that takes into account such factors as type of offense and prior convictions has obtained inconsistent findings: certain groups of female offenders appear to be treated chivalrously, whereas others clearly are not.

One would expect seriousness of offense and prior record to be strong predictors of sentence severity, but research reveals that this is more often the case for male offenders than for female offenders (Butler and Lambert 1983; Figueira-McDonough 1982). Although women typically commit less serious crimes than men, they do not fare as well as men in negotiating or bargaining for sentence reductions. Women are as likely to receive severe sentences for property crimes as for violent crimes (Myers and Talarico 1986; Figueira-McDonough 1982), and when placed on probation, their probationary period is typically longer than that of men convicted of similar crimes (Gold 1989).

Other studies have found that perceived "respectability" of the offender in terms of conformity to traditional gender norms influences the sentencing of female offenders more than male offenders. For example, Nagel, et al. (1982) discovered that married women were less likely than single or "independent" women to be sentenced to prison. In this study, marital status was unrelated to sentencing for male offenders, but we will see shortly that additional research contradicts this finding. Kruttschnitt (1982) and others (Sarri 1986; Schur 1984; Armstrong 1982; Parisi 1982) report that women who appear to conform to a traditional model of femininity—for example, economic dependence on a man, no evidence of drug or alcohol use, no evidence of sexual deviance—tend to receive lighter sentences than women deemed less "respectable" by the courts. Daly (1989) refers to this pattern of bias in judicial decision making as *familial-based justice*. She reports that defendants with family ties, especially those who are the primary caregivers to children, are treated more leniently by the courts than nonfamilied defendants. Based on interviews with court officials, she concluded that the protection of families and children, not the protection of women, influences much judicial decision making. This may also help to explain the recent inclination of criminal justice officials to prosecute pregnant drug addicts for passing drugs to their unborn children (*see* Chapter 12).

The female prostitute, of course, represents in many ways the antithesis of respectable femininity. She is independent and promiscuous so, not surprisingly, she is the victim of routine harassment within the criminal justice system, but her customers, although also guilty of breaking the law, are rarely prosecuted (Schur 1984; James 1982). Unfortunately, there is very little data available on male prostitution, to a large extent because researchers have focused on prostitution as exclusively a female crime (for an exception, *see* Luckenbill 1986). However, given that male prostitutes violate our culture's gender prescriptions for men, they, too, might be treated more harshly than the average male offender. Clearly, research that compares their experiences at the hands of criminal justice officials with those of female prostitutes would add to our understanding of the impact of gender stereotyping on the processing of offenders.

The age of the offender is also an important variable. For instance, the mere suspicion of sexual impropriety typically results in more severe sentences for juvenile female offenders relative to their male counterparts. Girls are more likely than boys to be charged with **status offenses** —that is, behavior which if engaged in by an adult would not be considered a violation of the law. These include, for example, running away from home, incorrigibility, truancy, being a "person in need of supervision" (PINS), and being in danger of becoming "morally depraved".

> But more to the point, the function of these offense categories in female
> delinquency cases is to serve as "buffer charges" for suspected sexuality. . . .
> Even if juvenile justice personnel are not themselves concerned about sexual
> misconduct, the uncritical acceptance of familial authority represented by these
> offense categories means that parents, who may well be anxious to control a
> daughter's sexuality, will bring her to court for behavior that they would ignore or
> endorse in their sons (Chesney-Lind 1982:90–91).

Many young women charged as runaways are attempting to escape from physically and sexually abusive homes. However, because of the juvenile courts' commitment to preserving parental authority, they frequently have forced these girls to return to their abusers, routinely ignoring the girls' complaints about abuse. Ironically, then, "statutes that were originally placed in law to 'protect' young people have, in the case of girls' delinquency, criminalized their survival strategies" (Chesney-Lind 1989:24).

Females charged with status offenses are more harshly treated at every step of criminal justice processing and are more likely than males to be institutionalized for status offenses. In fact, "results also show that young women have longer average confinements than their male counterparts, even though the vast majority of the males (82%) were criminal offenders" (Chesney-Lind 1982:94).

Sentencing reforms intended to reduce such disparities have benefitted female offenders in recent years. For instance, one federal policy, the Juvenile Justice and Delinquency Prevention Act of 1974, required states receiving funds for delinquency prevention programs to divert status offenders away from juvenile correctional facilities. Since girls are most frequently charged with status offenses, this policy at least initially helped to reduce their incarceration rates (Teilmann and Landry 1981). Unfortunately, in 1980, those rates again began to climb as a "get tough" attitude toward juvenile offenders started to take hold in the nation's family courts. In many jurisdictions, attempts were made to close what many viewed as "loopholes" permitted by the 1974 Act by reclassifying many status offenses as criminal offenses. Analysis indicates that this has impacted more negatively on girls than on boys (Curran 1984).

Similarly, several state and local jurisdictions have implemented sentencing guidelines for adult offenders so that sentences are neutral with respect to sex as well as race and social class. Evidence indicates, however, that these guidelines are often ignored or bypassed. In Minnesota, for example, where sentencing guidelines were established in 1980, the percentage of incarcerated female offenders rose by 32.8 percent compared with a 7.7 percent increase for males by 1983, although these increases were found to be unrelated to offense severity. In fact, low-severity property crimes, the crimes for which women are most likely to be convicted, showed the highest increase in incarceration in direct violation of the sentencing guidelines (Sarri 1986).

Sentencing guidelines have also been largely ineffective in reducing sentencing disparities between white and minority offenders. In general, incarceration rates in the United States rose steadily during the 1980s, but as we see in Table 9.3, the rate for minorities is disproportionately higher than that for whites, with the exception of Asian Americans who are the least likely group to be incarcerated. In 1987, for example, whites comprised 78.4 percent of the U.S. population and slightly more than half of the state and federal prison population. African Americans, however, constituted just 11.4 percent of the U.S. population, but 45.3 percent of the state and federal prison population. Similarly, Hispanics, who make up about 7.3 percent of the U.S. population, made up 12 percent of the state and federal prison population in 1987. According to Sarri (1986:96), "When one examines the rates for females, greater racial discrepancies are noted. Overall, the female rate is 22 per 100,000 [of the general population]—far below that for males [531 per 100,000 of the general population], but for white women it is 6 and for black women, 47." As criminologist Dorie Klein (1973) has observed, chivalry has never been extended to minority women.

To sum up, it appears that a number of extra-legal factors come into play in the administration of justice. As Chesney-Lind (1986:92) concludes, "Taken to-

TABLE 9.3
Prisoners under State or Federal Jurisdiction by Race and Sex, 1987*

Race	All Prisoners (%)		Male (%)		Female (%)	
White	291,606	(50.2)	277,229	(50.2)	14,377	(49.8)
Black	262,958	(45.3)	249,730	(45.2)	13,228	(45.8)
Hispanic	69,810	(12.0)	66,781	(12.0)	3,029	(10.5)
Native American	5,461	(00.9)	5,106	(00.9)	355	(1.2)
Asian American or Pacific Islander	1,997	(00.3)	1,909	(00.3)	88	(00.3)

*Percentages do not add to 100 due to rounding and the fact that in some jurisdictions, Hispanic prisoners are counted as Black or as race unknown.
Source: U.S. Department of Justice 1989:91–94.

gether, these research findings suggest that the criminal justice system has been involved in the enforcement of traditional sex-role expectations as well as, and sometimes in place of, the law." In some cases, if the offender is respectably feminine, this works to women's advantage. More often, though, females are at a disadvantage relative to males in the criminal justice system, especially if they are young and nonwhite.

This is not to say, however, that gender stereotyping is never applied to male offenders. According to Miethe and Moore (1986), married, employed men with no prior offense record—that is, those who conform to the gender prescription of "respectable" masculinity—are sentenced more leniently than single, unemployed men with previous arrests or convictions. This is especially true for black men; for instance, single black men are sentenced more harshly than single white men (*see also* Daly 1989). Interestingly, Myers and Talarico (1986:246) found that although severity of sentence increases with the seriousness of the offense as one would expect, the relationship is stronger for white offenders than for black offenders. They hypothesize that this may be because criminal justice officials hold whites to a higher standard of behavior simply because they are white; "black criminality could be more expected and tolerated than crime by whites." However, their findings, along with those of others (e.g., Flowers 1988; Berk 1985; LaFree 1980) indicate that the treatment that nonwhites receive in the criminal justice system is at least partially determined by the characteristics of their victims. In Myers and Talarico's study (1986:248), for example, "one district attorney dismissed assaults that involve 'just one nigger cutting up another,' as 'junk' cases," illustrating quite clearly the racism of some criminal justice personnel and the low value they attach to black lives. Those who victimize whites are sentenced severely. We will take up this issue again momentarily.

Importantly, the sexism we have observed in criminal sentencing carries over into corrections. Although women's prisons often are less secure and more physically attractive than men's facilities, they are also more geographically isolated and they offer far fewer educational and training programs (Gold 1989; Reid 1987). The lack of programs is sometimes justified in terms of cost efficiency; since females represent just 4.9 percent of state prison inmates and 6.3 percent of federal prison inmates, such programs would be uneconomical. But sexist stereotypes are also frequently at work; for example, there is the belief that men are in greater need of programs because they are primary breadwinners (Hancock 1986; Sarri 1986). In addition, researchers often express concern over the lack of adequate medical facilities in women's prisons as well as the overuse of psychotropic drugs. It is estimated that female inmates are two to ten times more likely than male inmates to be given such drugs, reflecting the traditional stereotype that female offenders, especially violent ones, must be "sick" or mentally disturbed (Chesney-Lind 1986; Edwards 1986; Shaw 1982).

At the very least, it seems that law enforcement agencies, the courts, and corrections personnel are applying a double standard of justice—one for men, another for women—that is exacerbated by racial and age-based discrimination. As we will see next, this double standard also affects the treatment of male and female crime victims.

CRIMINAL VICTIMIZATION: GENDER, POWER, AND VIOLENCE

Men are more likely than women to be victimized by crime in the United States. Data from the National Crime Survey, a semiannual federal study that questions a random sample of American households about criminal victimization, indicate that for most crimes of violence and for theft, men are the most frequent victims. It is estimated, in fact, that 89 percent of all males now twelve years old will be the victims of a violent crime at least once during their lifetime, compared with 73 percent of females. Contrary to popular thought, the elderly are the least likely to be victimized by crime, although they are among the most fearful of victimization (*see* Lindquist and Duke 1982, for an interesting analysis of this paradox). Rather, as we see in Table 9.4, it is the young, especially nonwhite males between the ages of twelve and twenty-four, who have the highest criminal victimization rates.

Studies have found that, despite their lower rates of victimization, women fear crime more than men do (Oretega and Myles 1987; Reid 1987). Some writers speculate that this may be because women are more conscious of crime, or the finding may simply be a reflection of women's greater willingness to talk about or admit victimization. In addition, though, women's fear may be more specific or focused than that of men. That is, women may not have a high fear of all crimes, but only of the particular crimes that are almost exclusively directed against them, such as sexual assault (Gordon and Rigor 1989; Reid 1987; Warr 1985).

Young women, particularly those who live in urban areas, are most fearful of

TABLE 9.4
Estimated Rate of Personal Criminal Victimization (per 1,000 persons in each age group) by Type of Victimization, Sex, Age, and Race of Victim, 1988

Sex, Age, and Race of Victim	Total Population	Crimes of Violence	Crimes of Theft
White Males			
12–15 years	5,383,160	70.1	96.4
16–19 years	5,999,440	84.7	129.2
20–24 years	7,667,050	77.3	142.0
25–34 years	18,268,210	36.9	86.1
35–49 years	20,683,440	22.8	62.5
50–64 years	13,783,060	11.3	42.4
65 years and older	10,814,820	5.7	19.9
White Females			
12–15 years	5,149,780	40.3	127.3
16–19 years	5,884,210	52.7	126.8
20–24 years	7,806,210	37.4	112.8
25–34 years	18,115,920	31.5	79.5
35–49 years	21,039,490	21.1	70.3
50–64 years	15,054,910	7.6	37.6
65 years and older	15,224,870	2.4	17.9
Black Males			
12–15 years	1,042,320	82.6	120.2
16–19 years	1,111,690	113.3	92.6
20–24 years	1,138,960	82.5	92.0
25–34 years	2,448,740	45.5	91.0
35–49 years	2,324,440	21.7	60.3
50–64 years	1,465,630	13.0	41.4
65 years and older	982,340	10.5*	11.9
Black Females			
12–15 years	1,017,840	46.1	114.2
16–19 years	1,105,130	72.5	79.5
20–24 years	1,375,260	58.7	104.8
25–34 years	2,901,780	44.2	69.5
35–49 years	2,848,370	20.8	68.2
50–64 years	1,816,170	16.6	34.1
65 years and older	1,448,100	5.1*	16.3

*Estimate is based on about 10 or fewer sample cases.
Source: U.S. Department of Justice 1990b:238.

rape. In fact, Warr's (1985) research indicates that it is the crime of rape that they fear more than any other. Their fear derives not only from the fact that rape is a serious crime but also because it is a crime associated with other serious offenses, such as robbery and homicide. In addition, women's high fear of rape is related to their perceived risk of being raped, and statistics on sexual assault indicate that their fears are hardly irrational. The U.S. Department of Justice (1987) estimates that one women in twelve will be the victim of rape or attempted rape during her lifetime. Sixteen rapes are attempted and ten women are raped every hour in the United States. The U.S. rape rate rose four times as fast as the total crime rate during the 1980s (U.S. House of Representatives 1990). Yet, sexual assault is one of the violent crimes *least* likely to be reported to the police; it is estimated that as few as 10 percent of all rapes committed are reported to the police (U.S. House of Representatives 1990). Rape also has one of the lowest arrest and conviction rates. For instance, although rape accounted for 6 percent of violent crimes in 1988, arrests for rape were only 1.8 percent of total arrests for violent crimes (U.S. House of Representatives 1990). Only about 1 in 150 suspected rapists is convicted (U.S. Department of Justice 1982). In 1986, 91,460 rapes were reported to police, but only 19,685 individuals were convicted of rape (U.S. House of Representatives 1990). In light of these startling facts, let us undertake a more careful discussion of the crime of rape.

Rape

Rape legally ocurs when a person uses force or the threat of force to have some form of sexual intercourse (vaginal, oral, or anal) with another person. This rather straightforward definition might lead us to conclude that the prosecution of rape cases is fairly simple, especially given current medical technology and modern evidence collection techniques. However, although at first it may appear that rape may be thought of in dichotomous terms (that is, a specific encounter either is or is not a rape), research indicates that what is defined as rape differs widely among various groups, including victims and perpetrators (Bourque 1989, Williams 1985). Unfortunately, the crime of rape is still prevalently viewed in our society in terms of a collection of myths about both rapists and rape victims (*see* Box 9.2). Rape victims face a predicament unlike that of victims of any other crime; it is often they who must prove their innocence rather than the state proving the guilt of the rapist (Estrich 1987). To understand this better, let's examine some of these myths more closely.

It is commonly believed that most rape victims have done something to invite or precipitate the assault. Therefore, in reporting the crime, complainants must first demonstrate that they are "real" or "worthy" victims. To do so successfully and thus have the complaint acted upon by the criminal justice system, victims must report the assault promptly, show emotional as well as physical trauma and, most importantly, convince authorities that they were in no way responsible for the crime (Bourque 1989; Schur 1984). This last condition is an

---

Common Rape Myths   **BOX 9.2**

Many people, both women and men, hold erroneous or false ideas about rape victims, rapists, and the crime of rape itself. These include beliefs that:

- Women enjoy being raped; they like to be "taken" by force.
- Only young, physically attractive women get raped.
- Many women provoke men by teasing them (e.g., by the way they dress or walk); therefore, these women "deserve" to be raped.
- A wife cannot be raped by her husband.
- Men cannot be raped.
- Most rapists are "sick" or mentally ill.
- Most rapes are interracial (i.e., the rapist and the victim are of different races).
- Most rapes take place on isolated streets or in dark alleys.

As the material in this section makes clear, the persistent and widespread belief in such myths has serious consequences in the treatment of rape victims, in the prosecution of rape cases, and in efforts to prevent the crime of rape.

---

especially difficult one to fulfill since even the slightest deviation from "respectable behavior" may be taken as evidence of the victim's culpability. Men, for example, are even less likely than women to report that they have been raped—after all, men are supposed to be able to defend themselves. If they are gay, reporting the assault may do more harm than good. Gays are rarely deemed "worthy" rape victims by virtue of their choice of a "deviant" lifestyle, and reporting could lead to harassment by the authorities and others.

Men, though, are estimated to constitute less than 10 percent of rape victims (U.S. House of Representatives 1990). It is women, then, who are routinely the double victims: first, by their assailants and second, by the criminal justice system. Because of the victim precipitation myth, female rape victims typically find that if they have violated any of the stereotyped standards of respectable femininity—if they were hitchhiking, drinking or using drugs, walking alone at night, visiting a bar unescorted, or dressed "seductively"—the probability increases that their complaint will not be prosecuted or, if it is, that their assailant will be acquitted (*see* for example, the *New York Times* 3 June 1990:30).

The victim precipitation myth also appears to render some groups of women unrapeable in a sense. Consider, for example, a 1986 California case in which a Superior Court judge dismissed charges of rape and sodomy brought by a thirty-year-old Hispanic prostitute against a white male with whom she agreed to have oral sex, but who subsequently became violent and forced her to engage in sexual intercourse and sodomy. Upon dismissing the case, the judge stated that a working prostitute could not be a rape victim even if she was forced to have intercourse, although the district attorney's office and a majority of the jury disagreed with this opinion (Bourque 1989). In October, 1990, it was reported that more than 200 sexual assault cases were being reopened in Oakland, California after the police chief there admitted that the cases had been closed without proper investigation because most of the victims were prostitutes or drug addicts. According to Gross (1990a:A14), rape complaints brought by prostitutes and addicts are routinely dismissed by police. "In New Haven, faced with a prostitute dressed for work, the police have said, 'What do you expect? Look at you.' In Houston, officers have shut their notebooks after a victim said that she was raped in a crack house. In the Atlanta suburbs, victims have been told they will be given a lie detector test and sent to jail if any part of their story is untrue."

Historically, the myths that women enjoy forced sex, that they really mean "yes" when they say "no," and that they often falsely accuse men of rape out of shame or revenge, led to strict rules of evidence in rape cases that essentially placed the burden of proof on the victim. For instance, the victim's testimony had to be supported by other witnesses, and the state had to establish that she had tried sufficiently to resist her assailant. Today, many of these requirements have been revised or abolished both in the United States and abroad. But despite legal reforms, both judges and juries still seem reluctant to believe rape victims and to convict and punish accused rapists (Bourque 1989; Herman 1988). Consider, for example, the instructions that one British judge gave to a jury just prior to its deliberation of a verdict in a 1982 rape trial:

> Women who say no do not always mean no. It is not just a question of saying no, it is a question of how she says it, how she shows it and makes it clear. If she doesn't want it she only has to keep her legs shut and she would not get it without force and there would be marks of force being used (quoted in Temkin 1987:19–20).

This quotation highlights the fact that in the majority of rape cases, the central issue is not whether the complainant and the accused engaged in sexual intercourse, but rather whether the complainant consented to the act. As most prosecutors know quite well, it is the victim's consent that is most difficult to disprove, particularly in cases in which she and the accused know one another (Schur 1984; Bloom 1981). A case involving a victim who knows or is familiar with her assailant is known as **acquaintance rape.** It is estimated that about 60 to 80 percent of rapes are date or acquaintance rapes. The younger the victim, the more likely she is to know her assailant; acquaintance rapes account for 63 percent of reported cases involving victims twelve to eighteen years of age, and 80 percent of cases in which the victim is under twelve (Kulp 1981). Yet the vast majority of acquaintance rapes go unreported; women raped by strangers are ten times more likely to report the crime than women raped by acquaintances (U.S. House of Representatives 1990). Acquaintance rapes are especially common on college campuses. In an extensive three-year survey of college students, for example, Koss and her colleagues (1987) found that one in eight female college students reported being victimized during the preceding twelve-month period; 84 percent of those who had been victims of completed rapes knew their assailants and two-thirds were assaulted by dates.

Acquaintance rapes are often treated as private squabbles or misunderstandings, rather than as prosecutable crimes (Bourque 1989; Estrich 1987). If a case reaches the courtroom, the complainant typically finds that among judges and juries "old myths die hard: if a women accepts a dinner-date from a man, she should be expected to hold up her end of the bargain later, or if she is friendly to the gas man or flirts with her neighbor at the laundromat, well what can she expect?" (Bloom 1981:7). Especially difficult are cases in which the victim and the assailant had a previous sexual relationship: "[judges and juries] might think that the rapist had certain 'rights' to the woman, or that, conversely, the woman gives up the right to say no when she just entered into a sexual relationship with him, or anyone" (Bloom 1981:6; Bourque 1989). This view is reflected in the law of at least five states in which, as of 1987, an exemption from prosecution for rape was extended to voluntary social companions with whom the victim had previously had sexual contact (U.S. House of Representatives 1988).

One form of sexual assault that has received considerable attention in recent years is *marital rape*. Historically, a husband could not be charged with raping his wife even if he used physical violence to force her to have sex with him, or even if they were legally separated. For the most part, this was because of the fact that a wife was considered the property of her husband; certainly no man could be prosecuted for a personal decision to use his property as he saw fit. It was not until 1977 the Oregon state legislature repealed the marital exemption to its rape statute. Two years later, James K. Chretien became the first person in the United States to be convicted of marital rape (Reid 1987).

Recent research indicates that marital rape is a common form of family violence. According to one study of 644 married women, 12 percent reported having been raped by their husbands (Russell 1990). Finkelhor and Yllo (1985) found in their study of 393 randomly selected women that half their sample reported more than twenty incidents of marital rape and 48 percent indicated that rape was part of the common physical abuse their husbands inflicted on them. It is important to emphasize that what we are discussing here is not a situation in which one spouse wishes to have sex and the other does not, but gives in out of love or to please. Marital rape is a brutal physical assault that may have a graver impact on a victim than stranger rape given that the assailant is a person whom she knows and, at least at one time, loved and trusted (Finkelhor and Yllo 1985). In fact, it is probably the severe level of brutality in these assaults that accounts for the high conviction rate: 85 percent in marital rape cases compared with just 2 to 5 percent in stranger rape cases (Reid 1987). Still, as of 1990, twenty-six states exempted husbands from prosecution for raping their wives under a variety of circumstances, largely because of lingering doubts about the ability to prove nonconsent in a marital relationship. For many, the marriage license continues to be viewed as a license for sex, forced or otherwise. However, in three states, the exemption from prosecution for rape extended to cohabitors as well (Small and Tetreault 1990).

Another factor that affects the prosecution and outcome of rape cases is the race composition of the offender-victim dyad. We have already noted that blacks accused of victimizing whites are treated more harshly within the criminal justice system. This is especially true in rape cases in which a black man is charged and convicted of raping a white woman (Flowers 1988). For example, sociologist Gary LaFree (1980) analyzed 881 cases of sexual assault in a large midwestern city, comparing official reactions to rape in intraracial cases (i.e., black offender/black victim; white offender/white victim) to those in interracial cases (i.e., black offender/white victim; white offender/black victim). LaFree found that black men suspected of sexually assaulting white women received the harshest treatment at various stages of criminal processing. They were more likely, for example, to have their cases filed as felonies (as opposed to the less serious category of crime, misdemeanors); to be sentenced to prison (rather than probation); to receive longer prison sentences; and to be incarcerated in a state penetentiary (as opposed to a local jail or minimum security facility). White men involved in interracial rapes were among those treated most leniently. However, black suspects in interracial cases were no more likely than other suspects to be arrested or found guilty; in fact, LaFree reports that less than 32 percent of all the suspects arrested were eventually convicted. LaFree concludes that "the severity of official sanctions imposed on men for the sexual violation of women will depend on the *relative power* of the victim and of the suspect, determined in part by the race of each" (pp. 852–853, emphasis added).

Over the last fifteen years or so, the treatment of rape victims has improved. Most police officers, for example, now receive special training to sensitize them to the trauma of victims, and there are innumerable victim support and advocate services throughout the country. None of this, though, has produced a measurable decrease in the rape rate, and rape is still typically viewed as a "woman's problem" with little attention given to the men involved (Johnson 1980). When rapists are discussed, they are usually depicted as psychologically disturbed individuals who need special medical treatment. Interestingly, however, researchers have been unable to uncover evidence of widespread psychological disturbance in rapists, nor can they consistently discriminate between rapists and non-rapists using psychological tests (Scully and Marolla 1985; Abel, et al. 1980; Rada 1978). In fact, as Herman (1988:702–703) points out, "The most striking characteristic of sex offenders, from a diagnostic standpoint, is their apparent normality. Most do not qualify for any psychiatric diagnosis." The psychopathologcal perspective serves largely to divert our attention and resources away from the structural causes of rape and encourages us "to ignore both the cultural meanings of the behaviors in question and the overall *context of power relations* within which the behaviors occur" (Schur 1984:147, author's emphasis; *see also* Herman 1988).

But if most rapists are not mentally ill, why do they rape? Herman (1988) has argued that the propensity to commit sex offenses should be viewed as an addiction similar to alcoholism. Perhaps she is correct, but her explanation begs the questions of how one becomes an addict and why some individuals become addicted to committing sexual assaults and others do not. Consequently, we think that an answer to the question of why rapists rape lies within the culture and social structure of a society. Consider, for instance, anthropological studies of societies that may be characterized as virtually "rape-free" (Reiss 1986: Sanday 1981; Broude and Green 1976). The most striking feature of these societies is their relatively egalitarian gender relations. Neither sex is viewed as more important or as more highly valued than the other, and both are considered powerful, although in different spheres of activity. Moreover, women in these societies are not socially and economically dependent on men; they control resources and act as autonomous decision makers. Finally, in rape-free societies, nurturance and nonaggression are valued traits in individuals, and women are highly regarded not for their sexuality, but for their wisdom.

Compare these societies with our own—one of the most "rape-prone" industrialized societies in the world (U.S. House of Representatives 1990; Scully and Marolla 1985). The contrasts are glaring. First of all, we live in an extraordinarily violent society. Not only is the rape rate exceptionally high, but also the United States has the highest homicide rate relative to its industrialized allies. Yet we know that violence is not condoned for everyone; it is expected of, even encouraged among men, not women. This is just one dimension of unequal gender relations in our society. Men control greater resources and, therefore, are more powerful than women. Not infrequently, they use violence to expand their power further. One of the few "bargaining chips" women have in our society is their sexuality, and male violence can deprive them of personal control over even that. As one convicted rapist told an interviewer:

> Rape is a man's right. If a woman doesn't want to give it, the man should take it. Women have no right to say no. Women are made to have sex. It's all they are good for. Some women would rather take a beating, but they always give in; it's what they are for (quoted in Scully and Marolla 1985:261).

This quote also reveals the "conquest mentality" toward sex that is part of American culture. Sex is something men get or take from women. Sometimes force is necessary to get women to "put out." It appears, then, that in the United States there is a very fine line between "normal" masculine sexual behavior and rape (Schur 1984). Indeed, the rapist quoted here, like most rapists, did not think he had done anything wrong. Importantly, a large segment of the U.S. public agrees with him. The fact that large-scale studies of high school and college students, for example, have found that a majority of young males and females believe that under some circumstances it is alright for a man to force a woman to have sex illustrates the extent to which sexual violence against women is an acceptable part of our culture (Koss, et al. 1987; Goodchilds and Zellman 1984; Ageton 1983).

Finally, the words of the rapist quoted here reflect the degree to which women are sexually objectified in our society. Unlike women in rape-free societies, women in the United States and similar countries are viewed as sex objects, and female sexuality itself is treated as a commodity. Clearly the most common form of objectified, commoditized female sexuality is pornography. We will now briefly discuss pornography and attempt to assess its relationships to the high incidence of violence against women in our society.

Pornography

In 1969, the President's Commission on the Causes and Prevention of Violence concluded in its report that media portrayals of violence can induce individuals to behave violently. In 1971, the Presidential Commission on Obscenity and Pornography concluded in its report that there is no causal relationship between exposure to pornography and subsequent sexual violence against women. Pornography, it said, is basically harmless. In 1986, the Attorney General's Commission on Pornography (also known as the Meese Commission) brought the issue full circle by concluding that violent pornography is causally related to both sexual violence and discrimination against women.

The inconsistency that characterizes these official reports reflects the general confusion that historically has clouded debates about pornography and its effects. Much of the problem stems from conflicting definitions of what is pornographic. Certainly, few would be willing to argue that any pictured nude or any description of a sexual act is pornographic, but where does one draw the line? As Supreme Court Justice Douglas once noted in an obscenity trial, "What may be trash to me may be prized by others" (quoted in MacKinnon 1986:69).

Still, we can discern important objective differences between pornography and what may be called *erotica*. Gloria Steinem (1978:54) provides us with a useful starting point:

> "Pornography" begins with a root [*porne*] meaning "prostitution" or "female captives," thus letting us know that the subject is not mutual love, or love at all, but domination and violence against women. (Though, of course, homosexual pornography may imitate this violence by putting a man in the "feminine" role of victim.) It ends with a root [*graphos*] meaning "writing about" or "description of" which puts still more distance between subject and object, and replaces a spontaneous yearning for closeness with objectification and a voyeur.

In contrast, *erotica* is derived from the root *eros* meaning "sensual love" and implying the mutual choice and pleasure of the sexual partners. We can see here, then, at least two distinct features of pornography. First, it depersonalizes sex and objectifies women. Second, and more importantly, pornography is not even about sex, per se, but rather the degradation of women and often children through sex. In fact, the sex depicted in pornography is secondary to the violence, humiliation, and dominance it portrays.

Significantly, the Meese Commission distinguished among four types of sexually explicit material: sexually violent material; nonviolent materials that depict degradation, domination, subordination, or humiliation; nonviolent and nonde-grading materials; and materials depicting nudity. In reviewing available evidence on the potentially harmful effects of such materials, the Commission concluded that with regard to the latter two categories, research indicates no causal connection to rape or other acts of sexual violence. However, the Commission maintained that material of these two types represents only a small percentage of the market. Instead, they argue that the market in sexually explicit material is largely composed of that which we have defined as pornography: sexually violent material and nonviolent but degrading materials (U.S. Department of Justice 1986).

At its most extreme, violent pornography takes the form of "snuff" and "slasher" films in which women are tortured, disfigured, murdered, or dismembered for sexual pleasure (Barry 1981). In addition, a common theme in these and other forms of violent pornography is rape. "[N]ot only is rape presented as part of normal male/female relations, but the woman, despite her terror, is always depicted as sexually aroused to the point of cooperation. In the end, she is ashamed but physically gratified" (Scully and Marolla 1985:253). Research indicates that this kind of pornography *is* harmful. Donnerstein (1983), for example, reports that exposure to *violent* pornography increases male subjects' sexual arousal and rape fantasies, lessens their sensitivity to rape, increases their acceptance of rape myths, and most importantly, increases their self-reported possibility of raping. "It is of further interest to note that these increases in arousal and changes in rape attitudes are also highly correlated with actual aggression against women" (Donnerstein 1983:141). As Scully and Marolla (1985:253) found in their interviews with convicted rapists, "The images projected in pornography contribute to a vocabulary of motive which trivializes and neutralizes rape and which might lessen the internal controls that otherwise would prevent sexually aggressive behavior. Men who rape use this culturally acquired vocabulary to justify their sexual violence."

What of material that may be considered nonviolent, but degrading? According to the Meese Commission, the bulk of available pornography comprises this kind of material and "depicts people, usually women, as existing solely for the sexual satisfaction of others, usually men, or that depicts people, usually women, in decidedly subordinate roles in their sexual relations with others, or that depicts people engaged in sexual practices that would to most people be considered humiliating [e.g., women are urinated or ejaculated on or shown having sex with animals]" (U.S. Department of Justice 1986:331). Although acknowledging that the evidence is more tentative than that regarding violent pornography, the Commission reached a similar conclusion: exposure to nonviolent but degrading pornography increases acceptance of rape myths. In addition, the Commission (U.S. Department of Justice 1986:334) concluded that "substantial exposure to materials of this type bears some causal relationship to the incidence of various nonviolent forms of discrimination against or subordination of women in our society."

Not surprisingly, the Meese Commission's report did little to settle the controversy surrounding pornography. To the contrary, it fueled the debate. Members of the Commission themselves disagreed with many of the majority's conclusions and filed a minority report of their own. In addition, some of the social scientists who testified before the Commission or whose work the Commission cited to support its conclusions publicly complained after the release of the majority report that their research was distorted so as to conform to the political or moral ideologies of some of the Commission members. The conclusions of the Commission also heightened the concerns of many who worry about potential infringements on the First Amendment right of free speech and who fear that the report could be used to legitimate government censorship of *any* sexually explicit material including information on contraception, "safe sex", and so on. Feminists themselves are divided over the question of whether pornography should be outlawed. There are those who maintain that pornography, even in portraying sadomasochism, is potentially liberating for women in that through it, women may become less puritanical and sexually passive and more open or aggressive about their sexual desires. Others label this approach male-identified and anti-woman. To them, pornography is itself "a form of forced sex, a practice of sexual politics, an institution of gender inequality" (MacKinnon 1986:65; Russo 1987).

It appears unlikely that the debate over pornography will be resolved any time soon. Meanwhile, however, the porn industry remains a multi-billion dollar enterprise that grossed over $7 billion in 1981 alone (Russo 1987). It has been argued that pornography has become more respectable with the proliferation of home video equipment. Viewers no longer have to visit seedy peep shows or adults-only outlets, they can watch X-rated video tapes from the neighborhood retailer in the comfort and privacy of their own homes. Producers are also trying to market more sexually explicit material to women, but importantly, to do so successfully they are finding they must develop a plot, reduce the number of close-ups, and add foreplay and afterplay to the sex scenes—in short, depict more affection, romance, and emotional relationships which research shows are sexually stimulating to women (Kristof 1986; Morgan 1978).

Nevertheless, despite this new "pornography for women," almost all pornography (as we have defined it here) continues to be produced, marketed, and purchased by men. However, as Edwin Schur (1984:179; author's emphasis) has pointed out, the "pornography-is-respectable" argument has some merit:

> This suggests that the link between pornography and the objectified uses of
> female sexuality in ordinary "respectable" advertising may be very close indeed.
> It could be that until women's bodies are no longer used to *sell* commodities, the
> treatment and sale of women's bodies *as* commodities through pornography is
> bound to persist [*see* Chapter 6].

Extending this position, we may argue that in a society in which women are regarded as sexual property and are denied equal access to wealth, power, prestige, and other resources, both rape and pornography are likely to flourish. The same can be said with regard to other forms of violence against women, as we shall see next.

Institutionalized Violence against Women: Custom or Crime?

The historical accounts left by colonists and missionaries along with the ethnographies of anthropologists testify to the extent to which violence against women has been an institutionalized component of the cultures of many societies throughout the world.

From the tenth to the twentieth centuries, for example, the Chinese engaged in the practice of binding the feet of young girls. This was accomplished by bending all of the toes on each foot (except the big toes) under and into the sole, then wrapping the toes and the heel as tightly together as possible with a piece of cloth. Every two weeks or so the wrapped feet were squeezed into progressively smaller shoes until they were shrunk to the desirable size of just three inches. Typically, the feet would bleed and become infected, circulation was cut off, and eventually one or more toes might fall off. Needless to say, the process was extremely painful and literally millions of women were crippled by it. Yet, they endured and perpetuated the custom—usually from mother to daughter—for 1,000 years in the belief that it made them beautiful, and beauty ensured a good and lasting marriage (Dworkin 1983a). In a society in which all roles other than wife and mother, or prostitute, are closed to women, we may expect them to pursue whatever means are necessary for personal and economic security.

It was the case that men did not look favorably on natural-footed women. For one thing, they felt that tiny feet were feminine, so that binding helped differentiate women from men. In addition, the immobile woman was a status symbol, "a testimony to the wealth and privilege of the man who could afford to keep her" (Dworkin 1983:181). Aspirations to higher status, however, prompted the lower classes to copy the tradition which originated with the nobility. And finally:

> Footbinding functioned as the Cerbrus of morality and ensured female chastity in a nation of women who literally could not "run around." Fidelity, and the legitimacy of children, could be reckoned on. . . . Women were perverse and sinful, lewd and lascivious, if left to develop naturally. The Chinese believed that being born a woman was payment for evils committed in a previous life. Footbinding was designed to spare a woman the disaster of another such incarnation (Dworkin 1983a:181–182).

A similar rationale was offered for *suttee* or widow burning, a custom practiced in India for approximately 400 years until it was officially outlawed in 1829. Suttee was a sacrificial ritual in which a widow climbed the funeral pyre of her deceased husband and set herself or was set on fire. Although the practice was supposed to be voluntary, records indicate that extreme measures were taken to prevent escape in case the widow changed her mind, such as "scaffolds constructed to tilt toward the fire pit, piles designed so that exits were blocked and the roof collapsed on the woman's head, tying her, weighting her down with firewood and bamboo poles. If all else failed and the woman escaped from the burning pile, she was often dragged back by force, sometimes by her own son" (Stein 1978:255). Since polygamy was also practiced and marriages between child-brides and men of 50 or older were not uncommon, some wives, still in their teens, were burnt alive with dead husbands they had rarely seen since their wedding day (Daly 1983; Stein 1978).

It appears that most women did not have to be coerced into suttee, especially in light of their alternatives. "Since their religion forbade remarriage [of widows] and at the same time taught that the husband's death was the fault of the widow (because of her sins in a previous incarnation if not in this one), everyone was free to despise and mistreat her for the rest of her life" (Daly 1983:190). Religious law required that unburnt widows live a life of extreme poverty, shaving their heads, wearing drab clothes, eating just one bland meal a day, performing the most menial tasks, never sleeping on a bed, and never leaving their houses except to go to the temple. Obviously, death might have seemed more appealing to many. Certainly, relatives and in-laws preferred it. Since it was widely believed that women were by nature lascivious, the widow was viewed as a possible source of embarrassment to her family and in-laws who feared she would become sexually involved with other men and perhaps even get pregnant. In addition, suttee ensured that she would make no claim to her husband's estate. Thus, the Indian widow had to decide between a miserable life of poverty and harassment or an honorable but excruciatingly painful death that elevated her status in the community:

> The widow on her way to the pyre was the object (for once) of all public attention. She distributed money and jewels to the crowd. Endowed with the gift of prophecy and the power to curse and bless, she was immolated amid great fanfare, with great veneration (Stein 1978:254).

For most, there was little choice.

Although, as we have noted, suttee was outlawed in the early 1800s, there is evidence that the cultural view of widows has not changed much in some regions of India. Daly (1983), for instance, reports that in some areas widows are still expected to abide by the old religious laws (e.g., living in poverty and shaving their heads), and that surveys indicate that a substantial portion of the population continues to approve of this tradition.

Another custom that has generated considerable controversy in recent years is *female circumcision.* Female circumcision actually takes several forms, the mildest being *Sunna,* in which the hood of the clitoris is cut analogous to the practice of male circumcision. The most extreme form, infibulation, involves the removal of the clitoris, labia minora, and most of the labia majora, after which the vagina is stitched closed save for a tiny opening to allow for the passage of urine and menstrual blood. The most common form, however, is excision whereby the clitoris as well as all or part of the labia minora are removed (Lightfoot-Klein 1989; McLean 1980). Currently, this custom is practiced in about forty countries, primarily in East and West Africa, and in many of these societies, it is not uncommon for as many as 90 to 98 percent of the female population to have undergone one form of the operation (Ebomoyi 1987; Renzetti and Curran 1986).

In the Western world, publicity regarding female circumcision has triggered angry protests by feminists who have denounced the tradition as oppressive and barbaric, and who have insisted that governments immediately outlaw it. Given the way the operation is often done and the serious medical problems that frequently result, their shock and indignation are understandable. More specifically, the circumcision is performed on young girls—sometimes as infants, but usually between the ages of seven and thirteen—by an elder village woman or traditional birth attendant using various nonsurgical instruments such as a razor, a knife, or a piece of broken glass. Typically, no anesthetics are available. Once the operation is completed, dirt, ashes, herbs, or animal droppings may be applied to the wound in the belief that they will stop the bleeding and aid in healing. Not surprisingly, complications are common and include shock, hemorrhage, septicemia, and tetanus (Lightfoot-Klein 1989; Ebomoyi 1987; McLean 1980).

Significantly, however, African women have criticized their Western sisters for sensationalizing this custom and for presenting it out of its cultural context (Graham 1986). To understand their perspective, consider the reasons given for female circumcision. For some, the custom is a religious obligation; for others, it has an aesthetic purpose—that is, the clitoris, believed to be a masculine organ in some cultures, is removed to ensure sexual differentiation and to enhance a girl's beauty and femininity by giving her a smooth and clean skin surface (McLean 1980; Epelboin and Epelboin 1979). For most women, though, the motivation to undergo circumcision derives from attitudes about moral purity and female sexuality. Among many practicing societies, there exists an elaborate mythology which serves to buttress firmly entrenched beliefs about the insatiable nature of female sexual desire. Circumcision, then, is a preventive measure taken to protect a girl from sexual temptations and thereby preserve her marriageability. Consequently, although some writers have argued that circumcision causes severe psychological trauma for a young girl, others have pointed out that remaining uncircumcised may result in far greater social and psychological damage. The uncircumcised are considered "dirty" and unmarriageable, making them unfit to fulfill what are considered in their societies to be women's two most valued roles, wife and mother (Renzetti and Curran 1986). As one Ghanian activist explained, "To put it cynically, not to go through mutilation is to commit economic suicide" (Graham 1986:18). No wonder, then, that the majority of women in practicing societies state that they will carry on the tradition with their daughters, although many are opting to have the operation performed under more sterile conditions in a hospital (Lightfoot-Klein 1989; Ebomoyi 1987; Myers 1986).

In sum, female circumcision, like footbinding and suttee, is a practice of institutionalized violence against women which many observers have labeled criminal (Morgan and Steinem 1980; Hosken 1979; Russell and Van de Ven 1976). Yet efforts to outlaw it rarely have been successful, and women themselves perpetuate this tradition. To most Westerners this appears irrational, but what we must consider is women's status in practicing societies. Female circumcision is one of the few means by which these women exercise power and achieve recognition. It is hardly surprising that women would cling to one of their only avenues of power and status, regardless of how damaging it may be. It may be argued, in fact, that their behavior is no less rational than that of Western women who very frequently seek harmful treatments or follow unhealthy diets for the sake of "beauty" (*see* Chapter 12).

If our goal, then, is the elimination of violence against women, laws banning particular practices are unlikely to be effective without simultaneous policies and programs to implement and ensure gender equality. In the final analysis, violence against women, whatever its form, is a direct outgrowth of the devaluation of women.

POWER, CRIME, AND JUSTICE

We have seen here that in societies that have accepted or condoned violence against women, whatever its form—rape, pornography, footbinding, suttee, or infibulation—women are viewed as innately inferior to men and are deprived of valued resources. Indeed, women may even participate in their own victimization as a means to exercise some power in their lives and to acquire a higher status.

Powerlessness, we have also suggested, may help to explain crime rates and the differential treatment of offenders by the criminal justice system. It is the relatively powerless—young, poor, minority men and women—who are disproportionately represented in the official crime statistics and who receive the harshest treatment within the criminal justice system. They, too, are most likely to be victimized by crime.

We have emphasized in this chapter that the content of laws and the way they are enforced have a lot to do with the values and interests of the powerful. The vast majority of lawmakers and law enforcement personnel are white men. In the next chapter, we will explore this issue further through an examination of politics and government.

KEY TERMS

acquaintance rape   an incident of sexual assault in which the victim knows or is familiar with the assailant

chivalry hypothesis   the belief that female offenders are afforded greater leniency before the law than their male counterparts

emancipation theory   posits that female crime is increasing and/or becoming more masculine in character as a result of the women's liberation movement

sentencing disparity   widely varying sentences imposed on offenders convicted of similar crimes, usually based on irrelevant factors, such as the offender's sex or race, or other inappropriate considerations

status offenses   behavior considered illegal if engaged in by a juvenile, but legal if engaged in by an adult

SUGGESTED READINGS

Bourque, L.B. 1989. *Defining Rape.* Durham, NC: Duke University Press.

Flowers, R.B. 1988. *Minorities and Criminality.* Westport, CT: Greenwood Press.

Guber, S., and J. Hoff (Eds.) 1989. *For Adult Users Only: The Dilemma of Violent Pornography.* Bloomington, IN: Indiana University Press.

Lightfoot-Klein, H. 1989. *Prisoners of Ritual: An Odyssey into Female Genital Circumcision in Africa.* New York: Harrington Park Press.

Morello, K.B. 1986. *The Invisible Bar.* New York: Random House.

Sanday, P.R. 1990. *Fraternity Gang Rape: Sex, Brotherhood, and Privilege on Campus.* New York: New York University Press.

Worrall, A. 1990. *Offending Women.* London: Routledge.

Chapter 10

Gender, Politics, Government, and the Military

In the spring of 1776, Abigail Adams wrote to her husband John, "I long to hear that you have declared an independency—and by the way in the new Code of Laws which I suppose it will be necessary for you to make I desire you would Remember the Ladies, and be more generous and favourable to them than your ancestors." But his response revealed that the designers of the new republic had no intention of putting the sexes on an equal political footing. "As to your extraordinary Code of Laws," John Adams wrote back to his wife, "I cannot but laugh. . . . Depend upon it, We know better than to repeal our Masculine systems" (quoted in Rossi 1973:10–11).

That Adams's sentiments were shared by his fellow revolutionaries is clear from their declaration that all *men* are created equal, although, at the same time, they considered some men (white property holders) more equal than others (blacks, Native Americans, the propertyless). Of course, it has been argued that the Founding Fathers used the masculine noun in the generic sense, but the fact remains that historically men and women have been accorded different rights and responsibilities as U.S. citizens solely on the basis of their sex. In this chapter, we will examine some of the differences and similarities in the political roles and behavior of the sexes, not only in the United States, but elsewhere as well.

As sociologists have repeatedly pointed out, when we speak about politics, we are essentially speaking about power—the power to distribute scarce resources, to institutionalize particular values, and to legitimately use force or violence. To the extent that men and women have different degrees of political power, they will have unequal input into political decision making and, consequently, their interests and experiences may be unequally represented in law and public policy. What is the political power differential between the sexes today? We will address that question on one level by assessing men's and women's relative success in winning public office and securing political appointments. In addition, we will examine the roles of men and women in defense and national security by discussing the issue of gender and military service. To begin our discussion, however, we will first take a look at differences in men's and women's political attitudes and participation, or what has become known in government circles as "the gender gap."

THE GENDER GAP: POLITICAL ATTITUDES AND ACTIVITIES

There are few certainties for political candidates on election day, but since women were granted full voting rights in 1920, there was one thing they could always count on: women and men would vote alike. Differences in voting patterns could be discerned among age groups, social classes, races, and educational levels, but within each of these subgroups, women and men tended to vote similarly—at least until 1980. It was not until the 1980 presidential election that women, for the first time in the sixty years they had been enfranchised, voted significantly differently than men: although 54 percent of the ballots cast by men went to Ronald Reagan, he got only 46 percent of women's votes. This eight-percentage-point sex difference might not seem like much, but as Table 10.1 shows, it was the largest difference recorded since polltakers began collecting such statistics in 1952. What is more, roughly equal percentages of women and men voted in 1980, but since women comprised 53 percent of the voting-age population, numerically more of them cast ballots—about 6 million more (Abzug 1984; Perlez 1984).

In the 1984 presidential election, some difference remained, although it was smaller than in 1980 and a larger percentage of women voted for Ronald Reagan than compared with the 1980 election. Moreover, in 1984, women constituted a slight majority of voters in every age group.

In 1988, a large sex difference in presidential voting again emerged: George Bush received 57 percent of men's votes compared with 50 percent of women's votes. Women were almost evenly divided in their support for Bush and Dukakis, but men were much more likely to support Bush. In 1988, women were again the majority of voters.

In short, it is these differences that since 1980 have stimulated the debate among politicians and analysts about the potential impact of what is called **the gender gap:** not only the different voting patterns of women and men, but also their differing opinions on key political issues.

At the heart of the gender gap are environmental, social welfare, and foreign policy issues. For instance, men and women tend to disagree over nuclear energy and the need for environmental protection. Although both show a trend toward supporting environmental protection, more women than men favor tougher laws

TABLE 10.1
The Gender Gap in Presidential Elections, 1952–1988

Election Year	Candidate Elected	%Women Supporting This Candidate	%Men Supporting This Candidate
1952	Eisenhower	58	53
1956	Eisenhower	61	55
1960	Kennedy	49	52
1964	Johnson	62	60
1968	Nixon	43	43
1972	Nixon	62	63
1976	Carter	48	53
1980	Reagan	46	54
1984	Reagan	56	62
1988	Bush	50	57

Sources: *New York Times* 10 November 1988:B6; CAWP 1987.

against pollution and nearly twice as many men as women favor construction of more nuclear power plants. In fact, about twice as many women as men (40 percent to 22 percent) report that they would like to see all nuclear power plants shut down within the next five years (Media General/Associated Press, January 12, 1989).

Sex differences with regard to social welfare issues are largely a reflection of the disparity in men's and women's economic positions that we discussed in Chapter 8. Thus, given the high percentage of women living in poverty, it is not surprising that more women than men disapprove of federal cuts in welfare spending and job training programs, and that more women than men think that the government should try to do more to reduce the income gap between the rich and the poor. Moreover, since women are a majority of Social Security recipients, we may expect them more than men to support increased government spending for Social Security (Bookman and Morgen 1988; Deitch 1988; Palley 1987; Abzug 1984).

The gender gap is widest on the issues of war and peace. For example, in the wake of the 1983 terrorist attack in Beirut that killed more than 200 U.S. Marines, considerably more women (62 percent) than men (34 percent) favored the withdrawal of U.S. troops from Lebanon (Abzug 1984). Similarly, following the U.S. invasion of Grenada, Ronald Reagan's popularity increased significantly, but only among men, 68 percent of whom approved of the military action compared with only 45 percent of women (Raines 1983). In 1990, when President Bush sent troops to the Persian Gulf in response to Iraq's invasion of Kuwait, women were 17 percentage points more likely than men to say that the President was too quick in committing troops to the Gulf and that he should have worked harder in arriving at a diplomatic solution to the crisis (Dowd 1990).

A number of analysts have offered explanations for the divergence of opinion between the sexes, with some arguing that women are innately more nurturant and peaceful than men are. Others, however, emphasize that differences in women's and men's political attitudes are chiefly a product of their differing life experiences as well as their historically and culturally specific social roles (Bookman and Morgen 1988).

What is perhaps more interesting is the sudden preoccupation with the gender gap by politicians and campaign strategists. After all, the gender gap is real with respect to certain issues, but it is not that new. With regard to war and peace, for instance, a gender gap can be traced as far back as World War I. In fact, women more than men considered the entry of the United States into both world wars to be mistakes and also voiced greater opposition to the Korean and Vietnam conflicts. In 1952 and 1956, more women than men voted for Dwight D. Eisenhower allegedly because he promised to end the Korean War and because of his success in keeping the United States out of the Suez Canal War (Abzug 1984; Baxter and Lansing 1983). Throughout the early seventies, opinion polls consistently showed women ahead of men in advocating peaceful rather than military solutions to international problems, and their "dovish" stance could further be seen in their greater opposition to the military draft and capital punishment as well as their support of strict gun control laws (Lynn 1984; Abzug 1984).

Part of the reason that the gender gap has received little attention until recently is because researchers studying political behavior have relied on gender stereotypes to interpret their findings. For example, if family members voted alike, it was simply assumed that men influenced their wives' and children's political choices. Equally plausible explanations—namely, that husbands were persuaded by their wives or that similarities in husband-wife voting are reflections of the fact that people tend to marry those like themselves—were rarely considered. However, if men and women voted differently, men's choices were viewed as rational, whereas women's were typically labeled irrational, moralistic, or parochial (Epstein 1983). "For years social scientists have perpetuated the myth that women are more 'irrational' than men, choosing candidates based on their good looks, personality, character, or style . . . [that] 'it was Eisenhower's personality or Kennedy's good looks that prompted greater appeal among women" (Baxter and Lansing 1983:61, 64). But as Cynthia Fuchs Epstein (1983:294) argues:

> [W]omen are as rational or irrational as men in voting their self-interest as well as their ideologies. For example, many women voted for prohibition because drunken husbands were poor providers and physically abused women and children in the home. Thus, it was not "moralism" but self-interest that determined their decision in some cases, and social awareness in others. This same reasoning may by applied to their opposition to more liberal divorce laws, which have been seen as threatening to women's economic interests. Furthermore, the "moral" positions said to be taken by women (e.g., being peace oriented) are often conceptualized as "liberal" when applied to men's political behavior. [*see also* Sears and Funk 1990]

Indeed, there is little evidence of greater conservatism among women voters. In Europe, for example, women at various times have been less supportive than men of authoritarian candidates, such as the National Socialists (Epstein 1983), and in recent U.S. elections, although more women than men identified with the so-called Moral Majority, fewer labeled themselves political conservatives or voted for conservative candidates (Baxter and Lansing 1983).

Epstein (1983) further cautions against comparing all women as a group with all men as a group when trying to discern voting patterns, for age, race, social class, religion, and education remain important intervening variables. For instance, in the 1984 elections, the woman most likely to go to the polls was white, college-educated, aged thirty or older, and living in the Midwest or the South. This contributed substantially to Ronald Reagan's victory that year even though fewer women voted for him. He was least popular among women with less than a high school education, divorced and separated women, and women living in the east. Significantly, black women comprise a substantial portion of each of these subgroups, which led analysts to predict that they would be least likely to cast ballots. Yet, black women have increased their voting rate faster than black men, indicating that they may become a constituency to be reckoned with in future elections (Baxter and Lansing 1983). As we see in Table 10.2, in the 1988 presidential election, black women voted significantly differently from white women. Poole and Zeigler (1985) have also pointed out that the voting differences between women who are full-time homemakers and women who work outside the home may be more significant than the gender gap between women and men. For example, when asked what issue they saw as of greatest importance, working women and working men indicated defense, whereas women who were homemakers cited

TABLE 10.2
A Statistical Portrait of the 1988 Electorate

	% Who Voted For:	
Voters	Bush	Dukakis
Men	57	41
Women	50	49
White Men	63	36
White Women	56	43
Black Men	15	81
Black Women	9	90
Married Men	60	39
Married Women	54	46
Unmarried Men	51	47
Unmarried Women	42	57
Men, 18–29 yrs old	55	43
Women, 18–29 yrs old	49	50
Men, 30–44 yrs old	58	40
Women, 30–44 yrs old	50	49
Men, 45–59 yrs old	62	36
Women, 45–59 yrs old	52	48
Men, 60 & older	53	46
Women, 60 & older	48	52
Men, < high school ed.	49	50
Women, < high school ed.	38	62
Men, high school grads	50	49
Women, high school grads	50	50
Men w/some college	60	38
Women w/some college	54	45
Men, college grads	63	36
Women, college grads	49	51

Source: Adapted from *New York Times* 10 November 1988:B6.

abortion. Women working outside the home felt that equality for women was the third most important issue, whereas women who were full-time homemakers gave this issue lowest priority in their rankings (Poole and Zeigler 1985). Obviously, then, the gender gap is not as simplistic as it is often made out to be; "particular subgroups of women are responsible for a pattern that is widely explained solely in terms of gender" (Bookman and Morgen 1988:23).

One final aspect of the gender gap that deserves our attention is the divergence of men and women on political party affiliation. From 1952 to the midseventies, there was a remarkable consistency in the party identifications of the sexes—as many women as men were likely to be Democrats, Republicans, or Independents. In 1976, however, a shift began: 5 percent more women than men called themselves Democrats. In 1980, the difference was only 4 percent, with women also 4 percent less likely than men to be Independents (Baxter and Lansing 1983). But by 1982, the overall gap had widened to 8 percent, and women in the eighteen to forty-four age group were about 33 percent more likely than their male counterparts to describe themselves as Democrats. In 1990, the gap had narrowed once again, but was largest among young women and men, the former group being significantly more likely to vote Democratic than the latter group. The age factor is especially important, since this is also the group of women that most outvotes their male peers. As one analyst commented, "For Democrats, this means that just on the basis of sex difference, their entire margin today is dependent on the vote of women" (quoted in Lynn 1984:404). In 1986, for instance, women's Democratic votes decided close congressional races in at least ten states and essentially gave the Democrats control of the Senate for the first time during Reagan's administration.

There are, though, many other forms of political activity besides voting. According to political scientist Lester Millbrath (1965), there are basically three levels of political activism. The lowest level, **spectator activities,** include wearing campaign buttons or putting a bumper sticker on one's car as well as voting. In the middle are **transitional activities,** such as writing to public officials, making campaign contributions, and attending rallies or meetings. The highest level, what Millbrath calls **gladiator activities,** involves working on a political campaign or taking an active role in a political party as well as running for public office (Lynn 1984).

Contrary to the popular myth that men are more interested and active in politics, there are actually few differences between the sexes in their level of political activism. In general, both women and men are fairly uninvolved in politics, and their levels of participation in traditional political activities have been declining since the 1960s. However, it appears that women are slightly more likely than men to engage in the spectator activities of wearing buttons and displaying bumper stickers, while men are more involved in transitional activities, especially contributing money to political campaigns (Lynn 1984). To a large extent, this latter difference has been due to the fact that women have had significantly less discretionary income than men, but there is evidence that women's campaign contributions are increasing as more of them join the ranks of the upwardly mobile professionals (Hacker 1986).

This difference, though, is also related to the fact that much of women's transitional political activism has been overlooked or devalued by researchers. Much of this activism has taken place at the grassroots community level by working-class and minority women. Recent studies also reveal that a substantial portion of this activism focuses on preserving and expanding government-funded services that the members of these communities depend on but that are threatened by budget cutbacks and retrenchment. Thus, during the 1970s, working-class minority and white women organized and led rent strikes, tenant unions, school boycotts, petition drives, and the like, in efforts to save essential social services, welfare benefits, and health care programs that were being withdrawn at the same time that the need for these services and programs was growing due to increasing unemployment and economic dislocation (Bookman and Morgen 1988). However, because the study of political activism has largely been limited to "the narrow realm of elections, candidates, and lobbying," these significant and often successful political challenges have gone unnoticed by most scholars (Bookman and Morgen 1988:9).

Indeed, a good deal of scholarly political research has focused on what Millbrath identified as the highest level of political activism, gladiator activities. Here the data are also mixed. Women, as Epstein (1983:290) observes, have long served as political "footsoldiers": canvassing for votes door-to-door or by phone, stuffing envelopes, distributing campaign literature, and so on. They continue to be almost twice as likely as men to work for a political party or a campaign (Lynn 1984). But although women are well represented among campaign staff and volunteers, men have traditionally dominated party conventions. This is noteworthy because:

> it is at party conventions that formal decisions are made about the major presidential candidates and the party platform, which spells out the party's positions on public issues. At conventions various factions come together to discuss common problems and to indulge in the bargaining and compromising that create the coalitions that comprise our national parties. At conventions party leaders interact with rank-and-file members to learn about concerns and potential troublespots in the coming election. For many party workers, a convention is viewed as a reward for years of faithful service (Lynn 1984:409–410).

As Table 10.3 shows, until 1972, neither major party had ever had more than 17 percent female delegates at their national conventions. In 1972, however, the Democrats instituted affirmative action regulations that helped to dramatically increase the representation of female delegates to 40 percent. Although their numbers dropped in 1976, women finally achieved equal representation at the 1980 Democratic National Convention. In contrast, the Republicans, who have

TABLE 10.3
Percentage of Female Delegates to the National Political Conventions, 1900–1988

Year	Democrats*	Republicans
1900	**	***
1904	**	***
1908	**	***
1912	**	***
1916	1	***
1920	6	3
1924	14	11
1928	10	6
1932	12	8
1936	15	6
1940	11	8
1944	11	10
1948	12	10
1952	12	11
1956	12	16
1960	11	15
1964	14	18
1968	13	17
1972	40	30
1976	34	31
1980	49	29
1984	50	44
1988	49	35

*Percentages do not necessarily reflect the proportion of convention votes held by female delegates; many Democratic delegates have held fractional votes.
**Less than 1 percent. Actual numbers: 1900, 1; 1904, 0; 1908, 2; 1912, 2.
***Less than 1 percent. Actual numbers: 1900, 1; 1904, 1; 1908, 2; 1912, 2; 1916, 5.
Source: CAWP 1988.

never adopted affirmative action rules for their conventions, continue to have delegations of 55 to 70 percent men (Center for the American Woman and Politics [CAWP] 1988).

What about male and female candidates and officeholders? This is the question to which we turn next.

PUBLIC OFFICE: FOR MEN ONLY?

Women and men, it seems, have a similar interest in politics if we use their voting rates and political activism as indicators. Yet, historically, men have had a virtual monopoly on public office holding and political appointments. Looking at Table 10.4, we see that this has been true for America's allies as well as the Soviet Union and the Eastern Bloc countries. Although women appear to have fared better outside the United States, nowhere have they "attained representation in political institutions which was equal to men. Rarely [are] they represented at the leadership level in proportion to their presence in the relevant population" (Lovenduski 1986:3; Lindsey 1987). As one senior British politician observed, "A few women, with a lot of luck, have achieved what they wanted. But women as a sex are still undervalued and under-used" (quoted in Lovenduski 1986:3).

During the eighties, women in the United States made considerable progress in the political arena at all levels—local, state, and federal—although they remained grossly underrepresented, especially in the federal government. Before we examine the numbers more closely, however, we will discuss some of the factors that may account for the disparity between the sexes in public officeholding.

One of the ways the gender gap in officeholding has traditionally been

TABLE 10.4
Women in World Politics, 1986

Country	% of Women in the National Legislature	% of Women in the Executive Cabinet	First Year Woman Held Office as President or Prime Minister*
Norway	34	47	1981
USSR	33	0	—
Sweden	32	24	—
Finland	31	18	—
Denmark	27	14	—
Yugoslavia	17**	n.a.	1982
Iceland***	15	10	1980
Australia	11	4	—
Canada	10	16	—
Ireland	8	7	1990
Israel	8	5	1969
Italy	7	3	—
United States	5	8	—
Great Britain**	3.5	0	1979

*Other countries for which data on female representatives in the national legislature or executive cabinet are unavailable but which have had a woman president or prime minister include: Sri Lanka (1960), India (1966), Argentina (1975), Portugal (appointed, 1979), Dominica (1980), the Philippines (1986), Nicaragua (1990), Bangladesh (1991), and France (1991).
**For Yugoslavia, the figures are from 1981 data; for Great Britain, the figures are based on 1983 data.
***The election of April 1987 resulted in a doubling of the number of women in Iceland's national legislature.
Sources: Berry 1987; Lovenduski 1986.

explained is in terms of boys' and girls' different socialization experiences. This argument maintains that dispositions toward politics are formed in childhood when boys are told they can grow up to be president some day; the best girls can hope for is to grow up to marry a man who may one day be a president. Consequently, children learn that politics is a masculine activity, and this is reflected in their adult behavior: women rarely run for public office.

This explanation has some appeal because, as we found in Chapter 4, early childhood socialization does have a powerful impact on the development of sex-typed attitudes and behaviors. Recent research, however, found no sex differences in the political views of school-age children (Epstein 1983). What is more, if differential socialization is at work, we would expect to find less similarity in men's and women's interest in politics than what we have seen here. Still, young women aspiring to political careers have had far fewer role models than their male counterparts. This is changing slowly, though, as more women each election year enter political races; the 1984 vice presidential nomination of Geraldine Ferraro is also reported to have had an impact (Engel 1985). Importantly, female officeholders frequently state that they were inspired and assisted in their political careers by other women. According to a report by the Center for the American Woman and Politics (1984), about 33 percent of female state representatives and 25 percent of state senators, county commissioners, and local council members had female role models.

A second explanation is that women have greater difficulty meeting the demands of public life given their domestic responsibilities. Like most employed women, female politicians shoulder a double work load; their spouses do not usually assume primary responsibility for housekeeping or childcare. It is not surprising, therefore, that women typically enter politics at a later age than men (after their children are grown), and that female political elites are more likely than men to be single, widowed, or divorced (CAWP 1984; Lynn 1984; Sapiro 1982). In Europe, too, Lovenduski (1986) found that women in public office are less often married and have fewer children than their male colleagues. This does not mean that men do not experience conflict between their political careers and their family lives. Recent research indicates that they do and that the tension may be high. However, men are more likely to pursue their political ambitions *despite* the conflicts, whereas women frequently try to manage the conflict by delaying their political careers or by giving up one role for the other. Hence, women more often than men have unfulfilled or suppressed political ambitions (Foderaro 1989; Sapiro 1982).

A third, although increasingly less frequent explanation is that men outnumber women in elected office because most women lack the necessary qualifications and credentials. It is certainly true that most female officeholders prior to World War II had inherited their seats and simply served out the terms of their deceased husbands or fathers. Even if they were elected, they usually had less education than the men, and because the legal and business professions were largely closed to them, they came to politics via different occupational backgrounds, typically teaching. In recent years, however, this has changed. Female officeholders, in fact, are more likely than male officeholders to have attended college, and black female officeholders are more likely than female officeholders overall to have attended college. The number of women in public office who are lawyers and businesspeople has also risen, as has the number with previous elective experience. Although female officeholders still are less likely than their male colleagues to have held previous elective offices, they are more likely to have had other types of political experience. For example, female officeholders are more likely than their male counterparts to have held previous appointed government positions and to have worked on political campaigns before running for office themselves (CAWP 1985, 1984; Carroll 1985; Gertzog 1984). Consequently, the "qualifications and credentials argument" is less tenable today than in the past.

A fourth argument is that women may be relatively scarce in public office because of prejudice and discrimination against them that may occur on two levels: among the electorate and within political office. Studies of sexism among the electorate have yielded mixed results. For example, in a 1989 opinion poll, 54 percent of respondents said they would vote for a qualified female candidate for president if such a woman were nominated by their political party (General Social Surveys 1989). Similarly, in a 1986 *U.S. News and World Report* opinion poll, a majority of voters (60 percent) reportedly favored a female presidential or vice presidential candidate for the 1988 election, and 55 percent said they would like to see more women in congressional and gubernatorial races. However, closer analysis revealed that only 22 percent really wanted a woman on the vice presidential ticket and just 9 percent wanted a woman to run for president; 36 percent of those surveyed said they would refuse to vote for a woman who ran for president (Mashek 1986; *see* Box 10.1, page 263). In a 1984 *Los Angeles Times* poll, a sample of citizens was questioned concerning whether or not they would vote for a hypothetical candidate for governor. Palley (1987:177) reports:

> One candidate was described as a business executive who was married, had two kids, and was a native New Yorker. The other candidate was presented as a lawyer who was married, had three children, and was a native midwesterner. For half of the sample, the New York native was described as "she." "She" lost to her opponent, the native midwesterner, 54 percent to 27 percent. For the other half of the sample, "she" was the native midwestern lawyer. "She" lost again, this time by a margin of 43 percent to 38 percent.

It is also the case that while a majority of voters say they think female candidates are as qualified as males (Rosenwasser, et al. 1987; Mashek 1986), female candidates are more closely scrutinized by the electorate and must present a carefully balanced image that is neither too traditionally feminine nor too masculine. As one observer explained:

> A woman candidate must be . . . assertive rather than aggressive, attractive without being a sexpot, self-confident but not domineering. She must neither be too pushy nor show reticence. The human qualities of compassion and sympathy

must not resemble emotionality. Because society tends to label active women as pushy, aggressive, domineering or masculine, voters may be more ready to see negative traits in a woman candidate. They may perceive determined women as shrill, strident or emotional. A woman is easily discounted by being labeled "just one of those women's libbers" (quoted in Carroll 1985:94).

The 1990s have been labeled by some analysts as the decade for women in politics. This is because as the Cold War ended at the start of the nineties, the political agenda in the United States began to shift to social issues, such as the environment, homelessness, education, and reproductive freedom. These are issues on which female candidates are thought to have had an advantage, since opinion polls show that voters perceive them as capable of handling such issues better than men (Toner 1990). Female candidates, though, did not fare well in the 1990 state elections. Although three of the seven female candidates for governor were successful in their election bids, only one out of eight won a senate race. As a result of the 1990 elections, the number of women in the House of Representatives declined by four. It remains to be seen whether a shift in national attention to the crisis in the Persian Gulf played any part in these election returns.

Prejudice and discrimination against female candidates can be found at a second level as well: within the political parties. Sexism within the political parties is well documented. The overwhelming majority of party leaders are men, many of whom subscribe to traditional gender stereotypes. Faced with the increasing demands of women for greater political roles, party leaders have sometimes responded by recruiting female candidates as "sacrificial lambs," that is, as candidates "in districts where the party's nominee has little chance of winning the general election" (Carroll 1985:36). However, other studies (*see* Welch, et al. 1982) have found this practice to be less problematic for women candidates than incumbency and access to campaign funds.

Incumbents, that is, those who hold political office and are seeking another term, have several advantages during an election, not the least of which are high public visibility, recognition among voters, and the opportunity to campaign throughout their term in office. Because fewer women are in office, when they do run it is more often as challengers rather than as incumbents and, not surprisingly, they lose more frequently when running against an incumbent than for an open seat. Incumbency certainly proved to be a formidable obstacle for candidates in the 1990 state elections (*New York Times* 8 November 1990:B6).

Incumbent or not, every political candidate needs money to run a campaign, and the more prestigious the office they seek, the more money they need. The significance of monetary power in elections is evident if one considers that in 1988, candidates for the U.S. Senate each spent on average more than $3 million. In effect, this means that to win a Senate seat, a candidate would have to raise $10,000 a week for six years (Common Cause 1989). In the 1990 congressional elections, more than $225 million was spent by candidates on television

How the American Public Views Male and Female Politicians

BOX 10.1

A number of polls have been conducted that question samples of American voters concerning their attitudes toward male and female politicians. The following are some of the results of those polls.

Do you associate the following qualities more with a woman or with a man running for public office?

	Women	Men	No Difference	Don't Know
Honesty	44%	12%	41%	3%
Toughness	19	55	23	3
Knowledge of Taxes	15	35	46	4

Do you agree or disagree with the following statement: Most men are better suited emotionally for politics than most women?

Agree:	28.3%
Disagree:	65.0%
Not sure:	6.0%
No answer:	0.5%

Are women candidates generally better qualified or less qualified than the men they run against?

Better:	13%
Less:	12
No Difference:	71
Don't Know:	3

For which office would you refuse to vote for a woman candidate?

State legislature:	3%
U.S. House:	4
U.S. Senate:	7
Governor:	8
Vice President:	21
President:	36

How likely do you think it is that a woman will be elected President of the United States in the next ten years?

	Women	Men
Likely	39	38
Unlikely	56	57
Don't know	6	5

Sources: compiled from General Social Survey 1989:244; Media General/Associated Press September 24, 1991; Mashek 1986:22.

advertising alone (*New York Times* 7 November 1990:B2). Of course, political parties provide some of the financial backing for their candidates, but increasingly, campaign funds come from other sources, and this has made fundraising especially difficult for women. For one thing, women typically have not been members of the interlocking professional, social, and political networks through which campaign contributions are frequently generated. Many elite private clubs, for example, have traditionally excluded women regardless of their occupations or status.

Women also have had difficulty securing funds and other resources from the more than 4,200 Political Action Committees (PACs) operating in the United States. PACs are basically lobbying groups that contribute to the campaigns of candidates whom they think will best represent their interests in government. In the period 1987–1988 alone, PACs contributed nearly $160 million to candidates for political office (U.S. Department of Commerce 1990). PAC representatives insist that the reason so few women receive contributions from them is that the candidates do not solicit them (*Women's Political Times* 1986a). This makes sense given that many PACs are parts of large corporations and professional associations in fields in which the percentage of women has been small. However, it does not explain why, even when contributions are solicited, female candidates are given less than their male counterparts (Carroll 1985).

There are indications that the political arena is changing, however. Courts have ordered the exclusive men's clubs to admit women, women's organizations have mobilized their memberships to support female or feminist candidates, women have established formal and informal political coalitions, and women have established their own PACs, such as the National Political Congress of Black Women's PAC and the Women's Campaign Fund, the oldest independent women's PAC (CAWP n.d.; Hacker 1986; *Women's Political Times* 1986b). And despite the many barriers that continue to stand in their way, record numbers of women are running for public office. How successful have they been in their election bids, and how far must we still go before the United States is equally represented in government by women and men? To find out, let's consider the relative numbers of men and women in specific elected and appointed offices.

Women and Men in State and Local Government

Table 10.5 shows the number of women holding selected state and local offices. Clearly, men continue to dominate state and local government as they constitute the vast majority of officeholders in every category. Still, it is at the state level that women have made their greatest political gains in recent years.

Most important perhaps is the increase in the number of female state legislators. Although men continue to hold 83 percent of all state legislative seats, the number of women legislators has more than quadrupled since 1969, increasing from 4 percent to 17 percent. However, the states with the highest numbers of

TABLE 10.5
Women in State and Local Government, Selected Offices, 1989

Public Office	Number of Women Officeholders	
Governor	3	
Lt. Governor	4	(of 42)
Secretary of State	15	
Attorney General	3	
State Treasurer	10	
State Auditor	6	
State Legislators	1,265	(17.0%)
County Governing Board Official	1,653	(8.9%)*
Municipal/Township Official	14,672	(14.3%)**
Mayor (cities with populations over 30,000)	115	(13.1%)***

*Based on 1988 data
**Based on 1985 data
***Of these, 31 serve in cities with populations over 100,000. Of the 100 largest U.S. cities, 17 have female mayors and 4 of these are among the 10 largest cities.
Source: CAWP 1989.

female legislators also have the lowest paid legislators. "In New Hampshire, for instance, a third of the seats in the State Legislature are occupied by women, the highest proportion in the nation. But that Legislature also has the lowest pay scale of any in the country" (Foderaro 1989:32).

It has been at the state level, too, that black and Hispanic men have made significant inroads. In 1989, for instance, there were 124 Hispanic state executives and legislators, up from 110 in 1983. For the same year, there were 417 black state legislators, an increase of 91 since 1981 (U.S. Department of Commerce 1990). This is especially significant because the state legislatures historically have served as the proving grounds for most politicians who aspire to higher office, particularly the U.S. Congress. However, this benefit may accrue only to white women and minority men since women of color continue to be grossly underrepresented in state legislatures. In 1989, minority women constituted just 1.8 percent of state legislators and 10.6 percent of female state legislators. Black women serve in the legislatures of thirty-two states, Hispanic women in seven states, Native American women in four states, and Asian-American women in three states (U.S. Department of Commerce 1990; CAWP 1989a). But there is reason to believe, as we will see next, that state legislative seats may not serve as stepping stones for female politicians, regardless of race, to the same extent that they do for men.

Women and Men in the Federal Government

Looking at Table 10.6, we see the number of women in the U.S. Congress from 1949 to 1990. What is most striking about the figures in this table is not so much the small number of women—most of you would probably predict that—but rather the lack of substantial improvement in these numbers over the forty-one-year period. It can hardly be said that there is a strong pattern of growth in the number of female elected officials, particularly in the Senate. In fact, at the rate women are currently being elected, it will be another 410 years before there is balance between the sexes in Congress. When race is taken into account, the disparity is even more dramatic: only five black women, two Asian-American women, and one Hispanic woman have ever served in the House of Representatives; no woman of color has ever served in the Senate (CAWP 1990).

TABLE 10.6
Women in the U.S. Congress, 1949–1989

Year	Congress	Senate	House
1949	81st	1	9
1951	82nd	1	10
1953	83rd	3	12
1955	84th	1	17
1957	85th	1	15
1959	86th	2	17
1961	87th	2	18
1963	88th	2	12
1965	89th	2	11
1967	90th	1	11
1969	91st	1	10
1971	92nd	2	13
1973	93rd	0	16
1975	94th	0	19
1977	95th	2	20
1979	96th	1	16
1981	97th	2	21
1983	98th	2	22
1985	99th	2	23
1987	100th	2	24
1989	101st	2	28*

*At the close of 1989, there were 27 women serving in the U.S. House of Representatives, but in early 1990, Susan Molinari (R-NY) won a special election and was sworn in to the seat previously held by her father.
Source: CAWP 1989b.

Although women have served in Congress since 1916 when Jeannette Rankin was elected to the House of Representatives, 45 percent of Congresswomen prior to 1949 came to office through **widow's succession.** We alluded to widow's succession earlier; it occurs when a congressman dies or becomes too ill to serve and his wife is appointed or elected to finish his term. Women who entered congressional office this way were sometimes reelected after their husband's term expired. For female senators especially, this has been the primary means to office; it was not until 1983 (the 98th Congress) that two women served in the Senate simultaneously without either of them having gotten their seats through widow's succession (Lynn 1984).

Although women are now coming to Congress through election in their own right, what happens when they get there remains problematic. More specifically, there are still no women in the high-ranking leadership positions and they chair none of the standing congressional committees. In the House of Representatives, for instance, to which women have had greater access than the Senate, no woman has served as House Speaker and only six women, all of whom served prior to 1977, have ever chaired House committees (CAWP 1989b). "[F]ew have served on, let alone headed, any of the four most coveted House committees—Appropriations, Budget, Rules, and Ways and Means" (Gertzog 1984:93). Women most often hold secondary positions, and although they can now be found as members of most structured congressional groups (e.g., bipartisan caucuses), they are still excluded from most of the unstructured groups (e.g., sporting groups). These latter groups are not insignificant, for apart from being social gatherings, they provide members with both an informal information network and opportunities to build alliances with colleagues.

Part of the reason for women's exclusion from some positions and committees is their lack of seniority. For example, most analysts agree that it takes a minimum of five terms in the House before election or appointment to a powerful position is likely; floor leaders typically serve eighteen years before securing that spot (Gertzog 1984; Lynn 1984). At the same time, there is evidence that sexism is also at least partly responsible, as Gertzog (1984:111–112) discovered in his conversations with Congressmen:

> Most Congressmen interviewed were disinclined to choose a congresswoman
> for a top leadership position. Selection of a woman for a secondary party role
> was one thing—election to a major leadership role was quite another. Some
> respondents said that they themselves might vote for a woman, but each added
> that their male colleagues were not ready to do the same. . . . A few noted that
> many of their colleagues believed that it was "in the nature of things" for men to
> have authority over women, not the other way around. Some added that House
> members were unaccustomed to working with or for a woman before they came
> to Congress. They saw themselves as the principal authority figure in their own
> households, and they were not prepared to accept a sharp departure from such
> arrangements in Congress.

We know that every chief executive of the United States has been male, as has every vice president. There has never been a female candidate for president from either of the major political parties, although Senator Patricia Schroeder sought the Democratic nomination in 1988. It was not until 1984 that a woman was nominated by a major party for the office of vice president. However, in considering the executive branch of the federal government, we must keep in mind that those elected to office also have the privilege of making a variety of high-ranking appointments. As one report emphasized, presidential appointments, particularly for women and minorities, are critical for three major reasons:

1. They provide young professionals with valuable career experience.
2. They set an example for private employers to follow in hiring personnel.
3. They offer opportunities for input into policy making from individuals with diverse backgrounds and interests (Pear 1987).

So how have the sexes fared relative to one another in recent political appointments? Although Ronald Reagan's support for women's rights was equivocal, it was to Mr. Reagan's credit that he appointed women to about forty posts which had never before been held by a female. These included several in nontraditional or stereotypically masculine areas: for instance, Elizabeth Dole to Secretary of Transportation, Constance Horner to director of the Office of Personnel Management, and Heather Gradison to chair the Interstate Commerce Commission. Nevertheless, Mr. Reagan had almost 300 federal judgeships to fill and appointed women to just 26 (8.7 percent) of them. This is of special significance because federal judges have an impact on law beyond the administration that appointed them since their terms are for life. At the same time, the number of minorities, male or female, receiving political appointments declined significantly between 1980 and 1986, from 44 to just 20 positions (Pear 1987).

President Bush has increased the number of presidential appointments to a record level for any U.S. president; 19.4 percent of Mr. Bush's appointments have been women (a total of 185 women). However, there are few women in his senior staff: nine women to forty men. The seven women who are deputy assistants to the president all work in areas traditionally considered "female fields". According to one report, President Bush is " 'a guy's guy' and his inner circle reflects that" (Dowd 1991:B6).

Perhaps the Bush administration's most highly acclaimed female and minority appointment was that of Antonia Novello as Surgeon General. But undoubtedly the most dramatic and well-publicized recent female presidential appointment was made by Ronald Reagan in 1981 when he nominated Sandra Day O'Connor as a Supreme Court justice. Historically, the all-male Supreme Court had done much to uphold sex discrimination. Well into the 1960s, their decisions in sex discrimination cases reflected the opinion of Chief Justice Waite who, in the 1875 case of *Minor* v. *Happersett,* declared that women, like children, are "a special category of citizens" in need of both discipline and protection (Sachs and Wilson 1978). This was essentially the Court's rationale for denying women equal employment opportunities and other civil rights. It was not until 1973 that the Court ruled that most of the discrimination against women was nothing more than "romantic paternalism" that, "in practical effect, put women not on a pedestal but in a cage" (*Frontiero* v. *Richardson*). Still, the Supreme Court has not struck down all forms of sex discrimination.

With O'Connor's appointment, many feminists were hopeful that a female justice would act to preserve the hard-won legal support of gender equality secured in recent cases. To a large extent, O'Connor has not disappointed them. In a substantial number of sex discrimination cases, O'Connor has supported equality, particularly in the area of employment. In addition, hers was the deciding vote in a 1983 case, *Arizona Governing Commission* v. *Norris,* in which the Court struck down insurance companies' discriminatory practice of paying women lower pension benefits than men because of their life expectancy. At the same time, however, O'Connor has been inconsistent with regard to protecting women's abortion rights and, in 1984, she voted to limit the Title IX liability of educational institutions (*Grove City College* v. *Bell; see* Chapters 5 and 12).

In 1990, President Bush had the opportunity to appoint another woman to the Supreme Court when Justice William Brennan, considered by many to be the leading liberal voice on the Court, retired. In fact, Edith H. Jones was one of the two finalists that the president interviewed for the appointment. Mr. Bush chose instead, the other finalist, David H. Souter, a white male. However, Justice O'Connor's behavior on the Court illustrates an important point: the presence of women in government posts is not enough to ensure that women's interests will be consistently represented or that gender equality will always be promoted. Indeed, as observers of British politics have noted, a female leader may oppose women's rights and gender equality, while some male leaders ardently support them. At the same time, most women in appointed government positions do not have an institutional mandate to actively work on gender-related issues, and even those who do must address them in the context of the administration's policy preferences (Boneparth and Stoper 1988). Still, it does appear that "a certain 'critical mass' of women must exist to enable the development of a group identity and the resistance of socialization into male norms of behavior" (Lovenduski 1986:243). It is also essential if gender stereotypes are ever to be broken down. The more sex segregated an institution is, though, the more difficult this is to achieve, as we will see next in our discussion of women and men in the military. National defense and the military are important aspects of government and, therefore, deserve our attention here.

WOMEN AND MEN IN THE MILITARY

We noted earlier that women tend to express greater opposition than men to military intervention and the draft, and in general, they appear to be more pacifistic. Clearly, this is not true for all women, nor has it ever been. Historical and cross-cultural research shows, in fact, that women have often supported militarism and have even engaged in combat and other military activities. During the nineteenth century, for example, in the West African nation of Dahomey (now Benin), the king had an all-female fighting force of between 4,000 and 10,000 soldiers as part of his standing army (Sacks 1979). More recently, Soviet women during World War II assumed combat roles and fought with men in first-line units; at least 100,000 of them were subsequently decorated for bravery. In December 1986, Denmark became the first NATO country to allow women to join combat forces; Danish women may volunteer for service on naval battle units.

In the United States, there are accounts of women who disguised themselves as men and fought at the front beside their husbands or brothers: Deborah Sampson, for instance, during the American Revolution; Lucy Brewer in the War of 1812; and Loretta Velasquez in the Civil War (Rustad 1982). Although women have been officially prohibited from combat duty in the U.S. armed forces, they were employed during World War II in espionage and as sabateurs behind enemy lines. According to one researcher:

> The role of females was not trivial, and it certainly was in no way token. Indeed, this female role subjected women to risks of death or torture exactly parallel to those for males. . . . The meager evidence we have from the performance of women in espionage and sabotage suggests that women can be as brave and as coldly homicidal as men, whenever their patriotism calls for it (Quester 1982:226, 229).

For the most part, however, these American women were an exceptional few. Warmaking has been and, to a large extent, remains a male activity and the military a male-dominated institution. In the United States, when women were first recruited for military service during World War I, it was to a limited number of nursing and clerical jobs that did not carry full military status and hence none of the benefits to which male military personnel were entitled. During the Second World War, the Women's Army Corps (WAC) was established and granted women full military status with benefits throughout the war and for six months afterward. Other military corps for women were also begun and included the Women's Reserve of the Navy (WAVES) and the Women's Air Force Service Pilots (WASPS). Yet their roles were strictly limited, and the War Department continued to adhere to a policy of recruiting men, no matter how uneducated, unskilled, or incompetent, before accepting women. Despite the fact that, especially as nurses, these women frequently faced dangerous and life-threatening conditions in war zones— some were wounded or killed—they were often derided by servicemen, civilians, and the press. Reporters seemed most interested in what the women were wearing right down to whether they were issued girdles, whereas the general public and servicemen typically viewed them as whores or lesbians in search of partners (Rustad 1982).

Until the late 1960s, women served as a reserve army in the truest sense for the military. Recruited as a cheap source of labor when manpower was low, they were dismissed as soon as men were available to replace them. Shortly after World War II, for instance, 98 percent of the Women's Army Corps was discharged, but because women had not been given the same civilian reemployment rights as men, they had greater difficulty finding work, and many were forced to take jobs well below their skill levels. "Representative of the remittable occupational roles was the plight of wartime women pilots who could find employment in the airline industry only as hostesses and typists" (Rustad 1982:34).

At the same time, women who joined the military had to meet higher enlistment standards than men; however, they were given fewer privileges and career opportunities and were subject to stricter regulations. For example, the 1948 Women's Armed Services Integration Act, while establishing a permanent place for women in the military, reserved 98 percent of the positions for men and placed a cap on the term of service and number of women who could be promoted to the rank of full colonel or navy captain: one. No woman could become a general or an admiral. As part of their training, women were instructed in how to maintain a "ladylike" appearance, how to apply makeup, and how to get in and out of cars in their tight-fitting uniform skirts. Unlike male military personnel, they had to remain childless—pregnancy was grounds for discharge—and, if married, they had to prove that they were their husbands' primary support in order to receive dependents' benefits (Stiehm 1985).

In the late 1960s and throughout the 1970s, a series of events took place that greatly expanded both the number and the roles of female military personnel. First, in 1967, Congress passed Public Law 90-30, which removed the limits on the number of enlisted women and the number of promotions for women officers. In addition, the Women's Movement was actively promoting the equal integration of women into all areas of life and, with the passage of the Equal Rights Amendment by Congress in 1972, many thought that this would extend to female military personnel as well. Also in 1972, congressional hearings were held on the role of women in the military, and the report that followed encouraged the Defense Department to recruit and utilize women on a more equal basis with men. In 1973, the military draft was replaced by the all-volunteer Force, causing worried military planners to turn to the recruitment of women as a means to keep enlistments up. Adding to this were several court cases, such as *Frontiero* v. *Richardson* (1973), in which the Supreme Court, in fairly strong language that we have already quoted, overturned the military's policy of awarding dependents' benefits to female personnel using different standards from those applied to male personnel. Later in a federal court, the navy's policy of barring women from sea duty was also struck down (*Owens* v. *Brown,* 1978). By 1976, ROTC was accepting women, as were the military academies, and air force women joined those in the army and navy in having flight schools open to them. Perhaps the most important change, though, occurred one year earlier in 1975 when the Defense Department lifted its ban on parenting for female personnel and made discharge for pregnancy available on a voluntary basis (Stiehm 1985).

In light of this dramatic turn of events, it is hardly surprising that the number of women who entered the military rose substantially during the 1970s. Between 1972 and 1976, the number of military women tripled; by 1980, it had increased almost fivefold. Most of the increase occurred in the enlisted ranks which, by 1980, accounted for 87 percent of female military personnel. However, like most men who enlisted, these women rarely stayed for more than one tour of duty and, in 1980, there were actually fewer women in the higher enlisted ranks (E-8 and above) than in 1972 (Stiehm 1985).

During the Carter administration, there appeared to be a strong commitment to recruit women for the military, and the president even favored requiring women to register for the military draft when registration was reinstated. Interestingly, despite Ronald Reagan's more "hawkish" attitudes and his support of military build-up, he took a more conservative stance toward women in the military and, shortly after his election, the Defense Department scaled down their recruitment of female enlistees (Quester 1982).

Nevertheless, looking at Table 10.7 we find that the number of women in the

TABLE 10.7
Men and Women on Active Military Duty, by Race, 1982–1990 [in thousands]

	1982	1983	1984	1985	1990*
Total	2,096.4	2,112.1	2,123.4	2,137.4	2,043.7
Men	1,908.1	1,915.9	1,922.6	1,928.0	1,816.7
Officers	267.1	273.7	274.9	278.8	262.4
White	237.5	245.7	248.2	251.4	n.a.
Black	13.7	14.4	15.3	16.1	n.a.
Hispanic	3.5	3.7	3.9	4.2	n.a.
Enlisted	1,641.0	1,642.3	1,647.6	1,649.2	1,554.3
White	1,094.8	1,164.2	1,177.7	1,181.1	n.a.
Black	351.7	341.4	334.5	331.7	n.a.
Hispanic	67.6	67.8	66.5	66.3	n.a.
Women	188.5	196.1	200.8	209.4	227.0
Officers	25.3	27.0	28.7	30.3	34.2
White	20.9	21.9	23.6	24.9	n.a.
Black	2.8	3.2	3.5	3.7	n.a.
Hispanic	.4	.5	.5	.5	n.a.
Enlisted	163.2	169.1	172.2	179.0	192.8
White	106.7	110.5	11.6	173.1	n.a.
Black	45.9	50.1	49.8	53.1	n.a.
Hispanic	5.2	5.7	5.4	5.7	n.a.

*The enlisted category for this year includes cadets and midshipmen.
Sources: U.S. Department of Defense 1990:7,16; U.S. Department of Commerce 1987:327.

military increased along with the number of men during the 1980s. Today, women make up 11 percent of the armed forces. We also see here that the number of minority women in the military has increased somewhat at least between 1982 and 1985. As Enloe (1987:533) points out, "It may well be that the militarization of American society in the 1980s is increasing the vulnerability of precisely those women who are most precariously positioned in the economic system, enhancing the appeal of the military's offers of shelter, health benefits for children, and a steady income." Given the exceptionally high unemployment rates of young minority men, we might expect Enloe's argument to apply to them as well, but as we see in Table 10.7, minority male enlistments decreased between 1982 and 1985. There were charges of racism in the military, however, when it was reported in January 1991 that, although one of eight Americans is black; one of four U.S. troops serving in the Persian Gulf was black. African Americans compose 11.3 percent of the civilian population over the age of sixteen, but at the outbreak of the war, they were 20.5 percent of military personnel on active duty and 24.6 percent of troops in the Persian Gulf (Wilkerson 1991).

Women in the military are still barred from combat positions, that is, positions that entail a substantial risk of being killed in action or captured as a prisoner of war. Nevertheless, they may hold "combat support" roles, which means that there are very few military jobs closed to them today. In the Air Force, for instance, 95 percent of positions are open to women including membership on the crews of reconnaissance and electronic warfare planes. In 1988, the Pentagon announced that it would open 4,000 military posts to women that had previously been closed to them. As a result, some observers argue that the difference between a combat role and a combat support role may now be more a matter of semantics than a reflection of the actual danger attached to the position. For example, "While [women] are not permitted to fly fighter aircraft, Air Force women regularly pilot KC-135 tankers that refuel the fighters and make an even more tempting target for enemy missiles" (Lamar 1988:27).

Indeed, female pilots engaged in aerial refueling operations during the U.S. raid on Libya in 1986. Women also actively participated in the U.S. invasion of Panama and, for the first time, a female army captain commanded U.S. soldiers in combat. One military official who reviewed the attack led by Capt. Linda Bray against Panamanian Defense Forces was quoted as saying that, "What has been demonstrated is the ability of women to lead, for men and women to work together as a team without distractions, and for women to react in an aggressive manner" (quoted in Gordon 1990:A12). In 1990 and 1991, women accounted for more than 10 percent of the military troops deployed in the Persian Gulf crisis. Ironically, in this last instance, U.S. female military personnel risked their lives—two, in fact, were taken prisoners of war—in defense of a country in which women are afforded few civil rights—where, in fact, they are still considered men's property.

Still, the Pentagon remains committed to its exclusion policy and maintains that if it is to be changed, it must be changed by legislation enacted by Congress.

It is uncertain, though, whether such legislation, even if passed, would become law, since President Bush supports the combat exclusion of women.

The exclusion of women from combat roles has important consequences for female military personnel. Combat positions command substantially higher salaries on average than support positions do. They are also critical for promotion to the highest military ranks, which helps to explain why women are concentrated at the bottom and middle ranks (Lamar 1988; Enloe 1987). In fact, a 1989 report to Congress from the General Accounting Office stated that combat exclusion constitutes women's greatest impediment in achieving promotions (Sciolino 1990).

This last point is important because it illustrates that what seems not to have changed much in the military is the rampant sexism (*see also* Box 10.2). All branches of the service have been accused of tokenism, and female military personnel remain underutilized and continue to be harassed, often sexually, by their superiors as well as their co-workers (Rustad, 1982). In one recent Navy survey, for instance, the majority of the 1,400 women who responded reported experiences of sexual harassment (Lamar 1988). In October 1990, four separate

---

BOX 10.2   Homosexuals in the U.S. Military

Other than the combat exclusion of women, the military also has a more general exclusionary policy on the basis of sexual preference. The policy, directive No. 1332.14, bars "persons who engage in homosexual conduct," or who "demonstrate a propensity" to do so, from military service on the grounds that such individuals "adversely affect the ability of the Armed Forces to maintain discipline, good order and morale." Furthermore, the directive maintains, homosexuals disrupt the system of rank and command, discourage heterosexuals from enlisting and remaining in the military, and endanger national security because they may be blackmailed into disclosing military secrets (Gross 1990b). Interestingly, two recent studies, commissioned by the Pentagon itself, call this policy into question. Neither study found evidence that homosexuals disrupt the armed forces and both urged the retention of gay and lesbian military personnel (Gross 1990c). The Pentagon, however, remains firmly committed to the policy and, in 1990, the U.S. Supreme Court, by refusing to hear two cases challenging the ban, upheld it.

According to Pentagon data, about 1,400 men and women are discharged annually from the military for violating directive No. 1332.14. It is not uncommon for them, and others suspected of being gay or lesbian, to be subjected to lengthy investigations and humiliating interrogations. Many, despite excellent service records, are discharged without benefit of judicial proceedings (Gross 1990b).

Although both male and female homosexual military personnel are subjected to such harassment, Pentagon data also show that lesbians are discharged at a rate almost ten times higher than that of gay men (Lewin 1988). It is unclear precisely why this is the case, but it is likely to be the product of sex discrimination coupled with homophobia.

reports of investigations of the United States Naval Academy found that "a 'considerable segment' of midshipmen, faculty and staff believe that women have no place there" and that " 'low-level sexual harassment can pass as normal operating procedure' in some classrooms or among groups of students" (Barringer 1990:A12). Similarly, in a major study conducted by the Pentagon, 64 percent of female military personnel and 17 percent of male military personnel out of more than 20,000 surveyed indicated that they had experienced some form of sexual harassment, ranging from teasing to sexual assault, from someone at work in the last year (Schmitt 1990).

It has been argued that "the changing nature of warfare, which is based on technology rather than on brute force, does not justify the exclusion of women" (Rustad 1982:230), and recent opinion polls show that more than 70 percent of the general public in the United States thinks that female military personnel should be permitted to serve in whatever roles they choose (Sciolino 1990). But the question remains, do women really want to fully participate with men in waging war? This question spotlights a feminist dilemma concerning the military roles of women and men. As Rustad (1982:5) has phrased it, "Does the inclusion of women in martial roles mean greater opportunities or does it mean only that women will have the same rights as males to perform strenuous, dangerous, and obnoxious tasks?" There are those who maintain that if women want full equality with men, then they must accept the fact that that status entails obligations, including defending their country, as well as privileges. Others concur that this may be the only way for women to prove that they deserve to be equal with men. Opponents of these views emphasize, in contrast, that feminism's goal is not to turn women into men, but rather to establish a new value system in which nurturing by both women and men is rewarded instead of aggression.

Although it is unlikely that this debate will be settled soon, there are at least two important points that should be kept in mind. The first is that there are some women who wish to participate on an equal footing with men in the military, just as there are men who would welcome the combat exemption now afforded to women. Inasmuch as feminism encourages individuals to exercise control over their lives, a feminist approach to the dilemma is to lobby government to allow both women and men the right to choose whether they will serve in the military as well as in what capacity they wish to serve.

At the same time, however, feminism does not mean adherence to total relativism. That is, feminists do not need to see every life choice as positive or beneficial simply because some individuals favor it. It is possible, therefore, to oppose militarism, but also hold that while the military establishment remains a central institution in our society, both women and men should be given equal roles in it. As the National Organization for Women has argued, "If we cannot stop the return to registration and draft, we also cannot choose between our daughters and our sons. The choice robs women as well as men. In the long and short run, it injures us all" (quoted in Rustad 1982:4).

THE POLITICS OF GENDER

The purpose of this chapter was to examine the different political roles and attitudes of men and women primarily in the United States, but in other parts of the world too. We have seen that women have been neglected in most discussions of government and politics. Denied the right to vote until 1920 and denied equal protection of the laws until the 1970s, American women have long been excluded from the practice of politics on the grounds that they were too stupid, too frail, too emotional, and too irrational.

As we have learned in this chapter, this situation is finally beginning to change. Once it was documented that women are as interested and active in politics as men are and, more significantly, that they are more inclined than men to vote, political analysts and campaign strategists began to sit up and take notice of female constituents and candidates. Differences in the political opinions of men and women received more careful study, and a gender gap on certain issues—environmental protection, social welfare, and foreign policy, in particular—was revealed. At the same time, we find more women now running for political office and obtaining political appointments, some in traditionally masculine-identified areas. By 1990, in fact, three states (Delaware, Iowa, and North Dakota) had enacted "gender balance" policies; that is, in those states, governors' appointments to boards and commissions must be equally divided between women and men (Gross 1990d).

Nevertheless, the percentage of women in government decision-making posts remains so small that it may take more than four centuries longer to achieve parity between the sexes in political representation. Although we have seen that women in the military have actually made greater progress in this regard, especially during the last twenty years, they are still far from securing equal status with military men.

In our discussion of women in Congress, we noted that some of their male colleagues have resisted electing or appointing them to leadership roles because they think female authority over men is not "in the nature of things." It is interesting that in trying to justify denying women equal rights, politicians and judges frequently claim that gender inequality reflects Divine will—that it is part of God's plan in other words. Indeed, in the United States, despite the constitutionally established separation of church and state, sociologists have long recognized that religion and politics are highly interactive. In this chapter we have examined the role of government in perpetuating and often justifying gender inequality. In the next chapter, we will consider the church's role.

KEY TERMS

gender gap   differences between the voting patterns and political opinions of men and
those of women

gladiator activities   the highest level of political activism in Millbrath's typology; include working on a political campaign, taking an active role in a political party, or running for public office

spectator activities   the lowest level of political activism in Millbrath's typology; include voting, wearing a campaign button, or displaying a political bumper sticker

transitional activities   the midrange of political activism in Millbrath's typology; include writing to public officials, making campaign contributions, and attending rallies or political meetings

widow's succession   occurs when a Congressman dies or is too ill to serve out his term and his wife is appointed or elected to finish it for him; prior to 1949, the primary means to seats in Congress for women

SUGGESTED READINGS

Barkalow, C., with A. Raab 1989. *In the Men's House: An Inside Account of Life in the Army by One of West Point's First Female Graduates.* New York: Poseiden Press.

Bookman, A., and S. Morgan (Eds.) 1988. *Women and the Politics of Empowerment.* Philadelphia: Temple University Press.

Enloe, C. 1990. *Bananas, Beaches and Bases: Making Feminist Sense of International Politics.* Berkeley, CA: University of California Press.

Lovenduski, J. 1986. *Women and European Politics.* Amherst: University of Massachusetts Press.

Mueller, C.M. (Ed.) 1988. *The Politics of the Gender Gap.* Newbury Park, CA: Sage Publications.

Russell, D.E.H. (Ed.) 1989. *Exposing Nuclear Phallacies.* New York: Pergamon.

In addition, the Center for the American Women and Politics (CAWP), National Information Bank on Women in Public Office (NIB), of the Eagleton Institute of Politics at Rutgers University (New Brunswick, NJ 08901), has available numerous fact sheets and other publications on gender-related issues in politics. The phone number of the Center is 201-828-2210.

Chapter 11

Gender and Spirituality

There is no doubt that religion or religious teachings play an important part in most people's lives. Consider, for example, that in the United States alone, there are currently more than 1,300 different religious denominations, sects, and cults; 70 percent of the population belong to a religious organization, and over 90 percent profess beliefs in a personal God (Robertson 1987). Western religious beliefs differ significantly from those held by people in other parts of the world, but regardless of the specific content of religious teachings, religion appears to be a cultural universal:

> Some form of religion has existed in every society that we know of. Religious beliefs and practices are so ancient that they can be traced into prehistory, perhaps as far back as 100,000 years ago. Even the primitive Neanderthal people of that time, it seems, had some concept of a supernatural realm that lay beyond everyday reality (Robertson 1987:397).

Why is religion so appealing? The answer lies in the fact that all religions, despite the tremendous variation among them, respond to particular human needs. First, virtually everyone seeks to understand the purpose of their existence as well as events in their lives and environments that seem unexplainable. Religion offers some answers to these puzzles, thus giving meaning to human existence and easing somewhat the psychological discomfort caused by life's uncertainties. Second, religion provides its followers with a sense of belonging, for it is not usually practiced alone, but rather, as the social theorist Emile Durkheim put it, in a "community of believers." And finally, religion lends order to social life by imposing on its adherents a set of behavioral standards. These include both prescriptions and proscriptions for how the faithful are to conduct themselves and relate to others. Importantly, however, religions typically establish different rules and often, different rituals for men and women, and it is upon these differences that we will focus in this chapter.

Obviously, given the sheer number of religions currently in practice, it is impossible for us to examine the gendered teachings of them all. Instead, we will limit our discussion to what many consider the major religious traditions in the world today: Judaism, Christianity, and Islam. Throughout this discussion we will find that historically, despite women's often greater religious devotion, the major religious traditions have been overwhelmingly patriarchal, according men higher spiritual status and privileges and frequently legitimating the subordination of women. But although religion has contributed to the oppression of women and other minorities, religious principles have also inspired many to work for social change as well as spiritual liberation. Therefore, this chapter would not be complete without a look at the efforts of both religious feminists and nonfeminists to influence not only religious attitudes and practices, but also social policies and social structure. We will begin with a general discussion of the relationship between gender and religion.

GENDER AND RELIGIOSITY

Sociologists use the term **religiosity** to refer to the intensity of commitment of an individual or group to a religious belief system. We noted at the outset of this chapter that 70 percent of persons in the United States claim affiliation with a particular religion. Importantly, however, church membership as well as one's level of commitment to a professed religion (i.e., one's religiosity) vary in terms of a number of factors. Looking at Table 11.1, for example, we find that most people, regardless of sex or race, hold some religious identification. Slightly more women (91 percent) than men (88 percent) identify themselves as members of a particular religion, and 5 percent fewer women than men state that they have no religious identification. Race is significant in terms of which type of religion one is likely to belong to. Black Protestants outnumber both white and Hispanic Protestants, whereas Hispanic Catholics outnumber both white and black Catholics. Nevertheless, almost identical percentages of each group state a religious affiliation.

These broad statistics, though, mask some important differences in religiosity among the groups listed in Table 11.1, particularly between women and men. Religiosity may be measured in a number of ways, but on most measures, women appear more religious than men. Table 11.2 shows differences between women and men on several measures of religiosity commonly used by sociologists. Here

TABLE 11.1
Religious Identifications by Race and Sex in the United States*

Religious Identification	All (%)	Men (%)	Women (%)	Whites (%)	Blacks (%)	Hispanics (%)
Protestant	56					
Baptist		48	52	70	29	2
United Methodist		43	57	97	3	1
Lutheran		48	52	98	1	3
Episcopalian		40	60	94	3	1
United Church of Christ		45	55	95	4	3
Disciples of Christ		47	53	94	5	4
Other		42	58	86	11	5
Unspecified		50	50	90	8	6
Catholic	28	49	51	86	4	17
Jewish	2	49	51	99	1	1
Other	2	n.a.	n.a.	n.a.	n.a.	n.a.
Unaffiliated	9	61	39	86	10	5

*Percentages do not add to 100 due to rounding and the way in which questions were asked on some surveys. Not all religions are included.
Sources: compiled from U.S. Department of Commerce 1990; Gallup and Castelli 1989.

TABLE 11.2
Comparing Religiosity by Sex

Church Attendance

Question: Did you, yourself, happen to attend church or synagogue in the last seven days?

Men: 38% Yes
Women: 46% Yes

Importance of Religion

Question: How important would you say religion is in your life—very important, fairly important, or not very important?

Men: 46% Very important
33% Fairly important
20% Not very important
1% Don't know
Women: 61% Very important
29% Fairly important
10% Not very important
<1% Don't know

Confidence in the Church or Organized Religion

Question: Would you please tell me how much confidence you, yourself, have in the church or organized religion—a great deal, quite a lot, some, or very little?

Men: 64% A great deal or quite a lot
Women: 69% A great deal or quite a lot

Belief in Religion as an Answer to Contemporary Problems

Question: Do you believe that religion can answer all or most of today's problems, or that religion is largely old-fashioned and out of date?

Men: 50% Can answer most of today's problems
32% Old fashioned/out of date
18% No opinion
Women: 65% Can answer most of today's problems
18% Old fashioned/out of date
17% No opinion

Source: Compiled from Gallup and Castelli 1989:32; Gallup 1988:268–269; 1987b:11; 1986:108,162,291.

we see that more women than men actually go to church or synagogue; that more women than men consider religion to be very important in their lives; that women have more confidence in the church or organized religion than men do; and that considerably more women than men believe that religion can answer all or most of today's problems. In short, for each of these measures, women show greater religiosity than men. Moreover, these data are supported by additional research that indicates that, when race is also taken into account, minority women have especially high levels of religiosity. In some black churches, for example, women make up from 70 to 90 percent of the congregations (Gallup and Castelli 1989; Grant 1986; Gilkes 1985).

One's religious beliefs may also strongly influence one's views on social and political issues. This is perhaps best seen in differences in attitudes toward sexuality and reproductive freedom. For instance, among those who say that religion is very important in their lives, 54 percent believe that premarital sex is wrong. In contrast, only 13 percent of those for whom religion is not an important part of their lives disapprove of premarital sex (Gallup 1985). Similarly, Luker (1984) found that the most significant difference between abortion rights supporters and anti-abortion activists is the extent to which they see religion as important in their lives; 75 percent of the pro-choice supporters in her study reported that religion was not an important part of their lives.

That religious beliefs bear such a strong relationship to our other attitudes and our behavior should not be too surprising. After all, religious values and concepts are among those first instilled in us as children, and such deeply ingrained ideas are hard to shake. Most, if not all, of us have been taught to pray to a male God, and to envision the deity as female probably seems silly, even unnatural, to many. Indeed, as Table 11.3 shows, most of us conceive of God in masculine terms. Most think of God as Father. Few image God as Mother, although research indicates that more women than men conceptualize God as Mother (Roof and Roof 1984). Interestingly, however, this was not always the case. There is, in fact, considerable evidence that in previous historical periods and in other cultures, images of God were feminine. We will now turn from contemporary Western images of the deity and venture to the time when God was believed to be a woman.

OF GODDESSES AND WITCHES

Astarte, Anat, Anahita, Asherah, Attoret, Attar, and Au are names few of us recognize today, but each name was intimately familiar to worshippers thousands of years ago. These are a few of the names in different languages and dialects for the Great Goddess, known also as the Queen of Heaven and the Divine Ancestress. Archeologists have discovered relics of worship to her among the cultural remains of peoples as disparate as the ancient Babylonians and pre-Christian Celts, at sites as distant as northern Iraq and southern France, and dating as far

TABLE 11.3
Gendered Images of God

Question: Which of the following images do you associate with God?	
Image	*Percent surveyed who image God this way*
Master	48.3
Father	46.8
Judge	36.5
Redeemer	36.2
Creator	29.5
Friend	26.6
King	20.6
Healer	8.3
Lover	7.3
Liberator	5.5
Mother	3.2
Spouse	2.6

Source: General Social Survey 1989:156–159.

back as 25,000 B.C. (Gadon 1989; Carmody 1979; Stone 1976). For example, at sites of what are thought to be "the earliest human-made dwellings on earth" belonging to the Aurignaican mammoth hunters (Upper Paleolithic period), archeologists have found stone, clay, and bone figurines of women they think were the idols of "a great mother cult" (Stone 1976:13). Similarly, among the ruins of later cultures, such as the Catal Huyak who, around 6000 B.C. inhabited part of what is now Turkey, excavators have recovered sculptures of women depicted in various life stages, leading them to conclude that "the principal deity was a goddess, who is shown in her three aspects, as a young woman, a mother giving birth or as an old woman" (quoted in Stone 1976:17).

That the females we have described so far were associated with fertility may lead one to mistakenly conclude that goddesses were only ascribed traditional feminine roles, such as mother. It is important to point out first that in goddess-worshipping societies, motherhood was not devalued like it is in our own society. Second, even in societies that also worshipped male gods, female gods were believed to wield as much and often more power than male gods, and were ascribed roles and traits, such as wisdom and courage, that only later were typed masculine. "Pre-Christian Celts, for example, worshipped Cerridwen as the Goddess of Intelligence and Knowledge. The Greek Demeter and the Egyptian Isis were lawgivers—wise dispensers of good counsel and justice. Egypt also celebrated Maat, the Goddess of Cosmic Order, while Mesopotamia's Ishtar was the

Prophetess, the Lady of Vision and Directoress of the People" (Carmody 1979:31).

Evidence of widespread goddess worship is abundant and convincing. What is less clear is why and how male or father-centered religions came to displace it. To better understand this change, some theorists draw on the factors that may have originally given rise to matriarchal religions. Matriarchal religions are thought to have emerged out of early humans' concern for survival as well as their desire to explain the generation of life and the phenomenon of death. Significantly, these early peoples did not understand the relationship between sexual intercourse and childbearing, and therefore assumed that women were the sole possessors of creative life forces. Women, then, were revered not only as producers of future generations, but also as the primal ancestor. In addition, since women alone were considered parents, children took the maternal name and traced descent along the mother's line. Although these theorists caution us not to romanticize or glorify this period as a golden matriarchal age, there is ample evidence that the status of women in these early human communities was high (Gimbutas 1989; Stone 1976).

The speculation follows that as the male role in reproduction came to be better understood, the appeal of matriarchal religions diminished. Once it was certain that the reproductive process could not take place without the help of a man, the status of the father became significant, and male generative power was more highly valued. With this realization occurred a concomitant decline in women's status. They came to be seen merely as the carriers and caretakers of future generations, whereas men provided the generative "seed," making them the true sources of life.

This, of course, is not the only theory of how patriarchal religions eventually supplanted matriarchal ones. Another plausible explanation, for instance, begins with the observation that female-centered religions were just one of many religious orientations adhered to in ancient societies. Besides monotheistic matriarchal religions, there were polytheistic religions that worshipped male and female deities; other monotheistic religions that worshipped a male deity; and even religions that worshipped the "sacred androgyne," a deity that was simultaneously female and male (Carmody 1979). It has been argued that the displacement of most of these religious traditions by one that favored the worship of a single male god may have been the result of ongoing political battles among various societies—for example, disputes over land or over who should rightfully rule, as well as military conquests aimed at empire building. The victors in these struggles would, in all likelihood, impose their own standards and traditions—including religious ones—on the vanquished (Gimbutas 1989; Christ 1983). The fact that members of goddess cultures tended to be pacifistic may have made them especially vulnerable to aggression from other societies (Gimbutas 1989; Carmody 1979).

Regardless of whether both or neither of these theories is correct, it is perhaps more significant that attempts to eradicate worship of female gods have never been completely successful. Research indicates that throughout history, groups continued to pay homage to a variety of female deities and spirits, although they were frequently forced to practice their rites and rituals secretly because of violent persecutions by those of the dominant faith (Gimbutas 1989). During early Christian times, for example, several groups claimed to be the disciples of Christ and wrote their own gospels of Christ's teachings. Among these were the gnostic Christian sects whose practices and beliefs were rich in female symbolism (Christ 1983). Some gnostic groups described God as a divine Dyad: the Primal Father and the Mother of All Things. Others spoke of the Holy Spirit as Mother, or as Wisdom, the female element in God. Women in the gnostic sects also held positions of authority; they were preachers and prophets and even ordained priests (Pagels 1979). However, other, more patriarchal sects, led by those who eventually established themselves as the Church Fathers, suppressed the gnostics and branded them heretics. Although researchers emphasize that the gnostics were not declared heretical simply because of the high status they accorded women, the practical effect of their suppression was the exclusion of much female symbolism and leadership from what became the recognized Christian Church (Christ 1983).

Scholars have argued, too, that **witchcraft** was a carryover of the beliefs and traditions of the Great Goddess religions. Although nowadays most people associate witchcraft with evil and devil worship, the meaning of the word *witch,* "wise one," hints at the truer character of this practice. Witchcraft was popular among plain, rural folk whose survival depended on good crops and healthy livestock. Because of women's long and close association with nature, fertility, and health, most witches were women. Their careful study of nature "enabled them to tame sheep and cattle, to breed wheat and corn from grasses and weeds, to forge ceramics from mud and metal from rock, and to track the movements of the moon, stars and sun" (Starhawk 1979:261). Appropriately, then, it was the witches who led the annual planting and harvesting celebrations. They also practiced folk magic and medicine, using herbs to cure the sick and relieve pain. Not surprisingly, many people sought their help and looked to them for comfort (Starhawk 1979; Ehrenreich and English 1973).

Interestingly, it appears that witchcraft peacefully co-existed with the established Christian churches for quite some time. Many people, it seems, elected to observe the traditions of both, and there is evidence that country priests were sometimes reprimanded by their superiors for participating in the seasonal "pagan" festivals (Starhawk 1979). Nevertheless, witchcraft clearly posed a threat to Church authority. Carol Christ (1983:93–94) explains:

> The wise woman was summoned at the crises of the life cycle *before* the priest; she delivered the baby, while the priest was called later to perform the baptism. She was the first called upon to cure illness or treat the dying, while the priest was called in after other remedies had failed, to administer the last rites. Moreover, if the wise woman had knowledge of herbs which could aid or prevent conception or cause abortion, she had a power over the life process which clearly was superior to that of the priest, and which according to official theology made her a rival of God himself. If, moreover, she appealed to pagan deities, some of them probably female, in the performance of divinations or blessings and spells

used to promote healing and ward off evil, then it is not difficult to see why she was persecuted by an insecure misogynist Church which could not tolerate rival power, especially the power of women.

Indeed, by the late fifteenth century, the Pope had officially declared war on witches. The two Dominican theologians who were put in charge of routing out and prosecuting the witches, Heinrich Kramer and James Sprenger, maintained that women were more attracted to witchcraft because they were less intelligent, more impressionable, and more lascivious than men. It was Kramer and Sprenger who most actively promoted the notion of witchcraft as a Satanic cult (Christ 1983). Tragically, in their zeal to rid the world of witches, Catholic *and* Protestant authorities tortured and killed between one half million and 9 million people during the fifteenth to eighteenth centuries, about 80 percent of whom were women (Nelson 1979; Starhawk 1979).

The worship of female deities survives today in some Native American religious rituals and in Australian aboriginal and various African societies, although Western anthropologists have typically devalued these practices, labeling them "primitive" (Carmody 1979). In addition, however, many feminists have revived or developed woman-centered spiritual traditions as part of their effort to make religion more responsive and relevant to female experience. But before we discuss feminist spirituality, let's examine the traditional teachings on gender espoused by the predominant patriarchal religions that we identified at the opening of this chapter.

TRADITIONAL RELIGIOUS TEACHINGS ON GENDER

In our attempt to summarize the gendered teachings of even the major religious traditions, we immediately confront a number of problems. For one thing, although many denominations and sects share a few basic tenets—for instance, all Christians believe Jesus was the Son of God—they tend to diverge considerably when it comes to more specific religious principles and practices, including those that concern appropriate roles for women and men. Southern Baptists, for instance, take a conservative stance regarding the proper role of women in religious and social life, but Quaker women have been called the "mothers of feminism" (Bacon 1986). Nonetheless, members of both groups are undeniably Christians. Similarly, the rules governing male and female behavior among Orthodox Jews are very different from those adhered to by Reform Jews, as we will see shortly.

Our brief discussion, therefore, is intended merely as an overview of the general attitudes toward men and women expressed in the teachings of three very broad religious traditions. We cannot address all the fine distinctions among the many sects and denominations that identify with a particular tradition, but we will try to show within each some gradations in attitudes—conservative, moderate, and liberal—with respect to three main topics: (1) appropriate behavior and rituals for the male and female faithful; (2) the regulation of sexuality; and (3) the relative positions of men and women as church leaders or authorities.

A second problem arises, however, in interpreting scriptures and religious teachings. We will find that a single passage of sacred text may be translated or edited to legitimate gender oppression or to promote gender equality. As Virginia Sapiro (1986:191) found, "The same Bible has proven to some people that women and men are equal and should take full leadership roles in religions and society, and it has proven to others that women are inferior, periodically unclean, dangerous, and subordinate to men." These contradictions are especially significant given that religious leaders cite scripture or other sacred texts as the source of their authority and as the foundation of church doctrine. Thus, in evaluating a particular religious teaching and the official rationale behind it, we must also consider alternative interpretations of the sacred writings on which church leaders claim it is based. These reinterpretations are often the products of feminist religious scholarship.

With these qualifiers in mind, then, let's examine the gendered teachings of Judaism, Christianity, and Islam.

Judaism

Jewish history spans more than 3,500 years. Throughout much of this period, Jewish women and men have been governed by a set of laws (*halakhah*) spelled out for them in the **Talmud.** The Talmud, thought to have been compiled around A.D. 200, records the oral interpretations of scripture by ancient rabbis and forms the crux of religious authority for traditional Judaism. However, in response to changing social conditions and political upheavals, such as diaspora and countless persecutions, Jewish leaders over the years have modified and reinterpreted Jewish law. In fact, as Paula Hyman (1979:112) points out, "Much of the strength of the Jewish tradition has derived from its flexibility and responsiveness to the successive challenges of the environments in which it has been destined to live."

Contemporary Judaism is largely congregational. That is, "public rituals [are] practiced in local synagogues whose congregations selected a mode of worship and expressed their preference for certain Jewish theological interpretations" (Pratt 1980:207-208). There are three major types of congregations: Orthodox, Conservative, and Reform. Orthodox Jews most strictly adhere to the traditional teachings of the Talmud, and we will begin our discussion with them. Then we will see how the practices and strictures of the Conservative and Reform congregations differ.

Orthodox men and women have separate and very clearly defined rights and obligations under Jewish law. As one commentator expressed it, "Men and women are expected to follow different routes in the pursuit of the ideal life that God has prescribed for them" (Webber 1983:143). Orthodoxy requires that men preserve and carry on Jewish tradition through communal worship and daily prayer at specified times, and especially through religious study. Theirs is clearly the spiritual realm. Women, in contrast, are exempt from these religious duties (*mitzvot*) on the ground that fulfilling them would interfere with their primary roles as wives, mothers, and homemakers. Women, then, control the domestic realm where they tend to the needs of their husbands and children. It is essentially because of his wife's household labor that the Orthodox man is free to pursue religious study and to fulfill his other *mitzvot*. Women must also see to it that their children, especially their sons, receive sound religious training. Orthodox women have their own *mitzvot* to fulfill, including separating bread dough in preparation for the Sabbath, lighting the Sabbath and holiday candles, assuring that the dietary laws are followed, and observing the rules of female bodily cleanliness—an issue to which we will return shortly (Pratt 1980; Carmody 1979).

It is important to emphasize here that Orthodox Jews do not see this separa-tion of roles as the relegation of women to an inherently unequal or inferior status. To the contrary, Orthodoxy maintains that in preserving the moral purity of their households, women engage in a form of religious expression comparable to that of men, and for this they are honored and respected both within the tradition and by their husbands and children. Nevertheless, critics have countered that the exemp-tions accorded to women effectively serve to exclude them from public ritual—"the real heartland of Judaism"—and, therefore, from full participation in the religious community (Webber 1983:143; Umansky 1985; Neuberger 1983). More-over, because of their lack of involvement in Talmudic study, "[it] is not un-usual . . . for Orthodox women to remain religiously, as well as secularly, unedu-cated" (Synder 1986:13).

These critical concerns usually intensify when considering the laws govern-ing male-female relations within the Orthodox family. Both women and men are permitted to acquire and inherit property, but wives may not bequeath their property while they are married without their husbands' consent. Women may not formally initiate marriage, although once wed they are entitled to adequate sup-port from their husbands (Webber 1983). Perhaps the most disabling laws for women, however, are those regulating divorce and remarriage. Within Orthodoxy, divorce is unilateral: only a husband may divorce his wife, not vice versa. A woman may institute divorce proceedings by charging her husband with "matrimo-nial offenses" before the religious court, which in turn can pressure the husband to grant his wife a *get* (a religious divorce). But until the husband grants the *get,* the Orthodox woman is not free to remarry according to Jewish law, even if she has obtained a civil divorce (Neuberger 1983).

Similar restrictions apply to the woman whose husband is "missing, pre-sumed dead." According to Jewish law, an *agunah* (the "forsaken wife") cannot remarry unless a witness testifies to her husband's actual death. Under strict Jewish codes, such a witness must be a male Jew, but it has not been uncommon, especially during wartime and persecutions, for rabbis to bend the rules a bit by "accepting the testimony, for instance, of women, minors, slaves, and non-Jews in this matter" (Neuberger 1983:136–137). Still, if the woman could not muster evidence of any sort, she remained married in the eyes of Orthodox authorities.

In light of what may be judged by many as rather repressive policies toward women, it may come as somewhat of a surprise that Jewish law recognizes the rights of both women and men to sexual fulfillment in marriage. Religious scholars, in fact, often contrast the positive attitude toward sexuality within Judaism with the more negative Christian view that we will discuss shortly. But others maintain that "it is precisely in this area that the second-class status of women within Judaism is highlighted," and they typically cite the laws of family purity to illustrate this point (Hyman 1979:110; Baskin 1985). These include the rules concerning female bodily cleanliness that we mentioned earlier. Paula Hyman's explanation of one of these laws and its effects is worth quoting at length:

> According to *halakic* prescriptions, the menstruating woman—or *niddah*—is to have no physical contact whatsoever with a man. Like the person suffering from a gonorrheal discharge, she is impure. Contact with her is permitted only after she has been free of her "discharge" for seven days and has undergone ritual purification in a *mikveh* [a bath]. During her period of impurity, anything she touches becomes impure. While the state of impurity is a legal rather than a hygienic concept and, according to rabbinic authorities, does not imply that the *niddah* is physically unclean or repugnant, it is clear that simple Jewish men and women throughout the ages have not interpreted the laws of family purity in such a disinterested manner. Even the mere fact of legal impurity for two weeks every month has involved many disabilities for women. And the psychological impact of the institution, especially in its strictest interpretations, upon a woman's self-esteem and attitude to her own body, would seem to be harmful (1979:110–111).

A number of reasons have been forwarded to justify such laws. It has been argued, for instance, that they protect women's health, that they "spiritualize" sexual relations, and that they help to "renew a marriage through a kind of monthly honeymoon" (Webber 1983:144; Hyman 1979). Less sympathetic observers have characterized them as the products of patriarchal religious leaders' fears and hatred of that which they could neither do nor understand.

In any event, such laws do seem to embody Judaism's emphasis on the physiological differences between men and women, which, it maintains, necessitates a literal "physical apartness" of the sexes (Webber 1983). This physical separation of men and women permeates virtually every area of Orthodox Jewish life (Baskin 1985). For example, in a small town in New York state, 600 male Hasidic students recently refused to ride buses to school because they were driven by women. Hasidism, an Orthodox Jewish sect, forbids interaction between the sexes apart from family life (*Philadelphia Inquirer,* 14 September, 1986:13C). Likewise, *mehitzah* mandates a seating division between men and women in synagogues. Orthodox women are relegated to the back of the synagogue, although this arrangement is considered an improvement over earlier practices whereby women were forced to sit "up in a gallery, or behind a curtain, or even in some Eastern communities in a separate room or outside the building altogether" (Neuberger 1983:138; Berman 1979).

Given what has been said thus far, it is not surprising that women are not permitted to be ordained Orthodox rabbis. Laying this issue aside, then, we may ask how else the participation of women and men in public Orthodox worship differs. We have already noted that women's exemption from particular *mitzvot,* especially the one calling the faithful to religious study, serves to curtail their active participation in public ritual. More specifically, women are not called to read the *Torah* during worship; even though no law prohibits this, it is not done to preserve "the dignity of the congregation" (Carmody 1979:103). Nor may women sing in the synagogue; "the ancient rabbis considered the female voice to be profane" (Pratt 1980:211). A woman also may not lead a prayer service; in fact, only men can be counted in a *minyan,* the quorum needed to hold a prayer service (Carmody 1979; Berman 1979).

Nevertheless, some Orthodox women have recently formed women-only *davening* (prayer) groups. Though technically not a *minyan,* members of a *davening* group gather to worship, to sing, and to read *Torah* and the rabbinical commentaries and to develop their own understanding of them. But judging by the negative reactions these groups have received from rabbis and members of their congregations, it appears that an equalization of the status of women and men within Orthodox Judaism will be painfully slow in coming (Snyder 1986). At times, women's attempts to pray as men do have been met by violence. In 1989, for example, a group of Jewish women attempting to hold a prayer service at the Wailing Wall in Jerusalem, considered the holiest Jewish site, were physically attacked by angry Orthodox men. The women, some of whom wore prayer shawls, were forced to flee from the wall after police fired tear gas at the men who were shouting insults and throwing heavy metal chairs at the women. Although the women vowed to return, Orthodox officials defended the ban on women's prayer services, arguing that it is a religious tradition that cannot be changed (*New York Times* 21 March 1989:A3).

Although the Reform Movement did not emerge solely in response to women's status under Orthodox Judaism, Reform Jews did call for equality between the sexes as early as 1845 (Neuberger 1983). By the turn of the century, Reform Judaism had made strides toward this goal. The *mehitzah* (seating division) was abolished; women were permitted to sing in synagogue choirs and to be counted in a *minyan*; girls were included in religious education programs and confirmed along with boys; and the prayerbook eliminated many of the blatantly sexist prayers, including men's daily thanksgiving that God had not made them women. The Reform Movement also established many social service and educational organizations in which women and men worked together. Women were even admitted to the rabbinical seminary, although when a woman first sought to become a Reform rabbi in 1922, authorities sternly rejected her (Briggs 1987; Pratt 1980).

It was not until 1972 that Reform Judaism opened rabbinical ordination to women. Today, there are more than 100 women rabbis in the United States. Moreover, on June 26, 1990, Reform Judaism's Central Conference of American Rabbis voted to accept sexually active homosexuals into the rabbinate (Goldman 1990a).

According to Norma Pratt (1980), Conservative Judaism grew out of the need for religious expression by Jews for whom Orthodoxy was no longer appealing, but to whom Reform seemed too radical. Conservatism lies midway between Orthodox and Reform Judaism in terms of how strictly it adheres to traditional Jewish law (Cummings 1986). It is understandable, then, that Conservative Judaism has moved considerably slower than Reformism toward equality between the sexes.

Early on, Conservatism permitted women and men to sit together during worship, and women were encouraged to participate in the religious education of children and in the care and upkeep of the synagogue itself. "Women, however, still were excluded from significant parts of the worship, for instance the rituals surrounding the handling and reading of the *Torah*" (Pratt 1980:213). In 1973, this also changed, and today women may be ordained as Conservative rabbis (Umansky 1985). In 1986, there were only five women Conservative rabbis in the United States, and just one of them served a major Conservative congregation (Cummings 1986). But their ordination was, nonetheless, an important step by Conservative Judaism toward equalizing the roles and statuses of its male and female believers. An even more significant step was taken in 1990 when the leadership of the Cantors Assembly, the professional organization of 400 Conservative Jewish cantors, voted to admit women. Cantors chant liturgy on behalf of the congregation during religious services and so are considered to play a more central role in worship than rabbis whose job it is to teach and preach (Goldman 1990b).

It has been argued that feminism is still somewhat suspect among many Conservative and even some Reform Jews. There are those, for example, who see feminism as a threat to the stability of the family and as overly critical of traditional gender relations. Also problematic is feminists' support of abortion and a woman's right to choose to bear children. As one Jewish observer cautioned:

> In an era when 6,000,000 Jews were killed—1,500,000 of them were children— we have to examine both sides of the abortion issue. . . . Stressing a woman's right to control her own body, and the legitimacy of considering the quality of life she and her children will have, should go hand in hand with emphasis on the sanctity of life and on the risk of devaluating it in unthinking or easy medical solutions (Greenberg 1979:188).

Nevertheless, opinion polls show Jews to hold the most liberal attitudes toward abortion (U.S. Department of Justice 1990b:163).

We have already discussed feminists' positions on reproductive freedom (Chapter 7), and later in this chapter we will examine the position of Christian religious conservatives on this issue. First, however, we will turn to the gendered teachings of two other major religious traditions: Christianity and Islam.

Christianity

It is not uncommon for Christian church leaders and theologians to cite the teachings of St. Paul when delineating the proper roles of Christian women and men. In one frequently quoted passage, for example, Paul instructs the Christians of Ephesus:

> Let the wives be subject to their husbands as to the Lord; because a husband is head of the wife, just as Christ is head of the Church, being himself savior of the body. But just as the Church is subject to Christ, so also let wives be to their husbands in all things (Ephesians 5:22–24).

Elsewhere, Paul explains why women must cover their heads at religious gatherings, but men need not:

> A man indeed ought not to cover his head, because he is the image and glory of God. But woman is the glory of man. For man is not from woman, but woman from man. For man was not created for woman, but woman for man (I Corinthians, 11:7–9; the latter two lines appear to be references to the Genesis creation story).

The sexism in Paul's writings, though hotly debated, is perhaps less important than the fact that they have been repeatedly used by church fathers and Christian theologians to legitimate and even promote the subordination of women.

There is considerable evidence that the leadership of the early Christian movement was shared by men and women. Both served as missionaries spreading the "good news of salvation." Both sheltered the persecuted, studied and interpreted scriptures, and prophesied (Carmody 1979; Schussler Fiorenza 1979). Within the first hundred years, however, an all-male hierarchical structure was firmly in place. Somewhere along the line, it seems, the example and teachings of their first leader, Jesus, were forgotten or ignored: "[T]here is nothing in his reported words that could be labeled antifemale, misogynistic, or sexist. . . . Rather, Jesus treat[ed] men and women simply as individuals who need[ed] his help, or as co-workers, or friends" (Carmody 1979:113, 115).

The rationale for the decision of male church authorities to exclude women from leadership roles remains open to speculation. We have already discussed their efforts to suppress gnosticism, which could have been related to it. Soon we will examine some of the more recent arguments in favor of continuing this exclusion. What is clear at this point, however, is the effect of their choice: women were relegated to a second-class citizenship within Christianity, a status that persists to this day.

Within the Christian tradition, both men and women have been characterized in contradictory ways. Men are supposed to be rational, authoritative, and in control, yet they are depicted as weak-willed when confronted with women's feminine charms. Indeed, women are portrayed as temptresses—"the devil's gateway" according to one church father—who will cause men to sin much the same way Eve supposedly led Adam into the original sin in the Garden of Eden. At the same time, though, the virgin, pure of heart and body, has been extolled by Christianity, as has the good (i.e., docile, modest, and long-suffering) mother. Both are exemplified by Mary, the mother of Jesus, who is said to have been both virgin and mother simultaneously. In 1988, Pope John Paul II reaffirmed this rather narrow view of Christian femininity. In an apostolic letter on the "dignity of women," the Pope characterized female identity in terms of the "vocations" of motherhood or virginity (Pope John Paul II 1988).

Such images hint at the Christian church's attitudes toward sexuality. Traditionally, sex has been discussed as an activity to be avoided if possible, except for the purpose of procreation. Celibacy has been regarded by many as a better way of life. For instance, "John Chrysostom, a very influential Eastern father, urged virginity because marriage was only for procreating, the world was then (about A.D. 382) filled, and therefore marriage was solely a concession to sin." Similarly, according to Augustine, a highly influential Western father, "marital pleasure is always a venial sin, and if procreation is not possible, as after menopause, it is a mortal sin. Therefore, a man should cherish his wife's soul, but hate her body as an enemy" (Carmody 1979:121, 122). The Protestant reformers, such as Luther and Calvin, were more temperate in their views of sex. While restricting sex to married couples, they recognized both husbands' and wives' needs for the "medicine for venereal desire." Still, they warned against "overindulgence" and reminded their followers that it was through childbearing that women could attain salvation (Carmody 1979).

Today, Christian teachings on sexuality remain mixed. Virtually all sects and denominations continue to frown upon nonmarital sex, although a 1987 report from the Newark, New Jersey diocese of the Episcopal Church urged that committed nonmarital sexual relationships not only be recognized, but also blessed by the church (Schaffer 1987). This report signaled a more open-minded attitude toward sexuality among some Christian leaders; this was especially significant for homosexuals who have been openly condemned and often persecuted by Christianity. It is unlikely that the condemnation of homosexuals will soon disappear from the teachings of most of the Christian churches (Berliner 1987; Heyward 1987). To the contrary, some fundamentalist sects are calling for greater repression, and at its 1988 General Conference, representatives of the United Methodist Church voted against the ordination of self-avowed, practicing homosexuals, arguing that "homosexuality is incompatible with Christian teaching" (Steinfels 1988:22).

Nevertheless, the statement in the 1987 Episcopal report that "homosexual couples should be able to find in the church 'the same recognition and affirmation which nurtures and sustains heterosexual couples in their relationships' " (Schaffer, 1987:6F), indicated that significant changes were in the making. In 1988, the United Church of Canada, that country's largest Protestant denomination, voted to admit homosexual men and women to its clergy, in 1989, an openly homosexual man was ordained an Episcopal priest, and in 1991, a lesbian was also ordained an Episcopal priest.

Even though some Protestant churches appear open to reconsidering their official teachings on sexuality, the Catholic Church represents a denomination that has remained steadfastly resistant to change in this area. The Catholic Church, in fact, speaks as one of the most conservative denominations in this regard. It recently reiterated its strong disapproval of homosexuality, calling it "an objective disorder" (Williams 1987). In addition, it continues to require celibacy on the part of clergy and nuns, and it prohibits the use of artificial contraception. Its opposition to abortion is well known, but the Vatican has also voiced objections to artificial insemination and *in vitro* fertilization (*see* Chapter 7). Church authorities hold that it is "the right of every person to be conceived and to be born within marriage and from marriage" (The Congregation for the Doctrine of the Faith 1987:703). Medical intervention is acceptable only when it assists "the conjugal act," not when it replaces it. That the semen needed for both procedures is typically obtained through masturbation is itself objectionable. But with regard to *in vitro* fertilization, the church also condemns the cultivation of "spare" zygotes that are subsequently destroyed or frozen if the initial implantation is successful. Catholic Church officials see the destruction of the extra fertilized eggs as analogous to abortion. Most recently, U.S. Catholic bishops condemned safe sex campaigns for the prevention of Acquired Immune Deficiency Syndrome (AIDS) (*see also* Chapter 12). Calling the use of prophylactics "technically unreliable" and a means, in effect, of "promoting behavior which is morally unacceptable," the bishops argued that chastity and marital fidelity are the best ways to prevent the transmission of AIDS (U.S. Catholic Bishops 1989).

The Catholic Church has also stood firm in its opposition to the ordination of women to the priesthood. Church authorities argue that Jesus called twelve men to be His apostles, not twelve women, nor twelve men and women. Moreover, priests act in the name of Jesus and represent Him physically; therefore they must be men. Besides, the church offers women other ways to do God's work: through religious sisterhoods and through Catholic laywomen's organizations. As Mary Jo Weaver (1985) convincingly demonstrates, however, these roles are usually confining and at best auxiliary. Nuns especially have been expected to remain the silent and obedient helpmates of bishops. At the same time, however, religious sisters have played a very active role in secular society. For instance, according to Briggs (1987:435), "Of all the women engaged in religious professions during the nineteenth and early twentieth centuries [American Catholic nuns] were the most powerful and usually the best educated. . . . They were disproportionately represented among women with higher degrees."

Since the early 1960s, a number of religious sisterhoods have sought greater independence and more input into the decision making that affects their lives, although the Vatican has either responded negatively or not responded at all (Weaver 1985). Catholic bishops, however, have urged that women be more quickly admitted to leadership positions in the church (except those requiring ordination to the priesthood). In a 1990 pastoral letter on women's issues, the bishops also condemned the "sin of sexism," which is manifested in economic discrimination against women, sexual exploitation, and violence against women (Steinfels 1990a). But although the bishops' statement is a significant one, official church teachings remain quite sexist and the leadership and authority of the Catholic Church continues to be a male stronghold.

Unlike the Catholic Church, virtually all the Protestant churches now ordain women to their ministries (Weaver 1985), and on February 11, 1989, the Episcopal Church consecrated its first female bishop, Barbara C. Harris, despite strong opposition from some Episcopal Church leaders. Table 11.4 shows the percentage of women clergy in U.S. Protestant denominations as of 1986. Of the major denominations, the United Church of Christ, which began ordaining women in 1853, has the highest percentage of women in its ministry and it is only 14.5 percent. Between 1977 and 1986, the number of ordained women ministers doubled, but relative to the overall number of ordained clergy, the percentage increase was from 4.0 percent to 7.9 percent (Jacquet 1988). However, there is evidence that more women are considering careers as ministers. The number of women enrolled in seminaries and divinity schools has been increasing, from just 10.2 percent in 1972 to 29 percent in 1989 (Jacquet 1990)

Still, women ministers know that their ordination has done little to eliminate the sexism prevalent in most Christian churches. These women continue to confront discrimination in access to leadership positions, ministerial assignments and responsibilities, and salary (Jacquet 1988; Briggs 1987; Carmody 1979). A recent study by the National Council of Churches, for instance, found that the median salary of clergywomen is $6,000 less than the median salary of clergymen, "even though their educational level is generally higher, with 90.8 percent having seminary degrees, three years beyond college, against 72.2 percent of the men" (*New York Times,* 29 March 1984:22). Importantly, however, a woman assumed a significant leadership role among the Protestant denominations in 1990 when the Rev. Joan Brown Campbell was named the general secretary of the National Council of Churches; she is the first female minister to hold the position in the organization's forty-year history (Goldman 1990c).

The inequality inherent in most Christian denominations leads one to wonder how church leaders can reconcile this with their professed concern for social justice. It has also caused many believers to question the relevance of organized Christianity to their own lives and to the contemporary world (Welch 1985). Consequently, some have abandoned the Christian faith altogether or at least have stopped practicing their religion in any formal sense. This is particularly true for Catholics who disagree with the Vatican's position on birth control (Hout and Greenley 1987). In a 1986 Gallup poll, a sample of U.S. Catholics was asked how well the church was handling the role of women within it. Only 37 percent reponded excellent or good; 60 percent said fair or poor (Gallup 1987). Nevertheless, other church members have chosen to stay and work for change from within their religious institutions by challenging church teachings and "depatriarchalizing" religious language, symbols, and ritual. This latter group, of course, includes Christian feminists.

We will address this issue again in a little while; now we will examine the gendered teachings of Islam.

TABLE 11.4
Women Clergy by Denomination, 1986

Denomination	Total Clergy	%Women Clergy
Advent Christian Church	568	3.0
American Baptist Churches	7,698	5.6
American Lutheran Church*	7,671	4.0
Apostolic Faith Mission Church of God	38	13.2
Apostolic Overcoming Holy Church of God	295	25.4
Assemblies of God	26,837	13.9
Baptist General Conference	1,700	0.1
Bible Church of Christ	40	40.0
Brethren in Christ Church	227	.9
Christian Church (Disciples)	6,806	10.9
Christian Congregation	1,455	19.9
Christian Nation Church, U.S.A.	23	8.7
Church of the Brethren	1,963	6.1
Church of the Nazarene	8,667	4.1
Conservative Congregational Christian Conference	424	0.2
Episcopal Church	14,111	4.5
Evangelical Lutheran Churches, Association of*	672	3.7
Evangelical Presbyterian Church	177	0.6
Free Methodist Church of North America	1,079	6.4
Friends United Meeting	595	10.1
Fundamental Methodist Church	23	4.3
General Association of General Baptists	1,444	0.6
International Church of the Foursquare Gospel	3,482	19.1
Lutheran Church in America*	8,586	5.6
Mennonite Church	2,399	2.0
Mennonite Church, The General Conference	365	9.0
Moravian Church (Northern Province)	174	7.5
Moravian Church (Southern Province)	83	3.6
Pentacostal Church of Christ, International	128	23.4
Presbyterian Church (U.S.A.)	19,514	7.8
Reformed Church in America	1,636	2.6
Reorganized Church of Jesus Christ of Latter Day Saints	16,535	5.2
Salvation Army	5,195	62.0
Seventh Day Baptist General Conference	69	2.9
Southern Baptist Convention	37,072	1.2
United Church of Christ	10,071	14.5
United Methodist Church	37,808	5.0
Wesleyan Church	2,596	9.8

*This body merged in 1987 to form the Evangelical Lutheran Church of America, which began operating January 1, 1988.
Source: Jacquet 1988:5–6.

Islam

One-fifth of the world's population follows the religious traditions of Islam; it is considered to be the world's fastest growing religion (Robertson 1987; Carmody 1979). Islam was founded by the prophet Mohamad around the year A.D. 610 in Mecca (now the capital of Saudi Arabia). Mohamad is said to have received over the course of his lifetime a series of revelations from Allah (God), which he in turn passed on to his followers in the form of rules of behavior. These are compiled in the **Qur'an** (Koran) which Muslims accept literally as the word of God. In addition, Mohamad's teachings and those of his immediate successors are recorded in the *Hadith,* which along with the Qur'an, serves as the basis for *shari a* (Islamic law). Taken together, these three sources constitute a religious framework that governs every aspect of Muslims' daily lives, including interactions between women and men. Indeed, 80 percent of the Qur'an is devoted to prescriptive and proscriptive verses concerning proper relations between the sexes (Haddad 1985).

It is clear that Islam radically altered male-female relations, although whether for better or for worse is a point still disputed by religious scholars. It appears that in the days of Mohamad, a variety of sociosexual arrangements coexisted. Some groups were decidedly patriarchal, valuing males above females (female infanticide was common) and allowing men as many wives as they could buy or steal irrespective of the women's consent or the men's ability to support them (Carmody 1979). Within other groups, though, women enjoyed considerable independence and practiced polyandry (had more than one husband). However, by the seventh century, there was movement away from gender equality among even some of these groups, particularly the ones in Mecca, as commercial expansion provided increasing contacts with northern societies whose religions (Judaism and Christianity) were already strongly patriarchal. Islam, some scholars maintain, consolidated this trend toward patriarchy, although Mohamad did not totally divest women of their rights (Ahmed 1986).

Mohamad declared that a woman's consent had to be obtained before a marriage and that she be paid the brideprice instead of her father. He also recognized women's conjugal rights, their rights to ownership of their jewelry and earnings, their right to initiate divorce, and their right to inheritance (although their share was half that of male heirs). Women, like men, were expected to adhere to the five "pillars" of Islam, which include prayer five times a day and fasting during the holy month called *Ramadan,* and they worshipped with men in the mosques (Carmody 1979).

Mohamad permitted men to have more than one wife, imposing a generous limit of four as long as they could be supported. He opposed female infanticide, but gave men unconditional custody rights to their children (boys at age two, girls at age seven). Moreover, despite the Qur'an's verses on the centrality of justice and the equal worth of all human beings, it declares men to be women's "guardians" and "a degree above" them (Ahmed 1986:678–679). A wife's duties, then, include obedience to her husband (Higgens 1985). According to the Qur'an, "Men are in charge of women because God has made one to excel over the other and because they spend their wealth" [referring to men's financial support of women] (quoted in Haddad 1985:294). Unfortunately, Mohamad's successors took these words to heart and used them to justify the suspension of many rights the prophet had allowed women, so that "by the second and third centuries of Islam, 'the seclusion and degradation of women had progressed beyond anything known in the first decades of Islam' " (Ahmed 1986:690).

Today, Islamic leaders maintain that men and women hold equal status, although they are quick to emphasize that this equality does not derive from sharing the same privileges and responsibilities, but rather from the *complementarity* of their roles. "In this world view men and women are equal before God, but they have somewhat different physical, mental, and emotional qualities, somewhat different responsibilities in the family and society, and therefore somewhat different rights and prerogatives" (Higgens 1985:491).

Men are the undisputed heads of both the sacred and secular realms, including the household. Theirs is the public sphere, where they conduct religious and worldly affairs and assume a variety of roles with few restrictions. Women, in contrast, are largely confined to the private sphere, the home, but even there they are not in charge. Their duties are to serve their husbands, to keep house, to bear many children, and to instruct the children in the ways of Islam. "Not only is [the Muslim woman] created to be pregnant [she is an "envelope for conception" according to one Islamic leader], but more specifically all her roles are defined by her relations to the men in her life. . . . Thus is created the ideal of a self-sacrificing individual whose existence is fulfilled only in the service of others and whose joy is completed by making others happy" (Haddad 1985:286).

Although Islamic doctrine continues to uphold the rights of both spouses to sexual pleasure and gratification, sex outside of marriage is condemned as harmful to the individual involved and as potentially dangerous to the moral fiber of Islamic society as a whole. Because women are thought to possess an innate capacity for sexual allurement, extraordinary measures (by Western standards at least) are taken to prevent them from tempting men. The most obvious examples of this are *purdah* and the *chador*. *Purdah* refers to the practice of severely restricting women's access to public life by secluding them in their homes and permitting them to venture out only in cases of emergency or out of necessity. In some Islamic societies, such as Saudi Arabia, women are prohibited from traveling alone and must be accompanied by their fathers, brothers, or a close male relative, unless they have written permission from one of these individuals that states they may travel alone (Ibrahim 1990). When a Muslim woman appears in public, she must dress "modestly" that is, veiled and clothed in a loose-fitting garment (the *chador*) that covers her from head to toe. Originally, such restrictions were imposed only on Mohamad's wives, but after his death they were extended to all Muslim women, a practice that continues today (Ahmed 1986; Haddad 1985).

This does not mean that there are no women in public life, but every effort is made to insure that they do not mingle with the opposite sex—that they are, in effect, invisible to men. There are female physicians, for instance, but they treat only female patients, just as female teachers instruct only female students (Darrow 1985; Higgens 1985). In Saudi Arabia, all banks have women's branches where only female tellers and lending officers work and attend to an all-female clientel (Ibrahim 1990) "In the Islamic nation of Oman, women are permitted to attend the country's only college—but they have to enter segregated classes through their own back door, and the entire campus has a system of overhead walkways for the exclusive use of women, so that contact with men can be avoided at all times" (Robertson 1987:320). Women are also excluded from the mosques and from most religious rituals, although they do make regular visits to the sanctuaries of Islamic saints where men, though permitted, rarely go (Crossette 1989; Mernissi 1977).

There are less orthodox sects of Islam, such as the Sufi and Qarmati, that are somewhat more liberal towards women, and in several Islamic countries, such as Pakistan and Saudi Arabia, women have begun to strategize on how to obtain more rights and freedom, including more job opportunities and the right to study the Qur'an at the mosque (Crossette 1989; Ibrahim 1989). In 1990, for instance, about seventy Saudi women dismissed their chauffeurs one afternoon and drove cars themselves in a protest against a ban on women driving. Although they argued that the right to drive would not cause them to break the laws of Islam, they were quickly arrested by the Saudi religious police, the Committee for Commendation of Virtue and Prevention of Vice. In addition, the Saudi Ministry of the Interior reaffirmed the ban, maintaining that, according to Muslim scholars, driving "degrades and harms the sanctity [of women]" (quoted in LeMoyne 1990:A19). Thus, in the majority of contemporary Islamic societies, fundamentalism remains the rule rather than the exception (Ibrahim 1990; Ahmed 1986; Carmody 1979).

Recent revolutions in some Islamic nations, such as Iran, have meant a return to orthodox practices after an interlude of Western modernization. Interestingly, there have been few signs of resistance to these changes among the Muslim women they have affected. Most, in fact, willingly donned the veil and *chador* to protest oppressive political regimes and Western imperialism in their countries (Darrow 1985; Higgens 1985). To them, the enemy is not male oppression, but rather outside forces, such as Zionism and U.S. imperialism, that threaten to destroy the Islamic way of life. Through their devotion to Islam, as evidenced by their adherence to its laws and customs, Muslim women see themselves on the front lines of the revolution (Haddad 1985).

In some ways the conservative politicization of Islamic women gives them more in common with American Christian fundamentalist women than would at first be thought. Both groups, though, have a particular vision of how their society should be structured—a vision informed by their religious beliefs, and both have undertaken political activity in an effort to have this vision realized. To understand this parallel better, let's look at some of the political beliefs and activities of various religious groups in the United States.

RELIGION, POLITICS, AND SOCIAL CHANGE

As we noted at the conclusion of Chapter 10, theoretically at least, the church and the government in the United States are supposed to constitute separate spheres of influence. Yet, sociologists have long recognized that the ideology of the separation of church and state is largely a myth. In practice, the affairs of the state and the interests of organized religion are closely and complexly intertwined. Historians tell us, for example, that Christian fundamentalists or "Evangelicals" as they are sometimes called, were active in the American Revolution, the abolitionist movement, the campaign for prison reform in the late 1700s, and a number of other political causes and social reforms (Pohli 1983).

Today, Evangelicals remain politically active, constituting what many refer to as the "New Right." It is estimated that the New Right as a political constituency comprises 25 percent of the U.S. adult population and that a large percentage of this group identifies itself as Evangelicals or fundamentalist Christians. Put another way, the Evangelical New Right has about 43 million members, which, although small relative to the total U.S. population, is still a sizeable number. More importantly, this group has taken a strong public stand on what it calls "family issues": for example, abortion and reproductive freedom, sex education, homosexual rights, and gender equality—in short, issues that feminists strongly support (Pohli 1983). Because of the New Right's political activism on these issues and the political impact it could have on any progress that has been made toward gender equality, it deserves our serious attention here. However, we will also see that while religion as represented by groups in the New Right seeks to preserve the status quo, it can also inspire resistance to oppression and promote liberating social change.

The Politics of Gender in the Evangelical New Right

Fundamentalist Christians or Evangelicals interpret the Bible literally, taking it to be truly God's word. At the same time, they believe that one can only attain eternal salvation by living one's life in accordance with the teachings of the Bible and thus developing a personal relationship with Jesus Christ. Evangelical leaders also exhort their congregations to be "soldiers of Christ" by combatting the erosion of biblical values in the secular world. According to the New Right, feminism, homosexual rights, and other liberal political and social movements are at the core of this erosion of values (Klatch 1988; Pohli 1983).

Not surprisingly, the fundamentalist Christian churches, along with other conservative Christian groups such as the predominantly Catholic Right to Life Movement, have been at the forefront of political opposition to feminist-supported policies and programs. For instance, they lobbied aggressively and successfully against the Equal Rights Amendment (*see* Chapter 13), and they have spearheaded campaigns to remove feminist and other types of "objectionable" books and materials from school libraries and classrooms. Since 1973, they have lobbied Congress for a Human Life Amendment that would overturn *Roe* v. *Wade* and once again outlaw abortion. In 1990, Catholic bishops in the United States even hired a public relations firm to present their anti-abortion message more favorably to the general public.

In the view of the religious New Right, feminism and its goals, as well as other movements such as gay rights, undermine the Christian family by promoting lifestyles and values inimical to "God's plan" for men and women. More specifically, they adhere strongly to the belief that a man's role is to provide for and protect his family, while a woman's appropriate place is at home caring for her husband and children. And just as men are subordinate to God, so are women subordinate to men (Klatch 1988; Connover and Gray 1983; Pohli 1983).

The religious New Right has won some impressive political victories, not the least of which was the defeat of the ERA as we have noted. Some analysts attribute this success to New Right leaders' masterful use of computer-generated mailing and telecommunications not only to promote their political positions, but also as fundraising tools. "Nearly a thousand American radio stations and eighty television stations are devoted to religious programming, most of which promote the fundamentalist message" (Robertson 1987:414). In a 1989 Gallup survey, nearly one-half of adults questioned reported that they had watched religious programming on television at least once, while 21 percent identified themselves as weekly viewers (Colasanto and De Stefano 1989). The Evangelicals' telecommunications network has also helped to generate contributions that provided the Moral Majority alone with a budget of more than $1.2 million (Connover and Gray 1983). It is those with the least discretionary income—older people, African Americans, and those who have not graduated from high school—who most often contribute, however.

Recent sexual and financial scandals involving New Right church leaders have damaged the movement's credibility in the eyes of its followers (Gallup 1989). At the present time, though, most feminists and gay rights activists continue to view the religious right as a powerful political foe—an issue we will take up again in Chapter 13.

Minority Churches: Resistance and Liberation

The Evangelical New Right represents a religious organization opposed to both liberal social change and social equality. For minority group members, however, the church has often been the source of inspiration and strength in their struggles to overcome discrimination and to secure equal rights and opportunities. The black churches, for example, have produced many prominent and influential political leaders and social activists, such as the late Rev. Martin Luther King, Jr., and the Rev. Leon Sullivan. A number of black politicians were first ministers in black churches: the Rev. Jesse Jackson, for instance, and Congressman William Gray of Pennsylvania. The black churches, in particular, have historically provided an organizational center within the black community where members could develop programs of action to overcome racial oppression; the Rev. King's strategy of nonviolent civil disobedience and direct action is an example (Lincoln and Mamiya 1990).

Minority churches have also been centers of social and political activism for women of color; as we noted earlier, they constitute the majority of members of many black church congregations (Grant 1986; Gilkes 1985). Yet despite their numbers and their level of participation in and support of their churches, minority women have encountered sexism and considerable resistance from black male church leaders to their assuming leadership roles within the church. "Most often this takes the form of barring women from a formally defined ministerial office even when they may already be performing its functions. Hence, in some Afro-American Pentacostal Churches, the male ministers hold the title 'preacher' but women ministers are called 'teacher' although their tasks may be identical" (Briggs 1987:411; Lincoln and Mamiya 1990; Grant 1986).

It is estimated that just 5 percent of black clergy are female (Lincoln and Mamiya 1990). Currently, African Americans represent just 6.8 percent of theological school enrollments, and 25 percent of these black students are females. However, almost half of the black female students are enrolled in only two-year programs. The numbers are similar for other racial minorites. Hispanics constitute 2.6 percent of theology students and Asian Americans 3.7 percent (Jacquet 1990; Briggs 1987).

It appears, then, that while minority churches have served as catalysts for social action against racial oppression, this has not typically extended to the problem of gender inequality within society or within the churches themselves (Grant 1986). This disparity has not lessened minority women's identification with their churches nor their community activism through their churches. In fact, minority churchwomen themselves have been reluctant to identify their activities and concerns as feminist, since they generally see feminism as a white, middle-class women's movement (Briggs 1987; *see also* Chapter 13). Nevertheless, although their numbers are small, minority feminist theologians have joined with white feminist theologians in critiquing the sexism of the dominant religious traditions and in working to depatriarchalize these religions. To conclude our discussion, therefore, we turn to an examination of these efforts.

CHALLENGES TO PATRIARCHAL RELIGIONS: FEMINIST SPIRITUALITY

It is really inaccurate to speak of **feminist spirituality** in the singular or to depict it as a unified religious movement, for within it one hears a plurality of voices professing different beliefs and advocating different strategies for change and reconstruction. Yet there are some common themes, perhaps the most important being the rejection of the *dualism* of patriarchal religions. More specifically, the major patriarchal religious traditions separate God and the world, and spirit and body (or nature), viewing them as distinct and placing human beings in tension between them. According to feminists, "This [dualistic model] is a model for domination, because [it divides reality] into two levels, one superior and one inferior" (Christ and Plaskow 1979:5). In contrast, feminists emphasize the unity of spirit and nature and see *experience* as the source of spirituality. Experience includes the events of the life cycle (e.g., menarche, coupling or marriage, parenthood, and so on) as well as developing an awareness of one's location in the social structure: recognizing oppression, confronting it, and acting to bring about liberation (Welch 1985; Ruether 1983; Christ and Plaskow 1979). It is over the issue of how to implement this principle, however, that feminist spiritualists part company with one another.

There are those who consider the Judeo-Christian traditions and other patriarchal religions as so hopelessly mired in sexism that they have abandoned them altogether. In their stead, some have turned to ecology, others are rediscovering the ancient prebiblical goddess traditions, and still others are reviving the practice of witchcraft (Adler 1983; Christ 1979; Starhawk 1979). Some advocate a complete break with men and all that is male-identified (e.g., Daly 1984; 1978), but many welcome women *and* men into their traditions on the ground that patriarchal religions may oppress members of both sexes through heterosexim, racism, and class bias, for example. From this perspective, women's experiences may provide the foundation for a feminist spirituality, but simply substituting female religious supremacy for male religious supremacy offers little potential for liberation for members of either sex.

Not all feminists, however, are completely disenchanted with the Judeo-Christian traditions. Some, often called "reformers," have chosen instead to challenge patriarchal religious forms and to reclaim Judeo-Christian history, language, symbols, and ritual as their own (Christ and Plaskow 1979). To them, Judaism and Christianity contain "the seeds of [their] own renewal" and, more importantly, "these feminists believe that the church [and synagogue are] *worth* renewing" (Weidman 1984:2, author's emphasis).

The first line of attack by this camp is to rename the elements of their religions so that they speak to women as well as to men (Chopp 1989). At the most basic level, this means divesting God-talk and religious symbolism of its he/man qualities—for example, depicting the deity as both female and male, referring to God as She or Mother, or using gender-inclusive or gender-neutral language such as Mother and Father or simply Holy One.

Once God is no longer imaged solely as male, the next step is to uncover women's contributions to Judeo-Christian heritage by critically rereading scriptures and examining other available evidence. From such careful study, we now know of the wealth of feminine imagery in the Old Testament and of the many ancient Hebrew heroines, wisewomen, and religious leaders: Deborah, Vashti, Esther, Huldah, and Beruriah are just a few examples (Brooten 1982; Gendler

1979; Goldfeld 1979; Trible 1979). Elisabeth Schussler Firoenza (1983) and others (e.g., Hilkert 1986) have rediscovered Jesus' female disciples and their central leadership roles in the early Christian church; among them were Junia who is referred to in Romans 16:7 as apostle, and Phoebe who was a missionary co-worker with St. Paul.

Finally, feminist reformers are restructuring religious ritual so that it is relevant to women as well as men. Jewish feminists, in particular, have been active in developing women's services and ceremonies for the Sabbath, Haggadah, Rosh Hodesh, Passover, and other holidays (Brozan 1990; Briggs 1987; Ehrenberg, et al. 1983; Agus 1979; Zuckoff 1979). Christian feminists have written women's prayers, organized women's prayer groups, and told women's stories and perspectives from church pulpits (n.a. 1982). In some cases, their efforts have resulted in changes in mainstream religious practices, such as the adoption of gender-neutral language in church services (*see,* for example, Canadian Bishops' Pastoral Team 1989).

Like those who have broken with Judeo-Christian traditions, religious reformers are split on the issue of whether feminist spirituality should be a women-only enterprise or a joint venture that includes members of both sexes. There are some who maintain that women need separate places and methods for worship, at least until they have fully reclaimed their religious heritage and reestablished a position of equal status and authority within Judaism and Christianity. Others argue, however, that separatism itself gives rise to and perpetuates inequality, and that the goal of feminist spirituality should be the building of a nonhierarchical human fellowship irrespective of individuals' sex, race, social class, or sexual preference.

Of course, it may be that this issue is unresolvable, but we do hope that through the struggle to come to grips with it, people will develop better ways to fulfill what appears to be a basic human need, religious expression. What we must keep in mind, however, is that a resurging religious fundamentalism threatens to negate even the most modest steps that have been taken toward gender equality. Religious fundamentalists—be they Jewish, Christian, or Muslim—vehemently oppose liberal trends, especially in gender relations, and they are becoming more active politically so as to get their position represented in civil as well as religious law. Increasingly, feminism is being held up as a devil to be combatted, rather than as a movement for liberation. In Israel, religious leaders are arguing that orthodoxy is a unifying force central to national security. In the Arab world, women's liberation is described as a United States-Zionist plot to weaken Islamic nations and eventually overthrow them. In the United States, pro-choice advocates are pitted against those who oppose abortion on religious grounds (Klatch 1988; Haddad 1985; Carmody 1979). Perhaps the underlying message in all this is that more can be gained by feminist spiritualists working together—women and men, homosexuals and heterosexuals, all races and social classes—than by each group going its separate ways.

KEY TERMS

feminist spirituality   a religious movement comprising diverse segments with differing beliefs and strategies for change, but unified in rejecting the dualism characteristic of traditional patriarchal religions; dualism is replaced with the theme of the unification of spirit and nature and the principle that human experience is the source of spirituality

Qur'an   (or Quran, variation of Koran) the book of sacred writings accepted by Muslims as revelations made to Mohamad by Allah; understood by Muslims to be literally the word of God.

religiosity   the intensity of commitment of an individual or group to a religious belief system

Talmud   constitutes the foundation of religious authority for traditional Judaism

witchcraft   naturalistic practices with religious significance usually engaged in by women; includes folk magic and medicine as well as knowledge of farming, ceramics, metallurgy, and astrology.

SUGGESTED READINGS

Gimbutas, M. 1989. *The Language of the Goddess.* New York: Harper and Row.

Lincoln, C.E., and L.H. Mamiya 1990. *The Black Church in the African American Experience.* Durham, NC: University of North Carolina Press.

Mernissi, F. 1987. *Beyond the Veil: Male-Female Dynamics in Modern Muslim Society* (revised edition). Bloomington, IN: Indiana University Press.

Plaskow, J. 1990. *Standing Again at Sinai: Judaism from a Feminist Perspective.* New York: Harper and Row.

Chapter 12

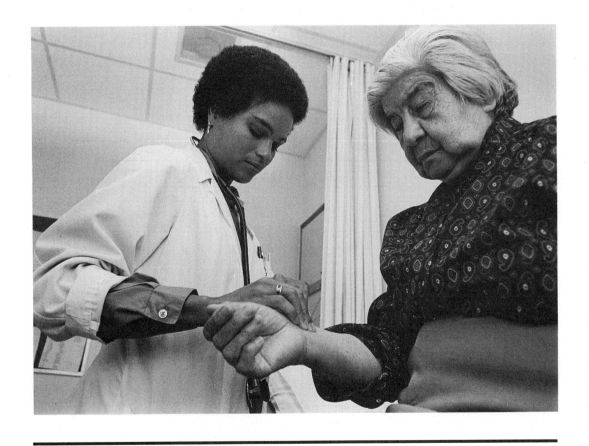

Gender and Health

Judging by media accounts alone, it seems that people across the United States are becoming increasingly concerned about their health. Some are trying to quit smoking and to consume less alcohol. Many have changed their diets, eating more fiber and less fat. And together they are spending billions of dollars a year on fitness club memberships and exercise equipment. This new health consciousness is due in large part to the results of recent studies, such as those released by the National Cancer Institute, that show a direct relationship between one's lifestyle and one's health. However, although this link is clear, we also cannot ignore the fact that lifestyle and therefore health are influenced to a considerable extent by a number of variables over which individuals have little or no control: most importantly, sex, race and ethnicity, social class, and age. In this chapter, we will examine how sex and gender relations impinge on health and how they interact with other factors—race, social class, age, and sexual orientation—in shaping both the physician-patient relationship and one's treatment by the health care system.

It is important to keep in mind that our conception of health encompasses more than simply the absence of illness. Health is, as the World Health Organization (1960:1) has told us, multi-dimensional. It is "a complete state of physical, mental, and social well-being." We will begin with a discussion of physical health. Later in the chapter we will take up the issue of mental health.

THE WEAKER SEX: MEN AND MORTALITY

One of the most consistent sex differences that can be observed across contemporary industrialized societies is that women, on average, live longer than men (*see* Box 12.1 for a discussion of sex and life expectancy in Third World countries). Looking at Table 12.1, we see first that the United States ranks low relative to many other countries in terms of both female and male life expectancy. (**Life expectancy** refers to the average number of years an individual may be expected to live from a given age or from birth.) The United States ranks eleventh (along with England and Wales) for female life expectancy and fifteenth (along with Italy) for male life expectancy. (The U.S. rankings declined during the 1980s.) However, in all the countries listed, women have a longer life expectancy than men. The gap is narrowest in Japan, but even there, the difference is more than six years.

As Table 12.2 shows, even though life expectancy for both sexes has improved over the decades, women's advantage has been increasing since the turn of the century. In the United States, for example, there was only a two-year difference in female and male life expectancies in 1900. By 1985, the life expectancy gap between the sexes had widened to seven years. Since 1970, this trend has slowed somewhat for women and men in particular age groups; for instance, "in 1980, the sex differential for persons aged 55 to 64 was lower than it was in 1970" (Cleary 1987:57). We also see in Table 12.2 that the gap is narrower between nonwhite men and women. Nevertheless, a significant sex difference in life expectancy persists regardless of age or race.

BOX 12.1   Sex and Life Expectancy in the Third World

In Third World countries, life expectancy in general is considerably lower than it is in developed and industrialized countries, and the gap between male and female life expectancies is narrower. Average male and female life expectancies in low-income (undeveloped) economies (excluding China and India) are 53 and 55 respectively, whereas in high-income (industrialized) economies they are 73 and 79 respectively (World Bank 1989).

It appears that sex differences in life expectancies in the Third World are related to gender norms and also to the feminization of poverty in these countries. This is not to say that men in the Third World are not poor; poverty touches the lives of Third World men as well as women. But as Doyal (1990b:509) points out, "it is women who must manage the consequences of poverty for the whole family" and this impacts on their life expectancy as well as their general health.

Consider, for example, that women in the Third World are responsible for securing water and fuel daily for their families. This usually means traveling great distances by foot and carrying back (typically on their heads) heavy loads while also often holding babies or small children. They also are involved in the production of food for their families, usually through subsistance agriculture, and because modern technology is rarely available to them, this means that they must cultivate and harvest their crops by hand or using crude tools, such as digging sticks. Grains must be husked and ground by hand, a process that takes many hours and is physically exhausting. In addition, cooking the food exposes the women to the hazards of inhaling wood smoke or emissions from biomass fuels, such as cattle dung. "Emissions from biomass fuels are major sources of air pollution in the home, and studies have shown that cooks inhale more smoke and pollutants than the inhabitants of the dirtiest cities" (Doyal 1990b:510).

Customs also contribute to sex differences in health and life expectancy. For instance, in some societies women are prohibited by religious and moral teachings from being seen defecating, so they must wait until dark to relieve themselves. This, though, can lead to constipation and other bowel and intestinal problems and also increases their risk of assault. In many countries, customs governing the distribution of food dictate that women and children will eat less than men. According to Doyal (1990b:511):

> In some cultures, it is common for boys to be breastfed considerably longer than girls and for girl children to be fed less well than boys, thus reducing their chances of surviving infancy. Adult men often sit down to eat before their women and children, who get what remains. . . . Thus, food which is itself in scarce supply is distributed according to the prestige of family members rather than their nutritional needs. As a result, many women become anaemic, especially during pregnancy, due to a lack of basic nutrients.

Consequently, it is hardly surprising that in some Third World countries, such as Bangladesh and Nepal, the sex difference in life expectancy is the reverse of that in industrialized countries; that is, in some Third World countries, men on average outlive women (World Bank 1989).

TABLE 12.1
Life Expectancy at Birth, by Sex, for Selected Countries*

Country	Female Life Expectancy (in years)	Male Life Expectancy (in years)
Japan	81.6	75.5
Switzerland	80.6	73.8
Sweden	80.2	74.0
France	80.0	71.8
Norway	79.9	72.9
Canada	79.9	73.1
Netherlands	79.8	73.1
Spain	79.8	73.2
Australia	79.6	73.0
Hong Kong	79.2	73.8
Finland	78.9	70.6
Greece	78.9	74.1
Italy	78.9	71.3
Federal Republic of Germany	78.5	71.9
United States	78.3	71.3
England & Wales	78.3	72.6
Denmark	77.8	71.9
Austria	77.8	71.0
Belgium	77.7	70.9
New Zealand	77.5	71.1

*Data cover the period 1985–1987.
Source: U.S. Department of Health and Human Services 1989:117.

A number of theories have been offered to account for the sex differential in life expectancy. At least part of the difference appears to be due to genetic factors. As we learned in Chapter 2, humans have 23 pairs of chromosomes, one of which determines sex. If an individual is male, his sex chromosomes are *XY;* a female has two *X* chromosomes. The *X* chromosome carries more genetic information than the *Y,* including sometimes defects that can lead to physical abnormalities. One might then expect females to be especially vulnerable to *X*-linked disorders, but instead they may have an advantage because of their "mosaic" nature:

> This refers to the fact that women have two sets of *X*-linked genes from which to choose, and different cells can operate on instructions from genes on different *X* chromosomes. That is why males more often suffer from *X*-linked defects, such as muscular dystrophy, which are usually recessive genes. If a female is heterozygous for the disease she can operate on the good gene, whereas if a man has

TABLE 12.2
Life Expectancy at Birth, by Sex and Race, 1900–1990

Year	All Races Male	All Races Female	White Male	White Female	Nonwhite Male	Nonwhite Female
1900	46.3	48.3	46.6	48.7	32.5	33.5
1920	53.6	54.6	54.4	55.6	45.5	45.2
1930	58.1	61.6	59.7	63.5	47.3	49.2
1940	60.8	65.2	62.1	66.6	51.5	54.9
1950	65.6	71.1	66.5	72.2	59.1	62.9
1960	66.6	73.1	67.4	74.1	61.1	66.3
1965	66.8	73.7	67.6	74.7	61.1	67.4
1970	67.1	74.7	68.0	75.6	61.3	69.4
1975	68.8	76.6	69.5	77.3	63.7	72.4
1980	70.0	77.4	70.7	78.1	65.3	73.6
1985	71.2	78.2	71.8	78.7	67.2	75.2
1988	71.4	78.3	72.1	78.9	67.4	75.5
1990*	72.1	79.0	72.7	79.6	67.7	75.0**

*Statistics for 1990 are projections.
**Life expectancies for nonwhites are projections for the black population only.
Sources: U.S. Department of Commerce 1990:72; 1987:69; U.S. Department of Health and Human Services 1986:84.

an *X*-linked gene for muscular dystrophy he will get it, since that is the only *X* he has (Holden 1987:159).

This is also thought to partially account for the higher number of miscarriages of male fetuses and the greater ratio of male to female infant deaths (146:100) and deaths at all ages due to congenital abnormalities (120:100) (Harrison 1984).

Some have hypothesized that hormonal differences between the sexes contribute to the life expectancy gap; however, research in this area has not produced consistent findings, so the role of hormones remains unclear (Holden 1987; Waldron 1986; Verbrugge 1985). What is more certain is that improvements in medical care and technology, while also benefitting men, have been particularly important in increasing women's life expectancy. Maternal mortality, for instance, has decreased from 73.8 per 100,000 live births in 1950 to only 6.6 per 100,000 live births in 1987 (U.S. Department of Commerce 1990). The widespread availability and use of PAP smears is estimated to have contributed to a 70 percent reduction in cervical cancer since World War II.

Marital status is also related to life expectancy, at least for men. In one recent study, for instance, researchers found that after controlling for crucial intervening variables, such as income, education, smoking, drinking, and obesity, men between the ages of forty-five and sixty-five who lived alone or with someone other than a spouse were twice as likely to die within ten years as men of the same age who lived with spouses. This relationship did not hold for women; women were more negatively affected by low income than by lack of a spouse. Although the researchers are not certain why marriage appears to be so important to the health of men, previous studies have shown that married men express a higher level of well-being than their nonmarried peers. There appears to be no difference, however, in the level of contentment expressed by married versus nonmarried women (Davis, et al. 1990; *see also* Hu and Goldman 1990).

We will examine the relationship between marital status and well-being later in this chapter (*see also* Chapter 7). Importantly, though, this relationship may be an indicator of another major component in men's and women's life expectancy differential: behavioral differences between the sexes. More specifically, we can observe a relationship between life expectancy and conformity to traditional gender stereotypes. To understand this better, we will examine male and female mortality rates for particular causes. (A **mortality rate** is simply the number of deaths in proportion to a given population.) Table 12.3 provides sex-specific mortality rates for a variety of causes. Let's look at some of these more closely.

Heart Disease and Stroke

Male deaths from heart disease, stroke, arteriosclerosis, and related causes are more than 65 percent higher than female deaths due to these causes. It is estimated that these causes of death combined account for 40 percent of the sex differential in mortality (Waldron 1986). Why is there such a prevalence of these particular diseases among men? Scientists maintain that a number of behavioral and cultural factors are responsible.

First, men are more likely to smoke than women. Twice as many men, in fact, are heavy smokers, and cigarette smoking does lead to and exacerbate heart disease. Still, "among middle-aged adults who have never smoked regularly the CHD [coronary heart disease] mortality rate exceeds that for women by 350 percent while for the total sample (including smokers) men's CHD mortality exceeds women's by 650 percent" (Waldron 1986:37). Obviously, cigarette smoking plays a major role, but other factors are also at work since the differential is substantial even among nonsmokers.

A second important factor appears to be that men are more likely to adopt the Coronary Prone Behavior Pattern, or what many call the Type A personality. Research indicates that Type A individuals are more than twice as likely as laid-back Type B personalities to suffer heart attacks, regardless of whether or not they smoke. Interestingly, the characteristics of Type A closely parallel those typical of traditional masculinity: competitiveness, impatience, ambition, and aggressiveness (Spielberger and London 1985). Not surprisingly, then, some physicians have reported that their coronary patients tend to appear more masculine in a negative sense than other men (Helgeson 1990).

TABLE 12.3
Age-Adjusted Mortality Rates for Selected Causes of Death by Sex and Race, 1987
(deaths per 100,000 resident population)

Cause of Death	Male		Female	
	White	Black	White	Black
All causes	668.2	1,023.2	384.1	586.2
Diseases of the heart	225.9	287.1	116.3	180.8
Cerebrovascular diseases	30.3	57.1	26.3	46.7
Chronic obstructive pulminary diseases	27.4	24.0	13.7	9.5
Malignant neoplasms (cancer)	158.4	227.9	109.7	132.0
Respiratory system	58.6	84.2	23.8	24.3
Colorectal	17.1	19.7	11.8	15.5
Prostate	13.7	30.1	—	—
Breast	—	—	22.8	26.5
Diabetes mellitus	9.5	18.3	8.1	21.3
Pneumonia & influenza	16.8	26.4	9.7	12.2
Chronic liver disease & cirrhosis	12.1	22.0	5.1	9.1
Accidents & adverse affects	49.7	66.8	18.6	21.0
Motor vehicle accidents	28.4	28.5	11.4	8.7
Suicide	20.1	12.0	5.3	2.1
Homicide & legal intervention	7.7	53.8	2.9	12.3
Human immunodeficiency virus infection (AIDS)	8.3	25.4	0.6	4.7

Source: U.S. Department of Health and Human Services 1989:121–122.

The findings with regard to Type A personalities are useful because they illuminate the detrimental impact that stress can have on health. However, the relationship between stress and heart disease is still poorly understood, and research is frequently colored by stereotypes. For example, early reports depicted heart disease as a health problem of executives, a middle- and upper-class disease, or as some referred to it, a "disease of affluence." Those most likely to be striken were said to be hardworking, successful professional men—men striving to "keep up with the Joneses" and to get ahead. Blue-collar workers and housewives were thought to be less susceptible, supposedly because they were less pressured, although it was predicted that women's rates of coronary heart disease would rise as more women entered professional fields (House 1986; Ehrenreich 1983).

Research based on such assumptions ignores the serious stressors confronted by blue-collar workers, for example, speed-ups, little or no control over work, and low rewards. This may partially account for the higher CHD mortality rate among African American men who, as a group, are underrepresented among white-collar professionals and overrepresented among unskilled laborers. In addition, as we noted in Chapter 8, female-dominated jobs have been found to be among the most stressful (LaCroix and Haynes 1987; Fleishman 1984), and female heart attack patients do report having experienced more stressful life events than male heart attack patients (Helgeson 1990). As will see in our discussion of mental health, the traditional homemaker role also can be debilitating for women (Doyal 1990a; Rosenberg 1984).

Significantly, though, while employed women face the doubly stressful burden of job responsibilities coupled with home and family care, there is no evidence that they are more likely than full-time homemakers to develop coronary heart disease. Indeed, empirical research indicates that just the opposite may be the case. Women employed outside the home appear to be healthier than non-employed women, even when employed women must fulfill multiple roles, such as worker, parent, spouse, and homemaker. According to LaCroix and Haynes (1987:103), "the employment role is the strongest correlate of good health for women," although it is unclear why; there is evidence that role *quality* may be more important for well-being than role occupancy per se (Barnett and Baruch 1987). More research is needed—for instance, on sex differences in social support networks among co-workers, relationships between supervisors and their employees, the socioeconomic benefits of working outside the home, and sex differences in access to and use of health care services—before the gender-specific relationships between stress and health are more fully understood.

Recent research also indicates that suppressed anger over racism may lead to elevated blood pressure and hypertension in African Americans, which in turn may contribute to their higher rates of death from CHD and related causes. A number of studies (e.g., Klag, et al. 1991; Armstead, et al. 1989) have shown that experiences of racism are an especially powerful trigger of anger in African Americans, but that the anger frequently is suppressed for fear of losing one's job, for example, or of being victimized by more overt violence. This suppressed anger, along with other risk factors prevalent among African Americans (e.g., a greater probability of retaining salt under emotionally stressful conditions) can, over a period of years, lead to hypertension, chronic high blood pressure, and CHD.

Cancer

Men's death rate due to cancer is more than 60 percent higher than women's cancer death rate, with the exception of breast cancer and other sex-specific cancers (e.g., ovarian cancer). Much of this difference is attributable to men's significantly higher rate of cancers of the respiratory system, especially lung cancer. Again, behavioral and social factors are chiefly responsible.

It is now a well-established medical fact that cigarette smoking causes respiratory cancers. Men's smoking habits are the primary reason for their higher cancer mortality. Not only do they smoke more than women, but also historically they have begun smoking at younger ages, they inhale more deeply, and they smoke more of each cigarette they light (Waldron 1986). There is some evidence that rates of smoking by both men and women are declining, although women's rates appear to be declining more slowly than those of men (Biener 1987; Cleary 1987), and the fastest growing group of smokers in the United States is young women under the age of twenty-three (U.S. House of Representatives 1990). It is estimated that each day, 2,000 young women start smoking (U.S. House of Representatives 1990). Moreover, the tobacco industry has moved aggressively to counter anti-smoking campaigns by marketing new brands of cigarettes to specific groups in the United States and abroad. In India, for example, the Golden Tobacco Company introduced a new cigarette brand, *Ms.*, in 1990 with advertisements aimed at Indian women who want to pursue a "modern, liberated" lifestyle—ads reminiscent of the *Virginia Slims* ad campaigns in the United States (Crosette 1990). Also in 1990, the R.J. Reynolds Tobacco Company test-marketed a new cigarette brand called *Uptown* targeted mainly at African Americans, a group that suffers from higher rates of all forms of cancer. However, after considerable government and public pressure, the company withdrew the cigarette.

Adding to the respiratory cancer risk are industrial hazards, especially the inhalation of dust and toxic fumes:

> Men who work with asbestos have up to eight times higher a risk of (broncho-genic) lung cancer than other men. This elevated risk affects primarily cigarette smokers. Asbestos is widely used in construction and insulation materials, and about one man in 100 is now or has been exposed to asbestos dust at his work. Thus, asbestos may be responsible for one in 20 male lung cancer deaths in this country. Metallic dusts and fumes elevate lung cancer risks between 20 percent and 130 percent for various categories of metal workers. About one man in 30 works or has worked in such an occupation. Thus, metallic dusts and fumes may be responsible for one in 50 male lung cancer deaths. Taken together, the established and suspected industrial carcinogens appear to be a factor in roughly one out of every 10 male lung cancer deaths (Waldron 1986:39).

Box 12.2 provides a list of known and suspected industrial carcinogens along with the occupations in which they are likely to be encountered. Although men predominate in these jobs, some, such as clerical work, are female dominated. Yet, less is known about occupationally related cancers and female mortality, since most research involving women has focused on their reproductive health. This is an important point that deserves further attention.

Common Carcinogens to Which Workers May Be Exposed in   **BOX 12.2**
the Workplace

There are about five million chemicals now in existence, more than 63,000 of which are listed as Toxic Substances under the Toxic Substances Control Act. Although most scientists maintain that the majority of the general population is unlikely to come into contact with more than a few of these chemicals, it is also the case that no toxicity information is publicly available for over 70 percent of the chemicals, so it is impossible to evaluate their potential effects on human health (Williams 1988).

The following are some of the toxic chemicals commonly encountered in the workplace, although exposure to some may also occur in the home.

asbestos   affects primarily the lungs; encountered in construction and the building trades, mining, milling, textile manufacturing, insulation, and shipyards

aresenic   affects the skin, the lungs, and the liver; encountered in mining, exterminating, tanning, and in the chemical- and oil-refining industries

auramine, benzidine, alpha-Naphthylamine, beta-Naphthylamine, magenta,
4-Aminodiphenyl, 4-Nitroldiphenyl   affect primarily the bladder; encountered in use and manufacture of dyestuffs and paint and by workers in rubber manufacturing

benzene   affects the bone marrow; encountered in the explosives industry, and by rubber cement workers, distillers, dye users, painters, and shoemakers

coal soot, coal tar, and other products of coal combustion   affect the lungs, larynx, skin, scrotum, and bladder; encountered by gashouse workers, stokers, and producers, coke oven workers, miners, and workers in the building trades

formaldehyde   may cause eye, skin, and lung irritations, menstrual disorders, toxemia and anemia in pregnancy, an increase in miscarriages, and reduced birth weight; a suspected carcinogen in humans; encountered by medical students, histologists, and many health service workers, and by mortuary workers; found as insulation in building materials, as a coating on automatic signature machines, as a fire retardant, and is released from disintegrating carpets

lead   may cause menstrual disorders, infertility, increased stillbirths and miscarriages, lowered birth weight, and congenital defects; may also affect the brain; encountered by smelters and battery manufacturers

ozone   affects the nervous system and lungs, and may also cause genetic damage; a suspected carcinogen in humans; encountered during photocopying and also emitted in exhaust fumes

vinyl chloride   affects the liver and the brain and may cause chromosomal abnormalities; encountered in plastics manufacturing and in the manufacture of plastic products

Sources: Fleishman 1984:63; Bellin and Rubenstein 1983:94–95; Julty 1979:131.

Occupational Hazards to Male and Female Workers

There's a certain irony in the phrase, "to work for a living," given that many workplaces are quite hazardous, even deadly. Historically, a recognition of this led to the enactment of laws prohibiting the employment of women in particular occupations. The stated rationale for such measures was not simply that women are "the weaker sex," but also that their childbearing function warranted them special protection so as to insure the health and viability of future generations. In practice, "protective" legislation has had two major effects: (1) legitimation of employment discrimination against women; and (2) neglect of the potential risks posed by workplace hazards to male workers' health, including their reproductive health.

The Pregnancy Discrimination Act of 1981 forbids employment discrimination against women workers solely on the basis of pregnancy. If a hazard can be shown to affect a fetus through either the mother *or* the father, then excluding only women from the workplace is illegal. It is estimated that over 14 million U.S. workers each year are exposed to known or suspected reproductive hazards in the workplace. Not surprisingly, then, reproductive disorders are among the ten most frequent work-related injuries and illnesses in the United States. However, little is known about the effects of most workplace toxins and other occupational hazards on the reproductive health of either sex, and male workers in particular have been virtually ignored (Blakeslee 1991; Paul, et al. 1989). Although it is true that "in the female reproductive system there are many more points at which, one can speculate, external agents could act," it is not implausible that workplace toxins could damage sperm or be transmitted through semen, causing visible congenital malformations as well as the possibility of childhood or adult cancer in the offspring (Bellin and Rubenstein 1983:90; Williams 1988; Hatch 1984).

Unfortunately, many researchers, employers, and policy makers traditionally operated under the assumption that women are more important than men in the reproductive process. Until 1991, most employers simply excluded women from certain hazardous jobs or employed only infertile or surgically sterilized women in such jobs (Willias 1988; Chavkin 1984a; Scott 1984). For instance, even low exposures to glycol ethers have been shown to have toxic effects on sperm, but a recent survey of Massachusetts companies that use glycol ethers in the production process indicated that none barred men from working with them. Similarly, jobs that involve radiation exposure may be more hazardous to men than to women because sperm cells are continually dividing, but eggs are not. Nevertheless, women, not men, have been routinely excluded from such jobs (Paul, et al. 1989). In other words, employers have typically addressed the problem by removing women from the workplace instead of rendering the workplace safe for both female and male workers. This is no solution at all, for the fact of the matter is that "toxic chemicals do not discriminate—they affect both female and male hearts, muscles, livers, and kidneys—and both female and male reproductive systems. . . . Men, women, and their offspring, are all at risk from toxic exposures;

we do not know whether these risks are sufficiently different to justify the selection of one of them as needing more protection than the other" (Bellin and Rubenstein 1987:87, 97).

We suspect that protection of women and their offspring has been less a motivating factor in the adoption of exclusionary policies than employers' concern with corporate liability and the advantages they accrue from a sex-segregated labor force (*see* Chapter 8). For one thing, exclusion from the workplace has not necessarily protected women from exposure to toxins. Men may transport residues home on their hair, skin, and clothes, with women being exposed through their daily unpaid activities as housewives (Rosenberg 1984; Robinson 1982). Indeed, housework itself is hazardous, but it is rarely considered in discussions of occupational health and safety because it is not recognized as "real work" (Chavkin 1984b; Rosenberg 1984).

Second, exclusionary policies have been common in male-dominated industries, but not in equally hazardous female-dominated occupations (Doyal 1990a; Goldhaber, et al. 1988; Scott 1984; Bellin and Rubenstein 1983). We know from our discussion in Chapter 8 that women, especially minority women, have always worked at dangerous jobs. In fact, racial discrimination in the workplace has meant that black workers of both sexes "have a 37 percent greater chance than whites of suffering an occupational injury or illness. Black workers are one and one-half times more likely than whites to be severely disabled from job injuries and illnesses and face a 20 percent greater chance than whites of dying from job-related injuries and illnesses" (quoted in Mullings 1984:122).

Recently, exclusionary policies have been successfully challenged in the courts. In March 1991, the United States Supreme Court reversed a lower court's decision that women could be barred from jobs that might potentially harm a fetus, ruling that such a policy constitutes sex discrimination. The case, *Automobile Workers* v. *Johnson Controls,* involved a battery company that prohibited fertile women, pregnant or not, from working at jobs that entail exposure to lead. The company argued that the exclusionary policy was not discriminatory because it is in the public's interest to protect the health of unborn children. However, the Supreme Court maintained that although employment late in pregnancy may sometimes pose a risk to the fetus, it is up to the woman to decide whether or not she will continue to work. Employers, ruled the Court, may not force a woman to choose between having a job and having a baby. Although this ruling is clearly a victory for female workers, it remains to be seen how employers will comply with it. They could make the workplace safer for employees of both sexes or they may simply leave it up to the workers themselves to decide whether or not to risk working in an unsafe, unhealthy work environment.

Other Causes of Death

For the remaining causes of death listed in Table 12.3, only two—specifically, diabetes mellitus, and pneumonia and influenza—are not associated with behavioral differences between the sexes. For example, chronic liver disease and cirrhosis of the liver are frequently caused by excessive alcohol consumption and related malnutrition. Since men are four times more likely than women to drink excessively—an issue to which we will return shortly—it is little wonder that their mortality rate from chronic liver disease and cirrhosis is nearly twice as high as women's (Waldron 1986).

Men's drinking habits also contribute to their higher accidental death rate. According to Waldron (1986), 50 percent of all motor vehicle deaths involve drunk drivers, mostly men. Even when not drinking, though, men drive more recklessly than women. Despite the unflattering stereotype of "the woman driver," women not only have fewer accidents than men, but they are also less likely to break traffic laws. This, at least in part, accounts for their lower rate of accidental deaths. Females, of course, are socialized to act safely, to seek help, and to avoid risks. Males, in contrast, are encouraged at an early age to be adventurous, independent, and unafraid of taking risks. Consequently, they, more often than females, are involved in the kinds of dangerous situations that may lead to accidental death (Waldron 1986; Harrison 1984).

Masculinity, we also know, is equated in many people's minds with aggressiveness. Men are expected, even encouraged, to behave violently, and this in turn is reflected in their higher suicide rate and their higher death rate due to homicide. Although women make twice as many suicide attempts as men, they are less likely to succeed in killing themselves, largely because the methods they use are less effective. More specifically, women tend to ingest drugs or poisons in their suicide attempts, whereas men typically shoot themselves. Some have interpreted this to mean that most women who attempt suicide do not really wish to kill themselves, but rather to seek help, while more men actually kill themselves because they have difficulty seeking help (Waldron 1986). Possibly, however, women and men attempt suicide using items from their environment with which they are most familiar and to which they have easiest access. "Masculine" items, such as guns, tend to be more lethal than "feminine" items, such as pills (Kushner 1985).

The mortality rates from homicide are particularly illuminating for they are products of the intersection of sexism, racism, and social class inequality. In general, men are nearly five times more likely than women to be murdered or to die from "legal intervention." Significantly, 84.5 percent of homicides involving male victims are committed by other men; 91.3 percent of female victims are murdered by men (U.S. Department of Justice 1990). Looking carefully at Table 12.3, though, we see that race is a more important variable than sex. Although black females are far less likely than black males to be murdered, they have a higher rate of victimization than either white males or white females. Most of the excess of male mortality caused by homicide, however, is accounted for by black male victimization. Indeed, since 1978, homicide has been the leading cause of death for young black males aged fifteen to twenty-four (U.S. Department of Health and Human Services 1989). In fact, according to a recent report issued by the Centers for Disease Control (CDC), "In some areas of the [United States], it is now more likely for a black male between his 15th and 25th birthday to die from homicide than it was for a United States soldier to be killed on a tour of duty in Vietnam" (quoted in Mydans 1990b:A26). This in no small part reflects their residential concentration in urban, high-crime neighborhoods and their disadvantaged economic position (Lee 1989). To paraphrase one observer, there appears to be incestuous relationships between racism, sexism, poverty, crime, and ill health (Holloman 1983).

Acquired Immune Deficiency Syndrome (AIDS)

Another fatal sex-linked disease for which the National Center for Health Statistics has only recently begun to report data is **acquired immune deficiency syndrome** or **AIDS.** The Centers for Disease Control reported the first cases of AIDS in June 1981. By March 1990, more than 128,000 AIDS cases had been reported in the United States; about 60 percent of these had already died. An additional 1.5 million Americans are estimated to have been infected and thus are carriers of the AIDS virus. Globally, it is estimated that 5 to 10 million people have been infected. Experts project that by 1994, 500,000 to 3 million more people worldwide will have developed the disease. In the United States alone, the prediction is that there will be 450,000 AIDS cases by the close of 1993 (Hilts 1990; Boffey 1988; Specter 1988).

It is important to keep in mind, though, that all estimates of the incidence of AIDS are *conservative* since they are based on the number of cases reported to authorities. There is evidence that a considerable number of cases go unreported. The CDC estimates that 10 to 30 percent of AIDS cases are not properly reported to health officials, although one recent study found that between 1986 and 1987, 40 percent of AIDS cases in South Carolina went officially uncounted (*New York Times* 28 November 1989:C15).

There are a number of reasons for this underreporting. For one thing, individuals infected may be unaware of it or may test negative. In addition, some physicians, concerned about the stigma attached to the disease, may decide not to report it to protect their patients. Underreporting is especially likely in the Third World where medical services are inadequate and recording is more difficult. Finally, since the disease has a five-to-ten-year incubation period, a tally of cases in 1990 only indicates the number of infections that occurred between 1980 and 1985, not the present rate of infection (Drake 1987; Lambert 1987).

An individual infected with the AIDS virus may show no physical symptoms of disease but is nonetheless a carrier who can infect others. Some develop AIDS-related complex (ARC) in which they display some symptoms of the disease (for example, swollen glands, loss of appetite, acute fatigue, and low resistance to infections), but have not yet developed any of the fatal diseases that result from full-blown AIDS. AIDS itself is a virus that attacks a person's immune system, destroying his or her ability to fight off other diseases, such as pneumocystis (a form of pneumonia) and tuberculosis. AIDS patients also often develop various cancers, such as Kaposi's sarcoma (a rare skin cancer) or suffer brain damage if the disease attacks the nervous system. The average time between diagnosis of full-blown AIDS and death is about eighteen months, although recent research has shown that early treatment with the drug AZT may prolong life and improve the quality of life of some patients. It is estimated that 30 to 50 percent of those infected will develop AIDS itself within five years (DePaulo 1987; Koop n.d.).

Despite the many myths, there are few ways one can contract AIDS. The most common way is through sexual contact with an infected person. The AIDS virus is found in several body fluids, but especially in blood, semen, and vaginal secretions. Consequently, anal intercourse is the riskiest form of sexual contact because it frequently results in tears in the rectal lining and blood vessels, allowing the virus to pass from the semen of the infected partner into the blood of the other partner. Vaginal sex, although less risky, is still a means of transmission. Another common way is through the use of contaminated needles by intravenous (IV) drug users. If an IV drug user injects himself or herself with a used needle or syringe that has even traces of blood containing the AIDS virus, the likelihood of contracting AIDS is extremely high.

About 3 percent of AIDS patients were infected by medical transfusions of contaminated blood. The majority of those with AIDS are homosexual or bisexual men (60 percent), IV drug users (21 percent), or members of both these groups (7 percent). Importantly, however, although only 5 percent of reported cases have been attributed to heterosexual sex, cases caused by heterosexual transmission are the fastest growing category of AIDS cases (Hilts 1990).

More than 80 percent of those who have contracted AIDS through heterosexual sex are female. This is due in part to the fact that heterosexual women have a greater probability than heterosexual men of being exposed to an infected sexual partner, since so many more men than women have been infected. Hispanic and African American women who are poor are especially at risk since impoverished minorities are more likely than whites to be IV drug users or to be the partners of IV drug users. In addition, health experts are concerned about the growing use of "crack" cocaine and the rising incidence of other sexually transmitted diseases in poor urban areas. Crack users, a large percentage of whom are women, tend to engage in promiscuous and risky sex either in exchange for the drug or because the drug itself tends to induce sexual arousal but inhibits sexual gratification. At the same time, the presence of other sexually transmitted diseases, such as syphilis, seems to facilitate transmission of AIDS (Hilts 1990). African American women constitute 54 percent of AIDS cases among women; Hispanic women account for 16 percent of these cases (Drake 1989).

Given the greater risk faced by minority women, it is not surprising that most pediatric AIDS cases are among nonwhite children. "Black children constitute 15 percent of the nation's children, yet account for 53 percent of all childhood AIDS cases. Hispanic children who represent 10 percent of U.S. children account for 23 percent of all pediatric AIDS cases" (U.S. House of Representatives

1989:1). A woman infected with the AIDS virus has a 30 to 70 percent chance of passing the disease to her child should she become pregnant. Currently, AIDS is the ninth leading cause of death among children aged one to four, but if present trends continue, it will become one of the top five causes of death for children in this age group by 1993 (U.S. House of Representatives 1989).

Presently, there is no vaccination against AIDS and no cure. Nevertheless, because researchers have learned how the disease is transmitted, they know it is preventable (*see* Box 12.3). The federal government, the CDC, and other organizations have launched AIDS education campaigns, but the level of misinformation among the general public is alarming and its consequences are often tragic: violence against gays has risen; parents have harassed school officials and families of AIDS victims to keep infected children out of school; AIDS patients have lost their jobs, and have been denied housing and insurance; the Rev. Pat Robertson, a candidate in the 1988 Republican presidential primaries, and Senator Jesse Helms (R, North Carolina) raised the possibility of quarantining the infected, and others have suggested identification cards or tatoos. Public anxiety about a disease like AIDS is understandable, but discrimination and violence against the afflicted is irrational and inexcusable. Perhaps former Surgeon General C. Everett Koop was correct in his prediction that discrimination against AIDS sufferers will probably end only when each of us knows someone with the disease. But according to another physician, "soon *everyone's* going to know someone who has it" (quoted in DePaulo 1987:140, author's emphasis).

Women, Men and Morbidity

We have seen that, on average, women outlive men by about seven years. But interestingly, despite their longer life expectancy and lower mortality rates, women have higher **morbidity** (i.e., illness) **rates** than men. Women have higher rates of illness from acute conditions and nonfatal chronic conditions. They are slightly more likely to report their health as fair to poor, they spend about 40 percent more days in bed each year, and their activities are restricted due to health problems about 25 percent more than men. In addition, they make more physician visits each year, and they have twice the number of surgical procedures performed on them as men do (Doyal 1990b; U.S. Department of Health and Human Services 1989; Cleary 1987; Waldron 1986). Cleary (1987:55) reports that "Those differences are largest during women's reproductive years (ages seventeen to forty-four) but even when reproductive conditions are excluded, there is a residual gender difference in short-term disability."

The higher morbidity of women may be related to their longer life expectancy. The older one is, the more likely one is to suffer from a chronic illness that restricts one's activities. Women comprise 59.3 percent of the population over 65 and 64.6 percent of those 75 and older (U.S. Department of Commerce 1990). Low income adds to the health problems of the elderly, particularly elderly women (Davis, et al. 1990). As we learned in Chapter 7, elderly women, especially

BOX 12.3   AIDS Prevention

Health officials have given us clear and simple advice with regard to preventing AIDS: practice safe sex, and if you are an IV drug user, do not share needles or other injection devices. Yet studies indicate that, with the exception of gay men, most people, including most college students, have not changed their sexual behavior or drug use habits to prevent AIDS (Johnson 1990b). At the same time, a sizable portion of the general public takes unnecessary "precautions" because they are misinformed about the disease.

Below are some facts about AIDS:

- AIDS is transmitted primarily through sexual contact—homosexual and heterosexual. You can help prevent infection by practicing safe sex: use a condom during (from start to finish) every act of sexual intercourse (vaginal as well as anal). Currently, there is little evidence that AIDS can be contracted through oral sex. However, the Surgeon General has advised that if you or your partner is at high risk for AIDS or either of you has sores or cuts in or around your mouth or genitals, oral sex should be avoided. There is no danger of contracting AIDS from kissing.
- Do not rely on a potential sexual partner's word as a safeguard against AIDS, especially if you are a woman. A recent study of sexually active eighteen- to twenty-five-year-olds in southern California found that 35 percent of the men surveyed admitted that they had lied to a woman in order to have sex with her. Twenty percent of the men said they would lie to a woman who asked if they had been tested for AIDS; they would say they had been tested and that the results were negative (Cochran and Mays 1988).
- Recently, a number of clubs and dating services have opened throughout the country for individuals who have tested negative for AIDS. This, however, is not a reliable indicator that a potential partner is free of AIDS for at least three reasons: (1) a small percentage of AIDS tests turn out to be false-negatives (i.e., the individual actually has the AIDS antibodies in his or her blood even though the test results are negative); (2) the individual may have been infected shortly before being tested, in which case the antibodies may not be detected, or he or she may become infected after the test; and (3) some individuals—no one knows how many—simply do not produce the AIDS antibodies detected by the tests even though they may have been infected.
- If you do not inject drugs, you have eliminated one of the main sources of AIDS infection. Anyone who does inject drugs should use only a clean, previously unused needle, syringe, or other injection device.
- There is no risk of contracting AIDS by donating blood. At the same time, the risk of infection from a blood transfusion is extremely low since all blood donors now are screened and blood donations are not accepted from members of high-risk groups. In fact, some health officials maintain that the blood supply is safer than it ever was because of the increased general screening.
- There is no risk of contracting AIDS through social contact, for example, hugging, shaking hands, crying, coughing or sneezing; sharing beds, cups, eating utensils, or other personal items; using toilets, telephones, swimming pools, furniture, or equipment. In short, you cannot contract AIDS from any nonsexual contact.

Sources: DePaulo 1987; Drake 1987; Koop n.d.

women of color, are significantly more likely than elderly men to live below the poverty line. There is a direct relationship between poverty and ill health (Holloman 1983). Moreover, official measures of poverty miss a considerable number of the elderly poor who are housed in public institutions and nursing homes. Almost 75 percent of nursing home residents are female (U.S. Department of Commerce 1990).

A second explanation of women's higher morbidity is that it is simply an artifact of their greater use of medical services. That is, men may experience as many or more symptoms as women, but they ignore them. Such behavior is again compatible with traditional gender norms: men are stoic and physically strong, while women are frail and need assistance (Calderwood 1985). There is some evidence to support this hypothesis. For example, although women delay as long as men before getting medical attention for some disorders, men tend to underestimate the extent of their illness more than women do, and they utilize preventive services less often (Waldron 1986). In addition, the medical community itself is not free of these gender stereotypes and may serve to reinforce them. Historical research, in fact, indicates that physicians have frequently equated normal femininity with the sick role (Ehrenreich and English 1986). To understand this better, however, we need to discuss the differential treatment of the sexes within the health care system.

SEXISM IN HEALTH CARE

Medical practitioners in the United States subscribe to a *functional model* of health which sees the human body as analogous to a machine. Illness temporarily disrupts the normal functioning of this "machine," preventing its owner from fulfilling his or her usual responsibilities. Curative medicine specializes in the scientific repair (i.e., diagnosis, treatment, and cure) of the malfunctioning human "machine." "Once 'fixed' the person can be returned to the community" (Rothman 1984:72).

Sociologist Barbara Katz Rothman (1984) argues that this model makes women especially susceptible to "illness labeling" by the medical establishment. This is because historically women in general have not been considered contributing members of society—"as people doing important things"—since their primary roles were performed outside the public sphere. "[W]omen were more easily *defined* as sick when they were not seen as functional social members" (1984:72, author's emphasis). This was particularly significant during the nineteenth and early twentieth centuries when physicians were competing with other healers for patients. The "nonfunctional" woman was a status symbol as well as a symbol of femininity. This image, though, was class- and race-specific; only middle- and upper-class white women (physicians' best paying customers) were viewed as delicate and frail. Poor and working class women, immigrant women, and women of color were thought to be more robust; it was argued that their less civilized nature made them strong and able to withstand pain. Of course, these women could hardly afford to be sick, even if their wealthy mistresses and employers had permitted it (Ehrenreich and English 1986; Rothman 1984).

At the same time, many women of that period did display symptoms of physical weakness, for example, fatigue, shortness of breath, fainting spells, chest and abdominal pains. These, though, were probably the consequences of stylishness:

> A fashionable woman's corsets exerted, on the average, twenty-one pounds of pressure on her internal organs, and extremes of up to eighty-five pounds had been measured. Add to this the fact that a well-dressed woman wore an average of thirty-seven pounds of street clothing in the winter months, of which nineteen pounds were suspended from her tortured waist (Ehrenreich and English 1986:285).

Physicians at the time, however, overlooked the effects of clothing styles on women's health and took these symptoms instead as further evidence of women's inferior constitutions. It was obvious to them that women needed special care, and they responded with the medical specialties of obstetrics and gynecology. Essentially, these specialties medicalized the natural biological events in women's lives: menstruation, pregnancy and childbirth, lactation, and menopause.

There is substantial evidence that early on, physicians' services were more detrimental than beneficial to women's health. Medical intervention in childbirth provides an excellent example. Prior to the nineteenth century, the birth of a child was looked upon as a family event, not a medical event. Women gave birth in the presence of female friends, relatives, and midwives who took a noninterventionist approach, letting nature take its course. For the most part, their role was supportive, trying to ease the labor of the birthing woman by making her as comfortable as possible. But when competition for patients began to intensify during the nineteenth century, physicians, who were virtually all men, began to deride midwives as uneducated "quacks." Physicians claimed to have scientific expertise in the area of childbirth. Only they had access to the specialized knowledge and medical instruments that would make childbirth safer, easier, and quicker. Eager for relief from the birthing trauma, women who could afford it increasingly gave birth with a physician, rather than a midwife, in attendance. The physician, having made his claims, felt pressured to "perform," especially if witnesses were present. "The doctor could not appear to be indifferent or inattentive or useless. He had to establish his identity by doing something, preferably something to make the patient feel better" (Wertz and Wertz 1986:140). These were the days, however, before asepsis, anesthesia, and other important medical developments, and the doctors' interventions were typically crude and harmful: for instance, bloodletting until the laboring patient fainted, the application of leeches to relieve abdominal and vaginal pain, the use of chloride of mercury to purge the intestines, and the administration of emetics to induce vomiting (Wertz and Wertz 1986).

Given these techniques, it is hardly surprising that births attended by physicians had higher maternal and infant mortality rates than those attended by midwives (Rothman 1984). Nevertheless, the physicians succeeded in convincing state legislators—men with socioeconomic backgrounds similar to their own—that midwifery was dangerous and unscientific. After 1900, the states enacted strict licensing laws that, in effect, drove midwives out of the business of birthing babies. Between 1900 and 1957, the number of practicing midwives in the United States declined dramatically from about 3,000 to 2 (Barker-Benfield 1976).

Today, obstetricians and gynecologists retain their virtual monopoly on women's health care. Women, in fact, are encouraged to obtain their general medical care from these specialists. Note that there are no comparable medical specialties devoted to "men's diseases" or men's reproductive health, but about 80 percent of obstetricians/gynecologists are men. The overwhelming majority are also white (American Medical Association 1990).

Advances in medical science and technology have clearly benefitted women and saved many lives, but much medical intervention into women's normal biological functioning continues to be unnecessary, and medical technology inappropriately used or inadequately tested harms, and often kills, thousands of women and their offspring each year. Consider, once again, medical intervention into pregnancy and childbirth. During pregnancy, women normally gain weight, retain fluids, and experience nausea. Doctors sometimes respond to these changes by prescribing special diets and medications. These may prove helpful, but not infrequently drugs, such as thalidomide and Bendectin, have produced severe fetal deformities and illness. The drug diethylstilbestrol (DES), a synthetic estrogen, was once widely prescribed to prevent miscarriages, but was taken off the market when it was found to cause cancer in the daughters of women who had taken it (Rothman 1984).

Studies also show that doctors may intervene in pregnancy for the sake of convenience—their own and the mother's. They may induce labor, for instance, if the pregnancy goes beyond forty-two weeks. Induced labor is more difficult and dangerous for both the woman and her baby. Moreover, if delivery does not quickly follow from induced labor, the physician may intervene further by performing a cesarean section (Rothman 1986). This, along with concern over malpractice suits, helps to explain the high rate of cesarean deliveries in the United States: almost one quarter of all births. The number of cesarean births has increased in recent years—from 5.5 percent in 1970 to 24.4 percent in 1987 (U.S. Department of Commerce 1990)—although many studies indicate that a substantial percentage of these are unnecessary. Some physicians and hospitals, for example, will not permit a woman who has had one cesarean delivery to attempt a vaginal delivery for a subsequent birth even though many experts claim such a policy is medically unfounded (Martin 1987). The widespread use of electronic fetal monitoring has also contributed to the rise in cesarean deliveries. Physicians, fearing malpractice suits, have taken to routinely using fetal monitors, even for low-risk deliveries, and are quick to intervene with a cesarean section at the first signs of "fetal distress" (Rothman 1986).

The medicalization of pregnancy and childbirth is just one example; there are numerous others. Menopause, for instance, is still viewed as a disease by many physicians who treat it as a hormone deficiency. Synthetic estrogens are frequently prescribed to help women overcome the side effects of menopause—for example, hot flashes, depression, irritability—even though some analysts have expressed concern that such drugs may increase the risk of endometrial cancer. Physicians tout these treatments in ageist as well as sexist terms, promising women eternal femininity and youthfulness (Fisher 1986; McCrea 1986).

Poor and minority women, however, have suffered the most at the hands of the medical establishment. Historically, these women have been treated by physicians as little more than training and research material. In fact, gynecological surgery was developed by physicians who first practiced their techniques on black and immigrant women. It has been documented, for example, that J. Marion Sims, the "father of gynecology" and one of the early presidents of the American Medical Association, kept a number of black female slaves for the sole purpose of surgical experimentation. "He operated [without anesthesia] on one of them thirty times in four years . . . After moving to New York, Sims continued his experimentation on indigent Irish women in the wards of New York Women's Hospital" (Ehrenreich and English 1986:291).

Researchers have also documented recent widespread sterilization abuse perpetrated against poor and minority women "because of the personal biases of physicians and social policies reflecting race and class discrimination" (Ruzek 1987:187). Davis (1981) reports, for instance, that in 1972 alone, 100,000 to 200,000 sterilizations took place under the auspices of federal programs. The majority of these involved poor minority women who allegedly underwent the surgery voluntarily, although evidence indicates that many had been misled or coerced. "Women were sterilized without consent, or consent was obtained on the basis of false or misleading information—commonly that the operation was reversible or that it was free of problems and side-effects. Information was given in languages women did not understand; women were threatened with loss of welfare or medical benefits if they did not consent; consent was solicited during labor; and abortion was conditioned upon consent to sterilization." (Committee for Abortion Rights and Against Sterilization Abuse 1988:27–28). Although the federal government issued regulations in 1979 to prevent involuntary sterilizations, research indicates that other more subtle, but nevertheless coersive conditions remain that encourage sterilization among the poor. One of these is the virtual elimination of federal funding for abortions. "The federal government assumes 90 percent of the cost of most sterilizations under Medicaid at the same time that it pays for only a miniscule number of abortions. This funding disparity amounts to a government policy of population control targeted at poor people and people of color" (Committee for Abortion Rights and Against Sterilization Abuse 1988:28). It is little wonder, then, that recently released statistics show the number of sterilizations of minority women still exceeding those of white women by a considerable margin (Alan Guttmacher Institute 1985; Hunter, et al. 1984).

Sexism in health care has been found in other medical specialties as well. For example, one recent study that sought to explain why women are less likely than men to survive heart bypass surgery found that female patients who undergo the operation usually are much sicker and slightly older than the male patients (Khan, et al. 1990). According to the researchers, most physicians do not respond as quickly to female patients' symptoms of heart disease as they do to male patients' symptoms. Frequently, women must "prove" that there is a genuine problem with their hearts by being significantly sicker (e.g., having had a heart attack or congestive heart failure) in order for their complaints to be acted upon by a physician. Additional research supports this: "In one study, only 4 percent of the women whose heartbeats became abnormal in exercise stress tests were sent to get angiograms, which provided pictures of blockages in coronary arteries. But 40 percent of men with abnormal heartbeats were directed to get angiograms" (Kolata 1990a:A15).

In short, research reveals a legacy of negative and stereotypic attitudes among physicians toward women, especially poor women, minority women, and elderly women. This, in turn, leads to the less than humane treatment that women receive within the health care system. Importantly, these prejudices are learned by physicians during their medical training. Medical textbooks and journals reflect the sexist tradition we have been discussing and thus help to perpetuate it. Gold (1983:136), for example, quotes a popular obstetrics and gynecology text that describes menstrual cramps as "evidences of personality disorders" and advises that the best way for both physicians and husbands to handle the problem is to be "firm in an understanding way." A recent study of advertisements in widely read medical journals found that women usually are portrayed as "stupid whiny sex objects," whereas men are depicted as physicians or as rational, busy patients (WIFP 1989g:6). In addition, much medical research, apart from that in obstetrics and gynecology, utilizes all-male samples. One well-known study found that taking an aspirin every other day could prevent heart attacks. However, since those studied were 22,000 men, it remains uncertain whether the aspirin regimen will have the same beneficial effects for women. This study was funded by the National Institutes of Health, which has as official policy the inclusion of women in biomedical research. Yet, NIH has been found to have funded several important studies recently that have excluded women (Kolata 1990b). (In response to this criticism, NIH established an Office of Research on Women's Health in September 1990, to ensure that their sex-inclusive policy is followed.) Finally, the role models available to medical students have also been steeped in this sexist tradition and many incorporate it into their teaching:

> An extreme example of sexism is the attending gynecologist who taught students to rub the woman's clitoris before doing a speculum examination in order to have her lubricate and thus have an "easier exam." Other examples include not respecting a patient's privacy, i.e., bringing in six people to watch a pelvic exam and even repeating it; talking about a patient to residents and students as if she were not there; and not explaining procedures and side effects to patients (Gold 1983:137; *see also* Fisher 1986).

Again, poor women most frequently experience such treatment since medical students still receive much of their training using clinic patients (Holloman 1983).

Clearly, the traditional doctor-patient relationship itself appears to be unhealthy for women seeking medical care. It has been argued, though, that this relationship will gradually change as more women enter the medical profession. According to some analysts, "Women physicians should be more capable of treating the health problems presented by women with respect, if only because the female body would be less alien and the female mind less mysterious" (Fee 1983:20; Klass 1988). Still, others are unconvinced by this argument and call for more radical changes. We will examine their alternatives shortly, but first let's look at the distribution of the sexes in the health care professions.

The Patriarchal Hierarchy of Health-Care Work

In Chapter 7, we discussed how functionalist sociologists, such as Talcott Parsons, differentiate between male and female roles as instrumental and expressive, respectively. Within the traditional patriarchal family, men are the instrumental leaders of the household and command greater power in decision making primarily because they are the breadwinners. Women, in contrast, are housekeepers and nurturers. Interestingly, critics of traditional medical practice in the United States draw parallels between patriarchal relations in the family and the male-female relations dominant in the delivery of health care. "The doctor/father runs a family composed of the nurse (wife and mother) and the patient (the child). The doctor possesses the scientific and technical skills and the nurse performs the caring and comforting duties . . ." (Fee 1983:24).

The sex distribution of workers across specific health-care fields makes this parallel even sharper. Health care historically has been an area of high female employment because many health-care jobs are viewed as an extension of women's roles in the home. Not surprisingly, therefore, women constitute over 89 percent of health service workers today, although they make up only 16.3 percent of practicing physicians (American Medical Association 1990). Women are concentrated in the "helping," "nurturing," and housekeeping jobs in health care. For example, they constitute 94.6 percent of registered nurses; 86 percent of dieticians and nutritionists; and 89.8 percent of nursing aides and attendants (U.S. Department of Commerce 1990). These positions have lower prestige and lower incomes than male-dominated health professions, such as physician, although the acute shortage of nurses during the 1980s did result in pay raises and other benefits for members of the nursing profession. Still, the least prestigious and lowest paying jobs are filled largely by minority women (Doyal 1990a; Aries and Kennedy 1986; McKinney 1986).

We have already seen how male physicians drove female health-care providers, such as midwives, out of practice early in this century. In addition, women and racial minorities historically were excluded from medical schools or discouraged from entering or completing medical training, either through blatant or, more recently, subtle forms of discrimination. Since 1971, however, the number of female and minority medical school students and graduates has increased significantly (*see* Table 12.4). There is evidence, too, that more women will be doctoring other women, given that female obstetrics and gynecology residents now outnumber males in these specialties (Commission on Professionals in Science and Technology 1989).

Although such trends are encouraging, some observers question the extent to which they will impact on sexism and other inequalities in health care. This skepticism stems from the recognition that female and minority medical students receive their training in the same sexist, racist, and class-biased system of medical education that white males do. What is more, they have very few role models other than white men from which to learn, since women compose 19.4 percent and minorities just 11.8 percent of medical school faculty, a distribution that has changed by only about 2 percent since 1975 (Commission on Professionals in Science and Technology 1989). Consequently, some analysts express concern that women, in particular, "are likely to be socialized into the 'physician role' as long as the role itself remains unaltered. Paternalism and authoritarianism are not genitally but structurally and culturally determined" (Fee 1983:24). In their view, then, the solution to the inequities in health care is not simply to put more women and minorities in positions of power within the current medical system, but rather to change that system itself. As we will see next, this goal is a cornerstone of the feminist health-care movement.

Feminist Health Care

The *feminist health-care movement* emerged during the 1960s as an outgrowth of the broader feminist struggle against sexism and gender inequality (*see* Chapter 13). Women meeting in small consciousness-raising groups began to relate their individual medical experiences, which contained some common themes: "[the doctor-patient relationship] was all too often characterized by condescension and contempt on the part of the doctor, and feelings of humiliation on the part of the patient . . ." (Marieskind and Ehrenreich 1975:39). Out of this grew the realization that "they had to begin by developing their own standards of normalcy based on study of their own and other women's bodies" (1975:38). By 1975, these early efforts had spawned more than 1,200 feminist health-care groups in the United States alone.

The feminist health-care movement combines self-help with political practice (Withorn 1986). According to health education specialist Sheryl Ruzek (1987:188), feminist health activists "educate themselves and other women about health issues, provide alternative services, and work to influence public policies affecting women's health." They accomplish these things in a wide variety of ways. With

TABLE 12.4
Minority and Female Medical Students, Medical Graduates, and Medical School Faculty, Selected Years, 1971–72 to 1988–89

	First Year Medical Students							
	Black		Hispanic		American Indian		Asian/Pacific Islander	
Year	#	%Female	#	%Female	#	%Female	#	%Female
1971–72	882	22.6	158	10.1	23	34.8	217	19.4
1981–82	1196	43.2	405	33.8	70	27.1	765	n.a.
1985–86	1117	52.1	467	35.9	60	50.0	1295	34.1
1988–89	1210	55.2	422	42.4	76	55.3	2100	n.a.

	Total Medical School Enrollment							
	Black		Hispanic		American Indian		Asian/Pacific Islander	
	#	%Female	#	%Female	#	%Female	#	%Female
1971–72	2055	20.4	328	11.3	42	23.5	647	17.9
1979–80	3627	42.7	1247	26.7	212	23.9	1777	29.2
1985–86	3849	46.6	1571	33.6	235	40.4	4289	7.4

	Medical School Graduates							
	Black		Hispanic		American Indian		Asian/Pacific Islander	
	#	%Female	#	%Female	#	%Female	#	%Female
1972–73	341	n.a.	49	n.a.	8	n.a.	n.a.	n.a.
1983–84	818	46.2	522	30.5	59	33.9	679	31.9
1985–86	824	42.5	322	33.9	49	30.6	909	32.5
1987–88	850	48.1	353	31.2	58	34.5	1119	35.1

	Medical School Faculty							
	Black		Hispanic		American Indian		Asian/Pacific Islander	
	#	%Female	#	%Female	#	%Female	#	%Female
1975	733	26.9	349	21.5	14	14.3	2383	18.6
1981	810	30.4	416	26.4	37	18.9	3319	22.7
1988	1103	33.8	548	24.6	52	19.2	4437	24.4

Source: Commission on Professionals in Science and Technology 1989:212–215.

regard to education, for instance, feminists have produced a large and impressive body of literature covering diverse health and medical issues in a nontechnical, highly readable style and format. Perhaps the best known example is the Boston Women's Health Book Collective's *Our Bodies, Ourselves* (1973). Feminist health activists have also organized "know-your-body courses" in which women not only learn about their bodies—thereby demystifying them—but also learn how to provide themselves with basic care through, for example, breast self-exams and pelvic self-exams. In the way of alternative medical care, women have opened their own clinics to provide a variety of services, such as gynecological care, pregnancy testing, counseling, and abortion services. The distinctive features of such clinics are twofold: (1) "the bulk of a patient's encounter, from initial intake to the final counseling, is with women like herself;" and (2) "the woman is not the object of care but an active participant" (Marieskind and Ehrenreich 1975:39). Finally, in terms of influencing public policy, feminist health activists have formed organizations, such as the National Women's Health Network, which has a membership of more than 20,000. Such groups lobby local, national, and international decision makers regarding policies affecting women's health throughout the world (Ruzek 1987).

The feminist health-care movement has not been free of problems. For one thing, women's clinics often face severe staffing shortages and funding difficulties. Such clinics are among the first to lose during government budget cuts (Withorn 1986). In addition, the movement in general has sometimes been criticized for not posing a more serious challenge to the medical establishment. "Many health activists believe that it is virtually impossible to create a truly humane health care system for women in a capitalist society. Yet none of the strategies used directly attack the underlying economic organization of society" (Ruzek 1987:195). Most still focus on individual treatment, rather than institutional change. And there is the added danger that an emphasis on self-care may simply serve to relieve the state of any responsibility for insuring the health of its citizens, female and male (Ruzek 1987; Withorn 1986).

Despite these difficulties, the feminist health-care movement is to be applauded for providing many women with safe, affordable, and affirming medical services. Equally important is the movement's central role in identifying and publicizing the inadequacies and inequities of our traditional health-care system. Although the movement's focus has been on women, its analysis of the problems inherent in traditional health-care delivery has also been beneficial to men, especially poor, working-class, and minority men who not infrequently are also subjected to inhumane and condescending treatment at the hands of an elitist medical establishment.

Another contribution of the feminist health-care movement has been to give women "a sense of pride and strength in their bodies" (Marieskind and Ehrenreich 1975:38). We will begin to explore this issue through a discussion of gender, physical fitness, and athletic participation.

GENDER, SPORT, AND FITNESS

Knowing the particular strengths and weaknesses of one's body, feeling fit and energized, being comfortable with and appreciative of one's body—all are empowering. What is more, developing one's physical potential instills a sense of achievement that encourages an individual to undertake other types of challenges (Lenskyj 1986). A recognition of this underlies the much quoted adage, "sports builds character." Unfortunately, the missing, but nevertheless understood adjective here has long been *masculine* character. Consider, for instance, the 1971 case of *Hollander* v. *Connecticut Conference, Inc.* in which a female student was barred from competing on her high school's boys' cross country team, even though she had qualified, because the state interscholastic athletic conference prohibited coed sports. In deciding in favor of the athletic conference, the judge stated, "Athletic competition builds character in our boys. We do not need that kind of character in our girls, the women of tomorrow" (quoted in Lawrence 1987:222).

The judge's statement reflects the traditional belief that athletics and fitness are masculine pursuits incompatible with our cultural standards of feminine beauty and female heterosexual attractiveness. In one sense, this is true; the ways in which sporting and fitness activities are typically organized and played out represent the antithesis of our culture's definition of femininity. The main ingredients of sport in our society are competition and domination, self-control and toughness, and violence and aggression. From their earliest encounters with sports, males are taught to develop a "killer instinct" on the playing field or court. Winning, they learn, is everything, and their success in sports is taken as an indication of their ability to succeed in the work world (Messner 1987; Sabo and Runfola 1980). Men and boys, in fact, typically approach sports and fitness as work. Exercise, for example, is a "workout" that must entail a certain degree of pain, exhaustion, and sweat to be satisfying (Sabo 1980). A few men—the professional athletes—even play sports as their jobs. And sports, we know, is big business, yielding about $25 billion a year (Sabo and Runfola 1980).

Females have not been excluded from sport and physical fitness activities altogether, but their participation historically has been limited. They have been encouraged to assume a supportive role as cheerleaders rather than as direct participants. Those who have participated directly have been channeled into "feminine sports," such as swimming and diving, skating, gymnastics, and aerobic dancing. Those women who seriously pursue sports have often done so under great stress, being labeled "mannish" and "unfeminine" or inept by others (Jarratt 1990). For instance, in one study, audience reactions to an announced basketball score (41–40) showed that when the audience was told that the players were women, they attributed the low score to lack of skill, but when they thought the players were men, the low score was explained in terms of strong defense (Cheska 1981). The exception, according to one writer, is the black female athlete who, in the black community, "can be strong and competent in sport and still not deny her womanliness" (Hart 1980).

Today, more women and girls than ever before are members of organized sports teams. However, recent research indicates that the majority still engage in sports and fitness activities alone or informally with friends (Lawrence 1987). Studies also show that females tend to approach sports differently than males, being more flexible and cooperative and having a greater concern for the fairness of a game rather than "winning at all costs" (Jarratt 1990; Gilligan 1982). In a sense, then, women and girls actually have been freer to approach sports in the way that at least theoretically they are supposed to be approached: in the spirit of play and for the purpose of personal enjoyment and enrichment.

In the early 1970s, a number of developments began to transform both women's and men's participation in sport and fitness activities. Perhaps the most important was the enactment in 1972 of Title IX of the Education Amendments Act. You may recall from Chapter 5 that Title IX prohibits sex discrimination in educational programs, including sports, that receive federal funding. In effect, Title IX forced United States educational institutions to broaden their athletic programs for women and to spend more money on women's sports. The effects have been significant: for example, the percentage of varsity athletes who were female rose from 16 percent in 1971 to 33.7 percent in 1989; the number of athletic scholarships awarded to women at the highly competitive NCAA Division I schools increased from 20 percent in 1977 to 26.4 percent in 1989; and the proportion of college athletic budgets earmarked for women's programs rose from 1 to 2 percent in 1972 to 18 to 46 percent in 1989 (Raiborn 1990; Dunkle 1987). Margaret Dunkle (1987:229) points to the success of U.S. female athletes at the 1984 Summer Olympic Games as evidence of the positive impact of Title IX. There, U.S. women outperformed their male peers, as measured by number of medals won. Significantly, "for the first time in history, and largely because of Title IX, athletic scholarships had financed the college education of many of the women members of the U.S. Olympic team . . ."

Also during the 1970s, research from the emerging fields of sports medicine and sports psychology helped to debunk many of the myths about the physical and emotional consequences of athletics for men and women. One of the first fallacies to come under attack, for instance, was the notion of "no pain, no gain" in exercise. Sports medicine specialists were quick to point out that men—more likely to subscribe to this tenet than women—by ignoring the signals their bodies send them through pain, were likely to injure themselves, sometimes permanently. Sports medicine researchers also demonstrated that participation in sports and vigorous exercise do not "androgenize" women's muscles, nor do they harm the female reproductive system. To the contrary, exercise may lessen menstrual discomfort and ease childbirth. Most importantly, studies from sports medicine showed that "there is more variation among individuals of each sex than the average difference, if any, between the sexes. . . . Sports medicine has finally taught us what should have been obvious all along: athletic training must be geared to the individual, not the sex" (Seldon 1983:133; Jarratt 1990).

Meanwhile, sports psychologists have found no evidence that athletic participation builds "character" or leads to work success or personal happiness. In fact, studies suggest that for men the opposite is true: sports frequently engender a sense of failure in men since so few ever reach the top of the athletic hierarchy. Messner (1987) notes, for instance, that only 6 to 7 percent of high school football players play in college and of those that do, about 8 percent are drafted into the pros, but only 2 percent eventually sign a professional contract. The odds are similar for basketball players. Moreover, even for those who reach the top, success may be shortlived: the average NFL career is 4 years, and the average NBA career is 3.4 years. Messner goes on to cite sports sociologist Harry Edwards, who has highlighted the disproportionate impact this has had on young African American men, since they are typically channeled into sports, but rarely have a "social safety net" to protect them if they "fail." Indeed, Edwards and others have played a major part in uncovering both the exploitation of African American athletes and the racism that continues to permeate organized sports. As one writer expressed it, "In sports, as in the plantation system of the Old South, the overseers are white and the workers are black" (Runfola 1980:83).

Developments such as these have prompted a number of reforms in athletic programs and have led many women and men to challenge the U.S. sport system itself "that too often glorifies violence, cheating, commercialism, and a win-at-all-costs mentality" (Lenskyj 1986:145). But despite the strides that have been made recently in "desexualizing" sports and exercise, there are indications that the gains are already being eroded. For example, women's increased interest and participation in fitness activities have been co-opted to a large extent by manufacturers and entrepreneurs who promote products and programs that promise youthfulness, thinness, and sex appeal rather than health and physical strength (Lenskyj 1986). As we will see shortly, the commercial tendency to imbue women (and increasingly, men) with insecurity about their bodies and appearance often results in serious psychological as well as physical harm.

THE POLITICS OF MENTAL HEALTH AND MENTAL ILLNESS

Up to this point, we have been discussing physical health and illness. We will now explore gender issues in *mental* health and illness.

Gender provides a strong link between physical and mental health since physicians have tended to view women's physical complaints as psychosomatic, that is, as "all in their heads." Research reveals a propensity on the part of physicians to see women's use of medical services as one of the ways women typically cope with psychological problems (Kurtz and Chalfant 1984). Consequently, physicians commonly prescribe psychotropic drugs for women who visit them with complaints of physical ailments. One study, for example, found that women receive 73 percent of psychotropic drug prescriptions; these are typically written by internists, general practitioners, and obstetricians/gynecologists rather than psychiatrists (Fidell 1980). This is an important point that we will take up again shortly.

Historically, it also has not been uncommon for physicians to assume that "malfunctions" in women's reproductive systems cause psychological disturbances. Around the turn of the twentieth century, for instance, physicians maintained that ovarian dysfunctions caused "personality disorders" in women—specifically, troublesomeness, eating like a ploughman, masturbation, attempted suicide, erotic tendencies, persecution mania, simple "cussedness," and dysmenorrhea. The "cure" physicians devised was ovariotomy (i.e., removal of the ovaries, or "female castration"). Ehrenreich and English (1986:290) report that:

> In 1906 a leading gynecological surgeon estimated that there were 150,000 women in the United States who had lost their ovaries under the knife. Some doctors boasted that they had removed from fifteen hundred to two thousand ovaries apiece. . . . Patients were often brought in by their husbands, who complained of their unruly behavior. . . . The operation was judged successful if the woman was restored to a placid contentment with her domestic functions.

Today, many physicians argue that menstruation and menopause precipitate personality disorders in women, ranging from depression to violent behavior, even though there is little, if any, evidence to support this and much to refute it (Gitlin and Pasnau 1990; *see also* Chapter 2). Drugs, such as synthetic hormones that have been found to cause cancer, have superseded surgery as "treatment."

The preceding examples highlight the difficulties we must consider in examining issues of mental health and illness: specifically, the problems of definition, identification, and appropriate treatment. First, psychiatrists themselves disagree as to what does and what does not constitute mental illness. At one extreme are those who claim that most mental disorders are objective conditions that have identifiable organic or genetic causes. In contrast, there are those such as Thomas Szasz (1974), who argue that mental illness is a political and moral label, not a medical one, and that mental institutions are not hospitals, but rather facilities to control those singled out as deviant.

Although most mental health specialists hold a position somewhere in between these two extremes, the disagreement itself makes it obvious that the identification of mental illness is a difficult enterprise at best. Just how difficult it is was demonstrated by D.L. Rosenhan and his colleagues in a classic experiment conducted in 1973. Rosenhan and seven associates were admitted to several different mental hospitals by claiming they were hearing voices. Their symptom, though, was contrived, as were the names and occupations they gave; however, they made no other changes in their life histories or regular behavior. Each of these pseudopatients expected to be identified quickly as an imposter by hospital personnel, but none was. Instead, the hospital staffs reinterpreted their normal behavior and previous life experiences to coincide with the mental illness diagnosis. They spent an average of nineteen days in the hospital, with all but one diagnosed schizophrenic.

The Rosenhan experiment illustrates that what is identified as mental illness "may be in the culturally filtered eye of the beholder rather than in the malfunction of the physiology or psyche of the person whose behavior is being judged" (Little 1983:345). Because mental health practitioners, like all other human beings, are not immune from social conditioning and therefore cannot be completely objective, we may expect their clinical judgments to reflect, at least in part, aspects of the culture to which they belong. Throughout this text, we have pinpointed a variety of cultural stereotypes regarding gender, sexual preference, race, age, and social class. How do such stereotypes impinge upon clinical assessments of mental health and illness? We will address this question now.

The Double Standard of Mental Health

More than fifteen years ago, a group of social scientists asked seventy-nine mental health professionals (forty-six men and thirty-three women) to describe "a healthy, mature, socially competent (a) adult, sex unspecified, (b) a man, or (c) a woman" (Broverman, et al. 1970:1). What they discovered was that the characteristics of mental health in the responses differed according to the sex of the person being described. More importantly, however, they found that traits considered healthy for an adult *person* were almost identical to those judged healthy for *men*, including independence, a sense of adventure, and assertiveness. In contrast, the healthy, mature, socially competent adult woman was described as submissive, dependent, excitable in minor crises, and conceited about her appearance. As Broverman, et al. (1970:5) concluded, "This constellation seems a most unusual way of describing any mature, healthy individual."

Since 1970, this study has been replicated a number of times under a variety of circumstances and with different subjects (Hansen and Reekie 1990; Philips and Gilroy 1985; Wise and Rafferty 1982; Brooks-Gunn and Fisch 1980). These replications have yielded results that support Broverman, et al.'s original findings. What we see here, then, is that stereotypical masculine behavior is assumed by many clinicians to be the norm or the ideal standard of mental health. This, in turn, puts women in a double bind. On the one hand, if they choose to behave as a healthy, mature adult, they risk being labeled abnormal (i.e., masculine women). On the other hand, women who follow the cultural script for the healthy, mature woman may find themselves unhappy, dissatisfied, and psychologically troubled.

Robertson and Fitzgerald's (1990) research demonstrates how this stereotype may also work against men who choose to deviate from traditional norms of masculinity. Robertson and Fitzgerald showed one of two versions of a videotaped conversation between a male patient (in reality, an actor) and his therapist to forty-seven other therapists. In one of the tapes, the patient stated he was an engineer with a wife at home who cared for their children. In the other tape, he indicated that his wife was an engineer and he stayed home with the children. Therapists who viewed the first tape attributed the man's problems to job or marital pressures or to biological causes. However, those who saw the second tape typically diagnosed the man as severely depressed and attributed the depression to his adoption of the domestic role, even though he reported to his therapist in the tape that his staying at home had worked out well for the family. In addition, these therapists tended to focus on the man's adoption of the domestic role as something to be treated through therapy and some appeared hostile toward the patient, questioning his notion of what it means to be a man. In short, this study indicates that men who choose not to adhere to the traditionally prescribed masculine role are at risk of being labeled mentally ill (*see also* Hansen and Reekie 1990).

In the sections that follow, we will examine several mental disorders that have a higher incidence among members of one sex than the other. We will pay particular attention to how traditional gender relations may foster these disorders and how gender stereotypes may affect clinicians' diagnoses and treatments of patients. In addition, we will consider how other factors, for example, a patient's race, age, social class, or sexual preference, may influence diagnosis and clinical outcomes.

Depression, histrionic personality, and agoraphobia   Each of us, at one time or another, has felt depressed. In everyday usage, *depression* refers to feeling down, "blue," or sad. Depression as a clinical syndrome, however, is more severe and prolonged. It entails persistent feelings of discontent or displeasure accompanied by at least four of eight symptoms (poor appetite or weight loss, insomnia or increased sleep, psychomotor agitation or retardation, loss of interest in usual activities, loss of energy or fatigue, feelings of worthlessness, diminished concentration, and suicidal ideation) that are present daily for at least two weeks without evidence of any other disorder (Rothblum 1982).

Women have consistently higher rates of depression than men, according to studies of both clinical populations and the general public. For every case of clinical depression among men, there are two among women (Cleary 1987), and this sex difference begins to emerge as early as puberty (Allgood-Merton, et al. 1990). "The life-time risk for developing depression ranges from 2 percent to 12 percent for men and from 5 percent to 26 percent for women" (Rothblum 1982:5). However, the incidence of depression among men and women also varies by race, social class, and marital status.

More specifically, minority women and poor women who head households (among whom racial minorities are disproportionately represented) have the highest rates of depression of any group (American Psychological Association 1985). Cannon and her colleagues (1989) report, though, that social mobility and race interact to have an impact on rates of depression among middle-class women. In their study of 200 female professionals and managers employed full-time, they found that black women who had been raised in middle-class households and white women who had been raised in working-class households had the highest levels of depressive symptoms. Their study also shows that single women and women with children are more likely to be depressed than married women or childless women.

However, other researchers have found that married women are more susceptible to depression than both never-married women and married men. Interestingly, the reverse is true for men: never-married men are more likely to suffer depression than married men. According to the American Psychological Association (1985:8), "marriage is associated with a 71 percent reduction in illness for minority men, 63 percent for white men, 28 percent for white women, and 8 percent for minority women." Also of special interest is the observation that among divorced women and men, the former experienced more depression during the marriage, whereas the latter grew depressed during the marital separation (Rothblum 1982).

A number of theories have been forwarded to explain these differences. One is that the difference is merely a statistical artifact of women's greater likelihood to seek help for their problems. There is evidence of bias among psychiatrists, especially male psychiatrists, toward diagnosing depression in women (Loring and Powell 1988). This, though, leaves unexplained women's higher rate of depression as reported in general community surveys in which respondents, regardless of sex, have not usually sought help (Cleary 1987; Weissman 1980). It also cannot explain the variation in depression by age, race, social class, and marital status.

A second argument focuses on hormonal differences between the sexes, but evidence in support of this is sparse. There is a strong relationship between postpartum hormonal changes and depression (*see* Chapter 2), but this can account for only a small portion of the rate variation between the sexes, nor does it explain the variation between white and minority women.

It seems more likely that social factors are responsible for the differences in depression rates that we have observed. There are two major psychological explanations: the *learned helplessness hypothesis* and the *social status hypothesis.* According to the former, females are socialized to respond passively to stress, but males are taught to respond assertively. Consequently, when confronted with a stressful life event, men are more likely to take some kind of action, whereas women tend to become depressed. At first glance, this argument is appealing, but if we look at it closely, we see that it amounts to little more than victim blaming. "Many women find their situation depressing because real social discrimination [not faulty socialization] makes it difficult for them to achieve by direct action and self-assertion, further contributing to their psychological distress" (Weissman 1980:102; Miller and Kirsch 1987). This is precisely the premise of the social status hypothesis, which also emphasizes that the traditional roles afforded to women (i.e., homemaker, mother) offer limited sources of personal satisfaction compared with the diversity of jobs available to men (Doyal 1990b). This explains why women who have high-income, high-status jobs also have high levels of psychological well-being and few symptoms of psychological distress, irrespective of marital status (Horwitz 1982). And if we consider the stress and disadvantages imposed by poverty, sexism, and racial discrimination, the depression so prevalent among low income and minority women is easy to comprehend.

Why do married men have a lower incidence of depression than never-married men? Research suggests that it is because they usually have someone available in whom to confide: their wives. Women, who are socially expected to give others emotional support, typically display a willingness to listen to their husbands' problems and try to help. Interestingly, husbands are not inclined to reciprocate when their wives are troubled (Lott 1987). In addition, as we learned in Chapter 7, men's traditional roles as husbands and fathers place relatively few demands on them in the home and permit them considerable control over the demands that are made of them. In contrast, women's traditional roles as wives and mothers afford them fewer options, thereby combining high demands with little control, an inherently stressful situation that obviously could foster depression (Doyal 1990b; Barnett and Baruch 1987).

Two other disorders that are more prevalent among women than men are histrionic personality and agoraphobia. *Histrionic personality* refers to what was formerly called *hysteria*. In ancient times, as well as more recent ones, hysteria was thought to be caused by the movement of the uterus through the body. Thus, by definition, all hysterics were women. More recently, the ratio of females to males exhibiting histrionic personality was estimated to be between 2:1 and 4:1 (Chambless and Goldstein 1980), although some psychologists continue to argue that the clinical description of histrionic personality in diagnostic manuals virtually guarantees that it will be applied more frequently to women than to men (Goleman 1990).

What are the characteristics of the histrionic personality? The histrionic personality is commonly described as demanding, dependent, manipulative, melodramatic, scatterbrained, and seductive but frigid. Hysterics may also exhibit a *conversion reaction:* that is, they exhibit a physical illness or disorder that has no apparent organic cause. Most frequently, this takes the form of pain, hyperventilation, fainting, violent fits and convulsions, and paralysis (Chambless and Goldstein 1980).

Given the close resemblance of the histrionic personality to our culture's conception of normal femininity, some analysts have argued that females are socialized into careers as hysterics. That is, because women have been taught to derive their sense of self worth from others' reactions to them, some may resort to extreme measures, such as the histrionic traits described previously, to attract attention and win approval (Wolowitz 1972). Although there is some support for this hypothesis, it is also possible that hysteria is a response to a highly stressful situation that an individual perceives to be extremely threatening but that he or she feels powerless to change. In other words, hysteria may be a form of rebellion, especially when conversion reaction is taken into account (Ehrenreich and English 1986). Consider, for example, that conversion reactions are most common among men during wartime. In addition, for the married woman, conversion reaction renders her "incapable of carrying out her responsibilities and renders her dependent on her family. These behaviors as well are more easily tolerated in women and may cause less conflict for the hysteric and her family than would an overt rejection of onerous duties" (Chambless and Goldstein 1980:116–117). In any event, care must be taken to insure that the terms *histrionic personality* and *hysteria* are accurately applied and not simply used to denigrate women or to dismiss their real physical symptoms as unfounded. A recent example of the latter is employers who maintain that the physical ailments of their female industrial workers are psychosomatic ("assembly-line hysteria") rather than products of an unhealthy working environment (Doyal 1990a; Harris 1983).

Agoraphobia is sometimes referred to as *anxiety hysteria.* Agoraphobia is commonly defined as fear of open spaces, but this may mean a fear of crowds, public places, expressways, being away from home—in short, "any situation in which escape to safe territory or to a trusted companion might be hindered; the more confining the situation, the more anxiety-provoking" (Chambless and Goldstein 1980:119). If agoraphobics perceive themselves to be in such a situation they often experience a panic attack, that is, an episode of terror during which they may hyperventilate, experience tightness in the chest, and a number of other symptoms that they interpret as evidence of "impending doom." In fact, Chambless and Goldstein (1980) hypothesize that agoraphobia is really not a fear of open spaces or of separation, but of panic attacks and the consequences. Thus, agoraphobics avoid places in which they think panic attacks will occur.

About 80 percent of agoraphobics are women, and it is estimated that more than one million women suffer from agoraphobia. Just why this is so remains speculative since systematic research only began during the 1970s. It may be that since females are not typically encouraged to confront fear in the way males are, they become "helpless in the face of stress and more easily trapped in situations from which they see no escape" (Chambless and Goldstein 1980:123). Agoraphobics tend to be passive and dependent and to have difficulty expressing their needs—traits fostered in females. In addition, researchers have noted that many agoraphobics are women in their twenties and thirties who are unhappily married and who have young children. Usually, these women have never been on their own, and their parents and husbands reinforce their dependency. Often, they are quite literally trapped in their marriages since they do not have the money or the skills to survive on their own. Even if the means to leave are available, the prospect of being alone—something they have never experienced—frightens them into remaining in their marriages. Agoraphobia symptoms may be the result of these circumstances (Chambless and Goldstein 1980).

Although these hypotheses are provocative, further research is needed to deepen our understanding of both agoraphobia and histrionic personality. Even more important, this research must examine race and social class differences, in addition to sex differences, among those afflicted.

Alcohol and drug addictions   We noted previously some researchers' claims that in reacting to stress, women tend to be passive, whereas men typically take some sort of action. In the extreme, males may respond by "acting out," for example, by fighting or becoming abusive, and by alcohol or drug abuse. Men have consistently higher rates of problem drinking and illicit drug use than do women.

With respect to alcohol use, men outnumber women among heavy drinkers, irrespective of race. The ratio of male to female heavy drinkers is estimated to be 4.5:1 among Native Americans, 4.3:1 among Hispanics, 3.5:1 among whites, and 1.4:1 among African Americans. Men do more public drinking than women, so they are less likely to drink alone. They also engage in more "binge drinking" or episodic heavy drinking (Leland 1984).

According to Morrissey (1986:159), "The availability of and accessibility of alcohol to specific groups is symbolic of the positions of those groups in a hierarchy." She notes that at the turn of the century, the sociologist Thorstein Veblen observed that the taboo against women drinking was one of the ways men in the United States symbolically demonstrated their higher status. In other words, drinking for men historically has been a kind of status symbol, and male dominance in society affords men greater access to alcohol which, in turn increases their likelihood of developing drinking problems.

Alcohol consumption certainly appears to be compatible with stereotyped masculinity (Lemle 1984). Two researchers found, for instance, that males who exhibit exaggerated masculinity ("hyper-masculinity") are more likely to be substance (i.e., alcohol and drug) abusers (Mosher and Sirkin 1984). Males also receive greater indirect social support for drinking. Parents, for example, are more tolerant of the drinking of adolescent sons than of adolescent daughters (Thompson and Wilsnack 1984). Similarly, wives are more tolerant of their husbands drinking than vice versa. About 90 percent of wives remain with alcoholic husbands compared with just 10 percent of husbands who stay with alcoholic wives (American Psychological Association 1985).

In recent years, there has been growing concern that the drinking behavior of men and women is converging. Many have argued that as traditional gender prescriptions change and more women occupy previously male-dominated positions, they will confront greater stress that may lead to increased drinking, or they may be encouraged to adopt male drinking patterns. Such concerns have been fueled by liquor advertisements designed to appeal to "liberated women" and by advice books that urge women seeking corporate success to keep up with the social drinking of their male colleagues (Morrissey 1986). There is, though, no evidence to support the *convergence hypothesis,* and there is much evidence that refutes it. For one thing, there has been no significant increase during the past twenty years in women's drinking or in the number of women with alcohol problems (Fillmore 1984; Thompson and Wilsnack 1984). Second, although employed women are less likely than unemployed women to be total abstainers, this does not mean that they engage in more stress-related drinking. Their drinking habits may simply reflect their greater opportunity to drink socially or their greater exposure to alcohol in both work-related and social settings (Biener 1987). In fact, success-oriented women appear the least likely to become substance abusers in reaction to stress (Snell, et al. 1987).

Also of concern is the low ratio of black males to black females who are heavy drinkers. Part of this is due to the relatively low percentage of heavy drinkers among black men (Biener 1987). Interestingly, however, although black women who drink are more likely than women of other racial groups to be heavy drinkers, they also are more likely to be abstainers. In other words, "black females tend to be concentrated at the extremes of abstinence and heavy drinking" (Leland 1984:71). Researchers have frequently utilized the concept of the "black matriarchy" (*see* Chapter 7) to explain rates of black male and female heavy drinking. Their argument is that the alleged black matriarchy promotes alcohol abuse "in men, by the emasculation resulting from women's economic independence and superior authority; in women, because their male-like role subjects them to stress and eliminates familial constraints, encouraging them to drink like men" (Leland 1984:83). However, as Leland goes on to point out, extensive research on African American families has led to the conclusion that the black matriarchy is a myth. If the black matriarchy does not exist, any theory based on it collapses. We must await unbiased race-specific research to get a better understanding of the similarities in black male-female drinking patterns, and to better understand cross-racial differences in drinking.

What is more clear is that when women do drink heavily, they suffer greater impairment. Recent medical research has shown that females have less of a stomach enzyme that helps the digestion of alcohol before it passes into the bloodstream. Consequently, more alcohol goes into women's bloodstreams than into men's, even if women drink the same amount as men relative to body size. More importantly, heavy drinking further inhibits the production of the enzyme, so that alcoholic men lose some of their ability to digest alcohol, but alcoholic women lose this ability completely because their stomachs have virtually none of the enzyme. As a result, women are more susceptible to liver damage and other physical problems if they become alcoholic (Freeza, et al. 1990).

Just as alcohol has been more readily available to men, so too have men had greater access to illicit drugs. Men, in fact, control the illicit drug trade in the United States and abroad, which is not surprising given their greater involvement in virtually all forms of criminal activity (*see* Chapter 9). It is also not surprising, then, that males use illicit drugs more than females and that they are more likely to be regular or habitual users. As is the case with alcohol consumption, there is no evidence that male and female patterns of illicit drug use are converging, although sex differences are smaller among youths than adults (Ferrence and Whitehead 1980). Recent evidence suggests that both sexes, especially among the middle class, appear to have decreased their recreational use of marijuana and cocaine (Treaster 1990). Women's use of heroin has increased more than men's use in recent years, but women still constitute only about 20 percent of known heroin addicts (Prather and Fidell 1978). However, women constitute a sizable number of "crack" cocaine users. Although it is estimated that there are almost two male crack users for every one female user, crack is a popular drug among women because it is easy to use (it does not have to be injected) and it is inexpensive (Hinds 1990).

Analysts sometimes argue that female drug abusers exhibit greater psychological maladjustment than their male counterparts; that is, they are "sicker" than male drug abusers. Recent research, however, fails to support this contention. Female and male drug abusers score similarly on tests of psychological adjustment and express similar motives for their drug use. The most frequent reason for beginning illicit drug use given by both males and females is peer or social pressures (Sutker, et al. 1981). For women, though, this pressure comes from men, primarily boyfriends, rather than same-sex peers (Prather and Fidell 1978).

Women increasingly are being subject to a sex-specific form of criminal prosecution for their drug abuse. As of February 1990, about thirty-five women in the United States had faced criminal charges—typically, delivering drugs to a minor—for having abused drugs (or alcohol) while pregnant. Only one woman, though, a twenty-five-year-old in Florida, has been convicted; she was sentenced to fifteen years probation. Prosecutors argue that they are motivated by a concern over the alarming increase in the number of drug-addicted babies being born in the United States—about one in ten live births in 1990. Criminal prosecution, they maintain, is a way to force drug-addicted women to get help for their problem, while simultaneously protecting the unborn infant.

Needless to say, this approach is controversial. Apart from the constitutional issues, what the prosecutors' argument seems to ignore is the lack of drug treatment programs for women, especially pregnant women. Out of approximately 7,000 drug treatment programs available nationwide, only about fifty provide female patients with obstetric and child care as well as special counseling (Diesenhouse 1990). In one survey of New York City programs, 54 percent excluded all pregnant women, 67 percent excluded pregnant women on Medicaid, and 82 percent excluded crack-addicted pregnant women on Medicaid (Chavkin 1990). Moreover, research indicates that women who enter treatment encounter opposition and less support from their families and friends than men who enter treatment (U.S. House of Representatives 1990). According to one researcher, only one woman in ten leaves her addicted male partner, whereas nine out of ten men leave addicted female partners (Hinds 1990). Thus, as one observer has argued, "Prosecuting [the female addict] for failing to get help no one would provide hardly seems fair" (quoted in Lewin 1990c:A14).

Significantly, the one form of drug addiction more common among women than among men involves the use of prescription drugs. Unlike illicit drugs, women have easy access to prescription drugs. We noted earlier doctors' propensity to prescribe mood-altering psychotropic drugs to women. The most frequently prescribed drugs are minor tranquilizers and sedatives, such as benzodiazepines, which according to Cooperstock (1980) may cause drug dependence even when taken in normal therapeutic doses. About half of all American women use psychotropic drugs; they constitute 70 percent of habitual tranquilizer users and 72 percent of antidepressant drug users (Gold 1983).

A final note: women are more likely than men to suffer *cross-addictions*— that is, simultaneous addiction to both alcohol and drugs. This appears to be due to women's greater likelihood to report alcohol-related problems to their physicians. The physicians, in turn, often prescribe tranquilizers, assuming that they will help women "cope" better and, therefore, stop drinking. Unfortunately, this frequently exacerbates the problem. Benzodiazepines and alcohol are the second most common overdose combination in the United States and Canada (Cooperstock 1980), illustrating clearly the tragic consequences of sexist health care.

Eating Disorders   In considering eating disorders, it is useful to think in terms of a continuum (Wooley and Wooley 1980). At one end is *obesity;* an individual is obese if he or she is 25 percent above the average weight for someone his or her age and height. More women than men are obese and the problem is especially acute for poor women and African American women (whom we know are disproportionately represented among the poor). According to Freedman (1986:151), "obesity occurs seven times more frequently in American women of the lowest socioeconomic levels than in those of the highest."

The obese are usually blamed for their condition. It is assumed that they lack self-control, are lazy, and engage in overeating. However, research indicates that often the obese eat no more than those who are thin; sometimes, they eat much less. It appears that for many, obesity is due to factors over which they have little or no control: heredity, metabolism, and nutrition (which helps to account for the social class dimension of the problem) (Bouchard et al. 1990; Stunkard, et al. 1990). Nevertheless, tremendous pressure is put upon the obese to lose weight. For example, they are discriminated against in the job market, made the brunt of jokes by the media and others, and judged by the general public to be sloppy, stupid, and ugly (Attie and Brooks-Gunn 1987; Freedman 1986; Wooley and Wooley 1980).

This last adjective is particularly important in understanding why the vast majority of people with other eating disorders are women. In the United States, fat is equated with ugliness, whereas thin is beautiful. More importantly, it appears that our cultural standard has idealized an increasingly thinner body since the 1920s (Attie and Brooks-Gunn 1987; Freedman 1976; Silverstein, et al. 1986). This is true for men as well as women, but men are given considerably more leeway with regard to their weight. Women, moreover, are frequently judged less by what they do than by how they look.

Not surprising, therefore, is the fact that women tend to evaluate their self-worth in terms of their appearance. Unfortunately, their estimates of themselves are often unrealistically negative. Women consistently express dissatisfaction with their bodies, and most frequently they couch this dissatisfaction in terms of weight. In one study, for example, 70 percent of the female college students questioned perceived themselves as slightly overweight or overweight, although only 39 percent actually were (Miller, et al. 1980). Interestingly, although women typically overestimated their weight, men tended to underestimate theirs. Mintz and Betz (1986), for instance, found in their study of college students that the majority of women felt that, on average, they were ten pounds *overweight,* whereas the majority of men considered themselves an average of three pounds *underweight.* The overweight men in this study perceived themselves to be thinner than they actually were, whereas the only women who judged themselves as being of normal weight were really slightly underweight.

This cultural and personal obsession with weight can lead to other types of eating disorders. One is *chronic dieting.* One of every two women reports being on a diet "most of the time" (Freedman 1986). Although this may not appear to be serious, it can have severe physical and psychological consequences (Attie and Brooks-Gunn 1987). The chronic dieter tries dozens of different diet plans—many of which are dangerously unhealthy—over the course of ten to forty years, often beginning as an adolescent. Ironically, the dieting may have the opposite effect of what was intended; restricting food intake can lower one's metabolic rate which, in turn, requires that the dieter eat even less to sustain further weight loss. This is why after one stops following some diets, one may regain lost poundage quickly, prompting the start of another diet (Polivy and Herman 1985). Thus, a vicious cycle ensues with the chronic dieter perpetually dissatisfied with her appearance:

> In its most extreme form, the effort to be slender becomes so central to self-acceptance that all other life activities are relegated to relative unimportance. If weight is too high, the patient will avoid seeing friends, refuse to attend social events, avoid sex, and postpone or dropout of training or careers. The plan is always to begin or resume these activities once weight is lost, but for many that day never comes, or, if it does, it is short-lived (Wooley and Wooley 1980:137).

Some people turn to eating as a way to handle stress. Women are more likely to do this than men are, perhaps because food shopping and preparation have been women's responsibilities and because women's magazines highlight food by presenting tempting recipes and advertisements (Silverstein, et al. 1986). However, since women also tend to be preoccupied by the fear of weight gain, some may develop the disorder known as **bulimia.** Bulimics engage in binge eating, consuming large quantities of food (usually "junk" food) in a short period of time. Afterwards, fearful that they will gain weight, they purge themselves of the food by fasting, taking laxatives (sometimes a dozen or two dozen a day), exercising excessively, and most commonly, by inducing vomiting (Sparkman 1985; Wooley and Wooley 1980).

Bulimia is difficult to detect because bulimics usually do not show extreme weight loss. Bulimia, though, causes serious psychological and physical damage. The binge-purge cycle may take on the character of an addiction, like alcoholism. Frequently, the gastrointestinal tract is damaged due to the overuse of laxatives, and the esophagus is harmed by the effects of repeated vomiting (Kmetz 1985; Wooley and Wooley 1980). Reports indicate that bulimia may currently be an epidemic, particularly on college campuses. Estimates are that from 4 to 20 percent of college students, virtually all of them women, are bulimic to some degree (Boskind-White 1985). Some researchers argue, in fact, that bulimia is becoming, in a sense, a "communicable disease" in that many bulimics report having been taught how to vomit by a friend or by media stories about the illness (Brumberg 1988; Attie and Brooks-Gunn 1987).

Finally, at the other extreme end of the eating disorders continuum is **anorexia.** Anorectics have a compulsive fear of becoming fat and literally starve themselves to prevent weight gain or to lose more weight. Anorectics—an estimated 90 to 95 percent of whom are women—have an exceptionally distorted body image, feeling or considering themselves to be fat even when they are emaciated. The symptoms of anorexia include a 25 percent loss of original body weight with concommitant refusals to eat (Freedman 1986; Sparkman 1985).

Most anorectics come from middle-class or wealthy families. The majority are young women in their teens and twenties, and most are white. In recent years, there has been an increase in the disorder among working-class and minority women (Root 1990; Rosen, et al. 1988) and among men. Researchers and therapists have found that anorectics often have difficulty expressing their personal needs and desires, and may feel they have little, if any, control over their lives. Their weight becomes the one thing they can control. Controlling their appearance is also a way to please others (Sparkman 1985). Although the early psychoanalytic literature claimed that female anorectics were trying to deny womanhood by making their bodies masculine (i.e., noncurvacious), it appears that these women actually embrace an exaggerated image of womanhood. "Anorectics are seeking beauty through body transformation (just as most 'healthy' women do). The goal is not to reject womanliness but to enact it by becoming thinner and lovelier than anyone else" (Freedman 1986:156).

In short, women receive contradictory messages about food and their bodies. Magazines and other media present models of thinness, but at the same time run articles, programs, and advertisements on food, cooking, and dining. One study found a ratio of 1179:10 food ads when comparing popular women's and men's magazines (Silverstein, et al. 1986). Our culture tells women they must be thin to be beautiful (i.e., appealing to others, especially men), but they also must fulfill their duty to cook delicious and elaborate meals for their families. At best, these contradictions generate dissatisfaction among women regarding their bodies; at worst, they lead to eating disorders with debilitating consequences. One recent study found that girls as young as twelve are experiencing clinical depression induced largely by their anxiety over whether they are physically attractive (Allgood-Merton, et al. 1990; *see also* Whitaker, et al. 1990). There is also evidence that men also are becoming increasingly discontent with their bodies (Richmond 1987). We wonder if the growth in the use of cosmetics, plastic surgery, and diet fads targeted at men is not just a further case of profit-oriented entrepreneurs twisting the notion of "liberation" into equality of exploitation.

Sexism and Mental Health Services

We noted at the outset of our discussion of mental health and illness that diagnosis and, therefore, treatment of psychological disturbances may be highly subjective processes. Clinicians bring to their work particular biases that derive from their personal backgrounds and characteristics, as well as from their training in a specific institutional system. We have already observed that clinicians tend to utilize a masculine model of mental health. That this persists today is not surprising given that the mental health professions, like medicine in general, are hierarchically structured and men predominate at the top of the hierarchy. For example, only about 22 percent of psychiatrists are women (American Medical Association 1990). What are some of the other salient features of traditional mental health care, and what are their implications for the treatment of female and male patients?

Critics of traditional mental health care have given special attention to what they see as its emphasis on conformity to dominant cultural standards and its corresponding intolerance of diversity or uniqueness (Ballou and Gabalac 1985). More specifically, mental health practitioners, while claiming to be objective medical experts, often function simply as upholders of the status quo. Their judgment of what constitutes mental health is conformity to dominant (i.e., white, middle-class, heterosexual, male) expectations, although for many individuals these are oppressive. Conversely, any departure from these norms is taken as a symptom of pathology or mental disorder. The traditional clinician, then, sees the source or cause of a problem as existing within the patient; the goal is to change the patient rather than the external conditions that may be affecting the patient. Treatment is considered successful when the patient "adjusts" to (i.e., uncritically accepts and conforms to) her or his circumstances. This can be accomplished with a variety of techniques, for example, psychoanalysis, behavior modification, or drug therapy.

Critics are quick to point out that this model is more progressive and humane than previous treatment models. It also seems to be a beneficial approach to the most severe cases of mental illness. However, it is not appropriate for the majority of patients who seek therapy or mental health care (Ballou and Gabalac 1985). Consider, for example, traditional clinical evaluations of homosexuals. Many gays and lesbians enter therapy because of low self-esteem and depression. Mental health practitioners frequently assess these troubles as resulting from homosexuality itself, rather than societal discrimination against homosexuals. To them, the first sign of "healthy adjustment" is for the patient to acknowledge his or her sexual preference as the problem or "disorder" to be treated. We have presented other examples throughout this chapter: alcoholism among blacks is attributed to the black matriarchy, anorexia in females is interpreted as an attempted denial of womanliness, and so on.

Even more disturbing is the high incidence of sexual abuse of patients by their therapists. Research reveals that about 10 percent of male therapists and 3 percent of female therapists have been involved in at least one "incident of intimacy" with a patient; 80 percent of male therapists have been intimately involved with more than one patient. In one study, half of the 1,320 clinical psychologists surveyed reported that they had treated patients who had had sexual relations with a previous therapist. Such patients frequently experience emotional problems similar to those of incest victims. About 10 percent of these patients are so severely affected that they must be hospitalized; 1 percent commit suicide (Sonne and Pope 1991). Not infrequently, victimized patients are children; more than 50 percent of youthful victims are females. One recent study showed that minor female victims ranged in age from three to seventeen and minor male victims ranged in age from seven to sixteen. The research indicates that neither threats of malpractice nor felony convictions have been effective in deterring therapists from having sex with their patients. However, more victimized patients are choosing to sue their therapists, and the courts have ruled that consent of a patient to sexual relations is not an acceptable defense for therapists. In addition, the American Psychological Association has established a new panel on sexual impropriety which is in the process of developing guidelines on appropriate therapist-patient interaction (Ethics Committee of the American Psychological Association 1988).

Feminist Therapy

Because more females than males make use of mental health services, the biases and problems inherent in the traditional system are especially detrimental to them. Recognizing this, some practitioners have sought to reform mental health care delivery through the adoption of *nonsexist counseling*. "Nonsexist counseling seeks to treat clients as human beings and actively to refute sex ascription in theory and in practice, that is, in options offered to the clients and in the values espoused by the therapist" (Ballou and Gabalac, 1985:30). Others, though, see nonsexist counseling as only the first step in a series of necessary changes. These practitioners are striving to remodel mental health care along feminist lines. To close this chapter, we will briefly examine their work.

Feminist therapy is part of the broader feminist health-care movement. As Ballou and Gabalac (1985) point out, no consensual definition of feminist therapy has been developed. Instead, we can identify several principles that form the foundation of this approach to mental health care.

First, feminist therapists establish egalitarian relationships with their clients. Rather than being someone to whom something is done by an expert, the client takes an active part in therapy, and the therapist engages in self-disclosure with the client. The therapy, then, is viewed as a shared learning process. A corollary to this is that the feminist therapist accepts the client's knowledge and personal experiences as valid, rather than interpreting them as defensive strategies. In other words, to the feminist therapist the client may be the best authority on her or his problem.

A second related principle is that feminist therapy assumes that external conditions, not individual interpersonal ones, generate most psychological difficulties, particularly those experienced by women. "The therapist facilitates the client's ability to understand, both generally and personally, the existence and impact of cultural conditioning and biased social/economic/cultural structures. . . . The goal is to build skills for coping and creating, to develop astute social analysis, and sophisticated consideration of the potential consequences of change" (Ballou and Gabalac 1985:31,33). A fundamental part of this process is the analysis of gender relations (Rawlings and Carter 1977).

Finally, feminist therapists are committed to working for broader social changes that benefit not only their individual clients, but all women and oppressed groups. For instance, they may lobby for adequate and affordable day care; for safe, sanitary and low-cost housing; and for shelters for battered women and the sexually abused. In short, feminist therapists are advocates for social change that will empower the disadvantaged and provide them with social and economic autonomy—factors these therapists recognize as essential for mental health (Ballou and Gabalac 1985; Rawlings and Carter 1977).

Although a goal of feminist therapy clearly is to assist members of oppressed groups, especially women, there is little empirical evidence attesting to its success in this regard. Future research should address this issue by determining to what extent feminist therapy is available to those most disadvantaged by the current social structure: poor, minority women and their children. To date, however, the impact of feminist therapy remains unassessed.

GENDER, HEALTH, AND ILLNESS: A SUMMARY

The data discussed in this chapter are alarming. Taken together, they indicate, to paraphrase Harrison (1984), that traditional constructions of gender are hazardous to our health.

With regard to physical health, traditional masculinity appears to put men at greater risk for a variety of physical conditions, such as heart disease and stroke, various forms of cancer, and chronic liver disease. Their greater likelihood to smoke, drink alcohol, and engage in violence renders them more susceptible not only to these diseases, but also to accidents, homicide, successful suicide, and alcohol and illicit drug abuse. In fact, it seems that the more a man conforms to traditional masculinity, the greater is the risk to his health.

The same appears to be true with regard to women who firmly adhere to traditional femininity. For them, however, the greatest threat appears to be to their mental health. Those who embrace the traditional feminine role are more prone to depression and other psychological disorders, such as histrionic personality, agoraphobia, bulimia, and anorexia. In addition, though women tend to live longer than men, their quality of life appears to be poorer. This is evidenced by mental health statistics as well as their higher morbidity, their higher number of restricted activity days, and their greater likelihood of institutionalization.

With few exceptions, minorities and the economically disadvantaged have poorer health than white, middle- and upper-class men and women. They also receive the poorest quality of health care from a system that is sexist, racist, and class-biased. As we learned in this chapter, this system of physical and mental health care has frequently done more harm than good, particularly to women, both historically and currently.

In response to the inadequacies and abuses of traditional health care, feminists have begun to offer alternative services. These have as their basic premises: a nonhierarchical structure; an egalitarian and mutually educational relationship between patient and provider; a recognition of external (i.e., societal rather than personal) causes for individuals' physical and psychological troubles; and a commitment to advocacy and action to bring about social change. Although the feminist model of physical and mental health care is not without problems of its own, it does hold the promise of transforming our traditional medical services into "forces committed to undoing damage [and] achieving and maintaining health" (Ballou and Gabalac 1985:169).

KEY TERMS

acquired immune deficiency syndrome (AIDS)   a virus that attacks a person's immune system, destroying his or her ability to fight off other diseases.

anorexia   an eating disorder in which an individual, because of an obsessive fear of becoming overweight, literally starves; characterized by a distorted body image, a 25 percent loss of body weight, and refusal to eat; 90 to 95 percent of anorectics are females

bulimia   an abnormal and constant craving for food, also known as binge-purge syndrome, in which the individual consumes large quantities of food in short periods of time followed by fasting, use of laxatives, or induced vomiting to purge the food; afflicts primarily young women fearful of gaining weight

life expectancy   the average number of years of life remaining to an individual at a given age

morbidity   the illness rate of a given population

mortality rate   the number of deaths in proportion to a given population

SUGGESTED READINGS

Ballou, M. and N.W. Gabalac 1985. *A Feminist Position on Mental Health.* Springfield, IL: Charles C. Thomas.

Barnett, R.C., L. Biener, and G.K. Baruch (Eds.) 1987. *Gender and Stress.* New York: The Free Press.

Brumberg, J.J. 1988. *Fasting Girls.* Cambridge, MA: Harvard University Press.

Graubard, S.R. (Ed.) 1990. *Living with AIDS.* Cambridge, MA: MIT Press.

Ratcliff, K.S. 1989. *Healing Technology: Feminist Perspectives.* Ann Arbor: University of Michigan Press.

Chapter 13

Restructuring Sex/Gender Systems

At this point we anticipate a few pangs of depression among some of our readers who were perhaps hopeful at the outset that sexism was, for the most part, a social problem of an earlier age. Unfortunately, the data we have examined here make it abundantly clear that gender inequality continues to be a pervasive and powerfully oppressive feature of both our society and most other societies throughout the world. Nevertheless, there is cause for optimism: many of the findings also attest to the significant dents that have been made in our patriarchal sex/gender system, particularly during the last quarter century. Although an inherently unequal infrastructure remains largely intact, it is safe to say that no major social institution—not the family, the school, the workplace, or the government—has been left untouched by collective efforts to eradicate gender-based inequities. What is more, surveys, and public opinion polls indicate that in the United States, the majority support greater equality of the sexes in most areas of social life.

Most of the collective activity to eliminate sexism has been organized and carried out by women for the benefit of women. To conclude the text, then, we will first turn our attention to the women's movement. Although typically discussed as a single, unified entity, **feminism** or **the women's movement** as we learned in Chapter 1 is actually quite diverse, comprising heterogenous factions with different interests, perspectives, and tactics or strategies to achieve various objectives. Importantly, this diversity has contributed to feminism's strength and resiliency in the face of backlash, but it has also generated some serious problems—an issue that we will explore in greater detail later in the chapter. We will briefly explore the history of feminism in the United States and then turn our attention to contemporary feminism. We will also discuss other social movements—the men's movement and the homosexual rights movement—that are also seeking to revise our social constructions of gender and to redefine cultural norms regarding appropriate relations between women and men. To begin, however, let's first examine the role of social movements in general in bringing about social change.

SOCIAL CHANGE AND SOCIAL MOVEMENTS

In each of the chapters of this text we have seen that gender inequality, along with other social inequalities, such as racism, classism, ageism, and heterosexism, are built-in features of our social structure. We may then feel that these are social problems beyond our control, that there is nothing we can do about them. Certainly there are no simple solutions, but as we emphasized in Chapter 1, what sets humans apart from other species is our ability to make rational choices and to transform our environment to better meet our needs. Two other social commentators describe that faculty in this way: our "highest freedom is not simply [our] ability to take [a] place on the social ladder, but the opportunity to assume control over and constantly reshape the basic institutions of society" (Buell and DeLuca 1977:26).

Social change is frequently initiated by those who perceive their needs as being left unmet under existing social arrangements and public policies. When a group of similar individuals shares this perception, a social movement may develop. A **social movement** is a group that has organized to promote a particular cause through collective action. Social movements form around specific issues, with movement members and supporters taking a stand for or against something and working together to get their position integrated into official public policy.

We find in our definition of a social movement, then, two important implied conditions for its emergence: (1) that individuals come to see the problems they are experiencing as *shared* by others like themselves; and (2) that they identify the social structure or a social institution as the source of the problem rather than blaming themselves. Of course, members of movements seeking social change typically encounter resistance to their efforts and goals. Those who benefit from the status quo and who see the objectives of a social movement as threatening their social position will likely resist change. Nevertheless, despite such resistance, history provides us with countless examples of how the direct collective actions of various social movements have brought about significant changes in our society. Feminism is one of these movements, and so we will turn our attention to it now.

THE WOMEN'S MOVEMENT IN HISTORICAL PERSPECTIVE

As we pointed out in Chapter 5, most of us have grown up uneducated with regard to women's history. If, in fact, we rely only on the information in standard history texts, we are left with the impression that the sole preoccupation and accomplishment of nineteenth and early twentieth century women was the right to vote. Not surprisingly, then, to some people, the word *feminist* is still synonomous with *suffragist*. Yet, "even a brief reading of early feminist writings and of the few histories that have dealt specifically with the woman movement (as it was called then) reveals that the drive for suffrage became the single focus of the movement only after several decades of a more multi-issued campaign for women's equality" (Hole and Levine 1984:533; Delmar 1986; *see also* Box 13.1 page 356).

As early as the 1780s, women could be found calling for equal rights with men, especially equal educational opportunities. These women, such as Judith Sargent Murray and Mary Wollstonecraft, were from the middle and upper classes. The men of their social station were espousing a political philosophy of individualism and democracy asserting that "all human beings had equal rights by nature; that man [sic] must never be used as a means to anything else but is considered 'an end in himself'; and that everyone should have an equal chance of free development as an individual" (Klein 1984:530). But none of this seemed to apply to women nor, for that matter, to anyone other than white men. Even as middle-class women acquired more education during the 1800s, they found most professions legally closed to them. Their alternative to filling hours at home with knitting and needlework was philanthropy and, as historian Lois Banner (1986) has observed, there were plenty of charitable voluntary organizations for them to join, particularly in the Northern states.

Of course, to the targets of these social reform groups, that is, African Americans and European immigrants, the poor and the working class, the goal of equal rights for women must have seemed irrelevant at best. Black women were enslaved with black men, both equal in a sense in their oppression, exploitation, and lack of any rights of citizenship. At the same time, while "the women of the upper and middle class claimed political freedom, the right to work, and improved educational facilities, working women wanted protection; while middle-class women were fighting for equality, working-class women demanded differential treatment" (Klein 1984:524). As we learned in Chapter 8, poor women were already working for wages outside the home—typically for $1 to $3 a week in unsafe, unsanitary, and overcrowded factories (Banner 1986). It is not difficult to understand, then, why the early feminists failed to attract broad-based support for their demands. (As we shall soon see, racism and elitism still plague some segments of the women's movement.)

Ironically, it was their experiences in antislavery organizations that converted many white, middle- and upper-class women to feminism. Work in other social reform groups equipped these women with valuable organizational and administrative skills, but their focus tended to be local and their interests diverse. Abolitionism brought geographically dispersed women together and united them for a common cause. In addition, it has been argued that the ideology of abolitionism provided these women with a framework for understanding their own inequality relative to men. However, it is also likely that the way they were treated by supposedly liberal male abolitionists helped greatly to politicize them. In 1840, for example, at the first international antislavery conference in London, women delegates were prohibited from speaking publicly and were segregated from the men in a curtained-off section of the convention hall. Understandably, the women were outraged, and many, such as Lucretia Mott and Elizabeth Cady Stanton, resolved to hold their own conferences in the United States—on women's rights as well as abolitionism (Banner 1986; O'Neill 1969).

Over the next twenty years, many such conferences were held, the most famous one being at Seneca Falls, New York, on July 19 and 20, 1848. There, led by Mott and Stanton, about 300 women and some sympathetic men—men originally were not to be admitted, but they ended up chairing the meeting—adopted a Declaration of Sentiments, deliberately modeled on the Declaration of Independence, along with twelve resolutions. The latter were mostly general statements in support of the principle of equality between the sexes and in opposition to laws and customs that preserved women's inferior status. All except one—specifically, "*Resolved,* That it is the duty of the women of this country to secure to themselves their sacred right to the elective franchise"—were adopted unanimously.

BOX 13.1   Early Feminists

Although the first wave of feminism in the United States is often depicted as a single-minded social movement aimed at securing suffrage for women, the activities of nineteenth and early twentieth century feminists in this country demonstrate otherwise. They were involved in a wide range of political and social reforms, including public health and hygiene, "moral uplift," abolition, and public education. We offer a small sampling of brief biographies of some of these women to illustrate the rich diversity in their backgrounds, ideas, and aims.

Elizabeth Blackwell (1821–1910)   The first female physician in the United States, Blackwell rejected marriage in favor of a career in medicine. She was a practicing physician, though, for only a short time before she moved into hospital administration and from there into public health. She was instrumental in the enactment and implementation of a number of public sanitation reforms that substantially improved the health and living conditions of the poor, the working class, minority Americans, and immigrants.

Charlotte Perkins Gilman (1860–1935)   As a professional writer, social critic, journalist, and public speaker, Gilman was one of the intellectual leaders of the first wave of feminism in the United States. She wrote and lectured on such topics as sex differences, social evolution, women and work, and child development. Although she preferred to be called a "sociologist" and not a "feminist," the influence of her work is evident in contemporary socialist feminist theory. At the turn of the century she advocated changes in traditional practices of child care and housework to relieve the double burden of women who worked outside the home. But as feminist scholar Alice Rossi (1973:570) points out, Gilman's ideas "were not centered on a narrow conception of 'women's rights'; they swept broadly across human history, social process, and institutional change."

Margaret Sanger (1879–1969) It is perhaps inappropriate to include Sanger here, since her work on behalf of women's right to control their own bodies spans more than five decades of the twentieth century. Nevertheless, her pioneering efforts during the early 1900s are especially significant because she carried them out at a time when contraceptive devices and even the dissemination of information about birth control had

Those who opposed the call for women's enfranchisement expressed concern that such a radical demand would weaken public support for the more reasonable proposals and would possibly discredit the entire movement. Nevertheless, the resolution was finally accepted by the majority, and the Seneca Falls Convention became known as the official launch of the campaign for women's suffrage (Hole and Levine 1984; O'Neill 1969).

Still, it was not until after the Civil War that the drive for women's enfranchisement became paramount. In the pre-war period, at women's rights conferences, before state legislatures, and in their own newspapers, feminists addressed a variety of issues: dress reform, changes in divorce and child custody laws, property rights, and the right to control their earnings. However, once the Civil War broke out in 1861, many feminists began to neglect the women's move-

Box 13.1 continued

been outlawed and deemed immoral; Sanger was arrested and prosecuted several times for her activities. Nevertheless, she remained committed to this cause throughout her life because she recognized that "without the means to prevent, and to control the timing of, conception, economic and political rights have little meaning for women" (Rossi 1973:517). While she is best known for her advocacy of reproductive freedom, Sanger also labored to improve employment and living conditions for the working class, and was politically active for many socialist causes.

Maria W. Stewart (1803–1879)   Orphaned at the age of five, this black woman was bound out as a servant to the home of a white clergyman and his family, where she stayed until she was fifteen. In 1832, she became the first woman born in the United States to deliver a public lecture. In a series of four lectures that she gave that year in Boston, she encouraged women domestics and laborers to educate themselves and to strengthen their talents, which she saw as being dulled by women's servitude and subordination. She also defended women's right to speak in public. Later, she became a teacher and in 1863 she opened her own school in Washington, D.C.

Sojourner Truth (1797–1883)   Born a slave in New York, Sojourner Truth was sold several times during her childhood and suffered many indignities at the hands of her masters, including rape. When slavery was outlawed in New York, she began traveling as an itinerant preacher, and in her homilies she advocated abolition, protection and assistance for the poor, and equal rights for women. During the Civil War, she visited Union troops, and following the war, she worked for freedmen's resettlement and relief.

Frances Williard (1839–1898)   Founder and early president of the Women's Christian Temperance Society (WCTU), Willard was active in a number of civic and moral reform movements, but is perhaps best known for her campaigning for strict laws regulating the sale and consumption of alcohol. As we noted in Chapter 10, many women, like Willard, joined the temperance movement motivated to protect women and children who were often abused by intoxicated husbands and fathers.

Sources: Compiled from Hill 1980; Gray 1979; Rossi 1973; Lerner 1972.

ment and instead devoted their time and energy to the war effort. Although some, such as Susan B. Anthony, were openly pessimistic about this strategy, the majority assumed that the Republican administration would reward them for their wartime support by granting women the right to vote. They were wrong. In the aftermath of the war, Congress not only failed to grant women equal rights, but it also added a sex distinction to the Constitution by using the word "male" in the second section of the Fourteenth Amendment. In addition, the Fifteenth Amendment was passed specifying only that suffrage could not be denied on the basis of race, color, or previous condition of servitude; the word "sex" was excluded (Banner 1986; Hole and Levine 1984; O'Neill 1969).

Disappointed and angry, feminists took up the fight for women's rights on a state by state basis, their first site being Kansas. In 1867, Kansas voters were called upon to decide two referendums, one to enfranchise blacks and one to enfranchise women. State Republicans supported the former, but openly opposed the latter. The Democrats, hardly friends of feminism, allowed their racism to get the better of them and campaigned for women's suffrage with the hope of defeating the referendum for blacks. Even though both measures lost at the polls, the Kansas campaign had serious repercussions within the women's movement. Feminists, such as Stanton and Anthony, who had sided with the Democrats, alienated many New England feminists who were appalled by the blatant hypocrisy and racism. Because of this as well as other disagreements over strategies and goals, the New Englanders formed an organization called the American Woman Suffrage Association (AWSA), which set as its sole objective the enfranchisement of women and blacks. At the same time, Stanton and her supporters organized themselves into the rival National Woman Suffrage Association (NWSA) which, despite its name, continued to lobby for a variety of causes, including marriage and divorce reforms. Neither group attracted a very large following, but it was the more radical NWSA that had the most difficulty winning favor with the general public. The advocacy by some of its members of such unpopular ideas as "free love" and Marxism helped give it an anti-American and anti-family image. Eventually, a sizable portion of its membership concluded that women's suffrage was more important than any "side issues," at least for the time being. By 1890, NWSA and AWSA merged to form the National American Woman Suffrage Association (NAWSA), whose sole objective was winning women the right to vote (O'Neill 1986). (Black men were enfranchised in 1870.)

Expediency characterized the movement by the turn of the century, and some feminists appeared willing to exploit virtually every prejudice and stereotype, no matter how harmful, if it helped garner support for their cause. They argued, for instance, that women voters would purify politics because they possessed a natural spirituality that made them not men's equals, but their moral superiors. In a similar vein, they capitalized on the growing anti-immigrant sentiment of middle-class, native-born whites. Stressing that native-born women outnumbered immigrant men, they "called upon American men to save themselves from alien domination by enfranchising their own women who were well born, well educated, capable, and yet 'the political inferiors of all the riff-raff of Europe that is poured upon our shores' " (O'Neill 1969:72). In the South, there were racist appeals: for example, "Just as surely as the North will be forced to turn to the South for the nation's salvation, just so surely will the South be compelled to look to its Anglo Saxon women as the medium through which to retain the supremacy of the white race over the African" (quoted in Hood 1984:194).

There were socialist feminists, such as Charlotte Perkins Gilman, who were active in mobilizing working-class women and men and new immigrants into suffrage organizations at the grass roots. According to historian Nancy Cott (1986:53), "As never before, men and women in discreet ethnic or racial or ideological groups saw the advantage of doubling their voting numbers if women obtained suffrage." Black women's organizations, such as the National Association of Colored Woman's Clubs, established suffrage departments or committees and conducted classes on civics and the Constitution to prepare women for enfranchisement (Lerner 1972). For black women, suffrage was more than a women's rights issue; it was a racial equality issue and a means to address the often violent subversion of black men's voting rights in the South. "[T]hey mobilized not only as a matter of gender justice but of race progress, despite [or perhaps because of] their awareness that white racist arguments were simultaneously being raised on behalf of woman's suffrage" and they were systematically excluded from white suffrage organizations (Cott 1986:53). NAWSA, for instance, discouraged black membership and typically segregated black women in its suffrage parades. Though O'Neill (1969) argues that toward the end of the suffrage campaign most white feminists were less openly racist and nativist, it is clear that by 1910, if not before, "mainstream feminism" was not every woman's movement, but rather an explicitly white, middle-class women's movement.

During the 1890s, several Western states enfranchised women, for example, Wyoming in 1890, Colorado in 1893, and Utah and Idaho in 1896, but no other states were won until 1910, owing largely to the efforts of anti-suffragists coupled with public apathy. NAWSA and other groups, such as Alice Paul's National Women's Party (NWP), continued to stage petition drives, demonstrations, and other media events, but ironically it took another war, World War I, to turn the political tide for women's enfranchisement.

Feminists supported President Wilson's position on the war and called for woman's suffrage as a "war measure." There was a presidentially appointed women's defense committee and women contributed to the war effort in many ways, leading feminists once again to demand the vote as their just reward. This time the president and Congress agreed and by June 1919, the Nineteenth Amendment was sent to the states for the two-thirds ratification process. Ratification took little more than a year; on August 26, 1920, 26 million American women finally won the right to vote (O'Neill 1986).

What followed can best be described as anticlimactic. For one thing, suffrage did not have the impact that feminists had promised, which is not surprising given that they had sold it as a panacea for virtually all of society's ills. Once the vote was won, women did not go to the polls as often as men and, when they did go, they voted similarly to men (*see* Chapter 10). More importantly, the vote cost feminism much of its active support since many women withdrew from the movement in the belief that equality had been achieved. Young women in particular ignored the women's movement or rejected it outright, depicting feminists as lonely, unmarried women who needlessly antagonized men. In the politically conservative postwar era, social activism fell into disfavor and the "cult of domesticity" was resurrected with a slightly new twist: the modern "emancipated" middle-class housewife was "to regard child-rearing and homemaking as complicated, lofty enterprises demanding a skilled mixture of exact science and aesthetic inspiration. . . . The housewife was no longer a mere drudge, but a 'woman administrator' or household manager, mobilizing the resources of her family and her community in the interests of an efficient, democratic domestic life" (O'Neill 1969:309–310). As O'Neill (1969:313) concludes, "femininity, not feminism, was increasingly the watchword."

Feminism did not disappear completely. For example, Alice Paul and her small following in the National Women's Party continued to advocate on behalf of women's rights, and in 1923, they managed to get the Equal Rights Amendment introduced in Congress (*see* Box 13.2 page 362). For the most part, however, feminism became dormant after the ratification of the Nineteenth Amendment and more than forty years passed before it reemerged as a major social movement.

The Second Wave of Feminism

Several factors contributed to the resurgence of feminism in the early 1960s. One important impetus was the publication in 1963 of Betty Friedan's book, *The Feminine Mystique.* Friedan voiced the unhappiness and boredom of white, educated, middle-class housewives. Isolated in suburban homes, which Friedan referred to as "comfortable concentration camps," these women found their personal growth stunted. After subordinating gratification of their own needs to those of their husbands and children, they were left with a profound sense of emptiness rather than fulfillment. This Friedan dubbed "the problem that has no name," but the real significance of *The Feminine Mystique* was Friedan's labeling this not an individual problem, but a *social* problem. The book quickly became a best seller, but more importantly, it served as a springboard for developing analyses of **sexual politics,** that is, the examination of gender inequality as rooted not only in the public sphere, but also "in the 'privacy' of our kitchens and bedrooms," in the intimate relationships between women and men (Stacey 1986:210). From such analyses has come the much-quoted feminist slogan, "The personal is political."

However, even before the publication of *The Feminine Mystique,* the federal government took action that drew attention to the problem of sex discrimination. In 1961, President John F. Kennedy appointed a Presidential Commission on the Status of Women at the urging of Esther Peterson, whom he later named as an assistant secretary of labor. Interestingly, Kramer (1986) reports that Peterson advocated the establishment of the commission to placate members of the National Women's Party and the Federation of Business and Professional Women's Clubs, who were intensifying their lobbying for the Equal Rights Amendment. In its final report, the Commission focused primarily on the persistent and severe discrimination experienced by women in the labor force. It subsequently provided the basis for the Equal Pay Act of 1963 (*see* Chapter 8), led to the appointment of two permanent federal committees on women's issues, and served as a model for the numerous state-level commissions that were established in its wake. The state commissions, in turn, became vehicles for gathering and disseminating information on women's issues (Kramer 1986; Freeman 1973).

The state commissions also helped give rise in a sense to the National

Organization for Women (NOW), which was founded in 1966 by Betty Friedan and twenty-seven others who were representing state women's commissions at a national assembly in Washington. The actual impetus for establishing NOW was provided by the executive director of the Equal Employment Opportunity Commission, the agency charged with enforcing Title VII, when he openly admitted that he did not consider sex discrimination a serious matter. Given that the word "sex" had been added to Title VII in the hope of defeating the measure altogether, it is not surprising that the EEOC did not vigilantly enforce the law. NOW took up the task of pressuring President Lyndon Johnson to strengthen the EEOC and of lobbying for a number of additional legal and economic reforms in women's interests (Kramer 1986). Importantly, NOW also became a model for a variety of other *reform-oriented* feminist groups, such as the National Women's Political Caucus, the Women's Equity Action League, the Congressional Caucus for Women's Issues, and the National Abortion Rights Action League.

Today, NOW has more than 200,000 members, and it probably represents what a substantial segment of the general public considers to be the women's movement. However, as was the case with the first wave of feminism, the contemporary women's movement is hardly homogeneous. In fact, as we emphasized in Chapter 1, it "makes more sense to speak of a plurality of feminisms than of one" (Delmar 1986:9). For example, at about the same time that NOW was being formed, a second, more militant branch of feminism was emerging from different sources. More specifically, this feminism had its origins in the political Left, centered largely on college campuses, and developed among women who were active in other social movements during the 1960s, such as the Civil Rights movement and the anti-Vietnam War movement. These latter social movements were male-dominated, but large numbers of women participated, voting, as O'Neill (1969:342) has phrased it, "with their feet"—that is, "demonstrating that they were prepared to run the same risks and fight for the same ends as men." Yet these women often found themselves relegated to traditional female roles, for instance as cooks, typists, and sexual partners. Indeed, what struck them was the glaring contradiction between the ideology of equality and freedom espoused by radical men and the men's sexist treatment of women (Shulman 1980; Evans 1979; Freeman 1973). By the late 1960s, these women had formed their own feminist organizations, less formally structured and more radical than NOW and similar groups. The focus of leftist feminism has been on developing a theoretical analysis of women's subordinate status as well as engaging in political activism to combat gender oppression.

Even within leftist feminism, different perspectives have developed. *Socialist feminists,* for example, reject the liberal reform orientation of NOW and its sister organizations. Whereas liberals press for formal legal rights and equal opportunities for women, socialist feminists seek "a transformation of production, reproduction, socialization, and sexuality. . . . Without a fundamental reordering of societal institutions and values, women cannot begin to achieve true parity in vocational opportunities, economic security, and social status" (Rhode 1986:158). Socialist feminists, then, see capitalism and gender inequality as reciprocally re-

---

BOX 13.2   What Happened to the Equal Rights Amendment?

The text of the ERA is short and simple:

> Section 1. Equality of rights under the law shall not be abridged by the United States or by any State on account of sex.
>
> Section 2. The Congress shall have the power to enforce, by appropriate legislation, the provisions of this article.
>
> Section 3. The amendment shall take effect two years after the date of ratification.

In contrast, the struggle over ratification of this amendment has been long and complex.

When Alice Paul and the National Women's Party succeeded in getting the ERA introduced in Congress in 1923, they saw it as the next logical move after winning suffrage and as a means to rally women around a single cause the way they thought suffrage had done. The effect, however, was just the opposite. Feminist reformers opposed the amendment because it would invalidate laws regulating wages and hours and other legislation that they felt gave women special protections. "Women ended up fighting each other over the value of protection rather than uniting to challenge the social and economic conditions that made protection so valuable" (Rhode 1986:157).

The amendment was less divisive in Congress—few legislators supported it. In 1946, the Senate did approve the amendment with a close vote, 38–35, but a two-thirds majority was needed for adoption. In 1950 and again in 1953, riders were added to the amendment stating that the ERA could not overturn protective legislation. These won it some support in the Senate, but exacerbated divisions among other proponents, further delaying consideration of the measure (Berry 1986).

In the 1960s, a second wave of feminism was building on several fronts, and pollsters were reporting increasing public support for women's rights. By 1970, the ERA was endorsed by both Lyndon Johnson and Richard Nixon, as well as a variety of prominent national organizations and federal committees. That same year, Rep. Martha Griffiths of Michigan got the amendment out the House Judiciary Committee and onto the House floor where it passed 350–15 after only an hour's debate on August 10. The Senate Subcommittee on Constitutional Amendments held hearings on the amendment in 1970, but the Senate did not vote on it until March 22, 1972. It passed the Senate by a vote of 84–8 (Berry 1986).

Before adopting the ERA, Congress set a seven-year limit on the ratification process. Given the overwhelming support for the amendment in Congress, however, ERA backers assumed that it would be relatively easy to secure the necessary thirty-eight state adoptions, Early on, it appeared that they were right. Within three months, twenty-two states ratified the ERA and by 1973, the state total was thirty. With only eight more states needed within the six remaining years before expiration, ratification prospects were bright. However, in 1974, only three states ratified; in 1977, only one; and in 1979, one more. Meanwhile, fifteen states voted against the amendment, some more than once, and other states that had ratified, tried to rescind (Hewlett 1986). ERA proponents did manage to convince Congress to extend the ratification deadline to

Box 13.2 continued

June 30, 1982, but ultimately the desparate battle to get legislators in unratified states to change their minds failed. What went wrong?

Analysts point to a number of factors as central in the ERA's demise. One of the most important is that the amendment's supporters grossly underestimated the power of their opposition and they failed to act accordingly until it was too late. Anti-ERA groups, such as Phyllis Schlafly's STOP-ERA, wisely targeted the southern and midwestern states in their campaign, whereas ERA proponents focused on national trends and ignored regional differences until relatively late in the ratification process (Berry 1986). Often, though, ERA backers misread even the national polls which indicated some significant contradictions in public attitudes. For instance, even though it appeared that at least 60 percent of women and men favored the ERA in the late 70s, 49 percent of these also said they would not vote for a qualified woman for president and 67 percent disapproved of married women's employment during periods of job scarcity. In short, the public was giving a socially expected response, that is, it opposed discrimination— but a large segment did not support real equality between women and men (Mansbridge 1986). ERA backers also overlooked the opposition of those Klatch (1988:686) has labeled laissez-faire conservatives. Laissez-faire conservatives viewed the ERA as a way to eliminate gender discrimination that was misguided because it implied the growth of big government. In other words, laissez-faire conservatives did not favor gender-based discrimination, but neither did they support the ERA since they saw it as the encroachment by government upon the liberty of individual citizens.

At the same time, although the anti-ERA groups frequently used scare tactics— for example, claiming that public toilets would become unisex and that the ERA would force full-time homemakers into the labor force to earn half their families' income—they did successfully persuade many Americans in unratified states to oppose the amendment. "These in turn convinced many legislators that they had nothing to lose politically by voting against ERA and much to gain. In other words, enough voters in their districts were against ERA or lukewarm so that they did not risk retribution in voting against it" (Berry 1986:83).

Recently, some ERA supporters have expressed mixed feelings about the amendment's defeat. Rhode (1986:158), for example, points out that, "Given the process and principal agents of constitutional adjudication, an abstract legal mandate is of itself unlikely to work major social transformation." What was of most value in the struggle to ratify the Equal Rights Amendment was that the process itself educated feminists, teaching them important lessons about political organizing. Some have vowed to continue to fight for adoption and ratification, although others maintain that the time is not yet right for another go round (Berry 1986; Mansbridge 1986). It remains to be seen, then, how well earlier lessons were learned.

---

lated and call for the elimination of both to achieve women's liberation (Hartmann 1984; Jaggar and Rothenberg 1984).

In contrast, *radical feminists* point out that women are oppressed in other types of societies besides capitalist ones, and therefore women's oppression by men is deeper and more harmful than any other form of oppression, including social class inequality. It is radical feminists who perhaps most strongly identify with the slogan, "The personal is political," for they point out that male domination of women permeates every aspect of life, including the home and interpersonal relationships. Women can be liberated only if they sever their ties with men, including their sexual ties. As one radical feminist explains, "Love can only exist between equals, not between the oppressed and the oppressor. . . . [Thus], lesbianism is not an oddity of a few women to be hidden in the background of the Movement. In a way, it is the heart of the Women's Liberation Movement" (quoted in Shulman 1980:599).

For still other women, none of these feminisms is relevant or appropriate. Working class women, for example, find it difficult to identify with groups like NOW whose liberal feminist agenda they quite accurately perceive as benefitting primarily educated middle-class housewives and professionals. At the same time, they have shown strong resistance and even hostility toward calls for lesbian separatism by some radical feminists. Socialist feminists, especially those in the labor movement, have forged strong ties with working-class women by actively supporting working women's struggles in factories and offices (Bookman and Morgen 1988; Briggs 1987). But the alliance has sometimes been strained by disagreements over political issues such as abortion rights, disputes over effective courses of action, and the not unfounded image of many socialist feminists as intellectuals rather than "real workers." Thus, *working-class feminism* has grown largely out of working women's involvement in trade unionism, as well as their activities at the grass roots level of their own neighborhoods. In contrast to the university-based feminism of the sixties, working-class feminism is rooted in the workplace and the working class community. It is oriented toward achieving practical concrete goals, such as the right to work, the right to unionize, equal pay and benefits, affordable child care, neighborhood health centers, and the like (Bookman and Morgen 1988; Maroney 1986).

A large segment of the working class is composed of women of color. Women of color, as we have seen throughout this text, confront a double oppression in the forms of sexism *and* racism, an oppression that frequently generates a third burden: poverty. Yet many minority women have approached the women's movement with suspicion and hostility—and with good reasons (King 1988). Historically, as we have seen, mainstream feminism has largely ignored the concerns of nonwhite women unless its own ends were also served by addressing them, and white feminists have not infrequently been racist. With the resurgence of feminism in the 1960s, for example, there was ample opportunity for white and black women to form alliances. Black women active in the Civil Rights and black power movements often found that despite their historical resistance to white domination, black male leaders expected them to assume a supportive, but subordinate position relative to black men (Hood 1984; Terrelonge 1984; Murray 1972). Yet white women, whom we noted had similar experiences with radical white men, typically failed to consider, let alone identify with, the difficulties of black women.

Women of color confronted such problems as forced sterilization, inadequate and unaffordable housing, and the degradation of welfare, and they struggled to raise their children, often alone and in poverty. They perceived white feminists pursuing liberation defined as "access to those thrones traditionally occupied by white men—positions in kingdoms which support racism" (Hood 1984:192; King 1988).

In addition, some minority women see feminism as divisive, that is, as pitting women against men. Their objective life experiences as nonwhites frequently lead them to conclude that they have more in common with nonwhite men, who also have been victimized by racism, than white women who, despite sexism, enjoy numerous privileges because of their race (King 1988). Still, many minority women identify themselves as feminists and, in recent opinion polls, they have expressed stronger support for the women's movement than white women. In a 1989 survey, for example, 85 percent of African American women and 76 percent of Hispanic women said that the United States continues to need a strong women's movement to press for changes that benefit women. In contrast, 64 percent of white women expressed this opinion (Dione 1989). More importantly, many women of color are actively working to expand the focus of feminism to include not only the fight against sexism, but also the battle against heterosexism, social class inequality, and racism—both in society and in the movement itself (Collins 1986; Allan 1986; Hohri 1986; Smith 1986; Quintanales, 1983).

Of course, our discussion of the divisions within feminism is, by necessity, overly simplistic. We will be the first to admit that it does not do justice to the multi-faceted character of a movement in which differences are rarely so clear cut and factions often overlap. Our intent, however, is merely to give our readers a sense of the rich diversity of feminism, a diversity that we pointed out earlier has given the movement strength and resiliency. Essentially, this diversity allows us to understand sexism and other inequalities from a variety of perspectives and to address these problems on many levels: in the home and the workplace; in the government and the church, and through law, demonstrations, boycotts, and strikes. This, in no small way, has contributed to the impressive list of achievements of the women's movement that we have hightlighted throughout this text. In short, "the women's movement contains as many diverse groups as most social movements, though these groups are united in their aims for changes that will create choice for women, that will create fulfillment of their individual potential, and that will improve the class position of women to one equitable with that of men" (Rowland 1986:681).

However, diversity also has generated problems for feminism. One of the most serious problems is what one analyst calls "a sclerosis of the movement" in which segments "have become separated from and hardened against each other. Instead of internal dialogue there is a naming of the parts: there are radical feminists, socialist feminists, Marxist feminists, lesbian separatists, women of color, and so on, each group with its own carefully preserved sense of identity. Each for itself is the only worthwhile feminism; others are ignored except to be criticized" (Delmar 1986:9). Under other circumstances, this problem might not be cause for alarm, but currently feminism is facing serious challenges from outside the movement that can perhaps best be addressed not only with openmindedness to alternative perspectives, but also a unity of purpose. To understand this better, let's consider some of these challenges.

The women's movement in the 1980s—The post-feminist era?   One challenge to the contemporary feminist movement is posed by antifeminists who have formed a coalition from the memberships of various politically conservative groups, including Phyllis Schlafly's STOP-ERA, the Moral Majority, and the National Right to Life Committee (*see* Chapters 7 and 11). Antifeminists maintain that there are biologically determined differences between the sexes that account for differences in male and female behavior, attitudes, and roles. By seeking equality, feminists are not only "opposing Mother Nature herself," but also threatening to deprive women of important "protections" (e.g., economic support from men and exemption from the military draft) that they deserve because of their inherent weaknesses. According to antifeminists, women's natural roles are wife and mother, and through these she can attain total personal fulfillment without ever leaving home. Feminists, though, are "women who have failed at being women and are trying, somewhat childishly, to spoil the happiness of others of their sex" (Marshall 1984:571). Thus, antifeminists (with considerable help from the media) have portrayed feminists as being bent on destroying marriage and the family, as antinatalist, and as communists seeking to replace democracy and individual freedom with their own programs and policies imposed by the state (Klatch 1988). Although research indicates that these claims are rarely based on direct contact with feminists (Rowland 1986; Pohli 1983)—and many are so inaccurate or exaggerated that they appear not to warrant a serious response—antifeminists have managed to attract considerable support and have organized themselves into a social movement with a substantial resource base. As we noted in Chapter 11, for example, some of these groups managed budgets of more than $1 million and effectively utilized computerized mailing lists and telecommunications networks to promote their positions. Resources such as these have aided antifeminist groups in achieving a number of significant political successes, including the defeat of the Equal Rights Amendment (*see* Box 13.2) and legal restrictions on abortion.

The fact that many antifeminists are women has led some to question what motivates them to "agitate for their own subordination" (Dworkin 1983b:xiii). Analyses of antifeminism indicate that it receives its greatest support from working class, nonemployed women; for these women, being full-time homemakers is a luxury in itself and a symbol of upward moblity. Antifeminists have successfully portrayed feminist programs, such as affirmative action, as threats to this lifestyle and to men's jobs (Klatch 1988). Feminists are depicted as " 'smooth-talking college women who have never seen a production line' and are thus far removed from and little concerned with the economic problems of working class women" (Marshall 1984:577). Moreover, in a period of economic recession, when single-income, working-class families are especially insecure about their financial futures and their ability to maintain their present standard of living, "it is easier to see the cause as a women's movement that insisted on 'changing things,' than as the social and economic structures operating in society" (Rowland 1986:681). In short, antifeminism appears to be an organized effort to preserve a particular lifestyle or cultural status which some groups, including many women, perceive as being threatened by the women's movement (Klatch 1988; Himmelstein 1986; Luker 1984).

Antifeminist groups present just one of the challenges facing contemporary American feminism, however. A second challenge to contemporary feminism is posed by the apparent lack of support for the movement among young women. Reports have recently appeared, primarily in the popular press, that indicate that among eighteen- to twenty-nine-year-olds, feminists are viewed as "radical, separatist, bitter" women who have "let themselves go physically," "have no sense of style," and "no sense of humor" (Wallis 1989; Hornaday 1983; Bolotin 1982). Feminists are seen as being out of touch with the concerns of this younger generation; these concerns revolve largely around the difficulties of obtaining a good job and, at the same time, caring for a family. These are issues, in fact, that cut across racial and social class lines, although they may be experienced differently by young women in different racial and social class groupings.

Research findings, however, qualify this negativism. In studies of college students' attitudes toward feminism, for example, researchers report that most young women do not hold negative views of feminists, and most recognize that gender-based discrimination is still a major problem in our society. In addition, they appear supportive of feminist ideals. Table 13.1 provides an example of some of these views obtained in one recent study of college-age women. Yet, at the same time, this research also indicates that the majority of these young women are reluctant to identify themselves as feminists and they stress individual rather than collective efforts to address sexism (Wallis 1989; Renzetti 1987; Komarovsky 1985).

Recent surveys of the general population also indicate that a reluctance to identify oneself as a feminist should not necessarily be translated as lack of support for the women's movement. A *Time* magazine/CNN survey of 1,000 women nationwide found that 77 percent of the respondents felt that the women's movement had made life better and 82 percent stated that it continues to improve women's lives (Wallis 1989). In a 1989 *New York Times* survey of 1,025 women, young women aged eighteen to twenty-nine were second most likely to agree that the United States continues to need a strong women's movement (71 percent); only women thirty to forty years old were more likely to express this position (72 percent) (Dione 1989).

Some within the women's movement have argued that both antifeminists and semi-supportive young women will eventually come around, especially when they personally experience sex discrimination. One analyst predicts, for instance, that "the movement will re-emerge within a few years—when young

TABLE 13.1
Attitudes of College Women Toward Feminism and Feminist Issues*

Statement	Strongly Agree/ Agree (%)	Strongly Disagree/ Disagree (%)
I consider myself to be a feminist.	27.3	49.6
Men tend to discriminate against women in hiring, firing, and promotion.	61.0	23.1
A woman should not let bearing and rearing children get in the way of a successful career if she wants it.	65.3	25.7
A woman can have a full and happy life without marrying.	83.0	9.5
Many women who do the same work as their male colleagues earn substantially less money.	79.5	13.1
If there is a military draft both men and women should be included in it.	27.9	57.5
When you get right down to it, women are an oppressed group and men are the oppressors.	27.2	55.6
In general, I am sympathetic with the efforts of women's liberation groups.	58.4	27.8

*These data are based on the responses of a sample of 398 full-time female undergraduates to a survey about attitudes toward feminism and awareness of gender inequality. The sample was drawn at a small, private university in the northeastern United States, so the data should be interpreted cautiously. Other researchers, however, (Wallis 1989; Komarovsky 1985; Bayer 1975) have obtained similar findings.
Source: Adapted from Renzetti 1987:267, 269.

women enter the work world with high hopes only to discover a severe gap between their expectations and reality" (Richardson 1981:267). Another writer warns: "Antifeminists may work to undermine all the positive changes women have made. But if they continue to support antifeminist men, they may lose more than they bargained for, and find, like Anita Bryant, that they have given men the ammunition they need to fire at *all* women—including homemakers" (Rowland 1986:691, author's emphasis).

There is, after all, evidence that personal experience of sex discrimination does increase support for the women's movement. But it is difficult for us to believe that none of these women has been discriminated against, despite their claims to the contrary. It is more likely that they simply do not recognize specific experiences as discrimination. As Renzetti (1987:275) has noted, however, "One of the most powerful forces in shaping and energizing the women's movement during the 1960s and 1970s was consciousness raising, which allowed women to see their experiences as inequality and to understand them in political rather than individual terms." Consequently, a useful starting point for addressing the challenges posed by both antifeminists and young, *potential* feminists may be a return to grass roots consciousness raising, not only among college women, but also among nonemployed working-class women, blue-collar as well as white-collar working women, poor white women, and women of color. If the movement is to remain strong and viable and, more importantly, if inequality in all its forms is to be eliminated, then the needs and experiences of these women must not just be taken into account by the "powers that be" within feminism, they must reshape the focus and course of the movement itself (King 1988).

It has been suggested by some mainstream feminists and leftists that feminism has been too antagonistic toward men, the family, and traditional feminine values, such as maternalism and sensitivity. It is this attitude, they maintain, that has turned many people off to the movement. Consequently, Betty Friedan (1981) and others (e.g., Kramer 1983; Elshtain 1981) urge feminists to adopt a more conservative pro-life, pro-family stance, to support the government's dismantling of the welfare state because it interferes with the "privacy" of families, and to abandon "unpopular" issues such as homosexual rights and abortion rights. However, in direct contradiction of this perspective, recent studies indicate that the Supreme Court's 1989 *Webster* decision upholding legal restrictions on abortion (*see* Chapter 7), has prompted a surge of support for the women's movement, especially among young women who justly perceive their reproductive freedom threatened. In addition, the research shows that contrary to wanting federal and state government out of the family support business, most women, particularly the young, want government to mandate programs such as public child care and parental leave benefits (Dione 1989; Wallis 1989). Finally, as sociologist Judith Stacey (1986:224), points out, so-called *conservative feminism* "discards the most significant contributions of feminist theory"—that is, a *structural* analysis of women's subordination in which a critique of the traditional nuclear family is central—"and provides in their place a feminism that turns quite readily into its opposite." Indeed, a close reading of conservative feminist literature quickly reveals that it is a misnomer to label it feminist at all. Yet, as Stacey rightly concludes, it presents another challenge to the movement, one that initiates a "struggle over what feminism will mean in the next historical period" (1986:208).

In addressing this particular challenge, one approach is to study and perhaps adapt to our own needs and experiences the strategies and tactics of European feminists, which we will discuss shortly. In addition, we agree with Stacey that there are at least three major issues that feminists need to reassess in order to effectively respond to the new conservatives, especially to their charges of antifamilism. Specifically, Stacey argues that in critiquing the traditional nuclear family, feminists have not given enough careful consideration to truly viable alternatives, and she urges them to begin doing so. Second, she feels that feminists have largely neglected the question of children's needs, and she calls on them to generate feminist theories of child development. Third, she sees the need for a fuller feminist analysis of heterosexuality (which up to this point has been inadequate): "We have done a better job of criticizing heterosexuality as institution and practice . . . than studying its history or appreciating its complexity and continued vitality, even for feminists" (1986:230).

Men are joining with women in addressing these and other significant issues. Some men, as we have learned in previous chapters, have come to recognize the serious limitations and detrimental consequences of traditional masculinity. Many realize, too, that they have a stake in equitably restructuring the present sex/gender system, and they have begun to evaluate their own roles in feminism. We will examine men's efforts by discussing what is usually called the men's movement. But first, it is important to discuss feminism beyond the boundaries of the United States, for feminism is clearly an international movement.

The Women's Movement Internationally

Although we have given considerable attention to feminism in the United States, the women's movement is virtually global. According to Staudt and Jaquette (1988:263), since 1975, "official programs for women's advancement have been established in 90 percent of national governments; progressive laws and policies are in place for women; and women's organizational growth has flourished." Not surprisingly, given the history of American feminism that we discussed earlier, the women's movement in Europe is both similar to and different from the women's movement in the United States, but Third World feminism is, in many ways, distinct from each of these.

Feminism in Europe   European feminism, like its counterpart in the United States, emerged out of particular social, political, and economic circumstances. The Enlightenment—with its emphasis on reason, progress, education, the fulfillment of the individual, and freedom from restrictions—has been identified as an important antecedent, although the major Enlightenment philosophers, such as Rousseau, were openly opposed to equal rights for women. Nevertheless, we can see the influence of Enlightenment ideals in the writings of early European feminists, such as Mary Wollstonecraft. In her 1792 treatise, *A Vindication of the Rights of Woman*, Wollstonecraft denounced traditional male authority and female subservience and called for equal educational opportunities for women as the means for their liberation and full development as individuals.

The French Revolution and the rise of liberalism also contributed to the emergence of nineteenth century European feminism. Women were actively involved in the French Revolution, leading protests and forming political clubs, and writers like Olympe de Georges argued vehemently for full economic and political rights for women under the new government. (Unfortunately, de Georges was beheaded by Robespierre, and the Revolutionary Assembly outlawed all women's organizations.) The writing of John Stuart Mill in *The Subjugation of Women* illustrates liberalism's emphasis on removing legal barriers to equal rights, although Mill was one of the few liberal male philosophers who took up the cause of women's rights. At the same time, socialists such as Auguste Bebel and Frederick Engels developed their critiques of the subordination of women in the family under capitalism and exhorted women to join the socialist movement to secure their emancipation.

With these diverse origins, it is not surprising that early European feminists tackled a range of issues, including the protection of women and children from battery and sexual abuse, prevention of the exploitation of women through prostitution, divorce reform, revisions in property laws, employment opportunities, equal access to education, and, of course, the right to vote, but their concerns were broader than formal legal rights. "Europeans focused as much or more on elaborations of womanliness; they celebrated sexual difference rather than similarity within a framework of male/female complementarity; and instead of seeking unqualified admission to male-dominated society, they mounted a widespread critique of the society and its institutions" (Offen 1988:124).

Still, European feminists exchanged ideas and experiences with their American sisters through participation in international feminist organizations, such as the International Council of Women, the International Women's Suffrage Alliance, and the Socialist Women's International (Lovenduski 1986). Indeed, the ideas and strategies of the women's movement in the United States were clearly influenced by the views of European feminists just as U.S. feminists made their mark on the development of feminism throughout much of Europe.

The success of European feminists' struggles depended to a large extent on specific conditions in the country in which they were waged. In most European countries, for instance, divorce laws were gradually liberalized during the nineteenth and early twentieth centuries, but in strongly Catholic-identified countries, divorce was prohibited until very recently. (For example, it was prohibited until 1985 in Ireland, and many restrictions still remain.) In addition, most European nations enfranchised women during or shortly after World War I, although some had granted women full suffrage rights much earlier (e.g., Finland in 1906) and others much later (e.g., France in 1944) (Lovenduski 1986).

The upheaval of war in Europe and increasing political conservatism in its aftermath helped to suppress feminism in many countries and to drive it underground in others. During the 1960s and 1970s, however, Western Europe, like the United States, experienced a resurgence of feminism. Although a variety of factors undoubtedly contributed to this, it was due at least in part to widespread dissatisfaction among women regarding how little genuine equality they enjoyed despite several decades of formal legal rights that had been secured largely through the efforts of nineteenth century feminists (Lovenduski 1986). This dissatisfaction has given rise to a multiplicity of feminist groups and organizations, which, like those in the United States, have diverse philosophies, strategies, and goals.

In Europe, there are liberal feminists, radical feminists, and socialist feminists just as there are in the United States. But some observers argue that, in general, contemporary European feminism can be distinguished from its American counterpart on the basis of the focus or emphasis of the two movements. As we have noted in this chapter, much of mainstream feminism in the United States is committed to securing legal rights for women. In contrast, consistent with its history, mainstream feminism in Europe for the most part has focused instead on securing social benefits, particularly for families. As Sylvia Ann Hewlett (1986:143-144) expresses it, "the overwhelming preoccupation of the American women's movement has been on equal rights and reproductive freedom, while the central focus of most European feminists has been on the material conditions of life, specifically on the support structures necessary to reconcile women's maternal and labor responsibilities."

Hewlett maintains that it is this difference in agenda that largely accounts for the effectiveness of feminism in securing important social welfare programs and policies, such as paid parental leaves, nationally mandated and subsidized child care, and a greater success in narrowing the gender gap in wages (*see* Chapter 8). Although the securing of equal legal rights often benefits primarily white middle-class and upper-income women, the social programs and policies instituted in Europe cut across social class lines and benefit women and men in diverse groups.

Some, such as Hewlett (1986), argue that a shift in emphasis in mainstream U.S. feminism from legal rights to social benefits would be valuable not only to women and men in general, but also to the movement itself. By addressing the needs of a broader constituency—racial minorities, the working class, and the poor—U.S. feminism can preserve its vitality as a social movement. It remains to be seen, however, whether a majority of feminists in the United States will take this advice, and similarly it is unclear whether such an emphasis could be successful in the United States given that the kinds of social programs and policies instituted in Europe are those that New Right antifeminists in the United States are mobilized strongly against. Certainly, though, U.S. feminists, by studying the ideas and strategies, and the successes and failures of European feminism, can gain some useful insights and fresh perspectives for their own movement just as their foremothers did in the nineteenth century.

Feminism in the Third World   Feminism is a more recent phenonmenon in the Third World than it is in the United States or Europe. For many people in the Third World—in many of the countries of Africa, Asia, and Latin America—the struggle for the liberation of women is inseparable from the struggle for national liberation from Western imperialism or the stuggle for liberation from political dictatorships. Indeed, as two analysts recently pointed out, we should perhaps think of women in these countries as *fourth world* women, that is, women as an oppressed group within an oppressed group (Awekotuku and Waring 1984).

In the impoverished Third World, daily economic survival usually takes precedence over any attempts to win formal legal rights for women. Third World men also are oppressed by imperialism, racism, and social class inequality, so that many Third World women view the goals of Western feminism as separatist and ethnocentric. As one South African observer noted, "In our country white racism and apartheid coupled with economic exploitation have degraded the African woman more than any male prejudices" (quoted in Bulbeck 1988:146–147). Nevertheless, women in these countries experience oppression not only because they are citizens of the Third World oppressed by international economic exploitation and racism, but also because they are women oppressed by patriarchy.

Consider, for example, economic development policies. Training and support programs, technology transfers, and agricultural extension programs typically benefit Third World men, rather than women, even though the women are responsible for much of the economic production (Rowbotham 1989; Curran and Renzetti 1987). Similarly, Asian women constitute a large percentage of the exploited labor force on the "global assembly line" (Ehrenreich and Fuentes 1981). In fact, in the international division of labor, "young women comprise 85–90 percent of workers in the Third World's Export Processing Zones of U.S. based multinationals" (Burris 1989:175). These women are unskilled and grossly underpaid. And it is Third World women who are the victims of sex tourism, the mail-order bride business, and the international prostitution trade (Matsui 1989).

In the Western world, as we have noted, one of the central feminist goals has been reproductive freedom. This largely has taken the form of freedom from childbearing. However, in the Third World, the issue of reproductive freedom sometimes has a different meaning. In some countries, where women are exhorted to bear many children to populate a small labor force or to staff revolutionary armies, reproductive freedom does often mean access to contraception and abortion. But in other countries where women gain status and material security through childbearing, they also often encounter pressures from Western agencies such as the World Bank and the International Monetary Fund, as well as from their own governments, to use contraceptives (some forms of which have not been approved for use in the West) or to undergo sterilization. In these countries reproductive freedom is the right to *have* children. And in still other countries, where women are weakened by pregnancies and births spaced too close together and where malnutrition and disease make it unlikely that most of their children will live into adolescence, reproductive freedom may simply mean the right to give birth to healthy babies whose lives may be sustained through adulthood (Bulbeck 1988).

Clearly, the concerns of Third World women are quite different from those of feminists in the developed world. This disparity has led some observers to question whether global unity is possible within feminism. We cannot hope to offer an answer to this sweeping question here, but we do think that a useful starting point, as others have argued, is for Western feminists to do their homework; that is, to learn about Third World women's experiences, to use these experiences to call into question the ethnocentrism and privilege inherent in their own positions, and to accept Third World women's analyses of their own oppression as valid rather than imposing Western analyses on them. As Bulbeck (1988:154) maintains, "The strength of feminism lies not in its ability to ape the unitary categories and Archimedean points of male theory, philosophy and politics; not to search for one position from which the 'truth' of all women can be seen, nor the one lever that will transform the whole female world, but to abandon the privileges of hierarchies for the multiple connections of the web and the quilt."

MEN AND LIBERATION

To some readers, the term *men's liberation* may seem a bit ironic. After all, much of the material covered in this text has documented male privilege, gained usually at the expense of women. It certainly would not be justifiable to argue that men are in need of liberation in the same sense that women are; yet, we have also seen that adherence to traditional prescriptions of masculinity is harmful to men. For example, their higher rates of ulcers, hypertension, and heart attacks, and their lower life expectancy have been linked to traditional masculinity (*see* Chapter 12). In addition, we have learned that the category "man" is as diverse as the category "woman." Although all men benefit to some extent from male privilege, the distribution of societal resources—most importantly, wealth, prestige, and power—varies among men according to their race and ethnicity, social class background, age, and sexual preference.

In the early 1970s, some men, mostly white, educated professionals, began to meet in small informal groups to discuss their experiences as men, their interpersonal relationships, and their notions of masculinity and how these impinge, for better or worse, on their lives. As one writer observed, the men's consciousness raising groups were "more introspective than political" (Katz 1974:153). Most became involved because of personal crises: their relationships with the women in their lives seemed jeopardized as the women themselves developed a feminist consciousness and grew increasingly dissatisfied with sexist gender relations. One group member expressed the sentiments of many when he wrote, ". . . I got myself into a men's group [because] I didn't want to get left behind—not only by [my wife], but by other people who seemed to be so much alive, including our own three children" (Levine 1974:157).

By the mid-seventies, there was an estimated three hundred men's groups in the United States meeting regularly "to explore the way in which sex-role stereotypes limit and inhibit them" (Katz 1974:152). Interestingly, however, these groups have not since coalesced into a full-fledged social movement akin to the women's movement. Today there is at least one national organization (The National Organization for Changing Men), several local and regional men's centers, men's studies programs in universities, and a number of newsletters and journals (e.g., *Changing Men, Men's Studies Review*). But the men's movement has not been politically active in the same sense as the women's movement (Astrachan 1986), and it has not attracted a broad-based following of either men or women. In fact, some recent analysts have argued that it is more accurately termed a social or political *network* than a movement (Carrigan, et al. 1987; Filene 1987).

Like the women's movement, though, the men's network contains not one, but several diverse perspectives. Harry Brod (1987), a leader in the new field of men's studies (*see* Chapter 5), has identified at least two strains of thought. The first he labels *male-identified,* and sees it as a corollary of mainstream liberal feminism. This perspective emphasizes that male privilege is really a double-edged sword that for most men bestows as many, if not more, disadvantages as advantages. Adherents to this approach maintain, however, that once men are made aware of this, most will recognize that it is in their interests to join with women in securing equal rights (*see also* Kanowitz 1981). The major strategy of this camp remains male enlightenment.

Another analyst of the men's movement, Anthony Astrachan, refers to this as the "pro-feminist" branch of the men's movement. Its focus, he argues, is largely on personal growth and development—"calls for pride in such traditionally masculine qualities as independence and courage and for changes in such traits as 'excessive involvement with work, isolation from our children, discomfort in ex-pressing emotions, lack of close friendships, excessive competitiveness and ag-gressiveness' " (1986:295). But although this profeminist segment of the men's movement expresses support for the struggle for equality of women and often of homosexuals, Astrachan criticizes it for failing to undertake a serious analysis of the issue of power and of how power impinges on men's relations with women and with other men.

A second branch of the men's movement has been labeled by Brod as *female-identified.* Members of this segment essentially agree that traditional mas-culinity is debilitating, especially for particular groups of men (e.g., minority men and the working class). Although it acknowledges that some men might be moti-vated to relinquish their male privileges because of this, most will not unless they are forced. It is this branch of the men's movement that takes up the issue of power, and proponents of this perspective advocate:

> revolution against, rather than a redistribution of, power. They aim to dismantle the power structures that damage male psyches, structures that liberal feminism leaves on the whole intact, generally seeking only greater access to them for women. Consequently, they hold out the greater possibility of men gaining from radical social reconstruction to alleviate or eliminate male and female role restrictions and debilities (Brod 1987:56).

For obvious reasons, Brod identifies this second perspective as a corollary of more radical or leftist feminisms.

In addition to these two approaches, considerable attention has also recently been given to "men's rights" groups, such as Free Men, a Maryland-based organization with chapters throughout the United States. Astrachan (1986) divides this branch of the men's movement into two segments. One segment is composed of divorce reformers who view most divorce and child custody laws as unfair to men. Groups such as Fathers United for Equal Rights have formed to provide divorcing men with an emotional support network and with legal assistance, but few of these groups have taken up political lobbying as a primary activity.

The second segment of the "men's rights" branch of the men's movement is called "the no-guilt wing" by Astrachan. No-guilt men's liberationists denounce traditional masculine stereotypes as harmful and destructive to men, but they also maintain that men should not feel guilty about gender privilege and domination. In their eyes, these are largely illusions given the advantages women enjoy in our society. Men's rights groups, therefore, concentrate their efforts on eliminating what they see as favoritism toward women in U.S. public policy—for instance in military exemptions, lower automobile insurance premiums, and "happy hours" or "ladies' nights" at bars and restaurants where women are offered drinks at reduced prices. Not surprisingly, such groups have staunchly supported the Equal Rights Amendment, but significantly, many of those involved in other branches of the men's movement disavow men's rights groups, viewing them as opposing rather than complementing feminism (Brannon 1981–82). This conclusion is not unfounded, for much of the men's rights literature is both reactionary and sexist, depicting men as the innocent victims of conniving and selfish women (Goldberg 1979; 1976).

Of course, it comes as no surprise that some, particularly women in the feminist movement, regard the men's movement in general with suspicion and skepticism. There is the very real concern, fueled by the actions of men's rights groups, that the men's movement or network is simply a strategy "for repairing men's authority in the face of the damage done by feminism . . ." (Carrigan, et al. 1987:100). Others share Barbara Ehrenreich's (1983) reservation that the net result of "men's liberation" will be to further encourage men to renege on their commitments—especially the financial ones—to women and children. And some question men's commitment to genuine social change in gender relations. As Astrachan (1986:290) points out:

> It's easy to see why the women's movement is so large and the men's movement is small. Women respond to their movement because they know first hand the injustices it wants to erase. They feel a passion to change the system that denies them true equality with men in access to power, economic opportunity, family life, personal autonomy. . . . Most [men] are the beneficiaries of existing political, social, and economic systems—in fact or in our own mythology. We are privileged compared to women, whom we often treat as an underclass.

Implicit in Astrachan's analysis is a question. Just as we asked with regard to antifeminist women, how they could not support the women's movement, we may ask of men's liberationists, why they should want to support a movement for equality. The challenge that confronts many men's liberationists, then, is how to mobilize men for social change when such a change may result in gains for women—but at the cost of some loss of privilege for themselves.

Still, despite these legitimate concerns, the men's movement has already provided us with reasons for optimism. For example, "The most dynamic aspect of the men's movement is its antiviolence component. Across the United States, dozens of men's groups are working with violent men to change their behavior," and the two largest groups have reported better-than-average success rates (Brod 1987:51). On an individual level, the men's movement has also generated "a good deal of quiet experimentation with masculinity" among men who wish to develop nonoppressive relationships with women and other men (Carrigan, et al. 1987:100).

One aspect of the men's movement that has drawn considerable criticism is the failure—some would say refusal—of some men in the movement to actively support the struggle for gay rights. "None of the 1970s books about men made a serious attempt to come to grips with gay liberation arguments or to reckon with the fact that mainstream masculinity is heterosexual masculinity. Nor did the 'men's movement' publicists ever write about the fact that beside them was another group of men active in sexual politics; or discuss their methods, concerns, or problems" (Carrigan, et al. 1987:83). Consequently, the gay liberation movement has remained, for the most part, separate and distinct from the men's liberation movement. However, it is a movement that, along with lesbian activism, deserves our attention.

GAY AND LESBIAN RIGHTS

Much of the information available about homosexual men and women has been produced by nonhomosexuals, and most, we know now, is heterosexist and grounded in myths and negative stereotypes (*see* Chapter 7). Because of the stigma attached to homosexuality, gays and lesbians themselves historically have been forced to remain silent and closeted, or suffer severe consequences, including imprisonment, violence, and the loss of their jobs.

This does not mean that there has been none but recent efforts to secure equal rights for homosexuals. For instance, accompanying the first wave of feminism in Europe was a simultaneous move to emancipate homosexuals (Carrigan, et al. 1987). In the United States, organizations were established as early as 1924 to combat prejudice and discrimination against homosexuals. Such efforts, though, were quickly repressed (Katz 1976). In the 1950s, new groups formed, such as the Mattachine Society for homosexual men and Daughters of Bilitis for lesbians. The goals of these groups were modest by today's standards, but radical for their time: to provide support for homosexuals, to correct widespread inaccuracies about homosexuals and homosexual lifestyles, and to promote tolerance of homosexuals among heterosexuals. It was not until the 1970s, however, that gays and lesbians became politicized and turned their attention away from tolerance to issues such as gay and lesbian pride and heterosexual oppression of homosexuals.

For gay men, harassment and violence at the hands of the police and the heterosexual public were major politicizing forces during the early seventies. Abuses led to demonstrations and organized political campaigns as gays demanded their rights as citizens as well as equal protection under the law (Marotta 1981). The women's movement also played a part by constructing a framework for analyzing oppression by heterosexual men. Gay liberationists began to emphasize that:

> the institutionalization of heterosexuality as in the family, was achieved only by considerable effort, and at considerable cost not only to homosexual people but also to women and children. . . . The gay movement's theoretical work, by comparison with the "sex-role" literature and "men's movement" writings, had a much clearer understanding of the reality of men's power over women, and it had direct implications for any consideration of the hierarchy of power among men (Carrigan, et al. 1987:86).

Most recently, the Supreme Court's decision in *Bowers* v. *Hardwick* (*see* Chapter 7), as well as the AIDS epidemic and its (mis)treatment by the medical establishment, the government, and the heterosexual public (*see* Chapter 12), have been powerful politicizers within the gay community.

We briefly discussed the philosophy underlying lesbian activism in our discussion of radical feminism. For lesbians, the feminist movement was central to their politicization as a group. As one writer explains, "Feminism gave lesbianism a female-oriented political movement and a political understanding of the basis of their persecution. . . . Feminist political activity gave lesbians places to meet outside of the bars through consciousness raising groups, women's centers, and services such as rape crisis and women's health centers" (Pearlman 1987:317).

A more open and supportive environment meant that lesbians could be visible and active. More women "came out" as lesbians and for many, their lesbianism was as much a political statement as it was a sexual preference. However, as lesbian feminists increased their participation in the women's movement and began to contribute their own critical analyses of heterosexual relations, straight feminists grew more defensive and argued that a visible and vocal lesbian presence would hurt the movement by delegitimating it. This eventually led to a *lesbian/ straight split* in the women's movement, with lesbian feminists forming their own organizations, such as Radicalesbians (Pearlman 1987; Bunch 1978). Although in recent years this split has been mended somewhat, there remains an uneasy alliance between lesbian and straight feminists within some segments of the women's movement.

Lesbian and gay activists have made important contributions to the restructuring of our inequitable sex/gender system. They have played a major part in antiviolence campaigns, with lesbians at the forefront of the effort to establish rape crisis centers and battered women's shelters. They have fought, though not always successfully, for the rights of homosexuals to adopt children and to retain custody of their own children. Gay men, in particular, have led the drive to educate the public about AIDS, to provide AIDS testing and counseling, and to insure that the rights of AIDS patients are protected. Nevertheless, sexual preference is still not a protected category under the Constitution; in fact, the *Bowers* v. *Hardwick* decision may be interpreted as official approval of heterosexist discrimination. The tragedy, of course, is that while we could continue to list the successes of gay and lesbian activism, it is clear that so much more remains to be done.

CARRYING ON

We conclude this text much as we began: with the observation that sex/gender systems are *social constructs*. What has been socially constructed can be socially reconstructed to better meet human needs (Lorber 1986). The social movements we discussed in this chapter are efforts toward that reconstruction. They are an expression of the shared grievances of disadvantaged and dissatisfied segments of the population who are working to change the status quo, and to remedy their grievances through direct collective action.

In this chapter and throughout the text, we have highlighted some of the successful challenges that these movements have posed to the present sex/gender system. Yet, we also know that existing institutions and most social relations remain fundamentally unequal. Although many overtly sexist policies and practices have been combatted through legal reforms, other more subtle, more insidious forms of sexism flourish, and heterosexism is as blatant as ever. Even the formal legal rights that have been won are subject to interpretation by a predominantly white, elite male judiciary which frequently produces less than desirable outcomes. Thus, for example, "the list of constitutional entitlements has been interpreted to include the right to bear arms or sell 'artistically redeeming' pornographic magazines, but not, if one is indigent, the right to obtain an abortion, child care, health services, or equal educational opportunities. Women are, at least in theory, protected from discrimination on account of sex in employment but not from discrimination on account of sexual preference or non-marital sexual activity" (Rhode 1986:154–155). These examples make clear that legal reform is at best a short-term solution to inequality. What must be changed is the inherently unequal social structure of which law itself is one part.

As we approach the twenty-first century, the issue of social change raises questions about the future. Can masculinity and femininity, homosexuality and heterosexuality, race, and social class ever disappear as hierarchical organizing categories in our society? Will the social movements we have discussed here overcome their individual differences and collaborate to achieve this goal? We share the sentiments of one group that wrote, "We feel that all liberation movements are equally important; there is no hierarchy of oppression. Every group must speak its own language, assume its own form, take its own action . . ." Our hope for the future, however, lies with the realization that "when each of these groups learns to express itself in harmony with the rest, this will create the basis for an all embracing social change" (Berkeley Men's Center 1974:174).

KEY TERMS

sexual politics   analysis of gender inequality as rooted not only in the public sphere, but also in the supposedly private sphere of the family and intimate male/female relationships

social movement   a group that has organized to promote a particular cause through collective action

women's movement (feminism)   a social movement that spans more than a century of U.S. and European history and which is represented today in most countries of the Third World; composed of many diverse segments, each committed to eliminating gender oppression as well as other oppressions

SUGGESTED READINGS

Astracan, A. 1986. *How Men Feel: Their Responses to Women's Demands for Equality and Power.* Garden City, NY: Anchor.

Bernard, J. 1987. *The Female World From a Global Perspective.* Bloomington, IN: Indiana University Press.

Cant, B., and S. Hemmings. 1988. *Radical Records: Personal Perspectives on Lesbian and Gay History.* New York: Routledge, Chapman, and Hall.

Jardine, A., and P. Smith (Eds.) 1986. *Men in Feminism.* New York: Methuen.

Mitchell, J., and A. Oakley (Eds.) 1986. *What is Feminism? A Re-Examination.* New York: Pantheon.

Solomon, I.D. 1989. *Feminism and Black Activism in Contemporary America.* New York: Greenwood Press.

Glossary

acquaintance rape   an incident of sexual assault in which the victim knows or is familiar with the assailant

acquired immune deficiency syndrome (AIDS)   a virus that attacks a person's immune system, destroying his or her ability to fight off other diseases

Affirmative Action   see **Executive Order 11246**

AIDS   see **acquired immune deficiency syndrome**

androcentrism   male-centered; the view that men are superior to animals and to women

anorexia   an eating disorder in which an individual, because of an obsessive fear of becoming overweight, literally starves her/himself; characterized by a distorted body image, and a 25 percent loss of body weight with a concommitant refusal to eat; 90 to 95 percent of anorectics are female

bipedalism   walking upright on two feet

brain lateralization (hemispheric asymmetry)   the theory that each hemisphere of the brain (the right and left halves) specializes in particular functions or skills

bulimia   also known as *binge-purge syndrome* because the individual consumes large quantities of food in a short period, and then, fearful of gaining weight, purges the food through fasting, laxatives, or induced vomiting; afflicts primarily young women

chivalry hypothesis   the belief that female offenders are afforded greater leniency before the law than their male counterparts

comparable worth   the policy of paying workers equally when they perform different jobs that have similar value

dissimilarity index (segregation index)   a measure of occupational sex segregation, reported as a percent, that indicates the proportion of workers of one sex that would have to change to jobs in which members of their sex are underrepresented in order for the occupational distribution between the sexes to be equal

double work load   a problem faced by women who are in the paid labor force but who also maintain primary responsibility for housework and child care

dual labor market   a labor market characterized by one set of jobs employing almost exclusively men and another set of jobs, typically lower paying and with lower prestige, employing almost exclusively women

economy   the system for the management and development of a society's human and material resources.

emancipation hypothesis   posits that female crime is increasing and/or is becoming more masculine in character as a result of the women's liberation movement

Equal Pay Act of 1963   forbids employers from paying employees of one sex more than employees of the opposite sex when these employees are engaged in work that requires equal skill, effort, and responsibility and is performed under similar working conditions, although exceptions, such as unequal pay based on seniority, merit, the quality or quantity of production, or any other factor besides sex, are allowed.

ethnocentrism   the view that one set of cultural beliefs and practices is superior to all others

Executive Order 11246 (Affirmative Action)   forbids federal contractors from discrimination in personnel decisions on the basis of sex, as well as race, color, national origin, and religion, and requires employers to take affirmative measures to recruit, train, and hire women and minorities; since 1978, implemented and enforced by the OFFCP

expressive family role   the role of women in the traditional nuclear family; according to structural functionalists, women's "natural" role; includes reproduction, housework, and caring for husband and children

feminism (women's movement)   a social movement that spans more than a century of American and European history, composed today of many diverse segments, each committed to eliminating gender oppression

feminist paradigm   explains gender in terms of the political and socioeconomic structure in which it is constructed; emphasizes the importance of taking collective action to eradicate sexism in sociology as well as the larger society and to reconstruct gender so that it is neither a harmful nor an oppressive social category

feminist spirituality   a religious movement composed of diverse segments with differing beliefs and strategies for change, but unified in their rejection of the dualism characteristic of traditional patriarchal religions; dualism is replaced with the theme of unification of spirit and nature, and the principle that human experience is the source of spirituality

feminization of poverty   the position that poverty is increasingly becoming a problem affecting primarily women and their dependent children

foraging societies (hunting and gathering societies)   small, technologically undeveloped societies whose members meet their survival needs by hunting and trapping animals, by fishing if possible, and by gathering vegetation and other types of food in their surrounding environment; characterized by highly egalitarian gender relations

formal curriculum   the set of subjects officially and explicitly taught to students in school

gender   socially generated attitudes and behaviors, the contents of which are usually organized dichotomously as masculinity and femininity

the gender gap   differences in the voting patterns and political opinions of men and women

gender stereotypes   oversimplified summary descriptions of masculinity and femininity

gladiator activities   the highest level of political activism in Millbrath's typology; include working on a political campaign, taking an active role in a political party, or running for public office

hemispheric asymmetry   see **brain lateralization**

heterosexism   the belief that heterosexuality is superior to homosexuality

hidden curriculum   the value preferences children are taught in school that are not an explicit part of the formal curriculum, but rather are hidden or implicit in it

homophobia   an unreasonable fear of and hostility toward homosexuals

human capital theory   explains occupational sex segregation in terms of women's "free choice" to work in jobs that make few demands on workers and require low personal investment in training or skills acquisition because women's primary responsibilities are in the home

hunting and gathering societies   see **foraging societies**

identification   a central concept of the Freudian-based theory of gender socialization; the process by which boys and girls begin to unconsciously model their behavior after that of their same-sex parent in their effort to resolve their respective gender-identity complexes

instrumental family role   the male role of breadwinner and protector in the traditional nuclear family; according to structural functionalists, men's "natural" role

isolated nuclear family   a family form in which the husband/father, wife/mother, and their dependent chidren establish a household separate from other kin and private in the sense that production no longer takes place there

life expectancy   the average number of years of life remaining to an individual at a given age

linguistic sexism   ways in which language devalues members of one sex

mentor   an older, established member of a profession who serves as a kind of sponsor for a younger, new member by providing advice and valuable contacts with others in the field

micro-inequities   subtle, everyday forms of discrimination that single out, ignore, or in some way discount individuals and their work or ideas simply on the basis of an ascribed trait, such as sex

modeling   a central concept of the social learning theory of gender socialization; the process by which children imitate the behavior of their same sex parent, especially if the parent rewards their imitation or is perceived by them to be warm, friendly, or powerful

morbidity rate   the illness rate of a given population

mortality rate   the number of deaths in proportion to a given population

no-fault divorce   a form of marital dissolution which allows either spouse to divorce the other on the ground of "irreconcilable differences" without fixing blame for the marital breakdown

occupational sex segregation   the degree to which men and women are concentrated in occupations that employ workers of predominantly one sex

patriarchy   a sex/gender system in which men dominate women and what is considered masculine is more highly valued than that which is considered feminine

PMS   see **premenstrual syndrome**

premenstrual syndrome (PMS)   a menstrual disorder, the exact causes of which are unknown, but for which there are up to 150 disparate physical, psychological, and behavioral symptoms

public/private split   the notion that the world of the family is private and, therefore, separate from and uninfluenced by the public world of work and other social institutions

Qur'an   the compilation of the revelations that the prophet Mohamad is said to have received from Allah and which is understood by Muslims to be literally the word of God

reflection hypothesis   the belief that media content mirrors the behaviors and relationships, and values and norms most prevalent or dominant in a society

reinforcement   a central principle of the social learning theory of gender socialization which states that a behavior that is consistently followed by a reward will likely occur again, while a behavior followed by a punishment will rarely re-occur

religiosity   an individual's or group's intensity of commitment to a religious belief system

schema   a central concept of the cognitive-developmental theory of gender socialization; a mental category that organizes and guides an individual's perception and helps the individual assimilate new information

segregation index   see **dissimilarity index**

semantic derogation   the process by which the meanings or connotations of words are debased over time

sentencing disparity   the imposition of different sentences on offenders convicted of similar crimes usually resulting in unfair or inappropriate sentences (i.e., sentences disproportionate to the severity of the crime or the offender's criminal history, and based instead on irrelevant factors, such as the offender's sex or race)

separation anxiety   the level of distress exhibited by a child if left alone by a parent, and the extent to which the child clings to its parent or seeks the parent's help when placed in novel situations; used as a measure of dependency in infants

sex   the biologically determined physical distinctions between males and females

sex/gender system   the institutionalized traits, behaviors, and patterns of social interaction that are prescribed for a society's members on the basis of their sex; composed of three interrelated components: the social construction of two dichotomous genders on the basis of biological sex, a sexual division of labor, and the social regulation of sexuality

sexism   the differential valuing of one sex over the other

sexual harassment   involves any unwanted leers, comments, suggestions, or physical contact of a sexual nature, as well as unwelcome requests for sexual favors

sexual politics   the analysis of gender inequality as rooted not only in the public sphere, but also in the supposedly private sphere of the family and intimate male/female relationships

socialization   the process by which a society's values and norms, including those pertaining to gender, are taught and learned

social movement   a group that has organized to promote a particular cause through collective action

spectator activities   the lowest level of political activism in Millbrath's typology; include voting, wearing a campaign button or putting a political bumper sticker on one's car

status offenses   behavior considered illegal if engaged in by a juvenile that would not be illegal if engaged in by an adult

structural functionalist paradigm   explains gender as being derived from the biological differences between the sexes, especially differences in their reproductive functions

symbolic annihilation   symbolically ignoring, trivializing, or condemning individuals or groups through the media

Talmud   thought to have been compiled around A.D.200; records the oral interpretations of scripture by the ancient Rabbis and constitutes the foundation of religious authority for traditional Judaism

Title IX   the provisions of the Education Amendments Act of 1972 that forbid sex discrimination in any education programs or activities that receive federal funding

Title VII of the 1964 Civil Rights Act   forbids discrimination in employment on the basis of sex, as well as race, color, or national origin, by employers of fifteen or more employees, although exceptions such as the BFOQ are allowed; implemented and enforced by the EEOC

transitional activities   the mid-range of political activism in Millbrath's typology; include writing to public officials, making campaign contributions, or attending rallies or political meetings

widow's succession   occurs when a Congressman dies or is too ill to serve out his term and his wife is appointed or elected to finish it for him; the primary vehicle to Congress for women prior to 1949

witchcraft   naturalistic practices with religious significance usually engaged in by women; includes folk magic and medicine as well as knowledge of farming, ceramics, metallurgy, and astrology

women's movement   see **feminism**

Bibliography

Abel, G., J. Becker, and L. Skinner 1980 "Aggressive Behavior and Sex," *Psychiatric Clinics of North America* 3:133–151.

Abplanalp, J.M. 1983 "Premenstrual Syndrome: A Selective Review," Pp. 107–123 in S. Golub (Ed.), *Lifting the Curse of Menstruation.* New York: Haworth Press.

Abzug, B. 1984 *Gender Gap.* Boston: Houghton Mifflin.

Adams, K.L., and N.C. Ware 1989 "Sexism and the English Language: The Linguistic Implications of Being a Woman," Pp. 470–484 in J. Freeman (Ed.), *Women: A Feminist Perspective.* Mountain View, CA: Mayfield.

Adler, F. 1975 *Sisters in Crime.* New York: McGraw-Hill.

Adler, M. 1983 "Women, Feminism, and the Craft," Pp. 388–397 in L. Richardson and V. Taylor (Eds.), *Feminist Frontiers.* Reading, MA: Addison-Wesley.

Administrative Office of the United States Courts 1990. *Annual Report on the Judiciary Employment Opportunity Program.* Washington, D.C.: Administrative Office of the United States Courts.

Ageton, S. 1983 *Sexual Assault Among Adolescents.* Lexington, MA: Lexington Books.

Agus, A. 1979 "This Month is for You: Observing Rosh Hodesh as a Woman's Holiday," Pp. 84–93 in E. Koltun (Ed.), *The Jewish Woman.* New York: Schocken Books.

Ahmed, L. 1986 "Women and the Advent of Islam," *Signs* 11:665–691.

Aiken, S. H., and K. Anderson, M. Dinnerstein, J. Lensink, and P. MacCaorquodale 1988 *Changing Our Minds: Feminist Transformations of Knowledge.* New York: State University of New York Press.

Alan Guttmacher Institute 1985 "Sterilizations Exceed One Million in 1983: Vasectomies Up Sharply," *Family Planning Perspectives* 17:43.

Allan, G. 1985 *Family Life.* New York: Basil Blackwell.

Allan, P.G. 1986 "Angry Women Are Building: Issues and Struggles Facing Native American Women," Pp. 407–409 in J.B. Cole (Ed.), *All American Women.* New York: Free Press.

Allgood-Merten, B., P.M. Lewinsohn, and H. Hops 1990 "Sex Differences and Adolescent Depression," *Journal of Abnormal Psychology* 99:55–63.

Alliance Against Women's Oppression 1986 "Poverty: Not for Women Only—A Critique of the 'Feminization of Poverty,' " Pp. 239–246 in R. Staples (Ed.), *The Black Family.* Belmont, CA: Wadsworth.

Alper, J. 1985 "Sex Differences in Brain Asymmetry: A Critical Analysis," *Feminist Studies* 11:7–37.

American Association of University Professors (AAUP) 1990 "Some Dynamic Aspects of Academic Careers: The Urgent Need to Match Aspirations with Compensation," *Academe* March–April:3–29.

American Medical Association 1990 *Physician Characteristics and Distribution in the United States.* Chicago: American Medical Association.

American Psychological Association 1985. *Developing a National Agenda to Address Women's Mental Health Needs.* Washington, D.C.: American Psychological Association.

Andersen, M.L. 1988 *Thinking About Women.* New York: Macmillan.

———1987 "Changing the Curriculum in Higher Education," *Signs* 12:222–254.

Andors, P. 1983 *The Unfinished Liberation of Chinese Women, 1949–1980.* Bloomington, IN: Indiana University Press.

Archer, C. 1984 "Children's Attitudes Toward Sex-Role Division in Adult Occupational Roles," *Sex Roles* 10:1–10.

Ardrey, R. 1966 *African Genesis.* London: William Collins.

Aries, N., and L. Kennedy 1986 "The Health Labor Force: The Effects of Change," Pp. 196–207 in P. Conrad and R. Kern (Eds.), *The Sociology of Health and Illness.* New York: St. Martin's Press.

Armstead, C.A., K.A. Lawler, G. Gordon, J. Cross, and J. Gibbons 1989 "Relationship of Social Stressors to Blood Pressure Responses and Anger Expression in Black College Students," *Health Psychology* 8:541–556.

Armstrong, G. 1982 "Females Under the Law: 'Protected' but Unequal," Pp. 61–76 in B.R. Price and N.J. Sokoloff (Eds.), *The Criminal Justice System and Women.* New York: Clark Boardman.

Arundel, J. 1989 "Stagflation for Female Engineers," *New York Times* 1 October: 32F.

Astracan, A. 1986 *How Men Feel: Their Responses to Women's Demands for Equality and Power.* Garden City, NY: Anchor.

Attie, I., and J. Brooks-Gunn 1987 "Weight Concerns as Chronic Stressors in Women," Pp. 218–254 in R.C. Barnett, L. Biener, and G.K. Baruch (Eds.), *Gender and Stress.* New York: Free Press.

Babcock, B.A., A.E. Freedman, E. Holmes Norton, and S.C. Ross (Eds.) 1975 *Sex Discrimination and the Law.* Boston: Little Brown.

Baca Zinn, M. 1989 "Family, Race, and Poverty in the Eighties," *Signs* 14:856–874.

Bacon, M.H. 1986 *Mothers of Feminism.* San Francisco: Harper and Row.

Baehr, H. 1980 "The 'Liberated Woman' in Television Drama," *Women's Studies International Quarterly* 3:29–39.

Baker, S.W. 1980 "Biological Influences on Human Sex and Gender," *Signs* 6:80–96.

Ballou, M., and N.W. Gabalac 1985 *A Feminist Position on Mental Health.* Springfield, IL: Charles C. Thomas.

Bandura, A. 1986 *The Social Foundations of Thought and Action: A Social Cognitive Theory.* Englewood Cliffs, NJ: Prentice-Hall.

Bane, M.J. 1986 "Household Composition and Poverty," Pp. 209–231 in S.H. Danzinger and D.H. Weinberg (Eds.), *Fighting Poverty: What Works and What Doesn't.* Cambridge, MA: Harvard University Press.

Banner, L. 1986 "Act One," *Wilson Quarterly* 10:90–98.

———1984 *Women in Modern America: A Brief History.* San Diego: Harcourt, Brace, Jovanovich.

Baran, S.J., and V.J. Blasko 1984 "Social Perceptions and the By-Products of Advertising," *Journal of Communication* 34:12–20.

Bardwell, J.R., S.W. Cochran, and S. Walker 1986 "Relationship of Parental Education, Race, and Gender to Sex Role Stereotyping in Five-Year-Old Kindergartners," *Sex Roles* 15:275–281.

Bardwick, J. 1973 "Infant Sex Differences," Pp. 28–42 in C.S. Stoll (Ed.), *Sexism: Scientific Debates.* Reading, MA: Addison-Wesley.

Barker-Benfield, G.J. 1976 *The Horrors of the Half-Known Life.* New York: Harper and Row.

Barnett, R.C., and G.K. Baruch 1988 "Correlates of Fathers' Participation in Family Work," Pp. 66–78 in P. Bronstein and C.P. Cowan (Eds.), *Fatherhood Today: Men's Changing Role in the Family.* New York: John Wiley.

———1987 "Social Roles, Gender, and Psychological Stress," Pp. 122–143 in R.C. Barnett, L. Biener, and G.K. Baruch (Eds.), *Gender and Stress.* New York: Free Press.

Barnhouse, R.T. 1977 *Homosexuality: A Symbolic Confusion.* New York: Seabury.

Baron, D. 1986 *Grammar and Gender.* New Haven: Yale University Press.

Barrett, N. 1987 "Women and the Economy," Pp. 67–99 in Sara E. Rix (Ed.), *The American Woman, 1987–88.* New York: W.W. Norton.

Barringer, F. 1990 "4 Reports Cite Naval Academy for Rife Sexism," *New York Times* 10 October:A12.

———1989 "Doubt on 'Trial Marriage' Raised by Divorce Rates," *New York Times* 9 June:A1, A28.

Barry, K. 1981 *Female Sexual Slavery.* New York: Avon.

Baskin, J. 1985 "The Separation of Women in Rabbinic Judaism," Pp. 3–18 in Y.Y. Haddad and E.B. Findley (Eds.), *Women, Religion and Social Change.* Albany: State University of New York Press.

Baxter, S., and M. Lansing 1983 *Women and Politics* (revised edition). Ann Arbor: The University of Michigan Press.

Bayer, A. 1975 "Sexist Students in American Colleges: A Descriptive Note," *Journal of Marriage and the Family* 37:391–397.

Beatty, R.W., and J.R. Beatty 1984 "Some Problems with Contemporary Job Evaluation Systems," Pp. 59–78 in H. Remick (Ed.), *Comparable Worth and Wage Discrimination*. Philadelphia: Temple University Press.

Beer, W. 1983 *Househusbands: Men and Household Work in American Families*. New York: Praeger.

Bell, R.Q., G.M. Weller, and M.F. Waldrop 1971 "Newborn and Preschooler: Organization of Behavior and Relations Between Periods." *Monographs of the Society for Research in Child Development*, Vol. 36, No. 142.

Bellin, J.S., and R. Rubenstein 1983 "Genes and Gender in the Workplace," Pp. 87–100 in M. Fooden, S. Gordon, and B. Hughley (Eds.), *Genes and Gender IV: The Second X and Women's Health*. New York: Gordian Press.

Bem, S.L. 1983 "Gender Schema Theory and Its Implications for Child Development: Raising Gender-aschematic Children in a Gender-schematic Society," *Signs* 8:598–616.

Benson, K.A. 1984 "Comment on Crocker's 'An Analysis of University Definitions of Sexual Harassment,' " *Signs* 9:516–519.

Benston, M. 1969 "The Political Economy of Women's Liberation," *Monthly Review* 21:13–27.

Berardo, D.H., C.L. Shehan, and G.R. Leslie 1987 "A Residue of Tradition: Jobs, Careers, and Spouses' Time in Housework," *Journal of Marriage and the Family* 49:381–390.

Bergman, B.R. 1986 *The Economic Emergence of Women*. New York: Basic.

Berk, R.A. 1985 "Racial Discrimination in Capital Sentencing: A Review of Recent Research," Paper presented at the Annual Meeting of the American Sociological Association, Washington, D.C.

Berkeley Men's Center 1974 "Berkeley Men's Center Manifesto," Pp. 173–174 in J.H. Pleck and J. Sawyer (Eds.), *Men and Masculinity*. Englewood Cliffs, NJ: Prentice-Hall.

Berliner, A.K. 1987 "Sex, Sin, and the Church: The Dilemma of Homosexuality," *Journal of Religion and Health* 26:137–142.

Berman, S. 1979 "The Status of Women in Halakhic Judaism," Pp. 114–128 in E. Koltun (Ed.), *The Jewish Woman*. New York: Shocken Books.

Bernard J. 1972 *The Future of Marriage*. New York: Bantam.

Berrill, K.T. 1990 "Anti-Gay Violence and Victimization in the United States," *Journal of Interpersonal Violence* 5:274–294.

Berry, K. 1987 "What the United States Has to Learn . . . About Women," *Ms.* (July/August): 164.

Berry, M. 1986 *Why ERA Failed*. Bloomington, IN: Indiana University Press.

Best, R. 1983 *We've All Got Scars: What Boys and Girls Learn in Elementary School*. Bloomington, IN: Indiana University Press.

Bezilla, R. (Ed.) 1988 *America's Youth: 1977–1988*. Princeton, NJ: The Gallup Organization, Inc.

Bielby, W.T., and J.N. Baron 1986 "Men and Women at Work: Sex Segregation and Statistical Discrimination," *American Journal of Sociology* 91:759–799.

―――― 1984 "A Woman's Place is with Other Women: Sex Segregation Within Organizations," Pp. 27–55 in B.F. Reskin (Ed.), *Sex Segregation in the Workplace: Trends, Explanations, Remedies*. Washington, D.C.: National Academy Press.

Biener, L. 1987 "Gender Differences in the Use of Substances for Coping," Pp. 330–349 in R.C. Barnett, L. Biener, and G.K. Baruch (Eds.), *Gender and Stress*. New York: Free Press.

Bishop, K. 1990 "Women's College Struggles to Keep Its Identity," *New York Times* 7 March:B5.

Blakeslee, S. 1991 "Research on Birth Defects Turns to Flaws in Sperm," *New York Times*, 1 January: 1, 36.

Blanc, A.K. 1987 "The Formation and Dissolution of Second Unions: Marriage and Cohabitation in Sweden and Norway," *Journal of Marriage and the Family* 49:391–400.

Blau, F.D. 1977 *Equal Pay in the Office*. Lexington, MA: Lexington Books.

Blaubergs, M.S. 1980 "An Analysis of Classic Arguments Against Changing Sexist Language," *Women's Studies International Quarterly* 3:135–147.

Bleier, R. 1984 *Science and Gender*. New York: Pergamon Press.

Blood, R.O., and D.M. Wolfe 1960 *Husbands and Wives.* New York: Free Press.

Bloom, A. 1987 *The Closing of the American Mind.* New York: Simon and Schuster.

Bloom, R.L. 1981 "Problems of Prosecution in Acquaintance Rape," *WOARpath* 7 (Fall):6–7.

Blum, L., and V. Smith 1988 "Women's Mobility in the Corporation: A Critique of the Politics of Optimism," *Signs* 13:528–545.

Blumstein, P., and P. Schwartz 1983 *American Couples.* New York: William Morrow.

Boffey, P.M. 1988 "Spread of AIDS Abating, but Deaths Will Still Soar," *New York Times* 14 February:1, 36.

Bohen, H.H. 1984 "Gender Equality in Work and Family: An Elusive Goal," *Journal of Family Issues* 5:254–272.

Bolotin, S. 1982 "Voices from the Post-Feminist Generation," *The New York Times Magazine*, 17 October:29–31, 103, 106–107, 114–116.

Boneparth, E., and E. Stroper 1988 "Introduction: A Framework for Policy Analysis," Pp. 1–19 in E. Boneparth and E. Stroper (Eds.), *Women, Power and Policy: Toward the Year 2000.* New York: Pergamon.

Bookman, A., and S. Morgen (Eds.) 1988 *Women and the Politics of Empowerment.* Philadelphia: Temple University Press.

Boskind-White, M. 1985 "Bulimarexia: A Sociocultural Perspective," Pp. 113–126 in S. Emmet (Ed.), *Theory and Treatment of Anorexia Nervosa and Bulima.* New York: Brunner/Mazel Publishers.

Boston Women's Health Book Collective 1973 *Our Bodies, Ourselves.* New York: Simon and Schuster.

Bouchard, C., A. Tremblay, J. Despres, A Nadeau, P.J. Lupien, G. Theriault, J. Dussault, S. Moojani, S. Pinault, and G. Fournier 1990 "The Response to Long-Term Overfeeding in Identical Twins," *The New England Journal of Medicine* 322:1477–1482.

Bourque, L.B. 1989 *Defining Rape.* Durham, NC: Duke University Press.

Bozett, F.W. 1988 "Gay Fatherhood," Pp. 214–235 in P. Bronstein and C.P. Cowan (Eds.), *Fatherhood Today: Men's Changing Role in the Family.* New York: John Wiley.

Bradbard, M.R. 1985 "Sex Differences in Adults' Gifts and Children's Toy Requests at Christmas," *Psychological Reports* 56:969–970.

Brannon, R. 1981–82 "Are the 'Free Men' a Faction of Our Movement?" *M.: Gentle Men for Gender Justice* 7:14–15, 30–32.

Brewer, R.M. 1988 "Black Women in Poverty: Some Comments on Female-headed Families," *Signs* 13:331–339.

Briggs, N. 1975 "Guess Who Has the Most Complex Job?" Pp. 203–205 in B.A. Babock, A.E. Freedman, E.H. Norton, and S.C. Ross (Eds.), *Sex Discrimination and the Law: Causes and Remedies.* Boston: Little Brown.

Briggs, S. 1987 "Women and Religion," Pp. 381–407 in B.B. Hess and M.M. Ferree (Eds.), *Analyzing Gender.* Newbury Park, CA: Sage.

Brod, H. 1987 "The Case for Men's Studies," Pp. 39–62 in H. Brod (Ed.), *The Making of Masculinities.* Boston: Allen and Unwin.

Bronstein, P. 1988 "Father-Child Interaction," Pp. 107–124 in P. Bronstein and C.P. Cowan (Eds.), *Fatherhood Today: Men's Changing Role in the Family.* New York: John Wiley.

Brooks-Gunn, J. 1986 "The Relationship of Maternal Beliefs About Sex Typing to Maternal and Young Children's Behavior," *Sex Roles* 14:21–35.

Brooks-Gunn, J., and M. Fisch 1980 "Psychological Androgyny and College Students' Judgments of Mental Health," *Sex Roles* 6:575–580.

Brooks-Gunn, J., and W.S. Matthews 1979 *He and She.* Englewood Cliffs, NJ: Prentice-Hall.

Brooten, B.J. 1982 *Women Leaders in the Ancient Synagogue.* Chico, CA: Scholars Press.

Broude, G., and S. Greene 1976 "Cross-cultural Codes on Twenty Sexual Attitudes and Practices," *Ethnology* 15:409–428.

Broverman, I.K., D.M. Broverman, F.E. Clarkson, P.S. Rosenkrantz, and S.R. Vogel 1970 "Sex-Role Stereotypes and Clinical Judgements of Mental Health," *Journal of Clinical and Counseling Psychology* 34:1–7.

Brown, J.D., and K. Campbell 1986 "Race and Gender in Music Videos: The Same Beat but a Different Drummer," *Journal of Communication* 36:94–106.

Brown, S. 1984 "Changes in Laws Governing Divorce," *Journal of Family Issues* 5:200–223.

Browne, A. 1987 *When Battered Women Kill.* New York: Free Press.

Brozan, N. 1990 "Telling the Seder's Story in the Voice of a Woman," *New York Times* 9 April:B4.

Brumberg, J.J. 1988 *Fasting Girls.* Cambridge, MA: Harvard University Press.

Buell, J., and T. DeLuca 1977 "Let's Start Talking About Socialism," *The Progressive* 41:24–27.

Bulbeck, C. 1988 *One World Women's Movement.* London: Pluto Press.

Bunch, C. 1978 "Lesbians in Revolt," Pp. 135–139 in A. M. Jaggar and P. R. Struhl (Eds.), *Feminist Frameworks.* New York: McGraw-Hill.

Burbridge, L.C. 1984 *The Impact of Changes in Policy on the Federal Equal Employment Opportunity Effort.* Washington, D.C.: Urban Institute.

Burris, B.H. 1989 "Technocracy and Gender in the Workplace," *Social Problems* 36:165–180.

Bush, D.M. 1987 "The Impact of Family and School on Adolescent Girls' Aspirations and Expectations: The Public-Private Split and the Reproduction of Gender Inequality," Paper presented at the Annual Meeting of the American Sociological Association, Chicago, IL.

Bussey, K., and A. Bandura 1984 "Influence of Gender Constancy and Social Power on Sex-Linked Modeling," *Journal of Personality and Social Psychology* 47:1292–1302.

Butler, A., and S. Lambert 1983 "Examining Sentencing Models for Two Midwestern Courts: Gender Differences," Paper presented at the Annual Meeting of the American Society of Criminology, Denver, CO.

Butler, M., and W. Paisley 1980 *Women and the Mass Media: Sourcebook for Research and Action.* New York: Human Sciences Press.

Byrne, J.M., and R. J. Sampson (Eds.) 1986 *The Social Ecology of Crime.* New York: Springer-Verlag.

Bystydzienski, J.M. 1989 "Women and Socialism: A Comparative Study of Women in Poland and the USSR," *Signs* 14:668–684.

Calderwood, D. 1985 "Male Sexual Health," Pp. 206–207 in C. Borg (Ed.), *Annual Editions 85/86.* Guilford, CT: The Dushkin Publishing Group.

Callahan, J.J. 1988 "Elder Abuse: Some Questions for Policymakers," *The Gerontologist* 28:453–458.

Campbell, A. 1984 *The Girls in the Gang.* Oxford: Basil Blackwell.

Canadian Bishops' Pastoral Team 1989 "Inclusive Language: Overcoming Discrimination," *Origins* 21 (September 21):1, 259–260.

Cann, A., and S. Palmer 1986 "Children's Assumptions About the Generalizability of Sex-Typed Abilities," *Sex Roles* 15:551–557.

Cannon, L.W., E. Higginbotham, and R.F. Guy 1989 "Depression Among Women: Exploring the Effects of Race, Class and Gender," Center for Research on Women, Memphis State University, Memphis, TN.

Canter, R.J., and S.S. Ageton 1984 "The Epidemiology of Adolescent Sex-Role Attitudes," *Sex Roles* 11:657–676.

Cantor, M.G. 1987 "Popular Culture and the Portrayal of Women: Content and Control," Pp. 190–214 in B.B. Hess and M.M. Ferree (Eds.), *Analyzing Gender.* Newbury Park, CA: Sage.

Carlen, P. 1988 *Women, Crime, and Poverty.* Milton Keynes, England: Open University Press.

Carmody, D.L. 1979 *Women and World Religions.* Nashville: Abingdon.

Carr, P.G., and M.T. Mednick 1988 "Sex Role Socialization and the Development of Achievement Motivation in Black Preschool Children," *Sex Roles* 18:169–180.

Carrigan, T., B. Connell, and J. Lee 1987 "Toward a New Sociology of Masculinity," Pp. 63–100 in H. Brod (Ed.), *The Making of Masculinities.* Boston: Allen and Unwin.

Carroll, B.A. 1979 "Political Science, Part I: American Politics and Political Behavior," *Signs* 5:289–306.

Carroll, J.W., B. Hargrove, and A.T. Lumis 1981 *Women of the Cloth.* San Francisco: Harper and Row.

Carroll, S.J. 1985 *Women as Candidates in American Politics.* Bloomington, IN: Indiana University Press.

Carter, D.B., and L.A. McClosky 1983 "Peers and the Maintenance of Sex-typed Behavior: The

Development of Children's Conceptions of Cross-gender Behavior in Their Peers," *Social Cognition* 4:294–314.

Center for the American Woman and Politics n.d. "Women Make a Difference: Women Supporting Women."

——1990 "Fact Sheet Changes Effective April 1990," 4 April.

——1989a "Women of Color in Elective Office 1989," fact sheet, December.

——1989b "Women in the U.S. Congress 1989," fact sheet, 20 September.

——1988 "Women at the Democratic and Republican National Conventions," fact sheet, 30 August.

——1987 "The Gender Gap" fact sheet, July.

——1985 "Black Women Officeholders," May.

——1984 "Women's Routes to Elective Office," June.

The Center for the Study of Social Policy 1986 "The 'Flip-Side' of Black Families Headed by Women: The Economic Status of Black Men," Pp. 232–238 in R. Staples (Ed.), *The Black Family*. Belmont, CA: Wadsworth.

Chafetz, J.S. 1988 *Feminist Sociology: An Overview of Contemporary Theories*. Itasca, IL: F.E. Peacock.

Chambless, D.L., and A.J. Goldstein 1980 "Anxieties: Agoraphobia and Hysteria," Pp. 113–134 in A.M. Brodsky and R. Hare-Mustin (Eds.), *Women and Psychotherapy*. New York: The Guilford Press.

Chapman, J.R. 1980 *Economic Realities and the Female Offender*. Lexington, MA: Lexington Books.

Chatters, L.H., R.J. Taylor, and H.W. Neighbors 1989 "Informal Helper Networks Among Black Americans," *Journal of Marriage and the Family* 51:667–676.

Chavkin, W. 1990 "Drug Addiction and Pregnancy: Policy Crossroads," *American Journal of Public Health* 80:483–487.

Chavkin, W. 1984a "Walking a Tightrope: Pregnancy, Parenting, and Work," Pp. 196–213 in W. Chavkin (Ed.), *Double Exposure*. New York: Monthly Review Press.

——1984b "Part 3, On the Homefront: Women at Home and in the Community, Introduction," Pp. 215–217 in W. Chavkin (Ed.), *Double Exposure*. New York: Monthly Review Press.

Cheska, A.T. 1981 "Women's Sports—the Unlikely Myth of Equality," Pp. 1–11 in J. Borms, M. Hebbelinck, and A. Venerando (Eds.), *The Female Athlete*. Basel, NY: Karger.

Chesney-Lind, M. 1989 "Girls' Crime and Woman's Place: Toward a Feminist Model of Female Delinquency," *Crime and Delinquency* 35:5–29.

——1986 "Women and Crime: The Female Offender," *Signs* 12:78–96.

Chesterman, C. 1990 "Women, Art, and Technology," *Refractory Girl* May:27.

Children's Defense Fund 1990 fundraising letter. 12 December.

——1988 *Teenage Pregnancy: An Advocate's Guide to the Numbers*. Washington, DC: Adolescent Pregnancy Prevention Clearinghouse.

——1987 *Adolescent Pregnancy: An Anatomy of a Social Problem in Search of Comprehensive Solutions*. Washington, DC: Adolescent Pregnancy Prevention Clearinghouse.

Chisler, J.C., and K.B. Levy 1990 "The Media Construct a Menstrual Monster: A Content Analysis of PMS Articles in the Popular Press," *Women and Health* 16:89–104.

Chodorow, N. 1990 *Feminism and Psychoanalytic Theory*. New Haven, CT: Yale University Press.

——1978 *The Reproduction of Mothering*. Berkeley: University of California Press.

Chopp, R.S. 1989 *The Power to Speak: Feminism, Language, and God*. New York: Crossroad/ Continuum.

Christ, C.P. 1983 "Heretics and Outsiders: The Struggle Over Female Power in Western Religion," Pp. 87–94 in L. Richardson and V. Taylor (Eds.), *Feminist Frontiers*. Reading, MA: Addison-Wesley.

——1979 "Why Women Need the Goddess: Phenomenological, Psychological, and Political Reflections," Pp. 273–287 in C.P. Christ and J. Plaskow (Eds.), *Womanspirit Rising*. San Francisco: Harper and Row.

Christ, C.P., and J. Plaskow 1979 "Introduction: Womanspirit Rising," Pp. 1–18 in C.P. Christ and J. Plaskow (Eds.), *Womanspirit Rising*. San Francisco: Harper and Row.

Christensen, A.S. 1988 "Sex Discrimination and the Law," Pp. 329–347 in A.H. Stromberg and S. Harkess (Eds.), *Women Working*. Mountain View, CA: Mayfield.

Churchman, D. 1985 "Paternity Leave is Up Sharply But Few Fathers are Taking It," *Philadelphia Inquirer* 13 January:51.

Cicirelli, V.G. 1983 "Adult Children and Their Elderly Parents," Pp. 31–46 in T.H. Brubaker (Ed.), *Family Relationships in Later Life.* Beverly Hills: Sage.

Clark, A., and D.N. Ruble. 1978 "Young Adolescents' Beliefs Concerning Menstruation," *Child Development* 49:201–234.

Cleary, P.D. 1987 "Gender Differences in Stress-Related Disorders," Pp. 39–72 in R.C. Barnett, L. Biener, and G.K. Baruch (Eds.), *Gender and Stress.* New York: Free Press.

Cohen, T. 1987 "Remaking Men," *Journal of Family Issues* 8:57–77.

Colasanto, D., and L. DeStefano 1989 "Public Image of TV Evangelists Deteriorates as Bakker Trial Continues." Princeton, NJ: The Gallup Polling Organization, Inc.

Cole, D. 1987 "The Cost of Entering the Baby Chase," *New York Times* 9 August:F11.

Colletta, N.D. 1981 "Social Support and Risk of Maternal Rejection by Adolescent Mothers," *Journal of Psychology* 109:191–197.

Collins, P.H. 1989 "A Comparison of Two Works on Black Family Life," *Signs* 14:875–884.

————1986 "Learning from the Outsider Within: The Sociological Significance of Black Feminist Thought," *Social Problems* 33:S14–S32

Collins, R. and M. Makowsky 1989 *The Discovery of Society.* New York: Random House.

Coltrane, S. 1989 "Household Labor and the Routine Production of Gender," *Social Problems* 36:473–490.

Combahee River Collective 1984 "A Black Feminist Statement," Pp. 210–214 in A. M. Jaggar and P. S. Rothenburg (Eds.), *Feminist Frameworks.* New York: McGraw-Hill.

Commission on Professionals in Science and Technology 1989 *Professional Women and Minorities.* Washington, DC: Commission on Professionals in Science and Technology.

Committee for Abortion Rights and Against Sterilization Abuse 1988 *Women Under Attack: Victories, Backlash, and the Fight for Reproductive Freedom.* Boston: South End Press.

Common Cause 1989 "Special-interest PAC Money in Congressional Elections," pamphlet.

Condry, J.C. 1989 *The Psychology of Television.* Hillsdale, NJ: Lawrence Erlbaum Associates.

Condry, J., and S. Condry 1976 "Sex Differences: A Study in the Eye of the Beholder," *Child Development* 47:812–819.

The Congregation for the Doctrine of the Faith 1987 "Instruction on Respect for Human Life in Its Origin and on the Dignity of Procreation," *Origins* 16:698–711.

Connor, M.E. 1988 "Teenage Fatherhood: Issues Confronting Young Black Males," Pp. 188–218 in J.T. Gibbs (Eds.), *Young, Black, and Male in America: An Endangered Species.* New York: Auburn House.

Conover, P.J., and V. Gray 1983 *Feminism and the New Right.* New York: Praeger.

Conrad, L.T. 1989 "Battling Postpartum Depression," *Philadelphia Inquirer* February 26:J1, J6.

Coombs, L.C. 1977 "Preferences for Sex of Children Among U.S. Couples," *Family Planning Perspectives* 9:259–265.

Cooper, S.E. 1986 "Introduction to the Documents," *Signs* 11:753–756.

Cooperstock, R. 1980 "Special Problems of Psychotropic Drug Use Among Women," *Canada's Mental Health* 28:3–5.

Corcoran, M., G.J. Duncan, and M.S. Hill 1984 "The Economic Fortunes of Women and Children: Lessons from the Panel Study of Income Dynamics," *Signs* 10:232–248.

Corsaro, W.A., and D. Eder 1990 "Children's Peer Cultures," Pp. 197–220 in W.R. Scott (Ed.), *Annual Review of Sociology, Volume 16.* Palo Alto, CA: Annual Reviews, Inc.

Corry, J. 1986 "As Violence Thrives, the Debate Goes On," *New York Times* 6 April:1

Cott, N. 1986 "Feminist Theory and Feminist Movements: The Past Before Us," Pp. 49–62 in J. Mitchell and A. Oakley (Eds.), *What Is Feminism? A Reexamination.* New York: Pantheon.

Couric, E. 1989 "An NJL/West Survey, Women in the Law: Awaiting Their Turn," *National Law Journal* 11 December:S1, S12.

Courtney, A.E., and T.W. Whipple 1983 *Sex Stereotyping in Advertising.* Lexington, MA: Lexington Books.

Cowan, C.P., P.A. Cowan, G. Heming, E. Garrett, W.S. Coysh, H. Curtis-Boles, and A.J. Boles III 1985 "Transitions to Parenthood," *Journal of Family Issues* 6:451–481.

Cowan, G., and C.D. Hoffman 1986 "Gender Stereotyping in Young Children: Evidence to Support a Concept Learning Approach," *Sex Roles* 14:211–224.

Cowan, R.S. 1984 *More Work for Mother.* New York: Basic Books.

Cox, M.J. 1985 "Progress and Continued Challenges in Understanding the Transition to Parenthood," *Journal of Family Issues* 6:395–408.

Craft, C. 1988 *Too Old, Too Ugly, and Not Deferential to Men.* Rocklin, CA: Prime Publishing and Communications.

Crawford, K. 1990 "Girls and Computers," *Refractory Girl* May:21–26.

Crites, L. (Ed.) 1976 *The Female Offender.* Lexington, MA: Lexington Books.

Croll, E.J. 1981a "Women in Rural Production and Reproduction in the Soviet Union, China, Cuba, and Tanzania: Case Studies," *Signs* 7:375–399.

———1981b"Women in Rural Production and Reproduction in the Soviet Union, China, Cuba, and Tanzania: Socialist Development Experiences," *Signs* 7:361–374.

Cron, T. 1986 "The Surgeon General's Workshop on Violence and Public Health: Review of the Recommendations," *Public Health Reports* 101: 8–14.

Crossette, B. 1990 "Women in Delhi Angered by Smoking Pitch," *New York Times* 18 March:18.

———1989 "In Pakistan, Women Seek Basic Rights," *New York Times* 26 March:9.

Cummings, J. 1986 "Woman in Conservative Rabbi Post," *New York Times* 3 August:24.

Curran, D.J. 1984 "The Myth of the 'New' Female Delinquent," *Crime and Delinquency* 30:386–399

Daly, K. 1989 "Neither Conflict nor Labeling nor Paternalism Will Suffice: Intersections of Race, Ethnicity, Gender, and Family in Criminal Court Decisions," *Crime and Deliquency* 35:136–168.

Daly, M. 1984 *Pure Lust.* Boston: Beacon Press.

———1983 "Indian Suttee: The Ultimate Consummation of Marriage," Pp. 189–190 in L. Richardson and V. Taylor (Eds)., *Feminist Frontiers.* Reading, MA: Addison-Wesley.

———1978 *Gyn/Ecology.* Boston: Beacon Press.

Danner, M.J.E. 1989 "The Implications of Feminist Theory for Cross-National Research on Women's Criminality," Paper presented at the Annual Meeting of the American Society of Criminology, Reno, NV.

Danzinger, N. 1983 "Sex-Related Differences in the Aspirations of High School Students," *Sex Roles* 9:683–695.

Darrow, W.R. 1985 "Woman's Place and the Place of Women in the Iranian Revolution," Pp. 307–320 in Y.Y. Haddad and E.B. Findly (Eds.), *Women, Religion and Social Change.* Albany: State University of New York Press.

Davis, A. 1981 *Women, Race and Class.* New York: Random House.

Davis, A.J. 1984 "Sex Differentiated Behaviors in Nonsexist Picture Books," *Sex Roles* 11:1–16.

Davis, K., P. Grant, and D. Rowland 1990 "Alone and Poor: The Plight of Elderly Women," *Generations* 14 (Summer): 43–47.

Davis, M., J.M. Neuhaus, D.J. Moritz, and M.R. Segal 1990 "Living Arrangement Influences Survival of Middle-Aged Men," Paper presented at the Annual Meeting of the American Public Health Association, Santa Barbara, CA.

Deaux, K. 1976 *The Behavior of Women and Men.* Monterey, CA: Brooks Cole.

Deaux, K., and M.E. Kite 1987 "Thinking About Gender," Pp. 92–117 in B.B. Hess and M.M. Ferree (Eds.), *Analyzing Gender.* Newbury Park, CA: Sage.

Deitch, C. 1988 "Sex Differences in Support for Government Spending," Pp. 192–216 in C.M. Mueller (Ed.), *The Politics of the Gender Gap.* Newbury Park, CA: Sage.

Delmar, R. 1986 "What is Feminism?" Pp. 8–33 in J. Mitchell and A. Oakley (Eds.), *What Is Feminism? A Re-Examination.* New York: Pantheon.

DeLoache, J.S., D.J. Cassidy, and C.J. Carpenter 1987 "The Three Bears are All Boys: Mothers' Gender Labeling of Neutral Picture Book Characters," *Sex Roles* 17:163–178.

deMause, L. (Ed.) 1974 *The History of Childhood.* New York: The Psychohistory Press.

DePaulo, L. 1987 "Love and AIDS," *Philadelphia Magazine* (May):105–111, 133–149.

Diamond, I. 1988 "Medical Science and the Transformation of Motherhood: The Promise of Reproductive Technologies," Pp. 155–167 in E. Boneparth and E. Stoper (Eds.), *Women, Power and Policy: Toward the Year 2000*. New York: Pergamon.

Dibble, U., and M.A. Straus 1990 "Some Social Structure Determinants of Inconsistency Between Attitudes and Behavior: The Case of Family Violence," Pp. 167–180 in M.A. Straus and R.J. Gelles (Eds.), *Physical Violence in Families*. New Brunswick, NJ: Transaction Publishers.

Diesenhouse, S. 1990 "Drug Treatment is Scarcer than Ever for Women," *New York Times* 7 January:26E.

Dione, E.J. 1989 "Struggle for Work and Family Fueling Women's Movement," *New York Times* 22 August:A1, A18.

Dobash, R., and R. Emerson Dobash 1979 *Violence Against Wives*. New York: Free Press.

Donnerstein, E. 1983 "Erotica and Human Aggression," Pp. 127–154 in R.G. Green and E.I. Donnerstein (Eds.), *Aggression: Theoretical and Empirical Reviews*. New York: Academic Press.

Dowd, M. 1991 "Bush Appoints More Women, But Most Top Aides are Men," New York Times 20 May:A1, B6.

———1990 "Americans More Wary of Gulf Policy, Poll Finds," *New York Times* 20 November:A12.

Downs, A.C. 1981 "Sex-Role Stereotyping on Prime-Time Television," *The Journal of Genetic Psychology* 138:253–258.

Downs, A.C., and S.K. Harrison 1985 "Embarrassing Age Spots or Just Plain Ugly? Physical Attractiveness Stereotyping as an Instrument of Sexism on American Television Commercials," *Sex Roles* 13:9–19.

Doyal, L. 1990a "Waged Work and Women's Well Being," *Women's Studies International Forum* 13:587–604.

———1990b "Hazards of Hearth and Home," *Women's Studies International Forum* 13:501–517.

Doyle, J.A. 1983 *The Male Experience*. Dubuque, Iowa: Wm. C. Brown.

Drake, D.C. 1989 "AIDS Now a Plague of the Poor," *Philadelphia Inquirer* 11 June:1A,12A.

———1981"Already, AIDS May Doom 4,000 Men in Phila.," *Philadelphia Inquirer* 1 March:1,10.

Draper, P. 1975 "!Kung Women: Contrasts in Sexual Egalitarianism in Foraging and Sedentary Contexts," Pp. 77–109 in R. R. Reiter (ed.), *Toward an Anthropology of Women*. New York: Monthly Review Press.

Dunkle, M.C. 1987 "Women in Intercollegiate Sports," Pp. 228–231 in S.E. Rix (Ed.), *The American Woman, 1987–88*. New York: W.W. Norton.

Dupre, J. 1990 "Global versus Local Perspectives on Sexual Difference," Pp. 47–62 in D.L. Rhode (Ed.), *Theoretical Perspectives on Sexual Difference*. New Haven, CT: Yale University Press.

Dutton, D.G. 1988 *The Domestic Assault of Women*. Boston: Allyn and Bacon.

———1987 "The Criminal Justice Response to Wife Assault," *Law and Human Behavior* 11:189–206.

Dweck, C.S., W. Davidson, S. Nelson, and B. Enna 1978 "Sex Differences in Learned Helplessness," *Developmental Psychology* 14:268–276.

Dworkin, A. 1983a "Gynocide: Chinese Footbinding," Pp. 178–186 in L. Richardson and V. Taylor (Eds.), *Feminist Frontiers*. Reading, MA: Addison-Wesley.

———1983b *Right-Wing Women: The Politics of Domesticated Females*. London: The Women's Press.

Dzeich, B.W. and L. Weiner 1990 *The Lecherous Professor: Sexual Harassment on Campus*. Boston: Beacon Press.

Eagan, A. 1983 "The Selling of Premenstrual Syndrome," *Ms.*, (October):26–31.

Eagly A.H. 1987 *Sex Differences in Social Behavior: A Social-Role Interpretation*. Hillsdale, NJ: Lawrence Erlbaum Associates.

Eagly, A.H., and V.J. Steffan 1986 "Gender and Aggressive Behavior: A Meta-Analytic Review of the Social Psychological Literature," *Psychological Bulletin* 100:309–330.

Ebomoyi, E. 1987 "Prevalence of Female Circumcision in Two Nigerian Communities," *Sex Roles* 17:139–151.

Eccles, J. 1985 "Sex Difference in Achievement Patterns," Pp. 97–132 in T.B. Sonderegger (Ed.), *Nebraska Symposium on Motivation 1984: Psychology and Gender.* Lincoln: University of Nebraska Press.

Eddings, B.M. 1980 "Women in Broadcasting (U.S.) *De Jure, De Facto," Women's Studies International Quarterly* 3:1–13.

Edelsky, C. 1981 "Who's Got the Floor?" *Language and Society* 10:383–421.

Edelson, J.L., Z. Eisikovits, and E. Guttmann 1985 "Men Who Batter," *Journal of Family Issues* 6:229–247.

Edwards, A. 1987 "Black Working Women: A Report from the Front," *Glamour* (July):162–163, 213–218.

Edwards, S.S.M. 1986 "Neither Bad nor Mad: The Female Violent Offender Reassessed," *Women's Studies International Forum* 9:79–87.

Ehrenberg, S., J.E. Lesley, D.B. Mandzuch, and S. Newman 1983 "Feminist Shabbat Service," Pp. 381–383 in L. Richardson and V. Taylor (Eds.), *Feminist Frontiers.* Reading, MA: Addison-Wesley.

Ehrenreich, B. 1983 *The Hearts of Men: American Dreams and the Flight from Commitment.* New York: Anchor-Doubleday.

Ehrenreich, B. and D. English 1986 "The Sexual Politics of Sickness," Pp. 281–296 in P. Conrad and R. Kern (Eds.), *The Sociology of Health and Illness.* New York: St. Martin's Press.

————1973 *Witches, Nurses, and Midwives: A History of Women Healers.* Old Westbury, NY: Feminist Press.

Ehrenreich, B. and A. Fuentes 1981 "Life on the Global Assembly Line," *Ms. Magazine* (January):53–59, 71.

Eiduson, B.T., M. Kornfein, I.L. Zimmerman, and T.S. Weisner 1982 "Comparative Socialization Practices in Traditional and Alternative Families," Pp. 315–346 in M.E. Lamb (ed.)., *Nontraditional Families: Parenting and Child Development.* Hillsdale, NJ: Lawrence Erlbaum.

Elshtain, J.B. 1981 *Public Man, Private Woman.* Princeton, NJ: Princeton University Press.

Enarson, E. 1980 "Sexual Relations of Production: Women in the U.S. Forest Service," Paper presented at the Annual Meeting of the Pacific Sociological Association.

Engel, M. 1985 "One Year After Ferraro: How are Women Doing? *Glamour* November:98.

Engels, F. 1942 *The Origin of the Family, Private Property and the State.* (1884) New York: International Publishers.

Enloe, C.H. 1987 "Feminist Thinking About War, Militarism, and Peace," Pp. 536–548 in B.B. Hess and M.M. Ferree (Eds.), *Analyzing Gender.* Newbury Park, CA: Sage.

Entwisle, D.R., and S. Doering 1988 "The Emergent Father Role," *Sex Roles* 18:119–142.

Epelboin, S., and A. Epelboin 1979 "Female Circumcision," *People* 6:26–31.

Epstein, C.F. 1983 "Women and Power: The Roles of Women in Politics in the United States," Pp. 288–304 in L. Richardson and V. Taylor (Eds.), *Feminist Frontiers.* Reading, MA: Addison-Wesley.

————1981 *Women in Law.* New York: Basic.

Erikson, E.H. 1968 *Identity: Youth and Crisis.* New York: Norton.

Estioko-Griffin, A. 1986 "Daughters of the Forest," *Natural History* 95(May):5.

Estrich, S. *Real Rape.* Boston: Harvard University Press.

Ethics Committee of the American Psychological Association 1988 "Trends in Ethics Cases, Common Pitfalls, and Published Resources," *American Psychologist* 43:564–572.

Etienne, M., and E. Leacock (Eds.) 1980 *Women and Colonization.* New York: Praeger.

Evans, S.M. 1987 "Women in Twentieth Century America: An Overview," Pp. 33–66 in S.E. Rix (Ed.), *The American Woman in 1987–88.* New York: W.W. Norton.

————1979 *Personal Politics: The Roots of Women's Liberation in the Civil Rights Movement and the New Left.* New York: Knopf.

Fagot, B.I. 1985 "Beyond the Reinforcement Principle: Another Step Toward Understanding Sex Role Development," *Developmental Psychology* 21:1097–1104.

Fagot, B.I., R. Hagan, M.D. Leinbach, and S. Kronsberg 1985 "Differential Reactions to Assertive and Communicative Acts of Toddler Boys and Girls," *Child Development* 56:1499–1505.

Faine, J.R., and E. Bohlander 1976 "Sentencing the Female Offender: The Impact of Legal and Extra-Legal Considerations," Paper presented at the Annual Meeting of the American Society of Criminology, Tucson, AZ.

Farley, L. 1978 *Sexual Shakedown.* New York: McGraw-Hill.

Fausto-Sterling, A. 1985 *Myths of Gender.* New York: Basic Books.

Fee, E. 1983 "Women and Health Care: A Comparison of Theories," Pp. 17–34 in E. Fee (Ed.), *Women and Health: The Politics of Sex in Medicine.* Farmdale, NY: Baywood.

Feinman, S. 1981 "Why is Cross-Sex-Role Behavior More Approved for Girls than for Boys?" *Sex Roles* 7:289–300.

Feldberg, R.L. 1984 "Comparable Worth: Toward Theory and Practice in the United States," *Signs* 10:311–328.

Fennema, E., and J. Sherman 1977 "Sex-Related Differences in Mathematics Achievement, Spatial Ability, and Affective Factors," *American Educational Research Journal* 14:51–71.

Ferguson, M. 1983 *Forever Feminine: Women's Magazines and the Cult of Femininity.* London: Heinemann.

Ferraro, B., and P. Hussey 1990 *No Turning Back.* New York: Poseidon Press.

Ferraro, K.J. 1989 "Policing Woman Battering," *Social Problems* 36:61–74.

Ferrence, R.G., and P.C. Whitehead 1980 "Sex Differences in Psychoactive Drug Use: Recent Epidemiology," Pp. 125–201 in O.J. Kalant (Ed.), *Alcohol and Drug Problems in Women, Vol. 5.* New York: Plenum.

Fidell, L.S. 1980 "Sex Role Stereotypes and the American Physician," *Psychology of Women Quarterly* 4:313–330.

Figueira-McDonough, J. 1982 "Gender Differences in Informal Processing: A Look at Charge Bargaining and Sentence Reduction in Washington, D.C.," Paper presented at the Annual Meeting of the American Society of Criminology, Toronto.

Figueira-McDonough, J., A. Inglehart, R. Sarri, and T. Williams 1981 *Females in Prison in Michigan, 1968–1978.* Ann Arbor: University of Michigan, School of Social Work.

Filene, P. 1987 "The Secrets of Men's History," Pp. 103–120 in H. Brod (Ed.), *The Making of Masculinities.* Boston: Allen and Unwin.

Fillmore, K.M. 1984 " 'When Angels Fall': Women's Drinking as Cultural Preoccupation and Reality," Pp. 7–36 in S.C. Wilsnack and L.J. Beckman (Eds.), *Alcohol Problems in Women.* New York: The Guilford Press.

Finkelhor, D. 1984 *Child Sexual Abuse: New Theory and Research.* New York: Free Press.

Finkelhor, D., and K. Yllo 1985 *License to Rape: Sexual Abuse of Wives.* Beverly Hills, CA: Sage.

Fisher, S. 1986 *In the Patient's Best Interest: Women and the Politics of Medical Decisions.* New Brunswick, NJ: Rutgers University Press.

Fleishman, J. 1984 "The Hazards of Office Work," Pp. 57–68 in W. Chavkin (Ed.), *Double Exposure.* New York: Monthly Review Press.

Flexner, E. 1971 *Century of Struggle.* Cambridge, MA: Belknap.

Flowers, R.B. 1988 *Minorities and Criminality.* Westport, CT: Greenwood Press.

Flynn, C.P. 1987 "Relationship Violence: A Model for Family Professionals," *Family Relations* 36:295–299.

Foderaro, L.W. 1989 "Female Politicians' Success Outside Cities is Limited," *New York Times* 1 April:29,32.

Foreit, K.G., T. Agor, J. Byers, J. Larue, H. Lokey, M. Palazzini, M. Patterson, and L. Smith 1980 "Sex Bias in the Newspaper Treatment of Male-Centered and Female-Centered News Stories," *Sex Roles* 6:475–480.

Frank, F.W. 1989 "Language Planning, Language Reform, and Language Change: A Review of Guidelines for Nonsexist Usage," Pp. 105–133 in F.W. Frank and P.A. Treichler (Eds.), *Language,*

Gender, and Professional Writing: Theoretical Approaches and Guidelines for Nonsexist Usage. New York: The Modern Language Association of America.

Franklin, D.W., and J.L. Sweeney 1988 "Women and Corporate Power," Pp. 48–65 in E. Boneparth and E. Stroper (Eds.), *Women, Power, and Policy: Toward the Year 2000.* New York: Pergamon.

Freedman, R. 1986 *Beauty Bound.* Lexington, MA: Lexington Books.

Freeman, J. 1973 "The Origins of the Women's Liberation Movement," *American Journal of Sociology* 78:792–811.

Freeza, H., C.D. Padova, G. Pozzato, M. Terpin, E. Baraona, and C.S. Lieber 1990 "High Blood Alcohol Levels in Women: The Role of Decreased Gastric Alcohol Dehydrogenase Activity and First-Pass Metabolism," *The New England Journal of Medicine* 322:95–99.

Freud, S. 1983/1933 "Femininity," Pp. 80–92 in M. W. Zak and P. A. Motts (Eds.) *Women and the Politics of Culture.* New York: Longman.

Friedan, B. 1981 *The Second Stage.* New York: Summit Books.

———1963 *The Feminine Mystique.* New York: W.W. Norton.

Friedman, R.C., S.W. Hurt, M.S. Aronoff, and J. Clarkin 1980 "Behavior and the Menstrual Cycle," *Signs* 5:719–738.

Frieze, I.H., J.E. Parsons, P.B. Johnson, D.N. Ruble, and G.L. Zellman 1978 *Women and Sex Roles.* New York: W.W. Norton.

Frodi, A., P. Ropert-Thome, and J. Macauley 1977 "Are Women Always Less Aggressive Than Men?" *Psychological Bulletin* 84:634–660.

Gadon, E.M. 1989 *The Once and Future Goddess.* New York: Harper and Row.

Gailey, C.W. 1987 "Evolutionary Perspectives on Gender Hierarchy," Pp. 32–67 in B.B. Hess and M.M. Ferree (Eds.), *Analyzing Gender.* Newbury Park, CA: Sage.

Gallup, G. 1988 *Public Opinion 1988.* Wilmington, DE: Scholarly Resources, Inc.

———1987 *Public Opinion 1986.* Wilmington, DE: Scholarly Resources Inc.

———1986 *Public Opinion 1985.* Wilmington, DE: Scholarly Resources Inc.

———1985 *Religion in America 50 Years: 1935–1985.* Princeton, NJ: American Institute of Public Affairs.

Gallup, G., and J. Castelli 1989 *The People's Religion.* New York: Macmillan.

Geis, F.L., V. Brown, J. Jennings (Walstedt), and N. Porter 1984 "TV Commercials as Achievement Scripts for Women," *Sex Roles* 10:513–525.

Gelles, R.J., and P.E. Maynard 1987 "A Structural Family Systems Approach to Intervention in Cases of Family Violence," *Family Relations* 36:270–275.

Gelles, R.J., and C.P. Cornell 1985 *Intimate Violence in Families.* Beverly Hills: Sage.

Gendler, M. 1979 "The Restoration of Vashti," Pp. 241–247 in E. Koltun (Ed.), *The Jewish Woman.* New York: Shocken Books.

Gerson, M., J.L. Alpert, and M.S. Richardson 1984 "Mothering: The View from Psychological Research," *Signs* 9:434–453.

Gertzog, I.N. 1984 *Congressional Women.* New York: Praeger.

Giddings, P. 1984 *When and Where I Enter.* New York: William Morrow.

Gilkes, C.T. 1985 "Together and in Harness: Women's Traditions in the Sanctified Church," *Signs* 10:678–699.

Gilligan, C. 1990 *Making Connections: The Relational Worlds of Adolescent Girls at Emma Willard School.* Cambridge, MA: Harvard University Press.

———1982 *In a Different Voice: Psychological Theory and Women's Development.* Cambridge, MA: Harvard University Press.

Gilmore, D.O. 1990 *Manhood in the Making.* New Haven, CT: Yale University Press.

Gilroy, F., and R. Steinbacher 1983 "Preselection of Child's Sex: Technological Utilization and Feminism," *Psychological Reports* 53:671–676.

Gimbutas, M. 1989 *The Language of the Goddess.* New York: Harper and Row.

Giordano, P., and S.A. Cernkovich 1979 "On Complicating the Relationship Between Liberation and Delinquency," *Social Problems* 26:467–481.

Gitlin, M.J., and R.O. Passnau 1989 "Psychiatric Symptoms Linked to Reproductive Function in Women: A Review of Current Knowledge," *American Journal of Psychiatry* 146:1413–1422.

Gjerdingen, D.K., D.G. Froberg, and P. Fontaine 1990 "A Causal Model Describing the Relationship of Women's Postpartum Health to Social Support, Length of Leave, and Complications of Childbirth," *Women and Health* 16:71–87.

Glamour Magazine 1987 "How College Women and Men Feel Today About Sex, AIDS, Condoms, Marriage, Kids," (August):261–263.

Glass, R. 1982 "Some Fear Abuses in Premenstrual Tension Decisions," *Philadelphia Inquirer,* 24 January:8C.

Glazer, N. 1980 "Overworking the Working Woman: The Double Day in a Mass Magazine," *Women's Studies International Quarterly* 3:79–95.

Glazer-Malbin, N. 1976 "Housework," *Signs* 1:905–922.

Glenn, E.N. 1987 "Gender and the Family," Pp. 348–380 in B.B. Hess and M.M. Ferree (Eds.), *Analyzing Gender.* Newbury Park, CA: Sage.

————1980 "The Dialectics of Wage Work: Japanese American Women and Domestic Service, 1905–1940," *Feminist Studies* 6: 432–471.

Gluck, S.B. 1987 *Rosie the Riveter Revisited.* New York: Twayne.

Gold, A.R. 1989 "Sex Bias is Found Pervading Courts," *New York Times* 2 July:14.

Gold, M. 1983 "Sexism in Gynecologic Practices," Pp. 133–142 in M. Fooden, S. Gordon, and B. Hughley (Eds.), *Genes and Gender IV: The Second X and Women's Health.* New York: Gordian.

Goldberg, H. 1979 *The New Male.* New York: Signet.

————1976 *The Hazards of Being Male.* New York: Nash.

Goldberg, S. 1974 *The Inevitability of Patriarchy.* New York: William Morrow.

Goldberg, S., and M. Lewis 1969 "Play Behavior in the Year-Old Infant: Early Sex Differences," *Child Development* 40:21–31.

Goldfeld, A. 1979 "Women as Sources of Torah in the Rabbinic Tradition," Pp. 257–271 in E. Koltun (Ed.), *The Jewish Woman.* New York: Shocken Books.

Goldhaber, M.K., M.R. Poland, and R.A. Hialt 1988 "The Risk of Miscarrige and Birth Defects Among Women Who Use Visual Display Terminals During Pregnancy," *American Journal of Industrial Medicine* 13:695–706.

Goldman, A.L. 1990a "Reform Judaism Votes to Accept Active Homosexuals in Rabbinate," *New York Times* 26 June:A1, A21.

————1990b "A Bar to Women as Cantors is Lifted," 19 September:B2.

————1990c "Ecumenist in Charge: Joan B. Campbell," *New York Times* 18 November:32.

Goldstein, L.F. 1979 *The Constitutional Rights of Women.* New York: Longman.

Goleman, D. 1990 "Stereotypes of the Sexes Persisting in Therapy," *New York Times* 10 April:C1, C10.

————1988 "Sex Roles Reign Powerful as Ever in the Emotions," *New York Times* 23 August:C1, C13.

Golub, S. 1980 "Premenstrual Changes in Mood, Personality and Cognitive Function," Pp. 237–246, in A. Dan, E. Graham, and C.P. Beecher (Eds.), *The Menstrual Cycle.* New York: Springer.

Gonzalez, A. 1982 "Sex Roles of the Traditional Mexican Family," *Journal of Cross-Cultural Psychology* 13:330–339.

Goodchilds, J., and G. Zellman 1984 "Sexual Signaling and Sexual Aggression in Adolescent Relationships," Pp. 233–243 in N. Malamuth and E. Donnerstein (Eds.), *Pornography and Sexual Aggression.* Orlando, FL: Academic Press.

Goodenough, R.G. 1990 "Situational Stress and Sexist Behavior Among Young Children," Pp. 225–252 in P.R. Sanday and R.G. Goodenough (Eds.), *Beyond the Second Sex.* Philadelphia: University of Pennsylvania Press.

Gordon, L. 1976 *Woman's Body, Woman's Right.* New York: Grossman Publishers.

Gordon, M.R. 1990 "Woman Leads G.I.'s in Panama Combat," *New York Times* 4 January:A12.

Gordon, M., and S.J. Creighton 1988 "Fathers as Sexual Abusers in the United Kingdom," *Journal of Marriage and the Family* 50:99–106.

Gordon, M.T., and S. Riger 1989 *The Female Fear.* New York: Free Press.

Gornick, V. 1982 "Watch Out: Your Brain May be Used Against You," *Ms.,* (April):14–20.

Gough, K. 1975 "The Origin of the Family," Pp. 51–76 in R.R. Reiter (Ed.), *Toward an Anthropology of Women.* New York: Monthly Review Press.

Gould, S.J. 1981 *The Mismeasure of Man.* New York: W.W. Norton.

_____1980 *The Panda's Thumb.* New York: Norton.

_____1976 "Biological Potential vs. Biological Determinism," *Natural History* 85:12–22.

Graham, E. 1986 "African Women Fight Clitoris Cutting," *off our backs* (June):18–19.

Graham, P.A. 1978 "Expansion and Exclusion: A History of Women in American Higher Education," *Signs* 3:759–773.

Grant, J. 1986 "Black Women and the Church," Pp. 359–369 in J.B. Cole (Ed.), *All American Women.* New York: Free Press.

Gray, F.D. 1989 *Soviet Women: Walking the Tightrope.* New York: Doubleday.

Gray, M. 1979 *Margaret Sanger.* New York: Richard Marek Publishers.

Greeley, A.M. 1990 *The Catholic Myth.* New York: Charles Scribner's Sons.

Greenberg, B. 1979 "Judaism and Feminism," Pp. 179–192 in E. Koltun (Ed.), *The Jewish Woman.* New York: Schocken Books, Inc.

Greene, K.W. 1989 *Affirmative Action and Principles of Justice.* New York: Greenwood.

Greenfield, P., D. Farrar, and J. Beagles-Roos 1986 "Is the Medium the Message? An Experimental Comparison of Radio and Television on Imagination," *Journal of Applied Developmental Psychology* 7:201–218.

Greer, W.R. 1986 "Violence Against Homosexuals Rising, Groups Seeking Wider Protection Say," *New York Times* 23 November:36.

Greif, G.L. 1985 *Single Fathers.* Lexington, MA: Lexington Books.

Gresham, J.H. 1989 "White Patriarchal Supremacy: The Politics of Family in America," *The Nation* 249 (July 24/31):116–122.

Gross, H.E., J. Bernard, A.J. Dan, N. Glazer, J. Lorber, M. McClintock, N. Newton, and A. Rossi 1979 "Considering 'A Biosocial Perspective on Parenting,' " *Signs* 4:695–717.

Gross J. 1990a "Prostitutes and Addicts: Special Victims of Rape," *New York Times* 12 October:A14.

_____1990b "For Gay People in Military, Lives of Secrecy and Despair," *New York Times* 10 April:A1, D20.

_____1990c "R.O.T.C. Under Siege for Ousting Homosexuals," *New York Times* 6 May:24.

_____1990d "At NOW Convention, Goal is Putting More Women in Office," *New York Times* 1 July:14.

Gruber, J.E., and L. Bjorn 1982 "Blue-Collar Blues: The Sexual Harassment of Women Autoworkers," *Work and Occupations* 9:271–298.

Gutis, P.S. 1989 "What is a Family? Traditional Limits are Being Redrawn," *New York Times* 31 August:C1, C6.

Hacker, K. 1986 "Campaigning to Win Power for Women," *Philadelphia Inquirer* 20 July:1, 8I.

Haddad, Y.Y. 1985 "Islam, Women and Revolution in Twentieth-Century Arab Thought," Pp. 275–306 in Y.Y. Haddad and E.B. Findly (Eds.), *Women, Religion and Social Change.* Albany: State University of New York Press.

Hale-Benson, Janice E. 1986 *Black Children: Their Roots, Culture and Learning Styles* (Revised Edition). Provo, UT: Brigham Young University Press.

Hall, R.M., and B.R. Sandler 1985 "A Chilly Climate in the Classroom," Pp. 503–510 in A.G. Sargent (Ed.), *Beyond Sex Roles.* New York: West.

Hancock, L. 1986 "Economic Pragmatism and the Ideology of Sexism: Prison Policy and Women," *Women's Studies International Forum* 9:101–107.

Hansen, F.J., and L. Reekie 1990 "Sex Differences in Clinical Judgments of Male and Female Thera-pists," *Sex Roles* 23:51–64.

Hanson, S.M.H. 1988 "Divorced Fathers with Custody," Pp. 166–194 in P. Bronstein and C.P. Cowan (Eds.), *Fatherhood Today: Men's Changing Role in the Family.* New York: John Wiley.

Haraway, D. 1989 *Primate Visions.* New York: Routledge.

———1978 "Animal Sociology and a Natural Economy of the Body Politic, Part II: The Past is a Contested Zone: Human Nature and Theories of Production and Reproduction in Primate Behavior Studies," *Signs* 4:37–60.

Harding, S.G. 1979 "Is the Equality of Opportunity Principle Democratic?" *Philosophical Forum* 10:206–223.

Harkess, S. 1980 "Hiring Women and Blacks in Entry-Level Manufacturing Jobs in a Southern City: Particularism and Affirmative Action," Paper presented at the Annual Meeting of the Society for the Study of Social Problems, New York.

Harlan, S., and B. O'Farrell 1982 "After the Pioneers: Prospects for Women in Traditionally Male Blue Collar Jobs," *Work and Occupations* 9:363–386.

Harmatz, M.G., and M.A. Novak 1983 *Human Sexuality.* New York: Harper and Row.

Harrington, A. 1987 *Medicine, Mind, and the Double Brain.* Princeton, NJ: Princeton University Press.

Harrington, M. 1962 *The Other America.* New York: Macmillan.

Harris, B. 1983 "The Myth of Assembly-Line Hysteria," Pp. 65–86 in M. Fooden, S. Gordon, and B. Hughley (Eds.), *Genes and Gender IV: The Second X and Women's Health.* New York: Gordian.

Harrison, J.B. 1984 "Warning: The Male Sex Role May be Dangerous to Your Health," Pp. 11–27 in J.M. Swanson and K.A. Forrest (Eds.), *Men's Reproductive Health.* New York: Springer.

Hart, M.M. 1980 "Sport: Women Sit in the Back of the Bus," Pp. 205–211 in D. F. Sabo and R. Runfola (Eds.), *Jock: Sports and Male Identity.* Englewood Cliffs, NJ: Prentice-Hall.

Hartjen, C.A. 1978 *Crime and Criminalization.* New York: Holt, Rinehart and Winston.

Hartmann, H.I. 1987 "Internal Labor Markets and Gender: A Case Study of Promotion," Pp. 59–106 in C. Brown and J.A. Pechman (Eds.), *Gender in the Workplace.* Washington, DC: The Brook-ings Institution.

———1984 "The Unhappy Marriage of Marxism and Feminism: Towards a More Progressive Union," Pp. 172–188 in A.M. Jaggar and P.S. Rothenberg (Eds.), *Feminist Frameworks.* New York: McGraw-Hill.

———1981 "The Family as the Locus of Gender, Class, and Political Struggle: The Example of Housework," *Signs*:366–394.

Hartmann, H.I., P.A. Roos, and D.J. Treiman 1985 "An Agenda for Basic Research on Comparable Worth," Pp. 3–33 in H.I. Hartmann (Ed.), *Comparable Worth: New Directions for Research.* Washington, D.C.: National Academy Press.

Hatch, M. 1984 "Mother, Father, Worker: Men and Women and the Reproduction Risks of Work," Pp. 161–179 in W. Chavkin (Ed.), *Double Exposure.* New York: Monthly Review Press.

Height, D. 1989 "Family and Community: Self-Help—A Black Tradition," *The Nation* 249 (July 24/31):136–138.

Helgeson, V.S. 1990 "The Role of Masculinity in a Prognostic Predictor of Heart Attack Severity," *Sex Roles* 22:755–774.

Hemmons, W.M. 1980 "The Women's Liberation Movement: Understanding Black Women's Atti-tudes," Pp. 285–299 in L.F. Rodgers-Rose (Ed.), *The Black Woman.* Beverly Hills, CA: Sage.

Henley, N., M. Hamilton, and B. Thorne 1985 "Womanspeak and Manspeak: Sex Differences and Sexism in Communication," Pp. 168–185 in A.G. Sargent (Ed.), *Beyond Sex Roles.* New York: West.

Henshaw, S.K., and J. Van Vort 1990 "Abortion Services in the United States, 1987 and 1988," *Family Planning Perspectives* 22:102–108.

Herman, J.L. 1988 "Considering Sex Offenders: A Model of Addiction," *Signs* 13:695–724.

Herzog, A. R., J.G. Bachman, and L.D. Johnston 1983 "Paid Work, Child Care, and Housework: A National Survey of High School Seniors' Preferences for Sharing Responsibilities Between Husband and Wife," *Sex Roles* 9:109–135.

Herman, J.L. 1988 "Considering Sex Offenders: A Model of Addiction," *Signs* 13:695–724.

Hess, B.B., and M.M. Ferree 1987 "Introduction," Pp. 9–30 in B.B. Hess and M.M. Ferree (Eds.), *Analyzing Gender.* Newbury Park, CA: Sage.

Hess, R.D., and I.T. Miura 1985 "Gender Differences in Enrollment in Computer Camps and Classes," *Sex Roles* 13:193–203.

Hewlett, S.A. 1986 *A Lesser Life.* New York: William Morrow and Company, Inc.

Heyward, C. 1987 "Heterosexist Theology: Being Above It All," *Journal of Feminist Studies in Religion* 3:29–38.

Higgins, P.J. 1985 "Women in the Islamic Republic of Iran: Legal, Social, and Ideological Changes," *Signs* 10:477–494.

Hilkert, M.C. 1986 "Women Preaching the Gospel," *Theology Digest* 33:423–440.

Hill, M.A. 1980 *Charlotte Perkins Gilman: The Making of a Radical Feminist, 1860–1896.* Philadelphia: Temple University Press.

Hiller, D.V., and W.W. Philliber 1986 "The Division of Labor in Contemporary Marriage: Expectations, Perceptions, and Performance," *Social Problems* 33:191–201.

Hilts, P.J. 1990 "Spread of AIDS by Heterosexuals Remains Slow," *New York Times* 1 May:C1, C12.

Himmelstein, J.L. 1986 "The Basis of Antifeminism: Religious Networks and Culture," *Journal for the Scientific Study of Religion* 25:1–15.

Hinds, M.D. 1990 "Use of Crack is Said to Stifle the Instincts of Parenthood," *New York Times* 17 March:8.

———1989 "Better Traps Being Built for Delinquent Parents," *New York Times* 9 December:11.

Hochschild, A.R. 1989 *The Second Shift.* New York: Viking.

Hodson, D., and P. Skeen 1987 "Child Sexual Abuse: A Review of Research and Theory with Implications for Family Life Educators," *Family Relations* 36:215–221.

Hoffman, F.L. 1986 "Sexual Harassment in Academia: Feminist Theory and Institutional Practice," *Harvard Educational Review* 56:105–121.

Hoffman, L.W. 1977 "Changes in Family Roles, Socialization, and Sex Differences," *American Psychologist* 32:644–657.

Hoff-Wilson, J. 1987 "The Unfinished Revolution: Changing Legal Status of U.S. Women," *Signs* 13:7–36.

Hohri, S. 1986 "Are You a Liberated Woman? Feminism, Revolution and Asian American Women," Pp. 420–425 in J.B. Cole (Ed.), *All American Women.* New York: Free Press.

Holden, C. 1987 "Why Do Women Live Longer than Men?" *Science* 238:158–160.

Hole, J., and E. Levine 1984 "The First Feminists," Pp. 533–542 in J. Freeman (Ed.), *Women: A Feminist Perspective.* Palo Alto, CA: Mayfield.

Holland, B. (Ed.) 1985 *Soviet Sisterhood.* Bloomington, IN: Indiana University Press.

Holloman, J.L.S. 1983 "Access to Health Care," Pp. 79–106 in President's Commission for the Study of Ethical Problems in Medicine and Biomedical Research, *Securing Access to Health Care.* Washington, D.C.: U.S. Government Printing Office.

Holmes, S.A. 1990a "House, 265–145, Votes to Widen Day Care Programs in Nation," *New York Times* 30 March:1,14.

———1990b "Day Care Bill Marks a Turn Toward Help for the Poor," *New York Times* 8 April:4E.

Hood, E.F. 1984 "Black Women, White Women: Separate Paths to Liberation," Pp. 189–201 in A.M. Jaggar and P.S. Rothenberg (Eds.), *Feminist Frameworks.* New York: McGraw-Hill.

Hornaday, A. 1983 "Why Are We Feminists Laughing?" *Ms. Magazine* (April):45–46.

Horner, M.S. 1972 "Toward an Understanding of Achievement-Related Conflicts in Women," *Journal of Social Issues* 28:157–175.

Horney, K. 1967 *Feminine Psychology.* New York: Norton.

Horwitz, A.V. 1982 "Sex-Role Expectations, Power, and Psychological Distress," *Sex Roles* 8:607–623.

Hosken, F. 1979 *The Hosken Report: Genital/Sexual Mutilation of Females.* Lexington, MA: Women's International Network News.

House, J.S. 1986 "Occupational Stress and Coronary Heart Disease: A Review and Theoretical Integration," Pp. 64–72 in P. Conrad and R. Kern (Eds.), *The Sociology of Health and Illness.* New York: St. Martin's Press.

Hout, M., and A.M. Greeley 1987 "The Center Doesn't Hold: Church Attendance in the United States, 1940–1984," *American Sociological Review* 52:325–345.

Howe, F. 1984 *Myths of Coeducation.* Bloomington, IN: University of Indiana Press.

Howe, K. 1985 "The Psychological Impact of a Women's Studies Course," *Women's Studies Quarterly* 13:23–24.

Hu, Y., and N. Goldman 1990 "Mortality Differentials by Marital Status: An International Comparison," *Demography* 27:233–250.

Hubbard, R. 1990 "The Political Nature of Human Nature," Pp. 63–73 in D.L. Rhode (Ed.), *Theoretical Perspectives on Sexual Difference.* New Haven, CT: Yale University Press.

———1979 "Have Only Men Evolved?" Pp. 7–36 in R. Hubbard, M.S. Henifin, and B. Fried (Eds.), *Women Look at Biology Looking at Women.* Cambridge, MA: Schenkman.

Hunter, K.I., M.W. Linn, and S.R. Stein 1984 "Sterilization Among American Indian and Chicano Mothers," *International Quarterly of Community Health Education* 4:343–352.

Hyde, J.S. 1984 "How Large are Gender Differences in Aggression? A Developmental Meta-Analysis," *Developmental Psychology* 20:722–736.

Hyman, P. 1979 "The Other Half: Women in the Jewish Tradition," Pp. 105–113 in E. Koltun (Ed.), *The Jewish Woman.* New York: Shocken Press.

Ibrahim, Y.M. 1990 "Saudi Tradition: Edicts from Koran Produce Curbs on Women," *New York Times* 8 November:A18.

———1989 "Saudi Women Quietly Win Some Battles," *New York Times* 26 April:A6.

International Labour Office 1990 *Yearbook of Labour Statistics.* Geneva: International Labour Office.

Isaaks, L. 1980 *Sex Role Stereotyping as It Relates to Ethnicity, Age and Sex in Young Children.* Unpublished doctoral dissertation, East Texas State University.

Ishiyama, F.I., and D.J. Chabassol 1985 "Adolescents' Fear of Social Consequences of Academic Success as a Function of Age and Sex," *Journal of Youth and Adolescence* 14:37–46.

Jacklin, C.N. 1989 "Female and Male: Issues of Gender," *American Psychologist* 44:127–133.

Jacob, H. 1989 "Another Look at No-Fault Divorce and the Post-divorce Finances of Women," *Law and Society Review* 23:95–115.

Jacobs, J.A. 1983 *The Sex Segregation of Occupations and Women's Career Patterns.* Unpublished doctoral dissertation, Harvard University.

Jacquet, C.H. (Ed.) 1990 *Yearbook of American and Canadian Churches 1990.* Nashville, TN: Abington Press.

———1988 *Women Ministers in 1986 and 1987: A Ten Year View.* New York: Office of Research and Evaluation, National Council of Churches.

Jaggar, A.M., and P.S. Rothenberg (Eds.) 1984 *Feminist Frameworks.* New York: McGraw-Hill.

———1984 "Theories of Women's Oppression," Pp. 81–90 in A.M. Jaggar and P.S. Rothenberg (Eds.), *Feminist Frameworks.* New York: McGraw-Hill.

James, J. 1982 "The Prostitute as Victim," Pp. 291–316 in B.R. Price and N. J. Sokoloff (Eds.), *The Criminal Justice System and Women.* New York: Clark Boardman.

Jarratt, E.H. 1990 "Feminist Issues in Sport," *Women's Studies International Forum* 13:491–499.

Jensen, M., and L.B. Rosenfeld 1974 "Influence of Mode of Presentation, Ethnicity and Social Class on Teachers' Evaluations of Students," *Journal of Educational Psychology* 66:540–547.

Jewell, K.S. 1988 *Survival of the Black Family: The Institutional Impact of U.S. Social Policy.* New York: Praeger.

Johnson, A.G. 1980 "On the Prevalence of Rape in the United States," *Signs* 6:136–146.

Johnson, D. 1990a "Milwaukee Creating 2 Schools Just for Black Boys," *New York Times* 30 September:1, 26.

———1990b "At Colleges, AIDS Alarms Muffle Older Dangers," *New York Times* 8 March:A18.

———1986 "Abused Women Get Leverage in Connecticut," *New York Times* 15 June:E8.

Johnson, J., and J. S. Ettema 1982 *Positive Images*. Beverly Hills, CA: Sage.

Johnson, L.B. 1981 "Perspectives on Black Family Research: 1965–1978," Pp. 87–102 in H.P. McAdoo (Ed.), *Black Families*. Beverly Hills, CA: Sage.

Johnson, P.J., and F.M. Firebaugh 1985 "A Typology of Household Work Performance by Employment Demands," *Journal of Family Issues* 6:83–105.

Jones, B.A.P. 1986 "Black Women and Labor Force Participation: An Analysis of Sluggish Growth Rates," Pp. 11–32 in M.C. Simms and J.M. Malveaux (Eds.), *Slipping Through the Cracks: The Status of Black Women*. New Brunswick, NJ: Transaction Books.

Jones, E.F. 1989 *Pregnancy, Contraception, and Family Planning Services in Industrialized Countries*. New Haven, CT: Yale University Press.

Julty, S. 1979 *Men's Bodies, Men's Selves*. New York: Dell.

Jurik, N.C. 1983 "The Economics of Female Recidivism," *Criminology* 21:603–622.

Kagay, M.R. 1989 "Homosexuals Gain More Acceptance," *New York Times* 25 October:A24.

Kamerman, S.B., and A.J. Kahn 1988 *Mothers Alone*. Dover, MA: Auburn House Publishing Co.

Kammeyer, K. C.W. 1987 *Marriage and Family*. Boston: Allyn and Bacon.

Kanowitz, L. 1981 *Equal Rights: The Male Stake*. Albuquerque: University of New Mexico Press.

Kanter, R.M. 1977 *Men and Women of the Corporation*. New York: Basic.

Kantrowitz, B. 1987 "How to Stay Married," *Newsweek* 24 August:52–58.

Katz, B.J. 1974 "A Quiet March for Liberation Begins," Pp. 152–156 in J.H. Pleck and J. Sawyer (Eds.), *Men and Masculinity*. Englewood Cliffs, NJ: Prentice-Hall.

Katz, J. 1976 *Gay American History*. New York: Crowell.

Kay, H.H. 1988 *Sex-Based Discrimination*. St. Paul, MN: West.

Kerber, L.K., C.G. Greeno, E.E. Maccoby, Z. Luria, C.B. Stack, and C. Gilligan 1986 "On *In a Different Voice:* An Interdisciplinary Forum," *Signs* 11:304–333.

Kessler-Harris, A. 1990 *A Woman's Wage: Historical Meanings and Social Consequences*. Lexington, KY: University Press of Kentucky.

———1982 *Out to Work: A History of Wage-Earning Women in the United States*. New York: Oxford University Press.

Khan, S.S., S. Nessim, R. Gray, L.S. Czer, A. Chaux, and J. Matloff 1990 "Increased Mortality of Women in Coronary Bypass Surgery: Evidence for Referral Bias," *Annals of Internal Medicine* 112:561–567.

Kimball, R. 1990 *Tenured Radicals: How Politics Has Corrupted Higher Education*. New York: Harper and Row.

Kimura, D. 1987 "Are Men's and Women's Brains Really Different?" *Canadian Psychology* 28:133–147.

King, D.R. 1988 "Multiple Jeopardy, Multiple Consciousness: The Context of a Black Feminist Ideology," *Signs* 14:42–72.

Klag, M.J., P.K. Whelton, J. Corech, C.E. Grim, and L.H. Kuller 1991 "The Association of Skin Color with Blood Pressure in U.S. Blacks with Low Socioeconomic Status," *Journal of the American Medical Association* 264:599–602.

Klass, P. 1988 "Are Women Better Doctors?" *The New York Times Magazine* 10 April:32–35, 46–48, 96–97.

Klatch, R. 1988 "Coalition and Conflict among Women of the New Right," *Signs* 13:671–694.

Klein, D. 1973 "The Etiology of Female Crime: A Review of the Literature," *Issues in Criminology* 8:3–30.

Klein, E. 1984 *Gender Politics*. Cambridge, MA: Harvard University Press.

Klein, V. 1984 "The Historical Background," Pp. 519–522 in J. Freeman (Ed.), *Women: A Feminist Perspective*. Palo Alto, CA: Mayfield.

Kmetz, J. 1985 "Combatting Compulsion: A Multidisciplinary Effort," *Image* (Winter):7–9.

Koehler, M.S. 1990 "Classrooms, Teachers, and Gender Differences in Mathematics," Pp. 128–148 in E. Fennema and G.C. Leder (Eds.), *Mathematics and Gender.* New York: Teachers College Press.

Koeske, R. 1983 "Lifting the Curse of Menstruation: Toward a Feminist Perspective on the Menstrual Cycle," Pp. 1–16 in S. Golub (Ed.), *Lifting the Curse of Menstruation.* New York: Haworth.

———1980 "Theoretical Perspectives on Menstrual Cycle Research," Pp. 8–24 in A. Dan, E. Graham, and C.P. Beecher (Eds.), *The Menstrual Cycle.* New York: Springer.

Kolata, G. 1990a "Study Finds More Women than Men Fail to Survive Heart Bypasses," *New York Times* 16 April:A15.

———1990b "N.I.H. Neglects Women, Study Says," *New York Times* 19 June:C6.

Komarovsky, M. 1985 *Women in College.* New York: Basic.

Konner, M. 1982 *The Tangled Wing: Biological Constraints on the Human Spirit.* New York: Harper Colophon Books.

Koop, C.E. n.d. *Surgeon General's Report on Acquired Immune Deficiency Syndrome.* Washington, D.C.: U.S. Dept. of Health and Human Services.

Kosberg. J.I. 1988 "Preventing Elder Abuse: Identification of High-Risk Factors Prior to Placement Decisions," *The Gerontologist* 28:43–50.

Koss, M., C. Gidycz, and N. Wisniewski 1987 "The Scope of Rape: Incidence and Prevalence of Sexual Aggression in a Sample of Higher Education Students," *Journal of Consulting and Clinical Psychology* 55:162–170.

Kramer, R. 1986 "The Third Wave," *Wilson Quarterly* 10:110–129.

———1983 *In Defense of the Family.* New York: Basic.

Kranichfeld, M.L. 1987 "Rethinking Family Power," *Journal of Family Issues* 8:42–56.

Krieger, S. 1982 "Lesbian Identity and Community: Recent Social Science Literature," *Signs* 8:91–108.

Kristof, N.D. 1990 "China Using Electrodes to 'Cure' Homosexuals," *New York Times* 29 January:A2.

———1986 "X-Rated Industry in a Slump," *New York Times* 5 October:1F, 6F.

Kruttschnitt, C. 1982 "Women, Crime and Dependency," *Criminology* 19:495–513.

Kuhn, D., S.C. Nash, and L. Brucken 1978 "Sex Role Concepts of Two- and Three-Year Olds," *Child Development* 49:445–451.

Kuhn, T.S. 1970 *The Structure of Scientific Revolutions.* Chicago: University of Chicago Press.

Kulp, K. 1981 "Acquaintance Rape," *WOARpath* 7 (Fall):2–3.

Kurtz, D. 1987 "Emergency Department Responses to Battered Women: Resistance to Medicalization," *Social Problems* 34:70–81.

Kurtz, R.A., and H.P. Chalfant 1984 *The Sociology of Medicine and Illness.* Boston: Allyn and Bacon.

Kushner, H.I. 1985 "Women and Suicide in Historical Perspective," *Signs* 10:537–552.

Kutner, N.G., and R.M. Levinson 1978 "The Toy Salesperson: A Voice for Change in Sex-Role Stereotypes?" *Sex Roles* 4:1–8.

LaCroix, A.Z., and S.G. Haynes 1987 "Gender Differences in the Health Effects of Workplace Roles," Pp. 96–121 in R.C. Barnett, L. Biener, and G.K. Baruch (Eds.), *Gender and Stress.* New York: Free Press.

Ladner, J. 1971 *Tomorrow's Tomorrow.* Garden City, NY: Doubleday.

LaFree G. 1980 "The Effect of Sexual Stratification by Race on Official Reactions to Rape," *American Sociological Review* 45:842–854.

Lake, A. 1975 "Are We Born into Our Sex-Roles or Programmed into Them?" *Woman's Day* (January):24–25.

Lamar, J.V. 1988 "Redefining a Woman's Place," *Time* 15 February:27.

Lambert, B. 1987 "AIDS Forecasts are Grim—and Disparate," *New York Times* 25 October:24E.

Lambert, H.H. 1978 "Biology and Equality: A Perspective on Sex Differences," *Signs* 4:97–117.

Langolis, J.H., and A.C. Downs 1980 "Mothers, Fathers, and Peers as Socialization Agents of Sex-typed Play Behaviors in Young Children," *Child Development* 51:1217–1247.

Larson, J.H. 1988 "The Marriage Quiz: College Students' Beliefs in Selected Myths about Marriage," *Family Relations* 37:3–11.

Lawrence, W. 1987 "Women and Sports," Pp. 222–226 in S.E. Rix (Ed.), *The American Woman, 1987–88.* New York: W.W. Norton.

Lawson, C. 1990 "Like Growing Numbers of Companies, I.B.M. is Building Child-Care Centers," *New York Times* 12 December:A20.

————1989 "Toys: Girls Still Apply Makeup, Boys Fight Wars," *New York Times* 15 June:C1, C10.

Lazier-Smith, L. 1989 "A New 'Genderation' of Images of Women," Pp. 247–260 in P.J. Creedon (Ed.), *Women in Mass Communication.* Newbury Park, CA: Sage.

Leach, W. 1980 *True Love and Perfect Union: The Feminist Reform of Sex and Society.* New York: Basic Books.

Leary, W.E. 1989 "In Vitro Fertility Clinics Vary Widely in Success Rates," *New York Times* 10 March:A16.

Leder, G.C., and E. Fennema 1990 "Gender Differences in Mathematics: A Synthesis," Pp. 188–200 in E. Fennema and G.C. Leder (Eds.), *Mathematics and Gender.* New York: Teachers College Press.

Lee, F.R. 1989 "Doctors See Gap in Blacks' Health Having a Link to Low Self-Esteem," *New York Times* 17 July:A11.

Leibowitz, L. 1975 "Perspectives on the Evolution of Sex Differences," Pp. 30–35 in R.R. Reiter (Ed.), *Toward an Anthropology of Women.* New York: Monthly Review Press.

Leland, J. 1984 "Alcohol Use and Abuse in Ethnic Minority Women," Pp. 66–96 in S.C. Wilsnack and L.J. Beckman (Eds.), *Alcohol Problems in Women.* New York: The Guilford Press.

Lemle, R. 1984 "Alcohol and Masculinity: A Review and Reformulation of Sex Role, Dependency, and Power Theories of Alcoholism," Paper presented at the Annual Meeting of the American Psychological Association, Toronto, Canada.

LeMoyne, J. 1990 "Ban on Driving by Women Reaffirmed by Saudis," *New York Times* 15 November:A19.

Lenskyj, H. 1986 *Out of Bounds.* Toronto: The Women's Press.

Lepowsky, M. 1990 "Gender in an Egalitarian Society: A Case Study from the Coral Sea," Pp. 169–224 in P.R. Sanday and R.G. Goodenough (Eds.), *Beyond the Second Sex.* Philadelphia: University of Pennsylvania Press.

Lerner, G. (Ed.) 1972 *Black Women in White America.* New York: Vintage.

Leung, J.J. 1990 "Aspiring Parents' and Teachers' Academic Beliefs about Young Children," *Sex Roles* 23:83–90.

Levant, R.F., S.C. Slattery, and J.E. Loiselle 1987 "Fathers' Involvement in Housework and Child Care with School-Aged Daughters." *Family Relations* 36:152–157.

Levine, S. 1974 "One Man's Experience," Pp. 156–159 in J.H. Pleck and J. Sawyer (Ed.), *Men and Masculinities.* Englewood Cliffs, NJ: Prentice-Hall.

Lewin, T. 1990a "California Lets Nontraditional Families Register," *New York Times* 17 December:A15.

————1990b "Suit Over Death Benefits Asks, What is a Family?" *New York Times* 21 September:B7.

————1990c "Drug Use in Pregnancy: New Issue for the Courts," *New York Times* 5 February:A14.

————1989 "View on Career Women Sets Off Furor," *New York Times* 7 March:A18.

————1988 "Gay Groups Suggest Marines Selectively Prosecute Women," *New York Times* 4 December:34.

————1986 "Statistics Have Become Suspect in Sex Discrimination Cases," *New York Times* 9 February:8E.

————1984 "A New Push to Raise Women's Pay," *New York Times* 1 January:F1, 15.

Lewis, D.K. 1975 "The Black Family: Socialization and Sex Roles," *Phylon* 36:221–237.

Lewis, M., and R.I. Simon 1986 "A Discourse Not Intended for Her: Learning and Teaching Within Patriarchy," *Harvard Educational Review* 56:457–472.

Liebert, R., J. Neale, and E. Davidson 1982 *The Early Window: The Effects of Television on Children and Youth.* New York: Pergamon Press.

Lightfoot-Klein, H. 1989 *Prisoners of Ritual: An Odyssey into Female Genital Circumcision in Africa.* New York: Harrington Park Press.

Lincoln, C.E., and L.H. Mamiya 1990 *The Black Church in the African American Experience.* Durham, NC: University of North Carolina Press.

Lindquist, J.H., and J.M. Duke 1982 "The Elderly Victim at Risk," *Criminology* 20:115–126.

Lindsey, R. 1987 "Women of 42 Nations Seek Leadership Roles," *New York Times* 15 March:28.

Little, C.B. 1983 *Understanding Deviance and Control: Theory, Research and Public Policy.* Itasca, IL: F.E. Peacock.

Lobel, K. (Ed.) 1986 *Naming the Violence.* Seattle: Seal Press.

Lockhead, M.E. 1986 "Reshaping the Social Order: The Case of Gender Segregation," *Sex Roles* 14:617–628.

————1985 "Women, Girls, and Computers: A First Look at the Evidence," *Sex Roles* 13:115–122.

Lofland, L.H. 1975 "The 'Thereness' of Women: A Selective Review of Urban Sociology," Pp. 144–170 in M. Millman and R.M. Kanter (Eds.), *Another Voice.* New York: Anchor/Doubleday.

Longino, H., and R. Doell 1983 "Body, Bias, and Behavior: A Comparative Analysis of Reasoning in Two Areas of Biological Science," *Signs* 9:206–227.

Lorber, J. 1986 "Dismantling Noah's Ark," *Sex Roles* 14:567–580.

Lorber, J., R.L. Coser, A.S. Rossi, and N. Chodorow 1981 "On *The Reproduction of Mothering:* A Methodological Debate," *Signs* 6:482–514.

Loring, M., and B. Powell 1988 "Gender, Race and DSM-III: A Study of Psychiatric Behavior," *Journal of Health and Social Behavior* 29:1–22.

Loseke, D.R., and S.E. Cahill 1984 "The Social Construction of Deviance: Experts on Battered Women," *Social Problems* 31:296–310.

Lott, B. 1987 *Women's Lives: Themes and Variations in Gender Learning.* Monterey, CA: Brooks/Cole Publishing Company.

Lovejoy, O. 1981 "The Origins of Man," *Science* 211:341–350.

Lovenduski, J. 1986 *Women and European Politics.* Amherst: University of Massachusetts Press.

Luckenbill, D.F. 1986 "Deviant Career Mobility: The Case of Male Prostitutes," *Social Problems* 33:283–296.

Luker, K. 1984 *Abortion and the Politics of Motherhood.* Berkeley: University of California Press.

Lunneborg, P.W. 1990 *Women Changing Work.* New York: Bergen and Garvey.

Lyall, S. 1987 "A Woman's College Looks to Men, Skeptically, for Survival," *New York Times* 26 April:E8.

Lynn, N.B. 1984 "Women and Politics: The Real Majority," Pp. 402–422 in J. Freeman (Ed.), *Women: A Feminist Perspective.* Palo Alto, CA: Mayfield.

Maccoby, E., and C. Jacklin 1974 *The Psychology of Sex Differences.* Stanford, CA: Stanford University Press.

MacDonald, K., and R.D. Parke 1986 "Parent-Child Physical Play: The Effects of Sex and Age on Children and Parents," *Sex Roles* 15:367–378.

MacKinnon, C. 1986 "Pornography: Not a Moral Issue," *Women's Studies International Forum* 9:63–78.

Madden, J., and J.A. Erikson 1987 "The Legal Remedy for Discrimination: The Real Challenge of the Sears Case," Paper presented at the Penn Mid-Atlantic Seminar for the Study of Women in Society, Philadelphia, PA.

Maguire, P. 1987 *Doing Participatory Research: A Feminist Approach.* Amherst, MA: The Center for International Education, School of Education, University of Massachusetts.

Mamonova, T. (Ed.) 1984 *Women and Russia: Feminist Writings from the Soviet Union.* Boston: Beacon Press.

Mansbridge, J.J. 1986 *Why We Lost the ERA.* Chicago: University of Chicago Press.

Margolin, G., and G.R. Patterson 1975 "Differential Consequences Provided by Mothers and Fathers for Their Sons and Daughters," *Developmental Psychology* 11:537–538.

Margolis, D.R. 1979 *The Managers: Corporate Life in America.* New York: Morrow.

Margolis, L., M. Becker, and K. Jackson-Brewer 1987 "Internalized Homophobia: Identifying and Treating the Oppressor Within," Pp. 229–241 in Boston Lesbian Psychologies Collective (Eds.), *Lesbian Psychologies.* Urbana: University of Illinois Press.

Marieskind, H.I., and B. Ehrenreich 1975 "Toward Socialist Medicine: The Women's Health Movement," *Social Policy* 6:34–42.

Marini, M.M., and M. Brinton 1984 "Sex Typing in Occupational Socialization," Pp. 192–232 in B.F. Reskin (Ed.), *Sex Segregation in the Workplace: Trends, Explanations, Remedies.* Washington, D.C.: National Academy Press.

Markides, K.S. 1990 "Risk Factors, Gender, and Health," *Generations* 14 (Summer): 17–21.

Maroney, H.J. 1986 "Feminism at Work," Pp. 101–126 in J. Mitchell and A. Oakley (Eds.), *What is Feminism? A Re-Examination.* New York: Pantheon.

Marotta, T. 1981 *The Politics of Homosexuality.* Boston: Houghton-Mifflin.

Marshall, S.E. 1984 "Keep Us on the Pedestal: Women Against Feminism in Twentieth-Century America," Pp. 568–581 in J. Freeman (Ed.), *Woman: A Feminist Perspective.* Palo Alto, CA: Mayfield.

Martin, C.L. 1990 "Attitudes and Expectations About Children with Nontraditional and Traditional Gender Roles," *Sex Roles* 22:151–165.

Martin, E. 1987 *The Woman in the Body.* Boston: Beacon Press.

Martin, M.K., and B. Voorhies 1975 *Female of the Species.* New York: Columbia University Press.

Martyna, W. 1980 "Beyond the 'He/Man' Approach: The Case for Nonsexist Language," *Signs* 5:482–493.

Mashek, J.W. 1986 "A Woman's Place is on the Ballot in '86," *U.S. News and World Report* 3 November:21–22.

Massé, M.A., and K. Rosenblum 1988 "Male and Female Created They Them: The Depiction of Gender in the Advertising of Traditional Women's and Men's Magazines," *Women's Studies International Forum* 11:127–144.

Matsui, Y. 1989 *Women's Asia.* London: Zed Books.

Mays, V.M., and S.D. Cochran 1988 "Issues in the Perception of AIDS Risk and Risk Reduction Activities by Black and Hispanic/Latina Women," *American Psychologist* 43:949–957.

McAdoo, H.P. 1986 "Societal Stress: The Black Family," Pp. 187–197 in J. B. Cole (Ed.), *All American Women.* New York: Free Press.

McAdoo, J.L. 1988 "Changing Perspectives on the Role of the Black Father," Pp. 79–92 in P. Bronstein and C.P. Cowan (Eds.), *Fatherhood Today: Men's Changing Role in the Family.* New York: John Wiley.

The McClintock Collective 1990 "Gender Inclusive Science and Technology Education," *Refractory Girl* May:34–36.

McConaghy, M.J. 1979 "Gender Permanence and the Genital Basis of Gender: Stages in the Development of Constancy of Gender Identity," *Child Development* 50:1223–1226.

McConnell-Ginet, S. 1989 "The Sexual (Re)Production of Meaning: A Discourse-Based Theory," Pp. 35–50 in F.W. Frank and P.A. Treichler (Eds.), *Language, Gender, and Professional Writing: Theoretical Approaches and Guidelines for Nonsexist Usage.* New York: Modern Language Association of America.

McCormack, A. 1985 "The Sexual Harassment of Students by Teachers: The Case of Students in Science," *Sex Roles* 13:21–31.

McCrea, F.B. 1986 "The Politics of Menopause: The 'Discovery' of a Deficiency Disease," Pp. 296–344 in P. Conrad and R. Kern (Eds.), *The Sociology of Health and Illness.* New York: St. Martin's Press.

McGuinness, D. 1985 *When Children Don't Learn.* New York: Basic Books.

McIntosh, P. 1983 "Interactive Phases of Curricular Revision: A Feminist Perspective," *Wellesley Working Papers Series,* no. 124. Wellesley, MA: Wellesley College Center for Research on Women.

McKinney, F. 1986 "Employment Implications of a Changing Health-Care System," Pp. 199–216 in M.C. Simms and J. Malveaux (Eds.), *Slipping Through the Cracks: The Status of Black Women.* New Brunswick, NJ: Transaction Books.

McLean, S. 1980 *Female Circumcision, Excision, and Infibulation: The Facts and Proposals for Change.* London: Minority Rights Group.

Mead, M. 1935 *Sex and Temperament in Three Primitive Societies.* New York: Dell.

Meigs, A. 1990 "Multiple Gender Ideologies and Statuses," Pp. 99–112 in P.R. Sanday and R.G. Goodenough (Eds.), *Beyond the Second Sex.* Philadelphia: University of Pennsylvania Press.

Mernissi, F. 1977 "Women, Saints, and Sanctuaries," *Signs* 3:101–112.

Messerschmidt, J. 1986 *Capitalism, Patriarchy, and Crime: Toward a Socialist Feminist Criminology.* Totowa, NJ: Rowman and Littlefield.

Messner, M. 1989 "Sports and the Politics of Inequality," Pp. 187–190 in M.S. Kimmel and M. A. Messner (Eds.), *Men's Lives.* New York: Macmillan.

———1987 "The Meaning of Success: The Athletic Experience and the Development of Male Identity," Pp. 193–210 in H. Brod (Ed.), *The Making of Masculinities.* Boston: Allen and Unwin.

Mezzacappa, D. 1986 "The New Motherhood: Science Creates Social Issues," *Philadelphia Inquirer* 22 June:1, 14.

Miall, C.E. 1986 "The Stigma of Involuntary Childlessness," *Social Problems* 33:268–282.

Miethe, T.D., and C.A. Moore 1986 "Racial Differences in Criminal Processing: The Consequences of Model Selection on Conclusions about Differential Treatment," *Sociological Quarterly* 27:217–237.

Miles, W.E. 1983 "How Many of These Laws Have You Broken?" *Ms.* (April):24.

Milkman, R. 1987 *Gender At Work: The Dynamics of Job Segregation by Sex during World War II.* Berkeley, CA: University of California Press.

———1986 "Women's History and the Sears Case," *Feminist Studies* 12:375–400.

Millbrath, L.W. 1965 *Political Participation.* Chicago: Rand McNally.

Miller, C.L. 1987 "Qualitative Differences Among Gender-Stereotyped Toys: Implications for Cognitive and Social Development in Girls and Boys," *Sex Roles* 16:473–488.

Miller, D.C. 1990 *Women and Social Welfare: A Feminist Analysis.* New York: Praeger.

Miller, S.M., and N. Kirsch 1987 "Sex Differences in Cognitive Coping with Stress," Pp. 278–302 in R.C. Barnett, and G.K. Baruch (Eds.), *Gender and Stress.* New York: Free Press.

Miller, T.M., J.G. Coffman, and R.A. Linke 1980 "Survey on Body-Image, Weight, and Diet of College Students," *Journal of the American Dietetic Association* 77:561–566.

Millman, M., and R.M. Kanter (Eds.) 1975 *Another Voice.* New York: Anchor.

Mintz, L.B., and N.E. Betz 1986 "Sex Differences in the Nature, Realism, and Correlates of Body Image," *Sex Roles* 15:185–195.

Mischel, W. 1966 "A Social-Learning View of Sex Differences in Behavior," Pp. 56–81 in E.E. Maccoby (Ed.), *The Development of Sex Differences.* Stanford, CA: Stanford University Press.

Mohr, J. 1978 *Abortion in America.* New York: Oxford University Press.

Money, J., and A.A. Ehrhardt 1972 *Man and Woman, Boy and Girl.* Baltimore: Johns Hopkins University Press.

Montgomery, R.J.V., and M.M. Datwyler 1990 "Women and Men in the Caregiving Role," *Generations* 14:(Summer):34–38.

Morello, K.B. 1986 *The Invisible Bar: The Woman Lawyer in America.* New York: Random House.

Morgan, R. 1980 "The First Feminist Exiles from the U.S.S.R.," *Ms. Magazine* (November):49–56, 80–83, 102–108.

———1978 "How to Run the Pornographers Out of Town (and Preserve the First Amendment)," *Ms. Magazine* (November):55, 78–80.

Morgan, R., and G. Steinem 1980 "The International Crime of Genital Mutilation," *Ms.* (March):65–67, 98–100.

Morrissey, E.R. 1986 "Power and Control Through Discourse: The Case of Drinking and Drinking Problems Among Women," *Contemporary Crises* 10:157–179.

Mosedale. L. 1987 "Now Hear This: Women's Voices Sell," *Glamour* January:96.

Mosher, D.L., and M. Sirkin 1984 "Measuring a Macho Personality Constellation," *Journal of Research in Personality* 18:150–163.

Mullings, L. 1984 "Minority Women, Work, and Health," Pp. 121–138 in W. Chavkin (Ed.), *Double Exposure*. New York: Monthly Review Press.

Murray, P. 1972 "Jim Crow and Jane Crow," Pp. 592–599 in G. Lerner (Ed.), *Black Women in White America*. New York: Vintage.

Mydans, S. 1990a "Science and the Courts Take a New Look at Motherhood," *New York Times* 4 November:6E.

———1990b "Homicide Rate Up for Young Blacks," *New York Times* 7 December:A26.

———1984 "Imbalances in Pay for Women Examined by City," *New York Times* 12 February:54.

Myers, M.A., and S.M. Talarico 1986 "The Social Contexts of Racial Discrimination in Sentencing," *Social Problems* 33:236–251.

Myers, R.A. 1986 "Female and Male Perceptions of Female Genital Operations in Six Southern Nigerian Ethnic Groups," *WID Forum*, 86-IX. East Lansing: Michigan State University.

n.a. 1982 *Spinning a Sacred Yarn*. New York: The Pilgrim Press.

Nagel, I.H., J. Cardascia, and C.E. Ross 1982 "Sex Differences in the Processing of Criminal Defendants," Pp. 259–282 in D.K. Weisberg (Ed.), *Women and the Law*. Cambridge, MA: Schenkman.

Nagel, S., and L.J. Weitzman 1972 "The Double Standard of American Justice," *Society* 9:171–198.

Nash, A. 1989 "Will Women Change Prime-Time TV News?" *Glamour* (October):242:245, 312–315.

Nazarri, M. 1983 "The 'Woman Question' in Cuba: An Analysis of Material Constraints on Its Solution," *Signs* 9:246–263.

Nelson, M. 1988 "Providing Family Day Care: An Analysis of Home-Based Work," *Social Problems* 35:78–94.

Nelson, M. 1979 "Why Witches Were Women," Pp. 451–468 in J. Freeman (Ed.), *Women: A Feminist Perspective* (2nd edition), Palo Alto, CA: Mayfield.

Neuberger, J. 1983 "Women in Judaism: the Fact and the Fiction," Pp. 132–142 in P. Holden (Ed.), *Women's Religious Experience: Cross-Cultural Perspectives*. London: Croom Helm.

Nevels, L. 1990 "Mentoring Relationships and Women," Paper presented at the Annual Meeting of the Mid-Atlantic Association of Student Officers of Housing, Women's Issues Group, Glasboro, NJ.

New York Times 1990 "Where French Course is Cause Celebre," 4 March:35.

———1990 "Domestic Violence is Target of Bill," 16 December:31.

———1990 "Nature of Clothing Isn't Evidence in Rape Cases, Florida Law Says," 3 June:30.

———1990 "Governing Party is Ousted in 14 States," 8 November:1A, B6.

———1990 "Winning a Seat in Congress in the 90s: High Costs, Changing Boundaries," 7 November:B2.

———1989 "Miller Beer Drops Ad After Protest," 13 March:D8.

———1989 "Juggling Family, Job and Aged Dependent," 26 January:B8.

———1989 "In New York City, There Are Many Ways to be Poor," *New York Times* 5 March:E6.

———1989 "Hasidim Attack Women at Prayers," *New York Times* 21 March:A3.

———1989 "Many AIDS Cases Go Unreported," *New York Times* 28 November:59.

———1988 "Portrait of the Electorate," 10 November:B6.

———1987 "Judges in Massachusetts Studying Spouse Abuse," 3 May:51.

———1987 "Supreme Court Reaffirms Rejection of a Reagan Tenet," 29 March:E1.

———1986 "Massachusetts to Look at Sex Bias in Courts," 10 August:37.

———1984 "Women in Clergy Called Low-Paid," 29 March:22.

———1984 "Supersexist?" 26 August:10F.

Nichols, P.C. 1986 "Women in Their Speech Communities," Pp. 140–149 in S. McConnell-Ginet, R. Borker, and N. Furman (Eds.), *Women and Language in Literature and Society*. New York: Greenwood.

Nicoloff, L.K., and E.A. Stiglitz 1987 "Lesbian Alcoholism: Etiology, Treatment, and Recovery," Pp.

283–293 in Boston Lesbian Psychologies Collective (Eds.), *Lesbian Psychologies*. Urbana: University of Illinois Press.

O'Brien. M., and A.C. Huston 1985 "Development of Sex-Typed Play Behavior in Toddlers," *Developmental Psychology* 21:866–871.

Offen, K. 1988 "Defining Feminism: A Comparative Historical Approach," *Signs* 14:119–157.

Ogden, A.S. 1986 *The Great American Housewife*. Westport, CT: Greenwood.

O'Hare, W.P. 1985 "Poverty in America: Trends and Patterns," *Population Bulletin* 40:1–42.

Older Women's League 1989 "Failing America's Caregivers: A Status Report on Women Who Care," *Mother's Day Report 1989*. Washington, D.C.: Older Women's League.

O'Kelly, C.G., and L.S. Carney 1986 *Women and Men in Society: Cross-cultural Perspectives on Gender Stratification*. Belmont, CA: Wadsworth.

O'Neill, W.L. 1986 "The Fight for Suffrage," *Wilson Quarterly* 10:99–109.

———1969 *Everyone Was Brave*. New York: Quadrangle.

Ortega, S.T., and J.L. Myles 1987 "Race and Gender Effects on Fear of Crime: An Interactive Model with Age," *Criminology* 25:133–152.

Owen, B.A. 1985 "Race and Gender Relations Among Prison Workers," *Crime and Delinquency* 31.

Pagelow, M.D. 1981 "Secondary Battering and Alternatives of Female Victims to Spouse Abuse," Pp. 277–298 in L.H. Bowker (Ed।)., *Women and Crime in America*. New York: Macmillan.

Pagels, E. 1979 "What Became of God the Mother?" Pp. 107–119 in C.P. Christ and J. Plakow (Eds.), *Womanspirit Rising*. San Francisco: Harper and Row.

Paige, K.E. 1975 "Effects of Oral Contraceptives on Affective Fluctuations Associated with the Menstrual Cycle," Pp. 193–204 in S. Hammer (Ed.), *Women: Body and Culture*. New York: Harper and Row.

Palley, M.L. 1987 "The Women's Movement in Recent American Politics," Pp. 150–181 in S.E. Rix (Ed.), *The American Woman 1987–88*. New York: Norton.

Paolantonio, S.A. 1987 "Abortion Law Hurts Poor, Study Says," *Philadelphia Inquirer* 15 February:10B.

Paradise, L.V., and S.M. Wall 1986 "Children's Perceptions of Male and Female Principals and Teachers," *Sex Roles* 14:1–7.

Parisi, N. 1982 "Are Females Treated Differently?" Pp. 205–220 in N.H. Rafter and E.A. Stanko (Eds.), *Judge, Lawyer, Victim, Thief*. Boston: Northeastern University Press.

Parlee, M.B. 1982 "New Findings: Menstrual Cycles and Behavior," *Ms.* (September):126–128.

Parry, B.L., S.L. Berga, D.F. Kripke, M.R. Klauber, G.A. Laughlin, S.S.C. Yen, and J.C. Gillin 1990 "Altered Waveform of Plasma Nocturnal Melatonin Secretion in Premenstrual Women," *Archives of General Psychiatry* 47:1139–1146.

Parsons, T. 1955 "The American Family: Its Relations to Personality and to the Social Structure," Pp. 3–33 in T. Parsons and R.F. Bales (Eds)., *Family, Socialization and Interaction Process*. Glencoe, IL: The Free Press.

Paul, M., C. Daniels, and R. Rosofsky 1989 "Corporate Response to Reproductive Hazards in the Workplace: Results of the Family, Work, and Health Survey," *American Journal of Industrial Medicine* 16:267–280.

Pear, R. 1987 "Number of Blacks in Top Jobs in Administration Off Sharply," *New York Times* 22 March:30.

Pearlman, S.F. 1987 "The Saga of Continuing Clash in the Lesbian Community, or Will an Army of Ex-lovers Fail?" Pp. 313–326 in Boston Lesbian Psychologies Collective (Eds.), *Lesbian Psychologies*. Urbana, IL: University of Illinois Press.

Peck, S. 1985 *Halls of Jade, Walls of Stone: Women in China Today*. New York: Franklin Watts.

Pedersen, F.A., and R.Q. Bell 1970 "Sex Differences in Preschool Children with Histories of Complications of Pregnancy and Delivery," *Developmental Psychology* 3:10–15.

Peretti, P.O., and T.M. Sydney 1985 "Parental Toy Choice Stereotyping and Its Effects on Child Toy Preference and Sex-Role Typing," *Social Behavior and Personality* 12:213–216.

Perlez, J. 1984 "Women, Power and Politics," *The New York Times Magazine* 24 June:22–31, 72–76.

Perrin, J.M., C.J. Homer, D.M. Berwick, A.D. Woolf, J.L. Freeman, and J.E. Wennberg 1989 "Variations in Rates of Hospitalization of Children in Three Urban Communities," *The New England Journal of Medicine* 320:1183–1187.

Perry, D.G., and K. Bussey 1979 "The Social Learning Theory of Sex Differences: Imitation is Alive and Well," *Journal of Personality and Social Psychology* 37:1699–1712.

Petro, C.S., and B.A. Putnam 1979 "Sex-Role Stereotypes: Issues of Attitudinal Changes," *Signs* 5:41–50.

Pfost, K.S., and M. Fiore 1990 "Pursuit of Nontraditional Occupations: Fear of Success or Fear of Not Being Chosen?" *Sex Roles* 23:15–24.

Philadelphia Inquirer 1986 "Won't Ride Buses Driven by Women," 14 September:13C.

Philips, R.D., and F.D. Gilroy 1985 "Sex-Role Stereotypes and Clinical Judgments of Mental Health: The Brovermans' Findings Reexamined," *Sex Roles* 12:179–193.

Phillips, F.B. 1978 "Magazine Heroines: Is *Ms.* Just Another Member of the Family Circle?" Pp. 116–124 in G. Tuchman, A.K. Daniels, and J. Benet (Eds.), *Hearth and Home*. New York: Oxford University Press.

Pillemer, K. 1985 "The Dangers of Dependency: New Findings on Domestic Violence Against the Elderly," *Social Problems* 33:146–158.

Pillemer, K., and D. Finkelhor 1988 "The Prevalence of Elder Abuse: A Random Sample Survey," *The Gerontologist* 28:51–57.

Pleck, J.H. 1983 "Husbands' Paid Work and Family Roles: Current Research Issues," Pp. 130–171 in H. Lopata and J.H. Pleck (eds.), *Research in the Interweave of Social Roles, Vol. 3, Families and Jobs*. Greenwich, CT: JAI Press.

Pogrebin, L.C. 1982 "Big Changes in Parenting," *Ms. Magazine* (February):41–46.

Pohli, C.V. 1983 "Church Closets and Back Doors: A Feminist View of Moral Majority Women," *Feminist Studies* 9:529–558.

Polivy, Janet, and C. Peter Herman 1985 "Dieting and Binging: A Causal Analysis," *American Psychologist* 40:193–201.

Polman, D. 1985 "A Backlash Against Gays as Parents," *Philadelphia Inquirer* 21 July:1F, 6F.

Poole, K.T., and L.H. Zeigler 1985 *Women, Public Opinion, and Politics*. New York: Longman.

Pope John Paul II 1988 "On the Dignity and Vocation of Women," apostolic letter, 15 August.

Prather, J.E., and L.S. Fidell 1978 "Drug Use and Abuse Among Women: An Overview," *The International Journal of Addiction* 13:863–885.

Pratt, N.F. 1980 "Transitions in Judaism: The Jewish American Woman Through the 1930s," Pp 207–228 in J.W. James (Ed.), *Women in American Religion*. Philadelphia: University of Pennsylvania Press.

Price, B.R., N.J. Sokoloff, and I. Kuleshnyk 1989 "Is Police Work Changing as a Result of Women's Contributions?" Paper presented at the Annual Meeting of the American Society of Criminology, Reno, NV.

Price-Bonham, S., and P. Skeen 1982 "Black and White Fathers' Attitudes Toward Children's Sex Roles," *Psychological Reports* 50:1187–1190.

Prinsky, L.E., and J.L. Rosenbaum 1987 "Leer-ics or Lyrics?" *Youth and Society* 18:384–393.

Project on the Status and Education of Women 1986a "Supreme Court Rules on Sexual Harassment," *On Campus With Women* 16(#2):5

———1986b "Studying Men . . . Formally," *On Campus With Women* 16(#2):11.

———1986c "Setting Their Sights on the Ministry," *On Campus With Women* 16(#2):4.

Purcell, P., and L. Stewart 1990 "Dick and Jane in 1989," *Sex Roles* 22:177–185.

Quester, G.H. 1982 "The Problem," Pp. 217–236 in N.L. Goldman (Ed.), *Female Soldiers— Combatants or Noncombatants?* Westport, CT: Greenwood Press.

Quindlen, A. 1987 "Baby Craving," *Life Magazine* (June):23–42.

Quinn, P., and K.R. Allen 1989 "Facing Challenges and Making Compromises: How Single Mothers Endure," *Family Relations* 38:390–395.

Quintanales, M. 1983 "I Paid Very Hard for My Immigrant Ignorance," Pp. 361–364 in L. Richardson and V. Taylor (Eds.), *Feminist Frontiers*. Reading, MA: Addison-Wesley.

Rada, R. 1978 *Clinical Aspects of Rape.* New York: Grune and Stratton.

Raiborn, M.H. 1990 *Revenues and Expenses of Intercollegiate Athletics Programs.* Overland Park, KS: The National Collegiate Athletic Association.

Raines, H. 1983 "Poll Shows Support for Political Gains by Women in U.S.," *New York Times* 27 November:1, 40.

Rankin, D. 1987 "Living Together as a Way of Life," *New York Times* 31 May:F11.

Rapp, R. 1982 "Family and Class in Contemporary America: Notes Toward an Understanding of Ideology," Pp. 168–187 in B. Thorne (Ed.), *Rethinking the Family.* New York: Longman.

Raskin, P.A., and A.C. Isreal 1981 "Sex-Role Imitation in Children: Effects of Sex of Child, Sex of Model, and Sex-Role Appropriateness of Modeled Behavior," *Sex Roles* 7:1067–1077.

Rawlings, E.I., and D.K. Carter (Eds.) 1977 *Psychotherapy for Women: Treatment Toward Equality.* Springfield, IL: Charles C. Thomas.

Raymond, J.G. 1990 "Fetalists and Feminists: They Are Not the Same," Pp. 257–261 in S. Ruth (Ed.), *Issues in Feminism.* Mountain View, CA: Mayfield.

Reid, P.T. 1982 "Socialization of Black Female Children," Pp. 137–155 in P. Berman (Ed.), *Women: A Developmental Perspective.* Bethesda, MD: National Institute of Health.

Reid, S.T. 1987 *Criminal Justice.* St. Paul, MN: West.

Reilly, M.E., B. Lott, and S.M. Gallogly 1986 "Sexual Harassment of University Students," *Sex Roles* 15:333–358.

Reinisch, J.M. 1983 "Influence of Early Exposure to Steroid Hormones on Behavioral Development," Pp. 63–113 in W. Everaerd, C.B. Hindley, A. Bot, and J.J. van der Werff ten Bosch (Eds.), *Development in Adolescence.* Boston: Martinus Nijhoff Publishers.

Reiss, I.L. 1986 *Journey into Sexuality: An Exploratory Voyage.* Englewood Cliffs, NJ: Prentice-Hall.

Rent, C.S., and G.S. Rent 1977 "More on Offspring-Sex Preference: A Comment on Nancy E. Williamson's 'Sex Preferences, Sex Control and the Status of Women' ", *Signs* 3:505–513.

Renzetti, C.M. 1988 "Violence in Lesbian Relationships: A Preliminary Analysis of Causal Factors," *Journal of Interpersonal Violence* 3:381–399.

———1987 "New Wave or Second Stage? Attitudes of College Women Toward Feminism," *Sex Roles* 16:265–277.

———1983 "One Step Forward, Two Steps Back: Women, Work and Employment Legislation," Pp. 395–404 in J. McCall and J. Des Jardins (Eds.), *Business Ethics.* Belmont, CA: Wadsworth.

Renzetti, C.M., and D.J. Curran 1986 "Structural Constraints on Legislative Reform," *Contemporary Crises* 10:137–155.

Reskin, B.A., and H.I. Hartmann (Eds.) 1986 *Women's Work, Men's Work: Sex Segregation on the Job.* Washington, D.C.: National Academy Press.

Rheingold, H.L., and K.V. Cook 1975 "The Content of Boys' and Girls' Rooms as an Index of Parents' Behavior" *Child Development* 46:459–463.

Rhode, D.L. 1990 "Theoretical Perspectives on Sexual Difference," Pp. 1–12 in D.L. Rhode (Ed.), *Theoretical Perspectives on Sexual Difference.* New Haven, CT: Yale University Press.

———1986 "Feminist Perspectives on Legal Ideology," Pp. 151–160 in J. Mitchell and A. Oakley (Eds.), *What is Feminism? A Re-Examination.* New York: Pantheon.

Rice, J.K., and A. Hemmings 1988 "Women's Colleges and Women Achievers: An Update," *Signs* 13:546–559.

Rich, A. 1980 "Compulsory Heterosexuality and Lesbian Existence," *Signs* 5:631–660.

Richardson, L.W. 1981 *The Dynamics of Sex and Gender.* Boston: Houghton Mifflin.

Richmond, P. 1987 "How Do Men Feel About Their Bodies?" *Glamour* (May):312–313, 369–372.

Riger, S. 1988 "Comment on 'Women's History Goes to Trial: EEOC v. Sears Roebuck and Company,' " *Signs* 13:897–903.

Ritzer, G. 1980 *Sociology: A Multi-Paradigm Science.* Boston: Allyn and Bacon.

Rix, S. (Ed.) 1987 *The American Woman 1987–88.* New York: W.W. Norton.

Roberts, H. 1981 "Women and Their Doctors: Power and Powerlessness in the Research Process," Pp. 7–29 in H. Roberts (Ed.), *Doing Feminist Research* London: Routledge and Kegan Paul.

Robertson, C., C.E. Dyer, and D. Campbell 1988 "Campus Harassment: Sexual Harassment Policies and Procedures at Institutions of Higher Learning," *Signs* 13:792–812.

Robertson, I. 1987 *Sociology.* New York: Worth.

Robertson, J., and L.F. Fitzgerald 1990 "The (Mis)Treatment of Men: Effects of Client Gender Role and Life-Style on Diagnosis and Attribution of Pathology," *Journal of Counseling Psychology* 37:3–9.

Robinson, C.C., and J.T. Morris 1986 "The Gender-Stereotyped Nature of Christmas Toys Received by 36-, 48-, and 60-Month-Old Children: A Comparison Between Nonrequested and Requested Toys," *Sex Roles* 15:21–32.

Robinson, J. 1982 'Cancer of the Cervix: Occupational Risks of Husbands and Wives and Possible Preventive Strategies," Pp. 11–27 in J.A. Jordan, F. Sharp, and A. Singer (Eds.), *Pre-clinical Neoplasia of the Cervix.* London: Royal College of Obstetricians and Gynecologists.

Robinson, J.G., and J.S. McIlwee 1989 "Women in Engineering: A Promise Unfulfilled?" *Social Problems* 36:455–472.

Rogers, L., and J. Walsh 1982 "Shortcomings of the Psychomedical Research of John Money and Co-Workers into Sex Differences in Behavior: Social and Political Implications," *Sex Roles* 8: 269–281.

Rogers, S.C. 1978 "Woman's Place: A Critical Review of Anthropological Theory," *Comparative Studies in Society and History* 20:123–162.

Rohter, L. 1987 "Women Gain Degrees, but Not Tenure," *New York Times* 4 January:E9.

Roof, W.C., and J.L. Roof 1984 "Review of the Polls: Images of God Among Americans," *Journal for the Scientific Study of Religion* 23:201–205.

Roos, P. 1985 *Gender and Work: A Comparative Analysis of Industrial Societies.* Albany: State University of New York Press.

Root, M.P.P. 1990 "Disordered Eating in Women of Color," *Sex Roles* 22:525–536.

Rosen, L.W., C.L. Shafer, G.M. Dummer, L.K. Cross, G.W. Deuman, and S.R. Malmberg 1988 "Prevalence of Pathogenic Weight-control Behaviors Among Native American Women and Girls," *International Journal of Eating Disorders* 7:807–811.

Rosenberg, H.G. 1984 "The Home is the Workplace: Hazards, Stress, and Pollutants in the Household," Pp. 219–245 in W. Chavkin (Ed.), *Double Exposure.* New York: Monthly Review Press.

Rosenfeld, R.A. 1984 "Academic Career Mobility for Women and Men Psychologists," Pp. 89–127 in V.B. Haas and C.C. Perrucci (Eds.), *Women in Scientific and Engineering Professions.* Ann Arbor, MI: University of Michigan Press.

Rosenhan, D.L. 1973 "On Being Sane in Insane Places," *Science* 179:250–258.

Rosenwasser, S.M., R. Rogers, S. Fling, K. Silvers-Pickens, and J. Butemeyer 1987 "Attitudes Toward Women and Men in Politics: Perceived Male and Female Candidate Competencies and Participant Personality Characteristics," *Political Psychology* 8:191–200.

Rossi, A.S. 1984 "Gender and Parenthood," *American Sociological Review* 49:1–18.

——— 1977 "A Biosocial Perspective on Parenting," *Daedulus* 106:1–31.

——— 1973 *The Feminist Papers.* New York: Bantam.

Rossi, A.S., and P.E. Rossi 1977 "Body Time and Social Time: Mood Patterns by Menstrual Cycle Phase and Day of the Week," *Social Science Research* 6:273–308.

Rothblum, E.D. 1982 "Women's Socialization and the Prevalence of Depression: The Feminine Mistake," *Women and Therapy* 1:5–13.

Rothman, B.K. 1989 *Recreating Motherhood.* New York: W.W. Norton.

——— 1986 "Midwives in Transition: The Structure of a Clinical Revolution," Pp. 345–353 in P. Conrad and R. Kern (Eds.), *The Sociology of Health and Illness.* New York: St. Martin's Press.

——— 1984 "Women, Health and Medicine," Pp. 70–80 in J. Freeman (Ed.), *Women: A Feminist Perspective.* Palo Alto, CA: Mayfield.

Rothschild, E. 1988 "The Reagan Economic Legacy," *New York Review of Books* 21 July:33–41.

Rowbotham, S. 1989 *The Past Before Us: Feminism in Action Since the 1960s.* London: Unwin Hyman.

Rowland, R. 1986 "Women Who Do and Women Who Don't, Join the Women's Movement: Issues for Conflict and Collaboration," *Sex Roles* 679–692.

Rubin, G. 1975 "The Traffic in Women," Pp. 157–211 in R.R. Reiter (Ed.), *Toward an Anthropology of Women*. New York: Monthly Review Press.

Rubin, J.Z., F.J. Provenzano, and Z. Luria 1974 "The Eye of the Beholder: Parents' Views on Sex of Newborns," *American Journal of Orthopsychiatry* 44:512–519.

Rubin, K. 1987 "Whose Job is Child Care?" *Ms.* (March):32–44.

Rubin, R.T. 1987 "The Neuroendocrinology and Neurochemistry of Antisocial Behavior," Pp. 239–262 in S.A. Mednick, T.E. Moffitt, and S.A. Stack (Eds.), *The Causes of Crime: New Biological Approaches*. New York: Cambridge University Press.

Ruble, D.N. 1977 "Menstrual Symptoms: A Reinterpretation," *Science* 197:291–292.

Ruether, R.R. 1983 *Sexism and God-Talk*. Boston: Beacon Press.

Runfola, R. 1980 "The Black Athlete as Super-Machismo Symbol," Pp. 79–88 in D.S. Sabo and R. Runfola (Eds.), *Jock: Sports and Male Identity*. Englewood Cliffs, NJ: Prentice-Hall.

Russell, D.E.H. 1990 *Rape in Marriage* (rev. ed.). Bloomington, IN: Indiana University Press.

———1986 *The Secret Trauma*. New York: Basic Books.

Russell, D.E.H., and N. Van de Ven (Eds.) 1976 *Crimes Against Women: Proceedings of the International Tribunal*. Mulbrae, CA: les Femmes.

Russo, A. 1987 "Conflicts and Contradictions Among Feminists Over Issues of Pornography and Sexual Freedom," *Women's Studies International Forum* 10:103–112.

Rustad, M. 1982 *Women in Khaki*. New York: Praeger.

Ruzek, S. 1987 "Feminist Visions of Health: An International Perspective," Pp. 184–207 in J. Mitchell and A. Oakley (Eds.), *What is Feminism? A Re-Examination*. New York: Pantheon.

Rytina, N.F., and S.M. Bianchi 1984 "Occupational Reclassification and Changes in Distribution by Gender," *Monthly Labor Review* 107:11–17.

Sabo, D.F. 1980 "Getting Beyond Exercise as Work," Pp. 291–299 in D.F. Sabo and R. Runfola (Eds.), *Jock: Sports and Male Identity*. Englewood Cliffs, NJ: Prentice-Hall.

Sabo, D.F., and R. Ronfola 1980 *Jock: Sports and Male Identity*. Englewood Cliffs, NJ: Prentice-Hall.

Sachs, A., and J.H. Wilson 1978 *Sexism and the Law*. New York: The Free Press.

Sacks, K. 1979 *Sisters and Wives*. Westport, CT: Greenwood Press.

Sadker, M., and D. Sadker 1985a "Striving for Equity in Classroom Teaching," Pp. 442–455 in Alice G. Sargent (Ed.), *Beyond Sex Roles*. New York: West.

———1985b "Sexism in the Schoolroom of the '80s," *Psychology Today* March:54–57.

———1980 "Sexism in Teacher-Education Texts," *Harvard Educational Review* 50:36–46.

Safir, M.P. 1986 "The Effects of Nature or of Nurture on Sex Differences in Intellectual Functioning: Israeli Findings," *Sex Roles* 14:581–589.

Saline, C. 1984 "Bleeding in the Suburbs," *Philadelphia Magazine* (March):81–85, 144–151.

Sanchez-Ayendez, M. 1986 "Puerto Rican Elderly Women: Shared Meanings and Informal Supportive Networks," Pp. 172–186 in J.B. Cole (Ed.), *All American Women*. New York: Free Press.

Sanday, P.R. 1981 *Female Power and Male Dominance: On the Origins of Sexual Inequality*. New York: Cambridge University Press.

Sanders, M., and M. Rock 1988 *Waiting for Prime Time: The Women of Television News*. New York: Harper Collins.

Sandler, B.R., and R.M. Hall 1986 "The Campus Climate Revisited: Chilly for Women Faculty Administrators, and Graduate Students," Washington, D.C.: Project on the Status and Education of Women.

Sapiro, V. 1986 *Women in American Society*. Palo Alto, CA: Mayfield.

———1982 "Private Costs of Public Commitments or Public Costs of Private Commitments? Family Roles versus Political Ambition," *American Journal of Political Science* 26:265–279.

Sarri, R.C. 1986 "Gender and Race Differences in Criminal Justice Processing," *Women's Studies International Forum* 9:89–99.

Saunders, D.G. 1989 "Who Hits First and Who Hurts Most? Evidence for the Greater Victimization of

Women in Intimate Relationships," Paper presented at the Annual Meeting of the American Society of Criminology, Reno, NV.

Sayers, J. 1987 "Science, Sexual Difference, and Feminism," Pp. 68–91 in B.B. Hess and M.M. Ferree (Eds.), *Analyzing Gender.* Newbury Park, CA: Sage.

Schaffer, M.D. 1987 "A Church Debate on Sexuality," *Philadelphia Inquirer* 22 March:1F, 6F.

Schmalz, J. 1986 "Pervasive Sex Bias Found in Courts," *New York Times* 20 April:1, 40.

Schmidt, W.E. 1989 "Study Links Male Unemployment and Single Mothers in Chicago," *New York Times* 15 January:16.

Schmitt, E. 1990 "2 out of 3 Women in Military Study Report Sexual Harassment Incidents," *New York Times* 12 September:A22.

Schneider, J., and S. Hacker 1973 "Sex Role Imagery in the Use of the Generic 'Man' in Introductory Texts: A Case in the Sociology of Sociology," *American Sociologist* 8:12–18.

Schur, E.M. 1984 *Labeling Women Deviant.* New York: Random House.

Schussler Fiorenza, E. 1983 *In Memory of Her: A Feminist Theological Reconstruction of Christian Origins.* New York: Crossroad.

———1979 "Women in the Early Christian Movement," Pp. 84–92 in C. P. Christ and J. Plaskow (Eds.), *Womanspirit Rising.* San Francisco: Harper and Row.

Schwager, S. 1987 "Educating Women in America," *Signs* 12:333–372.

Schwartz, F.N. 1989 "Management Women and the New Facts of Life," *Harvard Business Review* (January–February):65–76.

Schwartz, L.A., and W.T. Markham 1985 "Sex Stereotyping in Children's Toy Advertisements," *Sex Roles* 12:157–170.

Sciolino, E. 1990 "Battle Lines are Shifting on Women in War," *New York Times* 25 January:A1, D23.

Scott, H. 1974 *Does Socialism Liberate Women?* Boston: Beacon Press.

Scott, J.A. 1984 "Keeping Women in Their Place: Exclusionary Policies and Reproduction," Pp. 180–195 in W. Cahvkin (Ed.), *Double Exposure.* New York: Monthly Review Press.

Scully, D., and J. Marolla 1985 " 'Riding the Bull at Gilley's': Convicted Rapists Describe the Rewards of Rape," *Social Problems* 32:251–263.

Sears, D.O., and C.L. Funk 1990 "Self-Interest in Americans' Political Opinions," Pp. 147–170 in J.J. Mansbridge (Ed.), *Beyond Self-Interest.* Chicago: University of Chicago Press.

Seegmiller, B.R., B. Suter, and N. Duviant 1980 *Personal, Socioeconomic, and Sibling Influences on Sex-Role Differentiation.* Urbana, IL: ERIC Clearinghouse of Elementary and Early Childhood Education, ED 176 895, College of Education, University of Illinois.

Seldon, G. 1983 "Frailty, Thy Name's Been Changed: What Sports Medicine is Discovering About Women's Bodies," Pp. 129–133 in L. Richardson and V. Taylor (Eds.), *Feminist Frontiers.* Reading, MA: Addison-Wesley.

Serbin, L.A., D.K. O'Leary, R.M. Kent, and I.J. Tonick 1973 "A Comparison of Teacher Response to the Preacademic and Problem Behavior of Boys and Girls," *Child Development* 44:796–784.

Serrin, W. 1984 "Experts Say Job Bias Against Women Persists," *New York Times* 25 November:1, 32.

Shakin, M., D. Shakin, and S.H. Sternglanz 1985 "Infant Clothing: Sex Labeling for Strangers," *Sex Roles* 12:955–964.

Shapiro, L. 1990 "Guns and Dolls," *Newsweek* 28 May:56–65.

Shaw, N.S. 1982 "Female Patients and the Medical Profession in Jails and Prisons: A Case Study of Quintuple Jeopardy," Pp. 261–276 in N. H. Rafter and E. A. Stanko (Eds.), *Judge, Lawyer, Victim, Thief.* Boston: Northeastern University Press.

Sherman, B.L., and J.R. Dominick 1986 "Violence and Sex in Music Videos: TV and Rock 'n Roll," *Journal of Communication* 36:94–106.

Sherman, J.A. 1983 "Girls Talk About Mathematics and Their Future: A Partial Replication," *Psychology of Women Quarterly* 7:338–342.

———1982 "Mathematics the Critical Filter: A Look at Some Residues," *Psychology of Women Quarterly* 6:428–444.

———1978 *Sex-Related Cognitive Differences: An Essay on Theory and Evidence.* Springfield, IL: Charles C. Thomas.

_____1971 *On the Psychology of Women: A Survey of Empirical Studies.* Springfield, IL: C.C. Thomas.

Sherman, L.W., and R.A. Berk 1984 "The Specific Deterrent Effects of Arrest for Domestic Assault," *American Sociological Review* 49:261–272.

Shostak, M. 1981 *Nisa: The Life and Words of a !Kung Woman.* Cambridge, MA: Harvard University Press.

Shulman, A.K. 1980 "Sex and Power: Sexual Bases of Radical Feminism," *Signs* 5: 590–604.

Sichel, J., L.N. Friedman, J.C. Quint, and M.E. Smith 1977 *Women on Patrol.* New York: Vera Institute of Justice.

Sidel, R. 1986 *Women and Children Last.* New York: Penguin Books.

Sidorowicz, L., and G.S. Lunney 1980 "Baby X Revisited," *Sex Roles* 6:67–73.

Sifford, D. 1984 "Homosexuality: Not a Matter of Choice, But a Matter of Fact," *Philadelphia Inquirer* 19 March:8E.

Silveira, J. 1980 "Generic Masculine Words and Thinking," *Women's Studies International Quarterly* 3:165–178.

Silverman, I.J., M. Vega, and J. Accardi 1976 "Female Criminality in a Southern City: A Comparison Over the Decade 1962–1972," Paper presented at the Annual Meeting of the American Society of Criminology, Toronto.

Silverstein, B., L. Perdue, B. Peterson, and E. Kelly 1986 "The Role of the Mass Media in Promoting a Thin Standard of Bodily Attractiveness for Women," *Sex Roles* 14:519–532.

Simon, R. 1975 *Women and Crime.* Washington, D.C.: U.S. Government Printing Office.

Skelly, G.U., and W.J. Lundstrom 1981 "Male Sex Roles in Magazine Advertising, 1959–1979. *Journal of Communication* 31:52–57.

Skitka, L.J., and C. Maslach 1990 "Gender Roles and the Categorization of Gender-Relevant Behavior," *Sex Roles* 22:133–150.

Slocum, S. 1975 "Woman the Gatherer: Male Bias in Anthropology," Pp. 36–50 in R.R. Reiter (ed.), *Toward an Anthropology of Women.* New York: Monthly Review Press.

Small, M.A., and P.A. Tetreault 1990 "Social Psychology, 'Marital Rape Exemptions,' and Privacy," *Behavioral Sciences and the Law* 8:141–149.

Smart, C. 1982 "The New Female Offender: Reality or Myth?" Pp. 105–116 in B.R. Price and N.J. Sokoloff (Eds.), *The Criminal Justice System and Women.* New York: Clark Boardman.

Smith, B. 1986 "Black Lesbian/Feminist Organizing: A Conversation," Pp. 410–419 in J.B. Cole (Ed.), *All American Women.* New York: Free Press.

Smith, E. 1982 "The Black Female Adolescent," *Psychology of Women Quarterly* 6:261–288.

Smith, J. 1987 "Transforming Households: Working-Class Women and Economic Crisis," *Social Problems* 34:416–436.

_____1984 "The Paradox of Women's Poverty: Wage-Earning Women and Economic Transformation," *Signs* 10:291–310.

Smith, P.M. 1985 *Language, Society, and the Sexes.* New York: Basil Blackwell.

Smith, S.A., and M. Tienda 1988 "The Doubly Disadvantaged: Women of Color in the U.S. Labor Force," Pp. 61–80 in A.H. Stromberg and S. Harkess (Eds.), *Women Working.* Mountain View, CA: Mayfield.

Snell, W.E., Jr., S.S. Belk, and R.C. Hawkins II 1987 "Alcohol and Drug Use in Stressful Times: The Influence of the Masculine Role and Sex-Related Personality Traits," *Sex Roles* 16:359–374.

Synder, F. 1986 "Jewish Prayer Group Incites Rabbis' Ire," *New Directions for Women* November/December:13–14.

Sokoloff, N.J. 1988 "Evaluating Gains and Losses by Black and White Women and Men in the Professions, 1960–1980," *Social Problems* 35:36–55.

Sokoloff, N.J., and B.R. Price 1982 "The Criminal Law and Women," Pp. 9–34 in B.R. Price and N.J. Sokoloff (Eds.), *The Criminal Justice System and Women.* New York: Clark Boardman.

Sommer, B. 1983 "How Does Menstruation Affect Cognitive Competence and Psychophysiological Response," Pp. 53–90 in S. Golub (Ed.), *Lifting the Curse of Menstruation.* New York: Haworth Press.

Sonne, J.L., and K.S. Pope 1991 "Treating Victims of Therapist-Patient Sexual Involvement," *Psychotherapy* 28:174–187.

Sparkman, K. 1985 "Eating Disorders: Thin is In, but . . ." *Image* (Winter):6–7.

Specter, M. 1988 "U.S. Projects 450,000 with AIDS by '94," *Philadelphia Inquirer* 5 June:1A, 6A.

Speizer, J.J. 1981 "Role Models, Mentors, and Sponsors: The Elusive Concepts," *Signs* 6:692–712.

Spender, D. 1981 "The GateKeepers: A Feminist Critique of Academic Publishing," Pp. 186–202 in H. Roberts (Ed.), *Doing Feminist Research*. London: Routledge and Kegan Paul.

Sperry, R. 1982 "Some Effects of Disconnecting the Cerebral Hemispheres," *Science* 217:1223–1226.

Spielberger, C., and P. London 1985 "Rage Boomerangs," Pp. 77–79 in C. Borg (Ed.), *Annual Editions: Health 85/86*. Guilford, CT: The Dushkin Publishing Group.

Springer, S.P., and G. Deutsch 1985 *Left Brain, Right Brain*. San Francisco: Freeman.

Stacey, J. 1986 "Are Feminists Afraid to Leave Home? The Challenge of Conservative Pro-Family Feminism," Pp. 208–237 in J. Mitchell and A. Oakley (Eds.), *What is Feminism? A Re-Examination*. New York: Pantheon.

Stacey, J., and B. Thorne 1985 "The Missing Feminist Revolution in Sociology," *Social Problems* 32:301–316.

Stack, C. 1974 *All Our Kin*. New York: Harper Colophon.

Stanback, M.H. 1985 "Language and Black Woman's Place: Some Evidence from the Black Middle Class," Pp. 177–193 in P. Treichler, C. Kramarae, and B. Stafford (Eds)., *For Alma Mater*. Urbana, IL: University of Illinois Press.

Stanko, E.A. 1985 *Intimate Intrusions*. London: Routledge and Kegan Paul.

Stansell, C. 1986 *City of Women*. New York: Alfred A. Knopf.

Stanworth, M. 1983 *Gender and Schooling*. London: Hutchinson.

Staples, R., and T. Jones 1985 "Culture, Ideology and Black Television Images," *The Black Scholar* 16:10–20.

Star, S.L. 1979 "The Politics of Right and Left: Sex Differences in Hemispheric Brain Asymmetry," Pp. 61–74 in R. Hubbard, M.S. Henifin, and B. Fried (Eds.), *Women Looking At Biology Looking At Women*. Cambridge, MA: Schenkman.

Starhawk 1979 "Witchcraft and Women's Culture," Pp. 259–268 in C.P. Christ and J. Plaskow (Eds.), *Womanspirit Rising*. San Francisco: Harper and Row.

Staudt, K. and J. Jaquette 1988 "Women's Programs, Bureaucratic Resistance, and Feminist Organizations," Pp. 263–281 in E. Boneparth and E. Stoper (Eds.), *Women, Power and Policy: Toward the Year 2000*. New York: Pergamon.

Steenland, S. 1988 *Growing Up in Prime Time: An Analysis of Adolescent Girls on Television*. Washington, DC: National Commission on Working Women.

————1987 "Women in Broadcasting," Pp. 215–221 in S.E. Rix (Ed.), *The American Woman 1987–88*. New York: Norton.

Steffensmeier, D.J. 1982 "Trends in Female Crime: It's Still a Man's World," Pp. 117–130 in B. R. Price and N. J. Sokoloff (Eds.), *The Criminal Justice System and Women*. New York: Clark Boardman.

Stein, D.K. 1978 "Women to Burn: Suttee as a Normative Institution," *Signs* 4:253–268.

Steinbacher, R., and F.D. Gilroy 1985 "Preference for Sex of Child Among Primiparous Women," *The Journal of Psychology* 119:541–547.

Steinberg, R., and L. Haignere 1985 "Equitable Compensation: Methodological Criteria for Comparable Worth." Paper presented at the conference on "Ingredients for Women's Employment Policy," Albany, NY.

Steinberg, R.J., and A. Cook 1988 "Policies Affecting Women's Employment in Industrial Countries," Pp. 307–328 in A.H. Stromberg and S. Harkess (Eds.), *Women Working*. Mountain View, CA: Mayfield.

Steinem, G. 1978 "Erotica and Pornography: A Clear and Present Difference," *Ms. Magazine* (November):53–54, 75–78.

Steinfels, P. 1990a "U.S. Bishops Take a Harder Line in a Statement on Women's Issues," *New York Times* 3 April:A1, A21.

———1990b "Has Catholicism Lost a Chance to be Our Moral Clearinghouse?" *New York Times* 8 April:E1.

———1988 "Methodists Vote to Retain Policy Condemning Homosexual Behavior," *New York Times* 3 May:22

Steinmetz, S.K. 1978 "The Battered Husband Syndrome," *Victimology* 2:499–509.

Steinmetz, S.K., and D.J. Amsden 1983 "Dependent Elders, Family Stress, and Abuse," Pp. 173–192 in T. Brubaker (Ed.), *Family Relationships in Later Life*. Beverly Hills, CA: Sage.

Stiehm, J.H. 1985 "The Generations of U.S. Enlisted Women," *Signs* 11:155–175.

Stimpson, C.R. 1987 "Foreword," Pp. xi–xiv in H. Brod (Ed.), *The Making of Masculinities*. Boston: Allen and Unwin.

Stobaugh, S. 1985 "Housework: It Isn't Going to Go Away," *Philadelphia Inquirer* 1 September:I1, I4.

Stoddart, T., and E. Turiel 1985 "Children's Concepts of Cross-Gender Activities," *Child Development* 56:1241–1252.

Stone, M. 1976 *When God Was a Woman*. New York: Harcourt Brace Jovanovich.

Stoneman, Z., G.H. Brody, and C.E. MacKinnon 1986 "Same-Sex and Cross-Sex Siblings: Activity Choices, Roles, Behavior, and Gender Stereotypes," *Sex Roles* 15:495–511.

Stout, H. 1988 "Propping Up Payments at the Bottom," *New York Times* 24 January:4F.

St. Peter, S. 1979 "Jack Went Up the Hill . . . but Where was Jill?" *Psychology of Women Quarterly* 4:256–260.

Straus, M.A., and R.J. Gelles 1990 "How Violent are American Families? Estimates from the National Family Violence Resurvey and Other Studies," Pp. 95–132 in M.A. Straus and R.J. Gelles (Eds.), *Physical Violence in American Families*. New Brunswick, NJ: Transaction Publishers.

Straus, M.A., and C. Smith 1990 "Family Patterns and Child Abuse," Pp. 245–262 in M.A. Straus and R.J. Gelles (Eds.), *Physical Violence in American Families*. New Brunswick, NJ: Transaction Publishers.

Strauss-Noll, M. 1984 "An Illustration of Sex Bias in English," *Women's Studies Quarterly* 12:36–37.

Strober, M.H., and C.L. Arnold 1987 "The Dynamics of Occupational Segregation among Bank Tellers," Pp. 107–158 in C. Brown and J.A. Pechman (Eds.), *Gender in the Workplace*. Washington, DC: The Brookings Institution.

Strober, M.H., and A.G. Lanford 1986 "The Feminization of Public School Teaching: Cross-Sectional Analysis, 1850–1880," *Signs* 11:212–235.

Strober, M.H., and D. Tyack 1980 "Why Do Women Teach and Men Manage? A Report on Research on Schools," *Signs* 5:494–503.

Stunkard, A.J., J.R. Harris, N.L. Pedersen, and G.E. McClearn 1990 "The Body-Mass Index of Twins Who Have Been Reared Apart," *The New England Journal of Medicine* 322:1483–1487.

Sutker, P.B., A.T. Patsiokas, and A.N. Allain 1981 "Chronic Illicit Drug Abusers: Gender Comparisons," *Psychological Reports* 49:383–390.

Szasz, T.S. 1974 *The Myth of Mental Illness*. New York: Harper and Row.

Taeuber, C.M., and V. Valdisera 1986 *Women in the American Economy*. Current Population Reports, Series P-23, #146. Washington, D.C.: U.S. Government Printing Office.

Tannen, D. 1990 *You Just Don't Understand*. New York: William Morrow.

Tanner, N., and A. Zihlman 1976 "Women in Evolution. Part I: Innovation and Selection in Human Origins," *Signs* 1:585–608.

Tartre, L.A. 1990 "Spatial Skills, Gender, and Mathematics," Pp. 27–59 in E. Fennema and G. Leder (Eds.), *Mathematics and Gender*. New York: Teachers College Press.

Teachman, J.D., and P.T. Schollaert 1989 "Gender of Children and Birth Timing," *Demography* 26:411–426.

Teilmann, K.S., and P.H. Landry, Jr. 1981 "Gender Bias in Juvenile Justice," *Journal of Research in Crime and Delinquency* 18:47–80.

Teleki, G. 1975 "Primate Subsistence Patterns: Collector-Predators and Gatherer-Hunters," *Journal of Human Evolution* 4:125–184.

Temkin, J. 1986 "Women, Rape, and Law Reform," Pp. 16–40 in S. Tomaselli and R. Porter (Eds.), *Rape*. New York: Basil Blackwell.

Terrelonge, P. 1984 "Feminist Consciousness and Black Women," Pp. 557–567 in J. Freeman (Ed.), *Women: A Feminist Perspective.* Palo Alto, CA: Mayfield.

Terry, R.M. 1978 "Trends in Female Crime: A Comparison of Adler, Simon, and Steffensmeier." Paper presented at the Annual Meeting of the Society for the Study of Social Problems, San Francisco, CA.

Theroux, P. 1987 "TV Women Have Come a Long Way, Baby—Sort Of," *New York Times* 17 May:H35.

Thomas, C.S. 1982 *Sex Discrimination.* St. Paul, MN: West.

Thompson, C. 1964 *Interpersonal Psychoanalysis: The Selected Papers of Clara M. Thompson.* New York: Basic.

Thompson, K.M., and R.W. Wilsnack 1984 "Drinking and Drinking Problems among Female Adolescents: Patterns and Influences," Pp. 37–65 in S.C. Wilsnack and L.J. Beckman (Eds.), *Alcohol Problems in Women.* New York: The Guilford Press.

Thompson, L., and A.J. Walker 1989 "Women and Men in Marriage, Work, and Parenthood," *Journal of Marriage and the Family* 51:845–872.

Thorne, B. 1986 "Girls and Boys Together . . . But Mostly Apart: Gender Arrangements in Elementary Schools," Pp. 167–184 in W.W. Hartup and Z. Rubin (Eds.), *Relationships and Development.* Hillsdale, NJ: Lawrence Erlbaum Associates.

———1982 "Feminist Rethinking of the Family: An Overview," Pp. 1–24 in Barrie Thorne (ed.), *Rethinking the Family.* New York: Longman.

Thorne, B., and Z. Luria 1986 "Sexuality and Gender in Children's Daily Worlds," *Social Problems* 33:176–190.

Tidball, M.E. 1980 "Women's Colleges and Women Achievers Revisited," *Signs* 5:504–517.

Tiger, L., and R. Fox 1971 *The Imperial Animal.* New York: Oxford University Press.

Tobias, S., and C. Weissbrod 1980 "Anxiety and Mathematics: An Update," *Harvard Educational Review* 50:63–70.

Tolchin, M. 1988 "Many Rejected for Welfare Aid over Paperwork," *New York Times* 29 October:1,8.

Toner, R. 1990 "Gains Seen for Women, But Not Without Fights," *New York Times* 29 October:A13.

———1986 "Women in Journalism: A Global Perspective," *New York Times* 16 November:4.

Tong, R. 1989 *Feminist Thought: A Comprehensive Introduction.* Boulder, CO: Westview.

Townsey, R. 1982 "Female Patrol Officers: A Review of the Physical Capability Issue," Pp. 413–426 in B.R. Price and N.J. Sokoloff (Eds.), *The Criminal Justice System and Women.* New York: Clark Boardman.

Tracy, L. 1990 "The Television Image in Children's Lives," *New York Times* 13 May:M1, M5.

Treadwell, P. 1987 "Biologic Influences on Masculinity," Pp. 259–285 in H. Brod (Ed.), *The Making of Masculinities.* Boston: Allen and Unwin.

Treaster, J.B. 1990 "Bush Hails Drug Use Decline in a Survey Some See as Flawed," *New York Times* 20 December:B14.

Treichler, P.A., and F.W. Frank 1989a "Introduction: Scholarship, Feminism, and Language Change," Pp. 1–32 in F.W. Frank and P.A. Treichler (Eds.), *Language, Gender, and Professional Writing: Theoretical Approaches and Guidelines for Nonsexist Usage.* New York: The Modern Language Association of America.

———1989b "Guidelines for Nonsexist Usage," Pp. 137–278 in F.W. Frank and P.A. Treichler (Eds.), *Language, Gender, and Professional Writing: Theoretical Approaches and Guidelines for Nonsexist Usage.* New York: The Modern Language Association of America.

Treiman, D.J., and H.I. Hartmann (Eds.) 1981 *Women, Work, and Wages: Equal Pay for Jobs of Equal Value.* Washington, D.C.: National Academy Press.

Tresemer, D.W. 1977 *Fear of Success.* New York: Plenum.

Trible, P. 1979 "Depatriarchalizing in Biblical Interpretation," Pp. 217–240 in E. Koltun (Eds.), *The Jewish Woman.* New York: Shocken Books.

Tuchman, G. 1979 "Women's Depiction by the Mass Media," *Signs* 4:528–542.

Tuchman, G., A.K. Daniels, and J. Benet (Eds.) 1978 *Hearth and Home: Images of Women in the Mass Media.* New York: Oxford University Press.

Tyack, D., and E. Hansot 1990 *Learning Together: A History of Coeducation in American Public Schools*. New Haven, CT: Yale University Press.

Uchitelle, L. 1990 "Women's Push into the Work Force Seems to Have Reached Plateau," *New York Times* 24 November:1,28.

———1987 "America's Army of Non-Workers," *New York Times* 27 September: 1F, 6F.

Umansky, E.M. 1985 "Feminism and the Reevaluation of Women's Roles Within American Jewish Life," Pp. 477–494 in Y. Y. Haddad and E. B. Findly (Eds.), *Women, Religion and Social Change*. Albany: State University of New York Press.

Ungar, S.B. 1982 "The Sex Typing of Adult and Child Behavior in Toy Sales," *Sex Roles* 8:251–260.

Unger, R.K. 1981 "Sex as a Social Reality: Field and Laboratory Research," *Psychology of Women Quarterly* 5:645–653.

United Nations Commission on the Status of Women 1980 *Report of the World Conference of the United Nations Decade for Women*. Copenhagen, A/CONF.94/35.

U.S. Catholic Bishops 1989 "Called to Compassion and Responsibility: A Response to the HIV/AIDS Crisis," *Origins* 19 (November 30):1, 423–434.

U.S. Commission on Civil Rights 1979 *Window Dressing on the Set: An Update*. Washington, D.C.: U.S. Government Printing Office.

———1977 *Window Dressing on the Set: Women and Minorities in Television*. Washington, D.C.: U.S. Government Printing Office.

U.S. Dept. of Commerce, Bureau of the Census 1991 *Household Wealth and Ownership, 1988*. Washington, D.C.: U.S. Government Printing Office.

———1990 *Statistical Abstract of the United States, 1990*. Washington, D.C.: U.S. Government Printing Office.

———1989 *Statistical Abstract of the United States, 1989*. Washington, DC: U.S. Government Printing Office.

———1987a *Statistical Abstract of the United States, 1987*. Washington, D.C.: U.S. Government Printing Office.

———1987b *Child Support and Alimony, 1985*. Washington, D.C.: U.S. Government Printing Office.

———1985 *Statistical Abstract of the United States, 1985*. Washington, D.C.: U.S. Government Printing Office.

———1976 *Historical Statistics of the United States, Colonial Times to 1970, Part I*. Washington, D.C.: U.S. Government Printing Office.

U.S. Dept. of Defense 1990 *Military Manpower Statistics, September 30, 1990*. Washington, D.C.: U.S. Government Printing Office.

U.S. Dept. of Education, Center for Education Statistics 1986 *Digest of Education Statistics*. Washington, D.C.: U.S. Government Printing Office.

U.S. Dept. of Health and Human Services, National Center for Health Statistics 1989 *Health, United States, 1989*. Washington, D.C.: U.S. Government Printing Office.

———1988 *Health, United States, 1988*. Washington, D.C.: U.S. Government Printing Office.

———1986 *Health, United States, 1986*. Washington, D.C.: U.S. Government Printing Office.

U.S. Dept. of Justice 1990a *Crime in America*. Washington, DC: U.S. Government Printing Office.

———1990b *Sourcebook of Criminal Justice Statistics, 1989*. Washington, DC: U.S. Government Printing Office.

———1987 *Sourcebook of Criminal Justice Statistics, 1986*. Washington, D.C.: U.S. Government Printing Office.

———1982 *A National Crime Survey Report, NCJ-84015*. Washington, D.C.: U.S. Government Printing Office.

U.S. Dept of Justice, Attorney General's Commission on Pornography 1986 *Final Report*. Washington, D.C.: U.S. Government Printing Office.

———1990 *Occupational Projections and Training Data*. Washington, DC: U.S. Government Printing Office.

U.S. Dept. of Labor, Bureau of Labor Statistics 1991 Employment and Earnings. Washington, D.C.: U.S. Government Printing Office.

U.S. House of Representatives, Committee on Ways and Means 1989 *Background Material and Data on Programs within the Jursidiction of the Committee on Ways and Means.* Washington, DC: U.S. Government Printing Office.

U.S. House of Representatives, Select Committee on Children, Youth and Families 1990 "Victims of Rape," fact sheet, 28 June.

———1989 "AIDS and Young Children in Florida," fact sheet, 7 August.

———1988 *Women, Violence, and the Law.* Washington, DC: U.S. Government Printing Office.

———1987 *U.S. Children and Their Families: Current Conditions and Recent Trends, 1987.* Washington, D.C.: U.S. Government Printing Office.

U.S. Senate Special Subcommittee on Aging 1984 *Aging in America: Trends and Projections.* Washington, D.C.: U.S. Government Printing Office.

Vannoy-Hiller, D., and W.W. Philliber 1989 *Equal Partners: Successful Women in Marriage.* Newbury Park, CA; Sage.

Verbrugge, L.M. 1985 "Gender and Health: An Update on Hypotheses and Evidence," *Journal of Health and Social Behavior* 26:156–182.

Vogel, L. 1990 "Debating Difference: Feminism, Pregnancy, and the Workplace," *Feminist Studies* 16:9–32.

Vollmer, F. 1986 "Why Do Men have Higher Life Expectancy than Women?" *Sex Roles* 14:351–362.

Vrazo, F. 1983a "PMS: Its Misery and Its Mystery," *Philadelphia Inquirer* 19 June:1K, 8K.

———1983b "Feminists See PMS as a Step Back," *Philadelphia Inquirer* 19 June:1K, 8K.

Waldron, I.W. 1986 "Why Do Women Live Longer than Men?" Pp. 34–44 in P. Conrad and R. Kern (Eds.), *The Sociology of Health and Illness.* New York: St. Martin's Press.

Walker, L. 1979 *The Battered Woman.* New York: Harper Colophon.

Waller-Zuckerman, M.E. forthcoming. *Women's Own Companions: Two Hundred Years of Women's Magazines.* New York: Columbia University Press.

Wallis, C. 1989 "Onward, Women!" *Time Magazine* (December 4):80–89.

Ware, M.C., and M.F. Stuck 1985 "Sex-Role Messages vis-a-vis Microcomputer Use: A Look at the Pictures," *Sex Roles* 13:205–214.

Warr, M. 1985 "Fear of Rape Among Urban Women," *Social Problems* 32:238–250.

Weaver, M.J. 1985 *New Catholic Women.* San Francisco: Harper and Row.

Webber, J. 1983 "Between Law and Custom: Women's Experience of Judaism," Pp. 143–162 in P. Holden (Ed.), *Women's Religious Experience: Cross-Cultural Perspectives.* London: Croom Helm.

Weidman, J.L. (Ed.) 1984 *Christian Feminism.* San Francisco: Harper and Row.

Weissman, M.M. 1980 "Depression," Pp. 97–112 in A.M. Brodsky and R. Hare-Mustin (Eds.), *Women and Psychotherapy.* New York: The Guildford Press.

Weitzman, L.J. 1985 *The Divorce Revolution.* New York: Free Press.

———1981 *The Marriage Contract: Spouses, Lovers, and the Law.* New York: Free Press.

Weitzman, L.J., D. Eifler, E. Hokada, and C. Ross 1972 "Sex-role Socialization in Picture Books for Pre-school Children," *American Journal of Sociology* 77:1125–1150.

Weitzman, N., B. Birns, and R. Friend 1985 "Traditional and Nontraditional Mothers' Communication with Their Daughters and Sons," *Child Development* 56:894–896.

Welch, S., J. Clark, and R. Darcy 1982 "The Effect of Candidate Gender on Electoral Outcomes: A Six State Analysis," Paper presented at the Annual Meeting of the American Political Science Association, Denver, CO.

Welch, S.D. 1985 *Communities of Resistance and Solidarity: A Feminist Theology of Liberation.* Maryknoll, NY: Orbis Books.

Werthheimer, B.M. 1979 " 'Union is Power': Sketches From Women's Labor History," Pp. 339–358 in J. Freeman (Ed.), *Woman: A Feminist Perspective.* Palo Alto, CA: Mayfield.

Wertz, R.W., and D.C. Wertz 1986 "Notes on the Decline of Midwives and the Rise of Medical Obstetrics," Pp. 134–146 in P. Conrad and R. Kern (Eds.), *The Sociology of Health and Illness.* New York: St. Martin's Press.

Westley, L.A. 1982 *A Territorial Issue: A Study of Women in the Construction Trades*. Washington, D.C.: Wider Opportunities for Women.

Whipple, T.W., and A.E. Courtney 1985 "Female Role Portrayals in Advertising and Communication Effectiveness: A Review," *Journal of Advertising* 14:4–8, 17.

Whitaker, A., J. Johnson, D. Shaffer, J.L. Rapoport, K. Kalikow, B.T. Walsh, M. Davies, S. Braiman, and A. Dolinsky 1990 "Common Troubles in Young People: Prevalence Disorders in a Nonreferred Adolescent Population," *Archives of General Psychiatry* 47:487–496.

Whitehead, H. 1981 "The Bow and the Burden Strap: A New Look at Institutionalized Homosexuality in Native North America," Pp. 31–79 in S.B. Ortner and H. Whitehead (Eds.), *Sexual Meanings*. New York: Cambridge University Press.

Widom, C.S., and A. Ames 1988 "Biology and Female Crime," Pp. 308–331 in T.E. Moffitt and S.A. Mednick (Eds.), *Biological Contributions to Crime Causation*. Dordrecht: Martinus Nijhoff Publishers.

Wikan, U. 1984 "Shame and Honour: A Contestable Pair," *Man* 19:635–652.

Wilcoxon, L.A., S.L. Schrader, and C.W. Sherif 1976 "Daily Self-Reports on Activities, Life Events, Moods and Somatic Changes During the Menstrual Cycle," *Psychosomatic Medicine* 38:399–417.

Wilkerson, I. 1991 "Blacks Wary of Their Big Role in Military," *New York Times* 25 January:A1, A2.

Williams, B. 1987 "Homosexuality: The New Vatican Statement," *Theological Studies* 48:259–277.

Williams, J.A., Jr., J.A. Vernon, M.C. Williams, and K. Malecha 1987 "Sex Role Socialization in Picture Books: An Update," *Social Science Quarterly* 68:148–156.

Williams, J.E. 1985 "Mexican American and Anglo Attitudes About Sex Roles and Rape," *Free Inquiry in Creative Sociology* 13:15–20.

Williams, L.A. 1988 "Toxic Exposure in the Workplace: Balancing Job Opportunity with Reproductive Health," Pp. 113–130 in E. Boneparth and E. Stroper (Eds.), *Women, Power and Policy: Toward the Year 2000*. New York: Pergamon.

Williams, W.L. 1986 *The Spirit and the Flesh*. Boston: Beacon.

Williams, M., and J.C. Condry 1988 *Living Color: Minority Portrayals and Cross-Racial Interactions on Television*. unpublished manuscript.

Williamson, N.E. 1977 "A Reply to Rent and Rent's 'More on Offspring-Sex Preference'," *Signs* 3:513–515.

———1976a *Sons or Daughters*. Beverly Hills, CA: Sage.

———1976b "Sex Preference, Sex Control, and the Status of Women," *Signs* 1:847–862.

Wilson, E., and S.H. Ng 1988 "Sex Bias in Visual Images Evoked by Generics: A New Zealand Study," *Sex Roles* 18:159–168.

Wilson, M.N., T.F.J. Tolson, I.D. Hinton, and M. Kiernan 1990 "Flexibility and Sharing of Childcare Duties in Black Families," *Sex Roles* 22:409–425.

Wilson, W.J. 1987 *The Truly Disadvantaged*. Chicago: University of Chicago Press.

Wise, E., and J. Rafferty 1982 "Sex Bias and Language," *Sex Roles* 8:1189–1196.

Witelson, S.F. 1989 "Hand and Sex Differences in the Isthmus and Genu of the Human Corpus Callosum: A Postmortem Morphological Study," *Brain* 112:799–835.

Withorn, A. 1986 "Helping Ourselves," Pp. 416–424 in P. Conrad and R. Kern (Eds.), *The Sociology of Health and Illness*. New York: St. Martin's Press.

Wober, M., and B. Gunter 1988 *Television and Social Control*. New York: St. Martin's Press.

Wolowitz, H.M. 1972 "Hysterical Character and Feminine Identity," Pp. 307–313 in J. Bardwick (Ed.), *Readings on the Psychology of Women*. New York: Harper and Row.

Women's Institute for Freedom of the Press (WIFP) 1990a "Little Improvement Noted in Women's Page One Status," *Media Report to Women* May-June:3–4.

———1990b "NFPW Study" Women Grossly Underrepresented in Newspaper Content, Editorial Decisions" *Media Report to Women* July-August:2–3.

———1990c "Baseball Pitcher Uses Sexual Comment to Decline Interview with Reporter," *Media Report to Women* September-October:2–3.

———1990d "Fall 1989 TV Season 'Takes Two Steps Back,' Says NCWW/WOW," *Media Report to Women* January-February:4–5.

———1990e "TV Portrayal of the Childless Black Female: Superficial, Unskilled, Dependent," *Media Report to Women* March-April:4.

———1990f "Annual 'Visibility' Study of TV Reporters Shows Women Lagging," *Media Report to Women* September-October:6.

———1990g "Medical Ads Often Sexist: Women are Whiny Sex Objects," *Media Report to Women* July-August:6.

———1989a "Surveys of News Magazines Show Little News Coverage of Women," *Media Report to Women* November-December:1.

———1989b "Women Gain as Broadcast News Directors in New RTNDA Study," *Media Report to Women* September-October:6–7.

———1986a "Dorothy Jurney: Women Top Editors 11.1% in 1984, Rise to Only 11.7% in 1985; ASNE Sees New Attitudes," *Media Report to Women* March-April:7.

———1986b "British Women in Publishing Describe Subtle Forms of Discrimination Against Women's Issues," *Media Report to Women* July-August:7.

———1986c "1955 to 1985: Women in Prime Time TV Still Traditional, But New Treatment of Women's Rights Themes," *Media Report to Women* November-December:7.

———1986d "Women are Only 31% of TV News Staffs and 10% of News Directors: Both Radio and TV See Little Progress," *Media Report to Women* July-August:6.

———1986e "FCC Sees No Greater Programming Diversity Would Result from More Minority or Women Station Owners," *Media Report to Women* November-December:1,5–6.

———1982a "A.C.T.'s TV Study Shows 3.7% of Characters Black vs. 12% in Real Life; 16% Female vs. 52%," *Media Report to Women* 1 September:8.

———1982b "Public Trusts Women's Voices More Than Men's, Communication School Study Finds," *Media Report to Women* 1 September:9.

———1982c "NIMH Reports 10 Years of Studies on TV: TV Violence Doesn't Reflect Society," *Media Report to Women* 1 September:8.

Women's Political Times 1986a "Seeking Corp. PAC Money," 11 (Spring):6.

———1986b "Black Women Form PAC," 11 (Spring):6.

Woods, N.F., G.K. Dery, and A. Most 1982 "Recollections of Menarche, Current Menstrual Attitudes, and Perimenstrual Symptoms," Pp. 87–97 in S. Golub (Ed.), *The Transition from Girl to Woman.* Lexington, MA: D.C. Heath.

Wooley, S.C., and O.W. Wooley 1980 "Eating Disorders: Obesity and Anorexia," Pp. 135–158 in A.M. Brodsky and R. Hare-Mustin (Eds.), *Women and Psychotherapy.* New York: The Guilford Press.

The World Bank 1989 *World Development Report 1989.* New York: Oxford University Press.

The World Health Organization 1960 *Constitution.* Geneva: Palais des Nations.

Yen, M. 1988 "High-Risk Mothers," *Washington Post* August 23:18.

Young, S. 1990 "PMS Update," *Glamour* April:94, 98.

Zaretsky, E. 1976 *Capitalism, The Family, and Personal Life.* New York: Harper Colophon.

Zavella, P. 1987 *Women's Work and Chicano Families.* Ithaca, NY: Cornell University Press.

Zihlman, A.L. 1978 "Women and Evolution, Part II: Subsistence and Social Organization Among Early Hominids," *Signs* 4:4–20.

Zimmer, L.E. 1988 "Tokenism and Women in the Workplace: The Limits of Gender-Neutral Theory," *Social Problems* 35:64–77.

———1986 *Women Guarding Men.* Chicago: University of Chicago Press.

Zuckoff, A.C. 1979 "Jewish Women's Haggadah," Pp. 94–104 in E. Koltun (Ed.), *The Jewish Woman.* New York: Shocken Books.

Zuravin, Susan J. 1987 "Unplanned Pregnancies, Family Planning Problems, and Child Maltreatment," *Family Relations* 36:135–139.

Subject Index

Name Index